THE FIGHTING SHIPS
OF THE RISING SUN

By the same author

THE KOH-I-NOOR DIAMOND
THE KNIGHTS TEMPLAR

STEPHEN HOWARTH

THE FIGHTING SHIPS OF THE RISING SUN

The Drama of the Imperial Japanese Navy
1895-1945

'It must never be forgotten that the true use of history, military or civil, is, as Jacob Burckhardt once said, not to make men clever for the next time; it is to make them wise for ever.'
From *The Causes of War* by Michael Howard

ATHENEUM   NEW YORK   1983

Published in Great Britain under the title
Morning Glory: The Drama of the Imperial Japanese Navy

Copyright © 1983 by Stephen Howarth
Library of Congress catalog card number 83-45076
ISBN 0-689-11402-8

Manufactured by Fairfield Graphics, Fairfield, Pennsylvania
First American Edition

To the four seas, in brotherhood

This book was generously donated by

Dr. Kip Muir
***VMI Professor of History,
First Director of the John A. Adams '71
Center for the Study of Military History
and Strategic Analysis***

CONTENTS

Opening Fire with a Full Broadside	1
PART ONE: THE DARKNESS BEFORE DAWN 1853–1894	
1 'A new precedent . . . inconceivably disastrous to mankind'	5
PART TWO: THE SUN RISING 1894–1905	
2 'Slow to learn . . . but very sure'	19
3 'These bright dreams, these illusions'	26
4 'A great feeling of exhilaration'	36
5 'Allies, arms and intelligence'	39
6 'The national pleasure of building ships'	54
7 'Distant thunder . . . Death is near'	58
8 'A collection of stage properties'	82
9 'The day is fine, but the sea is high'	89
PART THREE: SUN OVER THE YARDARM 1906–1920	
10 'Bellicose rumours'	101
11 'To hold its own against any enemy'	113
12 'Signal success'	121
13 'Two formidable new Powers'	131
PART FOUR: ECLIPSE 1921–1936	
14 'Pacific intentions'	145
15 'Why should there be a war with Japan?'	158
16 'Different ideas of peace'	166
17 'Japan has never lost a war'	185
18 'Clouds over the sea'	198
PART FIVE: ZENITH 1937–1942	
19 'Dangerous toys'	211
20 'Paddling against the rapids'	228
21 'I shall run wild'	241

22 'The proper application of overwhelming force'	254
23 'The Imperial Navy takes this Territory'	262
24 'The enemy is unaware of our presence'	279

PART SIX: THE TROPICAL TWILIGHT 1942–1945

25 'These bright ministers of death'	291
26 'Change target!'	307
27 'Our chief object is to kill the enemy'	317
28 'I have grave news'	324
29 'The fate of the Empire'	331
30 'This proud success'	337
31 'This ultimate assignment'	341
32 'The fiercest serpent'	361

EPILOGUE: THE FOUR SEAS IN BROTHERHOOD

33 'Grim reflections . . . ominous of change'	369
34 'Evening faces'	372
Chronology of the Imperial Japanese Navy	375
Bibliography	385
Index	393

ILLUSTRATIONS

Between pages 110 *and* 111

Portrait of Togo
Portrait of Rozhdestvenski
The Battle of Tsushima, with Togo's calligraphy
Outside Port Arthur – an attempt to conceal the entrance
Inside Port Arthur
The battleship *Hatsuse* and her interior (1901)
Aspects of Etajima: submarine school
Aspects of Etajima: taking bearings with sextants
Aspects of Etajima: ceremonial parade on Navy Day 1941
Aspects of Etajima: signal practice on a 16-inch gun turret
Aspects of Etajima: inside a complete hangar, a lecture on aeronautics
Aspects of Etajima: firing practice
Aspects of Etajima: new recruits salute their parents
An officer serving his country's flag
Shanghai 1936
Shanghai – sunken steamers in the Whangpoo
Imperial Naval manoeuvres
The battleship *Kongo* in dry dock at Yokosura

Between pages 270 *and* 271

Japanese battleship *Hiei*, 5 December 1939
Japanese battleship *Tamato*, 30 October 1941
Japanese cruiser *Mogami*
Japanese aircraft carrier *Kaga*, circa 1936
Japanese aircraft carrier *Soryu*, January 1938
Japanese aircraft carrier *Hiryu*, 6 June 1942

Pearl Harbor – the destroyer *Shaw* in flames
Pearl Harbor – too little was destroyed
The Imperial Navy embarking
The Imperial Army invading
Port Darwin 1942
Coral Sea, 7–8 May 1942
Midway – the bursting of the steel balloon
Midway – *USS Yorktown* lists to port
Guadalcanal
Osaka 1945
'Debris all over the country greets our eyes . . .'

MAPS
(*drawn by Venture Graphics*)

The Japanese Empire	xiv–xv
Battle of Tsushima	92
Japan	169
Battle of Midway	304
Battle of Leyte Gulf	344

ACKNOWLEDGEMENTS

I would like to thank Manchester University Press for permission to quote extracts from *The Estrangement of Great Britain and Japan* by Malcolm Kennedy. For permission to quote extracts from Sir Winston Churchill's six-volume history *The Second World War*, I am grateful to both Cassell Ltd. and to Houghton Mifflin; for permission to quote extracts from G. A. Lensen's *The d'Anethan Despatches from Japan, 1894–1910*, I thank Sophia University, Tokyo; Constable Publishers, for permission to quote extracts from H. C. Bywater's *Sea-Power in the Pacific: A Study of the American-Japanese Naval Problem*; and Simon and Schuster, for permission to quote extracts from Joseph C. Grew's *Ten Years in Japan*. Japanese policy discussions before Pearl Harbor are reprinted from *Japan's Decision for War: Records of the 1941 Policy Conferences*, edited and translated by Nobutaka Ike, with the permission of the publishers, Stanford University Press, © 1967 by the Board of Trustees of the Leland Stanford Junior University; and finally, I am grateful to John W. M. Chapman, editor and translator, to quote extracts from *The Price of Admiralty: The War Diary of the German Naval Attaché in Japan 1939–1943 (Volume 1: 25 August 1939–23 August 1940)*. Further extracts from Wenneker's reports come from the National Archives, Washington, D.C., as do the diaries of Japanese soldiers and sailors, interrogations, and all magics.

My indebtedness to other authors will be apparent in the text and in the bibliography – my thanks to them all. Every effort has been made to trace all copyright holders, but the publishers would be interested to hear from anyone not here acknowledged.

In addition to written sources, many people in Great Britain, in Japan and in the United States helped me greatly. Firstly, I would like to record my gratitude to Tsukasa Tadayuki in Tokyo, who enabled me to meet many of the distinguished men listed below. In Washington, D.C., my work would have been much less effective without the help of Bruce Greenberg and Richard McGinnis, or the guidance of John E. Taylor through the Modern Military Archives. Dr Dean Allard of the Operational Archives, Naval Historical Center, was also helpful; and conversations, correspondence, and/or interviews were conducted with the following.

In the United States: Sgt. Lee Benbrooks, USAAF Retd; Fleet Admiral Arleigh Burke, USN Retd; Admiral Robert B. Carney, USN Retd; and Captain Roger Pineau, USN Retd. Useful advice was given by Professor Akira Iriye of the University of Chicago, and by Professor Roger F. Hackett of the Department of History, University of Michigan. *In Great Britain:* Cdr. Graham de Chair, RN Retd; Rear Admiral Royer Dick, RN Retd; Admiral Sir Frank Hopkins, RN Retd; Vice Admiral Sir Charles Hughes-Hallett, RN Retd; Captain Stephen Roskill, RN Retd; and Vice Admiral B. B. Schofield, RN Retd. Also of great value were conversations with the following British academic authorities: Dr J. W. M. Chapman, of the School of African and Asian Studies, University of Sussex; Dr I. T. M. Gow, of the Centre of Japanese Studies, University of Sheffield; and Professor I. H. Nish, of the London School of Economics and Political Science, University of London. *In Japan:* Lt.-General Azuma Tsuneo, JASDF Retd; Cdr. Chihaya Masataka, IJN Retd; Vice Admiral Fukuchi Nobuo, IJN/JMSDF Retd, Vice President *Mikasa* Preservation Society; Lt.-Cdr. Fukui Shizuo, IJN Retd; Captain Fukushima Osamu JMSDF; Furusawa Keiichi, observer during the *Prince of Wales*/*Repulse* sinking; Professor Ikeda Kiyoshi, of Sendai University, once an IJN submariner; Captain Kuzukara Shunsaku, JMSDF; Lt.-Cdr./Colonel Iki Haruki IJN/JASDF Retd; Lt. (jg) Kojima Kiyofumi, IJN Retd; Nagasue Eiichi, Paymaster IJN Retd, now Chief Whip of the Democratic Socialist Party; Nakamura Tsuneo, Constructor IJN Retd; Admiral Niimi Masaichi, IJN Retd; Professor Nomura Mineo, Chief of Naval History, Institute of Defence Research, Tokyo; Admiral Ohga Ryohei, JMSDF Retd; Vice Admiral Omuro Shoetsu, JMSDF; Shigihara Yoshiki, Paymaster IJN Retd and trained kamikaze pilot; Tachibana Koki, Constructor IJN Retd; Tsukasa Tadayuki, Ensign IJN Retd; Rear Admiral Uchi Tomio, JMSDF; Admiral Uchida Kazutomi, Chief of Staff JMSDF Retd; Rear Admiral Uotani Kiyohiro, JMSDF; and Captain Michael Forrest, RN, naval attaché at Her Britannic Majesty's Embassy in Tokyo.

And lastly, I would like to record my thanks to someone who perhaps should have been first: my wife, Marianne, who has seen this book grow from first to last. I could not have produced it without her.

Note: Throughout the text the Japanese names are given in Japanese order, that is the family name first and the given name second, as in 'Smith John'.

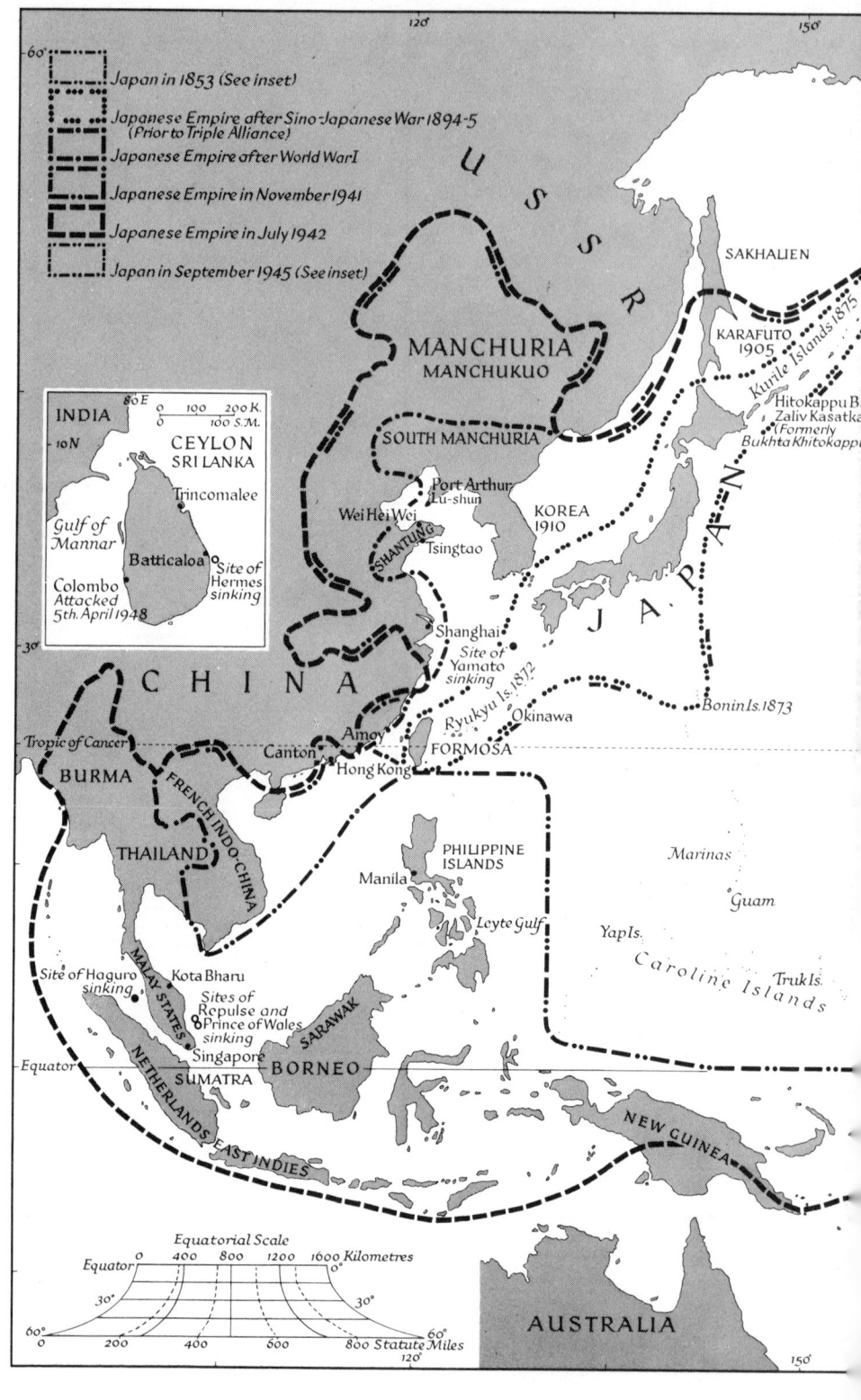

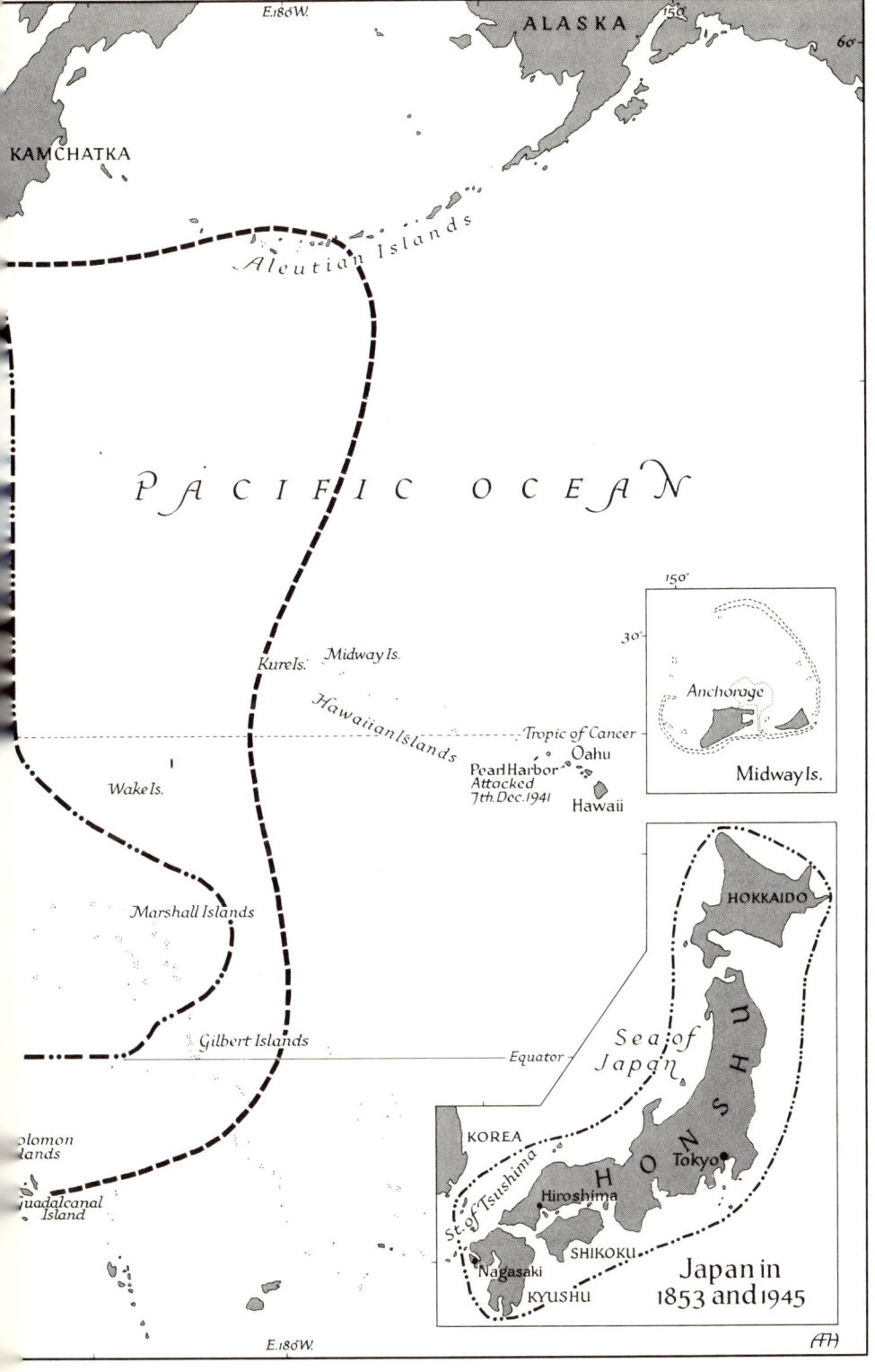

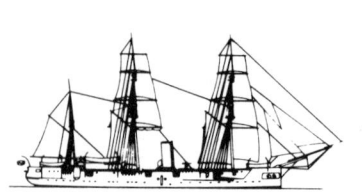

Unprotected Cruiser *Yamato* (1884)

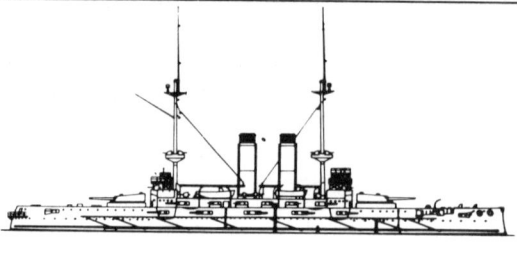

Battleship *Mikasa* (1902)

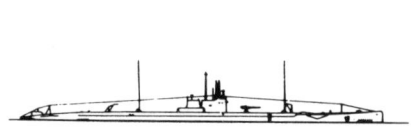

Submarine *I-51* (1924)

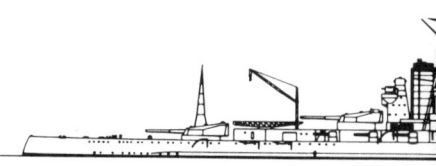

Battlec

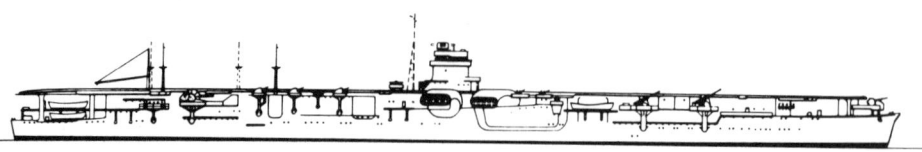

Aircraft Carrier *Hiryu* (1942)

Heavy Cruiser *Haguro* (1944)

Minesweeper *W19 Type* (1944)

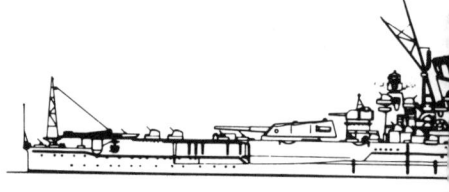

SCA

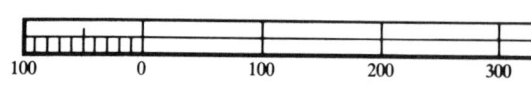

100 0 100 200 300

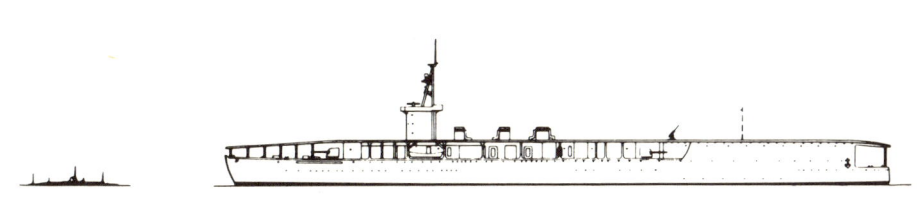

marine *Holland No. 6* (1907) Aircraft Carrier *Hosho* (1922)

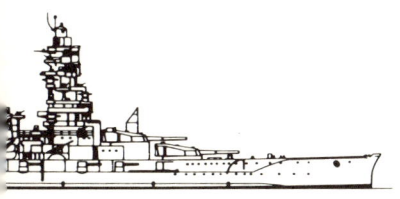
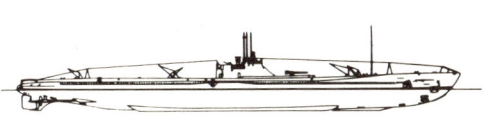

i (1940) Submarine *I-16* (1941)

Destroyer *Yukikaze* (1943) Light Cruiser *Yubari* (1943)

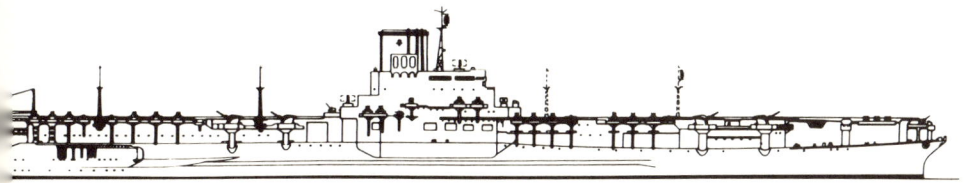

Super-battleship/Aircraft Carrier *Shinano* (1944)

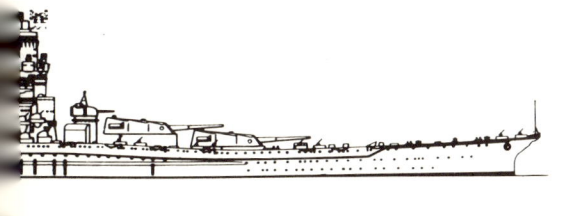
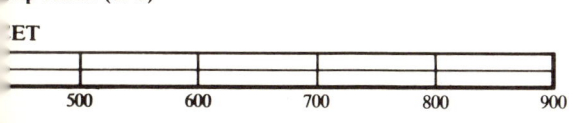

ship *Yamato* (1945) Minelayer *Kurosaki* (1945)

ET

500 600 700 800 900

Opening Fire with a Full Broadside

There has never been a navy like the Imperial Navy of Japan, and there never will be again. It is the only world-class navy in history which had a definite beginning and an equally definite end – at points, moreover, which can be established fairly easily and without too much argument not only as happening in a particular year or month, or on a particular day, but which can actually be brought down to nearly-exact minutes. The Imperial Japanese Navy began life as a fighting force very shortly before 8 a.m. on 25 July 1894; its fighting life ended at 2.23 p.m. on 7 April 1945 – a span, in other words, of just under fifty-one years, or very much less than a single average lifetime. And, despite its brief life, this was no tin-pot collection of second-hand battleships; the Imperial Navy rapidly achieved the status of the world's third greatest navy, and in its last years almost won an even higher position – but instead, in the final contest, lost everything.

The drama of its history is full of such extremes. It came from nothing, from absolute zero, and in a bare half-century to absolute zero it returned. Yet in its first decade it defeated the navies of two of the world's oldest and largest empires, China and Russia; at its zenith it possessed the biggest and most powerful battleships ever made, enormous sea-going fighting machines conceived, designed and built entirely by Japan; and once, in the space of three short days, it snatched control of seas and oceans which stretched in an unbroken line for 6,000 miles – a quarter of the Earth's circumference. It won some spectacular victories, and suffered outstanding defeats, culminating in history's largest naval battle. For three days, the Battle for Leyte Gulf blazed over an area more extensive than that of France, and in it a greater tonnage of ships and a greater number of men were used and destroyed than in any sea-battle before or since.

The Imperial Navy's history is, however, more than a chronicle of battles. In any naval history, battles must be of major importance, because it is in controlling the seas – and fighting other contenders to gain or maintain that control – that a navy proves its worth; and the Imperial Navy could certainly fight. Nevertheless, if that were the only criterion, the Imperial Navy might have to be judged ultimately worthless, for its final, total defeat ensured it would never rise again; today's JMSDF, the Maritime Self-Defence Force, is no phoenix, but a different bird altogether, with blunter talons and duller plumage. Still, it is impossible to say that the Imperial Navy was worthless. Its successes made Japan worthy of an alliance with Great Britain, then the world's number one naval nation; later, of participation in the highest levels of global diplomacy; later again, of an alliance with Hitler's Germany; and, lastly, of the longest-lasting, widest-ranging single naval effort that America has ever had to mount.

The historical worth, the continuing fascination, and the still-instructive value of understanding this most unusual navy lie not simply in the study of isolated sea-fights, but in the phenomenal nature of its rise and fall. How was it that a nation ignorant of the sea could achieve world eminence as a fighting sea-power in only ten years? And how could that navy then be defeated so completely, and so soon?

The answers to both questions lie essentially in the characters and minds of the men who crewed and commanded His Imperial Majesty's ships – and also in the characters and minds of the Emperor's allies and enemies: allies and enemies inside Japan as well as outside.

The people who were alive when Great Britain – in the epochal breaking of her 'splendid isolation' in 1902 – secretly allied herself with Japan are a very small and rapidly-dwindling group. But there are millions of people who remember the times when the Imperial Japanese Navy was a major figure on the world stage, and there are still many thousands who fought in or against the Combined Fleet. And from their comments and memories one vital aspect about it often emerges: unlike the Imperial Army, which fought hard and very dirty, the Imperial Navy fought hard and clean. There were exceptions, times when naval men committed vile atrocities, and they are in this book; but they *were* exceptions. Fundamentally the Imperial Navy was an honourable institution; this was its strength, its glory, and its weakness as well. For, trained by the British Royal Navy, the men of the Imperial Navy had a deep sense of the Western concept of honour – but deeper still lay their sense of the Japanese concept of honour, and the two were not always easily reconciled. This latent psychological tension existed even before the first shot of the Sino-Japanese War was fired on that summer's morning in 1894. Forty-seven summers later, in the troubled middle months of 1941, the leaders of the Imperial Army discovered they could exploit that internal divide. They did so, and the result was Pearl Harbor, the Pacific War, the Imperial Army's own defeat, and the obliteration of the Imperial Navy.

It may be that it need not have happened. Such speculation is often intriguing, and sometimes useful. But one thing is certain: it will not happen again; the world is too different. If it is unlikely that any nation other than Japan could have produced, and lost, such a great navy in so short a time, it is impossible that any nation – even Japan – could do it again. The Imperial Japanese Navy will remain a unique historical phenomenon forever.

PART ONE

*The Darkness Before Dawn
1853–1894*

*After two centuries of isolation,
Japan is painfully re-opened to the world.
In the interests of national security,
she recognizes the need for a navy
and immediately begins to create one.*

1

'A new precedent . . . inconceivably disastrous to mankind'

It seems extraordinary that Japan, an island nation, should not even have *begun* to possess a fighting navy until the late nineteenth century. Any other civilized nation surrounded by water, or with a substantial seaboard, had organized itself centuries earlier for maritime commerce, exploration and war. Britain, Spain, Portugal and Holland spring at once to mind: nations which long ago had understood that their well-being depended in large measure on sailing the world's oceans, charting, sounding, always exploring a little further. Those early sailors had a kind of bravery which is difficult to recapture today, voyaging as they did into completely unknown waters, with the belief that the world was flat, and the constant lurking fear that if they ventured too far, they might be swept off its edge. That terror was removed in 1519, when Magellan's voyage proved the world was a globe. With that, the dangers of the sea became finite and comprehensible – no less perilous than before, but conquerable by skill and seamanship – and the age of exploration could proceed seriously. And in 1542 Antonio de Mota, extending the line of Portuguese discoveries, made landfall at the southern end of the Japanese archipelago.

Traders and missionaries had followed, from England, Holland and Spain as well as Portugal. Prime amongst the missionaries was Francis Xavier of the Jesuits, whose preaching made converts by the thousands. By the early seventeenth century half a million Japanese professed Christianity; most of them were peasants. But to the majority of Japan's rulers the egalitarian religion seemed suspicious, and probably treasonable; and, since it was of the Jesuit brand, the Protestant Dutch and English regarded it with contempt and a considerable degree of wariness. It seemed a wily move on their part to suggest that the new religion was politically subversive, that conversion would lead to revolution – which it might well have done – and that, for the security of the realm, the Catholics should be banished, leaving the freedom of trade to their own good Protestant selves. The suggestion worked, but more thoroughly than anyone anticipated: all Christians, Protestant or Catholic, were thrown out of Japan. Native Christians were persecuted, and, to prevent the return of the foreign threat, in 1637 the borders of Japan were sealed. No foreign ships could enter; no Japanese ships could voyage abroad; and to build a vessel larger than a fishing-boat became a capital crime.

The only foreign enclave permitted to remain was a handful of Dutch merchants, who abased and humiliated themselves for the privilege of a trading monopoly; yet even they were confined to the tiny island of Deshima, near Nagasaki, and forbidden to set foot on the mainland. And so, while the rest of the world moved on, Japan remained where she was, a static, unchanging society. The sea was not a lifeline but a shield; ships were not a blessing but a curse, the bearers not of prosperity but of danger and insecurity.

The pyramidical, feudal power structure of Japan was already archaic to European eyes, and two centuries later it had still scarcely changed at all. Nominally ruled by the Emperor in Kyoto, in practice the country was ruled by the shogun, the most powerful of the daimyos – the regional military lords. Under this regime, internal trade grew slowly, and a merchant class emerged, but there was no scientific or technological invention, and even many old skills dwindled away. Sea-faring skills in particular, forbidden on pain of death, vanished almost completely.

Seventeenth-century Europe learned to recognize the world in scientific rather than religious terms. When the Christians were expelled from Japan, Galileo had just proposed that the Earth moved around the Sun, and incurred the wrath of the Inquisition for his heresy. But, by the end of the century, the Dutchman Huygens had invented the pendulum clock and had proposed the wave theory of light; Pascal had discovered the principle of hydraulics; Newton had conceived the theory of gravity and had published his *Principia Mathematica*; the speed of light had been measured, it had been proved that sound could not cross a vacuum, the steam engine had been invented, and both the Royal Society and Greenwich Observatory had been founded. Meanwhile, in Japan, the five-stringed *koto* had been adopted as the national musical instrument, and *haiku* poetry had reached its highest form.

And then the explosion of the Industrial Revolution came: the cotton gin, the spinning mule, anaesthetics, gas lighting, wire telegraphy, photography, electromagnetics, ultraviolet light, stellar parallax, the thermometers of Fahrenheit and Celsius, vaccination, geology, the atomic theory of elements, nitroglycerine and the Morse Code – all were invented or discovered in the space of 140 years. Meanwhile, in Japan, the use of colour printing was adopted.

In France, the Montgolfier brothers had already taken to the air. The miracle of the railway began in 1825; and in 1838, Brunel's *Great Western* opened the era of regular trans-Atlantic traffic. Yet Japan's ships were still the same as they had been two hundred years before – the little coastal fishing-boats, and nothing larger.

There had been hardly any social progress except in art. But, if any Japanese had been sufficiently curious to ask the Dutch traders about changes in the West, they would probably have felt they had the better end of the bargain. In that same period, the Western world had seen the English Civil War, the Thirty Years' War, the Anglo-Dutch War, the War of the Spanish Succession, the French Revolution, and innumerable other conflicts and trade wars on land and sea. Under the Tokugawa shogunate, and in comparison to the West, Japan had been an essentially peaceful country; there had been clan wars, small and localized by Western standards, but even they had been conducted between the *samurai*, the warrior class, since only they could carry swords. By 1853 this static society had existed relatively undisturbed for 215 years; and then on 14 July Perry came.

Commodore Matthew Calbraith Perry had been sent with a fleet of four steamships – the frigates *Susquehanna* and *Mississippi*, and the sloops *Plymouth* and *Saratoga* – by President Fillmore, with instructions to obtain from the Japanese a treaty guaranteeing protection for shipwrecked crews, coaling facilities and, if possible, a modicum of trade as well. Four ships, large ones, in a place where no true sea-going vessel had been seen for two centuries – ships with guns, and bearing armed men (some of whom, inexplicably and astonishingly, had black skins) – caused an immediate reaction of panic in the town of Yedo, and the population rushed for safety into the hills. A very natural reaction – the more sophisticated citizens of New York did exactly the same when Orson Welles brought news of alien invasion with his broadcast *The War of the Worlds*. Perry's uninvited visit was not an invasion, nor did he come from outer space; but the impact of his presence, and of his ships – funnels belching sparks and black smoke, engines throbbing, the vessels moving without wind – was just as great as if he had come from another planet. And in effect, that is what he had done.

Gradually it became apparent that Perry was not going to use force to achieve his objectives. But it was equally apparent that he could, if challenged – not only his ships, but also the letter of introduction made that clear. The letter was addressed to Fillmore's 'great and good friend' the Emperor of Japan, but it never got to him. Instead, intermediaries bore it from Perry's ship to the shogun, who as *de facto* ruler was the obvious recipient; and the shogun read of a nation over the sea which spanned a continent from ocean to ocean – a nation which was larger, richer and more powerful than his own – and which wished to 'live in friendship and have commercial intercourse' with Japan.

To give him his due, Fillmore was at pains to stress the peaceable nature of the mission: 'I have directed Commodore Perry to assure your Imperial

Majesty that I entertain the kindest feelings towards your majesty's person and government,' he said. 'The constitution and laws of the United States forbid all interference with the religious or political concerns of other nations. I have particularly charged Commodore Perry to abstain from every act which could disturb the tranquillity of your majesty's dominions.'

But it never occurred to Fillmore that the mere presence of foreigners in Japanese waters and on Japanese soil disturbed the tranquillity of the dominions more profoundly than anything else had for two hundred years. And Perry's own thoughts differed sharply from those of his pacific president: he acknowledged that every country had 'the right to determine for itself the extent to which it will hold intercourse with other nations', yet he reckoned that a country which did not help shipwrecked sailors but instead clapped them in prison (as Japan had done several times) might 'justly be considered as the common enemy of mankind'. It was a seaman's logic, and fair by those lights, for every seaman should help another in distress; but it was unfair and arrogant to expect that a nation in which sea-faring was forbidden should even be *aware* of a custom evolved by many generations of sailors. Nevertheless, the arrogance only reflected aspects of the age. There was rumoured to be coal in Japan, and Secretary of State Daniel Webster claimed in all seriousness that it was a 'gift of Providence, deposited by the Creator of all things in the depths of the Japanese islands for the benefit of the human family'. Japan also happened to be conveniently placed for refuelling on the newly-proposed steamer lanes from the West Coast to Asia, and Webster's conclusion – unstated but all the more powerful for being implicit and unconsciously received – was that if the Japanese refused 'the human family' access to the reported coal, they were attempting to go against Providence and the Creator. Likewise, when Perry's voyage was mooted, Secretary of the Navy John P. Kennedy commented that the Japanese government should be made aware of 'its *Christian* obligation to join the family of Christendom'. It clearly never crossed his mind to think, by the same token, of his own Confucian obligation to adopt the religion of Japan.

The comparison should not be taken too far, but the three motives of the American mission to Japan – trade, religion and the national purpose – were virtually identical to the motives which fired the First Crusaders. Inwardly desirable, spiritually and socially praiseworthy – it was a heady mixture, breeding in many Americans (as it had in many Crusaders) a certainty of their own moral, spiritual, cultural and material superiority. Their certainty of possessing far greater material power than Japan was justified, at any rate; and it was for this simple reason that the requested treaty was signed – although it took over a year for the signature to be exacted. Self-confident as they were, the Americans did not have a monopoly in arrogance and ignorance; the Japanese were at least as bad in that way, and these first encounters of the two worlds were marked by a lack of understanding that was mutual and very nearly total. As much as their unwelcome visitors, the Japanese believed their own country and their own habits to be superior to all others. Perry's nonchalant entrance proved unmistakably that that belief was at least partially false. However well-meaning Fillmore's letter had been, the method of its delivery and its very arrival were humiliating and destabilizing events.

Perry did not comprehend – perhaps could not comprehend – the convulsive turmoil which his presence produced in Japanese minds; but he, and the rest of the world, could see the physical turmoil which followed. The shogun signed the treaty in the interests of national safety. The Emperor, conservative and strongly xenophobic, would not ratify it. Unaware of his country's impotence relative to the nineteenth-century Western world, he was supported by daimyos as insular as himself, and civil disturbances broke out, slowly building up to full-scale civil war.

Thus, unintentionally but directly, the first gift of the West to Japan was fifteen years of strife and turbulence, murder and assassination, conspiracy and rebellion. It ended in 1868, with the Imperial party victorious – but the old Emperor was dead. The name the new Emperor took to symbolize his reign was Meiji: Enlightened Rule. And he did rule, for not only the old Emperor but the entire shogunate system was gone, overthrown as Japan was painfully reborn.

The most important part of the enlightened rule was *fukoku-kyohei*, a maxim meaning 'enrich the country, strengthen the army'. The phrase was old, but now was seen in a new light; the new leaders of Japan recognized from the examples of China and India that two paths lay ahead. Either their homeland, the land of the gods, could become a colony of Britain or America, economically, politically or both; or it could remain independent and free – if it could be as strong as its potential enemies.

Britain, Russia, France and Holland had all come running to share in the spoils when Perry's success was announced; and it was recognized that, if crossed, they could be formidable foes. Furthermore, they had all demanded treaties which allowed their nationals in Japan to be free of Japanese law. To Japanese people the implication was obvious: Japanese laws were second-rate, and therefore the people to whom they applied must be second-rate as well. On the other hand, the westerners considered their own laws appropriate for dealing with Japanese crimes: and nowhere was this demonstrated more clearly than at Kagoshima, in 1863.

A Briton named Charles Richardson, visiting from China, failed to give way before a group of Japanese horsemen, and unexpectedly he found his way into history, for the horsemen killed him. Telegrams to and from London produced the demand that his killers, men of the powerful Satsuma clan, should be handed over and the enormous indemnity of £100,000 paid.

The demand was refused, repeated, refused again; and on 14 August, with seven ships, Rear Admiral Kuper of the Royal Navy opened fire on the Satsuma capital.

'It was impossible to ascertain precisely the extent of the injury inflicted upon the batteries,' he reported afterwards, 'but considering the heavy fire which was kept up from the ships, at point-blank range, the effect must have been considerable. Many guns were observed to be dismounted, the batteries were several times cleared, and the explosion of magazines gave evidence of the destructive effects of our shells; one half of the town was in flames and entirely destroyed, as well as a very extensive arsenal or factory and gun foundry, and five large junks, in addition to three steamers . . . A heavy typhoon blew during the night, and the conflagration, increasing in proportion to the height of the storm, illuminated the entire bay.'

Kuper's account managed to sound at once both heroic and sanitary, as if his bombardment had destroyed nothing but guns, buildings and ships. 'You must remember,' he said when speaking to some Japanese ambassadors, 'that we are one of the first nations in the world, who, instead of meeting civilized people as you think yourselves, in reality encounter barbarians.'

His meaning was clear: barbarian lives, Japanese lives, counted for little or nothing; but one British life, taken in time of peace, counted for a great deal. The deliberate insult is astonishing, but like Perry's attitude it characterized the culture, and on 4 November 1863 was echoed in the pages of *The Times*. A Member of Parliament, John Walter, 'believed that at no distant period we should be at war with that skilful and interesting people the Japanese, probably at a great sacrifice of life, as it seemed to be a law of Providence that when civilization and barbarism met, the barbarians must be thrashed into good behaviour and submission'.

Others, more thoughtful, reacted differently. Lord Salisbury described Kuper's bombardment as a 'very fair specimen of English foreign policy towards the weakest Powers . . . overbearing, exacting, pushing every right to the extremest limit, and where the execution of a right is in doubt, cynically throwing a sword into the balance. In execution these principles are carried out with no diplomatic courtesy, and with no consideration of the feelings or wounded honour of those to whom they are applied, but rather with an ostentatious insouciance. It is throughout a tone by which the weak are made to feel their weakness, to drink the bitter, bitter cups of inferiority to the very dregs. This is not a character which the English people will be gratified to learn they have acquired.'

On the same day and on the same page as John Walter's brusque comment, this impassioned letter was published:

'TO THE EDITOR OF THE TIMES – Sir, – Of course, if a word be breathed against the doings of Admiral Kuper at Kagoshima, the usual stale cant will be talked about the cruelty of blaming public servants when not by to defend themselves . . . Now, as to the gallantry and decision of character shown by Admiral Kuper there can happily be no question; but as to the judgement and humanity shown in the burning of the town there is room, I think, for two opinions. It needs no stretch of the imagination to conceive the horrors of that day in the town of Kagoshima. Being built of wood and paper, wherever a shell lighted the flames must instantly have spread far and wide. The town contained 180,000 people . . . Sir, let it be remembered that in thus destroying the houses of unarmed inhabitants we are setting a new precedent, and one which may be inconceivably disastrous to mankind . . . Ought it not to be one of the first and foremost principles of British statesmanship that England should invariably be on the side of humanity? Let Russians fill Poland with blood; they have shown themselves to be but savages. But are we to take the lead in replacing among the usages of war the bombardment of unresisting towns?'

The writer, one Charles Buxton, had had the imagination to see through Kuper's sanitized account. Many thousands had been burnt to death at Kagoshima; scores of thousands more had been made homeless. A new precedent, 'inconceivably disastrous to mankind', had indeed been set.

Buxton was not only accurately prophetic, but accurate in writing of the past as well. 'Every principle of justice and of policy demanded gentleness and self-restraint,' he said. 'The Japanese did not seek – they abjured our company; they did their utmost to keep us from their shores. It was only the terror of our fleets which thrust our society upon them against their will.' But, naturally, the immediacy of Kuper's words and deeds had a far greater effect on them than letters in *The Times*, and they responded with *fukoku-kyohei* – enrich the country, strengthen the army; and not only the army but the navy as well, for the threats to the homeland came from beyond the seas. Wealth and power, the technology of the nineteenth century, the skills of a modern world, lay over the water and must be brought to Japan – but Japan had to be able to treat for them on equal terms, or remain a primitive, vulnerable, beggar state. At Shimonoseki the following year an international force repeated Kuper's exploit; and, over the ensuing decade, people like Charles Buxton must have been very surprised to see the broad trend of Japanese response. It was not rage and resentment, but admiration and apparent friendship. Belatedly, the Japanese had begun to understand that ships gave greater strength than swords. The sea-surrounded nations of the West had several centuries' start. In Japan, the ancient familiarity with the sea had long gone: it had to be revived, as quickly and thoroughly as political expediency allowed. From nothing, a navy had to be created, a navy to match the best that could be put against it; for, without it, Japan would never know security again.

It began quietly enough; when news got around in Great Britain and America that 'the Japanese deputation have come to buy ironclads', it caused more amusement than anything. That was in 1866; the American Civil War was only a year finished, the Japanese Civil War was at its height. Every political group in Japan had obtained a ship or two, the largest of which was a 1,445-ton ex-pirate ship; the smallest was a mere 250 tons. But, with the imperial restoration in 1868, the feudal fleets were abolished, their vessels were gathered together; the Imperial Japanese Navy came into being, and in 1872 was made a Department of State.

Ships were ordered from Britain. A naval training school was opened in Tokyo, and – since information from all sides, as well as the example of Kagoshima, had shown that the British Royal Navy was the most powerful in the world – Royal Naval officers were invited to become the instructors of the first generation of Japanese naval cadets. They did so, and that was not all: already the coasts of the island empire were being assiduously charted and marked by Britons. In 1869 the last beacon bonfires had been extinguished on Japanese capes; the old and primitive were thrown out, the new and modern welcomed in, and light-ships and catadioptical signals sprouted on every shoal and headland. In the space of a few years the physical profile of Japan changed from a model typical of the early seventeenth century to one of the late nineteenth century – which must have confused the coastal fishermen very considerably.

For Katsu Awa, the head of the Navy Department, the transformation could not be swift enough; he had a secret embarrassment to overcome. On a voyage to San Francisco in 1860 he had captained the very first Japanese ship to make an ocean crossing after Perry's disruptive visits. The ship was the *Kanrin Maru*, a 700-ton, 163-foot wooden schooner built in Holland. Her successful journey had been a source of intense pride to her captain and crew – or so, at least, said the official accounts for a full century afterwards. In fact, throughout the voyage, all the Japanese crew were constantly, dreadfully seasick, and Katsu himself only came out of his cabin two or three times. The work of sailing was done by a group of homeward-bound American passengers, who suddenly found that the only way of getting home was to sail themselves. But what was much more surprising was that every one of them kept the secret – except for one, who wrote it all in his diary, and left the journal with his family. A hundred years later the diary was published: but, by then, anyone who might have been embarrassed was long dead.

By 1872, however, Katsu's newly-created department had an impressive list of organizations in its wake: not only the Naval Academy, the Magazine (or the Arsenal, as it became), the Hospital and the Court-Martial, but also Yokosuka Dockyard and Workshop came under its jurisdiction. But behind the sonorous titles there were only seventeen ships; and, out of those, only two were iron-clads. The rest were of wood; and the whole lot together totalled less than 14,000 tons – an average of under a thousand tons' displacement for each ship.

Katsu and his colleagues promptly instigated a serious programme of naval building and acquisition, and in 1873, at Yokosuka, the keel was laid of a respectable 203-foot, 897-ton vessel. She was to be called *Seiki*, and she had a double function: in peace she was a despatch vessel, but she was armed for war as well, with three machine-guns and four breech loaders. Launched in 1875, she was the first wooden warship built in the new imperial Japan.

In any country, at any time, the launch of a ship has always been an occasion of mixed apprehension and anticipation for the builders, and a splendid entertainment for others; and 1877 was a great year for Japanese launches.

'This harbour [Yokohama] on a clear day is, perhaps, one of the brightest sights in the world', a *Times* correspondent wrote on 25 May. 'The high backgrounds stand out crisp and distinct, with an airy lightness peculiar to this bracing climate. The view is filled with steamers, ships and the native craft with their strange square sails; and there is Mount Fuji rising clear to its snow-covered summit at some 13,000 feet, giving a grandeur to the whole quite impossible to describe.'

A launch had been announced, and with some friends the writer had decided to spend a day at the Imperial Arsenal – 'quite a new place, extensive and neatly laid out'. The day was not bright, but the bay was calm and the weather balmy. The harbour reminded him of Balaclava – 'only that the hills are not built upon, and are covered with ferns and vegetation quite down to the water's edge'. The vessel, *Amagi*, was as graceful as her surroundings. Two hundred and fourteen feet of wood, she weighed just over a thousand tons, with three masts, a single funnel amidships, a long bowsprit and an elegant clipper bow – 'a beautiful model, but too fine in the stern'. Perhaps there had to be some qualification, for it was a French, not a British, design. There was, however, just enough drama in the actual launch to make it well worth attending.

'After lunch the master-carpenter took his stand at her fore-foot, and, waving the national flag – a red ball on a white ground, the rising sun – the shores were knocked down as he directed. A very full band, all Japanese, dressed in scarlet jackets, black jackets, and having short dirks, appeared on the scene, and struck up what a Frenchman told me was the national air, but which sounded to me uncommonly like "Yankee Doodle". All being ready at a quarter past 4, the dogs were taken out, daggers struck down – but she did not move on the ways; her forefoot was then wedged, but still she hung; at last a ram was brought into play, a few blows were struck, and steadily the vessel moved down, gaily decorated with nautical flags and trimmed from stem to stern with artificial camellias. From her bowsprit depended an enormous globe of evergreens and flowers.' Only one thing was missing: the observers 'listened in vain for a cheer, and saw no christening'.

But, even if no wine was spilt, it had been a memorable and pleasant day: and four weeks later, on the other side of the world, at the recently-established Samuda Brothers yard at Poplar, on the Thames, a full-scale 'proper christening' took place, with flags (but certainly no flowers); a bottle of good champagne smashed over the ship's bows; several speeches; and many toasts, 'drunk with three times three'. The event was the launching of the *Fuso*. At 220 feet in length and 48 feet in beam, she was not much bigger than *Amagi*; but she weighed nearly four times as much, for she was built of steel, and sported a belt of armour nine inches thick around her waistline.

Fuso was the first armoured ship built in England for Japan, and was quickly followed by *Kongo* and *Hiei*. Their armaments included not only machine-guns and breech loaders similar to those on *Fuso*, but a brace of torpedo-tubes each – weapons which some people viewed with concern. The Chinese ambassador to Britain was present at *Fuso*'s launch and, after proposing a toast to the ship and the Imperial Japanese Navy, he took the opportunity of adding the hope that they would 'never fire a shot except as an ally of China'. For, if Britain, France, Holland and – now that the Civil War was a memory – the United States as well were happy to provide ships for Japan, other nations pondered where those ships might be used.

But the climax of 1877 was a sober yet sensational article in *The Times* on 4 August: 'A fine ship, called the *Niigata Maru*, has arrived in the Thames from Japan. This is the first vessel bearing the Japanese flag which has entered the port of London.' She was built as a steamer, but her crew of thirty-four ('all of whom, with three or four exceptions, are Japanese') had sailed her the entire way from Japan. Their captain, a Briton named Walker, was full of praise for them, saying they 'behaved admirably, and in any emergency were always ready to do their part'. He was not being patronizing, but simply commending good seamanship. With a British crew, expected to be 'always ready to do their part', it might not have been necessary; but it must have flattered the young Japanese – men whose fathers had been forbidden to set sail on the sea at all.

Western seamanship, Western politics, Western economy – the new imperial Japan had determined to learn about them all, and all at once; there was a lot of ground to be made up. To Britain, America, France and Holland, Japanese seafaring meant only one thing – commerce, and therefore money, trade and employment. If anyone thought there might be a more ominous purpose behind it all, they ignored it, or were largely ignored themselves. Sir Rutherford Alcock, the British minister in China and Japan, suspected that Japan's sudden interest in the sea might not benefit the West in the end; and back in the days of pre-Perry seclusion – already they seemed so long ago – a British missionary had written in his diary his own thoughts about the Japanese. 'They'll take care,' he had said, 'to speak smoothly; but by her works Japan will be known as a malicious power for generations to come, unless she be subjected by power to obey the dictates of humanity.' But little notice was given to such Cassandras; speaking for Britain, *Times* correspondents showed that the old secretive Japan had been replaced in common thinking by a new country, tolerant, liberal and enlightened. 'They are highly intellectual, acute and reasoning,' said one. 'There is a rage amongst them for knowledge. A Japanese is full of eager interest and curiosity; there does not exist a more ingenious and industrious people; the bearing of the humblest peasant is marked by a natural courtesy, while that of the middle and higher classes is distinguished by a studied dignity and refinement.'

With enthusiastic agreement, another writer added, 'It is a wonderful country; beautiful hills with cultivated slopes and crests wooded with magnificent timber, surrounded by sea-like plains of rich black volcanic soil, bearing crops of every hue which vegetation can produce in a warm and humid climate.' A delightful place and an attractive people, it seemed; but most foreigners were more interested in commerce than in aesthetic appreciation, and over the next fifteen years more and more large ships rolled off the slipways of the world, bound for the Imperial Japanese Navy.

In 1885 there were the *Naniwa* and the *Takachiho*, the first steel cruisers in the Imperial Navy, and, at the time, the most powerful cruisers in the world. *Naniwa*, displacing 4,150 tons, was 500 tons larger than *Takachiho*, but both were 299 feet long and carried the same bristling armament – four torpedo-tubes, 14 machine-guns and 14 large guns, including two 10.2-inch Krupps. Furthermore, both ships were equipped with electricity and artificial ventilation, which, even at the *end* of the nineteenth century, were still thought worthy of comment. In the 1880s, they were astonishing, as an article in *Engineering* magazine revealed: the engine rooms were 'greatly enhanced in appearance by a liberal supply of electric incandescent lamps, which render the rooms as light as day, even with the fighting shutters closed'. The advantages of such an arrangement were obvious and staggering, and the report continued:

'It is a matter of regret that vessels of this character, whose want is so urgently felt in our own fleet, should not be about to increase the numbers of our lamentably deficient cruisers, but we can sincerely congratulate the Japanese Government on the acquisition of these fine ships.'

The Imperial Navy itself did not experiment then; but it took careful notice of all useful experiments around the world, and incorporated the best innovations as soon as possible, often long before they were used in the ships of their inventors' nations. The purpose was simple: to meet the modern world on its own terms, in the one place where a physical challenge could be met – at sea, with the best vessels available. Increasing percentages of the national budget were set aside for the navy; in 1882, 1886 and 1892 substantial programmes of buying or building were authorized, with, among other results, the satisfying news that the *Yoshino* – a 360-foot, 4,150-ton British-built cruiser – was the fastest in the world. Yet better still was the *Akitsushima*, another cruiser, 302 feet and 3,100 tons. She was only a third-class cruiser, neither as fast nor as heavily armed as *Yoshino*, but she promised more: built at Yokosuka, she was the last warship built in Japan of imported metal. Other ships for the Imperial Navy would still be built abroad, but never again would Japanese shipyards have to construct with foreign material.

1891 saw the launch of the first armoured ship to be built in Japan, the *Hashidate*, sister to *Naniwa* and *Takachiho*. She had taken six and a half years to build – not exactly a competitive speed, but progress all the same. Enough progress, in fact, for the British Admiralty to feel the need of collating and printing, 'for the use of Her Majesty's Officers ONLY', as complete a list as possible of all known Japanese war vessels. There were 13 armoured ships and 46 unarmoured – a fleet of 59 all told, ranging from torpedo-boats at 53 tons up to the great cruisers.

Already, it was a far cry from the rag-bag collection of fifteen wooden ships and two iron-clads which, a mere nineteen years before, had formed the first imperial fleet. Already, there was a generation near adulthood to whom the old prohibition on sea-faring was a story told by their fathers. Already, there were men verging on middle-age whose entire adult lives had been spent in the service of the sea. 'We managed to escape from the difficulties which beset us,' said an admiral, 'by throwing away the old system and adopting the new.' It had been a deliberate, conscious process; and now the ships were there, the men were there, the skills and knowledge of theory were there. But men trained for war and machines built for war have only one true testing-ground; and on 18 August 1894, by imperial edict, it was announced:

'We, the Emperor of the Empire of Great Japan, having ascended the throne by virtue of a lineal succession unbroken for ages eternal, fully assured of heavenly aid, do announce to all our brave and loyal subjects that we hereby declare war against China.'

PART TWO

*The Sun Rising
1894–1905*

*Like a child born into maturity,
in a single decade
the Imperial Navy defeats the navies
of China and Russia
and becomes the world's third greatest
maritime force*

2

'Slow to learn . . . but very sure'

In fact the war had already begun. It took a long time for the news to filter through to the West: when *The Times* said cautiously on 2 August, 'It now appears to be certain that war has been declared', the fighting had been going on for nine days. It had begun just before 8 o'clock in the morning on 25 July 1894, off the west coast of Korea; and it had begun by mistake.

Three Japanese warships – *Yoshino*, *Akitsushima* and *Naniwa* – met two Chinese warships, *Tsi-yuen* and *Kwang-yi*, coming out of the channel which leads to the town of Asan. No sooner had the vessels sighted each other than the *Tsi-yuen* made straight for the Japanese squadron at high speed – a standard preparation for a torpedo attack. Frozen for a moment in surprise, the Japanese then responded quickly: *Naniwa*'s captain gave the order to fire, her guns crashed out flame and smoke, the ship heeled under the shock, and *Tsi-yuen* at once replied, maintaining her course and speed directly towards her opponents. *Naniwa*'s companions joined in promptly, and as the range shortened, from 3,000 to 2,000 metres, down to a thousand and less, the deadly exchange of fire continued, each side flinging all it could at the other. Paradoxically, visibility diminished as the ships closed together, for mist and the heavy morning air kept the smoke of funnels and guns low on the water. It was the first time Japanese naval guns had been fired in anger against another modern fleet, and the first time Japanese captains and crews had come under such fire, and they could hardly see what was happening at all. But they could hear, all too clearly, the thunder of enemy guns, and the whistle of enemy shells; and then out of the vapour came one of the enemy ships, *Kwang-yi*, aiming herself at *Yoshino* with obvious intent to ram. *Yoshino* swung out of line, to avoid disaster: *Kwang-yi* vanished from sight: and at the same time *Tsi-yuen* was seen, severely battered, running up a Japanese Ensign and a white flag of surrender or truce.

But she did not surrender. Instead she turned and made for the friendly shore. *Yoshino* gave chase, still ready to fire; *Kwang-yi* reappeared; there was another brisk exchange of shots, and once more *Kwang-yi* turned and disappeared into the thickening fog. Perhaps through lack of preparation (since they had never come across such a situation before), perhaps through difficulties in visual communication, or possibly intentionally, the Japanese squadron broke up: *Yoshino* continued the pursuit of *Tsi-yuen*, *Akitsushima* took up pursuit of *Kwang-yi*, and *Naniwa* remained on the site of the battle. *Tsi-yuen* eventually escaped; but the only reason she survived was that many of the Japanese shells had proved to be duds, failing to explode on impact. Had they worked, she would certainly have sunk, and as it was, a large proportion of her crew was killed; yet on the Japanese ships there was not a single casualty, and even the ships were only slightly damaged. *Kwang-yi* ran herself heavily aground on a beach, to the astonishment of *Akitsushima*'s crew; and *Naniwa*, alone, suddenly found herself presented with a much more perplexing problem. Turning from the scene of the first action, her captain saw two more vessels in the distance – another Chinese man-of-war, accompanied by a merchant ship flying the British Red Ensign.

This was a serious development. The Chinese sloop had to be assumed to be aggressive; but what of the British merchantman? Before anything else, her real identity and purpose had to be established. It was possible that the Red Ensign was a Chinese hoax, placed on board to prevent the Japanese firing on her. Or it might be that, unknown to the Japanese sailors, a war had been declared between China and Japan, and Britain had sided with China. If it was a genuinely British, genuinely peaceful ship, she could be let go; but if her purpose was belligerent, then British or not she would have to be tackled. Taking the simplest part of the problem first, *Naniwa* stopped and captured the Chinese ship; and then for four hours the mysterious merchant ship was investigated and negotiated with.

It turned out she represented the most worrying set of factors possible. Despite her name, *Kowshing*, she was indeed British, under Captain Galsworthy; but she was carrying ammunition, fourteen field-guns, and eleven hundred soldiers for the Chinese Army – and Galsworthy swore that Great Britain and Japan were not at war. As senior officer present, *Naniwa*'s captain had to solve the riddle. He was out of touch with Tokyo, but after the first fight of the day he was obliged to accept that a *de facto* state of war existed between his country and China, whether or not it had actually been declared. *Kowshing* was carrying Chinese arms and soldiers: but, if he sank her, he ran the awful risk of setting his country at war with Great Britain. 'I knew,' he said later, 'that upon my action depended the future of my country – perhaps its very life. And I was quite ready to answer with my own life.' He could not let *Kowshing* proceed to her destination or return to her port of departure, and so he tried to make her follow him back to Japan. But the English captain was in just as great a dilemma; under protest, Galsworthy had been preparing to obey, when 'the generals gave orders to the troops on deck to kill us if we obeyed the orders of the Japanese or attempted to leave the ship. With gestures, they threatened to cut off our heads, to stab or shoot us; and a lot of men were selected to watch us and carry out the order'. Yet *Naniwa* could not back off and let *Kowshing* go free, even if Britain were neutral. Letting her go, the Japanese captain believed, might establish a fatal precedent: if Japan were ever at war, neutral ships could openly carry enemy men and matériel; and not even Britain, with the greatest navy in the world, should be allowed that.

So the decision, not easily arrived at, was made: and Captain Galsworthy, prevented from gaining the safety of *Naniwa*, saw and heard her guns flash out. In five minutes *Kowshing* was down by the stern; in thirty she had sunk. *The Times* called it piracy, and British papers were full of the 'insult to the British flag' and demands for the summary punishment of *Naniwa*'s captain. But nothing happened: lawyers in Britain and America vindicated him, saying that his conclusions had been correct and that no rights of neutrality had been infringed. As quickly as it had arisen, the international heat cooled off; but less easy to accept was *Naniwa*'s action as the waters of the Yellow Sea closed over the *Kowshing*. All reports said the same: 'the Japanese gun-boat stayed after the *Kowshing* sank and fired on the boats and people in the water . . .' 'The Japanese fired from the masts on the people swimming. Three boats put off with loads. The Japanese sank two.' 'No attempt was made to rescue the drowning Chinamen.' 'The fact is that the swimming men were fired at from the Japanese man-of-war *and from the sinking ship*, the men on board the latter one probably having the savage idea that if they had to die, their brothers should not live either.'

In Japan, denials have always been emphatic, but all other first-hand evidence agrees that the *Naniwa*'s long-boat rescued only three men – all Europeans – and left the Chinese thrashing through the sea to sink or swim, speeding the conclusion with a liberal addition of lead.

It happened; whether it should have happened is another question, never answered to universal satisfaction. On the one side is the ancient maritime custom that ships fight ships, not men, and that if circumstances permit, a victorious captain should rescue the crew of a sinking enemy vessel. On the other side is the fact that to take on board such a large number of very belligerent prisoners, and to have transported them back to Japan, would have been highly risky at best; that these were soldiers, not sailors, who had prevented Galsworthy from carrying out *Naniwa*'s orders, and who therefore had to take the consequences; and that, if they had been landed and allowed to go free, they would have simply rejoined their units as enemies of Japan – as, indeed, the survivors did.

But the saddest and most absurd thing about all the fighting that day was that none of it need have happened at all. No formal state of war had existed when *Tsi-yuen* charged the Flying Squadron. The charge forced the Japanese officers and men to the instant, perfectly reasonable, assumption that war had been declared unknown to them, and they had responded accordingly. But all that *had* happened was that, at the crucial moment, *Tsi-yuen*'s steering gear had got stuck. From the second of encounter to the moment when she was able to move back towards her base under a false flag of surrender, *Tsi-yuen* had been out of control.

The war had begun by accident. It is impossible to say what would have happened if the Chinese steering-gear had worked properly: perhaps the two squadrons would simply have steamed past each other cautiously, as in fact had happened in a similar meeting twenty-six days earlier. The Japanese fired the first shot, as it turned out, but they fired in the belief that a torpedo had already been launched towards them. And, if the intentions of *Tsi-yuen*'s captain had been entirely peaceful, he could have signalled his distress, and certainly would not have been so quick to respond to the trigger.

In any event, the incident did not precipitate a war that would not otherwise have taken place; it merely brought to a head passions and politics that had been festering for many years, needing only a pin-prick to break out. And, for the first time, it brought onto the world stage (to loud Japanese applause) a certain seaman of decisive character and great skill – the captain of the *Naniwa*. His name was Togo Heihachiro.

This exceptional man not only became one of the greatest leaders of the Imperial Japanese Navy (and, indeed, one of the great naval leaders of history), but also came to personify the navy which he served throughout his long life.

Born in 1847 of a samurai family in the Satsuma clan, he was just old enough to remember the furore created by Perry's arrival in the secluded homeland. Better than that, though, he remembered the British Admiral Kuper and the bombardment of Kagoshima ten years after Perry, for he had been there. He had served the guns in one of the forts – manhandling the stone shot for the primitive weapons, wearing his classic samurai outfit with its two swords (which must have got in the way terribly), and waving his matchlock musket in furious futility at the warships in the bay below. No one, least of all a still-impressionable youth of sixteen, would ever forget that day of terror and humiliation, nor the night which followed, as the typhoon blew and the town burned. Perhaps more deeply than with his elders, the lessons of Kagoshima burnt themselves into Togo's brain: the first, that Japan, as she was, was impotent when confronted with Western technology; the second, that naval strength must dominate an island nation; and the third – which any samurai understood and respected – that, for the sake of national respect and credibility, vital principles had to be established, defended and upheld, even if they involved extraordinary, disproportionate expense. The bombardment of Kagoshima after Richardson's murder had shown this to be a British belief at least, and Togo must have remembered the example when, in sinking the *Kowshing*, he braved the risk of setting his country at war with Britain.

But, in making that decision, Togo had the advantage of knowing something about Britain at first hand. He had begun learning English in 1870, and in 1871 had been one of a dozen junior naval officers sent for further training in Britain.

Even in the last years of the shogunate, other such groups had been sent there, although from the shogun's point of view this was illegal. In 1863, five young men had been smuggled aboard one of Jardine, Matheson's trading ships – with the owners' connivance – and had made their way to Britain. One of them, Yamao Yozo, spent three years in Glasgow, studying in a local college and working as an apprentice in a Clydeside shipyard. His unofficial enterprise was rewarded when he returned to post-Restoration Japan: in 1871 he became the first president of the Imperial College of Engineering in Tokyo. Togo's journey to Britain that year was only the second one officially sanctioned, but over the next fifty years many more cadets and young officers were sent to Britain, and many of them did just as Togo himself did.

Travelling via Hong Kong, the Straits of Malacca, the Indian Ocean, Suez and Gibraltar – British colonial possessions at every step of the long journey – he arrived in Southampton. Compared to Japanese houses, every English town seemed to be composed of castles, so solid were the buildings of stone and brick. In one of those, the young sub-lieutenant settled down to study European history, mathematics and mechanical drawing, before joining the training ship HMS *Worcester*. Time passed happily for him aboard this elderly, permanently-moored relic – she had been built in 1819 – and, despite the arduous work of British naval training, Togo always looked back on those days at Greenhithe with affection and nostalgia, corresponding with and sometimes meeting his old companions and tutors. He served two years aboard the old hulk, under Captain Smith, whom he later reckoned to have been the best teacher he had ever had in any subject; and then, returning by way of Cape Horn, aboard HMS *Hampshire*, he made a round voyage to Australia. This was tuition of the hardest and most complete kind, and he absorbed it all. 'Not what you would call brilliant,' said Captain Smith, 'but a great plodder; slow to learn, but very sure of what he had learnt.' Perhaps the most important thing he learnt was that a small nation could hold her own in the world – could, indeed, control half the world, in one colossal empire. All that was needed was an efficient, disciplined navy.

However, the final aspect of Togo's British training – perhaps, retrospectively, the most accurate cameo of the birth of a navy – was nothing to do with the Royal Navy. Someone in Japan (probably Katsu Awa, who has been called the father of the Imperial Navy) conceived the idea that, in this nascent force, officers and ships should grow together. And so, in 1876, Togo had been ordered to Poplar, there to watch the building of that first

British-constructed Japanese warship, *Fuso*. From the north bank of the Thames, he could see across to the Naval College on the south bank, and beyond to the Observatory. And it would be hard to say which side of the river influenced him more deeply; for, by an international agreement signed in Washington in 1884, Greenwich became the prime meridian of the world, the point from which all nations and all navies would measure their positions. Sailing back to Japan in 1878 aboard *Fuso*'s sister *Hiei*, the thirty-one-year-old Togo knew pretty well every nut and bolt in the vessel; but, throughout his life, Greenwich represented world-wide naval might, greater than any individual ship or man.

Certain things like this stood out in his methodical memory. Shortly before his departure for Britain, he had seen action at sea in one of the last spasms of the Japanese Civil War. A part of that action had been a surprise raid by a rebel vessel on Imperial ships at anchor. Aboard one of the Imperial craft, Togo had been profoundly impressed by the tactical advantages offered by a surprise attack. The rebel leaders lacked only one thing – discipline. The Imperialists suffered from the same lack and, in later years, when he was the venerated Commander-in-Chief of the Imperial Navy, Togo commented regretfully on the 'weakness and naivety' of the force of its early days, saying that its men knew 'not how to win but how to die'.

He returned from Britain to a mundane but essential task, the surveying of parts of the Japanese coast. Two sites had been chosen for future naval centres, for, while Tokyo had become the national focus of administration and commerce, it was recognized that other places were of greater strategic importance. Thus, in the same way that Togo had seen *Fuso* grow on her blocks, he witnessed the very beginning of the ports of Kure – on the Inland Sea, just a few miles south-east of Hiroshima – and Sasebo.

Sasebo lies on Japan's south-western point. About 150 miles north-west of it, across the Straits of Tsushima, the southern Korean coast begins: a place for Japan and her navy to look with concern and apprehension. Southwards there were no nations of any consequence; eastwards, the United States had proved to be reasonably friendly, despite the terrors that Perry had caused; but north-westwards lay the two ancient, malignant powers of Tsarist Russia and Manchu China. And in between them and Japan lay Korea, the Land of the Morning Calm.

Traditionally, China claimed Korea as a tributary state. Equally traditionally, Japan denied that claim: Korea was simply in too close proximity to be the base for another powerful nation. Russia, geographically the largest nation on earth, was also a major naval power, but her tradition was one of severe handicap: along all the thousands of miles of Russian sea-coast, there was no warm-water port free of ice the whole year round. Nosing southwards and eastwards, the giant nation was sniffing towards the warm waters around Korea.

Yet, to the still-inexperienced government in Tokyo, China was of more immediate concern. Six hundred years earlier, from Korean shores, Kublai Khan had launched his ill-fated fleet of a thousand ships, intent on the invasion of Japan. The fleet had been destroyed by a typhoon, acclaimed by the Japanese as a Divine Wind, a Kamikaze; nonetheless, he who ruled Korea could threaten Japan. And, while Japan could surely trust the gods to aid her in time of trouble, Perry and Kuper had shown that, in this modern nineteenth century, even the gods could use some help.

China's fleet had become an ominous threat, in tonnage far outweighing the Japanese Navy. From Peking, its corridor to the oceans was the Yellow Sea, bounded to the east by Korea. That alone would have been sufficient strategic reason for the Chinese to wish to keep Korea; but for them there was another reason – simple, but so deeply rooted it was almost unconscious, and therefore even more powerful.

For uncounted ages China had dominated the East, unchallenged leader of the yellow races; and, as always happens after long, easy supremacy, the Chinese had come to accept that dominion as a god-given right. Challenge was inconceivable; had it not been so, the Chinese might have taken the Tientsin Treaty of 1885 more seriously. This treaty confirmed Japan and China's agreement to notify each other before sending forces into Korea at any time; to permit the other to send an equal force; and to withdraw them simultaneously when the need was over. In 1894 the test of good faith came, and China failed it. There was insurrection in Korea; Chinese troops were called in; and, when notice was given to Japan, Korea was named once again – once too often – as a 'tributary state'.

The last straw is always, in itself, a trivial thing, and no one could count the number of domestic disputes, class quarrels and international wars which have begun from a silent implication, rightly or wrongly interpreted. The Chinese were probably doing no more than thoughtlessly using a customary form of words; but, to Japan, their implications were clear. Hegemony in the East remained where it had always been – with China; Japanese attempts at diplomacy were contemptible; her adoption of Western habits was at best misguided and at worst a betrayal of her race; and a threat to her security was a thing of no consequence.

Perhaps the Japanese were being over-sensitive. But it seemed a real enough threat to send the Imperial Navy's Flying Squadron, led by Vice Admiral Tsuboi Kozo and the future admirals Togo and Kamimura, off to Korea; and the *Tsi-yuen*'s faulty steering-gear made no real difference in the end. The war would have begun anyway, for by then the Japanese could see no other way to convince China that the way of the world was the way of the West, and that, on such a basis, Japan would soon be foremost in the East.

3

'These Bright Dreams, These Illusions'

'Japan is *not* a small country; it is one of the large countries of the world. Japan is not a weak country; it is one of the powerful countries of the globe. To make it out to be weak is to destroy the spirit of the people and to delight in servility. Is not this iron castle of ours and this impassable moat of ours made stronger by the wild waves and raging billows of the Red Sea and the Indian Ocean? Suppose by more or less violence we press the European and American powers; they positively can do nothing against us, if every one of their war-vessels and ships which cover the seas is indispensable for the safety of the mother country. . .'

In his room in Tokyo, the British Envoy Extraordinary Hugh Fraser read the hysterical article in the *Choya Shimbun* and reflected. Its language was extravagant, but its mood characterized much of Japanese public opinion. Treaties with Western nations were still, in 1891, unequal – foreigners in Japan were tried by their own laws, not by those of Japan. This and other signs of discrimination rankled deeply in Japan. Fraser considered that the changes wrought in Japanese society since the Restoration were interesting – the adoption of Western clothing, for example (although they often got it completely wrong, and in his opinion looked quite absurd, with top hats and straw sandals). Railways, usually an infallible index to modernization, were spreading over the country; telephones and the telegraph were slowly linking the various cities, and electricity was becoming available to subscribers in Tokyo. The army, modelled on the Prussian example, was much more efficient than ever before: the navy, too, which after a brief flirtation with French methods had wisely returned to learning from the Royal Navy. But it seemed unlikely to Fraser that any of these changes were more than skin-deep: the Japanese were quick to imitate, slow to innovate. Under the cosmetic alterations, Fraser believed the Japanese character remained essentially unchanged – jealous, proud, insular, militaristic. It seemed typical that their new constitution, promulgated in 1889, should be based, like the army, on the Prussian model; and that the War Minister and Navy Minister had to be chosen from amongst officers, not only independent of their civilian colleagues but also with direct access to the Emperor. Twenty years before, the right of the samurai to kill with impunity had been withdrawn, and in 1884 new titles of nobility had been transplanted from Europe; but the samurai kind and the samurai character remained. And, while that was so, Fraser believed there could be no revision of the original treaty with Britain.

Writing to his friend the Marquess of Salisbury, a once and future Prime Minister, Fraser said, 'It is true that Japan is a very strong country, although it may not be necessary to accept her own estimate of her strength to its fullest extent; that she is protected by the sea on all sides, is divided by thousands of miles of ocean from the stronger Powers, and contains a population of a distinctly war-like character. Although they have had little to do with foreign wars, I suppose no land on the globe has been so steeped in blood as Japan, or has so long or so barbarous a record of civil war in its history. The Japanese military and naval reserves have been concentrated since the deposition of the Shogun, and astonishingly well organized under European instruction. But whether the country would bear the brunt of a foreign war, or dissolve itself once more into anarchy under such a trial, is a question very difficult to answer. I hope it will never come forward in practical shape; but one cannot rely very confidently on the common sense of the Japanese. They are an attractive people on the whole, and have many good qualities; but they are eminently short-sighted, fierce, vain-glorious and excitable, and there is always danger of their committing a "coup de tête", doing childish wrongs, or giving childish provocation, in serious affairs.'

In the summer of 1894, against Fraser's advice, the Anglo-Japanese treaty was revised to give Japan effective equality with Britain in all things except tariff autonomy; that would come later. 'It had to be revised sooner or later,' *The Times* conceded, 'and the sooner it could be settled on terms affording even a fair prospect of a tolerable solution, the better for all parties concerned.' Britain was the first of the major powers to revise her treaty with Japan; the action was received as a major diplomatic triumph in Japan, and added greatly to the Japanese belief in British fairness. Nine days after the revised treaty was signed, *Naniwa* fired the opening shot of the Sino-Japanese War.

When the war broke out, Kabayama Sukenori had been a member of the Imperial Navy for exactly a decade, and was already Chief of the Naval General Staff. He was a Satsuma samurai, and a Vice Admiral – not because of any exceptional naval prowess, but because, before transferring to the navy, he had been a Major General in the army. In that Prussian-style organization, his training had been very different to what it would have been in the British-oriented navy, and he was typical of the hot-headed, seemingly unstable aggressionists whom Fraser deplored. And, in the tense days following the sinking of the *Kowshing*, he had more to do with the actual declaration of war than had any member of the Flying Squadron.

If war were declared, Japan faced the terrifying possibility of fighting on two major fronts at once, for the Minister in St Petersburg had reported to Tokyo that the imponderable weight of Russia might well come in behind China. In that case, the Imperial Japanese Navy would find itself caught between the Chinese fleet in the Yellow Sea – which by itself was believed to be far superior to the Imperial Navy – and the Russian Asiatic Fleet in Vladivostock.

The Emperor agreed to be advised by the Prime Minister; the Prime Minister chose to be advised by his military leaders; the leaders of army and navy gathered to debate a future which became more frightening with each word spoken; and as they discussed, cautiously and apprehensively, a war which instinct told them they could not win and for which they would be held responsible, Kabayama listened with scorn and spoke with sarcasm. Using informal, disrespectful words, he said, 'Can you gentlemen be talking with any hope of victory?' They were not; their fears were real, and they believed them to be realistic. Kabayama left the group in silence, and with one other man went to the Prime Minister and announced a 'unanimous decision' for war.

At 6.30 a.m. on 17 September 1894, Admiral Tsuboi's First Flying Squadron arrived off the shores of Haiyang, a small island in the centre of Korea Bay, the northern part of the Yellow Sea. Since the sinking of the *Kowshing* six weeks earlier and the skirmish before it, they had seen nothing at all of the Chinese fleet. Unknown to them, the Chinese ships had been ordered not to cross a line between the Shantung promontory and the mouth of the Yalu river – in other words, they were confined to the north-western corner of the Yellow Sea. At the same time, Tsuboi and the rest of the Imperial Navy had been occupied in convoying troops into Korea, operating along the Yellow Sea's eastern side; so to each fleet the sea appeared to be empty of enemies.

The Imperial Navy was not popular at home. The army, passionately proud of its traditional samurai role as the showcase of Japanese military strength, sneered at the sister force and complained of the amounts of iron and steel it claimed. Politicians baulked at its regular requests for more money, and very few of the general public understood the strategic principles it represented. On the other hand, everyone understood, in a deeply-ingrained and emotional way, the fighting value and prestige of an efficient army.

Reacting against this dissatisfaction, Admiral Ito Yukyo, Commander-in-Chief of the Navy, itched with impatience to show what his ships could do. Like Captain Togo of the *Naniwa*, Ito had been a youth at Kagoshima, beating a drum to encourage the others. Now, as an adult, he was sure his ships had a greater part to play than merely nursemaiding ungrateful soldiers across an empty sea. One fear had been allayed by Russia's eventual decision not to join in the struggle; Vladivostock was quiet, which was a relief. But so was Wei-Hai-Wei, the base of the Chinese fleet; and that was distinctly irritating.

A rumour, the slightest hint of a scent, reached Ito just after he had completed another shepherding operation on the Taidong river. Someone said (but no one could confirm) that Chinese ships were landing troops only a hundred miles away, on the eastern bank of the Yalu. The chances of getting confirmation were slim, but Ito needed none; leaving ten men-of-war (including two whose names would become famous, *Yamato* and *Musashi*) to aid the troops on shore, he set off with a dozen other vessels to sweep Korea Bay.

The ships were divided into two squadrons: Tsuboi's Flying, with its usual four, *Yoshino*, *Takachiho*, *Naniwa* and *Akitsushima*; and Ito's Main, with eight ships, including *Fuso* and *Hiei* – the very ships which the Chinese ambassador in Britain had toasted with the hope that they would 'never fire a shot except as an ally of China'. When built, they had been the most powerful cruisers in the world; now, twenty-seven years later, they were feeling their age. They could manage 12 knots each, panting along at full steam, but they were quite unable to go any faster. Potentially this was hazardous: the rest of the fleet could do 16 knots at least, and in the Flying Squadron 19 knots was possible, while *Yoshino*, at her full speed of 23 knots, could leave all the others trailing. But even *Fuso* and *Hiei* were not the weakest links; those ignominious positions were filled by the little *Akagi*, a gun-boat of 612 tons, and the *Saikyo*, 1,652 tons. The *Saikyo* was not even a warship, but a merchantman converted by the addition of a few guns. Admiral Ito would have been quite happy to have left her on troop duty, but he could not, for her commander was none other than the bellicose Kabayama. Since he had transferred from the Army, he was, despite his rank, relatively inexperienced at sea, and he flatly refused to stay out of any action, or to transfer to another, faster ship where he would not be in command.

At a speed dictated by the slowest vessels, 38,500 tons of Japanese shipping moved across Korea Bay, hoping to encounter the enemy. But, as the official report said, they 'did not by any means anticipate such a great battle as actually took place'.

Dawn on 17 September promised a beautiful day: the sky was the clear, pale blue of autumn, the sea almost completely calm, ruffled only by the lightest of breezes. Through the gathering light the ships approached Haiyang island: it lay on the starboard bow, gently illuminated by the first rays of the rising sun. In any one of its bays and inlets, an alien warship could be sheltering, even preparing for ambush, and every possible place of concealment was cautiously investigated. There was nothing, no deception in the island's air of somnolent tranquillity, and – perhaps somewhat disappointed – Admiral Ito gave the order to alter course towards Talu, an island roughly north-east of Haiyang and only a few miles from a known centre of enemy activity, the mouth of the Yalu river.

A little past nine o'clock Haiyang fell astern. For two and a half hours the fleet steamed onwards. Above and behind the ships, a dark cloud trailed up from their funnels; and then, far ahead, a second cloud appeared.

The fleets sighted each other at 11.40, the twelve Japanese ships matched by twelve Chinese. Ito put his vessels into line ahead; Ting, the Chinese admiral, had been surprised at anchor, and was only able to form a very ragged line abreast. Already the Japanese had an advantage, and, observing from *Yoshino*'s bridge in the vanguard of the fleet, Admiral Tsuboi could recognize his enemy and some further advantages. All the approaching craft were slower than his own – the fastest were two protected cruisers, *Ching-yuen* and *Chih-yuen*, which at their best could only manage 18 knots. The average tonnage of the Chinese fleet was much less than that of the Japanese; only two of the Chinese ships were over 3,000 tons. But those two were the great battleships *Ting* and *Chen*, built in Stettin, each armed with four giant 12-inch Krupps guns, and each displacing an impressive 7,335 tons – 80% larger than *Yoshino*, Japan's largest warship.

Togo, holding station as rearguard of the Flying Squadron and fourth in the neat, professional Japanese line ahead, knew exactly who and what he was about to fight. Three years earlier, in the summer of '91, this North China Fleet had paid an official visit to Yokohama, flaunting its formidable battleships. Togo had been aboard *Ting*, and had met her namesake admiral. Neither had impressed him. Admiral, officers and men seemed lacking in discipline; as for the ship, her powerful 12-inch guns were dirty, and had washing hanging over them. Togo inspected the ship in detail, and declared, 'I am not afraid of that wonderful Chinese warship. Guns are among the most important things aboard our ships. The Chinese seem more concerned about their laundry.'

At 12.03 the Japanese Imperial standard, a gold chrysanthemum on a red ground, was broken out: let battle commence. This was not the order to fire, but to prepare for firing. The battle which commenced at 12.03 was a battle of nerves. The fleets were still out of range of each other, but converging at a combined speed of 17 knots. As the distance shrank, the minutes stretched into what must have seemed the longest hour in many lives.

The Chinese nerve snapped first. At 12.45 Ting gave the order. Six thousand metres – nearly four miles – away, Ito, Tsuboi and Togo saw the flash of flame and the blast of smoke from a 12-inch muzzle; a moment more and they heard the shriek of the shell; another moment and they saw and heard the harmless splash as the first shot of battle fell inevitably short.

Instantly the entire Chinese line opened up, all forward guns squalling in an irregular cacophony, and all shots short. Not a single shot came from the Japanese line; instead, maintaining a precise distance from each other, the

First Flying Squadron increased speed to 14 knots. Ito's hunters, professionally trained for years for this moment, had found their prey and were closing for the kill.

The battle lasted five hours, and was only stopped by darkness. In those five hours, ninety Japanese were killed and over 200 wounded. No Japanese ships were lost. Chinese casualties numbered nearly a thousand. Of those, about 700 were deaths, and they were mostly by drowning, for five of the twelve Chinese ships were gone.

However, the bland statistics hide the horror and confusion that the battle brought to almost every ship. They hide the fire aboard the Chinese *Lai-yuen*, which 'burnt every scrap of woodwork in the ship', and, making the vessel glow nearly white-hot, roasted men to death; they hide the fate of her sister *King-yuen*, which, according to a Japanese account, 'began to roll very much indeed – first very heavily over one way, and then very heavily over the other way; she continued rolling like that, and one time she rolled and did not come back'. They hide the 300 hits on the *Ting*, the 400 on her sister *Chen*, and the single 12-inch shell which struck the Japanese *Matsushima*. It exploded some spare ammunition and created such heat that the uniforms, beards and hair of the crew burst into flames. The captain of *Tsi-yuen*, the only vessel which had faced the Japanese before, was so terrified that he turned tail and ran – or as the *North China Herald* said after, 'distinguished himself by his devotion to the white feather'. In his flight to Port Arthur, on the southern tip of China's Manchurian Liaotung peninsula, he rammed another Chinese ship, and for 'his villainous example' his 'head was promptly sheared off' when he entered the safety of the port.

Both sides claimed the victory. 'We hear that Our combined squadrons fought bravely in the Yellow Sea and obtained a great victory,' said the Emperor Meiji, 'and We perceive that their power will command the enemy's seas. Deeply appreciating the services of Our officers and men, We are delighted with the extraordinary results they have obtained.' At the same time, the Chinese ships that made it to Port Arthur had their guns draped in red – except for those of the *Tsi-yuen* – to celebrate success. But the real national mood was shown by a report in the *China Mail* of Hong Kong.

'One thing was evident at Port Arthur above all else,' it said, 'that is, that the officers and sailors did not seem very anxious to get their ships refitted for sea. For more than a week after the fight the wreckage was allowed to lie about, and aboard the *Ting* a decomposed body was discovered nearly a fortnight after. And the *Ting* is one of the crack ships of the Chinese Navy! Nothing more disgusting or likely to knock the heart out of a man could be imagined. The vessels that were lost might have been saved had it not been for cowardice and want of discipline.'

Interest all around the world was high: the political, technical, tactical and strategic lessons were fascinating and legion, for with the Pax Britannica still generally in force, there was usually little chance of any practical assessment of new naval theories, new naval building, or new political balances at sea. In Britain, Fred T. Jane, the founder of the celebrated *Jane's Fighting Ships*, was impressed by 'the astonishing amount of hitting that all these ships seem to have been able to stand' and concluded that mere penetrating shells were virtually useless: they had to be exploding ones if they were to achieve any real destructive power. He also dismissed the fear of fire in action as 'grossly exaggerated', reporting that the Japanese, 'one and all, say that they had no trouble with fire at Yalu'. Stemming from the typically Japanese trait of playing down set-backs, this was simply not true, although the Chinese had suffered more severely with their great quantities of decorative woodwork and inflammable paint. Even more characteristic of the prevailing mood of scientific detachment, though, was Jane's candid regret that not all the results wished for were available. The three largest Japanese guns had something wrong with them in the battle, 'and the consequence was that two fired about once each, and the third about once an hour. It is unfortunate that these guns did not secure at least one fair and square hit – the data of it would have been extremely valuable'.

Armchair authorities agreed it had not been a 'perfect' battle; tactical mistakes had been made on both sides. Ito, in his diagonal approach across the Chinese bows, had clearly expected Ting to turn to port, which would have put the two fleets in line ahead in opposite directions. For whatever reason, Ting had not done so. Some people said it was because his line abreast was so untidy, nothing much could be done with it; others said he had not yet learned about a line ahead. It may be that he held his formation, unsatisfactory as it was, because his ships had greater fire-power forward than laterally. But in the six weeks since the *Kowshing*, the Chinese fleet had not exercised at all, while the Japanese had done so constantly; and, in the long moments when Ito's starboard flank was exposed to Ting's forward batteries, Chinese fire control was so inefficient that they lost their temporary advantage. The Chinese advance came close to breaking the Japanese line and, had it done so, they could have swept through and around the Japanese ships; but they appear to have been working to a pre-arranged plan, for no signalled Chinese orders were made during the fight, and, disorderly from the start, their scrappy line became more and more disorganized. By contrast, Ito managed to recover from the weakness caused by crossing the enemy's line abreast, and, with swift signalling, had separated the Flying Squadron from the Main. The Main had doubled around the starboard wing of the Chinese line and had run down its back, while the

Flying Squadron had done a complete circle to port and had run down the Chinese bows. In other words, the two squadrons sandwiched the Chinese fleet between them. Successful as the final statistics showed this to be, it could have been still more successful; the North China Fleet *could* have been swept from the seas if the Japanese had been prepared to fight on as dusk fell.

The captain of the *Chen-yuen* was assisted by an American adviser, Commander Philo N. McGiffin, whose 7,300-ton battleship was one of the survivors. After it was all over, McGiffin wrote a racy account of the day, from which it seemed that he had been required not merely to assist the Chinese captain but to do his job for him.

'Commodore Lin was our captain,' said McGiffin, 'but he was not to be seen at Yalu. Clearing for action was more than he could stomach even – the fright of anticipation nearly killed him . . . I kept hearing a curious noise going on below me in the conning tower every time there was a lull in the firing, and going down there after a while, I came an awful header over Commodore Lin, lying flat on his stomach, cursing and grovelling, and praying to Buddha for all he was worth. He belonged to the Mandarin class, and they are all an effete race of arrant cowards.'

Able to see the Chinese weaknesses with his own eyes, McGiffin found the Japanese decision to break off action 'something of a mystery; had they stayed with us a quarter of an hour more, our guns would have been silent and the ships defenceless'. It was true, and a total victory would have shortened the war; but Ito was not to know that, after firing 138 rounds of heavy ammunition, the *Chen-yuen* had only twenty rounds left, and no smaller ammunition at all. Considering that, for most of his men, this was the very first battle they had fought in, Ito was right to feel they had done magnificently, and quite enough for one day.

Nit-picking aside, observers around the world agreed with him, and with the Emperor. In America, the redoubtable Captain A. T. Mahan announced that, on this showing, Japan would soon rank with the naval nations of Europe, and with America as well. In London *The Times* was scathing about the Chinese naval authorities, who, it said, 'appear to have formed their plans without the smallest appreciation of the elementary principles of warfare . . . it seems very doubtful if they can ever recover the advantages they have forfeited by ineptitude in counsel and delay in action'. And, even more bluntly, the *Deutsche Heeres Zeitung* – the *German Army Newspaper*, a powerful voice of Prussian militarism – assessed the Yalu as 'the most important event in the conflict between Japan and China. It secured to the Japanese Navy the supremacy in the Yellow Sea at the very outset'.

It did not, however, end the war. That came exactly seven months later, on 17 April 1895, when representatives of China and Japan signed the Treaty of Shimonoseki. By then the little island nation had won a series of stunning victories on land and sea against the vast, ancient empire – victories which were so completely unexpected to everybody else that countries around the world suddenly had to view Japan with a new and unfamiliar feeling of respect. On land, the army had taken Korea completely; then soldiers had been ferried across to the Manchurian peninsula of Laiotung, where two of the three major Chinese naval bases lay. The first, Talien Bay, was captured without a fight, and for the first time the Imperial Navy had a safe base on that side of the sea. The second was smaller but far stronger, and, guarding the mouth of the Gulf of Chihli, much more important. Port Arthur offered several square miles of harbour, and although it needed constant dredging it was surrounded by extremely good natural defences. Landward approaches were protected by two concentric arcs of rocky hills and mountains, while to seaward the port had only one entrance, and that a mere 250 yards wide. According to the Belgian representative in Tokyo, 'this fortress is fortified according to all the rules of modern military science, and with any enemy other than the Chinese would have been impregnable for many months, and a very long siege would have been necessary'. By itself, no nautical attack could have taken the place, but one day of fierce fighting – 21 November 1894 – in a combined army–navy operation scored a spectacular success. As an Italian writer, Zenone Volpicelli (writing, significantly, under the Russian pseudonym of 'Vladimir'), said shortly after:

'The foreigners in the Far East had been inclined to discount the Japanese victories. These had been won in obscure corners of Korea and the Chinese frontier, and they suspected exaggeration on the Japanese accounts. They also considered that China had not had time to put forth her whole strength, and imagined that with a few months of preparation the Chinese could repulse any Japanese attack on such a formidable fortress as Port Arthur. All these surmises were refuted by a day's fighting.'

Now it became apparent that Admiral Ito might have been too cautious at the Yalu. The Chinese fleet, patched up, inactive and unwilling to fight, was still a fleet in being, and had slipped over the Gulf of Chihli to its third base, just over a hundred miles south-east of Port Arthur: Wei-Hai-Wei, on the Shantung peninsula of the eastern China coast.

The harbour at Wei-Hai-Wei was big: six miles by three – eighteen square miles of deep water. But it faced north-east, and would be nothing but a large, exposed, uncomfortable mooring if it were not for an island in the middle of its entrance. This island, Liu-Kung, is about two miles long; behind it, a fleet could ride out the heaviest weather easily. The channels on either side of the island were protected by mines and nine-inch-thick steel hawsers; and Ting remained there, hidden, defended and trapped, for three months – from 18 November '94 to 11 February '95, when, facing total defeat, he drank an overdose of opium, and died.

The battle for Wei-Hai-Wei was arduous in the extreme, for defenders and attackers alike. For two weeks the Imperial Navy blockaded the harbour entrances – two weeks of the foulest possible weather, with prolonged blizzards, and days and nights of such intense cold that two crew-members actually froze to death at their posts. After the snow there had been nine days and nights of perpetual bombardment, accompanied by mine-sweeping operations, the cutting of part of one of the great steel booms, and daring night raids by torpedo-boats into the harbour itself. Torpedoes were still a relatively novel weapon, unreliable and untrustworthy; even if they ran true, they could still fail to explode, and these raids were considered so desperate that Japanese commanders resigned themselves to death, saying, 'Our boats and our bodies are the enemy's.'

For the Japanese sailors, the entire experience was a nightmarish and extremely hazardous test of seamanship. For Ting and his crews, hemmed in by the external blockade and by their own chosen defences as well, it can only have been a hell of icy despair. However hard they fought back – and they fought very hard – they must have known very quickly that defeat was inevitable.

Admirals Ito and Ting had actually been friends for many years before the war, and their mutual respect and liking were not altered by politics. Ito earnestly invited Ting to give up and come and live in Japan; and, after the surrender and Ting's suicide, Ito's fleet saluted the dead man. According to his last wish, Chinese survivors were allowed to leave in safety, to find their fate at home. Ting's corpse, borne upon one of his own ships, was sent in state to the neighbouring port of Chefoo; and, as it left Wei-Hai-Wei on its last voyage, the entire Imperial Fleet lowered their flags to half-mast, and fired the Admiral's salute.

4

'A Great Feeling of Exhilaration'

Victory in the Sino-Japanese War brought a great wave of pride and excitement to the Japanese nation. The army had lived up to tradition; in the three major battles of the Yalu, Port Arthur and Wei-Hai-Wei, the navy had brilliantly demonstrated its ability, and basked in the glow of far higher public status than before. At last it seemed that Japan had done something to win the respect of the West; but the painful process of jumping several centuries at once was not over. In 1873 in Berlin, Iwakura Tomomi was told by Bismarck that 'the only way for a country like Japan is to strengthen and protect herself with all her own might, and set no reliance on other nations . . . When international law is not to a nation's advantage, it is ignored, and resort is made to war'. Iwakura was chief adviser to the Emperor Meiji, and was the ear of Japan in Europe. He listened carefully to Bismarck and reported faithfully to the Emperor, and, had he not died in 1883, no doubt would have rejoiced loyally in the victory over China. But then he would have also shared in the shock, the disillusion and the disgraceful national shame which came immediately afterwards, for Germany (Bismarck's Germany no longer, but Germany all the same) was party to the notorious Triple Intervention of 1895.

Even before the Treaty of Shimonoseki had been ratified, France, Germany and Russia stepped forward together and 'advised' Japan that 'in the interests of Peace' one major part of the treaty should be dropped. Japan could keep Formosa and the Pescadores Islands, and claim her cash indemnity from China; but she should not, in fact could not, keep the Laiotung Peninsula – that key tongue of land with the harbours of Port Arthur and Talien Bay. In case Japan should try and keep the peninsula, as China had agreed, a dark reminder was given of the Russian fleet in Vladivostock. Japanese troops in Korea could be cut off from the homeland and, if that were insufficient, the three countries together would not flinch from a joint, direct attack. Thirty thousand Russian troops were already massed on the North Chinese border; all that was needed was the word and they would be in Korea, heading for Japan.

The cause of this sudden concern for the peace of the inhabitants of Laiotung was essentially Russia's passionate obsession with the search for a warm-water haven. Port Arthur was the one they had been working towards, and they were not prepared to see it snatched from under their noses by a presumptuous, upstart nation – especially one whose inhabitants were not only small but yellow as well. Any nation behaving so would have been bad enough in Russian eyes; but colour and stature became convenient pegs on which to hang malice and ambition. Egging on his cousin Tsar Nicholas, Kaiser Wilhelm produced a widely-publicized allegorical drawing in which improbably heroic European figures, dressed in a half-Roman, half-Viking manner, gazed with foreboding towards a distant Buddha. Thus, although Buddha must be the most peaceful of philosophers, the bogey of the Yellow Peril was created. Wilhelm's fear, widely shared in Europe, was probably genuine; but he had another reason to interfere in Far Eastern politics. Russia frustrated in the East would be more than likely to turn its attention westwards – to Germany – and the third intervening country, France, was already an ally of Russia. The two of them could have sandwiched Germany as neatly and effectively as Admiral Ito had sandwiched Ting's ships. The Germans therefore saw it as politic to join what most Japanese leaders saw as an unnatural alliance, and, in so doing, to deliver an extremely unwelcome practical version of Bismarck's theoretical lesson. Superior force, or its threat, could be used 'when international law is not to a nation's advantage'.

The Japanese had found themselves sucked willy-nilly into the whirlpool of European power politics and, faced with potentially insuperable opposition, could only give way with as much public grace as possible. The Europeans made and won their point; Japan, it seemed, had been successfully kept in her place.

But what none of the three intervening Powers understood in the slightest was how deeply their intervention offended and humiliated Japan. It was not simply a question of lost land and harbours won in fair fight; far worse was the national disgrace of being shown up, to themselves and the whole world, as weaklings who could still not hold their own. A national disgrace could only be reversed by a conscious national resolve. The interventionists would have understood this as an idea; but they would not have believed that Japan could actually do it. Yet, from the time the Russian admiral Stephen Makaroff flung his sword over the chart of Port Arthur and exclaimed 'Japanese? Never!', all Japan began to work towards one goal: to reclaim what it had won fairly and lost unfairly – a position of honour in the eyes of the world.

Empire, by definition, must include extensive territorial possessions. For an island, that means land beyond the seas, which in turn means a navy – a navy stronger than anything which can come within its sphere of influence. The logic was simple, and the Imperial Japanese Navy drew great benefit from the Triple Intervention. The naval budget for 1891 was 9.5 million yen;

in 1895 it was 13.5 million; and in 1898 it shot up to 58.5 million, no less, because with casual hypocrisy the Russians had forced the Chinese to grant *them* a leasehold on Port Arthur. In quick succession, Germany established a naval base at Kaiochow, just down the coast from Wei-Hai-Wei; France did likewise, at Kwangchow on the southern Chinese coast; and so did Britain, at Wei-Hai-Wei itself, which poor Ting had defended to the death.

If there was any distinction between their own and the Russian occupation of Port Arthur, the Japanese found it so fine as to be invisible. What was clear was that one needed to be very cunning and very muscular indeed to survive in this interlocked modern world. In next to no time, four potentially hostile naval bases had been established in an area which should by then have held none. That, at any rate, was the Japanese view, and analysis of the possible threats produced a fairly clear result. France's interests lay mainly in the south. Germany's presence appeared to be genuinely commercial and non-belligerent. Britain, with a world-wide empire to maintain, was similarly most interested in protecting its trade lanes to the East, and yet would be unlikely to send many more warships eastwards for fear of exposing British home waters to France and Germany. By the same token, British defences at Kowloon, Hong Kong and Wei-Hai-Wei were unlikely to be depleted.

So, out of the four, only Russia seemed a realistic threat. But that carried with it a three-fold strategic complication: the fleet at Vladivostock, the new naval base at Port Arthur, and the old Dual Alliance with France. Trying to regain face by attacking that three-pointed pincer would be to invite the extinction of the Japanese Empire; much more subtlety was needed. The core of the problem was that, economically bound to the West now, Japan was still isolated politically; none of her treaties was an alliance. Once that had been perceived, a new strategy emerged. Arms alone were not enough; equally essential were allies and intelligence.

5

'Allies, Arms and Intelligence'

All three were pursued with the diligence and national conscientiousness that are characteristically Japanese. An unsigned article in the newspaper *Jiji Shimpo* stated the national objective.

'We must continue,' it said, 'to study according to Western methods... If new ships of war are considered necessary, we must build them at any cost. If the organization of our army is found to wrong, it must at once be renovated. If advisable, our whole military system must be entirely changed. We must build docks to be able to repair our ships. We must establish a steel factory to supply guns and ammunition. Our railways must be extended so that we can mobilize our troops rapidly. Our oversea shipping must be developed so that we can provide transports to carry our armies abroad. This is the programme we have always to keep in view.

'What Japan has to do now is to keep perfectly quiet, to lull the suspicions that have arisen against her, and to wait, meanwhile strengthening the foundations of her national power, watching and waiting for the opportunity which must one day surely come in the Orient. When that day arrives, she will be able to follow her own course, not only able to put meddling Powers in their places, but even, as necessity arises, meddling with the affairs of other Powers. Then truly she will be able to reap advantages for herself.'

The anonymous author was Hayashi Tadasu, later ambassador to Great Britain; and he rounded off the clear, ominous list of Japan's needs with a note which foretold his own greatest achievement:

'If the continental Powers are going to continue the Alliance against Japan in order to curb our just aspirations, to fulfil which we have poured out life and money, then we too must endeavour to ourselves make an alliance which shall counteract their machinations.'

The diplomatic community took notice of such statements. Baron d'Anethan, the portly, balding, walrus-moustached Belgian representative in Tokyo, wrote one of his frequent despatches home: 'One must not lose sight of the fact that Japanese statesmen, counting on the rivalry of England and Russia in the Orient, believe that Japan is capable of waging war against Russia – alone.'

The twentieth century began with an astonishing diplomatic coup: on 30 January 1902, the Anglo-Japanese Alliance was signed. Cautious and painstaking negotiations between the British Foreign Secretary Lord Lansdowne and Ambassador Hayashi had been going on for nine months, in utter secrecy, and perhaps no other single event epitomizes so aptly the changes brought by the new century. Less than ten years earlier in Honolulu, the captain of HMS *Champion* had been embarrassed to find he had no Rising Sun flag with which to salute a visiting Japanese cruiser; he had had to borrow an ensign from an American ship anchored close by. Now the two island empires were allies in an essentially naval partnership, a union of immense political and historical significance. For Japan, the signatures meant a huge gain in prestige and status: the world's greatest navy was taking the world's newest navy seriously. And the Japanese felt they deserved to be taken seriously.

When the veil of secrecy was lifted in February 1902 with simultaneous announcements in London and Tokyo, everyone interested (which meant the entire world) knew that this marked the real end of Japan's ancient isolation; and it marked the end of isolation for Britain too, that 'splendid isolation' which had been the hallmark of empire. Britain had not had a full-scale alliance with any nation for almost a century. If the British acceptance of alliance was, for Japan, promotion into the élite club of politically powerful nations, for Britain it was a kind of demotion, a recognition that her era of maritime world-dominance was slowly fading away. And although there was certainly a degree of sentiment involved – a sense of kinship between two class-based, imperialist societies lying off the shores of large continents, and the sympathetic understanding between a willing tutor and an apt pupil – neither side would have entered into the agreement if it had not brought mutual benefits. For both, those benefits were the containment of Russian power. Britain gained a strong lever in the struggle to maintain the 'open door' policy in China trade, a door which, since the Boxer Rebellion of 1900, Russian had been trying strenuously to close to any other country. For this reason, the Alliance won considerable sympathy, though no official support, from America. And the Japanese gained something much more immediately valuable to them: the effective neutralization of the Franco-Russian Dual Alliance. The entire text of the Anglo-Japanese Alliance was composed of only six articles. One of them stated that if either Britain or Japan became involved in a war in defence of its interests in China or Korea, the other party would remain neutral. But the next article declared that, if such a war began and either ally was opposed by two nations or more, then the other ally would fight as well.

It was perfectly clear which nations were meant – France and Russia. So, if Russia and Japan went to war, Britain would remain neutral; but if, calling on the Dual Alliance, Russia dragged France into a war, then Britain would join in too. And it would be out of the question for France to try and fight far away in the East, and at home in the Channel.

Thus the Dual Alliance was checkmated; and, when the Russian Foreign Minister Count Lamsdorf suggested a revival of the Triple Intervention group, the German government replied truthfully (but quite unhelpfully, for the Russians) that its Eastern interests were purely commercial. The very idea of exposing its poorly-defended sea-lanes to attacks by the Royal Navy was absurd; moreover, to revive the Triple group might well prompt the United States to join Britain and Japan formally, which would create an exceedingly dangerous world-wide division. The German response was polite but very firm: in case of a Russo-Japanese war, Germany would remain strictly neutral.

It had taken slow, careful, patient work, but Japan had turned the diplomatic tables on Russia: now it was the Tsar's empire, not the Mikado's, which was politically isolated.

Lord Lansdowne, uncertain whether to trust Hayashi and suspecting correctly that similar negotiations were going on at the same time between Russia and Japan, had needed a great deal of persuading. Eventually King Edward VII intervened, indirectly but personally, to give Lansdowne the necessary impetus. Even so, the Alliance (which Hayashi called 'a great success for Japan') would have been even more difficult to achieve if Hayashi had not had the backing of an extraordinarily effective and widespread intelligence network. Quite simply, Hayashi probably knew much more about the British way of thinking and doing things than Lansdowne did about the Japanese, and this gave him a tremendous advantage. Parts of his knowledge he gathered himself, for he was a great Anglophile, and parts came to him through the Japanese intelligence network. 'Organization' would be too strong a word; the system was all the more effective for being largely unofficial. Its existence was one of the major reasons why Japan was able to transform so rapidly and thoroughly from a medieval to a modern state – and, indeed, why Japan since World War Two has been able to repeat that transformation, in the commercial rather than the military world. The idea – nowadays, sadly, rather old-fashioned – that every traveller is an ambassador for his country, had a counterpart in Japanese tradition: every traveller was an agent for his country.

In the early fourth century BC, the Chinese strategist Sun Tzu wrote his book *Ping Fa* – The Strategy of War. In the mid twentieth century AD, the great military historian Basil Liddell Hart said this book was 'the concentrated essence of wisdom on the conduct of war'. The Japanese had already held that opinion for two thousand years. One of the maxims it contained was: 'If you know yourself and know the enemy, you can win in battle . . . to defeat the enemy psychologically is the superior strategy; to defeat the enemy militarily is the inferior.' By the beginning of this century, espionage in Eastern and Western traditions was regarded quite differently: in the West, it was either romantic, or immoral and disreputable, though necessary; in the East, it was a patriotic and honourable profession, if not an honest one. (The Japanese *Who Was Who* contains the frank entry 'Ishikawa, Goichi: Spy. Born 1866 . . .') As far as the outer world was concerned, Japan under the shoguns totally forgot this principle, but domestically they never forgot it. Spying in the shogunate became a part of daily life, and at some point the natural extension occurred: when conducted by every household on its neighbours, the gathering of militarily valuable intelligence mingled with ordinary curiosity, and the two became virtually indistinguishable.

After the Restoration, reading Sun Tzu became obligatory in the Imperial Navy, as well as in the Army, and the English Japanophile Alfred Stead wrote: 'Everywhere throughout the world, the naval officers, attached to Legations or not, keep watch upon naval developments and write minute reports to their Government. All these lessons learned thoroughly are stored up ready for the time when necessity for action shall arise, when they will help greatly to insure successful plans of campaign.'

Espionage, though, was understood in the widest possible sense – the gathering of information, not necessarily for sinister purposes. After the Restoration, part of the Five Articles Oath for the forces stated specifically that 'knowledge shall be sought throughout the world'. And so it was; every Japanese abroad learned as much as possible about the strange world beyond the homeland, knowledge which made it less strange and easier to cope with, even if it was still difficult to understand. The customs and habits of other nations were just as useful to know about as were their technologies, and everything that could be observed – from ships' boilers to table-manners – *was* observed, remembered, and reported to an authority back home. In doing this, even the humblest student could be confident that he was fulfilling a patriotic duty; for the more important part of the oath was the reason for gathering knowledge. Again, it was specific: 'Knowledge shall be sought throughout the world, so as to strengthen the foundations of Imperial Rule.'

It is perhaps inconceivable that such a command could be accepted, taken seriously, and acted upon by an entire nation. But in imperial Japan at the beginning of the century, the Emperor and the nation were indivisible; loyalty to the Emperor was not only undeviating but was also completely conscious, and, without that, modern Japan might never have existed. Only their intense, pragmatic nationalism enabled the Japanese to take on the world on its own terms, and to prevent their islands being conquered, colonized or cut up by the Western nations. It had happened in China and

India; the only reason it did not happen in Japan was that every Japanese believed, as naturally and easily as breathing, that his country was something very special indeed; that to be born Japanese was an honour he should always live up to, a privilege and a blessing he should always try to repay; and that the best way to fulfil the obligations of his fortunate birth was to serve and obey the divine Emperor. Once again, imperial guidance was specific, given in one of the Emperor Meiji's most important utterances – the Rescript to the Army and Navy in 1882.

'Our Forces have been commanded by the Emperors in person from time immemorial. Since the Emperor Jimmu, in personal command of the troops of Otomo and Monomobe, put down the rebels of Chugoku and ascended the throne, more than twenty-five centuries have elapsed. During that interval, our military organization has undergone frequent changes, in accordance with the changes of the times.

'. . . We undertook to reform our military organization and to extend the influence of our country, and now, after fifteen years, We have permanently established the Army and Navy on their present bases.

'The supreme command of the Army and Navy is held always by Ourselves, while its detailed functions are entrusted to you. That command in chief shall remain always in Our hand, and never be put in yours. This principle shall therefore be transmitted to Our posterity and held inviolable, namely, that the Emperor alone wields the great civil and military powers. You will, We trust, never fall into the errors of past ages.

'Soldiers, sailors, We are your Commander-in-Chief. Therefore We regard you as Our limbs, and you, on your part, will look upon Us as your head, and thus our mutual relations will be ever closer. Soldiers, sailors, it rests entirely upon your faithful discharge of your duties whether, by guarding our country, We can requite the grace of Heaven and the benevolence of Our forefathers.'

The Rescript continued with the instructions on conduct, and on the first virtue, loyalty. This was 'the chief duty of the soldier and sailor. While there can be no man in this land destitute of the feeling of patriotism, such a feeling is essentially a part of the duty of a soldier or sailor, for without it he is useless to his country . . . Remember always that the defence of a country, and the maintenance of its prestige, depend entirely on its military and naval forces, and that in proportion as they remain efficient or deteriorate so will the whole nation flourish or decay. You must never allow yourselves to be led astray by public controversies or influenced by politics, but you must be guided by loyalty alone. This is indeed your principal duty. Keep well in mind that your duty outweighs death itself as much as a mountain outweighs a feather. Never allow your good name to be tarnished by any violation of principle.'

Then there were exhortations to fidelity, conscientiousness, simplicity and frugality in habits, and courage. But most important after loyalty were obedience and courtesy: 'Soldiers and sailors must be courteous in their demeanour . . . juniors must obey their seniors while those of lower rank must obey those set over them, remembering that in so acting they do but obey Our own direct commands.

'. . . And thus all ranks shall be united harmoniously into one body in the service of their country. If no decorum, no respect towards superiors, no consideration for inferiors, and hence no bond of unity, exist among soldiers and sailors, not only are they plague-spots on the army and navy, but also they are traitors to their country.'

The full Rescript in English is only about 2,000 words long, but it is one of the most important single documents in the history of the Imperial Navy, and hence in the history of modern Japan before 1945. All naval cadets learned it by heart, with its clumsy flattery, its religious overtones, its explicit demands and its final, implicit threat; and, one and all, they did their best to live up to it, accepting it in its entirety as the product of a man better than themselves, yet obscurely related to them – a man descended from gods; a man who embodied the Land of the Gods, their own homeland; a man and a land in whose service no duty was too onerous, nor any sacrifice too great.

British people began to admire Japan greatly, even if they had never visited the distant country: it was 'one of the pluckiest little nations in the world', said a typical absentee commentator. Alfred Stead, who not only visited but lived in Japan, retained a more detached view nonetheless, and said that 'the love of the Japanese for their country is a real, active force, which is shown in every action, and which colours all the national development'. The accurate, guarded comment hinted at a power that could be directed at will towards any chosen objective at any chosen time.

One of the places where this 'real, active force' was most clearly in evidence, even to a casual observer, was Etajima – the academy for naval officers. The surroundings are exquisite; the establishment was efficient. Established in 1888 on an island in the Inland Sea, the academy lies a few miles away from the naval port of Kure, which Togo had helped to create. Places like this make one understand why Japan, to the Japanese, is the land of the gods, and why the first gods of all gods chose Japan as their homeland. Water, mountains and trees predominate, as in all Japan's countryside. On a fine spring or summer day, the sun glittering on the sea, the sea studded with islands, the islands mountainous and covered with trees, the Inland Sea is a magnificent sight. In autumn the maples come into their own, fiery and vivid; and even in winter the mingled sea- and landscape has an oddly haunting beauty, muted and somewhat ghostly, when the rocky shores are covered and softened by mists. Looking across the bay from Kure, it is not immediately obvious that Etajima is markedly different from any of the hundreds of other islands which fringe Japan's coastline; its wooded hills and cultivated valleys, dotted with small concentrations of houses, are typical, though none the less attractive for that. The jetty is unpretentious – one wonders what each year's new cadets thought they were coming to. The island's secret is its shape, roughly that of a Y; the academy is located within the fork of the two arms. From the jetty, the road over the low hills in the island's centre is rather an anti-climax after the exhilarating sea-passage from Kure; the only really noticeable element is the heap of Mount Furutaka off to the north. The village of Etajima is similarly undistinguished; but that only makes the academy, when one arrives at its gates, the more impressive.

From the start, a new cadet approaching the wide parade-ground and classical Western-style buildings knew that he was someone special – not only a Japanese, but one picked from rigorous and highly-competitive nation-wide examinations to become part of the Emperor's foremost fighting arm: thirty, and sometimes over forty, youths between the ages of sixteen and nineteen applied for every vacancy in the academy. With few exceptions, they were products of the non-compulsory middle-school system; the exceptions were the rare enlisted men who had been able to pass the rigorous examinations. These went on for five days annually. The first day involved a stringent medical examination, which disposed of about half the applicants straight away – nothing less than perfect health would do, and even bad teeth could be enough to fail a candidate. The next three days contained a daunting series of written tests, on physics, chemistry, mathematics, geography, the histories of Japan, China, Europe and America, Japanese and Chinese classics, and the Japanese and English languages. Passing those, a candidate could still fail the ensuing oral interview if he spoke a dialect, or stammered; and, if he got through that, a character and reputation check by the police – not only on him, but on his whole family – might also fail him. He might even have got as far as the very gates of the academy, and still be refused entry, for at the gates there was a final medical, which sometimes weeded out an unlucky few more. Even so, the four years spent at Etajima were years of such strenuous physical training that one in ten of the new cadets – already paragons of fitness – had to leave before their course was over.

Once the cadet was securely within the walls of the academy, and assuming his health stood up to the arduous régime, he hardly left the place in all his four years. There were seven weeks of holiday each year – four in the summer, three in the winter – and one day off – Sunday – each week. During the annual vacations most cadets went home, where they very naturally relaxed completely – sleeping a great deal, enjoying home cooking, walking, fishing, and able (as one cadet put it) to 'accept a beautiful clear and silent influence from Nature'. It was the only chance they had; on Sundays, they were still restricted to the island. Some then would climb Mount Furutaka, 465 metres high, but the majority would use the eight hours of liberty to lounge in their clubs in the little town, dozing, listening to music or eating chocolate – luxuries denied them all the rest of the week.

Otherwise they were on the go sixteen hours a day, from 5.30 a.m. to 9.30 p.m. in the summer, 6.00 a.m. to 10.00 p.m. in the winter. Between those times, every day, they had about eight hours of class-work and three hours' hard exercise. Three hours were allotted for meals, and seventy minutes for free-choice activities, but everything else was done with the maximum of speed, discipline and efficiency. For instance, after reveille, the cadet was allowed a minute and a half to leap from his iron bed, strip it, fold the blankets in a neat pile and stand to attention. If he was slow or untidy, he might well be cuffed fairly hard and certainly had to repeat the process; but there was no further physical punishment – the disgrace of inefficiency was punishment enough. Regular discipline was stern, slaps and blows being common, and, more rarely, squads being made to stand to attention in sun, rain or snow for several hours at a stretch. But this was not much stricter than ordinary discipline in many Japanese homes and, if it was ever resented, incidents of insubordination were almost non-existent.

This was quite simply because the cadets were Japanese. From their early years, the habit of conformity had been inculcated into the young men – conformity to the family, their parents and grandparents, to the authorities of their home village or town, and on up through the social strata to the Emperor himself, and therefore to the nation and the gods. In the days of the shogunate, the ordinary Japanese conformed, or died on the edge of a samurai sword; and, if conformity came easily under those circumstances, it came willingly after the Imperial Restoration. Appreciative of the natural beauties of their homeland; profoundly aware that they were members of a people, and inhabitants of a land, of particular antiquity and benediction; conscious too that in the unquestioned social hierarchy they were at the beginning of a ladder that could lead to national, even imperial recognition and respect, few cadets were ever satisfied with doing less than their best. And each day they would read or hear again 'that in so acting they do but obey Our own direct commands'.

But even that is not enough explanation. Central to any account of the Imperial Japanese Navy must be these questions. Why was Japan after Perry able to overturn more than two centuries of her history, and able to create a good navy virtually overnight? Why was the Imperial Navy so victorious at first, so utterly defeated in the end? Why did its strategies first succeed magnificently, then fail miserably? Why could its men – epitomized, perhaps, by the Kamikaze pilots of World War Two – be so obedient that they would deliberately court death? And why, given that obedience and the specific imperial command that naval men should not become involved in politics, why were naval officers in the 1930s able to murder and assassinate senior officers and politicians, and then be publicly seen as heroes? To a Japanese it is enough to say, 'because they were Japanese'. There is no riddle, no inconsistency. To a Westerner it is not so obvious. Some explanation is needed of how the Japanese thought, and why they thought as they did; of how and why Imperial Navy thinking differed from civilian and military thinking.

In trying to understand the phenomenon of the Imperial Navy, in trying to answer these questions, one has to look at the dramatic events in its brief life not just as observable historical facts, but as keys to its viewpoint and mentality. Knowing something about the forces which formed the Japanese mind, a Westerner can review the old stories of victory and defeat, treachery, deceit and honour, and see them in a rather different light – from something approaching a Japanese point of view. For a Westerner to answer these questions properly and comprehend that point of view requires a certain leap of the imagination. And so it is probably better to edge delicately towards answers, as it were, rather than try and give them directly – to establish some of the basic roots of Japanese thinking, and especially naval thinking, and then, as the historical events unroll, to remember those roots. In that way it becomes possible to understand why an assassin may be a hero, deceit may be a virtue, and suicide the greatest good of all.

If one steps, then, for a little while into the mind of a typical cadet at Etajima in 1902, the 34th year of Meiji, one can see that there were three main areas which distinguished him from his counterpart in the West – society, service and strategy. All three were so interconnected that to separate them is artificial; but it makes their discussion easier.

He is seventeen or eighteen years old, neither a boy nor a man; but to a Western observer – his English teacher, for example – he sometimes seems astonishingly adult, and sometimes very childish, because when it is demanded of him (that is, most of the time), he is polite, diligent, conscientious, and very serious. But, when he can relax, he finds pleasure in simple, unsophisticated ways, and laughs a great deal, often at puerile jokes and situations; yet with a foreigner he is hardly ever completely relaxed and, rather than make an embarrassing linguistic mistake, will remain silent, unless social duty obliges him to speak. About some things he seems innocent and naive; he is very conservative; about his work, he is narrow-minded and dedicated to the point of obsession; if he is uncertain of what he is expected to do, he becomes tense, nervous and embarrassed; if he knows what he has to do, but does not know how to do it, he will do it all wrong rather than reveal his ignorance. He has a strong sense of patriotism, even of nationalism; he is much prouder than the average British or American youth of his country, and of being a member of it; he gives to his emperor a double dose of devotional fervour, combining in one a Westerner's emotional loyalty to the flag – the national symbol – and whatever the Westerner's symbol of God on Earth may be. He is very aware of his heritage.

His tenseness when uncertain, his concentration when directed, and his simplicity when relaxing, are all because he is permanently in debt to many people. He knows it, and he knows that some of the debts are ones he will never be able to repay. The debts are not financial, but moral and spiritual, and that makes them all the harder to live up to; indeed, there are eighteen different kinds of debt, ranging from debts to his own name – the protection of his personal honour – to unpayable debts to his parents and, beyond them, to the Emperor. They are so precise and universal, these debts, that they could be tabulated; and he knows them all, and is always aware of them.

The debts, and the duties to repay or attempt to repay them, have always been there – many of them he incurred by the simple honour of being born Japanese. But he did not know about them until he was six or seven, and from then on he began to learn about them in the most painful way – by neglecting a duty, or offending against a code of behaviour, and being made to feel deeply ashamed. Before that age he was able to do very much as he liked, playing with other children, an unconcerned but full member of the community. Bit by bit, he had to take on his obligations; and, if he failed in any of them, his parents warned that the world would laugh at him. They would say this in those exact words; and, if the child broke some rule badly or repeatedly, the punishment could be worse than physical – he could be rejected by the family, perhaps having to live somewhere else. This would only be temporary, for ten days or so, but the sense of loss was profound, and so was the sense of shame.

The society was founded on shame, rather than on guilt, as the ultimate moral sanction, and, because the social system was universal, the sanction was remarkably effective. The young Japanese would be extremely sensitive to slights or insults, real or imagined, and felt honour-bound to redress them. This was so well understood by everyone that, even if it led to violence, such violence was not reckoned to be aggression.

Another of the mainstays of the young man's thinking was Shintoism, with its particular understanding of divinity and its assessment of life after death. A few of the cadets might be Christians; this could, and sometimes did, lead to terrible moral dilemmas in wartime. The typical cadet, however, would have only the vaguest and most confused knowledge of the foreign religion, if any. The things he would remember about it would be its paradoxical highlights – an omnipotent and omniscient God who allowed free will and demanded penitence; who loved all, yet was vengeful as well; who created the world, yet condemned large parts of it. Shintoism, by contrast, would seem comprehensible, fair and eminently practical. The original creator was unimaginably far back in time, and was not, therefore, the object of daily worship – that honour went to a more understandable group of beings, the *kami*. The word is usually translated as 'gods', but the overtones of that word are inappropriate; more exactly, *kami* means above, or superior, and the idea it conveys is better expressed as a tutelary spirit – a guiding, guarding spirit of place. *Shinto*, in turn, means the way or teaching of the kami. The dead become spirits and, if they are especially honoured, may be named kami; as such, they may affect the living for good or ill, and might need propitiation; but they need neither to hope for heaven, nor fear hell, for neither exists. Instead, spirit and matter co-exist, and for the spirits of dead warriors there is a special meeting place – the Yasukuni shrine in Tokyo. There the living could pray for protection, or seek inspired advice – and this was actually not vastly different from the old Royal Navy question, 'What would Nelson have done?' If they had been Japanese, Nelson, Shakespeare and Washington would have made very good kami, and it may have been that feeling of honour, respect and indebtedness which made the young Togo burst into tears when he attended the Trafalgar Day ceremony on the deck of HMS *Victory* in Portsmouth.

Shintoism has no scripture like the Bible or the Koran, in the most important sense of written words believed to be the revealed wisdom of God; the nearest comparable thing, which is not an equivalent, is the *Kojiki*, a 1,200-year-old collection of the early oral traditions. The same difference occurs in that area of fundamental importance to Christianity and Islam, the 'spark of faith' which carries the believer over all the hurdles of rationality. For the Shintoist those hurdles were never erected, because his beliefs tapped and exploited the simplest, most common feelings. Shintoism makes no appeal to reason; it carries its own built-in spark of faith, the feeling of believing without knowing why. The beauty of the moon, the delicacy of a flower, the pleasure of health, the satisfaction of efficiency, the thrill of fighting were all equal proofs that its beliefs were correct and good. The feeling is nebulous, but authentically religious, and well expressed by an ancient Japanese poem: 'Unknown to me who resideth here; tears flow from a sense of unworthiness and gratitude.'

This indefinite, non-dogmatic but supremely human faith has no founder; its roots lie in Japan's most distant past, several centuries before the beginning of the Christian era, when Ninigi, grandson of the sun, built a palace on Mount Takachiho and founded the dynasty which has continued in unbroken descent to the present. It was Ninigi's grandson Jimmu who became the first Emperor of Yamato, ancient Japan, on a date given with charmingly improbable precision – 11 February 660 BC. In 1902 AD the Emperor Meiji was the 123rd emperor in direct line. In the twenty-five centuries between Jimmu and Meiji, Buddhism and Confucianism had been imported, living side by side with the indigenous Shintoism, and contributed to it – filial piety, uprightness, sincerity and ancestor-veneration. But the most famous, and most important, aspect of revived Shintoism was a nineteenth-century invention. Emperor-worship was not advocated until 1871, as another part of the total programme to create national unity, and to avoid the partition of Japan into either petty principalities or foreign colonies. The idea was contained in the phrase *kazoku kokku*, the 'family state': the Emperor was the father of the nation, so, as in the domestic family, all his children expected his protection and owed him their support.

In 1889 the principle of freedom of religion was set up in the new constitution, but Shinto remained as a unifying element – no longer a state religion, but transmuted by deft politicians into a state ethic. So, theoretically at least, a person could be a good Christian, Buddhist or whatever he chose, and still, as a good Japanese, follow Shinto and adore the Emperor. The very idea of being part of a tradition more than 2,500 years old is clearly seductive, and the novelty of emperor-worship – barely a generation old when the Anglo-Japanese Alliance was signed – did not diminish its effectiveness. Writing in 1939, Cecil Bullock, one of the last native-speaking English teachers in the Imperial Naval academy, said:

'Reverence for the Imperial House is shown in many striking ways at Etajima, but in picturesqueness there is nothing, to my way of thinking, which quite matches the *Kigensetsu* procession up Mount Furutaka, *Kigensetsu* being the anniversary of the accession of Jimmu, the first Emperor, some 2,600 years ago . . . The cadets get up at about 4.30 when it is quite dark, and with their officers climb to the top of Furutaka-yama, the highest point on the island. They wend their way up the long zig-zag path by the light of pine torches carried at the head of each group. At the top they face East, the direction of the Imperial Palace in Tokyo, and await the sunrise in silence. As the sun appears, they bow deeply in homage and sing together the "Kimigayo" [the national anthem].

'I attended this ceremony once, and I found it very impressive. Sunrise and sunset over the Inland Sea of Japan are very beautiful . . . The cadets, like all Japanese, are very sensitive to the beauties of their country, and I have no doubt that they experience a great feeling of exhilaration at this lovely scene, which is diverted into patriotic channels.'

In this way the union of religion and patriotism gave the Imperial Navy, and the country as a whole, a certain advantage – at least in that period – over the nominally Christian countries of the West, and a distinct advantage over Russia. For them, the traditional Western distinction between affairs of religion and affairs of the state did not exist. Instead of making different demands which could conflict, the two were mutually supportive – land and people, emperor and gods, were all aspects of one whole, a splendid interlocking unity of duty.

To a person brought up in this manner, the historic moral dilemma of Christianity in wartime simply did not occur. Conscientious objections to fighting and killing were impossible concepts, described typically by a destroyer captain as 'simply folly, caused by their stupid religion'. He was being generous; if a Japanese had had such scruples, it would have been seen as unthinkable selfishness, an attempt to set himself up against everybody else's beliefs. Or, worse, it would have been thought plain cowardice, an unwillingness to give all of himself for the good of the Emperor, the personification of everything Japan held dear. That would have inevitably brought disgrace and shame, and life for a disgraced person would have been well-nigh intolerable. *Hara-kiri* or *seppuku*, honourable suicide, was logically the only way of repaying the debt incurred, the only valid 'apology to the Emperor'; and, by the same token, life could be held lightly, and death, if not actively sought, could be accepted willingly. The highest virtue was not the freedom to do what one wanted, but having the strength of will to conquer personal desires and submit to the group ethic; and, the more demanding the ethic, the greater the strength needed to submit, and the greater the virtue of submission and obedience. In later years, Japanese war propaganda films did not show the 'glories' of war, with valiant charges and the home-coming of heroes; instead they showed all the physical and emotional pains and horrors. To Westerners they almost seemed to be anti-war films; but the film-makers knew their audience, and what the audience saw were men of such spirit that they could endure the horrors, because it was their duty. Indeed to die, especially in action for the Emperor, could literally be the apotheosis of the individual – a man could become not merely a spirit, but one of the gods.

Society demanded service, and the new naval recruits of 1902, all around eighteen years old, had known nothing else. They could, and did, believe themselves to be the inheritors of Japan most ancient, and the exemplars of Japan most modern. In that mood, then, they gave themselves – literally body and soul – to the service of the Navy, knowing themselves to be doubly élite, and determined to succeed in their gruelling timetable of work.

They learned mathematics, physics, chemistry, English and either French or German, philosophy, psychology, logic, leadership, law, hygiene, economics, Chinese classics and Japanese literature; seamanship, navigation, gunnery, torpedo work, communications, signalling, strategy, tactics, naval organization and military history (but, significantly, little naval history); rifle, revolver and bayonet practice, with landing-party work and drill (because there was no separate Marine force); rowing, swimming, rugger, soccer, basket-ball, baseball, tennis, judo, kendo (a relic of the samurai sword-fighting, with four-foot staves instead of swords), sumo wrestling and *botaoshi*. One understands why sixteen hours a day, six days a week for four years was necessary.

All four of these last, essentially Japanese, sports in the academy revealed further aspects of the Japanese character – aspects which affected the Imperial Navy especially deeply, and which contributed, invisibly but certainly, to its eventual downfall. In judo, of course, the strength of the opponent is used against him. In European fencing, it is usual to whittle away the opponent's strength by repeated small strikes; in kendo, the objective is to land a single deadly blow – a blow that would have been deadly with a samurai sword – on one of five designated places: the top of the head, the right arm, the neck, or either side of the body. In sumo, unlike European wrestling, the fighters never descend to grappling on the ground, but win on points – and not by *gaining* points, but by making the opponent *lose* points. Finally, botaoshi: this was an Etajima invention, played in the academy and nowhere else. The cadets were very proud of it, and an especially honoured visitor might be invited to watch a game.

It was very simple. The players were divided into two teams, and each team was divided into attackers and defenders. Two poles, about eight feet high and topped with flags, were placed a hundred yards or so apart. The objective of the contest was merely to pull down the opponents' pole.

The defenders grouped around their pole in two tiers, the lower ones linking arms and the upper ones standing on their shoulders. On the signal of a bugle call, the attackers charged from opposite ends of the field, shrieking like maniacs. They tussled in mid-field, and those who broke through leapt bodily onto the opposition defenders, with no holds barred except scratching and biting. The first lot to pull down a pole were the winners, and the whole thing was over in three or four minutes, often with a couple of unconscious bodies being dragged out from under the scrambling heap. It was extremely vicious, incredibly exciting, and swiftly finished – one quick, decisive battle.

The principles of all these distinctive sports, handed down or invented, were absorbed by every Imperial Navy officer in the most formative part of his naval career, and they were fine as sports. But, in the minds of this dedicated, loyal, élite group, their principles of sport became, unconsciously or consciously, their principles of war. Throughout its life, the fundamentals of Imperial Navy strategic thinking could be traced back to the games at Etajima. The seeds of thought in every navy officer's mind were there: the beliefs that they could tackle an enemy, however strong, by using his strength against him; that a single, well-calculated blow was always worth more than a score of smaller ones; that they could always win, not by overwhelming force, but by inflicting greater losses than they sustained; and finally – an eternal conviction – that it would all be over in one final, decisive battle.

Also traceable to Etajima was another fatal mental straitjacket. The very dedication to duty that produced such fine professional sailors, men of unquestioning loyalty to their group, also produced a severe narrow-mindedness, an inability to improvise against the unexpected, a phobia of doing the wrong thing, a reluctance to operate without exact orders for every eventuality, and a generalized contempt for the army. The army returned this contempt, with interest; all too often the devotion to the respective services produced not cooperation, but bitter rivalry.

However much conscious awareness the new young officer leaving Etajima had of these elements in his mental make-up, he would not have seen their inherent flaws. By the end of his four years of intensive training, he would be 'just about as fit physically as it is possible for anyone to be', as Cecil Bullock remembered. Those four years, at such a crucial time of life, had provided friendships that would last till death – even today, among the very oldest, long-retired survivors of the Imperial Navy, this is true; loyalty to their contemporaries and class-mates never dies.

The passing-out ceremony was a profoundly solemn occasion, a time of deep emotion held rigidly in check, for it was led by one of the imperial princes – or even, from time to time, by the Emperor himself. And, immediately it was finished, a new life began: the young men boarded cruisers, and set off on training voyages around the world – leaving the small island and the secluded academy, and of course leaving the homeland too, probably for the first time in their lives. This was such a moving and momentous event that even the most reticent felt the urge to express themselves.

'I shall never forget one cadet on this occasion,' wrote Bullock. 'He was an unusually quiet and reserved fellow, and had never, as far as I could remember, volunteered to speak a single word of English during his whole four years at Etajima. With flushed face and eyes full of emotion, he came up to me, and said, "Sir, I am Snotty Suzuki. Thank you for your kindness to me. Goodbye!"'

6

'The national pleasure of building ships'

When the class of Meiji 34 (1902) passed out of Etajima, they were well on the way to becoming fully professional officers, and the Navy they went to work in included some of the world's best matériel. 'Japan blossomed forth like her own chrysanthemum,' the *Navy and Army Illustrated* said in Britain. 'Now we see what a Navy and what resources she possesses – battleships perhaps the finest in the world, armoured cruisers which are equal to the best, destroyers that are like our own, and dockyards, arsenals, and harbours of great extent and admirably equipped.' The programme of naval expansion commenced under the premiership of Ito Hirobumi had almost come to an end; only one vessel remained to be delivered, a ship which would be called *Mikasa*. Built in England by Vickers of Barrow, completed on 1 March 1902, *Mikasa* represented an abiding Japanese predilection: for her time, she was the biggest, strongest battleship in the world. Four hundred feet long between perpendiculars, her beam was 76 feet, her draught just over 27 feet. Her motive power came from vertical triple expansion boilers of the Belleville type, not one of the latest, but one of the most reliable kinds available. With them she could steam at up to 18 knots, and with a maximum fuel capacity of 2,000 tons of coal her theoretical maximum radius without refuelling was 9,000 sea miles at 10 knots. Allowing for higher speeds and the variable conditions and manoeuvres of battle, this meant that in war she would be able to go for around 4,000 miles between one coaling and the next – in other words, even if moving all the time, she could be independent of the shore, or colliers, for at least ten days and perhaps more than two weeks at a stretch. Her armament was impressive: four 12-inch guns, two for'ard and two aft; fourteen 6-inch and twenty 3-inch quick-firers; a dozen 47-millimetre guns, the small 2½- or 3-pounders; and four underwater torpedo-tubes. To match her own armament, she was heavily armoured as well with Harvey-nickel steel in a nine-inch belt around her waterline, ten inches around the gun turrets, and fourteen inches around the barbettes (the platforms on which the turrets stand) and the conning tower. Her flying bridge, however, was open and unprotected.

Today, she is preserved in Yokosuka, a unique memorial to the spirit of the Imperial Navy. From the open bridge, she appears to be afloat; yet, sadly and rather pathetically, she is not even in a dry dock, but embedded in concrete. As one climbs her ladders, peering into her cabins, walking her decks, she seems a genteel little old lady now, steeped in memories: there is the admiral's cabin, with its high bunk and little basin, and, next door, the simplest possible bathroom; the officers' wardroom, still solid, comfortable and companionable; the men's hammocks, slung by their guns, just as they would have been in Nelson's time. There are also a couple of distinctively Japanese touches, essential to any Imperial Navy ship: in the elegant staff cabin, there is a space reserved for the portrait of the Emperor, and amidships there is a little Shinto shrine. It is all, to a modern eye, pocket-sized and homely, and to some extent it must have been so, for with a total crew averaging around 840 it would not have been difficult for any one crew member to have been on nodding terms at least with everyone else. But there are two things about her which bring home her old reality – firstly, everywhere there are areas large and small painted with red stripes, on deck, hull, funnels, even on the guns themselves; and every one of these striped areas marks a hit she received in battle. And, secondly, there are the big guns. Even today a 12-inch naval gun is a fairly impressive sight – especially from the wrong end – and in 1902 there was hardly anything to beat those guns, on land or sea.

Since Trafalgar in 1805, naval technology had developed at a greater rate than ever before, and in the last quarter of the nineteenth century the speed of development had accelerated so much that ships were sometimes obsolete before they were completed. The explosive shell had replaced the ancient cannon-ball; the armoured wooden hull, and then the steel hull, had naturally followed. Breech-loading guns had replaced muzzle-loaders; their range, accuracy and hitting power had increased; and so ships had come to be built with fewer and larger guns. These had to be able to turn from side to side, instead of remaining fixed in one direction; so sails and rigging had had to go, because they got in the way. The British had marked the beginning of the end of the steamer-sailer battleship in 1873 with HMS *Devastation*, the first ocean-going ship without any sails, eleven years after the USS *Monitor* (which was not ocean-going) fought the CSS *Virginia* in the first battle between iron-clads. In the 1870s, *Devastation* was so distinctive that she and her immediate successors were called mastless ships; but guns, armour and steam machinery progressed so swiftly that by 1884 a new term, recognizing these developments, had entered the English language. 'Battleship' was an appropriate abbreviation, faster and more punchy than the old sailing phrase, a 'line-of-battle ship'.

At the same time the Royal Navy was beginning to labour under the strain of maintaining its 'Two Power' policy, by which it reckoned to be able to match the fighting ability of any two other fleets, and to perform the thankless task of policing the world's oceans and keeping the peace at sea. It had become a huge, almost innumerable, heterogeneous fleet, widely scattered and of very varying fighting ability; its superiority was more a matter of numbers than of generally superior ships. The Imperial Navy of Japan was very different. Without a world-wide empire to patrol, Japan needed far fewer vessels; and, starting from scratch, she was able to build a much more homogeneous fleet, a relatively standardized navy in which all ships could work together.

The Imperial Navy's first battleship in the modern sense was *Fuji*, completed with her sister *Yashima* in 1897. *Fuji* displaced 12,533 tons, *Yashima* slightly less, but both were 374 feet long, had a main armament of four 12-inch guns, and could do 18¼ knots. Their cruising range was much less than *Mikasa*, a theoretical maximum of 4,000 miles giving them a war maximum of more like 1,800. *Shikishima* and *Hatsuse*, completed in 1900 and 1901 respectively, were longer, heavier, and more heavily armed than the earlier pair, and with a somewhat greater cruising radius; but it was left to *Shikishima*'s sister *Asahi*, completed in 1900, to combine length, strength, weight and power with enormous radius. *Mikasa* and *Asahi* were virtually identical, but *Mikasa* was two years younger, two years newer; and she became the flagship of the Imperial Navy, the pride and emblem of maritime Japan.

All those ships were built in Britain, where a sense of mingled pride and chagrin prevailed – pride that British yards could produce such splendid craft, and chagrin that there were not more like them in the Royal Navy. Comparing the products of Britain, America and Japan herself became something of an international hobby: evaluating *Takasago*, a second-class British-built cruiser, against her equivalent in the Royal Navy, *Engineer* magazine discovered 'an increased proportion of 50% of striking energy in favour of the Japanese . . . scarcely a pleasing reflection', then proceeded to add that *Takasago* was also 'a much better ship than her American-built sisters *Kasagi* and *Chitose*'. But *Chitose* could do a quarter of a knot more, and 'that', said her American designer, 'knocks the record, and she can beat anything afloat today'. Willing to give praise where it was due, provided it was not to America, *Engineer* commented that Japan herself had now learned 'the national pleasure of building ships', and had begun to produce cruisers 'practically on a par with Elswick designs'. By this the magazine meant designs as good as the world's best; and one way and another – through a little building, a lot of buying, and adding in a few vessels captured in the war against China – the Imperial Navy at the beginning of the 20th century numbered no less than 74 ships.

Cruisers and destroyers, like battleships, were offspring of the age of steam. Before then, the only essential characteristic shared by all ships used as cruisers was speed, since their function in war was to scout ahead of the fleet; but, as the battleship developed, so the cruiser developed separately and became a distinct type of warship in its own right. Top of the categories that slowly sorted themselves out were armoured cruisers such as *Kasuga*, completed in 1903, and one of only two Italian-built ships in the Imperial Navy. Next came belted cruisers, with a waterline belt of armour, followed by second-class cruisers with light armour, and finally third-class, with a relatively small amount of armour but proportionately higher speed. *Suma*, completed in 1896, was a third-class cruiser – 295 feet long, but displacing only 2,657 tons, and able to speed along at 20 knots. Fast and light, she was typical of her class, and she was the first armoured warship built in Japan, with Japanese materials, to Japanese plans. With her white-painted hull and the imperial chrysanthemum on her bow, she looked a smart, sleek ship, but she was unstable, and turned out to be a bad seaboat.

As for destroyers, their origin is revealed in their original name – torpedo-boat catchers, or torpedo-boat destroyers. The torpedo took its name from the torpedo fish, which gives an electric shock. The weapons first known as torpedoes were explosive charges moored to the seabed and triggered by an electrical impulse from the shore. These, of course, came to be called mines – 'infernal machines', in some British opinion – while the same kind of electrically-triggered explosive, mounted on the end of a long pole projecting from the bows of a small craft, was named the spar torpedo. Other primitive versions of the weapon were towed at an angle behind their mother craft, but the ancestor of the modern torpedo was created by the Englishman Robert Whitehead in 1867. Its charge was a mere 18 pounds of dynamite, its speed 6 knots and its range an erratic and chancy few hundred yards. But, when it was refined and put into small, fast vessels for launching, every naval country in the world realized that this was a weapon of tremendous potential. The Russians sank a Turkish cutter with one in 1878; in 1891 the torpedo seemed to prove itself, by sinking a *battleship* in the Chilean war. Everyone rushed to build and buy more torpedoes, stronger and faster still; and, to counter this, the Royal Navy felt obliged to invent the torpedo-boat destroyer. The first was HMS *Havock*, 250 tons and 27 knots, with four guns and three torpedo tubes, and able to outrun and outgun any torpedo-boat around. She was completed in 1893. A year later, when the war with China began, the Imperial Japanese Navy already had a few similar vessels – they were not slow to take up a good idea; and ten years after that, in 1904, the Imperial Navy included a large collection of both torpedo-boats and destroyers: ready, and waiting to be used.

7

'Distant Thunder . . . Death is Near'

The war that was about to break out would become the most heavily documented conflict in history to that date. Foreign correspondents from all over the world flocked to Japan and Manchuria to cover it, with very varying degrees of accuracy. The chancelleries and admiralties of all the powerful nations observed it with the keenest interest. Special monthly magazines were created to publicize the victories and defeats, the mistakes and successes, and their editions sold out as soon as they were printed. Many of the participants kept diaries, or wrote their memoirs later if they survived; sometimes, if they did not, their letters home were published posthumously. Many more Russians, who lost, wrote about it than did the Japanese, who won – victory does not need as much public explanation as defeat.

The Russo-Japanese War of 1904–5 was a huge experiment, and a true child of the twentieth century: a small nation, new to modernity, challenged the right of another – physically one of the largest, militarily one of the strongest – to invade, take over and control lands situated in between the two; the right to extend arbitrarily its sphere of direct influence; the right to threaten with its dominion a large section of the globe. If Britain had met similar opposition two hundred years earlier, the British Empire might never have existed; and the Russo-Japanese War was one of the symptoms of the end of the age of successful, overt imperialism.

It was not only politically experimental, it was experimental in its weapons as well. The war took place on land and sea, but its location meant that control of the sea was crucial; and the weapons at sea, the ships and men of both sides, were not unknown quantities but of unknown qualities. Outside the fleets, no one was really sure how well they would work, or how the matériel and personnel would stand up to actual war. It had been nearly ten years since the Imperial Navy's baptism of fire against the Chinese; it was far longer since the last major Russian naval war. So, many of the men were novices, and technical progress had been so rapid that many of the weapons were new to war as well. Inside the fleets, two contrary feelings generally prevailed: among the Russians, mistrust of their commanders, their weapons and their own ability; among the Japanese, complete confidence in all three.

In 1898, one British apologist wrote of Russia that 'as a naval power, she now stands third among the great States of the world . . . the creation of the modern fleet since the Turkish war of 1877–78 must be regarded as an achievement unparalleled in her history'. But then he added cautiously: 'Only the test of war can show whether the Russian people have been fully able, in the words of Peter the Great, "to conquer the art of the sea".' He, however, was almost alone in his admiration; the more common foreign attitude was put by Bennet Burleigh, the *Daily Telegraph* war correspondent, in a way that would find many echoes today: 'If they [Russia] covet a country,' he said, 'or a township, or a house, they will, if they can, reach out and take it without a touch of febrile self-consciousness.'

The country they had taken, during the Boxer Rebellion, was Manchuria, and they had Korea under the quizzing-glass – the country whose independence Japan had guaranteed with the Treaty of Shimonoseki in 1895. These incursions, plus the Russians' refusal to move out again, were the essential causes of the war. Nervous as ever at the risk of being approached too closely, Japan had attempted to find a diplomatic solution, but moves and counter-moves were ineffective, and on 6 February Russo-Japanese diplomatic relations were broken off. Four days later came the Japanese declaration of war, righteous, hurt, and largely correct:

'We cannot in the least admit that Russia had from the first any serious or genuine desire for peace. She has rejected the proposals of our Government. The safety of Korea is in danger. The interests of our Empire are menaced. The guarantee of the future which we have failed to secure by peaceful negotiations can now only be obtained by an appeal to arms.'

But by the time the declaration was made – just as in the Sino-Japanese War a decade earlier – the war had already begun; and, this time, there was no accident about it at all.

The man in control was Togo Heihachiro – the same Togo who as captain of the *Naniwa* had triggered the Sino-Japanese War, who as a student had learned his profession with the British Royal Navy, and who as a youth had fought from the medieval ramparts of Kagoshima. After the Sino-Japanese War he had been promoted to Rear Admiral, and one of his first deeds as such was to run his new ship, *Yoshino*, onto a rock – an act which would have caused many of his countrymen to commit suicide. Unperturbed, however, he had simply transferred his flag back to *Naniwa*, a ship he was fond of in any case; and before the end of 1895 he had been made a member of the Council of Admirals, and President of the Naval Technical College – a fair measure of the regard in which he was held, despite the accident. He was certainly helped by the fact that he was a Satsuman; even before Perry, the Satsuma clan had been pre-eminent at sea, and in the new Imperial Navy many Satsumans held high office. At the turn of the century, both the Minister and Vice Minister of Marine were Satsumans, as was Ito Yukyo, the victor of the Yalu, and now the Chief of Naval Staff. But Togo went on to become far more than a member of a clan – he became the embodiment of the entire Imperial Navy, with the world-famous nick-name of 'the Japanese Nelson'.

Nevertheless – and despite the frequently deliberate modelling of his life in Nelson's image – his character remains far less clear than that of the British admiral. When Nelson was talkative, Togo was reticent to the point of silence rarely broken; when Nelson wrote copiously, vainly and vividly of his thoughts and plans and feelings, Togo wrote very little, apart from official reports (which one commentator found to be 'just as dull' as any Royal Navy official report), poetry, and the occasional terse exhortation to his colleagues, pungent with naval wisdom but revealing little of the man. Physically he was about average height for a Japanese then – about five foot three – with rather round shoulders, sparse grey hair and an even sparser grey beard (both of which turned white during the course of the 1904–5 campaigns). 'A quiet, silent man,' said Lord Redesdale, who met him in 1905, 'with a rather melancholy face, lighted up, as the spirit moves him, by one of the sweetest of smiles.' His only striking features were his eyes, more round than usual among Japanese (which prompted one of his officers to refer to 'his European face, though he is not to be blamed for that') – eyes which were black, piercing, and captivating.

Nor is there any evidence that the Imperial Navy loved him in the same way that the Royal Navy openly and unashamedly adored Nelson – although such expression would have been difficult, since the Japanese language does not actually contain a word to parallel the Western understanding of love. Words expressing degrees of respect and affection are legion, however, and though some of his men were understandably overawed and even a little afraid of him – 'I am very glad,' said a destroyer captain, 'to be at a certain distance from him . . . he is an unpleasant neighbour for his inferiors' – the Imperial Navy's affection for Togo was great; and its respect for him was boundless.

Without the Russo-Japanese War it would have been different; he would have slipped away into obscurity, vaguely remembered as a good fighter in the struggle against China. The affection and respect came because, even if they have no word for it, the Japanese, like everyone else, love a winner; and Togo, even if he did not win the naval war single-handed, led his fleet to a sensational and annihilating victory. A popular song of the time, absolutely typical of the Japanese attitude, ended with the words, 'We shall show the world what we can accomplish.' Showing the world what Japan could do, Togo showed the Imperial Navy that it could exceed its own best expectations, and, in so doing, astonish everyone.

Togo really did not look the type for such deeds. Captain Smith, his old tutor back on HMS *Worcester*, gave an accurate description when he called the unprepossessing little student 'a great plodder; slow to learn, but very sure of what he had learnt'. Using a book by Fred T. Jane, Togo played chess, because, he said, 'it makes the mind alert and is good for those who study tactics'. Of course he studied tactics, and Russian tactics in particular, reading and re-reading a book on the subject by a certain Admiral Makaroff – the same Makaroff who had flung his sword over the chart of Port Arthur. Togo regarded the book so highly he had it translated and put on to the officer cadets' compulsory reading list. He also studied coastlines, especially those of southern Japan and Korea, as well as the strait in between, named Tsushima after the island in its middle. Cruising off Korea in 1899, he noted a bay called Chinhae, near Masampo, and underlined its name in his notebook. Nobody knew the reason, and no one dared ask him; it took them six years to find out.

After being Commander-in-Chief of the naval bases of Sasebo in the south-west and Maizuru on the coast of the Sea of Japan, he became C-in-C of the navy's Main Squadron, and a Vice Admiral; and on 15 October 1904, summoned to a three-hour meeting in Tokyo's Navy Department, he was informed of yet further promotion. All the Imperial Navy's ships were gathered in one Combined Fleet, and he was Commander-in-Chief. Moments like that must have brought home the speed of the navy's growth, even to one who had spent all his life in it. Forty-one years earlier young Togo had waved a sword and pushed stone and iron round-shot into the muzzles of smooth-bore cannon, then the best in Japan; now he was in charge of ships which were equal to the best in the world. Yet after his interview he said absolutely nothing about it – but a colleague noticed his step was more sprightly, and his round black eyes sparkled.

Preparations had been going on for years, not only in the mind of the new Commander-in-Chief, but across the nation. Back in 1898, the portly Belgian representative, Baron d'Anethan, had noted that 'in spite of the rather difficult present financial situation, the naval and military budgets have not been cut. On the contrary, the government does all it can to hasten the construction of ships in England, and has placed large orders for cannons in Germany and France'; and only eighteen months later, in the spring of 1900, he wrote:

'When I visited the state arsenals recently, I ascertained how busy they were. They work night and day to forge cannons, make cartridges, cast bullets and bombs, build and equip torpedo-boats, etc. On all sides of the Inland Sea new forts are being built and batteries established. Much ammunition and many cannons also come from England. Large quantities of coal have recently been purchased from Cardiff [ironically, Welsh coal was of better quality than Japanese, the original American reason for breaking Japan's isolation] and installed in the arsenals of Kun and Sasebo. Japan shrinks from no expenditure and spares no effort to prepare for any eventuality.'

With Togo in charge of Sasebo, d'Anethan added: 'The great naval manoeuvres decided upon a year ago have just begun. More than forty warships, not counting torpedo-boats, are taking part. The plan of the manoeuvres is kept secret; not one foreign naval attaché has been invited. There is no doubt, however, that the exercises are being held in the south, not very far from the Korean coast.'

Without foreknowledge, d'Anethan could only record the development of events around him. Read today, his despatches trace the slide towards war with a dreadful inevitability.

'19 June 1900 – Japan now has nine warships in the China Sea, and is sending a corps of 3,000 troops, infantry, artillery and cavalry.'

'20 March 1901 – I do not say that war is imminent, but it is far from improbable. In the present state of mind in Japan, it would be popular and undertaken with confidence. It is believed here that the fleet is superior to that which Russia can send now, and in a very short time at least 200,000 men could attack the Russians in Manchuria, or in Korea. In the military world the idea is now expressed loudly and publicly that the present time would be most favourable for making war, and that one must not wait until Russia has built the formidable fleet that she will have in a few years.'

'2 May 1901 – The Japanese Fleet, mobilized for April manoeuvres, is ready for action. Gathered at Sasebo and Kure it can radiate to the coasts of China and Korea. Besides the ships at Taku, there are cruisers at Shanghai, Amoy and Chefoo. A squadron will soon be sent also to the South China Sea.'

'5 June 1903 – The Japanese Parliament has voted the projects presented by the Government to increase the Navy considerably. The expenses over a period of ten years will amount to 115 million yen . . . and, on the other hand, there will be no reduction in the budget of the Ministry of War, that is, the Army.'

'1 July 1903 – Had Russia not pledged herself to evacuate Manchuria [a pledge she had not fulfilled], thereby forcing Japan to content herself with a diplomatic victory two years ago, we would have seen arise at that time the danger that is the more threatening today . . .'

On 10 October 1903 d'Anethan's wife, who was Rider Haggard's sister, wrote in her diary with the calmness of certainty: 'Japan and Russia are on the eve of a war. It is difficult to see how it can be averted. It does not look as though Russia, in spite of her promises, seems inclined to give up the occupation of Manchuria . . . The Japanese are most bellicose and equally indignant. Russia thinks that the latter are playing a game of bluff, but they are mistaken, and there is not the slightest doubt that the Japanese are in deadly earnest.'

And on 22 January 1904, the Baron confirmed his wife's fears. 'Japan,' he wrote, 'is in a position to begin hostilities without a moment of delay. The time has passed when Japan can content herself with any last-minute Russian promises, unless the promises are backed by the withdrawal of the enormous fleet that Russia has assembled at Port Arthur.'

Japanese intelligence had given the Naval Ministry a clear picture of Port Arthur, its defences and personnel, because one in ten of the thousands of Oriental coolies, servants and labourers was a spy – either a subverted Chinese or a Japanese in disguise. And their reports, pieced together, did reveal an enormous fleet: seven battleships, half a dozen cruisers, a pair of torpedo gunboats, a pair of minelayers, and twenty-five destroyers – forty-two vessels, all told. Against them, Togo's Combined Fleet could range half a dozen battleships, fourteen cruisers, fourteen torpedo-boats and nineteen destroyers. Those were his First and Second Squadrons; the Third Squadron had, in addition, a pair of battleships, seven cruisers, half a dozen gunboats, a coast defence ship and a dozen torpedo-boats. But all the Third Squadron vessels were old, long past their best; and, apart from a few despatch boats and nineteen merchant ships chartered for special services, that was the sum total of the Imperial Navy. And, although the Japanese yards would be able to cope with repairs, they would not be able simultaneously to build more ships. The Port Arthur squadron, on the other hand, was only one of several in the Russian Navy. In Vladivostock there were another four cruisers and seventeen torpedo-boats; in the Black Sea there was a totally separate fleet, though that could be discounted, since international agreements forbade it to cross the Bosphorus; and in the Baltic, which the Russians tended to regard as another private lake, there was yet a further fleet, of unknown strength – a fleet which no agreement held in check.

As for land forces, Japan's army numbered 270,000, with a reserve of 200,000 older men, against Russia's forces in the Far East of around 80,000. But again, Japan's total of less than half a million trained men was the sum total of her army; and in Russia, at the other end of the single-track Trans-Siberian Railway, there were almost unlimited forces available – a million to start with, and after that as many more as anyone could wish, pressed into service from among the steppe-dwelling peasants.

The Imperial Navy's prime task was to establish and maintain communications from Japan to Korea and Manchuria; to contain, or better still to destroy, the squadrons at Port Arthur and Vladivostock, so that the Imperial Army could be landed safely and swiftly, and thereafter supported. Command of the sea was essential, and it had to be achieved rapidly.

Constant drills and manoeuvres had gone on during January, but at that stage few were aware of their purpose, although everyone was deeply aware of the high-pitched national and international tension. One officer wrote, 'I must say I would like to know whether we are manoeuvring for its own sake, or whether the Mikado has anything serious in view;' and a group of officers verged on insubordination when they approached the Commander-in-Chief himself and demanded that the fleet should stop playing around and go to war at once. It gave Togo the opportunity for a splendidly Nelsonian remark: 'Have confidence in Togo,' he said – and they did. And, on 6 February, their confidence was rewarded: 'The commander of the destroyer flotilla could hardly speak for emotion, and only managed to utter one single word: "Mobilisation!" He couldn't keep still, and kept jumping from one place to another, twisting his legs and laughing, without coming to the point. More explanations were unnecessary; we knew all.'

Aboard *Mikasa* Togo had read out the Emperor's order to his assembled squadron and divisional commanders, and then had added: 'I intend, with you officers, to crush the enemy, and thus set His Majesty's heart at rest.' And some of the officers had wept, bursting with pride and pleasure, and fear for their ancient empire.

At 11 p.m. on 8 February the Viceroy's Chief of Staff in Port Arthur received a telegram from St Petersburg with the comforting news that negotiations were going well – 'any fear of armed conflict is mere fancy.' The night was dark, the sea outside the harbour moderate with a light mist over the water; and twenty miles away, advancing at 13 knots, their decks waxed to slide ammunition boxes, their tubes ready with Whitehead torpedoes, there were ten Japanese destroyers. One of the commanders remembered Togo's last briefing – 'The attack must be delivered with the greatest energy possible,' he had said, 'because, gentlemen, we are at war, and only he who acts fearlessly can hope for success.' The commander, Lieutenant Tikovara, had complete confidence in his sixty-man crew – 'they cannot be improved upon . . . nothing can surprise us.' He had confidence in his ship as well, the 220-foot, 363-ton, turtle-bowed *Akatsuki*, completed in England only two years before. She drew less than six feet, and with a maximum speed of 31 knots had considerable power in reserve. Her armament was four 57-mm and two 3-inch quick-firers and a brace of 18-inch torpedo-tubes; and the torpedoes were Tikovara's only worry. They had been fitted with net-cutters, in case the Russian ships had anti-torpedo nets out, and Tikovara was not sure the cutters would work.

As the destroyers closed on Port Arthur, the sight in front of them was a raider's dream. All the ships except one in the roadstead outside the harbour were lit up; 'the lighthouse situated between the outer and inner roadsteads was throwing out its brilliant beams; the town was also completely lit up . . . those poor devils, then, had no presentiment, and apparently were wrapped in peaceful slumber.'

Two patrolling Russian destroyers had spotted the flotilla, but without wireless the best they could do was to sweep into Port Arthur first, attempting to deliver a worse than useless warning: the ships they were guarding, seeing them enter, paid no attention to those which followed. Later, one anonymous Russian remembered that some officers had invited some ladies back to their ship.

'The boat with the ladies in it was nearly run down by a destroyer, making lamp signals, and going very slow. It escaped being run down; but it passed so close that one in the boat said he could hear men whispering in a strange tongue. "It is the Japanese monkeys come to attack us!" said one in jest, and all laughed; and as they laughed there came a great explosion, two other explosions very loud, then a pause of silence, then firing. Then ships were seen moving, and the lights of one went out, and all was confusion and terror . . .'

The attack was immediate world news, by some never forgotten, by others forgotten until 1941, when the Imperial Navy sprang its third surprise assault. Like Pearl Harbor, the strike on Port Arthur was not completely effective. In 1941, the American carriers were at sea, and the naval workshops and oil farms were not bombed – omissions which left the Pacific Fleet in partial being, and enabled the Hawaiian garrison to repair and rebuild with the utmost rapidity. In 1904, out of the seven Russian battleships at anchor, only three were hit – torpedo nets had been hung on some of the target ships, and, as Tikovara had feared, the cutters did not do their work. As searchlights swung back into the control and Russian shells began to scream out – 'it is impossible,' he said, 'to grudge them praise for the great speed with which they ran to their guns' – he saw 'any number of bubbles rising from the water alongside their nets, which held the torpedoes firmly suspended by their heads . . . the antiquated net-cutters were no use whatever.' Yet, though the Russian warships in 1904 were far less severely mauled than the American ones in 1941, the effect of the two attacks could hardly have differed more greatly. The terrible shock of Pearl Harbor snapped America into national, united retaliation; the shock of Port Arthur, no less terrible to Tsarist Russia, did almost the exact opposite. War took wing at once, indeed, and the rickety Trans-Siberian Railway was overloaded with troops heading east; but, in Port Arthur itself, more than four thousand miles from St Petersburg – so far, the two were like separate nations – the official reaction was, 'Risk nothing.'

An order more damaging to morale could hardly have been invented – especially since, given the chance, many of the younger naval officers would have willingly fought to the death. Years later, survivors still recalled their orders with utter fury: 'Why not admit that we might very easily have been sent to the bottom, one by one, if our men had not been at their stations and had not done their duty conscientiously? . . . their [the Russian commanders'] sole objective was, so far as possible, to keep their matériel, their personnel, and above all their own precious skins out of harm's way.'

Twenty-six-year-old Andrew Petrovich Steer was a lieutenant on the cruiser *Novik*, the only Russian ship to show consistent daring throughout the long months of war, and he could not be said to have spoken for everyone; but he must have echoed the thoughts of many when he wrote of the daylight action on the 9th, the day after the night attack. About a dozen ships, including *Novik*, emerged cautiously from the battered harbour. Eighteen miles offshore, Rear Admiral Dewa Shigeto had returned with four cruisers to take a look at the handiwork of the destroyers the night before. Signalling Togo, he recommended a follow-up, and Togo, taking another Nelsonian cue, ordered his crews to dinner while the fleet came up. At 11.45 a.m. they had the Russians in range, and a signal fluttered up to *Mikasa*'s mainmast, a signal which, had it been visible and translatable to them, the few English people in Port Arthur would have found very familiar: 'Victory or defeat will be decided by this one act. Let every man do his utmost.' With slight variations, this signal was to be repeated at moments of crisis throughout the Imperial Navy's life, and it never really lost its power to put sailors on their mettle. Seeing it for the first time that day, one officer on *Mikasa* felt as if his soul had suddenly been pickled in red pepper.

By the afternoon, however, it might have seemed a little premature. The action took just over an hour, with little achieved on either side. Many shells were fired and most of the ships were hit, but none was sunk, or even permanently damaged. Of the Russians, only *Novik* made a quick dash out; all the rest followed Viceroy Alexieff's craven orders to remain within the shelter of the shore batteries. Lieutenant Steer watched the Imperial Navy's enviable discipline and chafed against the viceregal orders in an agony of frustration:

'The entire Japanese fleet steamed past us in one well-kept line ahead, the cruisers bringing up the rear, always following in the wake of their battleships, then very quietly steamed away, complete in numbers, after they had traversed the arc of fire of our guns ashore and afloat. Any sea officer with the slightest idea of what war meant, or simply possessing some energy, would not have hesitated to fall upon this tail of the line, so as to cut it off from the main body, which would then have been obliged to turn back. Everyone was expecting this manoeuvre . . . to the present day I remain convinced that if instead of obstinately sticking to a passive defence we had shown the slightest spur of enterprise, things might in the end have perfectly well turned out to our advantage.'

In a way Togo's signal had been right: that day's act did decide victory or defeat, not for the war as a whole, but for the naval war at Port Arthur. It showed both sides who had the upper hand, both in training and morale; and, for almost the entire time until Port Arthur fell, the Russians laboured under that yoke, and the Japanese operated with that conviction.

Ten years earlier, when it had been Chinese property, Port Arthur had fallen to Japan in a single day, and Baron d'Anethan had written, 'With any enemy other than the Chinese . . . a very long siege would have been necessary.' In 1904, demoralized, ill-trained and badly led as they were, the Russians proved d'Anethan correct: they held out until the end of the year.

Reactions around the world to the night-time torpedo attack depended, naturally, on point of view. In America, opinions ranged from weak protests to cautious admiration; in Britain it was seen as daring and dashing, 'destined to take a place of honour in naval annals'. Only two months later Britain and France would sign the Entente Cordiale, but many Frenchmen denounced the attack as treacherous, saying that nothing better could be expected from an ally of 'perfidious Albion' – the French press actually used the phrase – and, in St Petersburg, Tsar Nicholas wrote unhappily and not very hopefully in his diary, 'This without a declaration of war. May God come to our aid.'

Rubbish, said *The Times*' leading article – 'Our ally put her navy in motion with a promptness and courage that exhorted the admiration of the world, and her action in doing so before war had been formally declared, so far from being an international solecism, is in accordance with the prevailing practice of most wars in modern times.'

A torpedo in the guts of a battleship is at least an unequivocal statement of intent, but in fact the first shots of the war had been fired by a Russian ship – not in Port Arthur, but 300 miles east of there, in the Korean port of Chemulpo. The culprit was a gunboat, the *Koreetz*. In company with the cruiser *Varyag*, at 2.30 p.m. on 8 February, she had suddenly found herself face to face with an ominous Japanese squadron of five cruisers and four torpedo-boats. The frightened, rather pathetic little gunboat had loosed off a couple of small-calibre shells. What had followed could not be called a battle. The Japanese commander, Rear Admiral Uriu, blithely fulfilled his orders and landed troops in what was technically a neutral port, then stood out to sea and requested that Russian captains to run the gauntlet or be sunk at anchor. With a bravery that was to prove typical of most ranks except the highest, the challenged captains did both. The two vessels came out, gave a hopeless fight, then, heavily damaged, returned to port where their crews scuttled *Varyag* and blew up *Koreetz*.

But, once it had started, the question of who started it was immaterial. 'War does not always begin with the firing of guns,' said one Russian admiral. 'In my opinion the war began long ago.'

What was important to both sides was Togo's limited success in the first night attack; there was still nothing, except the Imperial Navy and the fearful attitude of the Port Arthur admirals, to stop the rest of the squadron coming out, fighting, and interfering with the landings of Japanese troops in Korea – or even cutting their communications with the homeland. Moreover, from the moment war opened, the Japanese had to assume that sooner or later news would come that the Russian Baltic Fleet had set sail. If the two Russian fleets joined they would certainly be an overwhelming force; and, if Port Arthur did not fall, it would give the Baltic Fleet its one other necessity, a strong base. At the very least, therefore, Togo had to contain the Port Arthur squadron and render the port unusable.

Achieving this was, if anything, rather more difficult than it would have been in the days of sail. Nelson at Toulon and Cornwallis at Brest had instituted blockades which had lasted years. They had been tedious tests of high seamanship, vessels keeping station in interminable patrols; but the blockading ships could at least run for rest and shelter whenever a strong on-shore wind sprang up, because they knew the enemy ships were then unable to come out of port. In the age of steam, the risk of mines and torpedoes made close blockade far more dangerous; the blockaders, instead of cruising back and forth for as long as they needed to, were dependent on fuel supplies; and, if they relaxed their vigilance, the blockaded ships could slip out at any time, whichever way the wind was blowing. Worst of all from the Japanese point of view was the sense of urgency, the lack of time. A sailing fleet in the Baltic would have been a negligible additional threat; a steam fleet could, it seemed, come to Japan only too easily.

The answer was to use Port Arthur against itself, to exploit the narrow entrance and high hills which, to the Russians, had seemed so protective. If the ships would not come out to fight, very well then, keep them in – not only by distant blockade, but by sealing the entrance – and then shell them at will, from sea or land. The bombarding ships outside would be sheltered by the very hills which were meant to protect the ships bombarded; and, if an army took the same hills, it would have a splendid bird's-eye view of the quarry below.

That, essentially, became the Japanese approach, and in the end it worked. But Port Arthur was far easier to defend than to conquer; by the time of its surrender, more than 28,000 Russians had died, and almost 58,000 Japanese.

One of those who died at sea was the Russian admiral Stephen Ossipovich

Makaroff, the strategist whose book Togo had had translated. Physically a huge man, with a colossal forked beard, Makaroff inspired almost as much respect among the Russian sailors as Togo did among the Japanese. Slightly younger than Togo, he had achieved his rank through ability, not – as had most of his colleagues – through influence, a fact which must have contributed to his popularity with his juniors. But his main virtue was that he could put theory and practice together in a way that was particularly apt for the beleaguered squadron at Port Arthur. He was a noted hydrographer, and had invented an ice-breaker that was used in Vladivostock; his very distinguished service in the Russo-Turkish war of 1877–78 had included the launching of that successful torpedo attack. Even better, he had studied torpedo tactics exhaustively thereafter, and had become a recognized authority on the subject; and, best of all, he was a *fighting* admiral. He arrived to take over from the faint-hearted Admiral Stark on 7 March 1904, and he was just what the squadron needed. He 'shook up the whole of Port Arthur', said one officer. Another added: 'The great mass believed in Makaroff, believed that he was the right man in the right place . . . the squadron had at last found its proper leader, and its old spirit arose anew.' Not everyone agreed; he was 'a clever man with many ideas', one embittered sailor acknowledged, 'a famous fighter of the old days, but a silly old man, of no great use to us as we were . . . he was like most of our admirals, too old'.

In most eyes, though, Makaroff's age was no disadvantage – affectionately, he was nick-named 'Old Beardy' and 'Little Grandfather' – and in any case he could do nothing about it. What he could change was the attitude and the ability of the fleet in his command, and he set about that at once, visiting all the ships, checking and inspecting them, talking to the officers and the men as well, familiarizing himself with local conditions, and constantly exuding energy, efficiency, authority and confidence.

'Gradually a change took place,' Commander Vladimir Semenoff recalled in after years. Makaroff and he had worked together at the naval base of Kronstadt; Semenoff admired the Admiral intensely, and in Port Arthur had been made second-in-command of the cruiser *Diana*. 'There arose the spirit that leads to victory – faith in the leader at whose command one gladly faces death. It only remained to instil into the men the fact that death was not the main thing, but victory; that it was not sufficient to be able to die, but that one had to know how to fight. They had to learn to fight, and to grasp the necessity for keeping everything on board ship, down to the smallest detail, in good order and readiness for war. Gradually their dullness and discontent gave way . . . It was no easy matter serving for Makaroff. Often there was no time either for eating or sleeping; but for all that it was a splendid life.'

In reviving the squadron's spirits, Makaroff's masterstroke was to show them in one move that they would not be ordered to do anything he would not do himself. On 18 February, Togo had made his first attempt to seal the harbour, sending a flotilla of five old merchant ships, loaded with rocks and explosives, to sink themselves in the narrow entrance. Picked out by searchlights as they approached, they had failed in their task almost completely: only two had been able even to get close to the entrance, and between their wrecks there was still a substantial channel. Three days after Makaroff's arrival, a pair of destroyers out on reconnaissance were returning towards this channel when they ran into a Japanese patrol twice their size. A battle began immediately. In Port Arthur, the Admiral's flagship was not yet ready for him; and Makaroff amazed everyone by jumping aboard the third-class cruiser *Novik* and racing out to the rescue. As it happened, he was too late; he arrived on the scene to find one destroyer sunk and the main Japanese fleet bearing down on him, and he was obliged to turn back. But his return was a triumph: thousands of his sailors had run to viewpoints to stare at, and cheer, this admiral who would actually lead a rescue attempt himself. 'The old maxim "risk nothing" was buried at that moment, and a new principle arose in its place,' said Semenoff. 'The Admiral had conquered all hearts at one stroke . . . every one was his, body and soul.'

Makaroff had reminded his men that both he and they were sailors, and that they shared a tradition prouder than that of any army: they would not be *sent* into action, they would be *led* into action, with the Admiral and his flagship in the position of most danger.

Now, more than ever, the subjugation of Port Arthur became an urgent necessity for the Imperial Navy. On 27 March, in the early hours of the morning, a second blockship attack took place. In this attack a god was born.

Again the ships were old merchantmen – four this time. Again they were loaded with rocks and explosives, and this time cement as well. Again there were more volunteers than could possibly be accepted; and, this time, one of them was a survivor of the first attempt, a young lieutenant-commander named Hirose Takeo. With the captains of the other blockships and their escorting destroyers and torpedo-boats he received his orders from Togo personally, and a final note of encouragement: 'If one acts with determination,' said the Commander-in-Chief, 'even gods and devils give way. Courage is the greatest protection . . . this must lead to a great success.' After hearing that, Hirose went to his blockship and wrote a poem:

> 'Would that I could be born seven times,
> And sacrifice my life for my country –
> Resolved to die, my mind is firm,
> And again expecting to win success,
> Smiling, I go on board.'

The four ships and their escorts left the Main Body at 7.30 in the evening of 26 March, passing through an honour guard of battleships and cruisers. Seven hours later they were close off the port, the sea calm and misty, the night lit only by a sliver of moon and the flickering beams of the Russian searchlights ahead. The escort fell away, the blockships rumbled ahead; then, two miles from the entrance, a searchlight passed over them, came back, and fixed. A Russian who had been similarly trapped described the feeling – the light not only blinded, but confused and disoriented the person in its beam. 'This blinding process simply paralyzes one: there is no choice but to shut one's eyes until the horrid rays have left one.' It was Lieutenant Steer of the *Novik*, watching, with some sympathy, from the port. Around him the shore batteries opened fire, and he saw first one, then a second, then a third of the blockships anchor near the entrance and explode with flashes briefer but almost as bright as the searchlight beams. The fourth blockship ploughed on through the barrage alone. 'Beautiful view,' said its commander, Hirose, to his warrant officer. The poor warrant officer was terrified, and Hirose calmed him with a ludicrous but effective piece of advice: 'Put your hand in your groin,' he said, 'and feel your testicles. If you're frightened, they'll be shrunken and stuck to the top; if you're calm, they're stretched, and dangle. If they dangle, you'll win; if they're shrunken, you'd better run.' Such an experiment might take one's mind off things, but the warrant officer probably never had the chance to try, for moments later the ship was hit by a torpedo and blew up; and, when the smoke cleared, he was nowhere to be seen. Hirose searched for him as a life-boat was lowered; and then, as the lieutenant-commander stepped unwillingly into the boat, a shell exploded close by and blew him to pieces. Nothing remained but a small piece of flesh; and the blocking of the entrance had failed again.

Japan, and the Imperial Navy, needed a hero, and Hirose became it. The little scrap of flesh was taken home and buried with full honours, and the dead lieutenant-commander was promoted: he became not only a commander, but the first *gunshin* – divine soldier, war-god – of the Russo-Japanese War.

One more ship in the right place would have done it. The channel was now only 200 feet wide. Inside the harbour – almost, now, another Russian lake, but unbearably cramped – Makaroff discovered how appallingly ignorant his officers were. They could not even move their ships in company; one junior officer admitted, 'It is painful to have to declare that not one of our captains had any conception of this.' When the Japanese columns passed by outside, they made 'never the least hesitation, never a mistake. Compared with this, what must have been Admiral Makaroff's feeling when he wanted us to take up our first formation? The signal was hardly down before things were at sixes and sevens, and two battleships, who had not understood what was required of them, promptly rammed one another'.

Even so, 'Little Grandfather' managed to instil sufficient spirit and skill into the squadron to make bold forays through the half-closed entrance, forays which the Imperial Navy could only admire. 'Experience up to the present,' said the Official History, 'had shown that the enemy, as soon as they saw us, bolted as fast as they could, and never dared to stand up to us . . . In comparison with their usual behaviour of bolting like rats whenever they saw our destroyers, this was a distinct advance towards recovering face; we saw that the enemy still had a fleet which could not be despised.'

The bombardment over the hills was intensified, yet even under the steady rain of Japanese shells it was a mark of Makaroff's morale-boosting presence that many of his men joked about it, laying bets on where the next hit would fall. Others showed their improved mood differently: 'When one has to act as a target, a good battle seems a hundred times better. For my part, I know of nothing which is such a trial to the nerves as to remain at anchor waiting for a 12-inch shell to fall on top of one, especially when said projectile weighs about 800 pounds . . . however problematical the result may be, it is a good satisfaction to be able to hit back, intead of twiddling one's thumbs, waiting to be hit.'

Makaroff did hit back, organizing a retaliatory fire across the hills, with spotters on top to direct the shots. Discomforting as these exchanges were to both fleets, however, there were three weapons which both feared more than the noisy, usually visible shells – the silent and invisible weapons of underwater: torpedoes, mines and submarines. Throughout the war, torpedoes and mines were used, the former with limited effect, the latter with great effect. No submarines were involved at all, but from their agents in the port the Japanese knew that pre-war Port Arthur had at least contained the materials to build a few, and they were never absolutely sure that none had been realized. As for the Russians, they remained convinced for years after that the Imperial Navy used submarines all the time, deployed in the most sly and cunning manner. It was a complete myth, fostered by a natural but unreasoning fear of a secret weapon which no one knew much about and nobody understood at all. Captains were issued with farcical instructions in case they encountered one; they were 'to seize the submarine by its periscope, then to smash it by blows with a mallet, so as to blind its crew; better still, to wrap a flag or a piece of canvas around it; or lastly (which would have been the best of all), to tow the said submarine by its periscope into the inner harbour'. Mercifully, no one had to attempt such a kidnap, since there were no submarines around; and, in any case, the state of the art was such that a British admiral of the time, Sir Cyprian Bridge, described the machines as 'nothing but handicapped torpedo-boats'. Despite their occasional successes, torpedoes too were chancy things at the best of times. It was the mines which did the real damage, and for both sides scored some of the most important kills of the war.

On 12 April, Togo ordered minelaying to begin outside the port. The same day, Makaroff ordered all his destroyers to investigate a point seventy miles north of the port, where the Japanese were believed to have a base. By 10.30 p.m., when the destroyers had still not returned, Makaroff began to worry that they were lost; so, when a searchlight operator reported movements out to sea, the Admiral assumed the vessels were his own, holding off their return until daylight in case they were mistaken for Japanese. In fact the ships seen by the searchlight operator *were* Japanese, and on the smooth sea, in drizzle and biting cold, they were calmly carrying out Togo's orders.

At dawn on the 13th, four of the minelayers' destroyer escort found to their astonishment that anchored in their midst there was a single one of Makaroff's destroyers. The Russian had indeed got lost and separated from his companions, just as Makaroff had feared. Wandering around in the dark, he had sighted the Japanese, thought they were his lost comrades, and happily settled down for the night with them. The Japanese took no notice, and they had lain all night together without realizing it. In the morning, at the instant of stupefied recognition, a hot fight began, and inevitably the Russian was sunk; but Makaroff, repeating his exploit of the previous month, came racing out from Port Arthur. This time he was aboard the 10,960-ton first-class battleship *Petropavlovsk*. With him came the *Petropavlovsk*'s sister *Poltava* and four cruisers. By then, six cruisers under Rear Admiral Dewa had augmented the Japanese destroyer force; but, when three further Russian battleships emerged, Dewa turned and ran, apparently in full flight.

It was not going exactly to plan, but the effect was just as Togo had intended: to draw out the Russian fleet and set it up for a decisive battle. Hidden by mist, he was approaching with six more cruisers and six battleships – but, fifteen miles from the port, the mist lifted. For the first time the two Admirals sighted each other's fleets at sea. The trap had failed: against the superior force, Makaroff turned for home, and what should have been a battle degenerated into a chase as the fleets streamed towards the distant shore. On the bridge of *Mikasa*, Togo grimaced in disappointment and stared at the fleeing enemy – then suddenly everyone on deck saw *Petropavlovsk* heel over sharply. Seconds later they heard a dull explosion. Aboard *Novik*, closer to the stricken ship, Lieutenant Steer saw and heard everything clearly:

'In quick succession, a series of perfectly deafening explosions, and the big ship, literally broken up into several parts, began to go down fast, head foremost. We saw by degrees the propellors, still revolving, appear out of the water, then her bottom, painted bright green, whilst positive sheets of flame ran along the upper deck, like lava pouring down the slopes of a volcano . . . [she] finally disappeared in a veritable geyser of steam and columns of water [and] lasted barely a minute and a half . . . It was *awful*, all the more awful since we could do nothing in the way of rendering assistance to the victims or in any way arrest the appalling catastrophe.'

In less than ninety seconds, the battleship, 'Little Grandfather', and all his crew had vanished under the sea.

'We were astonished,' said the captain of *Shikishima*. 'When the smoke somewhat dispersed, we saw nothing at all on the sea. One would have thought that a mast would show, but there was nothing.'

On the battleship *Asahi*, a British observer described the dead silence which hung for some moments over the Japanese fleet, and then 'was broken by an involuntary burst of cheering and hand-clapping, succeeded by sympathetic murmurs as the awful probable significance was realized'.

In Port Arthur the Russians were stunned by the tragedy, and an ordinary bosun expressed their wretchedness and misery. 'What's a battleship?' he groaned. 'They are welcome to sink another one, and even a couple of cruisers. That's not it; but we have lost our head. Oh, why had it to be him?'

Far away from the daily business of war, the people of Tokyo and Nagoya held candle-lit processions to honour Togo and mourn Makaroff; and, although the processions became good propaganda, they undoubtedly sprang from a genuine emotion: there had been no personal quarrel with Makaroff, and he had fought bravely; and, to the Japanese, an enemy who dies after fighting with all his might is no longer seen as an enemy.

Aboard *Mikasa*, staff officers suggested that a message of condolence be sent to the bereaved squadron, but Togo vetoed it. Their intention, he said, had been to sink a Russian capital ship, 'and having succeeded beyond expectation, it would be insincere to offer condolences in a simulated spirit of chivalry'. This was honest, at least; but it was also a reflection of the new century, and the new warfare.

From that day on, the fall of Port Arthur was a matter of time. A German doctor living in Tokyo found the national confidence 'almost uncanny', and complained that there were no lanterns to be had; all the shopkeepers said 'they could take no further orders, since their entire stock had been pre-empted for the Port Arthur festival'. In the port itself, the squadron's fragile morale went down to the bottom with Makaroff, and never surfaced. And yet, almost incredibly, they managed to endure for another eight months – a tribute to Port Arthur's natural strength. Those were months in which a third attempt to block them in was made, no more successfully than before; in which Admiral Togo lost seven of his limited fleet, including two battleships; and in which the major sea-battle of this phase of the war was fought.

After Makaroff's death, Togo was able to redispose his fleet for a time; a squadron was sent north to Vladivostock, to keep in the ships there as the summer thaw threatened to release them. A second squadron was sent to assist the Imperial Army's crossing of the Yalu river, and a third reconnoitred the mouth of the Taidong river, where the 10th Army was due to land. But, while Port Arthur remained in Russian hands and Russian ships remained afloat inside it, a substantial part of the Combined Fleet was tied down; and cruising outside the port, in the space of six days, the Japanese suffered more losses than ever before – without a single shell being fired. Despite the blocking attempts, Port Arthur was still open, and both sides began to lay and sweep mines assiduously, so that the mine-fields were constantly shifting. Some mines, moreover, broke loose and drifted as currents took them, and the Russians started laying others, illegally, in international waters, so no part of the sea was quite safe for anyone. On 12 May a Japanese torpedo-boat struck one and sank; on the 13th, a gunboat; on the 14th, in thick fog, two battleships were mined and a cruiser rammed – all sank; the same day a gunboat was run heavily aground, and was severely damaged; two days later a destroyer was mined and sank; and finally, in another collision, a despatch boat went down. Even the smallest of these counted for something, and the two battleships counted for a third of the Imperial Navy's total battleship force. A month later the Vladivostock squadron broke out briefly, raided the coast of Japan itself, and sank three transports containing railway engines destined for Korea and several 11-inch howitzers destined for the land assault on Port Arthur. The stretching and weakness of Japanese communications had never been more evident; but Togo's officers reported that they never saw the slightest sign of perturbation in the Admiral's face. In Tokyo, Baron d'Anethan recorded the same apparent lack of concern: 'The calm – I would say, indifference – with which the government and the population have learnt that the Russian squadron threatened the coasts of Japan is truly extraordinary. So absolute is the confidence concerning the outcome of the war, the taking of Port Arthur and the defeat of [the Russian general] Kuropatkin, that some material damage is regarded as insignificant.'

Dreadful battles still had to be fought ashore before the fortress fell, battles in which the navy took part. To stand for all of them, one, which took place on 20 September, was described by a destroyer captain, watching from his ship eight miles offshore. A dawn chorus of heavy guns from the cruisers and battleships awakened him:

'And at the same time General Nogi's army, which had already taken many of the positions which dominate the line of Russian forts, was employing all its guns against the town and forts . . . Dense clouds of smoke marked the discharge of each gun, and as I looked towards the town through my glasses, I could see masses of far thicker smoke which now and again burst into terrible conflagrations. After an hour and a half of this fiendish din, which filled one's imagination with a vivid picture of this world during the volcanic period, we heard the deafening roar of a terrible explosion. A huge sheet of flame breaking through a dense, black bank of smoke marked the position . . . we made out that one of the powder magazines had exploded. Minutes and hours went by, yet the intensity of fire never flagged; most of the time more than thirty heavy projectiles a minute were falling into the besieged city . . . It was the most gorgeous sight I have ever witnessed in my life.'

By then the squadron's last sea-battle had been fought and lost, and it was trapped in harbour, its guns dismounted and taken ashore to keep up the land defence. Makaroff had been succeeded by a man much more typical of the Russian naval high command, Vilgelm Karlovich Vitgeft, the mirror image of the dead fighting admiral. One of the first things Vitgeft said to his officers after his appointment was, 'Gentlemen, I expect you to assist me with words and deeds. I am no leader of a fleet.' And yet he was a Rear Admiral. Despite his admitted incompetence, however, he did his poor best. At first he had refused to take the squadron to sea, wishing to act solely in defence; this prompted the sarcastic comment that 'for the rest of the war, the squadron will observe the strictest of neutrality'. Eventually the Viceroy, safe in Vladivostock, ordered Vitgeft to try and break out of Port Arthur and reach him. Vitgeft complied with the utmost reluctance, his only consolation the belief that Russian mines and redistribution of the fleet had considerably reduced the nearby Japanese forces. On 23 June the break-out came, beginning at four in the morning: six battleships, five cruisers, and seven destroyers. It took them twelve and a half hours to sweep a passage through the mines. Just before 6 p.m., the weather still clear in the long mid-summer afternoon, the eighteen ships sighted the 'reduced' Japanese fleet – 53 vessels. Vitgeft proceeded, his heart no doubt in his mouth, until 6.45. They were still only twenty-three miles from harbour. Whether they continued or turned back, the danger seemed equally great; but the thought of a night engagement made up Vitgeft's mind, and he turned tail for the old familiar port. He made it, too, in the gathering darkness, with Japanese destroyers and torpedo-boats roaring and hissing a thousand yards and less behind him. Togo would not risk his heavy ships in the mine-infested waters, and results vindicated this caution: although not one of the torpedoes hit, the battleship *Sevastopol* hit what might have been one of the Russians' own mines, and limped back into her refuge with a hole in her hull.

This extraordinary non-battle was seen by the British naval observer on *Mikasa*, William Pakenham, as 'one of the most remarkable victories in history'. He regarded it as a personal battle of nerves and will: 'Here were Togo and a Russian admiral face to face. The man Vitgeft quailed and retired before the man Togo. Is it possible to conceive of triumph of armed and numerous force more personal to an individual?

It was certainly a psychological victory of the kind approved by Sun Tzu, but, with the ever-present threat of the Baltic Fleet joining Port Arthur, Togo required the 'inferior' victory as well, and Vitgeft had not the least intention of giving him the chance for that. It took a personal order from Tsar Nicholas to get the Russian admiral out of harbour again; and when, on 10 August, the squadron weighed anchor for the last time, the admiral's signal was an apologetic shrugging off of responsibility: 'The fleet is informed that His Majesty has ordered us to proceed to Vladivostock.' In October 1903 this same admiral had said, with the confidence of a true desk-sailor, 'Our fleet cannot be defeated by the Japanese fleet, whether in the Gulf of Korea or the Yellow Sea.' Now he sent quay-side well-wishers away with the gloomy prophecy that they would meet again 'in the next world'.

Later on, one of the officers remembered that the squadron 'started with the firm conviction that it was going to meet with disaster'. Every moveable ship was going out, but some of them were not even sea-worthy, let alone battle-worthy. One of the battleships, hit in harbour below the water-line, was taking in water from the moment she got under weigh. Another had a wooden replica in place of a gun too badly damaged to be repaired; and two of the Russian-built cruisers, victims of drawing-board inefficiency which (in the name of 'improvements') altered a ship's design again and again during her actual building, were 'just about fit to act as targets'. The squadron for the Vladivostock run totalled eighteen vessels: six battleships, four cruisers and eight destroyers. The destroyers and one cruiser, *Novik*, were in the van, the other cruisers in the rear, with Admiral Vitgeft in *Tsarevich* leading the centrally-placed battleships. Against these the Imperial Navy, despite its collisions and mining disasters, could still muster four battleships, 19 cruisers and 46 destroyers and torpedo-boats, as well as the old second-class battleship *Chen-yuen*, captured from the Chinese ten years earlier; but they were widely scattered. Six of the cruisers were far away with Admiral Kamimura in the Sea of Japan, keeping the Vladivostock squadron in harbour. Eleven more of the cruisers were located to the east and west of Port Arthur. The huge quantity of torpedo craft could only be used to real advantage after dark, and the antique *Chen-yuen*'s value was mainly for display; so what it came down to, when, at 11.30 a.m., the two admirals sighted each other's ships once again, was a fairly even balance. Vitgeft's great hope was to get away without a fight, or at least without more than a skirmish at long range, and then to elude – or, with his material superiority, to defeat – the six cruisers in the Sea of Japan. Togo's intention at the same time was to lure Vitgeft on until he was so far from Port Arthur he could not return, but not so far that he could escape.

With the sky clear, a light breeze dispersing the mist and the sea calm, the Japanese fleet felt it was 'perfect weather for a fight'. They almost lost the opportunity. After an hour's manoeuvring, with occasional exchanges of fire at over 8,000 yards, Togo was on the brink of crossing the Russian T – the classic move in which all the attacking fleet's guns are brought to bear simultaneously on the single ship that leads the enemy line. Togo believed firmly that the flagship should always lead. *Mikasa*, accordingly, was at the head of the Japanese line, when Vitgeft unexpectedly swung away to port, a move which left Togo with two choices. Either he could about-turn all his ships together, which would place *Mikasa* in the rear, or he could keep her in the van by turning the fleet in succession, all ships following him. But that would take time, and, with the Russian ships making 14 knots and the distance between the fleets increasing at every moment, the idea of escape to Vladivostock became a real possibility – if only Vitgeft could maintain his lead until dark. Faced with this quandary, Togo stuck to his beliefs; the fleet turned in succession.

When the evolution was complete, the nearest things in sight were the sterns of the Russian rear-guard cruisers, making off as fast as they could towards the horizon. Togo's dilemma seemed even worse. The Russian battleships, far ahead, had to be destroyed or turned back; merely bagging a few of the rear-guard cruisers would still leave a force capable of beating the Kamimura cruisers in the Japan Sea. But if Togo's ships came up straight astern of Vitgeft, then, once the rival battleships were in range of each other, the Russian cruisers would also be able to challenge the Japanese battleships, while the *Japanese* cruisers would still be too far away to join in. It was even conceivable that, if Togo gave direct chase, Vitgeft might choose to relinquish part of his lead, make a sharp turn, and cross the Japanese T.

What happened next thoroughly confused everybody – except, presumably, Admiral Togo. He altered course to starboard, increased his speed to 15 knots, and began to pull away from the Russian line. As the range gradually increased, the firing – which had been sporadic – diminished further, and shortly after 3 p.m. ceased altogether. By then the fleets were so far apart the Russians could see nothing more than the enemy funnels and superstructures jutting above the horizon. Togo seemed to have given up.

The Russian crews relaxed and were ordered to go and eat, more hopeful and optimistic than they had been for many months, 'glad to be away from Arthur and the constant quarrelling, which made one ready to look for death as a relief'. 'We were advancing markedly,' another recalled. 'Our road was clear. If only our battleships had been able to go the speed they possessed on paper!'

In the Japanese boiler-rooms, stokers were slaving in 130° Fahrenheit, pressing the engines to the maximum. The notion that Togo had given up was an idle hope. What he was doing was charging forward as fast as possible in a great ellipse, curving out from the Russians to overtake their cruisers outside their range, and curving in again to meet the battleships with his own. By 4.30 p.m., the ellipse had been made: the opposing battleships were less than five miles apart. At 4.45 the battle recommenced, and Admiral Vitgeft began the last hour of his life. He ordered his cruisers to steam two miles to port of his battleships, parallel with them; Togo did likewise with his cruisers, sending them off to starboard; and so the battle which developed became that rarity in the age of steam – a duel between fleets of battleships in line ahead. It was also a race between the fleets and against the sun, a deadly competition in which the Japanese had two advantages – their own confidence, and the Russian smokeless Pyroxyline shells. Every Japanese hit, with clouds of brownish-black gas and smoke, was visible from any deck – 'it gave one in the first moment the impression that it had produced some catastrophe,' said a Russian – but the Russians could not see their own hits. In fact their shooting was far better than the Japanese had been expecting, and *Mikasa* came in for much of it – there were hits below decks, on the after funnel, on the water-line, and one so close to the bridge that 'a junior officer had the honour of receiving in his body a fragment which would otherwise have killed our Admiral'.

In such circumstances it was extremely difficult for any individual to have a clear idea of what was going on; as a Russian lieutenant wrote, 'the brain overflows . . . Occupied with the search for means to stop the sudden inrush of water somewhere below, one unconsciously shudders at the dull roar of a big projectile passing overhead, or at the groans of some wounded close by; the stampede of the stretcher party hustles you; the deafening sound of our own guns momentarily obliterates the distant thunder of those of the enemy. The agonizing thought that death is near, or that it will be your turn next to be mutilated, grips you by the throat and to some extent clouds your brain . . .'

Another Russian found he would react quite differently: 'The sea was boiling . . . Of course we were firing like mad. Our guns were roaring incessantly. To this was added the noise of the bursting shell. Clouds of smoke and gigantic columns of water arose all around us. What chaos! And yet this picture of the elements let loose was beautiful. I heard the call for stretcher parties, saw that blood was streaming on the deck; but this was unable to break the spell. These things seemed trivialities which could not be helped.'

Like Togo, Vitgeft was on the bridge of his flagship *Tsarevich*; both were exposed in positions of extreme danger and able to see the damage inflicted on their own ships, but Vitgeft could not see the damage his guns inflicted in return. At 5.45, though, he must have been aware that, if only he could hold on for another half-hour, darkness would begin to fall, and safety for himself and all his fleet would be at hand. But it was at that instant that two 12-inch shells hurtled down, exploded on impact without penetrating the decks, and, blowing a furious shock-wave of shrapnel, gas and smoke in every direction, brought down *Tsarevich*'s foremast and shattered her conning-tower. And, when the smoke cleared, a single piece of one leg was all that could be found of Admiral Vitgeft.

Within moments the Russian fleet was in utter confusion. Not only Vitgeft but his second-in-command was dead; the ship's captain was unconscious; and the wheel was jammed over with bodies that had been flung against it. *Tsarevich* circled crazily; some ships followed, thinking the movement intentional, while others hesitated, since no signal had been made. It took the senior surviving officer – Rear Admiral Prince Ukhtomski aboard the battleship *Peresvyet* – several minutes to realize he *was* the senior surviving officer, and several more minutes to put any kind of order back into the turmoil. When he did, his instruction was the simplest possible – 'Follow me' – and the direction he led the fleet was back to Port Arthur. Not everyone obeyed: *Peresvyet*'s topmasts had been shot away, and the signal had to be attached to the rails of her upper bridge, where it was almost invisible. But, even when all had understood Ukhtomski's intention, several ships decided to obey the Tsar rather than the Prince: 'As soon as it is dark,' said the captain of the cruiser *Diana*, 'we shall separate from the squadron, and, if it is possible, go to Vladivostock.' None made it. *Tsarevich* and three destroyers got to Tsingtao, *Diana* to Saigon, the cruiser *Askold* and a destroyer to Shanghai. All were interned. *Novik* made it as far as Sakhalien, where two fast cruisers caught and sank her, and a single destroyer was driven ashore near Wei-Hai-Wei.

Even when the whole war was over, many Japanese considered this, the Battle of the Yellow Sea, to have been their most important naval engagement. As darkness fell on 10 August, Togo sent in his torpedo-boats to harry the fleeing remnants, but once again caution prevented him from letting his battleships measure themselves against their rivals in the mined coastal waters. Yet he was probably not too regretful; at last he could be certain that the squadron would not re-emerge.

Next day, the victory confirmed, the Imperial Navy was jubilant. 'At last we have had our battle!' one officer wrote in his diary. 'The Russian squadron has been vanquished, just as China was at the Battle of the Yalu. Japan is absolute mistress of the sea!'

In the opinion of a British admiral, the double hit on *Tsarevich* was 'the most critical minute of the war'. One Russian sailor wrote with philosophical sadness, 'It is quite clear that he [Ukhtomski] should never have been made a flag officer, but having been made it, one was bound to take him as he was . . . One cannot *order* anyone to be a hero.' But most of the Russians were filled with rage and bitterness, and some even believed that the Prince had run away from certain victory:

'. . . So we came back, and thanked God that we had got inside without meeting the fate of Makaroff, which was luck more than anything else, for no one took precautions and no one cared. Our chance was gone; the ships were too damaged ever to go out again!'

8

'A collection of stage properties'

'And after all this an Admiral came,
A terrible man with a terrible name,
A name which we all of us know very well
But no one can speak and no one can spell.'

Zinovi Petrovich Rozhdestvenski was the name. Physically, the man was as imposing as the name suggested. He was a Rear Admiral, Chief of the Russian Naval General Staff; and in 1905, in his fifty-seventh year, he was in charge of the biggest, most unwieldy fleet that Russia had ever put to sea. The voyage of the Russian Baltic Fleet – the Japanese Navy's nightmare through all those months of blockade and battle around Port Arthur – began in comedy, ended in tragedy, and was marred throughout by incompetence and inefficiency. But it was also an epic achievement, one of history's great voyages, which no one could fail to admire. A fleet of almost fifty ships travelled nearly 20,000 miles without loss, and with scant assistance. An old-fashioned sailing fleet, drawing its power from the wind, might actually have found less challenge in such distances; the modern fleet, dependent on coal to move at all, needed regular fuel supplies from shore or from other ships – and, from the Baltic to Japan, the Anglo-Japanese Alliance effectively prevented Rozhdestvenski's ships from coaling ashore. So with few exceptions, when the French broke the international embargo, all coaling operations were undertaken at sea; and, each time, as much as possible was taken on, with every available space filled. Cabins, bathrooms and deck areas all overflowed, with the extra weight pushing the ships' armour bands below sea-level and making the vessels dangerously top-heavy. But that was only one among many severe problems, the two worst of which were the very components of the fleet: the ships and the men. The former ranged from those so out-dated they were virtually obsolete, to those so new they had not completed their trials. The majority broke down repeatedly, forcing the rest to wait while repairs were made, and sometimes reducing the fleet's progress to an infuriating three knots or less. Hardly one of them matched any other, in speed, armour, armament or range, and the fastest and strongest – which were good – were constantly handicapped. 'The difficulties of handling a fleet so composed,' said Fred T. Jane in an untypically supercilious manner, 'are more immense than any civilian can possibly grasp.' Jane's passionate interest in all naval matters, and the fact that he was one-eighth Russian, led to the slanderous rumour in Britain that he was a Russian spy. And even his publication in 1899 of a book on the Tsar's navy, written after he had visited several Russian naval bases, did little to dispel the rumour, because the navy he described seemed too hopeless to be true. Far from being a fledgling fifth columnist, however, he was simply reporting the facts.

The Russian Navy was an organization based on favouritism, preferment, bribery and graft – an occupation fashionable for officers, who bought their commissions with smart uniforms to show off in the cities, and incomprehensible to the ordinary ratings, who were generally farming peasants taken unwillingly from their villages, and not at all at home on the sea. 'In appearance,' said Jane, 'the Russian executives struck me as differing chiefly from their English brethren in that some of them wore moustaches; otherwise there was a wonderful similarity.' But, he added, this 'does not necessarily prove that their efficiency is equal . . . as a class the Russian junior engineer officers are very inefficient, continually causing minor accidents through ignorance; they have a weakness for turning taps off and on in a casual way. Every officer does not become one for love of a sea-life, and in consequence is very anxious to secure a shore-going billet . . . Foreign service comes to be looked upon as a sort of exile to be avoided as much as possible'. As for the men, in comparison to the British, Jane found that 'Ivan is not over-clean. In fact, he stands much where our men stood a hundred years or more ago. He comes, too, from a different and lower class; the young British blue-jacket has to be a very respectable youth. *He* is a sailor, too, from boyhood; the Russian joins as a man of 21, and joins because he is told to, not because he wants to'.

Jane repeated this again and again – it had been one of the things which impressed him most deeply about the Russian Navy. 'The sluggish, good-tempered moujik can hardly comprehend hot blood and passion on the battlefield. He fights as he ploughs – because he is told to. They would accept war more with a dogged determination to do their best than with a conviction of certain success . . . Ivan realizes that he exists *to be shot at*; Jack, that he exists *to shoot at* others, and this psychological difference is all the difference in the world.'

The Baltic Fleet, renamed the Second Pacific Squadron, weighed anchor on 15 October 1904 and set off to relieve the squadron trapped in Port Arthur, twenty thousand miles away. It had taken the authorities over eight months to reach this decision; and within five minutes of starting, one battleship had run aground and another had been rammed by a torpedo-boat. In the North Sea the fleet came within an ace of precipitating a conflict with England when they fired on and sank some trawlers fishing off the Dogger Bank – a minor tragedy in the scale of war, but in the scale of peace 'a most dastardly outrage', as King Edward wrote. Although it was finally accepted that the Russians had just been nervous and trigger-happy, it was, in *The Times*' words, 'almost inconceivable that any men calling themselves seamen, however frightened they might be, could spend twenty minutes bombarding a fleet of fishing boats without discovering the nature of their target'. The Russians had believed there were Japanese torpedo-boats lurking amongst the trawlers and, though they apologized formally and paid a hefty cash sum in compensation, that belief never altered, however improbable it seemed to everyone else.

In fact they had some reason for their suspicion. Only a year before, in September 1903, two lieutenant-commanders of the Japanese Navy working as clerks in the offices of the Potemkin Shipping Company in St Petersburg had been arrested – correctly – on charges of espionage. Their names were Akiyoshi Seiko and Kamamura Kenzo. The arrests took place the day before Kamamura was due to marry a Russian girl, and, in time-honoured style, his fiancée turned out to be a member of the Ochrana, the Tsarist secret police. The incident had enabled the Imperial Navy to change its intelligence codes, without which the Port Arthur strike would not have remained secret. It also enabled them to capitalize on the misgivings of Russian intelligence for, realizing that the Russians knew there were other naval agents scattered throughout Europe, the Imperial Navy network 'let slip' an occasional titbit, including the idea of a North Sea ambush. This was not revealed until after the war was over, and at the time only one Briton knew of it – Edgar Wallace, correspondent for the *Daily Mail* in Vigo. When Rozhdestvenski's fleet called there, Wallace met and interviewed two petty officers who explained how Russian intelligence had had warning of the 'ambush'. Wallace's editor in London disbelievingly sent him on to Tangiers, the fleet's next port of call, to obtain confirmation, which came in a macabre manner: between Vigo and Tangiers the two informants were executed and buried at sea. Wallace may have made it all up – not surprisingly, neither the Russians nor the Japanese offered corroboration; but on the whole it seems far more likely that the Imperial Navy had remembered Sun Tzu, and duped the Russians with a masterly piece of disinformation.

Speaking shortly after the Dogger Bank incident, at least one of Rozhdestvenski's officers thought it was a pity war had not broken out between Russia and England there and then, 'because then they would have scattered us directly we had got outside. Now we have to go all that distance to meet the same fate'.

With men of that calibre under his command, Rozhdestvenski probably knew he was doomed from the start. On 21 April 1905 the German ambassador to Washington, who was very friendly with Theodore Roosevelt, wrote prophetically to the President. 'The Russians are on the big horse again,' he said, not quite colloquially, 'but Togo is bound to knock them out of the saddle. Suppose the smashing up of the Russian battleships will occur near the bases of Japan.'

By 26 May, more than seven months after leaving the Baltic, Rozhdestvenski had shepherded and bullied his ill-assorted ships and worse-assorted crews to the mouth of the Sea of Japan. He had tried unsuccessfully to shed the oldest, weakest and slowest ships by sending them through the Suez Canal, while he, with the main squadrons, proceeded via the Cape of Good Hope. In Madagascar he had quelled an incipient mutiny, and on the night of 5 January had received the 'bitter and humiliating' news that Port Arthur, the objective of his voyage, had fallen on the 2nd. Somewhere in Russia, Vladimir Lenin wrote: 'The capitulation of Port Arthur is the prologue to the capitulation of tsarism.' Very far from Russia, Admiral Rozhdestvenski had sent his own assessment of the situation in an uncompromising telegram to his Admiralty: 'I have not the slightest prospect of recovering command of the sea with the force under my orders. The despatch of reinforcements composed of untested and in some cases badly built vessels would only render the fleet more vulnerable. In my view the only possible course is to use all force to break through to Vladivostock and from this base to threaten the enemy's communications.'

'I do not see,' said one of Port Arthur's survivors, 'why the Baltic Fleet should fear defeat, if only good attention is paid to shooting.' It was just as well, for this man's equanimity, that he had not heard Rozhdestvenski's Order of the Day on 27 January. It was long, angry and depressed, and in part it went as follows:

'The manner in which the battleships and cruisers weighed anchor yesterday showed that after four months in the squadron the results which might have been expected have not been reached as yet. This operation took about one hour, but even at the end of a full hour the ships had not yet taken up their respective stations . . .

'If we have not learnt to work together during the four months we have been in company, we are hardly likely to do so by the time we may, under God's will, expect to meet the enemy . . .

'The firing yesterday was extremely slow . . . the expensive 12-inch shells were fired away without anything like the same proportion of hits as the guns of other calibres . . . practice with the 12-pounder Q.F. [quick-firing] guns was very bad . . . As regards the firing of the 6-pounder Q.F. guns, which are intended to repel torpedo attacks, one really feels ashamed to speak of it . . . the entire squadron did not score *one single hit*, although the targets were stationary.'

And yet, however much he agonized over expense and inefficiency, Rozhdestvenski later admitted that throughout the seven-month voyage 'the admirals were never called together to discuss a detailed plan of battle, and, speaking generally, no such plan was drawn up'. The only admiral who had no need of such plans was Baron Dimitri von Felkerzam: on 25 May, aboard his flagship *Oslyabya*, he died at sea. For the sake of morale his death had not been announced to the fleet, and on the night of the 26th, as the ships ploughed through a low mist, and a waning moon shone in a clear sky, Felkerzam's coffin lay, sinister in the ghostly light, on his flagship's upper deck, while his flag still flew from her stern.

Rozhdestvenski at that point had three possible routes for the last leg of the immense voyage, now extended to Vladivostock. Crossing the Indian Ocean his ships had gone 4,500 miles without being seen. Even then, wrote one commander unhappily, they 'only managed with difficulty to maintain something in the shape of a formation in clear weather and under the most favourable navigational conditions . . . only one formation ever succeeds: the formation of "huddled-up-mass". A sad sight!'

The choices ahead of them were the Tsugaru Straits, between Japan's main island, Honshu, and the more northerly Hokkaido; the Straits of La Pérouse, between Hokkaido and Sakhalien; or the Straits of Tsushima, otherwise known as the Straits of Korea, between Korea and Japan's south-western tip. Tsugaru was discounted immediately; the straits were sometimes only seven miles wide, had strong currents, and had a naval base on their southern shore matched by an army base on the northern. The authorities in St Petersburg, whom fleet officers vilified as 'patent strategists', recommended La Pérouse, blithely ignoring the extra distance it entailed and the mind-boggling problems of coaling in secret off the enemy coast. One officer wrote in exasperation that the clumsy fleet was expected 'to pass the Kuriles in a thick fog, safely get into the funnel of La Pérouse, avoid Kamen Opasnosti [a very dangerous shoal], and then, on reaching the open sea, to endeavour to get to Vladivostock! I beg leave to point out that I am now discussing the question purely from the navigator's point of view, in which I leave out any consideration regarding possible interference by the Japanese'. No; it had to be Tsushima, the widest and most direct. Rozhdestvenski sent a pair of cruisers off around Japan's east coast with instructions to make as much of a nuisance of themselves as possible, and give any ships they encountered the impression that the entire fleet was behind them. But they saw no Japanese warships at all, for the simple reason that there were none in the area. Rozhdestvenski had also sent his colliers to Shanghai, a clear advertisement that he intended to take the shortest route, and after a period of intensive refitting, repairing, and yet more training, the battle-seasoned Japanese Main Fleet was waiting, only a little anxiously, off the island of Tsushima.

As he smoked his pipe, silent and alone in his cabin on *Mikasa*, Admiral Togo's anxiety was prompted not by the thought of battle, but by the worry that a battle might not take place. He knew as well as Rozhdestvenski the alternative routes available to the Baltic Fleet, and from an identical reasoning process had worked out the Russians' choice; but he also knew their colliers had arrived in Shanghai in the afternoon of 25 May, and he had expected the fleet to appear in the Tsushima Straits by the 26th at latest. By nightfall there was still no sign of them, and he began to face the possibility that they might after all have gone eastwards to La Pérouse. Provided news came in time, he could probably steam up the Sea of Japan to intercept them as they crossed; but, if he failed, there was the dreadful spectre of a hugely reinforced Vladivostock squadron; another interminable siege by land and sea; threats to Japanese communications, and perhaps to the homeland itself; and such a revival of Russian strength and morale in the Far East that Japan's resources of men and money would be drained away entirely. A foreign observer in Japan had noted in admiration that 'the whole country is sending its best flesh and blood without a whimper or a murmur to feed the war . . . the country may bleed to death internally without the world knowing it. O Japanese! You are a wonderful people, and mighty fighters'. Civilians faced not only the loss of friends and relatives, but steep inflation induced by the war; wages in 1905 were 2.3% higher than in 1903, but prices of daily necessities had shot up by 21%. There might be a limit to national solidarity; there was certainly a limit to war capability. The hundreds of thousands of lives, the millions in cash, could not go on indefinitely, and the Baltic Fleet in Vladivostock could win the war for Russia. The whole of Japan was depending on its fleet; the fleet was depending on Togo; and, as the night of 26 May wore on, Togo grew less and less sure that he was in the right place.

Yet all he could do was wait. A picket-line of 16 ships had been stationed over the straits' hundred-mile width, and charts of the area had been divided into numbered squares so that any sighting could be reported swiftly and accurately; but, as midnight passed and no signal came, the mist over the sea thickened to fog and visibility dropped to two miles. At any moment, the picket-ships could survey less than two-thirds of the straits.

Aboard Rozhdestvenski's flagship, the battleship *Suvoroff*, the admiral had fallen asleep in an armchair on the bridge. Beside him, the ship's commander paced silently up and down, from time to time staring gleefully out – the fog was so thick he could not even see the sternmost ships. 'How can they find us in this?' he asked a colleague nearby. 'It's 200,000 to one against anyone running into us accidentally! We've been going for twenty-four hours without being seen. If it's the same tomorrow, we'll give them the slip! They are on the move, and keep calling each other up, and they haven't come on us! They'll have to wait for our second coming, out of Vladivostock! That'll be a different tale. My! What a stew they must be in! What fun!' And he began to laugh so much he had to stuff his handkerchief into his mouth, to avoid disturbing the admiral.

At 2.45 a.m., forty miles west of the Goto Islands, Captain Narukawa's converted merchant cruiser *Shinano Maru* was patrolling her section of the picket-line. Nothing had been seen all night; then someone spotted three vertical lights, white, red and white, glowing softly through the mist. Whatever ship they were on, it could not be seen clearly, and Narukawa moved in to have a closer look.

Aboard the hospital ship *Orel* the startled look-out suddenly saw an unfamiliar vessel approach, then move away rapidly.

For more than an hour Narukawa cautiously shadowed *Orel*, uncertain of her identity. She had the lines of a Russian auxiliary, but it was so extraordinary that she was carrying lights he could hardly bring himself to believe it. At 4.30, as the sky began to lighten, he approached again, saw she had no guns, and recognized her as an enemy hospital ship. During the night a damp, penetrating breeze had sprung up, and just as Narukawa identified *Orel*, at 4.45, the mist swirled aside. Not a mile away he saw ten warships or more, and the smoke of many others. The signal went out: 'Enemy is in square 203.'

Twenty minutes later, relayed from the Third Squadron, the message arrived aboard *Mikasa*. The conquest of 203-Metre Hill had ensured the fall of Port Arthur. It had to be a good omen, even though it was mere coincidence. In the suddenly electric mood on the flagship, an officer remembered one thing in particular: Togo laughed, as cheerful as a child. Moments later his own message was flashed to the Minister of the Navy in Tokyo, terse and supremely confident: 'The Russian fleet has been sighted. I am going to attack it and annihilate it.'

9

'The day is fine, but the sea is high'

'By combining with the squadron led by Admiral Nebogatoff, our squadron is not only equal in strength to the enemy's, but we are superior in number of battleships. The Japanese, however, have had more experience of war than we, and are more skilled in gunnery and warfare. You must not forget this. Though they may fire with greater rapidity than we, we must not imitate them and waste ammunition. The Japanese are of unparalleled loyalty to their Imperial Family and state. They are a nation who hate dishonour and think nothing of sacrificing their lives in the cause of heroism. But we have made an oath to the Lord of Heaven . . . we shall wipe away with our blood the shame which has so far been brought to our fatherland.'

That was one of Admiral Rozhdestvenski's Orders of the Day to his fleet – accurate, but hardly calculated to inspire bravery or confidence. Admiral Togo's Order of the Day on 27 May 1905, factually as accurate, could not have been more different in mood.

'The combined squadrons are at last to meet the enemy. We have developed a high fighting efficiency, and now that we are to defeat the enemy there is little more that I can say to you. But in order that in this final battle there may be no misunderstanding I wish to give you a few final instructions.

'In a battle the most important thing is caution. We must not fear a formidable enemy, or make light of a weak one [here he echoed the Imperial Rescript of 1882], and we must not be taken by surprise. Those who have little experience in fighting are apt to feel that the enemy is strong and we are weak; this is because while we cannot see the damage done to the enemy's vessels, the damage to ours is always before our eyes . . . The most important point in battle is to do to the enemy what we would not wish him to do to us.'

When Togo received Captain Narukawa's alert, *Mikasa* was anchored with the Main Body of the fleet in Chinhae Bay – the very bay whose name Togo had underlined in his notebook six years before, in his time as Commander-in-Chief of Sasebo. This was not prescience, of course; he had simply noted the virtues of the place and remembered it in case it should ever prove useful. But it was just such attention to detail and possibility that enabled him to give that marvellous comment in his Order of the Day – 'now that we are to defeat the enemy there is little more I can say to you.' To have such implicit and utter confidence in the men and ships in his command must be the hope of every fighting admiral; and to be given such confidence must have thrilled and galvanized every man in Togo's fleet.

At dawn the Russian fleet was 150 miles from Chinhae Bay. At 5.20 a.m., Narukawa lost sight of the enemy in the rising morning mist. For forty-five minutes more they went unobserved, when another glimpse allowed Narukawa to estimate their course and speed; and from 6.45, when Admiral Kamimura took over surveillance with his six-year-old armoured cruiser *Izumo*, they were watched almost constantly. Togo decided to give battle in the vicinity of Okinoshima, an island east of Tsushima, and over the next seven hours he received unceasing reports through the still-novel medium of the wireless. Even he found the experience impressive. 'Though a heavy mist covered the sea and visibility was only five miles,' he said later, 'the enemy's disposition was as clear to us, many tens of miles away, as if we had seen it with our own eyes.'

That disposition was certainly curious. Beginning with a cruising formation of two parallel lines, Rozhdestvenski, with considerable difficulty, got his ships into the battle formation of line ahead. Accidentally, or from sheer fright, one of the ships loosed off a 12-inch shell at the enemy cruisers observing from five miles away, and all the rest of the Russian fleet instantly joined in. On *Suvoroff*'s bridge, as tense as his men, Rozhdestvenski bellowed with anger and a signal was hurriedly run up: 'Ammunition not to be wasted.' But the crews were ecstatic, and congratulated each other, for the Japanese were vanishing, moving away into the mist. The men were ordered to dinner; and, by the time they were finished, the Admiral had decided that a line abreast might be better than a line ahead. The change was only half done when the enemy cruisers suddenly reappeared. With neither one formation nor the other, Rozhdestvenski tried to pull his ships back to line ahead, which produced such confusion that he ended up with something like a cruising disposition – two parallel lines, the starboard slightly ahead of the port, and each masking the other's guns. It was no battle fleet, but a mob – 'this is the only adequate word,' exclaimed Admiral Nebogatoff despairingly.

Behind the cruisers, Togo and the Main Body were approaching at 14 knots. The ships, painted light grey, were almost invisible; but, for some bizarre reason, Rozhdestvenski had decreed long ago that every funnel in *his* fleet should be painted brilliant yellow. In harbour, above the black hulls, they had looked very smart to an unprofessional eye; on a misty sea, just before battle, they looked like invitation cards.

At 1.39 p.m. the Japanese Main Body saw them. Even with the confidence of past victories it was a daunting apparition. William Pakenham was aboard the battleship *Asahi* and saw that 'in the right column the four biggest battleships loomed enormous, dwarfing all others into insignificance. It was not easy to realize that the battleships of Japan were probably producing at least equal effect on the minds of the Russians'. But they were; to the inexperienced Russians they seemed like monsters, and aboard the battleship which had fired that first inadvertant shot 'dead silence prevailed. It seemed as if the crew were in a state of suspended animation'.

It had taken the Russians a few minutes longer than the Japanese to make out their enemy fleet. In those minutes Togo had altered course, and the Russians' first sight of *Mikasa* was as she steamed nonchalantly across Rozhdestvenski's T. The battleships in her wake held station so well it looked as if they were chained together; and, as the Russian officers and gun crews watched, a signal fluttered up to *Mikasa*'s yardarm – the Z flag, quartered in red, black, yellow and blue. It was another memory of Nelson, a slight variation of the signal at Port Arthur, and the most celebrated signal in Japanese naval history: 'The fate of the empire depends on this battle. Let every man do his utmost.'

Another turn brought the Japanese onto a course opposite and parallel to the Russians'; and then, in a move so audacious it became known as 'the Togo turn', *Mikasa* wheeled hard to port, followed in succession by all the others. If it succeeded the manoeuvre would mean that the two fleets would be steaming parallel and in the same direction; but turning in succession meant that each successive ship passed over the same area of water, and in doing so masked the guns of those behind her – and the turning area was within Russian range. 'How rash!' said an officer on *Suvoroff* in amazement. 'Why, in a minute we'll be able to roll up the leading ships!' Another officer, a veteran of Port Arthur, felt his heart beating faster than it had ever done during the siege, and prayed – 'If we succeeded! God grant it! Even if we didn't sink one of them, if we could only put one out of action!'

And, three minutes later, the firing began.

The Battle of Tsushima – or the Battle of the Sea of Japan, as it is known in Japan – was the first major sea battle since 1827, when a combined British, French and Russian fleet decisively defeated a Turco-Egyptian fleet at Navarino Bay in Greece. Tsushima was also the first major battle between steam ships, much larger, more decisive and of far greater consequence than the Battle of the Yalu in 1894; and, in comparison, the Battle of the Yellow Sea in 1904 had been a mere rehearsal. Tsushima bore out Japan's confidence in her navy and its Commander-in-Chief, Togo's confidence in his men, their confidence in him, and his own confidence in himself. As nearly as made no odds, the Russian Baltic Fleet was annihilated, just as Togo had promised. Out of the 38 Russian ships which entered the battle, nineteen –

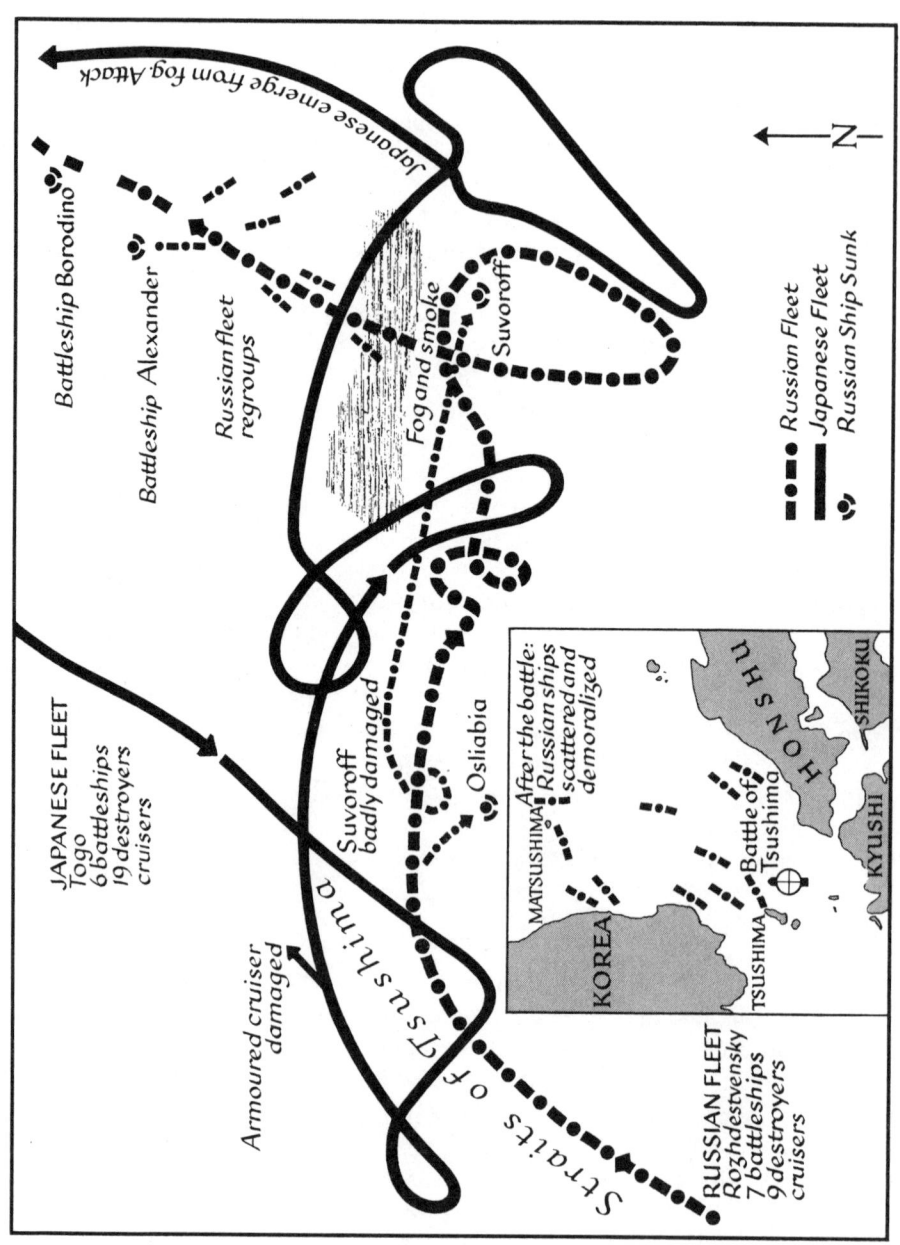

exactly half – were sunk. Seven were captured; six were interned in neutral ports; two scuttled themselves; one escaped to Madagascar; and three ships – two destroyers and a cruiser – were all that was left to take the news to Vladivostock. 4,830 Russian sailors died. So many were wounded that no tally was taken of them. 5,917 became prisoners-of-war in Japan, and a further 1,862 were interned with their ships in neutral ports. Japanese losses were 117 killed, 583 wounded, and three torpedo-boats sunk – not a single capital ship was irreparably damaged.

This was naval victory on the grandest scale imaginable, and the Russians firmly believed that the Japanese must have used submarines, at Tsushima if nowhere else; but they had not. The Russo-Japanese naval war was the last major sea-war fought in two dimensions, on the surface only. As the reports of Tsushima were slowly pieced together, every naval nation studied them with intense interest. Perhaps the most important result of these studies was the launch in February 1906 of the British battleship *Dreadnought*, the order for which had been stormed through Parliament and the Admiralty by the eccentric and irascible First Sea Lord, Admiral Jacky Fisher. The analysis he demanded immediately after Tsushima came up with two revolutionary conclusions. The first was that, to a modern fighting fleet, speed was absolutely vital; Togo's advantage of only a few knots had been one of the crucial elements in his victory. If one battleship could manage 16 knots while another could do only 12, the effect was just as if the slower was standing still while the faster moved at 4 knots and chose its firing position at will. The second conclusion was that, if a battleship's big guns could be shot accurately at long range, the smaller guns were superfluous, an unnecessary waste of space and weight. Fisher's naval analysts commented: 'If, as seems probable, the lesson is equally appreciated and acted on by other maritime powers, it is evident that all existing battleships will shortly become obsolescent, and our preponderance of vessels in that class will be of little use.' Fisher had already begun a programme of total modernization of the Royal Navy before the report came in, and on it he wrote: 'How glad we ought to be that we dropped out the battleships and armoured cruisers last year! Why, they are now as obsolete as the Ark!' HMS *Dreadnought*, armed with ten 12-inch guns and, against torpedo-boats, only 27 little 12-pounders, inaugurated the age of the 'all-big-gun' battleship. She ran on steam turbines, the first major warship to do so, which gave her 17,900 tons a maximum speed of 21 knots and a cruising range of 6,620 miles at 16 knots. And Fisher was right: she made every other battleship 'as obsolete as the Ark'. Historically, this meant that, only nine months after their cataclysmic victory at Tsushima, the warships of the Imperial Japanese Navy were already on their way to museums and dry docks. It also meant that the Battle of Tsushima was unique, not only in Russian and Japanese history, but in world history, because it was the only test and proof of nineteenth-century naval development. In those terms, it was the end of one age and the beginning of another, and it could not be repeated.

Nevertheless, many of the individual experiences of the combatants were not much different to those of sea-battles before and after. In all the complex manoeuvres, culminating at 2.25 p.m. in Togo's second crossing of the T – this time *within range* – no single person, not even the Commanders-in-Chief, could see everything that was happening, and most people, most of the time, could see very little. Outside, mist, sometimes thickening to fog and always augmented by smoke, swirled across every man's vision. Whenever a gun fired there was the brilliant flash of flame, flaring yards out of its muzzle; the roar that burst some men's eardrums, and left them deafened for whatever remained of their lives; the thump and shudder that passed through the entire ship. Underfoot, the decks were vibrating and pitching as the engines strained and the helmsman swung the wheel from one side to the other; overhead was the whine and shriek of the enemy's shells, the deluging waterspouts of near-misses, the shattering, blazing impact of hits, the hiss and rattle of white-hot shrapnel as it flew and struck – 'an inferno of noise' was how one young officer remembered this horror. And below-decks was no less hellish: the stink of blood, vomit and antiseptics in the sick-bay, of coal and oil in the engine-rooms, the stunning concussions on the hull, the dead and the living and the almost-dead thrown bodily across cabins, along corridors, down ladders – and, perhaps worst of all, the special terror that the ship might become a tomb for them all. This was one of the dreadful novelties wrought by the Russo-Japanese naval war: however perforated a wooden ship was, it generally remained more or less afloat; but, despite its stronger build, a battered steel ship could sink like a stone. And at Tsushima, of course, nineteen of them did. In each of the nineteen, as a Russian survivor said, 'anyone familiar with the details of naval life can imagine what went on in the bowels of the doomed ship'.

'When she turned turtle, the men inside must have been flung from floor to roof with all objects that were not firmly attached; and this in absolute darkness, save for the glow from the furnaces not yet extinguished, while human cries mingled with the clash of inanimate objects.' Many ships went down with their engines still working, and 'those who fell into the machinery and were *brayed* to death were perhaps more fortunate than the rest. For the entrance of water into those sealed depths must have been very slow . . . many of the men may still have been alive when the vessel touched bottom.'

Personal reactions under fire depended very much on experience. William Pakenham began observing the Imperial Navy at war in March 1904; by the time of the Battle of Tsushima, he had not stepped ashore for fourteen months, and, clad immaculately in a white uniform which he changed whenever it became too blood-stained, he witnessed the entire battle from a wicker armchair on *Asahi*'s bridge. Out of the surviving combatants, more Russians than Japanese wrote about it, frequently in order to criticize the régime and the leaders which had brought them to such a pass. But their tragic memoirs had other, non-political, motives – the simple wish to tell a story; the urgent personal need to exorcize the ghosts and stop the nightmares; and the wider need to warn others, through description, of the horrors of naval warfare. No one had warned *them* what to expect – few people, least of all the Russians, knew what war with the new weapons would be like, and the Russian crews were devastated by it. One officer was so frightened and excited that he signalled 'full speed' to the guns and 'commence firing' to the engine rooms, but that was the lightest aspect. The effects of the shells had been far greater than anyone had imagined possible: a ship's deck under a single hit 'opened like stretched paper struck by a fist'. Commander Vladimir Semenoff, veteran of Port Arthur and the Battle of the Yellow Sea, had intended to note the times and places of all hits upon his ship, as he had done on the Yellow Sea – 'but how could I make detailed notes when it seemed impossible even to count the number of projectiles striking us? I had not only never witnessed such a fire before, but I had never imagined anything like it . . . After six months with the Port Arthur squadron I had grown indifferent to most things, but this was something new. It seemed as if these were mines, not shells, which were striking the ship's side and falling on the deck. They burst as soon as they touched anything – the moment they encountered the least impediment in their flight. Handrails, funnel guys, topping lifts of the boats' derricks, were quite sufficient to cause a thoroughly efficient burst. The steel plates and superstructures on the upper deck were torn to pieces, and the splinters caused many casualties. Iron ladders were crumpled into rings, and guns were literally hurled from their mountings . . . In addition to this, there was the unusual high temperature and liquid flame of the explosion, which seemed to spread over everything . . .'

In one minute the Russian guns could deliver 500 pounds of high explosive. But in the same time the Japanese guns, with superior control and far better quality shells, could retaliate with no less than 7,500 pounds. One of those shells, bursting upon the upper deck of a battleship, showed this modern way of killing in an image of such ghastliness that those who saw it were never able to forget:

'The bosun was knocked down by the wind of a shell. He rose, uninjured, and caught sight of something which, surrounded by grey smoke, was jumping like a young bear. A torpedo hand, with both legs shot off at the knee, was in the death-struggle. His eyes anguished, his face twisted, he was bounding on the red stumps that were left him, trying (it seemed) to run, and fighting desperately for breath. A moment later he fell into the pool of his own blood. "Brothers, the ironclad is flying up into the clouds, up into the clouds," he cried . . . the bosun fled in search of a refuge from the nightmare vision.'

The battle lasted till shortly after noon on 28 May – almost a whole day, with a torpedo assault during the night and a rounding-up of strays next morning. Its outcome was decided, however, after the first half-hour; but even when the firing had completely stopped, and Admiral Nebogatoff had surrendered on behalf of the wounded and unconscious Rozhdestvenski, there were some who were convinced it was still going on. The cruiser *Oleg* was one of the ships which escaped to internment, and as she limped towards the safety of Manila, constantly pumping out water, almost all of the officers and men could hear guns booming around them, as clearly as when they were in the thick of battle. And, in what they could only say afterwards must have been an extraordinary mass-mirage, at the very moment of Admiral Nebogatoff's surrender, they sighted and identified his flagship heading for the Straits of Formosa. When they eventually learned the truth, they were at first profoundly shocked; Rozhdestvenski had specifically ordered that all ships should be scuttled rather than surrendered. Their reaction was oddly Japanese – defiant suicide was infinitely better than meek surrender; but then they shrugged sadly, and remembered that Nebogatoff had only commanded a flagship once before, at Kamranh Bay, and then for a mere fifteen minutes.

In America, President Roosevelt did not believe the first reports of the battle. But as confirmation arrived, 'I grew so excited,' he said, 'that I myself became almost like a Japanese, and I could not attend to official duties. I spent the whole day talking with visitors about the battle.' One of the visitors was the Japanese naval attaché, and, as he left the President's office, the Secretary of the US Navy turned to Roosevelt and said, 'Well, there goes a happy man. Every Japanese, but perhaps above all every Japanese naval man, must feel as if he were treading on air today.'

In Tokyo, Baron d'Anethan was equally filled with admiration: 'Admiral Togo made a triumphal entrance into Tokyo, cheered by millions of spectators who had come from all parts of the Empire. The most perfect order was maintained throughout by this huge throng, which had only one thought: homage to a hero who had brought such high renown to the fleets put under his command . . . The same enthusiasm was aroused at the Naval

Review held by His Majesty in Tokyo Bay. All the combined fleets assembled between Yokohama and Tokyo – 166 vessels! The captured Russian vessels could be recognized by the different colour of the chimnies. I believe we witnessed a unique spectacle in history – the victorious fleet comprising, after a naval war, the same number of vessels as at the beginning of hostilities.'

The battle had taken place on the birthday of the Japanese Empress and the anniversary of the coronation of the Russian Tsar and Tsarina. When the news of the awful defeat arrived, the Russian royal couple were enjoying a family picnic. Nicholas wrote bitterly in his diary of 'the terrible news about the destruction of almost the entire squadron', and then added, 'the weather has been wonderful.' In the streets of St Petersburg and in their houses, peasants and officers wept with shame and rage and sorrow, and, as some of the dead of Tsushima had predicted, the revolutionary movement found new strength and supporters.

On some occasions Admiral Togo's emulation of Lord Nelson was certainly deliberate. His triumphant return to Tokyo took place, from his own choice, on 21 October 1905 – the hundredth anniversary of the Battle of Trafalgar. It may be, too, that in his understandable desire to echo Nelson, still the spiritual apogee of admirals, Togo had hoped he might actually die during his greatest battle. As it was starting, his officers had tried to persuade him to leave the bridge for the greater security of the conning-tower, but he had refused, saying, 'I am getting on for sixty, and this old body of mine is no longer worth caring for.' That he survived was pure luck; he himself was wounded slightly, and men were killed so close beside him that his beard was splashed with their blood. And if he missed the chance of rephrasing Nelson's last words, 'Thank God I have done my duty', which would have been both legitimate and appropriate, then at least the Japanese nation was also able to avoid echoing Captain Blackwood's words of a hundred years earlier – 'On such terms, it was a victory I never wish to have witnessed.'

Such was Togo's fortune that he lived to enjoy the honour and glory, the nation's frank adulation and the Emperor's respect, for another twenty-nine years; and he did so with modesty. 'One has to believe,' he said, 'that the small number of our casualties was due to the protection of the spirits of the Imperial Ancestors.' Perhaps the praise he most appreciated was from Jacky Fisher who said: 'In the fleet the Admiral's got to be like Nelson – "the personal touch", so that "*any silly ass can't be an admiral*" [as Nelson himself once said]; and . . . so it was that Togo won that second Trafalgar.'

Yet, although the Imperial Review of the Combined Fleet on 23 October was spectacular and inspiring, that great public celebration was not the climax for the officers and men of the navy and for the relatives of the dead. That came six days later, on 29 October, in a comparatively small, strictly naval religious ceremony, when Admiral Togo paid tribute to the dead. It took place in Aoyama Cemetery. Standing bare-headed in front of an altar, speaking to the empty air, Togo expressed the universal, eternal wish of the living to those dead whom they have loved or respected – the wish 'to tell you of all we feel towards you'. As he spoke, the birds stopped singing; and, when he had finished, a slight breeze sprang up, stirring the leaves and branches of the surrounding trees. And, as they thought of their dead, none of the living found it hard to believe that the spirits might actually have heard the Commander-in-Chief, and had assembled beside him on the way to the Yasukuni Shrine.

PART THREE

*Sun Over the Yardarm
1906–1920*

*After two victorious wars,
Japan faces the modern world
with a disturbing mixture
of assertiveness and defensiveness.
Perceiving a new age of
maritime opportunity,
she continues to expand her navy,
as do Germany and America.
Limited participation in the Great War
secures considerable benefits;
but a fatal rivalry with America begins
in the Pacific Ocean.*

10

'Bellicose rumours'

When the armoured cruiser *Asama* bore the Emperor Meiji proudly up and down the assembled ranks of His Majesty's Imperial Fleet, one particular vessel was very conspicuously absent. Among the scores of ships were the *Beduivy*, on which Nebogatoff had surrendered and Rozhdestvenski had been taken prisoner, and the *Chen-yuen*, on which Ting had committed suicide; d'Anethan noted that both of these 'fired triumphant salvoes as the Emperor passed'. But *Mikasa*, the one ship which should have been at the review, was lying stern down and decks awash in Sasebo harbour.

It was ironic that one of Japan's major naval calamities in the Russo-Japanese War should have occurred just after the war had actually finished. It may have been accidental, as the official records say; but it may in fact have been deliberate and, if so, it was a very Japanese act. *Mikasa* had blown up at her moorings on the night of 11/12 September. By the grace of the Imperial Ancestors, Admiral Togo had gone ashore a few hours earlier and was on his way to Tokyo; but 590 officers and men were killed or wounded in the explosion. There were various explanations; at first it appeared that some unstable ammunition had ignited spontaneously and set off a chain reaction. Later it seemed possible that a group of sailors, celebrating their victory, had got drunk on industrial alcohol, spilt some in the bilges, and tried to get rid of the smell by burning of the spillage. But many thought then, and many think now, that it was a deliberate act of sabotage, a patriotic protest against a dishonourable peace; and that may very well be the truth of it.

Peace between the warring nations had been signed the week before at Portsmouth, New Hampshire, on 5 September. The treaty had ignited riots at Hibiya Park, and from the 6th to the 9th, Tokyo was under martial law. The newspapers carried the popular reaction – 'The authorities should resign,' said the *Jiji Shimpo*. 'The start of a coup d'état,' cried the *Yorozu Choho* – 'The Unpardonable Crime,' squawked the *Hochi Shimbun*; and, in its lead article, the influential *Asahi Shimbun* said with grim solemnity: 'We now positively declare that our authorities have made a mistake in their business of government.'

The problem was not peace, but the details of its achievement. The war as a whole, on land and sea, had been vastly expensive; the people as a whole had been well aware of this, and had expected a large cash indemnity from the Russians as part of the peace settlement. But what few people knew was how close the war had brought Japan to national bankruptcy, and still fewer knew that, on the question of an indemnity, Tsar Nicholas was absolutely obdurate. His man at Portsmouth, Count Sergei Witte, had agreed to give up the Russian lease on Port Arthur and the Kwangtung Peninsula, to evacuate Manchuria, and to recognize Korea as being within Japan's sphere of influence. He was also prepared to cede to Japan half the island of Sakhalien, which Russia had possessed in entirety since 1875; and all that, Nicholas felt, was quite enough, without paying a $600,000,000 indemnity as well. The Tsar believed he could continue the war if the point was pressed, and he may have been right; the Japanese delegate at Portsmouth, Komura Jutaro, believed that Japan could also continue the war, and he was almost certainly wrong. Both Witte and Komura were under instructions from their capitals, and peace was achieved because Witte, at a crucial moment, chose to ignore his instructions, while Komura obeyed his. Against his inclination, Witte had been told at one point to give up and come home. Komura wanted to do just that, and it was against his own inclination that he was told to remain and see the negotiations through, even if it meant renouncing the indemnity. Fortunately for the two countries, the Japanese delegate obeyed Tokyo, while the Russian disobeyed St Petersburg. Both men stayed in Portsmouth, working towards agreement, and peace was achieved; but neither delegate came home to a hero's welcome, and to Western eyes the uproar in Japan over what seemed to be simply a question of money appeared vulgar and degrading.

The Japanese naturally saw it differently. Western-style diplomacy was still a novel art to them, and the idea of a certain amount of give and take was not widely held: winner takes all seemed to be the logical outcome of a war. Within four months the government in Tokyo had resigned. But at the same time, said d'Anethan, 'in spite of the Alliance with England, and the sacrifices of the war, the build-up of the navy does not stop. At the dockyards of Kure and Yokosuka, three cruisers and one battleship are now under construction, and two others will soon be begun. In England the ships ordered before the war are being finished. The conclusion of peace thus will not lead to any reduction in naval expenditures, and Japan will continue to take all necessary measures to retain command of the Pacific and of the seas which bathe her territories'.

By 'command of the Pacific', d'Anethan probably meant command of the areas now within Japan's acknowledged control, the limited waters immediately around the homeland; there was, as yet, no Japanese dream of full oceanic power. But to the dominant white countries around the Pacific – America, Australia, New Zealand – these were ominous words; the possibility that they were meant literally seemed great enough to be worrying, because nobody else in that part of the world had a navy as good as the Japanese.

In this period, the nine years between the end of the Russo-Japanese War and the beginning of the First World War, three points came to the fore, points which were destined to have a profound effect on the history of the twentieth century. The first was a simple fact; the second was a character trait; and the third was an abstract phenomenon, in part resulting from Togo's victory at Tsushima.

The first, the simple fact, was that Japan was becoming overpopulated. The total area of Japan proper is about 145,000 square miles; its population, in the early 1980s, was about 117.65 million. For the purposes of comparison, France, at the same time, had an area of about 211,000 square miles – fifty per cent *more* than Japan – and a population of just over 54 million – less than half Japan's. Similarly, California was roughly comparable to Japan in area, with 158,000 square miles; but only 23.66 million people lived there – less than a fifth of Japan's population. Moreover, conditions of climate and geography in Japan mean that only about fifteen per cent of the country is comfortably habitable. Now, throughout the Tokugawa era, the national population remained almost static, at approximately 30 million; but, as soon as the Restoration came, it began to increase steadily, and by 1890 – one generation – had risen by one-third, to nearly 40 million. Japan was beginning to be a crowded country. With too many people in too little space, any breakdown of strict orderliness can lead all too easily to chaos, rage and the mutual cutting of throats, and it is conceivable that this crowding is one root of Japanese punctiliousness, self-restraint and conformity. What is more certain, though, is that the Japanese themselves recognized the problem of overcrowding very quickly, and throughout the life of the Imperial Navy searched, peacefully or belligerently, for population outlets.

The second emerging point of the period, the character trait, was something recognizably, though not uniquely, Japanese – a combination of assertiveness and defensiveness. Brashness might be the nearest single word, and anyone can observe it, in any individual or group which has been put upon; which has then, against the odds, achieved success; but which has not yet achieved the certainty that its success will not be whisked away. Japan, put upon by Perry and the great Powers, achieved success against China; was put upon again by the Triple Intervention; achieved success again against Russia; and she was by no means certain in 1906 that she would not be put upon yet again by the world's established power chain. The result was an assertiveness – 'we shall show the world what we can do' – combined with defensiveness, the urge to disprove the parental warning that 'the world will laugh at you', by being so strong that the world would not dare laugh. And, because the fleet and the army were the visible products of this insecure brashness, a divergence of interpretation sprang up between Japan and the rest of the Pacific world, a divergence which existed until fleet and army were finally defeated. The other countries saw aggressive intent in the development of Japan's armed forces; the Japanese saw it – or claimed to see it – as purely defensive, an expression of the natural wish for greater security. If, as seems likely, this view was to begin with genuine, then later it undoubtedly contained an element of double-think; yet, even today, retired officers of the Imperial Navy protest, with every appearance of frankness and conviction, that all their opening moves in war were in self-defence – pre-emptive perhaps, but always with limited, solely defensive intentions.

Both these aspects of the Pacific condition emerged as realities to be reckoned with at about the same time, just after the Russo-Japanese War, and have remained. Japan is still a vastly over-populated country; and, if her fleet and army are now quite different to their Imperial equivalents, the defensive-assertive mood which made them grow so large still exists to a great extent, and is still subject to the same divergence of interpretation. But the third aspect of the period, the abstract phenomenon, occurred then and then only – at least as far as the Imperial Navy was concerned. It was opportunity.

The maritime world was shifting on its axis. As one diplomat said after Tsushima, Russia had been 'erased from the list of naval nations for a long time'. The lumbering, world-scattered British Royal Navy was becoming rapidly out-dated; and, to those who had not followed the first years of its development, the Imperial Japanese Navy seemed to have burst upon the twentieth century like Pallas Athene, fully-armed and adult from the moment of birth. In this state of flux, this breaking down of the past century's sea-order, there was an opportunity which had not existed since Trafalgar – the opportunity for *any* nation with the will and the wealth to forge ahead in the naval stakes, and build itself a place of power. By the same token, any nation which did not take the opportunity was going to slip behind, perhaps irrevocably; for chances of that kind do not occur often.

With Tsushima, Admiral Togo had partially created this opportunity, and he recognized it. On 21 December 1905 the Combined Fleet was formally disbanded, in a purely naval occasion, and placed on a peace-time footing. But of course the Imperial Navy, as distinct from the wartime Combined Fleet, was continuing to expand; and, on 21 December, Togo's speech of disbanding was memorable for its specific reference to the Royal Navy, and for its insistence that, even in peace, war readiness should be maintained.

'The war of twenty months' duration is now a thing of the past,' he said, 'and our Combined Fleet, having completed its function, is to be herewith dispersed. But our duties as naval men are not at all lightened for that reason. To preserve in perpetuity the fruits of this war; to promote to an even greater height of prosperity the fortunes of the country, the navy – which, irrespective of peace or war, has to stand between the Empire and shocks from abroad – must always maintain its strength at sea and must be prepared for any emergency.

'The triumphs recently won by our Navy are largely to be attributed to the habitual training which enabled us to garner the fruits of the fighting . . . A warrior's whole life is one continuous and unceasing battle, and there is no reason why his responsibilities should vary with the state of the time.

'. . . If men calling themselves sailors grasp at the pleasures of peace, they will learn the lesson that however fine in appearance their engines of war, these, like a house built on the sand, will fall at the first approach of the storm. From the day in ancient times when we conquered Korea, that country remained for over 400 years under our control, only to be lost immediately our Navy declined. Again, when under the sway of the Tokugawa in modern days our armaments were neglected, the coming of a few American ships threw us into distress, and we were unable to offer any resistance to attempts against the Kuriles and Sakhalien. On the other hand, if we turn to the annals of the Occident, we see that at the beginning of the nineteenth century the British Navy, which won the battles of the Nile and of Trafalgar, not only made England as secure as a great mountain, but also – by carefully maintaining its strength and keeping it on a level with the world's progress – has throughout the long interval between that era and the present day safe-guarded the country's interests and promoted its fortunes.

'. . . We naval men who have survived the war must take these examples deeply to heart, and, adding our actual experiences in the war to the training which we have already received, must plan future developments . . . Heaven gives the crown of victory to those who by habitual preparation win without fighting, and at the same time deprives of that crown those who, content with one success, give themselves up to the ease of peace. The ancients were right when they said: "In the hour of victory, tighten the straps of your helmet."'

The idea of perpetual preparedness is commonplace today and was no novelty when Togo stated it. But, coming with the authority of victory in that time of naval flux, it began to alarm the white Pacific nations. The Admiral probably did not intend this effect, and he may not even have intended the speech for foreign consumption; but, inevitably, it was widely reported, and, inevitably, others drew their own conclusions.

Outside Japan, there were only three important people who really read the stars correctly – who saw the naval opportunity, and who had the ability to take it. The first was Britain's Jacky Fisher, who, by instituting the *Dreadnought* programme and cutting away the dross in the Royal Navy, enabled Britain to retain her maritime supremacy for a few more decades.

The second was Germany's Alfred von Tirpitz. He had joined the

Prussian Navy at the age of sixteen, in 1865, coming into a fleet which, stocked with wooden sailing ships with auxiliary steam engines, was hardly in better shape than the contemporary Japanese. But his own talent, together with the advent of the torpedo and the creation of a torpedo arm needing new officers, gave Tirpitz accelerated promotion, faster than any other Prussian naval officer ever had: by the age of forty-three, in 1892, he was chief of staff to the supreme naval command, and four years later – just after the Triple Intervention – he was C-in-C of the German Far East Squadron. Charged with reaping the fruits of intervention, he was busy setting up the German port of Tsingtao, in Kiaochow Bay. From this direct experience of the East came interest in the progress of the Japanese Navy; from that in turn came recognition of opportunity, when it arose; and by 1906, under his master Kaiser Wilhelm, he was well advanced with plans for the High Seas Fleet – the fleet which, ten years later, would face British dreadnoughts in the Battle of Jutland.

Fisher in Britain, Tirpitz in Germany; and the third man in this clear-sighted trio was the American President, Theodore Roosevelt. At the start of the Spanish-American war in 1898, he was Assistant Secretary of the Navy, a post which three more Roosevelts would hold over the next thirty-eight years. Coming from the vice-presidency to the supreme office after McKinley's assassination in 1901, he was one of America's 'accidental' presidents; yet he was a man of great historical vision, not only in assessing the past, but the future as well, and – despite considerable national inertia and active opposition – he became one of the main architects of American naval policy in the Pacific.

The peace which existed between Japan and the white nations of the Pacific from 1905 to 1941 was at its best an uneasy peace. The seeds of unease were sown in 1898, with the American annexations of Hawaii and the Philippines: imperial America found not only the pride, but also the fear and vulnerability, that comes with distant possessions. And, as British squadrons were withdrawn from the Far East after the Anglo-Japanese Alliance, colonial Australia and New Zealand likewise found the fear that comes with distant dependency.

'The Mediterranean era died with the discovery of America,' said Roosevelt in 1903. 'The Atlantic era is now at the height of its development, and must soon exhaust the resources at its command; the Pacific era, destined to be the greatest of all, is just at its dawn.'

The question was, on which nation would the rising sun of the Pacific dawn shine? Mastery of an ocean required a navy; there was only one really great navy in that ocean; and Japan's native problem, vice and virtue – her over-population, her assertive-defensiveness, and above all her continually expanding fleet – did nothing to diminish the fears of other nations that, after Russia, they might be next.

In June 1904, writing to his friend Sir Cecil Spring Rice – then Secretary at the British Embassy in St Petersburg – Roosevelt said, 'I am well aware that if they [the Japanese] win out, it may possibly mean a struggle between them and us in the future; but I hope and believe not.' Almost exactly a year before, before the Treaty of Portsmouth was signed, he referred to Japan in a letter to the Republican senator, Henry Cabot Lodge, as 'this formidable new power – a power jealous, sensitive and war-like, and which if irritated could at once take both the Philippines and Hawaii from us, if she obtained the upper hand on the seas'. Deeply impressed by Admiral Mahan's book *The Influence of Sea Power Upon History*, Roosevelt had spotted the opportunity of the time, and the expansion of American naval strength and authority became a pet project; but lesser politicians, shying away from such expensive investment, constantly blocked his efforts in that direction. Meanwhile, across the ocean, Japan was actively encouraging emigration, especially to America. In 1902 Yoshimura Daijiro, long resident in the United States, wrote a typically well-publicized paean in praise of his adopted new world.

'Picture yourself,' he said to young Japan, 'boarding a huge ship of over ten thousand tons, crossing the Pacific Ocean in 15 or 20 days . . . arriving in America, entering the spacious city lined with stone buildings 13 or 14 storeys high, walking on clean stone pavements, observing the development of machinery which can build tall buildings with only a handful of men . . . going to a college where men *and women* engage in education . . . riding a train at the speed of 50 or 60 miles an hour through the interior of the country, where all you see are vast spaces without a trace of man – and compare this with life in Japan, where you will be living on a modest income of 30 or 40 yen a month, fighting with your neighbours over a foot or two of land, or involved in lawsuits to obtain water for irrigating a small plot. Before you know it you will be opened up, your horizon broadened, and your narrow provincialism will melt like a block of ice in the sun.'

It was a captivating image, to which tens of thousands of Japanese responded. Their new Californian neighbours, however, did not; and with the easy identity-tag of race, reviving the Kaiser's Yellow Peril, a series of legal fence-posts were erected to restrict Japanese immigration.

'It isn't the exclusion of a few emigrants that hurts here [in Japan],' said George Kennan, a friend of the president, to Roosevelt in April 1905. 'It's the putting of Japanese below Hungarians, Italians, Syrians, Polish Jews, and degraded nondescripts from all parts of Europe and Western Asia. No proud, high-spirited and victorious people will submit to such a classification as that, especially when it is made with insulting reference to personal character and habits.'

President Roosevelt found the West Coast attitude wildly irritating: 'the Senators and Congressmen from these very states,' he said in May 1905, 'were lukewarm about the navy last year. It gives me a feeling of contempt and disgust to see them challenge Japanese hostility and justify by their actions any feeling the Japanese may have towards us, while at the same time refusing to take steps to defend themselves against the formidable foe, which they are ready with such careless insolence to antagonize.'

The question of restricting Japanese immigration to America simmered on until 11 October 1906 when a San Franciscan school board passed a resolution to the effect that all Japanese students should be removed from the regular schools and segregated into separate institutions – in order to prevent 'these lascivious Orientals sitting next to our Californian maids'.

Had the Californians been privy to Imperial Navy thinking, they might have acted differently. At the end of 1906, in a draft paper to the General Staff, the Imperial Army declared its belief in two areas of national expansion – firstly through the extension of national interests abroad, secondly through the acquisition of land for Japan's excess population. The first of these, they reckoned, could be achieved peacefully; the second might need force; and, in order of preference, the Army recommended three places for possible exploitation. These were Siberia, Manchuria and Mongolia; the American-owned Philippines, the Dutch East Indies and the South Sea Islands; and Central and South America. The Army thought that war with the United States was improbable; but the Imperial Navy disagreed, and listed Russia, America and France in that order as Japan's possible enemies.

The school board resolution did not in itself precipitate the war scares which formed the background to Japanese-American relations in following years; it merely increased the heat under existing tensions and brought them into a wider public arena. But in one way the resolution became one of the roots of twentieth-century naval power; because on 22 October 1906, reacting to the San Franciscan slur, the *Mainichi Shimbun* newspaper said: 'The whole world knows that the poorly equipped army and navy of the United States are no match for our efficient army and navy. It will be an easy work to awake the United States from her dreams of obstinacy when one of our great Admirals appears on the other side of the Pacific . . . why do we not insist on sending ships?'

Roosevelt had already been trying for a long time to persuade his fellow Americans to see the naval opportunities, and naval dangers, in front of them. In February 1906 he had even taken the unusual step of publishing Admiral Togo's last speech to the Combined Fleet in one of his own General Orders of the Naval Department, praising the speech as a model for America; but it took the thought of an imminent Pacific war to get the message through. At last others, apart from Admiral Mahan and the

President, began to believe that America should have a strong navy, and should display it for Japan and all the world to see. Someone started the rumour that only four battleships were worth showing, and Mahan wrote anxiously to the President, pointing out that such a trifling display would be worse than none at all. Roosevelt's tart reply was: 'I have no more thought of sending four battleships to the Pacific while there is the least possible friction with Japan than I have in going thither in a rowboat myself.' 'Congress,' he wrote to his son Kermit, 'has greatly hampered me in building up the navy.' Now, however, he had his chance – a splendid demonstration could hardly fail to make the whole country pro-navy, and in June 1907 he decided on the form the show should take: a round-the-world cruise of the entire battleship fleet.

One very good reason for this was that the American navy, based mainly on the East coast, knew little about other waters. To Senator Lodge the President said: 'It became evident to me, from talking with the naval authorities, that in the event of war they would have a good deal to find out in the way of sending a fleet to the Pacific. Now, the one thing I won't run the risk of is to experiment for the first time in a matter of vital importance in time of war. Accordingly I concluded it was imperative that we should send the fleet on what would practically be a practice voyage.' Sixteen days later, on 26 July, he wrote to Secretary of State Elihu Root: 'If the Japanese attack us now, as the German, English and French authorities evidently think they will, it will be nakedly because they wish the Philippines and Hawaii – or, as their heads seem to be swollen to a marvellous degree, it is possible they may wish Alaska.' Then he added, with greater confidence than most Americans would have then dared, 'I do not think they will attack us.' Root replied more cautiously: 'I think the tendency is towards war – not now, but in a few years.'

Both men were right. For, while the British admiralty and the German Naval General Staff were laying bets on the outcome of a Japanese-American war, giving odds of five to four in Japan's favour; while West Coast reporters announced that 'anti-Japanese agitation is growing', as Japanese people were harassed and Japanese restaurants were burnt; and while the American fleet was making ready for its historic cruise, an American adviser in Korea observed that the Japanese themselves were 'thinking of other things than war'.

This was true. The *Mainichi*'s jingoistic comments had been very much in the minority: in January 1907 the Minister of War in Tokyo had 'wished it distinctly understood that Japan's completion of her armaments were not aimed at any Power. It was intended solely to preserve the peace and security of the Empire'. At the same time, *The Times*' Tokyo correspondent reported that 'Japan is perfectly calm. In this country there is absolutely no talk of war. All the excitement, all the bellicose rumours emanate from the

American side. Japan from the outset has maintained and still maintains unshaken faith in the American spirit of justice'. The resulting immigration problem had not been resolved, but the Japanese had never generally thought of it as a *casus belli*: not only were they sure it could be solved diplomatically, but they also recognized the right of any country to admit only those foreigners it wished. That, after all, was exactly what they had done under two centuries of Tokugawa rule. In their eyes the problem was one of discrimination: after a working lunch with Admiral Yamamoto Gombei and Ambassador Aoki Shuzo, Roosevelt noted that Yamamoto 'kept insisting that the Japanese must not be kept out, save as we keep out Europeans'.

At the beginning of the century, Roosevelt had been an ardent imperialist. By the end of the Russo-Japanese War, however, he had begun to see the liabilities, as well as the assets, of overseas possessions; and in a letter of August 1907 to Elihu Root he admitted 'that in the physical sense I don't see where they [the Philippines] are of any value to us, or where they are likely to be of any value . . . The Philippines form our heel of Achilles. They are all that makes the present situation with Japan dangerous'. His assassinated predecessor, William McKinley, had recognized the same thing after Commodore George Dewey had sunk the Spanish ships in the Philippines in 1898. McKinley had said with prophetic understatement: 'If only old Dewey had just sailed away when he smashed the Spanish fleet, what a lot of trouble he would have saved!'

By 1907 the American public was coming to the same uncomfortable conclusion. It made no difference if Durham Stevens, an American living in the Far East, said: 'The acquisition of the Philippines has never figured in Japanese plans'; Americans living in America had convinced themselves otherwise. The bogey of Japan victorious after being so long disdained was a fearsome one. The Combined Fleet may have been put on a peace footing, but the Imperial Navy was continuing to expand. Admiral Togo may not have called for war in so many words, but he had called for permanent war readiness. Japanese spokesmen may have denied any interest in the Philippines, but Japan needed a population overspill, and the islands were difficult for America to defend; and so, 'speaking softly and carrying the "Big Stick"', as Roosevelt described it, the United States' 'Great White Fleet' sailed on 16 December 1907 from Hampton Roads, where the Chesapeake flows into the Atlantic. The Panama Canal was yet to come, so down the east coast of South America they went, around Cape Horn, and up to San Francisco; then across to Hawaii, where there was as yet no American naval base; and on 20 August 1908 *The Times*' correspondent in Sydney wrote an ecstatic report.

'No better day could have been deliberately devised for welcoming the American fleet to the Empire's finest harbour. Sydney's winter climate was

Togo: 'A quiet, silent man with a rather melancholy face, lighted up, as the spirit moves him, by one of the sweetest of smiles' *(Mansell Collection)*

Rozhdestvenski: 'I have not the slightest prospect of recovering command of the sea with the force under my orders' *(BBC Hulton Picture Library)*

The Battle of Tsushima, with Togo's calligraphy: 'The fate of the empire depends on this battle. Let every man do his utmost' *(BBC Hulton Picture Library)*

Outside Port Arthur – an attempt to seal the entrance: 'This blinding process simply paralyzes one there is no choice but to shut one's eyes until the horrid rays have left one' *(Mansell Collection)*

Inside Port Arthur: 'The poor devils, then, had no presentiment, and apparently were wrapped in peaceful slumber' *(National Archives 165.RJ.41)*

The battleship *Hatsuse* and her interior (1901): 'We can sincerely congratulate the Japanese Government on the acquisition of these fine ships' *(BBC Hulton Picture Library)*

Aspects of Etajima: *above left* Submarine school; *above right* taking bearings with sextants; *below* a ceremonial parade on Navy Day 1941, the 36th anniversary of Tsushima *(all Pictorial Press Ltd)*

Aspects of Etajima: *above left* signal practice on a 16-inch gun turret; *above right* inside a complete hangar, a lecture on aeronautics; *below* firing practice — a part of landing party drill
(all Pictorial Press Ltd)

Aspects of Etajima – new recruits salute their parents: 'The inheritors of Japan most ancient...'
(Pictorial Press Ltd)

An officer serving his country's flag: '... and exemplars of Japan most modern'
(Pictorial Press Ltd)

Shanghai 1936, before the China Incident and the Tripartite Alliance: 'I shall try to draw a line from Rome to Tokyo, and the system will be complete' *(Mansell Collection)*

Shanghai – sunken steamers in the Whangpoo: 'In the view of the Japanese Navy, China was only a means to an end, only a step on the way to a final reckoning with *England*' *(Mansell Collection)*

Imperial Naval manoeuvres: 'It is a magnificent sight! We seem to overpower the South Pacific Ocean' *(Pictorial Press Ltd)*

The battleship *Kongo* in dry dock at Yokosuka during her first reconstruction, 29 November 1930: 'The empire should complete its naval defence by whatever means it deems best' *(Imperial War Museum MH 6158)*

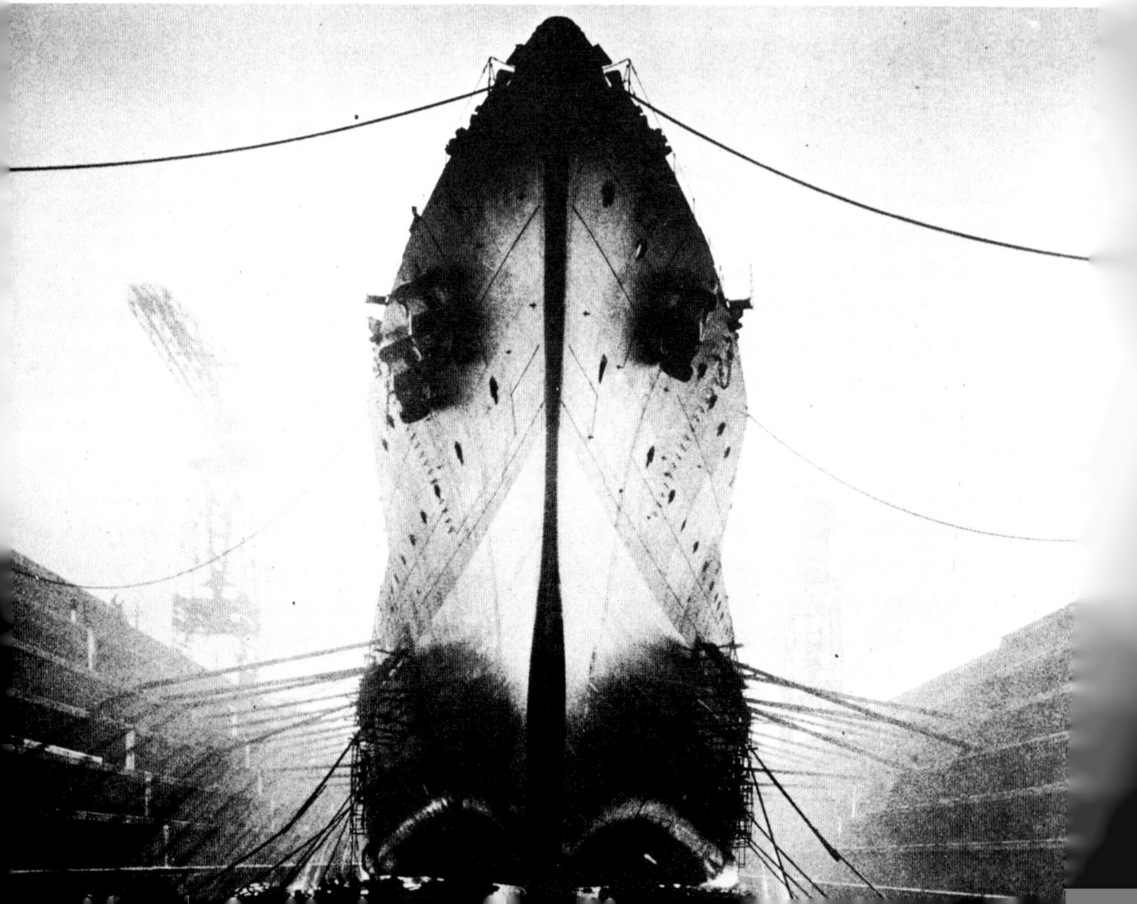

at its best, which is hard to beat anywhere in the world. A slight haze veiled the coast and foreshore till shortly after the fleet's arrival, when a clear sky, bright sun, and cool breeze perfected the holiday for the spectators, and enhanced the natural beauties of the harbour for the incoming fleet. More than half a million people had come to welcome the ships. They covered the cliffs, the headlands and the foreshores, or were afloat in vessels of all descriptions, and nowhere was there the slightest discomfort, mishap or muddle . . . Australia's first sight of modern battleships has proved even more impressive than was expected.'

Ten days earlier they had been in New Zealand, where, according to the *Auckland Herald*, the nation 'welcomes the visit, because the fleet stands for the racial integrity of every English-speaking state in the Pacific'. The Australian reaction was the same – the fleet there was seen as a 'Monroe Doctrine for the Pacific'. And yet, paradoxically, the fleet's next major destination after Australia was Japan: a formal invitation had been issued on 18 March.

'I suppose they will have to go,' was Roosevelt's gloomy comment. 'I had hoped they would not be asked, because there is always the chance of some desperado doing something that will have very bad effects.'

He need not have worried. When the fleet arrived in Yokohama on 18 October, the welcome it was given was even more rapturous than that given to Togo after Tsushima; and the American officers and sailors responded with delight. Baron d'Anethan was still there, observing and reporting, and as he said, 'The reception accorded to the fleet not only by the Emperor and his staff but by the entire nation has great political significance. It will strengthen more intimately than ever the relations of amity and confidence between the two countries. Far from giving umbrage or inspiring any fear in Japan, this deployment of forces is regarded as a guarantee of peace.'

The name of the American commanding officer gave a curious echo of that first foreign fleet to anchor in Tokyo Bay, back in 1853. Admiral Charles S. Sperry anchored his sixteen ships alongside the same number of Japanese vessels, in an agreed display of equality; and, while he and his men enjoyed themselves in the strange country, he wrote a letter to his son.

'In Yokohama and Tokyo there were countless entertainments for them; normally a sort of garden party in a park, with exhibitions of juggling, dancing, wrestling, theaters, etc., and booths where they could get light beer, very good beer, and luncheon. There were thousands of chairs about the grounds for those who would sit. The city of Tokyo gave one party of this kind for 2,500 men at once, and sent them up and back in three special trains . . . There was literally nothing in the way of comfort or convenience that was not provided.'

The festivities went on for a week, and the 14,000 American sailors were entranced. The flag officers were the Emperor's guests in the Shiba Palace;

all the high officers were invited to dine with the Mayor of Tokyo, the Tokyo Chamber of Commerce, the Navy Minister and Admiral Togo himself; and Sperry was given an Imperial audience. But perhaps the most extraordinary event was described by a young ensign named William F. Halsey. In a most unusual show of goodwill, Admiral Togo – the greatest living admiral in the world, and by then a sedate sixty-one years old – allowed the young Americans to toss him up in the air and catch him in a blanket. 'If we had known what the future held,' said Admiral Halsey many years later, 'we wouldn't have caught him the third time!'

In October 1908, however, as the sailors of both fleets celebrated, the Pacific seemed a large ocean, quite large enough for both navies. The Japanese discovered that their guests had spent so much that Tokyo actually made a small profit out of the exercise; and, after eight days' junketing, the American sailors departed – a little dazed, very content, and feeling that the Japanese were not nearly so bad as they had thought before.

11

'To hold its own against any enemy'

Eighteen months after the visit of the American fleet, a small tragedy took place in the Inland Sea – the kind of accident of which naval legends are made, and which sailors everywhere respond to with sympathy and admiration. Submarines had made their belated entry into the Imperial Navy, but they were still primitive, experimental machines, far more dangerous and far less reliable than any surface vessel. On 15 April 1910, Lieutenant Sakuma took his submarine, with her crew of fourteen, out from Hiroshima on one of the navy's standard training manoeuvres. They never returned; and, when the wreck of the ship was salvaged, and the bodies of its commander and crew were taken ashore, a manuscript was found which described the accident in harrowing detail. It was in Sakuma's handwriting, and it was addressed to the Emperor.

'Words of excuse fail me for having lost Your Majesty's submarine Number 6,' he had scribbled. 'My subordinates are perishing by my fault. But it is with pride that I inform you that the crew fulfilled its duties, without exception, with the greatest coolness, until the last moment, as befits sailors.

'We now are sacrificing our lives for our country, but I fear lest this disaster affect the future development of submarines. That is why I hope that nothing will stop your determination to study the submarine until it has become a perfect machine, absolutely trustworthy. If this be the case, we can die without regret.

'In submerging with the gasoline engine, the ship sank deeper than desired, and in our efforts to close the watertight door, the chain broke. We tried to stop the entrance of water with our hands, but too late – the water came in at the stern and the ship sank at an angle of 25°.

'When it touched bottom, it was at an angle of 13°. The stream of water flooded the electric generator, extinguishing the light, and the electric wires burnt.

'In a few minutes there developed bad gas which made our breathing difficult. It was 10 a.m., the 15th of this month, when the ship sank. Surrounded by poisonous gas, the crew tried to pump water. As soon as the ship had sunk, we started pumping out the water from the main tank. The electric light was out, and the leak invisible, but it seems the water from the main tank was pumped out completely.

'The electric current has now become useless. We cannot produce air, and the handpump is our only hope. The ship is in the dark, and I write these notes by the light which comes from the turret, at 11.45 a.m.

'The crew is now wet, and it is extremely cold. It is my opinion that men who embark on submarines must have the qualities of coolness and nerve, and be tireless; it takes courage and daring to handle the ship. One can make fun of this opinion, seeing my failure, but it is the truth.

'We have worked hard to pump the water, but the ship is still in the same position. *It is now noon.* The depth of the water here is about ten fathoms.

'The crew of a submarine must be chosen from the bravest, and those who have the most presence of mind. Otherwise they would be useless at a moment of crisis like the one in which we are. My brave men do their best.

'I always expect death when I am away. Consequently my last will is prepared. It will be found in my chest, and these are my private affairs. I hope that Mr Taguchi will be so good as to send it to my father.

'A word to His Majesty the Emperor. It is my fervent hope that Your Majesty will furnish the means of existence to the poor families of the crew; this is my only wish, and I am very anxious that it should be realized.

'My respects and best remembrances to the following persons – to Admiral Saito, Minister of the Navy; to Vice Admirals Shimamura and Fujii, to Rear Admirals Nawa, Yamashita and Narita – *the air-pressure is so light that it seems to me that my eardrums will burst* – to Captains Oguri and Ide, to Commander Matsumura, to Lieutenant-Commander Matsumura (the latter is my elder brother), to Captain Funakushi, to Mr Marita and Mr Ikeda – *it is now 12.30* – my breathing is so difficult and painful – I thought I could turn off the gasoline, but it poisons me – to Captain Nakano – *it is now 12.40 –*'

And then the scribble trailed away, and stopped; Sakuma must have died a few minutes later, choking in the gas-filled hull sixty feet underwater. His poignant document was published in full in Japan and elsewhere, and made a profound impression. To Japanese people it became a tale of classic endurance, of men fulfilling their duty to the end. To people who knew nothing of the sea it conveyed a vivid image of the dangers of modern naval life. But to naval people outside Japan it delivered two more important messages – firstly, a little information about possible problems underwater, and secondly, a look into a Japanese naval officer's mind. There was no doubt that the information Sakuma left was valuable, and brought some good out of the tragedy; but surely, at ten fathoms, it should have been possible for some, if not all, of the crew to survive. Western navies were not quite sure what to make of the sinking of No. 6. Once the loss of the ship was certain, the commander's next duty, in their eyes, would have been to do everything he could to save the lives of his men and himself. Sakuma's coolness was certainly admirable; but with his apparent submission, and calm recording, he almost seemed to see himself as part of a huge experiment, a continuing process.

In fact such deaths – not necessarily inevitable – occurred again and again in the history of the Imperial Navy; and the thinking that led to them had two roots. One was derived from the Japanese ideal of submission of the individual to the whole, the repayment of a debt (specifically, the lost ship) to the Emperor, and the belief that the spirit would continue to support its living comrades with no loss of strength. But the second source was a rather pathetic misunderstanding. Taught from the beginning by the British Royal Navy, the Imperial Japanese Navy had great respect for the traditions of its tutor, and adopted many of them. Somewhere along the line, Japanese officers had learnt that an honourable commanding officer went down with his ship. This tallied so well with their established concept of honourable suicide that the idea was taken on board at face value: if a ship sank, it was not only an honour, but a duty, for the captain to die as well. Yet that was not what the Royal Navy meant at all; rather, if a British captain's vessel was going down, his duty was to be *the last to abandon ship*. If that meant he went down with his ship, then down he went, and his death was honourable; but living, if he survived, was honourable too, and death was not a duty.

Clearing up the misunderstanding takes none of the dignity from Sakuma's death, nor from the voluntary, unnecessary deaths of later Japanese captains, like the one in World War Two who saw all of his men into lifeboats, then returned to the bridge to admire the beauty of the moon, while plentiful minutes remained for escape. But, when such deaths as Sakuma's, in time of peace, were held as examples to be emulated, such deaths in war meant the useless loss of trained, experienced men.

The original Anglo-Japanese Alliance of 1902 had been renewed for ten years in 1905, shortly before the Peace of Portsmouth was concluded; its renewal played a part in the Russian Count Witte's determination to secure peace. The new form differed from the original in two important ways: its physical range had been extended to include India, and, whereas the original treaty could only have been invoked if two enemies had combined against one of the allies, now only one enemy was necessary. If either Britain or Japan was attacked by a third country, now, theoretically, the victim's ally would come to her aid at once. The motive for this change had been to ensure there would be no Russian revenge-attack on Japan, and to that extent it worked – indeed, by 1907, Russia and Japan had amicably agreed on their respective spheres of interest in Manchuria and Mongolia. But what applied to Russia, in terms of the Alliance, applied to everyone else as well, and on 17 July 1911 the *Auckland Star* voiced the obvious fear – that 'should

Japan and the United States go to war, then the British Empire would automatically become involved with hostilities with the US'. Two years earlier, also in New Zealand, the *Evening Post* had given expression to an equally unwelcome phantom. Watching Tirpitz's build-up of the High Seas Fleet, the newspaper suggested the frightful notion that at some future date the German Navy might take command of the English Channel. What then would happen to the British Empire? New Zealand and Australia, the paper speculated, 'might possibly have the choice between the Kaiser and the Mikado for their sovereign'.

Perhaps these were just the paranoid ramblings of a racially-conscious, defenceless island; but the fears they expressed were real enough, and not only for New Zealanders; and they had, moreover, a fair basis in fact. Japanese respect for Royal Navy technology had risen higher than ever since the victory of Tsushima, and the Imperial Navy had lapped up whatever information it could from its 'elder brother'; but it had not given much in return. This state of affairs became so noticeable that even Fisher, who had praised Togo so highly, said in February 1910, 'I don't think anyone appreciates what intense benefit the Japs have derived from our Naval secrets – especially Fire Control and the scientific use of the Big Gun'; and at the same time, Vice Admiral Sir Alfred Winsloe, C-in-C of the China Station, informally arranged with his French counterpart for mutual assistance. As Fisher became increasingly reluctant to divulge naval secrets, and Winsloe looked to the French rather than to the Japanese, the Royal Navy took on a new mood of wariness: a strong ally was welcome, but *too* strong an ally was not. And, apart from the tragic death of Sakuma and his crew, 1910 was something of a red-letter year for Japan and her navy; for in that year the country annexed Korea (another foreboding symptom, to white Pacific eyes, of yellow expansionism), while the navy ordered *Kongo* and launched *Kawachi*.

Kongo's importance was that she was both a first and a last. Ordered in 1910, built by Vickers in Barrow, launched in 1912 and completed in 1913, she was the Imperial Navy's first battle-cruiser, and the last of its capital ships to be built outside Japan. The battle-cruiser concept (originally Fisher's idea) combined the speed of a cruiser with the fire-power of a battleship, at the sacrifice of some of the battleship's weight in protective armour; and, even though *Kongo* was not a dreadnought, she showed vividly how much a thing of the past the warships of Tsushima had already become. With the water-line length of 659 feet, a beam of 92 feet and a draught of almost 27 feet, she dwarfed even the once-mighty *Mikasa*. She was also bigger than Japan's first true dreadnoughts, *Kawachi* and her sister *Settsu*. Built respectively at Kure and Yokosuka, launched in 1910 and 1911, these ships were not only of Japanese construction, but also the first completely independent Japanese designs. *Kawachi*'s launch on 15 October was a day of unabashed naval glory and unprecedented ceremonial; now both branches of the navy, the creative as well as the destructive, had shown the world what they could do. By then, the unfortunate *Mikasa* had been raised from her ignominious submersion at Sasebo, and restored to service, and many years remained to her; but, henceforth, she would always be outclassed, as the pride and energy of the Imperial Navy poured out in ever larger and more powerful warships.

American fears about Japan had been mitigated to some extent, partly by the visit of their fleet to Japan, partly by agreements in 1907 and 1908 which had clarified the two countries' commercial interests in China, and partly by the fact that, at the end of Theodore Roosevelt's second administration in 1909, the US Navy totalled 496,000 tons – more than four times what it had been when he took office in 1901. Nevertheless, even the Japanophile Roosevelt did not feel the country's security was necessarily guaranteed – as he said to Secretary of State Philander C. Knox on 8 February 1909, 'with so proud and sensitive a people, neither lack of money nor possible future complications will prevent a war if once they get sufficiently angry'.

It was just such considerations which kept anxiety in the southern Pacific very much alive. A New Zealand journalist wrote: 'Japan may wait until 1915 when the Treaty expires before she shows her hand. She may, I say; but if Australia or New Zealand would be useful places for her to discharge her millions of people into, what an advantage it would be to her to get hold of America first . . . Is it to that end she is working?' The fear was taken from the fantastic to the credible by the assumption that the entire British Empire would be fighting willy-nilly with Japan. To counter that fear, the Alliance was renewed four years ahead of time, in 1911, with the specific exclusion of America from the nations against which Britain would fight on Japan's side; yet even that did not help. For Australia and New Zealand, the problem was already approaching, as Japanese emigrants moved on to the island of New Caledonia, 900 miles east of Australia. They were mostly labourers, gone to work in the island's nickel mines; but a reporter especially sent by the *New Zealand Herald* wrote that the native islanders 'would not be a tiny bit surprised to see the red sun of Japan floating over the government buildings'. And, probably only in the interests of journalism, he made a sinister suggestion: that Japan was using New Caledonia in the same way as Hawaii – 'as a sort of base, a barracks which shall bring her closer, shall make a connecting link between her own little island and the bigger island that may be her objective – Australia or New Zealand.'

In 1911 it was easy to find reasons to make scare-mongering sound like responsible reporting. An Imperial Navy officer named Sato Tetsutaro, nicknamed 'the Mahan of Japan', had cogently argued in favour of increasing the Navy at the Army's expense. He said, fundamentally, that to build up the Army was a waste of time and money, since it could only be used against

Russia, while other powers were developing their navies 'with inevitable implications for Japan's security'. However, he did not imagine either a Japanese- or an American-dominated Pacific Ocean; instead, he thought, keeping the Pacific peaceful would be a responsibility shared by both. His ideas became especially influential when Britain refused to guarantee Japan support in the event of a conflict with America: the conviction took shape that Japan's navy must be strong enough to stand alone if need be.

The Emperor's edict in 1882 had said: 'You must never allow yourselves to be led astray by public controversies or influenced by politics.' But the peculiar structure of the government meant that, even if they wished to avoid it, navy men were bound to be involved in politics. The Commanders-in-Chief of both Army and Navy had direct access to the Emperor; the constitution stated that Army and Navy Ministers should be acting officers; and it also stated that, if either of these posts were empty, no Cabinet could exist. If, therefore, one of the Forces Ministers resigned from a Cabinet, the Cabinet could either try to persuade the appropriate Force to nominate another candidate, or it could itself resign as well.

In any case, being the rival recipients of limited governmental financial allocations as well as the instruments of national strategy, both Forces would always be passively political at the very least; and, if either felt inclined to become actively political, which indeed happened more and more as time went on, they could quickly convince themselves they were not disobeying the Imperial edict. For the rest of that sentence in the Emperor's edict said: 'You must be guided by loyalty alone.' And of course, they believed they always were.

One of the earliest active, effective pressure groups was the Kogetsukai, formed before the Russo-Japanese War began. The express aim of this belligerent combination of Army and Navy officers meeting in the Kogetsu restaurant, ostensibly just to dine, had been to activate the politicians and force a war. Of course it would have started anyway, sooner or later, but, even after peace had been declared, the taste for applying political pressure remained; and in September 1911 all the birds came home to roost – the rivalry of the Forces, the contradictions of the edict, and the limitations of the budget.

The Navy's stance was that, in order to defend the nation even without Great Britain, the fleet had to be as large as possible. The desirable nucleus was the 'eight-eight' fleet – eight battleships and eight cruisers, supported by appropriately enormous numbers of other vessels, including some submarines. This was pure Sato; but, under the cabinet of Saionji Kimmochi, the Army's idea of a fleet as large as possible was much more modest. Only four cruisers were being built at the time, at the Vickers, Yokosuka, Kawasaki, and Mitsubishi yards, and to fulfil the Navy's requests by their stipulated date – 1918 – would require £40 million. In the event only £9 million was allocated; and, angry and disappointed, the navy men precipitated a political crisis which lasted through 1912 and into 1913. The Saionji cabinet was obliged to resign; in a General Election in May 1912, the Army Minister, General Uehara, became premier. He demanded that the Army be increased by two divisions. The cabinet refused; he resigned; the Army refused to present another nominee as their Minister; the cabinet resigned. Another Army man, General Katsura, was appointed premier, whereupon the Imperial Navy refused to nominate a Navy Minister. Katsura, in some desperation, called on the Emperor to command a naval nomination, and was publicly censured for bringing the throne into politics. On 24 December 1912 the Diet, the parliament, was suspended; it did not sit again until 5 February 1913, and on 10 February the new cabinet resigned, and Admiral Yamamoto Gombei was declared Prime Minister. The strangest aspect of this stormy period was that, in the middle of it, the Emperor Meiji died; yet the wrangle continued unabated.

Meiji was replaced by his only son, Yoshihito, whose reign-name – Taisho – meant 'Great Righteousness'; and the reign opened with the commissioning of the super-dreadnought *Yamashiro*. She was sister to the *Fuso*, commissioned two years earlier out of the stingy £9 million of 1911. The first *Fuso*, that first British-built contribution to the Imperial Navy back in 1877, had been struck off the active list in 1908 and broken up in 1910. But the name continued, and in its new incarnation was given to a mightily impressive craft. The first *Fuso* displaced 3,800 tons; the second, 35,900. The first had been 220 feet long; the second was 630. Other relative figures were: beam, 48 feet and 94 feet; speed, 13 knots and 22½ knots; horsepower, 3,500 and 40,000; complement, 250 and 1,193. Hearing of the great new ship, W. F. Massey, the Prime Minister of New Zealand, sounded a warning:

'Japan is building at the present moment what will be one of the strongest and most powerful battleships afloat. When we see what is going on there, is it not time for New Zealand to think that she should be doing something in the way of naval defence? Is Japan building all these battleships and cruisers and torpedo-boats for toys? Are they intended for holiday-making purposes, or do they mean business? Japan has become one of the greatest naval powers in the world. Neither New Zealand or Australia, nor New Zealand and Australia combined, could hope to successfully contend with Japan. I do not think we can hope, for many years to come, to build a fleet sufficient to hold its own against the Japanese fleet; but that is no reason why we should not do everything we possibly can to provide for our own defence, and at the same time strengthen the [British] imperial fleet . . . I say, as a citizen of New Zealand, that I shall never be satisfied until I see a British fleet in the Pacific, whether it be made of ships from Canada, ships from Australia, ships from New Zealand, or British ships, or all four combined . . . able to hold its own against any enemy, white or yellow, that may happen to come along.'

Fuso and *Yamashiro* marked another advance in Japan's ship-building skills: they were the first battleships built there using not only Japanese materials but also Japanese-made weapons. Yet it was not their 14-inch guns which were the real threat to New Zealand and the rest of the British Empire; that threat was taking shape on the other side of the world, only a few score miles from the shores of England, in the dockyards and workshops of Germany. And, when a Japanese warship entered Wellington harbour in October 1914, it was not as an enemy, but as a desperately needed friend.

12

'Signal success'

On 15 August 1914 the Japanese Foreign Minister Kato Takaaki sent an ultimatum to Count Rex, Germany's Ambassador in Tokyo.

'We consider it highly important and necessary in the present situation to take measures to remove the causes of all disturbances of peace in the Far East and to safeguard general interests as contemplated in the agreement of alliance between Japan and Great Britain. In order to secure firm and enduring peace in eastern Asia, the establishment of which is the aim of the said agreement, the Imperial Japanese Government sincerely believes it to be its duty to give advice to the Imperial German Government to carry out the following two propositions: 1 – to withdraw immediately from Japanese and Chinese waters German men-of-war and armed vessels of all kinds, and to disarm at once those which cannot be withdrawn; 2 – to deliver on a date not later than 15 September to the Imperial Japanese authorities, without condition or compensation, the entire leased territory of Kaiochow with a view to the eventual restoration of the same to China.

'The Imperial Japanese Government announces at the same time that, in the event of its not receiving by noon of 23 August an answer from the Imperial German Government signifying unconditional acceptance of the above advice offered by the Imperial Japanese Government, Japan will be compelled to take such action as it may deem necessary to meet the situation.'

The advice was worded in a very similar way to the Triple Intervention of 1895, and, because of that, many people in subsequent years have seen Kato's ultimatum as a piece of exquisite, long-awaited revenge for the degradation forced on Japan by the Interventionists. It would be hard to deny that there must have been a certain degree of satisfaction in being able thus to return tit-for-tat; but it is easy to make too much of it, and imagine the Japanese nation as patiently awaiting its chance. That had happened with the Russo-Japanese War; the German-Japanese War, as Japan's part in World War One was known, was undertaken much less eagerly, prosecuted much less willingly, and fired by much less passion. When it was wholehearted, it was effective, and helped the Allied cause; but, in the end, it helped Japan more than all the rest of the Allies put together.

The year 1914 began in Japan with the disclosure of a stupendous financial scandal. Three years earlier, at the beginning of the eight-eight fleet political crisis, the British naval attaché, Sir Douglas Brownrigg, had written caustically: 'There are some confiding idiots who fancy that [Japan] is run on the non-squeeze principle; all I have to say to that is that it shows them either to be absurdly credulous or lamentably ignorant! as there is not a move made of any sort or kind in the Armament or Machinery line or of course in the ship-building line generally, without very large sums of money being diverted from their intended destination!'

Such behaviour was all very well when it was exercised discreetly; but someone overstepped the boundaries of caution, and on 22 January the lid was blown off a system of bribery in naval circles – a system so habitual that it was regular in all but law. It is scarcely surprising that the revelation did not originate in Tokyo; instead it emerged in a court in Berlin, and became one of the clues which explained, to the British, Japan's inconsistent attitude in the Great War.

The scandal was international; the British firm of Vickers, the German firm of Siemens and the Japanese Mitsui company all admitted bribing Imperial Navy officers to win contracts. Instead of the unsavoury word 'bribery', the more sanitary term 'commission' was used as often as possible; but just one per cent of the cost of a battleship would be a hefty sum, and the coy terminology attracted such derision that even Tokyo school-children added 'commission' to their English vocabulary. For the government under Admiral Yamamoto Gombei – a founder of the Imperial Navy, and a Satsuman, like the naval officers involved – it was a poor joke; the Diet refused to let the issue go quietly, and on 24 March Yamamoto resigned. The merry-go-round of cabinets came to a temporary halt with the installation of a coalition government, a weak and uncertain creature in which a man of determination could lead beyond his rank; and so it was that, at the outbreak of World War One, the government's initial declaration of neutrality was overturned by Foreign Minister Kato within four days.

The unusually long deadline given in Kato's ultimatum – seven days, rather than the more common twenty-four or forty-eight hours – was because the German Ambassador was not in direct touch with his own government, and a rapid reply could not reasonably be expected. But Kato also hoped that Germany might settle out of court, so to speak – that his advice might actually be taken, Kiaochow handed over, and German warships in the area either removed or disarmed. There was not the faintest possibility of such agreement: to the governor of Kaiochow, Kaiser Wilhelm said, 'It would shame me more to surrender Kaiochow to the Japanese than Berlin to the Russians.' The Japanese had anticipated as much, and when noon on 23 August came and went without a word from Germany, the Imperial Navy was already steaming towards the blockade of Kiaochow.

The operation would result in one of the Allies' first major victories of the war.

The land surrounding Kaiochow Bay was rough and inhospitable, but the bay itself gave Tsingtao the best and deepest harbour on the China coast. The town was garrisoned by about 3,500 German soldiers, aided by German-trained Chinese soldiers; the Japanese force began with 30,000 men. When they arrived off Kaiochow on 24 August, a British blockade – the battleship *Triumph* and the destroyer *Usk* – had already been in position for two weeks. The Japanese took over, and on 2 September attempted their first landing. It was literally a wash-out; abnormally heavy rains brought floods which made any advance impossible. Lungkow, the site of that effort, was some eighty miles north of Tsingtao; the second choice, Laoshan Bay, was fifteen miles north-west. A landing was made there on 18 September, and four days later the Japanese were joined by a British expeditionary force from Shanghai.

One of the officers in the British contingent was thirty-one-year-old George Gipps. When the war began he was in Peking, and had gone as quickly as possible to Shanghai. Along the way 'everybody was talking of war', and by the time he arrived he was itching for action; but, to his amazement, he was not needed. Able only to while away the time with tennis and polo, 'useless days spent doing nothing in particular', he began to wonder if he could do anything more than die of boredom; and then he was ordered to join *Triumph*. Joyfully he did so, and on 22 September saw the thrilling spectacle of the landing at Laoshan.

'The Beach generally presented a most inspiring scene – British and Jap flags crossed, outside Base Commandant's office erected; long trains of ammunition and stores moving off in one continual stream, with an occasional Howitzer battery interposed; rail head being rapidly pushed along . . . The work of pile-driving and pier-building goes on incessantly, with continual landing of all kinds of men, horses and material.'

'All kinds of men' was an apt phrase – the rather unlikely combined force included Japanese, Sikhs, and South Wales Borderers. As for ships, the Japanese were joined by the British vessels *Triumph*, the cruiser *Yarmouth*, five destroyers and the French cruiser *Dupleix*; and this international group, for the first time ever, was under Japanese command. Aboard the cruiser *Iwato* – a 10,000-ton veteran of the Russo-Japanese War – Vice Admiral Tochinai was doing his best to solve the problems of alliance. He sent over to *Triumph* five thousand Japanese cigarettes and some sake – 'unsmokable and undrinkable,' said Gipps, 'however very nice of him' – and tried to work out some way to stop his men arresting the Welshmen on suspicion of being German. Armbands were the answer; and, after these initial complications, the attack on Tsingtao got under way. The Germans there hoped to hold out for six months, assuming, like so many others, that by then the war would be over. By 12 October they were surrounded; on 7 November they surrendered. By then, the Japanese infantry had made a decision whose influence would hang on for decades – that the British troops were not much good. On the maritime side, the Imperial Navy offended *Triumph*'s Captain Fitzmaurice by asking him to leave at the very end, so that only Japanese ships would be seen victorious; but naval relations were mostly good and, after Tsingtao's defeat, the allies exchanged messages of congratulation. Captain Hubert Brand, naval attaché at the Tokyo embassy, wrote with particular enthusiasm to Vice Admiral Kato Sadakichi, commander of the Second Fleet.

'After three months' service in ships under your command,' he said, 'I am more than ever confident that in the Japanese Navy, Great Britain has a most faithful and very valuable Ally. I shall take an early opportunity of reporting to the British Admiralty on the cordial state of relations between our two Navies during the late operations off Tsingtao.'

However, the most significant aspect of the whole operation, in the long run, was something about which comparatively little was said at the time: since Tsushima, only nine years before, war had gone beyond two dimensions. Now air-power was beginning to play a part. In the autumn of 1913, the British Lieutenant-Commander A. Longmore had dropped the first armed Whitehead torpedo from a Short floatplane, and on 26 October of the same year Winston Churchill had already envisaged an ideal air force – it would include 'an overseas fighting seaplane to operate from a ship as base, a scouting seaplane to work with the fleet at sea, and a home service fighting aeroplane to repel enemy aircraft'. The Japanese at Tsingtao had what Gipps called an 'aeroplane ship' – a 7,700-ton one-time British merchant ship, converted to carry seaplanes, which were winched over her side to take off from and land on the sea. She carried four seaplanes; but she was very much a last-minute job, for her conversion from merchant ship to carrier was only completed on 17 August – one week before the blockade of Tsingtao began. During the operations, moreover, she 'bumped a mine and had to be beached to prevent her sinking'; and the event which most succinctly characterized the state of the art was noted by Gipps with sailorly amusement: a duel between a Japanese and a German pilot. Flying noisily around, they shot at each other with pistols. It must have been very frightening, and great fun; but neither was hurt at all.

While these little auguries of future wars were emerging, the Imperial Navy was busy elsewhere, to the nation's profit and the Allies' annoyance. Scattered over the Pacific Ocean was a chain of German radio stations, based on various German-owned islands. On 30 August New Zealand forces had taken Samoa; on 13 September Australian forces had taken New Guinea; and, during September and October, Japanese forces took all the islands in the Marshall, Carolina and Mariana groups. And, once they had got them, they would not let them go – nor would Britain, keen to encourage further Japanese help in Europe, do much to take the islands over, despite repeated protests from mistrustful Australians who felt threatened by so close an approach. The argument rambled on until the end of the war; and, after the war, Japan retained the islands, with all the strategic advantages they represented. North of the Equator there was only one exception – the little island of Yap was given over to Australian command.

Australians were worried not only by the relative proximity to their shores of Japanese bases, but also by the loss of trade with the northern isles. The British, on the other hand, were eager for Japanese naval aid not only in European waters but in the Pacific itself – for the German East Asiatic Squadron, under Vice Admiral Graf Maximilian von Spee, was harrying British merchant shipping from India to South America.

The German armoured cruisers *Gneisenau* and *Scharnhorst*, and the light cruisers *Diana*, *Emden*, *Leipzig* and *Nürnberg*, had all been based in Kaiochow. Cruising at the outbreak of war, they had left harbour even before the British blockade began. *Emden* had gone west to India, the others east to South America. On 22 September, combined Japanese and British cruisers came close to catching *Emden* near Madras, after she had shelled oil installations there. Between the start of the war and 9 November, when she was finally destroyed by the Australian light cruiser *Sydney*, she sank or captured 23 merchant ships, totalling over 100,000 tons; and, when she herself was finally sunk, the Imperial Navy claimed that, although they had taken part in the hunt, the British Admiralty had prevented them sinking her. As for the rest of von Spee's squadron, the presence and superiority of the Imperial Navy in the Western Pacific sent him to South America, where, before he met his fate in the Battle of the Falklands, he sank the British armoured cruiser *Good Hope* and the cruiser *Monmouth*, commanded by Admiral Sir Christopher Cradock. Thus, the full extent of the Imperial Navy's involvement against von Spee was entirely passive, limited to shooing him out of the Western Pacific; and the knowledge that they could have done a great deal more provoked much bitterness in Britain.

'It is preposterous to speak of the services rendered by their navy,' said Ernest Morrison, *The Times*' correspondent in Peking. 'Did their navy save Cradock's fleet? Did their navy assist in the Battle of the Falkland Islands? Have they no commerce of their own to protect? One would think, when one reads of the wonderful services they have rendered in the Far Eastern Seas, that they are doing this solely in the interests of British commerce. Did they check the depredations of the *Emden*? Or was a bargain struck that the activities of this raider would not be interfered with so long as they did not molest the Japanese flag? Whatever they boast, the fact remains, that the Japanese have not exchanged a single shot with any enemy ship . . . In the operations at Tsingtao, a fort of very inferior strength defended by 6,000

Germans hastily gathered together, and containing a large percentage of clerks, pot-bellied cooks and such-like, was after a short siege reduced by a gigantic Japanese force whose casualties were quite insignificant . . .'

Morrison went on to complain that, out of what he regarded as a too-famous victory, Japanese awards included two baronies, 380 decorations for nurses, hundreds of promotions for officers, and 145,000 medals. Although the general tone of his comments reflected much of British opinion, not long afterwards, Churchill, as First Lord of the Admiralty, gave the official attitude.

'It has been a matter of the greatest satisfaction to me', he wrote to the Japanese attaché in London, Admiral Oguri Kobaburo, 'that the signal success which has been achieved between the navies of Japan and Great Britain has been reflected in the relations established between the two Admiralties. When the history of this great war comes to be written, the ungrudging and whole-hearted assistance of Japan will form a striking chapter, and the cordiality that has united the naval staffs of both countries will endure as one of our pleasantest memories . . .'

This was considerably exaggerated – but it was necessary to achieve an effect. He went on: 'For the moment, our attention is turned to the naval operations in the North Sea and the Mediterranean, but we know that should ever the need arise we can rely with confidence upon the powerful aid of the navy of Japan.'

In that skilful slide from flattery to suggestion, his purpose came clear: to try and persuade the Imperial Navy to come to Britain's aid in the north.

He did not have much success – nor, for that matter, did anyone else in the British Admiralty. Japan's entry into World War One had been undertaken officially not because of the Alliance but because of the spirit of friendship brought about by the Alliance. Unofficially, but practically, it had been undertaken largely out of self-interest, as a carefully estimated risk, with the intention of clarifying Japan's relationship with China. Since Tsingtao, two things had occurred to cool Japanese enthusiasm, never hot at best, for the foreign war. The first was that it had become apparent that the world conflict was going to be long drawn out, a state of affairs temperamentally unattractive to the Japanese, especially since some new Pacific possessions had been acquired. The second was that, on 18 January 1915, Japan had presented to China the infamous Twenty-One Demands, a paper of considerably greater interest to the country.

The name 'Twenty-One Demands' is a Western one, because, although in effect that is what they were, they were not regarded as such in Japan. There, the list was seen more as sixteen strong proposals and five desires; but given their nature, and that China's agreement could be won by force if necessary, 'Demands' seems fair enough. The first group dealt with the Shantung peninsula, which, since the conquest of Tsingtao, was occupied by Japanese troops, and which the Japanese wished to remain under their administration. The second group covered Manchuria; the Japanese leases there were due to expire in 1923, and an extension was deemed advisable. The remainder mostly involved Japan in China's programme of modernization, including everything from docks to heavy industries; while the last group – the 'desires' – suggested that Japanese advisers should be employed in Chinese military, financial and political fields.

As always, interpretation depended on point of view. China, and most of the rest of the world, saw the package as a barely-warranted interference in Chinese home affairs; Japan saw it as a fair repayment for ousting Germany from Tsingtao, and pointed out that no territorial claims were involved, but merely economic preferences. Either way, it says a good deal for the Japanese assessment of China and the rest of the world that the Demands were acceded to – after much Chinese opposition, and some Japanese revision – on 9 May. But it was all clumsily done, and Kato's part in it, as Foreign Minister, was particularly inept; and though, as an exercise popular in Japan itself, it gave the country some welcome political stability, it unnecessarily tarnished the nation's hard-won reputation abroad for fair dealing in foreign affairs, very much more than either the Sino-Japanese or the Russo-Japanese War had done.

Meanwhile, the British hope of bringing the Imperial Navy into the European sea war was faring poorly. A request early in the war for a squadron to be sent to the Mediterranean was refused in September 1914; a second request for help in the Baltic was also refused, although assistance was offered if Britain should actually be invaded. (The idea that by then it would be too late did not seem to occur.) In November 1914 the Baltic request was repeated accidentally, through a slip-up in the British Foreign Office. This time the Imperial Army vetoed it, on the basis that the Japanese national interest was not at stake. That at least was the surface reason; the deeper reason was more intriguing, and recognizably Japanese. Forty years or so earlier, the Imperial Army had been trained by the Prussians. The training had held up well in two wars, and the Imperial Army had the same kind of respect for the German Army as the Imperial Navy had for the Royal Navy. The prospect of fighting the German Army in World War One was, for the Imperial Army, a dilemma which could only be refused; for defeat would be intolerable, and victory against Germany would be unthinkable. This may give another insight into the differences between Army and Navy thinking in Japan: at war in 1915, the Army refused to fight its tutor, and forbade the Imperial Navy to assist *its* tutor, maintaining that the national interest was not at stake. In 1941, on the brink of a war it estimated to be unwinnable, the Imperial Navy reluctantly agreed to fight Britain, because the Army, now allied with Germany, saw the Second World War as being in Japan's national interest.

The requests for naval aid came up again in 1916. On 9 February, Sir Edward Grey, the British Foreign Secretary, formally asked for a cruiser squadron to go to the Indian Ocean, and a destroyer flotilla to the Malacca Straits. The reply non-plussed everyone: Japan agreed, but on various conditions. This bargaining was a governmental, rather than a naval, response; the Imperial Navy was actually keen to extend its range beyond local waters, and pressed the government to permit its involvement. Very early in the war, on 21 August 1914, two Imperial Navy ships – the battle-cruisers *Ibuki* and *Chikuma* – had ventured as far as Singapore, where they had joined the British squadron. With von Spee's ships still at large, ANZAC troops – the Australia and New Zealand Army Corps – had been unable to set forth for Europe, and it was *Ibuki* which had joined the ANZAC convoy in Wellington on 16 October 1914 – the only occasion on which a Japanese ship escorted ANZAC forces, and, for most Australians and New Zealanders, the only occasion on which they saw a Japanese warship actually in one of their harbours.

Since then the Imperial Navy had kept a low profile in the Indian Ocean, and was very willing to alter that position. Their government acceded to the British request, and it became India's turn to feel nervous, fearful lest the Indian Ocean should become a Japanese patrol-ground. In fact relations between the Royal and Imperial Navies during World War One were at their best in the Indian Ocean; but, if Japan's navy was willing to assist, its government had put so many obstacles in the way that getting Japanese assistance was almost more trouble for Britain than it was worth. On 30 December 1916 the First Sea Lord, Admiral Jellicoe, gave his commendably restrained opinion: 'It cannot be said that the attitude of Japan has been entirely satisfactory. It is true that in certain respects they are much handicapped owing to the antagonism between the United States and Japan, but the trouble lies far deeper than that . . . Apart from the selling of guns and ammunition to the Russians and ourselves, Japan is not taking a full share in the war.'

New requests were met with new bargaining; the British felt more and more strongly that they were in the disagreeable position of having to ask favours, and of accepting whatever Japan's terms might be. At the beginning of 1917 two cruisers were asked to patrol the Cape of Good Hope, while it was requested that a flotilla of Japanese destroyers be sent to Malta to protect merchant shipping and counter the ever-growing menace of submarines in the Mediterranean. This was so far from home waters that, like the government, the Imperial Navy began to have doubts – doubts that divided its officers into two lobbies, the *hakensetsu* and the *hantaisetsu*, respectively for and against the sending of ships. The *hantaisetsu* was led by Commander Nakamura Ryozo, head of the first operations section of the general staff, whose very Army-style argument against sending ships so far off was that such action would denote a complete change in national policy. He was right; but it was the *hakensetsu*, led by Rear Admiral Akiyama Saniyuki, who had actually toured the battle-fronts of Europe, which prevailed.

The Japanese price was British support for their presence in Shantung and the ex-German Pacific islands; and when the British, out of necessity, agreed to this, they had a pleasant surprise. Two third-class sister cruisers, *Niitaka* and *Tsushima*, were sent to the Cape, as requested, while to the Mediterranean went more than double the number of requested ships: two flotillas of destroyers, and also the cruiser *Akashi*, something of an historic ship, being one of the first two vessels built in Japanese yards with domestic materials to domestic plans. Such data was of little interest to the Royal Navy in the Mediterranean; but even an old cruiser was a welcome addition, and the extra destroyers were very handy.

Yet, by the end of April, even more destroyers were needed. Another dozen were asked for; the Imperial Navy, however, had four ships undergoing repair in dock, and in all honesty felt under strength. The request was refused, repeated, and eventually granted as far as possible. Four vessels were all that could be spared, but they were four of the best in Japan – brand-new ships, and the most advanced of their type. Indeed, they were the sum total of their class. Their names were *Momo*, *Kashi*, *Hinoki* and *Yanagi*. Each was 275 feet long, weighed just over 800 tons, could do 31½ knots, and, unlike any other destroyer in the Imperial Navy, was armed with two sets of triple torpedo-tubes. On 23 May it was agreed to send them. The youngest, *Yanagi*, had been completed only eighteen days before. Even *Momo*, the oldest, had been in use a mere five months; and, in thanks for the contribution, an official statement was made in the House of Commons.

'These services to the Allied cause,' said Lord Robert Cecil, 'gratifying and important as they are themselves, gain additional value as showing the spirit of every one of our Allies, and indicating the greatness of the assistance which we may expect from them in the future.'

Japan and the Imperial Navy, however, would give no more; nor would they even sell anything. In the autumn of 1917, despite the entry of American in the war, there were still too few Allied ships in European waters. Urgently needing more, the British government considered asking Japan for the loan of two battle-cruisers; but, after the difficulties encountered over destroyers and ordinary cruisers, and given the likelihood that Japan would exact some exorbitant political price, the idea was dropped. Someone made the slightly sour-grapes comment that, even if the loan was proposed and agreed, Japanese officers and men would not be up to German standards. Then, more constructively, came a brain-wave: Britain would offer to *buy* the battle-cruisers. So desperate was the need for these fast, heavily-armed ships that the Admiralty offered to include two battleships in the bargain if necessary, the battleships being even stronger, though slower. Since Japan's only enemy was Germany, and the German navy had been swept from the Pacific, it seemed an admirable solution and an excellent deal for Japan; and so when, on 5 October, Japan refused the offer, the reaction in Britain was mistrustful. Jellicoe's predecessor as First Sea Lord, Admiral Jackson, had voiced the same feeling over a year before: Japan's attitude, he considered, 'gives rise to some suspicion as to her action after the war, when we may be exhausted by our war efforts, so the transfer of any of her best fighting units to our Navy would be all in our favour, if she breaks the alliance with us and leans towards our possible future enemies'.

After that rebuff, Britain never asked for any further Japanese naval assistance in World War One. The Mediterranean squadron, under Admiral Sato Kozo, continued to operate in conjunction with other Allied forces until the end of the war, as did the Japanese ships in the Indian Ocean. In neither case were officers of other navies allowed to command Japanese men; instead, a system was established whereby British ships invited the collaboration of the Japanese. Collaboration in practice was automatic and, as far as it went, the arrangement worked well, so that after the war the mood in Britain became generous and hopeful. The Japanese Mediterranean Squadron was invited to visit Great Britain, and did so; Winston Churchill later said that during the war he 'did not think that the Japanese had ever done a foolish thing'; and in March 1919, on its final visit to Malta, Lord Methuen reviewed the Squadron. Paying tribute to 'its splendid work in European waters', he expressed the pious hope that 'God grant our alliance, cemented in blood, may long endure'.

But the Anglo-Japanese Alliance was decaying. Both allies felt that too much was asked by the other, and not enough given in return; and diplomatic pressures, especially from America, were working towards its end. Jackson's fears of 1916 would be realized through the 1920s – Japan would lean more and more closely 'towards our possible future enemies' – and yet it was Britain, not Japan, which would eventually break the alliance.

13

'Two formidable new Powers'

When peace was proclaimed in Europe, the citizens of Tokyo celebrated as enthusiastically as those of Paris, London or Washington. But, while the Western allies held nationwide festivities as they welcomed home their menfolk, the Japanese countryside was undisturbed – for one of the peculiarities of World War One, as far as the people of Japan were concerned, was that many of them had had no idea it was taking place at all. Malcolm Kennedy, a British Army captain seconded to the Japanese Army, discovered this in 1917:

'While the War was still in progress, I actually came across Japanese peasant folk who had not even heard that there was a war. They were frankly incredulous when I assured them, that not only was there a war, but that Japan was taking part in it. Their incredulity was based on the fact that the young men of the village had not been called up for service. If Japan was really at war, they argued, surely all the male youth of the country would be summoned to the colours.'

A year later, the same peasants may have been very well aware that a war was on; for the second peculiarity of Japan's part in World War One was that her fighting did not finish in 1918, but instead intensified, in a strange and frequently forgotten postscript to the World War: the Siberian Intervention. Being mainly a land operation, this was more an Army than a Navy affair; but the Imperial Navy had some direct involvement, and indirectly was deeply affected: the international mistrust which characterized the episode contributed to the air of high tension in the Pacific – tension which grew through two decades of nominal peace to such a level that a Pacific War was needed to clear it.

The need, as the Western Allies saw it, for the Siberian Intervention began in December 1917, when the newly-successful Soviet Government signed its armistice with Germany. The action began in January 1918 with the arrival in Vladivostock of one British and three Japanese warships; and it did not end until October 1922, when the last Japanese troops withdrew. The Soviet-German armistice threatened to release thousands of German troops from the Eastern Front; it also stranded fifty or sixty thousand Czech troops in Siberia. Thus, the Intervention started with a double purpose: to rescue the Czechs, and to prevent the Germans from returning to fight on the Western Front. But for America it became an early Vietnam, an unwinnable war against popularly-supported Bolshevism; and for Japan it became an opportunity for out-and-out expansion.

Since Japan and America fought side by side throughout the campaign for different objectives, it started with bad relations between them and ended with worse. On 30 December 1917 the British Ambassador in Tokyo forwarded a message from Vladivostock to London:

'December 24 at Habarosk commissioner of provisional government for eastern Siberia handed over his powers to meeting of representatives of the peasantry organizations and town register. Meeting decided in view of chaotic conditions of country and the absence of central authority to form standing committee of six, being one from each province and one from each Cossack district to carry on local administration. This decision caused direct conflict with council of soldiers and workmen's delegates who support Lenin government . . . I request instructions by telegraph with utmost urgency. General situation is bad but will be very seriously aggravated in the near future . . . I repeat that the presence of Allied warships is necessary for protection of goods lying there. Visit of Japanese ship of war alone might provoke disagreeable situation. Infinitely preferable that British or other Allied ship be sent simultaneously. This question should be decided immediately.'

At once the British Admiralty ordered a cruiser up from Hong Kong. The Japanese had already expressed the wish that they alone should be involved, since the prospect of a revolutionary government in control of shores so close to their own affected them more immediately than Britain or America, and since they had more men available than the other Allies. Their ambassador in London was therefore informed of the British action, and the Imperial Navy immediately sent a cruiser of its own, which arrived in Vladivostock two days before the British *Suffolk*, and was followed by two Japanese battleships. These, the *Iwami* and the *Asahi*, were both old vessels, veterans of Tsushima. In that battle they had fought against each other, for the *Iwami* had been one of Rozhdestvenski's fleet, captured, repaired and made over to the Imperial Navy. At last, thirteen years too late, re-named and with a different ensign, she had made it to Vladivostock.

Suspicious from the start of Japan's intentions, President Wilson had refused to allow the intervention to be solely Japanese; and yet no American ship was sent until late February 1918, and no active American assistance was given on the spot until 11 July. By then the British and Japanese had both made two landings, to protect the 600,000 tons of Allied supplies and munitions in Vladivostock and to supply them to the Czechs in the region. In the early part of the summer the city changed hands backwards and forwards between Czech and Bolshevik, until Wilson authorized the despatch of

7,000 American troops, to be accompanied, he said, by an equal number of Japanese. The seven thousand Americans arrived; and, by the end of October, they had been joined by *seventy* thousand Japanese.

Wilson had attempted to limit Japanese involvement because he believed that Japan wished to take over the Russian Maritime Provinces; and that was exactly what happened. Within a short time the Japanese troops had taken control of a thousand miles of the Chinese Eastern Railway through Manchuria, and 1,200 miles of the Trans-Siberian Railway through the Maritime Provinces. And so began the years of Allied anti-Bolshevist war in Russia: years in which the tide of territory ebbed and flowed, the Czechs at one time advancing further westward than the Urals, and at last – in November 1920 – being forced to evacuate Russia eastwards through Vladivostock.

In 1920 as well, the massacre of Nikolaievsk took place. This town, situated on the mouth of the river Amur, was home to numerous Japanese nationals – mainly fishermen and their familes – and contained a consulate. On 25 May, Red partisans, who had taken temporary control of the town, slaughtered the Japanese population – Western figures gave the deaths at over 700; Japanese figures claimed ten times that amount. The incident shocked the Japanese nation greatly, and in guarantee of its settlement Japan took control of the northern half of the island of Sakhalien, the southern half of which Tsar Nicholas had reluctantly ceded in 1905. Such were the trials and prizes of intervention – the loss of life, the gain of land. And oil-rich Sakhalien offered Japan more than land: the country was now able to supply its Navy with the three basic essentials – men, steel, and fuel.

But these steps forward for Japan were accompanied by steadily deteriorating relations with America, the Pacific's other Great Power. Acquiring Germany's Pacific islands had put a line of Japanese territory between America and the Philippines. Japan's actions in Siberia seemed to fulfil all too clearly Wilson's predictions of expansion; and the independent fuel supply of Sakhalien promised worse to come. By the end of 1920, the confidence generated in the white Pacific nations by Roosevelt's Great White Fleet was a thing of the distant past; and President Taft's comment of June 1907 seemed like an echo from another age. 'War with Japan!' he had said then. 'Don't you believe it. Never mind the news that keeps coming. We will have no war with Japan, you may rest assured of that.'

On 6 January 1919, Theodore Roosevelt died in his sleep. In one of his last letters he wrote: 'I regard the British Navy as probably the most potent instrumentality for peace in the world . . . I think the time has come when the United States and the British Empire can agree to a universal arbitration treaty. In other words . . . under no circumstances shall there ever be a resort to war between the United States and the British Empire.'

But the Great War had changed the balance of the world, perhaps more than the ageing Roosevelt ever realized. At a meeting of the Committee of Imperial Defence in December 1920, Lloyd George tried to foretell the future. 'A European enemy could be ruled out,' he said. 'There were, however, two formidable new Powers in the world – formidable today and possibly overwhelmingly so in a few years' time.' He meant Japan and America; and, shortly afterwards, the Canadian prime minister echoed his opinion with the comment that 'there were only three major Powers left in the world: the United States, Britain and Japan'. To lend credence to their claims, all three nations depended ultimately on their navies. Japan's naval losses in the war had been minimal – two light cruisers and one destroyer, a battleship and a battlecruiser by accident. Britain's, in comparison, had been enormous – accidental losses included a dreadnought, a pre-dreadnought battleship and a cruiser; losses in action included a dreadnought, ten pre-dreadnoughts, three battle-cruisers, a dozen cruisers, a dozen light cruisers, 67 destroyers and 54 submarines. Losses of other types brought the Royal Navy total loss to 312 ships. And then there was America. In the years from the Battle of Tsushima to the Treaty of Versailles, the United States Navy had undergone almost as radical a transformation as the Japanese Navy had at the turn of the century; thus, by 1920, the three fleets' respective total tonnages (exclusive of gunboats and auxiliary vessels) were: Britain, 4,153,000 tons; America, 1,370,000 tons; and Japan, 686,000 tons. And their projected additions were even more frightening. By the end of 1924, America intended to have added 820,000 tons to her navy; by the same date, Japan intended to have added no less than 946,000 tons to hers. The naval race was on, and no one wanted to give an inch. Typical of the feeling in each nation's Admiralty or Navy Department was the statement of Admiral Beatty, the First Sea Lord, on 14 December 1920: 'The loss of the year 1921–22 would be nothing less than disastrous to our chance of retaining our equality with the strongest naval power.'

Tonnage alone, however, is not a final index of naval power; to put it extremely, 120 500-ton vessels are not the same as a single 60,000-ton vessel – not that any warship, in 1920, was anywhere near such a weight. In that year the world's largest war vessel weighed in at a gross displacement of 38,500 tons – and it is not, perhaps, surprising that once again this was a Japanese battleship, the *Nagato*. Completed on 25 November 1920, she was also the first ship in the world to be armed with 16-inch guns, and the latest example of the Imperial Navy's eternal wish: to possess the biggest, most powerful ship afloat. The sight of a big warship always brings a surge of pride to the nation which owns it, and an equal surge of dismay to those which do not, if they have nothing to equal it; but there was a more practical reason than that for the Imperial Navy's undying love affair with big ships. Every naval person who travelled abroad – and that meant all the officers, in their training cruises at least – knew perfectly well that Japan's industrial resources could not hope to compete with those of Britain or America. Japanese strategists therefore reasoned that, within a limited capability, they should have one of the most powerful rather than three or four less powerful ships. But – and it was a very big but – the superiority of a surface vessel lay only in the inferiority of other surface vessels. Its armament was designed to cope with horizontal threats, as it were; vertical threats, from above or below, were another matter altogether, for which the warships of 1920 were not designed. Their armour-plating was getting more substantial all the time; *Nagato*, for example, had a water-line belt 11.8 inches thick at its maximum, the same around the barbettes, seven inches on the deck, fourteen on the turrets and 14.5 on the conning tower. However, the increases over the years had been in mere fractions of an inch – *Mikasa*'s armour, back in 1905, had not been very much less than *Nagato*'s fifteen years later – and even in 1920 it was still mainly concentrated around the water-line, despite the losses sustained by both sides to mines outside Port Arthur. There it had been shown that a very expensive warship could be lost to a very cheap underwater weapon; and by 1920 there were other cheap weapons which could attack the vulnerable points of a surface vessel.

These, of course, were submarines and aircraft, both of which had advanced considerably during World War One. The years 1915–18 had seen a number of aircraft 'firsts', all of which, as it happened, were British achievements: on 12 August 1915, as the grouse season was opening in Scotland, Flight Commander C. H. K. Edmonds became the first man to launch an aerial torpedo against an enemy ship. The incident took place in the Sea of Marmora, north-east of the Dardanelles. The ship was a Turkish merchantman; the aeroplane was a Short 184 float-plane. Flying at 75 mph, Edmonds came down to within fifteen feet of the sea and launched his torpedo at 300 yards to score a direct hit. It turned out later that the merchantman had actually been put out of action four days earlier by a submarine attack; but, as if to emphasize his point, on 17 August Edmonds had another first with a successful launch against a supply ship under weigh; and on the same day, within an hour of Edmonds' hit, his colleague, Flight Lieutenant G. B. Dacre, torpedoed another moving ship, a Turkish steam tug. And both of these operations were carried out with aircraft so new, they were untested prototypes, sent straight into the Dardanelles action.

The day before those hits, on 16 August, Flight Lieutenant W. L. Welsh flew his Sopwith Schneider float-plane off the 120-foot flight deck on the converted Cunarder *Campania* as she steamed into the wind at 17 knots – the first successful take-off from a ship; and three months later, in November 1915, Flight Lieutenant H. F. Towler took off in a Bristol C Scout biplane from the seaplane-carrier *Vindex* – the first take-off from a specially-designed ship, foretelling all the great carriers of World War Two. Taking off was one thing; but landing was quite another. The US Navy airman

Eugene Ely had managed to land aboard USS *Pennsylvania* in 1912, but no one had ever landed on an operational ship until 2 August 1917, when Squadron Commander Dunning did it, flying a Sopwith Pup from the flight deck of HMS *Furious*, a battle-cruiser converted to the role of carrier by the addition of a 228-foot flight deck. In fact Dunning did it twice; but on his third attempt, a few days later, he drowned.

By then, the first submarine had been sunk by air attack, when, on 20 May 1917, Flight Sub-Lieutenant C. R. Morrish, flying an H.12 flying-boat, spotted and destroyed the U-boat UC36. And, in the last months of the war, there was a particularly spectacular aircraft first: on 19 July 1918, seven 2F.1 Camels took off from *Furious*. Each was armed with two 50-pound bombs. Launched off the Schleswig coast, they flew eighty miles over sea and land to bomb the German airship sheds at Tondern.

'Captain Jackson dived right onto the northernmost shed,' said one of the pilots later, 'and dropped two bombs, one a direct hit in the middle and the other slightly to the side of the shed. I then dropped my one remaining bomb and Williams two more. Hits were observed. The shed then burst into flames and an enormous conflagration took place rising to at least 1,000 feet, and the whole of the shed being completely engulfed. After dropping, Jackson went straight on, Williams to the left and I to the right.'

Ten minutes later, the other four pilots attacked in an equally successful second wave. Dickson, the narrator, was one of only two able to return directly to *Furious*, and both these pilots were obliged to ditch alongside, deck-landing still being very experimental. Of the other five, one was lost at sea and four landed in Denmark; but the first carrier-launched air strike against a land target had been achieved, and was a notable victory – largely because, like a much more notorious carrier-launched air strike in December 1941, it was totally unexpected. Perhaps the line that led to Pearl Harbor could be traced back to the Schleswig coast in 1918; yet, to the victims at Tondern, air attack from the sea may have been even more terrifying and horrific than it was to the victims of Pearl, because, by 1941, everyone knew that such a thing was at least theoretically possible. Certainly, to the people in Oahu anyway, the Pearl strike was unexpected, but it *was* conceivable. Those at Tondern in 1918, in contrast, found themselves on the receiving end of an absolutely unprecedented style of attack. Clearly such things happen in every war, when new weapons, untested in the battlefield, are put into action for the first time; and from the first use of gunpowder to the first use of the atom bomb, from the 12-inch shells at Tsushima to the Exocet missiles in the Falklands, the reaction of victims must have always been the same – blind horror, in the face of the unimagined.

Submarines had gone through a similar evolution. The US Navy had bought its first submarine, the *Holland*, in 1900; the Royal Navy launched its first in November 1902, a primitive little craft displacing only 166 tons submerged, capable of five knots, and armed with a single torpedo-tube. In 1904, on 18 March, a disaster similar to the Japanese Lieutenant Sakuma's struck the Royal Navy when a new model submarine, the *A.1*, sank with all hands after being struck by a passing passenger liner; but still work progressed. In 1906 Germany's *U.1* was completed; in 1909 the British *D.1*, the Royal Navy's first diesel-driven ocean-going boat, was completed; and, on the fateful 22 September 1914, the German *U.9* sank the cruisers *Aboukir*, *Cressy* and *Hogue*. These were not the first of the U-Boats' victims in the Great War, but their loss was terrible and significant: in less than an hour, three 12,000-ton warships were sent to the bottom by one small, obsolescent submarine firing five torpedoes, and nearly 1,400 lives were lost.

The first sinking of a battleship by a submarine was claimed by Britain three months later, when the *B.11*, under Lieutenant Norman Holbrook, sank *Messoudieh* off Cape Helles, at the mouth of the Dardanelles. On 7 May 1915 the *Lusitania* went down; and, by October 1916, the rate of destruction of Allied shipping by U-boats had exceeded 300,000 tons *a month*. The tragic figures rose and rose: by March 1917, over half a million tons of Allied ships were being lost to U-boats each month, and the peak was reached in April 1917. The total for those four weeks is known with awful exactness: 834,549 tons. Twenty-two years later Winston Churchill remembered that nightmarish time, recalling how he 'watched with a fear that I never felt at any other moment of that struggle, the deadly upward movement of the curve of sinkings over the arrival of new construction . . . That was, in my opinion, the gravest peril that we faced in all the ups and downs of that war'. Indeed, at that point the Allies were facing defeat, and it was only the wide introduction of the convoy system, and America's almost simultaneous declaration of war on Germany, which turned the losses.

At the end of the Great War, the Royal Navy had 132 submarines. Germany surrendered 150, and in the course of the war had lost 199. Britain had lost 54; neither Japan nor America had lost any. Two years later it seemed that America had learnt the extraordinary value of the submarine, for by then the US Navy possessed 91 coastal submarines, ranging from 106 to 569 tons; the largest and newest of these could do 14 knots for 4,000 miles, and were armed with a 3-inch gun and four torpedo-tubes. America was also part-way through a building programme of 51 ocean-going vessels displacing 850 tons, armed like the coastal vessels, but capable of 16 knots for 5,000 miles. Against these numbers it is surprising that, at the same time, the burgeoning and ambitious Imperial Japanese Navy possessed only twenty-six submarines altogether. Fifteen of those were coastal vessels, the smallest being a minute thing of 62 tons; and, of their eleven ocean-going boats, only two were as large as 1,000 tons, and able to do 16½ knots for 7,500 miles. With the worth of this arm of the navy proved beyond doubt by the exploits of the U-boats, such neglect seems uncharacteristic of the Imperial Navy;

and the use of naval aircraft was even more neglected. In 1920 the Imperial Navy had only one aircraft carrier, and she was nothing special – merely the old *Wakamiya*, the ex-British freighter which had been present at Tsingtao. This undistinguished vessel with her canvas hangars had a flying-off deck fitted over her forecastle, and with that less than sensational alteration was, on 1 April 1920, reclassified from seaplane-carrier to the proud role of sole aircraft carrier in Japan's fleet. The phrase 'flying-off deck' is important: the first take-off was made from *Wakamiya* in June, by a British-built Sopwith Pup; but the plane could not return and land on board – it was still obliged to come down on the water and be winched into its hangar.

If they had rarely been inclined to experiment, the Imperial Navy had never been slow in taking up the best of others' weaponry, and, in retrospect, it seems strange at first that in 1920 they had not seriously adopted submarines and aircraft – especially when one remembers the devastation wrought by Japan's carriers, and her use of unrestricted submarine warfare, in World War Two. But it was that war which taught naval planners how vulnerable a surface vessel without air protection was to vertical attack; and what was obvious in 1945 was not at all clear in 1920. It was not stupidity or short-sightedness which caused the Imperial Navy to neglect these two vital elements at that time – or, at any rate, no greater stupidity or short-sightedness than in other navies. And, far from being uncharacteristic of the Imperial Navy, this neglect was most probably a product of typical Imperial Navy traits. Firstly, despite the proofs given in World War One, agreement outside Japan on the value of submarines and aircraft was by no means universal; it is likely that the Japanese were waiting to see which way the wind would blow, before making the commitment for future development. The debate over the relative virtues of the battleship versus submarines and aircraft stretched back to the beginning of the century; on 7 July 1901 in Britain, the *Sunday Times* had written with more perspicacity than most:

'If we want to retain our supremacy of the sea we must be supreme in the later and more effective, as well as the older and now less effective, though huger, engines of destruction. What is the use of our going on building great and powerful battleships if another country has a boat which can destroy them without its presence being discovered or even suspected?'

In contrast, the *Army and Navy Gazette* said cheerfully a few months later, 'We have a somewhat robust belief that these submarine vessels are likely to delude those who depend upon them;' and, the previous year, the First Lord of the Admiralty, George Goschen, was calmly dismissive: 'The submarine boat, even if practical difficulties attending its use can be overcome, would seem . . . to be eventually a weapon for Maritime powers on the defensive.'

Many people doubted the morality of submarine warfare, declaring that an underwater warship was unfair, unsporting, and, in Vice Admiral Sir

Arthur Wilson's memorable phrase, 'a damned un-English weapon'. Wilson campaigned ardently for the abolition of submarines even before they really got started, and in Parliament proposed a suitable text for the purpose: 'As certain foreign nations had devoted considerable sums to the construction of submarine boats, and shown their intention of making use of this *underhand* method of attack in future wars, HM Government considers it would be to the advantage of all the Maritime nations of the world if the use of submarine boats for attack could be prohibited.'

Of course it never came to that; yet how much distress and misery would have been avoided if Wilson's proposal had been accepted, and enforced, world-wide. Commenting on the proposal, Vice Admiral Archibald Douglas said, 'I am not apprehensive of submarine boats ever proving very formidable;' and, if many people disagreed with Wilson, many others disagreed with Douglas. Whether the Wilson proposal was based purely and genuinely on moral grounds, or whether he had discerned in the submarine a weapon which threatened the fundamentals of British supremacy, Arnold Foster – Parliamentary Secretary to the Admiralty – said pointedly, 'Our moral objection to any weapon will not prevent a foreign power using it against us, if it can be used to our injury.' And, following up the same train of thought, it was Jacky Fisher who said in 1904, 'More submarines! At once!'

In 1920, shortly before he died, it was Fisher again who wrote of the Royal Navy: 'Why keep any of the present lot? All you want is the present naval side of the air force! – That's the future navy!' That comment, it should be remembered, came from the man who had said of the nineteenth-century Royal Navy, 'Scrap the lot!', and who had then kept Britain on top of the world with HMS *Dreadnought* and her descendants. Fisher was always far-sighted, always iconoclastic, even when the icons were his own creation. But the all-big-gun dreadnought battleships were so splendid to look at, so obviously powerful, so inspiring – especially in contrast to the invisible, 'underhand' submarines and the puttering aircraft of the day – and Fisher's own personality was so abrasive, that the failure of his second attempt at naval revolution was almost inevitable. Moreover, he had been retired from the Navy, with a peerage, in 1910 – thinking of his turbulent, demanding spirit, one officer said then, 'So Jacky is growing roses, is he? Well, all I've got to say is that those roses will damned well have to grow.' After his retirement, Fisher's opinions carried progressively less weight – the image of the half-crazy old lord in his rose-garden made it ever easier for his critics to discredit him. But, if he died disappointed with his second revolution, in his lifetime he had achieved one thorough-going reorganization of the world's largest navy; and not many individuals could claim that.

Waiting, then, to see which way the long-standing debate would end – to see if aircraft would be exploited or submarines abolished – was one reason for the Imperial Navy's neglect of the possible third dimension, the vertical element of sea warfare. The other two reasons were closely interlinked, and one of them was of such compelling interest to the Imperial Navy that it alone would have deflected attention from the new weapons.

The majority of senior naval officers in any navy have almost always been men of legendary conservatism – which is partly why Fisher, and his contribution to the Royal Navy, were so outstanding. Most Japanese naval officers were no exception to the general rule, and in their case, being Japanese, there was a double dose of conservatism; a proved advance would be adopted with alacrity, but if there was any doubt about it, their innate dislike of change was even stronger than that of their Western counterparts. And, as it happened, 1920 saw the realization of a long-standing dream – parliamentary approval for the new eight-eight fleet. Eight battleships and eight cruisers – next to that, anything else paled into insignificance.

In 1905, Kato Tomosaburo had been Chief of Staff to Admiral Togo. By 1914 he was Minister of Marine, and remained in that post until 1923. Under him the Imperial Navy had lobbied constantly for the eight-eight fleet – to such an extent that it became an obsession, stifling support for the cheaper, less grand underwater and air weapons. The eight-eight plan was endorsed by the Diet in 1914, but modified to eight-four; approved in 1917, but in 1918 amended to eight-six; and presented in full again in 1918, when the proposal collapsed after the Diet's dissolution. By contemporary standards it was a huge project, spread over ten years, at the end of which the existing fleet would become a back-up to the new eight battleships and eight cruisers; and, with a typically naval blend of conservatism and romanticism, officers stuck to the grand plan with passionate determination, even when their efforts might have been better directed elsewhere. At last, under a new Diet, it was all approved, on 7 July 1920. Eight days earlier, *Mutsu* had been launched; with her sister *Nagato*, already nearing completion, these battleships were the largest vessels of their kind in the world.

And then paradoxically, just when the ten-year project was secured, the Imperial Navy underwent a radical change of mood, as did, simultaneously, the British Admiralty and the American Navy Department. All three countries were building at fantastic rates, and if all their programmes were realized, the proliferation of warships around the globe was likely to have only one logical result – another war, probably between at least two of the three nations. A couple of years before, they had all been fighting together in 'the war to end wars'. Suddenly it began to seem absurd that erstwhile allies should be running so enthusiastically in a race that seemed bound to result in yet further conflict. And, more practically, budgets were being overstretched. From both points of view, something had to be done to end the race.

But, whatever the future held for them – war or bankruptcy – at the end of 1920 the Imperial Navy could look back on its achievements with considerable satisfaction. Their day, as a fighting force, had dawned in 1894; by 1905 they had 'shown the world what they could do'. In 1906 their sun had risen over the yardarm, and in the full meaning of that traditional maritime saying, a period of relaxation, assessment and planning had begun. Experience had been used and extended, strategic territories had been gained, their latest ships were the biggest and best in the world, and Japan now occupied one of the five permanent seats in the League of Nations, reserved for the countries with the largest navies. All that in a single generation; the future must have looked very bright.

PART FOUR

*Eclipse
1921–1936*

*The 'Oceanic Powers'
– Japan, Britain and America –
agree on naval limitation;
but Japan seems to have two voices,
civil and military.
Struck by natural disaster and
economic depression,
facing hostility from its own armed forces,
Japan's inexperienced democracy
struggles through the 1920s.
The 1930s begin with a wave
of terrorism inspired by the army and navy,
and the policy of naval limitation
is formally rejected.*

14

'Pacific intentions'

On the evening of 3 March 1921, a 16,000-ton battleship moved out of Yokohama harbour and, attended by a group of destroyers, headed for the open sea. They had not gone many miles down the coast when the battleship, *Katori*, slowed her engines and stopped. The destroyers moved further out to sea. A small, slightly-built man wearing an admiral's uniform came out onto *Katori*'s deck, gazed towards the darkened shoreline three miles away, and bowed deeply. Apart from him, the deck was empty. He remained bent over for five minutes; then, as he straightened, the beat of the engines picked up and the battleship moved on. Despite his admiral's uniform, the solitary man on deck was only twenty years old: he was Crown Prince Hirohito, the Emperor Meiji's grandson, and he was doing something no heir to the Japanese throne had ever done before – he was leaving Japan. Somewhere behind him, invisible in the darkness, was the beach palace of Hayama; and somewhere in the palace was his father Taisho, ageing, ill, and slowly going mad. At least, it was said he was going mad; the instance that was always cited as proof was the occasion of his speech to the Diet. On that embarrassingly memorable day, Taisho, with all due gravity, had looked at his parliamentarians, looked at his speech, rolled the speech up into a tube; then, using the rolled-up speech like a telescope, he had peered through it from side to side, while his distinguished audience sat rigid with shock. No one knew quite what to do – especially since it may have been a fair comment on them all.

Mad or not, the Emperor Taisho was certainly physically ill, and Hirohito at twenty was already accustomed to standing in for his father on ceremonial occasions. Because of this, the young man's historic departure from Japan had been in the balance for some time. But eventually it had been organized and, twenty-five years after it was over, in 1946 – when he had presided over more dramatic history than anyone could have foretold – Hirohito still remembered his single journey to Britain and Europe as the happiest period of his life.

It lasted exactly six months, from 3 March to 3 September. Hirohito was head of state in all but name, and yet, though the six months were hedged around with fuss and protocol, it was – compared to Hirohito's childhood and adolescence – all so informal that a holiday itself could not have been better. Apocryphal or not, there is a story about King George V which typifies the mood Hirohito found in England. At breakfast-time on Hirohito's first day in Buckingham Palace, the king came into the prince's suite, clad in trousers and braces, an open-necked shirt, and carpet slippers. Patting Hirohito on the back, King George said, 'I hope, my boy, that everyone is giving you everything you want. If there's anything you need, just ask. I'll never forget how your grandfather treated me and my brother when we were in Yokohama. No geishas here though, I'm afraid; her Majesty would never allow it.'

Arriving in Britain on 9 May, Hirohito left on the 29th to visit France, Belgium, Holland and Italy. As an exercise in foreign relations, the trip as a whole was a considerable success, and this was fortunate for Japan; for in 1921 the Anglo-Japanese Alliance was due to be renewed, and at the same time – the height of the post-war arms race – the Japanese economy was desperately stretched, with 48% of the total national budget allocated to the armed forces.

The argument over battleships versus aircraft had still not been resolved. The year before, the British Admiral Beatty had said: 'The latest type of capital ship is so well protected that she can be hit by a considerable number of the most expensive torpedoes now existing without being sunk . . . the Admiralty are of the opinion that there is nothing in the present offensive qualities of aircraft which render them a menace to the capital ship.' The American Navy General Board echoed this view, seeing the function of aircraft and carrier vessels as being limited to scouting and gathering information; and, in Japan, official thinking was ambivalent and uncertain. In 1918 the Minister of Marine, Admiral Kato Tomosaburo, had succeeded in passing a Bill to add 140 new aircraft to the infant Naval Air Service; then the following year he had said: 'The more we study the lessons of the war, the stronger does our conviction grow that the last word in naval warfare rests with the big ship and the big gun.'

But in July 1921, while Hirohito was in Europe, the American Billy Mitchell had sunk the 22,440-ton battleship *Ostfriesland* in tests, as well as a cruiser and a destroyer, using only bombs dropped from aircraft. The ships were all German ones, surrendered after the war; General Mitchell and his colleagues dropped 67 bombs on *Ostfriesland*, scoring sixteen hits and three near-misses. Down she went; and Mitchell returned to discover that, as far as the 'blue water' sailors were concerned, he had proved nothing. It was pointed out that the ship had not been moving; that she had had no crew to effect repairs; there had been no anti-aircraft gunfire; the pilots had been able to choose their optimum height, speed and direction without interference; and that, in any case, *Ostfriesland* was obsolete, since she had no anti-bomb deck armour. Mitchell and the air lobby countered by saying that, if the ship had been active, the presence on board of explosives and high-pressure steam in the boilers would have made her more vulnerable, not less; and still no one was persuaded.

One of the clearest-thinking writers, however, was a Japanese who would have agreed with Mitchell. Studying theoretical Pacific strategy, Nakamura wrote:

'It would be within the power of a superior naval opponent to strangle our commerce and cut off our supplies without sending a single ship into the Sea of Japan. The majority of the merchant ships entering Japanese ports traverse certain steamer lanes which the enemy would have no difficulty in closing. Having established a blockade, he would certainly endeavour to undermine our resistance by attacking exposed parts of the coast with his battleships, submarines and aircraft. Many of our great commercial and naval harbours would be open to attack, and the enemy, being well informed as to our resources, would know in what direction to concentrate his efforts. On the Pacific coast the capital of Tokyo, the huge entrepôt of Yokohama, and the naval arsenal of Yokosuka would lie open to the visitations of hostile flying machines. Osaka, the heart of our national industry, would not be beyond an enemy's reach, and the swarming industrial hives of Kyushu would present him with innumerable targets. Our coast defences, submarines, and torpedo-boats might be able to prevent the near approach of hostile armourclads, but they could do nothing against an invading air fleet. The sole defence against this form of attack is a battle fleet of sufficient power to sweep the outer seas and make it impossible for the enemy to send out his aircraft-carrying vessels. Sea-power and air-power have become synonymous terms.'

Nakamura's theoretical analysis now seems almost uncannily accurate, a virtually exact prediction of the last months of the war in the Pacific a generation later.

'Above and beyond all,' he concluded, 'we must provide ourselves with an adequate battle fleet if the safety of the Empire is to be assured.'

It seemed obvious that Nakamura's idea of an 'adequate battle fleet' would include aircraft carriers, and while Crown Prince Hirohito met monarchs, presidents and the Pope – and, incidentally, fell in love with the game of golf and imported a new national passion into Japan – the Imperial shipyards were hammering and riveting enthusiastically; but not a single carrier was being built. The Imperial Navy's shopping list that year was long and expensive. Building had commenced on twelve destroyers and eight light cruisers; half a dozen submarines had just been completed, and 22 more were at various stages of construction. At Kawasaki a 26,000-ton battleship was well on the way; and six battlecruisers, each with ten 16-inch guns and weighing around 40,000 tons, were racing to completion – one each at Yokosuka and Kure, two each at Kobe and Nagasaki. This meant that in

1921, while America was building a mere handful of destroyers, and in the whole British Empire only a single submarine was authorized, Japanese yards were engaged in building over 343,000 tons of major war-ships; and still not a single one of those tons would be part of an aircraft carrier.

Nevertheless, the Imperial Navy was interested in aircraft, and in their possibilities as weapons. The Army had a slight start on the Navy; in January 1919 they had started taking lessons from a French military aviation mission. Malcolm Kennedy, the British army captain, remembered the autumn manoeuvres of 1918 as 'very indifferent'; by November 1919 he noted a 'marked improvement in air reconnaissance and aerial combat'; and the Navy had no wish to be left behind. 1921 saw the despatch from Britain of a semi-official naval air mission, composed of some thirty officers and men under Sir William Forbes-Sempill. Perhaps it was because of Sempill; perhaps because of Nakamura; perhaps because of the Army's example; or perhaps because, in September 1921, Billy Mitchell repeated his exploit and sank the old battleship *Alabama* – whatever the reason, on 13 October 1921, there was a sudden change to an order at the Tsurumi shipyard. A humble tanker named *Hosho* – 510 feet long, 7,500 tons – was redesigned as an Aircraft Depot Ship. An island bridge was put on her starboard side; a flight-deck 519 feet long capped her; and Japan's first flat-top carrier was on the water, to be completed in December 1922.

Political as well as technical changes were in the air in the summer of 1921. Between 20 June and 5 August, at the Imperial Conference in 10 Downing Street, William Massey, the New Zealand Prime Minister, predicted that 'the next naval war will be fought in the Pacific', an opinion seconded by his Australian counterpart William Hughes, who said, 'We *must* have such naval defence as is adequate for our safety.' But now Hughes dared to face an important truth – that 'Britain was no longer able to maintain her navy at the strength necessary for the complete protection of the Empire'. With the Anglo-Japanese Alliance due to be renewed or scrapped, practical necessity forced Hughes to admit – unpleasant as it must have been for him – that 'no man can deny that it is a thing more precious than rubies that we should have an alliance with the greatest Power in the East' – even if the people of that Power were racially unacceptable as citizens of Australia. Now he saw 'the case for renewal as very strong, if not overwhelming'; and Massey supported him entirely.

This view was shared throughout Britain's dominions; at the Imperial Conference, only the Canadian Prime Minister expressed strong disapproval of the renewal of the alliance. Such widespread support for renewal embarrassed the British Admiralty, where official opinion considered 'a continuation of the Alliance in its present form neither necessary nor desirable'; and this in turn embarrassed the British Foreign Office. There, Lord Hardinge had confidently commented that 'with the growing strength of the Japanese Navy there can be little doubt that the Admiralty will press for a renewal'; and the Foreign Secretary, Lord Curzon, had stated the ominous alternative: 'if we leave Japan alone, she will quickly drop into the arms of Russia and Germany.'

The Imperial Navy in 1920–21 would have been a highly desirable ally for any nation; apart from its ambitious building programme, it contained 2,750 executive officers and 73,500 other ranks and ratings – a total of 76,250 men, with an immediately accessible reserve of 41,000. In the same year, Royal Navy personnel numbered 124,009; and the US Navy had 139,010 officers and men. In terms of ships, either the British or the American Navy far outweighed the Japanese. But Japan had by far the greatest number of ships in the Extreme Orient, and, counting her reservists, the differences in the three navies' personnel numbers were fairly negligible. And, as a Japanese flag officer said in the heady days after the Russo-Japanese war, 'You can do anything with our sailors, and get them to do anything for you.'

That, in a nutshell, was the root of the problem, the triple dilemma, which Britain faced at the beginning of the 20s. The Imperial Navy, which Britain had done so much to assist, had become *too* successful. Patrolling the sea-lanes of the British Empire became ever more costly for the Royal Navy, and under the Alliance Japan's navy and strategic location offered an easy way of decreasing the burden on Britain and her dominions. But, on the other hand, American suspicion of the Alliance was so great that it seemed hardly worth continuing; and then again, if the Alliance were terminated, in order to satisfy American opinion, Japan's navy and its intentions would have to be thoroughly reviewed. Instead of being allies, they would have to be put on the list of possible enemies, requiring a corresponding increase in Eastern defence expenditure. There seemed no obvious way out of the tangle; and it was not made any easier when the Japanese position was taken into account.

'What is the purpose of [America's] colossal Navy,' asked a member of the Diet, 'if it is not to make her power supreme in every part of the Pacific? American statesmen profess an undying devotion to peace, and meanwhile they are building warships on a scale unparalleled in history. They preach the doctrine of racial equality and equal opportunity, and yet refuse to admit educated Japanese immigrants to American citizenship. They disclaim all intention of meddling with foreign politics, and at the same time continue to bombard us with arrogant notes about our policy in Manchuria, Siberia and Sakhalien. In these circumstances' – and it had to be admitted, privately if not publicly, that they were all true – 'America has only herself to blame if sober Japanese are beginning to suspect her of designs upon their country and its most cherished interests.'

Yet a number of similar criticisms could have been, and were indeed, made in reverse; and so it was with some gloom that Lord Curzon said, late in 1920: 'When we come to draw up the terms of a possible new instrument for prolonging the alliance, the dominating factor for us will have to be the necessity of not antagonizing the United States.'

Such thinking was not easy to swallow in imperial Britain. Captain Kennedy remembered how, just before the semi-official Sempill air mission, an official Japanese Navy request for British flying teachers had been turned down. 'The reason?' he snorted with contempt. 'Fear of upsetting the Americans . . . Instead of standing shoulder to shoulder with the United States as equals, our policy was to stand behind her like a well-trained dog, eager only to carry out the wishes of its master.'

1921 opened with no happier omens. In January, Secretary of the Navy Josephus Daniels reiterated the American stance: that there was no chance of America reducing its armaments while Britain and Japan were still allied. In February, with joyless certainty, Winston Churchill said to Arthur Balfour: 'Britain is in danger of becoming not only a second but third naval power in a few years' time;' and at the Imperial Conference in Downing Street that summer the point was underlined yet again that 'the worst situation with which the British Empire could be faced would occur if Japan seized the opportunity for aggressive action in the Pacific at a time when the situation at home was threatened from another quarter'. Actually, Admiral Kato Tomosaburo, Japan's Navy Minister, actively favoured a reduction in his country's expensive naval programme, and he was supported by no less a figure than the venerable Togo; but as a member of the British Foreign Office said, 'All Japanese, I think, are at heart anti-foreign; it is a question of which foreign country they dislike most for the time being. It is America's turn at present' – and so, even with Togo's support, Kato could do little about it. At the same time British interests were torn both ways; thus, it was left to America to make the first move. And when that move came, in July 1921, it was completely novel and highly imaginative: representatives of all the major naval countries should come together in Washington to work out a mutually satisfactory programme of arms limitation.

Today, the idea of mutual limitation is no novelty, even if it is more necessary than ever before; yet before the Washington Naval Conference of 1921–22 nobody had ever seriously suggested that potential antagonists should do such a thing as sit down and talk, and prevent a war before it had even started. But then, the preparation for war – or rather the preparedness, that dreadful phrase invented by the armed forces as a job-preservative – had never been so expensive before.

In Japan, where modern military and naval glamour had found such fruitful soil for transplantation, the proposal was received with uncertainty and some scepticism. Knowing all too well the American objections to their activities in China and Manchuria, and believing (with much reason) that post-war Britain was excessively influenced by America, the Japanese suspected that the conference might turn out like a world court, with themselves as the accused. But it gave the liberal Admiral Kato his chance, and with Prime Minister Hara and Admiral Yamashita, the Chief of Navy General Staff, he was received by the Emperor Taisho, Prince Hirohito still being away on his travels. Perhaps the half-dotty emperor had a flash of sanity; perhaps the two admirals and the prime minister were simply going through the correct motions in order to have imperial authority for a decision they guessed would be unpopular; but, whether Taisho understood it or not, the American invitation to confer in Washington was accepted. And, if the young Hirohito had been there to act on his father's behalf, the answer would certainly have been the same.

In the four months between the American proposal and the beginning of the actual conference on 21 November, the editor of *Dai Nihon*, Kawashima Saijiro, published an intriguing little pamphlet entitled 'On the Eve of the Washington Conference'. Its basic point was to prove Japan's perpetual ill luck in being forced into repeated wars of self-defence. The British Foreign Office acquired a copy, and – quietly and privately – commented that 'some of Mr Kawashima's dicta border on the comic: "Even the so-called militarists . . . harbour no intentions whatever to annex a foreign territory without some good reason"; "the 21 Demands" are "an emphatic statement of the urgent necessity of China-Japan friendship"; and "the Japanese . . . know no racial discrimination."'

'Qui s'excuse, s'accuse,' said the Foreign Office sardonically. But, at the time, nobody recorded a comment on the part which retrospectively seems much more interesting. In a discussion on aggressiveness and defensiveness, it became clear that Kawashima – who was an average Japanese – understood aggressiveness as meaning a stronger country going to war against a weaker one. Since China in 1894 had been believed to be, and Russian in 1904 certainly was, more powerful than Japan, this made Japan's opening acts in those two wars defensive, and not aggressive at all. Perhaps the lack of British comment on this interpretation may be taken to indicate agreement. If so, there must have been a painful revision in 1941. Kawashima's pamphlet had been out of print then for twenty years; but, for Japan, its interpretation of defensiveness had not ceased to be valid.

The Japanese delegates were chosen carefully. Leading them was Prince Tokugawa, president of the upper house of the Diet; he was more for show than for work. The Navy Minister Admiral Kato was the second, though in practice the more important, delegate; and Japan's ambassador to Washington, Baron Shidehara, was third in line. Prime Minister Hara decided that, during Kato's absence, he himself would act as Navy Minister. For a political man to take over a function traditionally held by a naval officer was unheard of. Hara's decision caused great consternation and much opposition – more, as it happened, from the Army than from the Navy. The chief dissenter was Field Marshal Yamagata, a leading elder statesman and head of the Army's most militarist section. Eventually, with reluctance, Yamagata accepted the decision, on the strict understanding that such treatment would never be applied to his, the War Department. On 2 November 1921 Prince Tokugawa and Admiral Kato arrived in Washington; and, two days later in Tokyo, Prime Minister Hara was stabbed to death.

The official comment – that there was no connection between the events – was probably true; but, in later years, Hara's assassination took on the aspect of a sinister overture, the beginning of a particularly unpleasant habit: it was only the first in a series of political assassinations.

With the nations gathered in Washington, Secretary of the Navy Hughes gave a blunt, dramatic opening to the conference: 'The way to disarm,' he said, 'is to disarm.' From the outset of this first-ever arms limitation assembly, the intention was genuine; an opportunity was offered for Britain and Japan to cut the cost of defence and avoid the possibility of war with the United States – but only if the Anglo-Japanese Alliance was ended. Robert Craigie (later, as Sir Robert Craigie, British ambassador to Tokyo) was then First Secretary of the British Embassy in Washington. He remembered how in 1902 the Alliance had 'electrified the world . . . the danger of aggression from without was to be shared – and therefore halved'. Now, nevertheless, he was optimistic, and believed that to end the Alliance would bring in 'a period full of hope for the Orient'. But, for differing reasons, other people, British and Japanese, were much less buoyant. Malcolm Kennedy was one of those.

'Most of the British out here,' he wrote in his Japanese diary, 'are dead against the renewal of our alliance with Japan and are doing their best to prevent it, not realizing that by doing so they are playing into Germany's hands; for if the alliance ends, it is a thousand to one that Germany will step in and form a Japan-Germany alliance, and may eventually get Russia to join in also. If that happens, there is going to be hell for the world within a few years.'

Kennedy also noted the opinion of an acquaintance of his, the Japanese Military Attaché to London, who said to him: 'You will lose far more than you gain by giving up one friend to win the favour of another.'

And when Prime Minister Hara's successor, Takahashi Korekingo, was asked his views on the Washington Conference, he remarked rather sadly that 'if Great Britain, Japan and the United States were able to come to an agreement, it could not be denied that the need for the Anglo-Japanese Alliance was diminished; but, if the alliance became superfluous, it also became harmless'. Given that, Takahashi concluded that he 'could not see why the United States should object to Great Britain and Japan recording their friendship in a formal agreement'.

The point that few British people, and still fewer Americans, had grasped was the *emotional* importance of the Alliance to the Japanese. Essentially a naval link, it had been the first full-scale alliance with a Western nation, the first proof of Japanese equality in the modern world. If their navy had outgrown the need for the Royal Navy, much of the old respect and admiration remained; and if the old link were severed, sooner or later, somewhere or other, another East-West alliance would take its place. But in Washington in 1921 the practical need for cutting costs was so pressing that, to achieve it, the American condition of termination had to be met as well, for good or ill.

Admiral Kato, the second delegate, had been Togo's Chief of Staff at Tsushima. During World War One he had succeeded to the leadership of the fleet. Now, from Washington, he telegrammed the Navy Vice Minister Ide in Tokyo and set out a clear picture of his approach to the conference.

'Generally,' he said, 'what has governed my thinking at the conference has been the need to improve the bad relations between Japan and the United States. That is, I should like to set to rights the many anti-Japanese opinions in America . . . We could not in any circumstances oppose the American proposals on principle. If we were to oppose them, Japan would pay dearly for it later. What would happen if there was no success over naval limitation, and naval competition continued on the lines laid down in the existing programmes? Though Britain has not the power any longer to expand her great navy, she would certainly do something. Although American public opinion is opposed to the expansion of armaments, America has the power, if once she feels the need, to expand as much as she wants.'

World War Two would prove Kato an accurate prophet. He continued by saying that, if Japan proceeded with her own naval programme, 'the United States would not ignore Japan's new building without herself making a fresh plan. Japan must make up her mind that the United States *would* do this. While Japan was experiencing the greatest financial difficulties in completing her own 8-8 programme, she could not cope with further naval expansion. It would be difficult for us to pursue a plan to expand the 8-8 fleet after

1927. Thus, the gap between American and Japanese naval strength would widen more and more and we could do nothing to narrow it. Japan would therefore be seriously threatened'.

The British point of view was put forward by Anthony Balfour, head of his country's delegation. To continue the Alliance in its current form would be, he estimated, 'very unpopular in the United States of America, and will render the conclusion of a satisfactory and enduring arrangement for the limitation of armaments extremely difficult to negotiate'.

Kate could only agree; and so, on Japan's behalf, he and his colleagues accepted the end of the Alliance. With remarkable despatch the old union was allowed to pass into history; and, in its stead, the equally famous 5:5:3 ratio of warships was established.

The formula is always known as '5:5:3', although in its full form it was actually 5:5:3:1.67:1.67. The two 1.67s were the proportions allowed to France and Italy, the other participant nations; and perhaps it was because of the small allowance that the French were cynical about the whole business. In their opinion, an official American report noted, 'the talk of disarmament had little reality, and . . . the real purpose of the United States in calling this Conference was to marshal the white world for an inevitable conflict with the yellow races'.

During the conference, Britain, with her first-hand knowledge of the destructive power of submarines, had once again advocated their abolition. None of the other nations had agreed, however; nor had any agreement been reached on light craft. The agreed ratios affected battleships and aircraft carriers; some were to be scrapped, some retained, and none built for ten years. The figures are most easily read in table form:

	Ships retained	*Tonnage*
British Empire	22	580,450
United States	18	500,610
Japan	10	301,320
France	10	221,175
Italy	10	182,800
	Ships scrapped: old	*Building*
British Empire	19	4
United States	15	15
Japan	10	6

By 1931, the intention was that the figures would be stabilized at:

	Units	Tons	Ratio
British Empire	15	525,000	5
United States	15	525,000	5
Japan	9	315,000	3
France	unfixed	175,000	1.67
Italy	unfixed	175,000	1.67

Aircraft carriers were dealt with separately from battleships. For the British Empire, the United States and Japan the ratios were the same as for battleships; for France and Italy they were slightly increased, and by 1931 were to be stabilized at:

	Tons	Ratio
British Empire	135,000	5
United States	135,000	5
Japan	81,000	3
France	60,000	2.22
Italy	60,000	2.22

Agreement was also reached on the maximum displacement and gun calibre of future warships: capital ships were to be limited to 35,000 tons with 16-inch guns; carriers were to be no larger than 27,000 tons, with 8-inch guns; and other ships were limited to 10,000 tons, also with 8-inch guns.

It had been a grand concept, imaginatively thought out and industriously carried through; yet perhaps its most apt epitaph is that it seemed a good idea at the time. Many years later, in hindsight, Admiral of the Fleet Lord Chatfield wrote that the end of the Alliance 'had turned a proved friend . . . into a potential and powerful foe'. Frederick Moore, an American adviser to the Japanese government before World War Two, agreed: 'It opened the way psychologically for co-operation with Germany', he wrote, 'when that nation recovered military might. It weakened the influence of the Naval men, and gave the Army men the dominant prestige.' And, also with hindsight, Ambassador Craigie said the same of the dead Alliance: 'With it was swept away one of the main buttresses against the pursuit by Japan of a policy of adventure and aggression.'

'The all-important question of "face" intervened,' he added. 'It was felt that the procedure used in terminating the treaty had been unnecessarily formal and abrupt . . . it was our *friends* in Japan who considered, quite unjustly, that they had been left in the lurch, and resented it bitterly. On all sides the mischievous accusation was made – and did not die easily – that Great Britain had discarded the Alliance like an old shoe once it had served its purpose. From now onwards the influence of our friends in Japan – and incidentally of the friends of America also – was on the wane.'

As for the 5:5:3 ratio, Craigie considered that 'no reasonable Japanese could maintain in practice that the defensive needs of Japan, securely tucked away in the north-west corner of the Pacific, were commensurate with the needs of the far-flung British Empire . . . but at all events the Japanese extremists and expansivists, who in reality wanted a navy for offensive and not defensive purposes, found ready to hand a lever to prise open Pandora's box of megalomania and false pride.'

It was indeed so; and although it would be fair to say that the men who framed the Washington agreement, and who demanded as a precondition for arms limitation the end of the Anglo-Japanese Alliance, could have known better – although it would be fair to say that they could have acceded to Prime Minister Takahashi's wish that Britain and Japan should still be permitted to 'record their friendship in a formal agreement' – although it would be fair to speculate that, then, subsequent Anglo-Japanese-American relations could have been much better – despite all these suppositions, it would not be fair to say that the American politicians *should* have known better. They were not seers or prophets; and they cannot really be blamed if the limitations of their cultural understanding meant that a good idea went wrong, and became the launching-slip, twenty years later, for the greatest war their country has known.

Nevertheless, one final thing has to be said about the American approach to this conference: they did not deal fairly. Just before the conference, they had succeeded in breaking the Japanese diplomatic code. Kato Tomosaburo's telegrams to Tokyo, revealing his innermost thoughts on Japan's relative weakness, lay before the American delegates during the negotiations. Without these telegrams, the Americans might have taken a less firm line – some 'formal agreement' recording British-Japanese friendship might have been accepted; and Japan, then, might never have joined the Axis.

But after Washington, the Japanese had actually gained a great deal. From the start, a lower ratio seemed to many of them to signify a lower status; and later, when it became apparent that a lower ratio would have to be accepted, many senior officers of the Imperial Navy had argued for a 10:10:7 ratio, rather than the finally agreed 5:5:3. The difference may seem slight, but it would have meant an extra fifty thousand tons of war shipping for Japan; and so to make the lower figure acceptable, Japan and her navy were granted important concessions. Conditional to Japan's acceptance of the 5:5:3 ratio were guarantees that the status quo of fortifications and naval bases in the Pacific should be maintained; that there should be no American base west of Hawaii; and that there should be no British base north of Singapore. Fulfilment of these conditions meant that Japan was assured a very large measure of security in her home islands and waters – for the first time since 1853 – and, moreover, enjoyed an unbreakable naval supremacy in the western Pacific.

Furthermore, the practical effect of the Washington Conference on the actual limitation of naval arms was more apparent than real; for with the non-abolition of submarines, and the lack of agreement over light craft, the Conference's main result was to limit the construction of two very costly types of ships – battleships and aircraft carriers – whose relative fighting value had still not been determined. In other words, the Conference gave formal limitation to ships which argument and expense would probably have limited anyway; and, to achieve that dubious result, it sacrificed one of the mainstays of East-West political stability.

Nevertheless, when the Washington Conference disbanded on 6 February 1922, the politicians of America were able to feel that they had done what they intended to do, and had changed the world for the better. On 9 February, the American delegation reported to the President; and in their report they made a small, probably unintentional play on words.

'To stop competition,' they wrote, 'it is necessary to deal with the state of mind from which it results. A belief in the pacific intentions of other Powers must be substituted for suspicion and apprehension. The negotiations which led to the Four-Power Treaty were the process of attaining that new state of mind, and the Treaty itself was the expression of a new state of mind. It terminated the Anglo-Japanese Alliance and substituted friendly conference in place of war as the first reaction from any controversies which might arise in the region of the Pacific.'

Pacific intentions: on the one hand, it meant the desire for peace; on the other, it meant the desire to rule a great ocean. If anyone remembered it twenty years later, it must have seemed a very macabre pun.

15

'Why should there be a war with Japan?'

It was two minutes to noon when the earthquake hit. The first day of September 1923 had begun as a pleasant autumn morning, and, as the last seconds of that morning ticked away, families throughout Japan were preparing for lunch, stoking fires in their flimsy traditional houses – for even Tokyo, the capital, was still largely a city of wood and paper. It was a bank holiday, and Captain Kennedy, with his wife and their infant son, had left the city for a few days in the country. Like everyone else, he and his family were about to eat when the earth shook, the house fell, and all three were buried in the ruins.

They were lucky; they all survived, and dug their way out during the afternoon. That night they camped under the stars, and in the darkness 'saw a strange glare over the hills: we wondered what it could be. It was not until the following morning, when a steady flow of refugees began straggling through the village, that we learned the cause. It was the reflection of the fires raging through Yokohama, eighty miles or so away'.

The earthquake's epicentre was in Sagami Bay, sixty miles south of Tokyo, but it became known as the Great Kanto Earthquake, after the district in which Tokyo, Yokohama and Yokosuka lie; for it devastated the entire region.

'In a matter of seconds,' Kennedy discovered, 'the flourishing port city of Yokohama, and large parts of Tokyo and of the naval base of Yokosuka had been reduced to ruins.' If anyone cared to ponder the matter, it gave a bizarre perspective to the arguments over ships versus aircraft; the natural world could still destroy cities faster and more thoroughly than any machine could. For uncountable years Japan had been accustomed to earthquakes; it was their very frequency that brought about the wood and paper style of building. The houses were easily destroyed, but they were easily rebuilt as well; yet this resilience had its price too, for with earthquakes there were always fires. The cycle was so common that in Tokyo, originally called Edo, fires after earthquakes were nick-named 'the flowers of Edo'. In 1923, when twentieth-century technology lay side by side with seventeenth-century domestic architecture, the flowers bloomed their savage brightest as the tanks in the naval oil farm burst. Kennedy heard from the refugees how 'streams of blazing oil from the nearby storage tanks had poured through the stricken city and spread over the harbour waters. These were soon a vast sheet of flame, setting boats on fire and bringing death to the luckless seamen struggling to escape'.

He did not return to Yokohama until early October – over a month after the disaster – but then he saw for himself how complete the destruction had been.

'The recently thriving port city had ceased to exist. In its place was a fantastic expanse of rubble and burnt-up débris, with here and there a blackened wall or the skeleton framework of a building still standing; all else had been levelled to the ground. What remained was a veritable city of the dead, with numberless decaying corpses under the great piles of rubble and fallen masonry, giving off a stench in the hot humid air that was indescribable.'

In Tokyo, Yokohama and Yokosuka at least 140,000 died; obviously, it was a national disaster of the first magnitude. One of the areas hardest hit was the Imperial Navy base at Yokosuka. Established in 1868, at the very end of the Tokugawa Shogunate, it had been handed over to the new Imperial Navy in 1872. Then, the base covered eighteen acres and employed less than a thousand men; by 1921 it had grown to 120 acres in area, and 11,000 men worked there. There had been six building slips; one for a battlecruiser, two for dreadnought-size battleships, and the remainder for gunboats, torpedo-boats and submarines. There had been five dry docks, including two big enough for dreadnoughts; and, just as important, there had been two years' supply of oil in the storage tanks. Now, 'in a matter of seconds', all that had gone – oil, docks, slips, many of the ships and boats, and many more of the men, the workers, sailors and officers.

But out of the tragedy the navy and the country learned one vital lesson. With the destruction of the nation's major oil stock, the navy, the merchant marine, aviation, motor transport and industry were suddenly and severely crippled. The loss of oil was rapidly made good by foreign supplies; but it brought home to everyone how dependent modernized Japan was on those suppliers – and on their goodwill. If Japan had been at war when the earthquake struck, those first few seconds would have cut off the country's fighting ability more effectively than any human enemy.

In that same year, by unhappy coincidence, the Imperial Navy suffered a loss and a disappointment: Kato Tomosaburo died, and the British Royal Naval College at Greenwich ceased admitting Japanese naval architect officers.

Admiral Kato's unexpected, though natural, death at the age of sixty-four affected the navy, and the nation, more than the death of any other admiral could have – except that of Togo, who, at seventy-six, was still going strong, recently retired from tutoring Prince Hirohito and now – like Jacky Fisher –

finding pleasure in roses. Kato's untimely death affected the nation immediately for the simple reason that since June 1922 he had been Prime Minister; it affected the navy equally deeply, but in a more subtle, more enduring, and ultimately more harmful manner.

Kato Tomosaburo's main achievement had been his contribution to the Washington Naval Conference; and that, as he himself said, had been governed by 'the need to improve the bad relations between Japan and the United States.' He was wise enough to recognize that war was a sign of failure, not of success; that Japan could not hope to win a naval building race against America; and that deterrence was a better, more modern policy than provocation, since a modern war would be total. Fortunately he had the authority and the leadership necessary to impose his moderate views; unfortunately, he had a rival, a man of spirit and determination, whose views exactly opposed his own – a spokesman for the numerous officers and men left angry and embittered by the Washington ratios and the end of the Alliance. And, in a curious counterpart, this man was also called Kato – Vice Admiral Kato Kanji.

A decade later, in 1933, the Prime Minister, Saito Makoto – a former Navy Minister and a retired admiral – said, 'The present commotions have their roots in Kato Kanji's antipathy to Plenipotentiary Kato Tomosaburo at the time of the Washington Conference.' Kato Kanji himself went further, and said that in his opinion Japan's part in World War Two could be traced back to the same conference, and the same antipathy. And there is much truth in this, for the battle between the two Katos – they were not related – began with Washington, and only ended with the elder Kato's death. After that, and through the 1920s and 1930s, the younger Kato's views (which had never lacked supporters) were felt more and more. The Kanto Earthquake brought about a new assessment of Japan's strategic needs; the death of the elder Kato removed a moderating influence; and the refusal of the Royal Naval College to accept any more Japanese naval architect officers stood, for some parts of the navy, as an emblem of their apparent rejection by Great Britain.

Indeed, the growing dominance of the younger Kato's views during the 1930s was attended by increasing polarization as naval factions shifted, reformed and shifted again, cutting across obvious divisions and creating new ones – and thus not gaining but actually losing political influence, while the Army grew in power.

Meanwhile, following the navy's triple tragedy, the shocks of 1923 were not yet over. Admiral Yamamoto Gombei – ex-Navy Minister, ex-Prime Minister – became Prime Minister again. Unfortunately, his short, politically moderate, administration ended as it began – in dramatic circumstances: during the earthquake, he was injured by falling masonry, and his investiture was delayed for twenty-four hours; then, on 27 December, barely four months later, an attempt was made on the life of Prince Hirohito. It may have been inspired by the emerging left wing; but, while Hirohito survived, Yamamoto – politically at least – did not. Overcome with shame and embarrassment, resignation was the only course he felt he could take.

1924 opened with the best omen possible for an imperial nation – the marriage, on 26 January, of the Crown Prince. During that day of rejoicing and celebration, Hirohito – still fresh from Admiral Togo's tuition – was saluted by his father's warships in Shinagawa Bay; and Japan's unusual democracy – parliamentary government under the ultimate rule of the Emperor – seemed set fair for progress. Yet within a few months came another shock. Baron Shidehara, the third delegate at Washington, became Foreign Minister on 1 July, and on the same day – an inauspicious start for his new post – America's Quota Immigration Act was announced in Japan. This overturned the 'Gentlemen's Agreement' of 1908, which had worked tolerably well; it reduced the number of Japanese who could settle in the States each year to about 150 in theory, and to virtually nil in practice; and, by classifying the inhabitants of Japan along with all other Asians as 'undesirable aliens', it brought back into Japan's newspaper headlines all the old accusations of racism and discrimination.

In that same year Matsukata Masayoshi died. He had been one of the *genro*, the elder statesmen whose political lives had begun with the Emperor Meiji. As Meiji's advisers, imbued with the authority of age and association, their influence remained strong, and their counsel had favoured moderation. But, when Matsukata died in 1924, there was only one of the old band left. This man – Prince Saionji Kimmochi – lived on until 1940; in his time he had been Prime Minister, and he was always a firm supporter of parliamentary democracy. Nonetheless, he had only become an adviser to Meiji in the last year of the Emperor's life. Afterwards, therefore, his influence was weaker than that of the other *genro*; and after 1924 he was isolated. Slowly but surely, then, the counsellors of moderation were dying off; equally slowly, equally surely, as a new generation arose which felt Japan was losing ground in the world, the counsellors of extremism gained strength.

'But why should there be a war with Japan?' Winston Churchill asked the Prime Minister, Stanley Baldwin, early in 1924. 'I do not believe there is the slightest chance of that in our lifetime.'

During 1925, the twentieth anniversary year of the Battle of Tsushima, the shocks to Japan's navy and political system continued. The Peace of Paris in 1919 had already forced Japan's withdrawal, in 1922, from the Shantung Peninsula; in 1925 her troops were removed from Sakhalien as well, and the island reverted to Russia. The war of 1904–5 had been fought against the Tsarists, not the Soviets, and the Soviets had never recognized the Peace of Portsmouth. This left them as a theoretical possible enemy; and the idea of fighting the Russo-Japanese War all over again was so unattractive, so impossibly expensive, that Foreign Minister Shidehara accepted the Soviet price of peace. In return for giving Sakhalien back, he won not only Soviet recognition of the Portsmouth treaty, but also important commercial concessions in fishing, coal, timber and oil. But the Army and Navy did not want concessions for oil, which could be cut off – they needed *ownership* of the precious oil-fields. And the Navy's chagrin at seeing this most valuable resource thrown to the winds was multiplied by two other roughly simultaneous events: Britain began to refortify Singapore, and America held massive naval manoeuvres in the Pacific. In London, the Foreign Secretary, Austen Chamberlain, said to the Committee of Imperial Defence:

'I cannot conceive of any circumstances in which, single-handed, we are likely to go to war with Japan. I cannot conceive it possible that Japan, single-handed, should seek a conflict with us. The only case in which I think Japan (which is an uneasy and rather restless power whose action is not easy to predicate) might become dangerous is after a regrouping of the European powers.'

But, back in 1913, a German naval officer in Tokyo had written that his Japanese counterparts were 'astonishingly self-confident. However, whether this readiness to attempt the impossible is a characteristic of the class from which they spring, or whether it is deliberately inculcated by their teachers, I am unable to determine. Their easy victories over China and Russia may have contributed to it. In any case, they firmly believe themselves and their Navy to be invincible'.

He also said they were 'readier for war than any other navy'. Coming from a German naval officer just before World War One, this was a striking admission; and he ended with a comment which might have changed Chamberlain's mind: 'their confidence knows no bounds, and I verily believe that the Navy would cheerfully engage in a war against a coalition able to outnumber it by three to one.'

On Christmas Day 1926, the Emperor Taisho died. There could be no break in continuity, and, at the moment Taisho breathed his last, Hirohito became the god-ruler of Japan. He was twenty-five years old, already experienced in the demands his new role would make on him: since his return from Europe in 1921, he had acted as his father's Regent. The young man, grandson of the great Meiji, was quiet, studious, introverted – temperamentally quite unsuited for the imperial throne. But, like every Japanese, he was duty-bound to accept his obligations, however unwelcome, and he did so. And he has lived longer, and ruled longer, and in the end has turned out to be both a lesser and a greater man than his illustrious grandfather. And, like all the emperors before him, he chose a new name for himself which he hoped would characterize his reign – Showa. The name means 'Shining Peace'.

In 1925, a young US Navy language officer named William Sebald began a tour of duty in Japan. It was his first visit to the country; more than twenty years later, he would return as his nation's ambassador, and of the year 1927 he wrote: 'As my facility in Japanese increased I accompanied the US naval attaché, Commander George McC. Courts, on inspection trips throughout the country. The Japanese authorities showed us only what they wanted us to see, and only in strict exchange for the same privileges extended to Japanese attachés in the United States. Nevertheless, we were able to acquire a considerable amount of circumstantial evidence which convinced us that the Japanese Navy, even then, was violating the strict limitations on naval tonnage imposed by the Washington Treaty.'

Presumably Sebald and Courts were not allowed into the yards at Yokosuka, Kure, Nagasaki or Kobe. If they were, there must have been one area in each yard that was screened off from them; but the Americans had guessed correctly, for in each yard there were either one or two cruisers building that were at least 20% above the 10,000-ton limit of the Treaty. Yokosuka concealed the *Myoko*, Kure the *Nachi*, sisters that weighed in at 12,374 tons each. Their keels were laid down in 1924 – two years after Hirohito, as Regent, had ratified the Treaty. Nagasaki and Kobe held two further sisters to these ships – respectively, the *Haguro* and the *Ashigara*, both begun in 1925; and in 1927, again in Yokosuka and Kure, work began on a separate class of cruiser, represented by *Takao* and *Atago*. Each displaced 12,986 tons – very nearly 30% over the Washington limit. The fact that these ships were being built was not a total secret – absolute secrecy in Japan's shipyards would come later, when, in Kure and Nagasaki, keels were laid for the biggest battleships in history. But what *was* secret about the cruisers was their weight, which was given as 10,000 tons or rather less. After the war to end wars, and the first-ever conference to limit naval arms, an international cruiser-building race began, as Britain, America, France and Italy followed Japan's lead, and tried to build to the limits of the Treaty.

Early in the 1923 London Imperial Conference, a message of condolence and sympathy had been sent to earthquake-torn Japan, a message which referred to Japan as the 'old and faithful ally' of the British Empire. A grateful reply was received, and without any appearance of insincerity the Imperial Conference promptly launched into a lengthy debate over the possibility of war with the 'old and faithful ally'. With changes of government in Britain, the question of the refortification of Singapore during the 1920s was an on-off affair; but in 1924 Admiral Beatty gave evidence to a Cabinet committee that Britain 'existed in the Far East on the sufferance of another power'. If a base was not established at Singapore, he maintained,

Japan could at any time 'destroy our oil fuel storage and the ports of Colombo, Trincomali, Madras and Rangoon. She could exercise complete control of the sea communications in the Indian Ocean for 42 days, and at least a year in the Pacific. All trade in the Indian Ocean would cease . . . and the coast of India would be open to attack'. He was right, of course; even with a fortified Singapore, that was almost exactly what happened in 1941 and 1942.

Against this background of secrecy and duplicity on one side, prophecy and double standards on the other, the Geneva Conference of 1927 must have been entertaining for Japan's delegates. The conference met to review the 1921–22 Washington Conference; its general intention was to extend the limitations agreed there. The Japanese proposals at Geneva amounted initially to a complete cessation of all naval building; the suggestion was, as far as anyone could tell, completely genuine, and it may have been so. But it was far too much for either Britain or America to swallow; their interest lay in the further limitation of cruisers, destroyers and submarines. However, the two groups found it impossible to agree on what that limitation should be; the British view, thinking always of the world-wide empire, proposed a far higher number and tonnage of cruisers than the Americans were prepared to concede. Informally, the British and Japanese agreed that Britain and America should be allowed half a million tons of cruisers each, while Japan should have 325,000 tons – a ratio of 10:10:7 – and that the ratio of cruisers at 10,000 tons should be 12:12:8, the difference being made up with smaller cruisers. But in no way would the American delegation agree either to those ratios, or to the originally proposed British figures, which would have given cruiser superiority to Britain at America's expense. The conference broke up in mutual British-American recrimination; the British accused the Americans of 'exasperating obstinacy', while the Americans continually saw the original British proposals 'grinning at us . . . after the false whiskers were removed'.

The disagreement on which the conference foundered was basically the differing manner in which the British and the Americans interpreted each other's defensive needs; and the Japanese were the only ones to emerge with any credit. As a modern British authority, Captain Stephen Roskill – not renowned for any pro-Japanese bias – has said, 'during the conference, the Japanese delegates strove hard to produce an acceptable compromise'. That they did not succeed was not their fault; the British-American disagreement was so profound that no one then could have succeeded in resolving it. The British delegate, William Bridgeman, noticed that one of the Japanese, Admiral Saito Makoto, was 'almost in tears' when it was eventually acknowledged that the conference had failed; and yet there must have been a certain back-handed satisfaction in it for the Japanese. The failure was certainly not because of any lack of effort, or any intransigence, on their part; they had put more into the search for compromise than either the British or the Americans. So two things had been revealed: that there was not, as the Japanese delegates to Washington had suspected, a combined Anglo-American front designed to do Japan down; and that, if anyone had 'pacific intentions', in the sense of the wish for peaceful cooperation, it was – rather surprisingly – Japan.

16

'Different ideas on how to achieve peace'

Naval genius sometimes arises in the most unexpected places. In 1758, in the little village of Burnham Thorpe in Norfolk, the rector's wife gave birth to a boy. The rector, the Reverend Edmund Nelson, christened his new son Horatio, and carried on with his contented ministry, never imagining what future fame his wife nursed in her arms. A hundred and twenty-six years later, on the other side of the world, another historic birth took place. In 1884 the wife of a schoolmaster in southern Japan bore a son. There was samurai blood in the family, but the Takano family were as humble as the Nelsons. It was not an auspicious heritage, and the family name would hardly be remembered in the same way as Nelson; but father Takano gave his son a name that millions would know: Isoroku. It means fifty-six – the father's age when the son was born.

In 1900, aged sixteen, Takano Isoroku entered the Naval Academy at Etajima. On leaving in 1903, he was seventh in his class; like the rest, he spent the next year on a sail training cruise. Like many others, he was an ensign at the outset of the Russo-Japanese War in 1904, and, posted to the cruiser *Nisshin*, he took part in the legendary Battle of Tsushima.

'When the shells began to fly above me I found I was not afraid,' he wrote to his family. 'The ship was damaged by shells and many were killed. At 6.15 in the evening a shell hit the *Nisshin* and knocked me unconscious. When I recovered I found I was wounded in the right leg, and two fingers of my left hand were missing. But the Russian ships were completely defeated, and many wounded and dead were floating on the sea. However, when the victory was announced at 2 a.m. even the wounded cheered . . .'

After the battle, he accompanied Admiral Togo to the hospital where Rozhdestvenski lay bandaged, and heard Togo's apology to the Russian – in war, said Togo, someone had to lose.

In 1930, an observant reporter might have noticed that one of the group of Japanese disembarking at Southampton Docks was missing two fingers on his left hand. It was the same Takano Isoroku; but now he was a captain in the Imperial Navy, and he had a new family name. In 1914, at the age of thirty, Takano had been adopted into a family prominent in his neighbourhood – not an unusual practice in Japan, where a family without a son may continue its name by adoption at any age – and now he was called Yamamoto.

In 1917, three years after his adoption, Yamamoto Isoroku had gone to America. There he had spent two years at Harvard as a languages officer. Although he was a short man, he gave an impression of height and great strength, for he was broad-shouldered and barrel-chested; and, with his open, attractive face, his charming social manners, and his passion for and skill at card games, he was a popular man. Back in Japan, between 1921 and 1923 he had risen from instructor at the Naval Air College to executive officer at the naval air training school at Kasumigaura, thirty miles northeast of Tokyo. In 1923–24 he had returned to the States on an inspection tour, and from 1925 to 1927 he had been naval attaché in Washington. While there he was deeply impressed by Billy Mitchell's exploits; in Japan again, he began to propound the virtues of air power, predicting in 1928 that sooner or later air power would become the mainstay of every serious navy. And, for the angry, unsettled Imperial Navy in the days after the Washington limitation, he had other far-sighted comments – 'Anyone who has seen the auto factories in Detroit and the oil-fields in Texas,' he said, 'knows that Japan lacks the national power for a naval race with America;' and 'the 5:5:3 ratio works just fine for us – it is a treaty to restrict the *other* parties'.

Middle-aged in 1930, Captain Yamamoto was a man who knew his work well; but what made him a real professional was that he also knew – accurately – how his work affected his country, and other countries, and how the countries affected one another. As a member of Japan's delegation to the 1930 London Naval Conference, he was ideal; and, when he stepped off the gangplank in Southampton and boarded the train for London, he, at least, was quite sure that naval limitation was essential.

The delegation was headed by a civilian, Wakatsuki Reijiro. Accompanying him were the Navy Minister, Admiral Takarabe; Admiral Sakonji, Admiral Abo – who was naval attaché in London – and two diplomats, Matsudaira Tsuneo and Nagai Matsuzo. They came prepared to insist on an increase of the Washington ratios in Japan's favour, from 5:5:3 to 10:10:7 – 70% instead of 60%. The day they left Tokyo, 30 November 1929, had been cold and harsh. That day another admiral and Captain Kennedy had watched their departure. 'Looks like snow,' Admiral Kobayashi had murmured to Kennedy; then he had added, 'Well, it will help to keep our delegates cool-headed.'

Baron Shidehara, veteran of the Washington Conference, was still Japan's Foreign Minister. His slogan was: 'We offer no menace to any nation. We submit to menace from none.' One man who accepted this as true was the British naval attaché in Tokyo, Captain Varyl Robinson. He told Kennedy that he believed Japan was the only country with a purely defensive naval policy, and that he agreed with the demand for a 70% ratio 'absolutely, and my sympathies are entirely with Japan in this matter. America's demands can only be regarded as aiming at sufficient strength to interfere in Far Eastern waters if ever she wishes to do so, and this just makes nonsense of the principles worked out at Washington'. Robinson had once tackled his American counterpart, Captain Ogan, to find out why America wanted so many heavy cruisers.

'We want them,' said Ogan, 'because we have no bases for capital ships in Far Eastern waters.'

'That,' Robinson replied, 'can only mean that you want them for use in distant waters and therefore for aggressive action.'

Captain Kennedy noted that Ogan merely shrugged his shoulders, and would say no more.

The first Plenary Session of the London Naval Conference opened on 21 January. With the delegates of five nations, expert advisers, technical staff and secretaries, over 150 people were gathered in the Royal Gallery of the House of Lords. Less than three months earlier the Wall Street Crash had taken place; the psychological shock was still vivid, the financial implications had yet to be fully understood, and governments around the world were eager, once again, to cut costs. The Hamaguchi cabinet in Tokyo was no exception; naval limitation was a major part of its programme of retrenchment, intended to stabilize Japan's economy against the anticipated depression. But Prime Minister Hamaguchi also had to find a position on naval armaments that could avoid both internal and international complications; for Admiral Kato Kanji – the younger Kato, now Chief of the Naval General Staff – was making his opinions felt in a forceful, disturbing manner. Backed by his Vice Chief, Admiral Suetsugu, Kato represented the militant side of Japan's post-Washington navy. It was these men, the so-called 'Fleet school', who saw Japan's inferior ratio as a national humiliation and a strategic error, and who were determined to reverse it. In Tokyo they had argued consistently for a ratio of complete parity with Britain and the United States. Prime Minister Hamaguchi, Captain Yamamoto, and the moderate chief delegate Wakatsuki knew perfectly well that there was no chance of achieving parity, and that Kato's alternative – abrogation of the Washington Treaty – could only result in a race which Japan could not afford to enter. The cabinet decision to go for 70% was a large nod in the Fleet school's direction, a compromise whereby Hamaguchi hoped to avoid both the international disruption of treaty abrogation, and the internal disruption of naval discontent. Equally importantly, it was a gauntlet, a challenge to decide whether the political parties, or the navy and army militants, were to be the effective rulers of 1930s Japan.

Along with the London Conference proposals for an increased Japanese ratio went proposals for an overall decrease in armaments – unlike at Washington, cruisers, destroyers and submarines were to be included in the limitation. Japan would thus have a larger share of a smaller market. The British still hoped to ban submarines altogether – King George V, remembering World War One, stigmatized the submarine as 'this terrible weapon', for during that war, the blockade had, at one time, brought Britain's fuel stocks down to a mere eight weeks' reserve. At the naval conference of 1930, however, the French delegates (as ever) utterly refused to concede the abolition of submarines, which they saw as the ultimate defence of small navies. Japan's Admiral Takarabe supported France in this; at the fourth plenary session on 11 February, he said: 'With this comparatively inexpensive war craft, [Japan] can contrive to look after her extensive waterways and vulnerable points. Japan desires to retain submarines solely for this purpose . . . Japan gives her full support to an undertaking to outlaw the illegitimate use of this legitimate and defensive agency of war.'

Two days later, on 13 February, the entire Japanese delegation submitted a pious memorandum to the conference: 'Japan is determined to contribute her full share in bringing about an all-round reduction in the naval weapons of war, to the end that human happiness may be increased and the financial burden of the peoples may be lightened.'

Not everyone believed them; Robert Craigie, of the British Foreign Office, felt certain that they were 'cloaking some offensive design'. Someone who did unexpectedly believe them, however, was American Secretary of State Henry L. Stimson. 'I take my hat off to them,' he said on 13 May. 'No amount of talk about cost of building could minimize what they have done. No country is so poor that it cannot be frightened into competitive building.'

By then the conference had reached a successful conclusion. Japan had been denied her 70% – but only by a small fraction. The final compromise agreed upon gave her 69.75% overall; 60.02% in cruisers, to be raised to 70% in 1935; and equality in submarines, at 52,700 tons. It was a considerable diplomatic victory, and had been accepted on 22 April; but, the very day before its acceptance, Kato Kanji had heard about it, and he, predictably, was furious.

'The Navy General Staff *cannot* accept the London Naval Treaty,' he fulminated, 'because of the inadequacy of the tonnage of auxiliary vessels permitted to us by the treaty, when compared with the minimum necessary for imperial defence.' Compared, that is to say, with the minimum he considered necessary – and he threatened to resign.

Presumably considering that Kato's resignation would be no bad thing, Prime Minister Hamaguchi had gone ahead and accepted the treaty. Kato was as good as his word; he *did* resign, but not until 10 June. Perhaps he wanted to retain his post through 27 May. That was the twenty-fifth anniversary of the Battle of Tsushima; Admiral Togo was still alive at eighty, and the day was a huge national celebration. Certainly being Chief of the Naval General Staff would put Kato in the front line.

Acceptance of the Treaty in the teeth of militant opposition was definitely a trick for Hamaguchi, and for parliamentary government. But he probably would not have won it if he had not taken the post of acting Navy Minister, during Admiral Takarabe's absence in London – just as Prime Minister Hara had done when the elder Kato had been at Washington. Hamaguchi must have remembered Hara's death under the assassin's knife, and he must have known that, if the trick was won, the game was far from over.

On 23 July, the next cards were played. The budget before the Diet did not give the Navy enough money even to rise to its treaty limits, and word came to Hamaguchi that, if the allocation was not increased, Admiral Takarabe would be forced to resign as Navy Minister, and his resignation would bring down the cabinet. The same day, the 'official reply to the Throne' of the Supreme War Council was approved by Hamaguchi. In it the Navy's budgetary demands were met, and attention was drawn to the fact that both the Washington and London Treaties would expire at the end of 1936. After that date, said the official reply, 'the empire should complete its naval defence by whatever means it deems best'.

One trick to Kato Kanji and the militants – for, although Kato had resigned the leadership of the Navy General Staff, he was still a member, and a very vocal one, of the Supreme War Council.

On 1 October the Treaty was ratified by Hirohito's Privy Council and became a national commitment – another trick to Hamaguchi.

On 3 October the Fleet school informed Navy Minister Takarabe that he was to resign. They did not, however, choose to bring the cabinet down. Instead a replacement minister was found, Admiral Abo Kiyokazu. He was installed the same day, and his political colour may be gauged from his action four days later: on 7 October he pressed for, and won, the 'First Supplemental Building Programme'. A later Vice Navy Minister, Kobayashi Seizo, revealed the Fleet school's intentions: 'to avail ourselves of the seeming concessions [of the London Treaty] as a golden opportunity to fill deficiencies that had heretofore plagued the navy, and to effect a substantial increase in our naval strength.'

The 'First Supplemental Building Programme' was to run from 1931 to 1936, and it was to produce four cruisers, 27 non-restricted vessels, and a doubling of the naval air force. The cruisers were the *Mogami* class – *Mogami*, *Mikuma*, *Suzuya* and *Kumano*. *Mogami* and *Mikuma*, which were somewhat more powerful than their sister ships, could do 37 knots and were armed with fifteen 6.1-inch guns, eight 5-inch guns, eight smaller guns, rotating torpedo-tubes, three aircraft and two launching catapults. Their weight placed them within the treaty limits for light cruisers; but before the treaty had expired, they would both be rebuilt as heavy cruisers.

Several tricks, it could not be denied, had fallen Kato's way; the last one of the rubber still remained. At 8.55 a.m. on 14 November, Prime Minister Hamaguchi was waiting to board a train in Tokyo station. Close by was a member of the *Aikokusha*, the 'Patriotic Society'. Pushing through the crowd, he came up to Hamaguchi, pulled out a Mauser, and shot the Prime Minister.

Hamaguchi did not die at once, but lingered on for ten painful months, until 26 August 1931. By then the cabinet succeeding his, under Shidehara, had also collapsed. That was in April 1931, after a stormy spring session in the Diet; rashly, Shidehara had tried once more to restrict the naval budget. *His* successor was Wakatsuki Reijiro, the chief delegate to the London Naval Conference. He was appointed premier in May, and on 24 August – two days before Hamaguchi finally died – a memorandum was passed around the British Foreign Office.

'As regards Japan's future system of government,' it said, 'I see every prospect of Japan evolving some kind of a party system such as ours . . . there is no doubt whatever that the naval and military authorities are rapidly losing the enormous influence they formerly had in internal politics, while the Cabinet are more and more taking over control of higher policy.'

That optimistic statement could scarcely have been more mistaken. On 18 September what came to be known as the Manchurian Incident began: the Imperial Japanese Army took part of the national foreign policy into its own hands.

The 'incident' was triggered by the blowing up of part of the Japanese-owned railway in Southern Manchuria. At first it appeared that Chinese Nationalists were to blame, and the story was accepted by other countries which had fallen victim to similar anti-foreign attacks; but eventually it turned out that the Japanese Army in Manchuria had put itself into the role of *agent provocateur*, and had blown up its own railway as an excuse for invasion. And as a direct consequence, early in December, the Wakatsuki cabinet fell.

With the new year, the navy joined the action, as, on 18 January, the 'Shanghai Incident' commenced. Shanghai was the centre of foreign investment in China; the two greatest traders were Britain and Japan, with 37% and 35% respectively of China's total foreign trade. Every nation had its enclave there, and no place could have been better chosen to divert world attention from Manchuria. A small riot was staged between Chinese and

Japanese, in which a Japanese civilian died. Escalation was swift as Admiral Shiozawa brought his Yangtze squadron in to protect the lives and property of Japanese nationals. It was a very noticeable force: five cruisers, twenty destroyers, two gunboats, a seaplane carrier and a minelayer were anchored off the city, while two aircraft carriers, *Hosho* and *Kaga*, cruised offshore. Navy militants were as willing as the army to show their strength – even if the show was excessive.

On Monday 25 January all the ships were in position. The Chinese Nationalist leader, Chiang Kai-Shek, had sent no reinforcements from Nanking; not a shot had been exchanged, but an attempt had been made to burn down the Japanese consulate, and the city was taut with apprehension. On Tuesday the Supreme War Council in Tokyo ordered Shiozawa to 'exercise the right of self-defence'; on Wednesday, the Tokyo Navy Office, describing anti-Japanese agitation as 'warfare without arms', warned that the Navy might have to intervene; and on Thursday, seeing the ships' guns trained on his city, the Chinese Mayor Wu informed Shiozawa that the municipal government would do whatever the admiral told them. But around midnight Shiozawa sent in his sailors – those with marine-style training – and the fighting began in earnest.

Before first light on Friday the aircraft carriers despatched their planes, and small, thirty-pound bombs were dropped at random over the Chinese civilian areas of the city while shelling began from the sea. The indiscriminate shelling of civilians was nothing new; Britain's Admiral Kuper had done it at Kagoshima, back in 1863, to Buxton's protests of 'a new precedent . . . inconceivably disastrous to mankind'. But the indiscriminate *bombing* of civilians *was* new, and, for his precedent, Shiozawa was dubbed 'the baby-killer' in Western newspapers. Cynics, however, noted that the emotional label only appeared when Western business interests were threatened.

Apparently disconcerted by developments, Navy Minister Osumi disowned Shiozawa's actions, saying that 'Manchuria is a matter of life and death for Japan. Shanghai is only a passing incident, which we are anxious to close as soon as possible'.

On 2 February, Kato's successor to the leadership of the Navy General Staff was replaced in his turn, by a cousin of the Empress, Admiral Prince Fushimi Hiroyasu. A similar appointment had already taken place in the Army General Staff; this meant that, within five months of the outbreak of the Manchurian Incident, the general staffs of both forces were headed by imperial princes – and therefore were beyond popular criticism in Japan. It made little difference in Shanghai. There, Shiozawa was finding the Chinese more formidable opponents than he expected. A ceasefire had been negotiated by the British and American consuls on 29 January; but, in the way of ceasefires, it had been all too tenuous, and on 2 February, when Prince Fushimi became Chief of the Naval General Staff, fighting had broken out again. Admiral Sir Howard Kelly, the British Commander-in-Chief of the China station, warned Shiozawa that, if Japanese bombers continued to fly low over his flagship HMS *Kent*, they would be shot down, and the British ambassador in Tokyo issued his gloomy verdict – that it would 'inevitably lead to war . . . they are as mad as March hares'.

By 5 February a clear measure of the incident's international seriousness lay offshore. In addition to Shiozawa's fleet, HMS *Kent* was there with the Fifth Cruiser Squadron; close by was USS *Houston*, flagship of the American Asiatic Fleet, with ten destroyers; and equally close were three French and two Italian warships. Admiral Kelly, much to his annoyance, had been ordered to promote a ceasefire; Shiozawa took no notice. The Chinese were fighting back far too hard for the Japanese admiral to contemplate something so close to surrender. On 9 February, the Chinese delegate to the League of Nations, Dr Yen, called a meeting of its council; the council appealed to the Japanese government, with no effect at all; and, on 14 February, the Imperial Army sent in reinforcements.

Shiozawa must have been unbearably embarrassed to have to call upon the Army for help. It came in only forty-eight hours: 10,000 men, 60 guns, 15 tanks and a dozen crated aircraft, as well as sundry motor vehicles, anti-aircraft guns and other equipment. Not only that, but the operation required no more than 60,000 tons of shipping; and a rueful British estimate suggested that, for the Royal Navy to do the same, 215,000 tons of shipping would have been necessary – more than three times as much.

Dr Yen summoned another meeting of the League of Nations council: 'We are on the eve of a big battle,' he said, 'in which hundreds of thousands of men with modern armaments and with forty Japanese warships will be engaged'; and he accused Japan, quite understandably, of breaking the Covenant of the League.

Not so, retorted the Japanese delegate – 'the Covenant applies only to organized States, not to anarchies like the Chinese. There is no such thing as a responsible Chinese government – if there had been we would have acted differently . . . The Covenant does not fit the realities of the Far East. Japan cannot see in the League an effective safeguard of her rights. She cannot abandon Shanghai and entrust her rights to the Chinese.'

It had to be admitted, he had a point; the turmoil of the civil war in China between the Nationalists and the Communists meant that there was no real government. But Yen was as quick: 'Is Japan,' he asked, 'with her army and navy running amok, an organized country? She makes a promise one day and breaks it the next. Is that a test of organization? And, if China is an anarchy with which there can be no negotiations, why has Japan negotiated with it?'

Touché; but the moral condemnation of the League of Nations affected Japan not a whit. On 7 March Lord Grey, the Vice President of the League, said: 'There are people who ask, could not the League of Nations have done more? I will ask, what more could it have done? . . . I do not like the idea of resorting to war to prevent war.'

Gradually, however, and anti-climatically, the Shanghai Incident passed – or, more exactly, appeared to pass, and life there returned to what was considered normal. But, if the incident itself faded away – the opposing forces ceased hostilities, and the Japanese troops withdrew – its effects lingered long; Japan's militants never lost their interest in China and, before the decade was over, the two countries would be locked again in open but undeclared war. And, while the troops were still in Shanghai in 1932, two events with a similar ring of prophecy took place in distant countries. In London, on 12 March, a report was submitted to the Committee of Imperial Defence from the Joint Planning Committee. It concerned Singapore and gave a new urgency to Admiral Beatty's warning of 1924.

'If the protection of our important naval bases is not provided for on an adequate scale in time of peace,' the report said, 'there will be little hope of rendering them during the very limited time available after it becomes probable that an emergency may arise.'

It was less elegantly phrased than Admiral Togo's demobilization speech in 1905, but the message was the same: readiness was all. Just over a year later, on 26 April 1933, the same committee reiterated its advice, saying, 'the experiences of 1932 have shewn that we cannot rely upon receiving any intelligence of the collection, despatch and movements of Japanese military expeditions, or of the Japanese Main Fleet'.

Not only readiness, but readiness for the unexpected; and early in 1932 the American Admiral Harry Yarnell showed precisely what the unexpected could be. In the spring Pacific manoeuvres, 12 battleships, 17 cruisers, 33 submarines and three carriers were sent over from the East Coast. This meant that 199 ships, the greater part of the US Navy, were west of Panama; and, with Oahu in Hawaii as the objective, Yarnell tried out a new mode of attack: a task force. Instead of a large, easily detectable fleet of battleships and cruisers, only two carriers and a few destroyers were employed. Poor weather conditions, radio silence and sailing without lights all helped to keep Yarnell's movements secret – until, at dawn on a Sunday, he launched his planes. Unobserved, he had approached from the north to within sixty miles of the island. Surprise was complete, and the verdict was simple: theoretically, he could have destroyed Pearl Harbor, and most of its ships and installations.

At about the same time as Yarnell dropped his theoretical bombshells over Oahu, the militant Admiral Kato Kanji in Tokyo set the clock ticking on one of his own bombs. He arranged the appointment of Takahashi Sankichi, a protégé of long standing and like mind, to the post of Vice Chief of the Naval General Staff; and he set Takahashi to revive an old favourite plan. Ten years earlier, they had devised a project to extend the authority of the Naval General Staff. But then the elder Kato had been alive, and the younger Kato, knowing there would be no chance of success, had never presented the proposals. Now the elder Kato's restrictive moderation had gone; the London limitations had stirred the militants even more than those of Washington had done; and, as ties with the Royal Navy faded away, increasing numbers of young Imperial Navy officers went to work in Japan's Berlin embassy. In peacetime, as things stood, the Navy Ministry had the right of naval command; the Chief of the General Staff took over that right in wartime. During the Shanghai Incident, Shiozawa and his cronies had had their actions severely restricted by this. The Kato–Takahashi plan was to transfer the right of command permanently to the Navy General Staff – in peace as well as in war – and thus to free the Navy from political authority. To put it another way, they were hoping to place the Navy on a permanent war footing, ready to act at any moment, without the irritating constraints of politicians to bind them.

At this time, too, the US Navy decided to update its 'War Plan Orange'. Orange was the code-name given to Japan; Britain was 'Red'. Navy war games were sometimes aimed at Red – 'just to be able to say,' one participant commented, 'that we weren't always fighting the Orange Fleet.' But Orange figured far more frequently. For some years the plan had been 'to advance into the Western Pacific at an early date and to establish there an advance fleet base from which to operate against Orange, while at the same time denying to Orange the establishment of an advance base in waters near to the continental United States.' On 4 May 1932, seeing that Japan had 'a progressive and balanced building programme' in hand, the US General Board said that 'the estimate of the situation should immediately be revised up to date'.

Ten days later, a new American ambassador left the States for Japan: Joseph C. Grew. On the Overland Limited from Chicago to San Francisco he pondered his new appointment.

'Many interesting questions present themselves,' he wrote in his diary. 'Will Japan be content with safeguarding her present rights in Manchuria or, as some would have it, does her programme include ideas of far-flung empire throughout Asia, with Korea as the first step and Manchuria the second? Can she avoid a clash with Soviet Russia, with America? The big issue is whether this irresistible Japanese impulse is eventually going to come up against an immovable object in world opposition and, if so, what form the resultant conflagration will take, whether internal revolution or external war.'

The very next day newspaper headlines flared out the latest: JAPANESE PREMIER SLAIN – SERIOUS REVOLT – PALACE IN PERIL.

In Tokyo, the *New York Times* correspondent Hugh Byas had slowly pieced together the story and prepared his report. 'I would not say "officers",' he wrote later. 'I could not believe that officers, especially officers of the navy, were getting into political murder. I need not have been so particular. They were officers all right, officers in uniform.'

A total of forty-one conspirators – twenty civilians, eleven military cadets and ten naval officers – had attacked simultaneously in various parts of the capital. The oldest of the naval men was aged twenty-eight; their victim was Inukai Tsuyoshi, the seventy-six-year-old Prime Minister. One group had ineffectively attacked the city's power stations. A second had bombed the headquarters of the ruling Constitutionalist party; a third had thrown a hand grenade, which did not explode, at the home of the Lord Privy Seal. The fourth group – a naval reserve lieutenant, five army cadets, and three naval airmen from Kasumigaura – had been to the Yasukuni Shrine and prayed to their dead colleagues. Their professed motives, said Byas, were 'definite and appallingly simple'. Translating them into English, Byas felt they were 'crude, silly and inadequate'; but he was assured that his translation was correct. The ring-leader, naval 1st Sub-Lieutenant Koga, explained that 'the Japanese delegates to the London Naval Conference were influenced by financiers and therefore they failed [to achieve armament parity]. The political parties are the tools of financiers; the nation was asleep and Japan failed because of the lack of united force . . . the condition of the country could not be improved unless blood was shed'.

Earlier in the year, the same group had killed a former finance minister and a prominent capitalist. After the murder of the Prime Minister, the killers went of their own accord to the police and gave themselves up, certain that, because their motives had been for the good of Japan, they would be treated leniently. And indeed some people who should have known better, such as Admiral Nomura Kichisaburo, later ambassador to the United States, took an almost dismissive attitude towards the killing. 'I was once a hothead myself,' said Nomura, 'and I grew out of it. They usually do.' Nomura's assessment of the situation was wildly inaccurate: the direct result of the 15 May Incident, as it came to be called, was the end of constitutional party political government in Japan. From then on, prime ministers were not the elected heads of parties, but appointees in charge of coalitions. In the nine years leading to the Pacific War, there were nine separate cabinets, and only three of the appointed premiers were civilians.

'One thing is certain,' noted the newly-arrived Ambassador Grew on 13 June, 'and that is that the military are distinctly running the Government and that no step can be taken without their approval.'

Four weeks later he wrote a strictly confidential letter to Secretary of State

Stimson: 'A prominent peer recently said to a member of my staff, referring to the military: "I hope they will change their minds before they wreck the country."'

In Manchuria the Japanese Army had set up a puppet government under the last descendant of the Manchu emperors. On 25 August Japan recognized the new country of Manchukuo. The League of Nations, however, did not consider that the new government represented a genuine popular movement or that it could have come to power without Japanese support, and therefore, with some nervousness, refused to recognize it.

'We must explain to Japan,' said the British Foreign Secretary, Sir John Simon, in November, 'that the course we take is *pro*-League and not *anti*-Japan . . . we must strive to be fair to both sides. But we must not involve ourselves in trouble with Japan.'

Although the League had been largely an American brain-child, the United States had not joined it. Perhaps because of that, the US Minister to China, Nelson Johnson, was able to express his impatience at the League's pussy-footing.

'When I was a boy in Oklahoma,' he said in January 1933, 'the only influence that had any effect on the gentlemen who used to come to town on Saturday, get drunk, and then take command of the streets with their guns, was a public opinion that was willing to step out in the street equally armed with a gun and do some shooting. Perhaps there is no parallel. But I have a feeling that in so far as Asia is concerned, the Japanese have within the past years made ashes in the mouths of every thinking European.'

'Their policy', wrote Grew in his diary on 20 February, 'is to face the world with one *fait accompli* after another. The military are still supreme and form a dictatorship of terrorism . . . I am afraid we are in for a very bad time ahead.'

The question had also been raised of Japan's continued control of the Mandated Islands, the ex-German Pacific colonies taken over during World War One. On 22 February 1933 the Tokyo Navy Office stated its attitude to these explicitly and uncompromisingly: 'The Mandated Islands are Japan's lifeline on sea as Manchukuo is on land. Japan will never surrender them.' The next day, Ambassador Grew affirmed his own analysis:

'A considerable section of the public and the Army, much influenced by military propaganda, believes that eventual war between either the United States and Japan or Russia and Japan or both is inevitable. The military and navy machines are in a state of high efficiency and are rapidly being strengthened. They possess complete self-confidence and arrogance. The Navy is becoming more bellicose. In the present temper of the Army and

Navy and the public there is always the risk that any incident tending to inflame public opinion might lead Japan to radical steps without counting the cost thereof.'

On 24 February, after a 42 to 1 vote in the League of Nations against Japan remaining in Manchuria, the Japanese representative said simply – but very truly – that 'Japan and other members obviously had different ideas on how to achieve peace in the Far East'.

And just over four weeks later, on 27 March, the same man, Matsuoka Yosuke, announced to the assembly his government's intention to withdraw from the League. This had been feared for some time, but the assembly did not ask Matsuoka to reconsider; instead its president noted that Japan had decided 'to follow her own policy into isolation'.

It seemed that Japan in the 1930s had, indeed, one single policy – aggressive expansion, by land or sea or both. While this was broadly true as far as the Army was concerned, it was not so for the Navy. Many Americans and Britons thought then, as many think today, that the entire nation acted with one agreed impulse, like a huge moving monolith. In fact there was much friction, discord and disagreement over which was the best path to follow. Between the militants in the Army and those in the Navy there was the basic argument over whether to strike north, towards the continent of Asia and on to the Russian provinces, or south across the sea to the mineral-rich, fertile colonies of America, Holland and Great Britain. And beyond that division was a deep split in the Navy; for while the Army was generally united in its wish to press forward from Manchuria into China and further, there was a large and important section of the Navy which was pacifist, opposed to any aggressive expansion south or north – but particularly south, for aggressive expansion southwards seemed a prelude to an inevitable war with the nations whose colonies would be overrun. And the pacifist element of the Navy was perfectly convinced that such a war could not be won.

Prominent among the naval pacifists, spiritual descendants of the elder Kato, were Captain (later Admiral) Inoue Shugemi, chief of the First Section of the Naval Affairs Bureau; Rear Admiral Yamamoto – he had been promoted after the 1930 London Naval Conference, and became commander of the First Air Fleet; Admiral Yoshida Zengo, a class-mate of Yamamoto's who distrusted aircraft so much that he adamantly refused ever to set foot in one; Admiral Koga Mineichi, shortly to become Vice Chief of the Navy General Staff; Admiral Nomura Kichisaburo, sometime naval attaché and future ambassador to Washington; and Admiral Yonai Mitsumasa, four years older than Yamamoto – a naval intelligence officer specializing in Russian, a future foreign minister and later Prime Minister of

Japan. They were, in short, a powerful group of men in influential positions, who had travelled widely and who knew the calibre of their country's potential enemies. But, to avoid a fatal clash abroad, they had first to deal with their enemies at home.

Prime amongst these was the infamous Kato Kanji. A former Vice President of the Naval Academy and President of the Navy War College, Kato, in 1920, had made an inspection tour of Europe – just three years before Yamamoto made his tour of the States. But, while Yamamoto returned soberly impressed with America's potential, if not its actual, strength, Kato returned with a passionate admiration of defeated Germany. His reports from Europe were strongly pro-German, and in that country he had seen much to praise in its submarine and optical technology. He was certain that Germany could teach Japan a great deal in those fields, which was true; yet there was more than a cool assessment of fact behind his judgement. The pacifist Admiral Yonai, a man of an older generation than Kato, had also visited Germany – indeed he had spent two and a half years there, shortly after World War One – and everything *he* had seen and heard convinced him that, if Britain had in the end proved a poor ally and had 'cast Japan off like an old shoe', Germany would nevertheless prove worse. In later years he read Hitler's disjointed, monomaniacal book *Mein Kampf*, and in its pages found nothing to make him change his mind.

Yamamoto, Yonai and their like-minded colleagues presented facts, plain statements comparing Japan's capability with those of Britain and America; and to anyone who listened and believed them, the conclusion was obvious that Japan was not in a condition to wage a successful war against such opponents. Her natural resources and her industrial limitations were simply not up to the challenge. But, when they spoke to the mind, Kato Kanji spoke to the heart; and, in the domestic battlefield which the Imperial Navy had become, the weapons of the mind could not compete with the challenge of the heart.

To be charitable, one could call Kato a romantic; but his romanticism was of the same kind as Hitler's, a bewitching dream of blood and steel and the unconquerable spirit of a master race – a dream of power in which spirit overcame any material superiority. To those who heard Kato and believed *him*, the conclusion was as apparent as the pacific conclusion was to others – for was not Japan the land of the gods, the first-created homeland? Was the Emperor not a god incarnate, the direct descendant of the first gods and emperors? And, since the time when Hirohito's grandfather Meiji had wisely created the Imperial Navy, had not that navy brought about the defeats of two mighty empires?

Yamato was one of the regions of ancient Japan; the name has the same kind of archaic, poetic and influential overtones that Albion has for England – except that in the '30s 'Yamato' was (and still is today) a much more common part of Japanese thought than 'Albion' has ever been to Britons. So when Kato talked of the 'unparalleled Yamato spirit' everyone knew what he meant: in a single phrase he could encapsulate all that made Japan Japanese. In that context, when he went on to speak of 'Japan's mission to purify world thought', it seemed not only comprehensible but logical. And he turned aside the inescapable facts of Anglo-American physical superiority in the same deft but crooked manner: Westerners, unlike Japanese, were effete and degenerate; Westerners, unlike Japanese, had no will-power or determination; above all, Westerners – by their very nature – did not share the Yamato spirit; and, with all these advantages, Japan could not fail in 'turning an impossibility into a possibility'. It was clever, because it was quite unproveable unless put to the test. Yonai and Yamamoto could point out that Japan had won her wars against China and Russia by the skin of her teeth; that neither enemy had had active allies; or that both had lacked the organizational ability, the naval discipline, the sheer coherence that either Britain or America would undoubtedly be able to bring against Japan. But Kato could counter them by saying that the pacifists were Americanized, and with that broadside would suggest – and later would say openly – that to be a pacifist was to be un-Japanese, unpatriotic, and downright cowardly.

If he had been alone, he would have been much less effective. But there were other flag officers who agreed with him: Takahashi Sankichi, his protégé who had become Vice Chief of the Naval General Staff; Suetsugu Nobumasa, Kato's own ex-Vice Chief, who in November 1933 became Commander-in-Chief of the Combined Fleet; Osumi Mineo, who had been Navy Minister at the time of Shanghai and returned to that post in 1933; and Nagano Osami, the confusingly-named successor to Osumi and a later Chief of the Naval General Staff. Their positions, obviously, were no less influential than those of the pacifists. But Kato and Suetsugu, jointly and separately, enjoyed the all-important support of many of the Navy's *junior* officers as well. To these young men of the new, post-Tsushima generation, the hair's-breadth war successes of '95 and '05 were magnified into smashing, irresistible victories. Tsushima itself had become legend to them; it was not merely a decisive win in a long-drawn-out campaign which had nearly bankrupted the country, but in their minds had become a hammer-blow of total, undiluted conquest. Of course it could be repeated, come who might to challenge. They hero-worshipped Kato, they adored him as the man who held the banner of Japan's naval power and pride steadfastly aloft; and, against such passions, there was little chance for pacifist rationality.

On 8 July 1933, Ambassador Grew was received aboard USS *Houston*. Anchored in Yokohama harbour, her anti-aircraft guns and fire-control stations were carefully concealed from prying eyes, for they incorporated some novelties which the American Navy was not anxious to reveal. Grew asked Captain Bagley if his other guests, some Japanese naval officers, had asked to inspect the ship. They had not, Bagley replied – 'presumably because they would not be willing to return the courtesy when the American admiral visits Yokosuka.' But both men noticed that aircraft with photographers flew low over the ship.

On Japanese-American relations, Grew was hopeful: they were certainly far better than a year previously. Late in July, he and most of his staff were guests with various high admirals of the Japanese Navy at a geisha evening, given in the Koyokan naval club by an American naval captain.

'A good deal of sake is consumed during the evening,' Grew confided to his diary, 'although the sake cups are very tiny, and thus a mere thimbleful is taken at a time. It made me enjoy the evening thoroughly, and there are no uncomfortable effects whatever in the morning – if you don't put whisky on top of it . . . it certainly helped to make a gay and highly amusing party that was convivial but never obstreperous, intimate yet always dignified, formal and restrained . . . Admiral Takahashi, who sat next me, observed that if international conferences could take place in such an atmosphere there would never be the slightest difficulty in reaching agreements. I concurred.'

Six days later, through the medium of Prince Fushimi, the revived, ten-year-old Kato–Takahashi plan began to work. Seven weeks later, on 21 September, the Emperor suggested to his chief aide-de-camp that the details of the proposed change in the naval staff regulations should remain secret; and on 25 September the plan received imperial approval. From then on the right of command of the navy lay with the Chief of the Naval General Staff in peace as well as in war. Now it was he, and not the Navy Minister, who determined the level of strength necessary to defend the empire. In effect, from that day onwards, the Imperial Navy was on a permanent war footing. It was 'a great reform for the rebirth of our Imperial Navy', said Prince Fushimi; but Captain Iwamura Seiichi, the Navy Minister's senior aide, saw it quite differently and remarked that, if anything, it increased the danger of war.

In 1933 another Roosevelt became President of the United States of America. On 19 August F.D.R. learnt to his dismay that the US Navy 'was and probably is inferior to the Japanese Navy'. In cruisers, destroyers and submarines this was true; Japan had built almost up to the treaty limits, while American vessels of the same classes were still of World War One vintage. On 19 September, Admiral of the Fleet Sir Ernle Chatfield said: 'I am firmly convinced that unless we are prepared to steadily increase our navy estimates, we are bound to go under. We literally have not got the income to keep up a first-class Navy.' In the same year, the budgets for the Imperial Navy and Army amounted to 72% of Japan's total revenues.

Moreover, 'it would hardly be an exaggeration,' wrote Hugh Byas, 'to say that between 1931 and 1936 more political meetings were being held in officers' quarters than in the rest of the country.' 1933 saw the inaugural public meeting of the 'Association of Friends of Peace in the Far East'. One of the speakers was a navy captain, Mizuno Kokohu, who happened to be that very un-Japanese phenomenon, an active Christian. An outspoken supporter of pacifism, he became a typical victim of militant criticism. 'Pamphlets poured from the War and Navy offices in Tokyo during the decade 1931–1941,' Byas noted. 'The pamphleteers promulgated the idea of impending crisis.' The Association of Friends of Peace was countered by the 'Association for the Study of Measures to meet the Situation that will arise after 1936' – when the treaties of Washington and London expired – and Mizuno was denounced: any officer, said the 'Study' pamphlet, who 'supports the peace theory is a rank defeatist and should be banished from society'. This may seem to have been an empty threat; but, if one remembers how a disobedient Japanese child might be banished for a time from his family (as Togo had been), the threat was, emotionally, right on target.

On 20 September Ambassador Grew recorded an account of an interview given by Prime Minister Saito to an American journalist. The journalist, whose name Grew concealed, asked Saito 'about the rumours of war between the United States and Japan. I told him that both navies seemed to have the jitters, but I couldn't see any prospect of war. He said: "Don't be too sure of that, Mr __. Always remember that those whose careers depend upon war always want war." I asked him, "Do you mean the Navy, Your Excellency?" "Oh no, no, no," he said. "The Navy is all right; but the Army knows very little about the world."'

About the same time, the ambassador himself wrote an article for the *Japan Times*. 'I can see no reason,' he said, 'why the coming Pacific Era, whose destiny lies so largely in our [joint] hands, should not be one of peace and friendliness, consecrated to the promotion of the welfare of the world, and it is in our combined power to make it so.' A truly Pacific Era was indeed in Japan and America's power; but privately Grew could see many reasons why it might not take place.

14 October: Hitler announced Germany's withdrawal from the General Disarmament Conference and the country's intention to leave the League of Nations.

16 October: at the regular 'Five Ministers' conference in Tokyo, Navy Minister Osumi said: 'If the United States should take a strong stand in opposition to our fundamental policy, we must resolutely repel it, and with this in view we must proceed to complete our preparedness.'

21 October: the 128th anniversary of Trafalgar – Commander Ishikawa Shingo of the Naval General Staff submitted a memorandum to his chief, arguing that naval parity was essential for Japan in order to prevent a trans-Pacific American offensive, and proposing a novel manner of achieving parity, and more. His proposal was that Japan should build fighting ships bigger than any the world had ever seen – giant battleships twice as big as those allowed by the treaties of Washington and London. Such weapons, he pointed out, would 'at one bound raise our strength from the present ratio of 60% of US strength to a position of absolute supremacy'. As for air power, Japan in 1932 already had seventeen shore-based air squadrons; the 'First Supplemental Building Programme' had provided for fourteen further squadrons – 472 aircraft; the 1934–35 estimates would include another eight squadrons, bringing the total by 1938 to 590 shore-based and 400 ship-based aircraft, including reserves.

On 3 November 1933 the Director of the British Naval Air Division underlined the contrast with his country's Fleet Air Arm.

'The full measure of the weakness of our air power in the Far East,' he said, 'will be realized when it is pointed out that our one carrier in China [HMS *Eagle*] has a capacity of 21 aircraft . . . if we do not expand the Fleet Air Arm, air superiority, with all its great advantages, will go to the Japanese Fleet. This will entail continuous torpedo-bombing and dive-bombing attacks, and uninterrupted air-spotting . . . day and night reconnaissance of our fleet and night attacks by air assisted by destroyers . . . The need for a more adequate Fleet Air Arm is, therefore, sufficiently plain.'

But there were still three full years to run before the Washington and London limitation treaties came to an end.

17

'Japan has never lost a war, and never will'

The new year, 1934, did not begin happily. On 16 January Grew reported on an article – 'a pretty jingoistic utterance' – by the new Commander-in-Chief Combined Fleet, Admiral Suetsugu, printed in the magazine *Gendai*.

'He says,' wrote Grew, 'that Japan fought the Sino-Japanese and the Russo-Japanese wars and took over Manchuria in order to preserve peace in the Far East – which to every Japanese, of course, means simply Japanese dominance, yet they say it with apparently genuine sincerity.'

According to Suetsugu, the Americans 'are now bringing airplanes to Canton in large numbers; they are reinforcing the air lines at Shanghai, Hankow, etc. . . . What are the Americans doing now? They are continuing since then surveying along the Aleutians [America's islands in the north Pacific] on a large scale, making use of survey corps, telegraph corps, aviation corps, etc. What does all this point to? Then they have resumed diplomatic relations with Soviet Russia . . . they may have had in view the possibility of surrounding Japan in all directions with their warlike preparations . . . We must expect a large air force will be brought by the large fleet across the Pacific. We are preparing for such an eventuality'.

A secret report from the British naval attaché in Tokyo, Captain G. Vivian, revealed one aspect of these preparations. On 21 November 1933 he noted that Imperial Navy appointments had been made earlier than usual that year. 'The outstanding feature of the appointments,' he reported, 'is the posting to important commands of high officers who are known to be opposed to the provisions of the London Naval Treaty of 1930 and the relegation of those officers who were in favour of this Treaty to nominal appointments on the active list.'

Beginning in 1933 under Navy Minister Osumi, this process – the notorious 'Osumi purge' – continued into 1934, and by the time it was over most of the pacifist 'treaty faction' officers had been either retired or placed on the reserve list. One of its victims, Vice Admiral Hori Teikichi, was commonly acknowledged as the most brilliant man in the Imperial Navy. As head of the Naval Affairs Bureau he had been one of those who had steered the 1930 London Conference to its successful conclusion. In the opinion of the pacifist Admiral Inoue, his loss was a more serious blow for the Imperial Navy than a

20% reduction of its fleet ratio would have been; and Admiral Yamamoto, on hearing the news, revealed the depths of his pessimism. 'Perhaps,' he said, 'there is no way to rebuild the Navy, until, by such outrages, it has wrought its own ruin.'

Any attempt to reconcile such overtly political actions with the Emperor Meiji's specific prohibition of such involvement must seem, to outsiders, to be nothing but sophistry. 'You must never allow yourselves to be led astray by public controversies or influenced by politics,' Meiji had said in 1883. But it was his addition – 'you must be guided by loyalty alone' – which unintentionally gave the way out. Anyone could do anything and say anything, however outrageous or hurtful, and maintain that they were acting only through loyalty. On 1 February 1934, Osumi gave official sanction to this kind of double-think. In an article in the *Japan Weekly Chronicle*, he said, 'Navy officers and men are forbidden to submit petitions, hold meetings, or make public their views of the administration.' And then he added, 'But still, they could discuss matters relating to national defence.' This, of course, they had been doing for years. Back in 1913 a German naval officer in Tokyo had said that his Japanese counterparts were 'intensely interested in politics. I find them remarkably well versed in current world affairs; but while they hold strong views on questions of foreign policy, they are chary of expressing themselves to foreigners'. Likewise by 1934, in his review of sea-power in the Pacific, the commentator Hector C. Bywater felt obliged to say:

'One would credit the people of Japan with too much intelligence not to perceive the dangers to which an aggressive foreign policy must expose their Empire. There are, however, unmistakable signs that wide circles of the nation have become imbued with the political doctrines of the Prussian school and hypnotized by the shibboleths which lured Germany to her ruin. The old cry of *Weltmacht oder Niedergang* – World Power or Downfall – has been taken up by the military caste, and is echoed with equal or greater conviction by "intellectuals" and hard-headed men of business.'

It has to be said, too, that as the pacifist-militant division festered within the Navy, and as the Osumi purge did its work, there was not only less and less moderate guidance from the senior naval officers, but apparently more and more toleration for destructive mischief from those who were left. The trials of Prime Minister Inukai's murderers had begun with a navy court martial on 24 July 1932 and an army court martial the following day – the civilians were tried separately. All the accused were allowed to say as much as they wanted, and they used the opportunity to harangue the nation. Navy ensign Mikami, assistant to the ringleader Koga, proclaimed that 'our revolution is intended to bring about . . . harmony between ruler and ruled', adding that 'as we intend to establish direct Imperial rule, we are neither rightists nor leftists'. The man who fired the first shot at Inukai was the only one to express any regret: 'I felt sorry,' he said, 'but I thought his death unavoidable, as he had to be sacrificed at the shrine of national reformation.' During the trials it emerged that part of the plot had been to steal some navy planes and bomb Tokyo itself – the objective had been to bring about martial law, which the conspirators confused with military government. With such revelations, it was natural that people might look to Admiral Togo for guidance; and, when asked for his opinion, the eighty-six-year-old hero said, on 16 September: 'All of the officers in the Imperial Navy must be prudent in speech and action.' Such a comment was so prudent as to be completely unhelpful; and it was Togo's last public counsel to the fleet.

The army court martial ended on 19 September 1933, the navy one on 9 November. The sentences did not appear to be stern: the army cadets were given four years, the navy flight officers from one to fifteen years, depending on the degree of their involvement. And, as events turned out, the army cadets were released in the New Year amnesty of 1935, and only three of the navy officers served more than a few months. As for the civilians, they were sentenced on 3 February 1934; but some were amnestied only two weeks later. More regained their freedom in November, and, apart from those actually involved with the killing, most of the rest were freed in 1935.

Since then, some Westerners have argued that this lenience is evidence of a deliberate policy, stemming from the highest powers in 1930s Japan, to inculcate a warlike mood throughout the country. But the tradition of Caesarian murders was an ancient one in Japan. The idea that, whatever his motive, a murderer was culpable, was by contrast a weakly-rooted Western import. The judges could no more have gone against the unwritten law than they could have flown to the moon. However, in the contest between modern political democracy and Japan's old habitual military rule, the democrats must have known that they had lost yet another round.

At the same time, preparations were being made for further multilateral naval talks. These were to begin towards the end of the year, again in London, and were themselves preliminary to the 1936 conference in which both the Washington and London treaties would be reviewed. The London treaty would need to be renewed then, if it were to continue; the Washington treaty, however, would run on automatically, unless one or more of the signatory nations abrogated it. Because of the naval race that everyone expected would follow, abrogation did not seem probable. But, in 1934, the spectre of 1936 already presented a dilemma to Japan's navy men, militant or pacifist. To extend the naval building holiday meant, to the pacifists, extending unemployment; to the militants it meant continuing with a shamefully inferior ratio. On 3 February – the day Inukai's civilian assassins were sentenced – Navy Minister Osumi expressed the official view of the problem.

'If Japan says she is not afraid to risk a naval construction race,' he stated, 'she will be accused of adopting a challenging attitude; if she indicates she is anxious for an agreement, she will be considered timid and treated accordingly.' Therefore, concerning Japan's intentions at the naval conference, he concluded that 'with the immediate situation extremely delicate, it is best to maintain the utmost silence'.

In America, General Mitchell was certainly not maintaining silence; as former head of the Army Air Force, he was convinced that the outcome of the next war would be decided by the bombing of enemy nerve centres. And, leaving his listeners no room to doubt where he thought those nerve centres would be, he announced specifically: 'Our most dangerous enemy is Japan.'

Despite his certainty, many of Mitchell's countrymen thought him unduly alarmist; and, in Britain, the Defence Requirements Committee report of 28 February verged on being anti-American. 'We cannot overstate the importance we attach to getting back, not to an alliance,' they said, 'but at least to our old terms of cordiality and mutual respect with Japan . . . There is much to be said for the view that our subservience to the United States of America in past years has been one of the principal factors in the deterioration of our former good relations with Japan.'

It was too late, however, for that kind of hope and regret; on 17 April, the Tokyo Foreign Office issued the Amau statement. It was nothing less than a Monroe Doctrine for the Far East, a repudiation of the right of any country other than Japan to guide the political relations and military safety of the entire area. 'It is difficult these days,' commented Ambassador Grew, 'to judge whether Amau is regarded in Japan as an *enfant terrible* or a hero; it rather depends on whether you seek opinions from the camp of the moderates or that of the chauvinists.' And he appended an unofficial translation of the statement: 'This country considers it only natural that, to keep peace and order in east Asia, it must act single-handed and upon its own responsibility. In order to be able to fulfil this obligation, Japan must expect its neighbour countries to share the responsibility of maintaining peace in east Asia, but Japan does not consider any other country, except China, to be in a position to share that responsibility with Japan.'

To put it simply, Japan was to rule east Asia, and Western countries were to mind their own business. Unfortunately east Asia contained a great deal of Western business.

Sometimes, though, even an ambassador could shake off the worries of the time and, five days after the Amau statement, Grew experienced 'a grand red-letter day'. At 7.45 in the morning he and his wife boarded the destroyer *Shimakaze* for a trip to Shimoda. At 25 knots, the voyage took three and a half hours.

'The day was lovely,' he wrote in his diary, 'and the sea quite smooth, thank heaven (yesterday the trip would have been appalling), but even so, there was a marked swell when we got out of Tokyo Bay and some of the ladies looked rather green, while Debuchi [Japan's ambassador to America] and [Count] Kabayama passed out completely. (Which reminds me that the Japanese press solemnly spoke of the ceremonies that were to be held at the grave of the five sailors of Perry's expedition who had "passed out" – not "passed on"!) . . . The little harbour of Shimoda is lovely – high, thickly-wooded shores and pretty little islands . . . we were profoundly moved by the significance and solemnity of it all.'

When one thinks of all the adventures that had taken place since Perry had first come to Japan, the significance of Grew's day-trip is astonishing: it was the eightieth anniversary of the signature of Japan's treaty with Perry. So much had happened in that short time; and, as if to emphasize its brevity, an unusual meeting took place, when Ambassador and Mrs Grew were introduced to the man who, as a child, had been houseboy to Townsend Harris, the first American envoy to Japan. Harris had arrived in 1856; in 1934, the venerable Baron Masuda and Mrs Grew were practically able to talk about old times – for Mrs Grew was a grand-daughter of Commodore Perry himself.

But those who had known the early days, who remembered the reality of near-defeat against China and Russia, who still felt the pride of the British alliance and respect for the Royal Navy – these men were becoming fewer and fewer; and on 30 May the greatest of the old heroes died. One foreign correspondent awoke early that morning in Tokyo, unable at first to make out what had stirred him, for everything was absolutely quiet. Then he realized that it was precisely that – the silence – which had disturbed him, for Tokyo is never totally quiet, at any time of day or night. No one needed to tell him what had happened; he knew, as well as every citizen of the capital, that for days past Togo Heihachiro had been gently slipping away. At 7 a.m. the revered old admiral had finally weighed anchor on his last voyage; and, before they wept, the people of Tokyo stood in silent homage as his spirit sailed past to the Yasukuni shrine.

The funeral took place on 5 June and lasted from dawn till dusk. Prime Minister Admiral Saito was there; he had been Navy Minister when Togo had been Chief of the Naval General Staff. Admiral Uriu was there, and laid flowers on the bier; he was the last survivor of Togo's flag officers at Tsushima. For a week, a dozen of Togo's junior Tsushima officers stood as a guard of honour over the grave, three at a time in eight-hour shifts. At Shinagawa, the battleship *Ise* fired a nineteen-gun salute and the foreign ships responded with minute guns. Togo, said a British commentator, 'lived and died in the service of Japan, but though his career was chiefly associated with warfare, he did not believe that it was a solution to the world's problems ... If Togo's name is kept fresh in the minds of young Japan in this way, there are good prospects of peace remaining undisturbed in the Pacific'.

But, if Togo was dead, the Imperial Navy continued; the day after his death, the light cruiser *Mikuma* – second of the *Mogami* class ordered under the militants' 'Supplemental Building Programme' – was launched at Nagasaki. The British Admiral Sir Frederic Dreyer had been present at Togo's funeral; and in his opinion, the naval-political situation in Japan began to deteriorate further once the old Admiral was dead. On 11 August Dreyer said: 'It is a cold fact that war cannot be waged against a resolute, warlike and well-equipped country like Japan, without adequate ships, troops, naval bases and aircraft, all fully supplied with weapons, ammunition, fuel, stores and all manner of equipment, as well as food.'

During June and July, the militants had been busy. Admiral Togo was barely cold before Kato Kanji began lobbying fleet commanders to support a new prime ministerial candidate – naturally, Kato himself – who would put through all the appropriations they wanted, at the Army's expense if need be. To further this plan – which did not work – Kato and Suetsugu revealed to their colleagues the secret proceedings of the Supreme War Council. On 8 June, Suetsugu expressed his belief to the Council that only the power of the Imperial Navy had 'beaten off' the League of Nations – a comment characteristic of the militants, for in a sense there was some truth in it. Kato seconded the notion and took it further, describing the Washington treaty as a 'cancer'; if it were abrogated, he claimed that 'the morale and self-confidence of our navy would be so bolstered that we could count on certain victory over our hypothetical enemy, no matter how overwhelming the physical odds against us'.

On 16 July, there was Kato again, this time at a conference of senior naval leaders, to whom he said that parity with America was essential if the junior officers of the Navy were to be kept under control; and, three days later, the message was repeated when the Chief of Naval General Staff, Prince Fushimi, presented a sealed envelope to his cousin the Emperor. He explained that it contained the wishes of the Navy; and, amongst other things, the paper said: 'There is no other choice but to discard the existing system of ratios and vigorously pursue a policy of equality; otherwise, the Navy will not be able to control its officers.' It is no surprise to learn that the paper was drafted not by the Prince, but by his Vice Chief – Admiral Takahashi, Kato's protégé.

What is much more surprising to Westerners is the apparent willingness of senior naval leaders to admit that they could not control their own subordinates – that they themselves were, in other words, incompetent. It is difficult to imagine such an admission being used in a Western country as a serious argument in favour of a radical and risky change in national policy. Yet, though Hirohito rejected Fushimi's letter, it was not because of its contents, but merely because the Prince presented his message in an irregular manner. The message itself was perfectly recognizable; for, just as Caesarian murders were a part of Japanese tradition, legitimized by their frequency in the past, so was *gekokujo*. Japanese translators tend to give the English meaning of the word as 'rule from below'; English translators often favour the bluntly negative overtones of 'insubordination'. That, indeed, is just what *gekokujo* is; but, from the Japanese point of view, the vital distinction between straight disobedience, insubordination, mutiny or rebellion and *gekokujo* is that, while insubordination is generally done for selfish motives, *gekokujo* is disobedience undertaken for the good of the country. This, of course, has occurred from time in time in Western history; its outstanding naval practitioner was Nelson, at the battles of Cape St Vincent in 1797 and Copenhagen in 1801. At the former, Nelson was a commodore; at the latter he was an admiral, second-in-command to Admiral Sir Hyde Parker; and in neither battle did he do as he was told. At Cape St Vincent, before any order for individual action had been given, he saw the Spanish ships were able to escape and, on his own initiative, wore his ship out of line and cut them off. At Copenhagen he deliberately disregarded Hyde Parker's order to break off a heavy action, giving his famous remark that, since he had only one eye, he had a right to be blind sometimes. He emerged the victor and, back home in England, replaced Hyde Parker as commander-in-chief. Had he not been victorious, he would certainly have accepted the consequences, which would have been death in battle at best, and demotion and degradation at worst; and, in somewhat the same way, an unsuccessful attempt at *gekokujo* would entail the natural consequence of hara-kiri. So it might be said that *gekokujo* equals initiative, and in a limited way that would be true; but again there is a vital distinction which renders the translation inadequate. What it comes down to is that successful *gekokujo* is initiative, while if unsuccessful it is insubordination; yet – and this is the translator's problem – even if unsuccessful, *gekokujo* is still respectable. Perhaps this is more just than the Western approach – but it assumes good intentions, and, cloaked with the spurious authority of tradition, it was all too easy in 1930s Japan for a dishonest, an ill-intentioned or quite simply an irrational junior officer to push his seniors around, and get away with it. It was also all too easy for a senior officer to incite his juniors, and then claim to his own seniors that there was a powerful feeling amongst the juniors which had to be listened to.

It was because of this that the moderate Rear Admiral Sakano, a pro-British, pro-Royal Navy friend of Captain Kennedy, said to Kennedy in the summer of 1934, 'We cannot afford to ignore the aftermath of the London Treaty, or what happened on 15 May two years ago' – when the young naval officers murdered Inukai. And for the same reason, at the Five Ministers' conference of 24 July, when the Prime Minister, the Army Minister, the Foreign Minister and the Finance Minister all said to Navy Minister Osumi that abrogation of the Washington Treaty would have to await the outcome of the impending London talks – for the same reason, Osumi was able to look his four colleagues in the eye and say that naval circles could 'hardly be pacified by such an explanation'.

Claiming that any attempt to 'suppress the general wishes of the navy' was a recipe for 'utter disaster', Osumi appeared to be very nervous about the whole business. He may actually have been so; but he may also have been skilfully manipulating the *gekokujo* tradition in order to place the blame, if anything went wrong with the militant dream, squarely on the shoulders of his juniors.

Whatever the truth of that episode, the cabinet gave in to militant pressure. On 7 September, the delegates for the London talks were instructed to denounce the ratio system, replace it if possible with a common upper limit for all navies, and get Japan out of the 'Washington, London and other treaties which are not of advantage to us'. It was a curious irony that the man charged with seeing these belligerent proposals through was one of the main opponents of a Japan-America war, the newly-promoted Vice Admiral Yamamoto Isoroku. The suggestion has been made that he was given the task because of the good connections he had and the respect in which he was held in America – that he was to trade, under a mask, on old friendships. That is possible. It has even been suggested that his emphatic pacifism had been a blind from the start; *that* seems highly unlikely. But if no one today can know the whole story, it is only a reflection of those days; for no one knew it all then – not even, it would appear, highly-placed politicians in Japan itself. Some time after the cabinet's September decision to abrogate the Washington and London treaties, Ambassador Grew noted the comments of Hirota Koki, the Foreign Minister.

'While the difficulties of solving the naval problem with foreign powers were no doubt considerable,' Hirota had said, 'they were not so difficult as the domestic problem which he had to face in dealing with the chauvinists . . . he had great hopes of some solution of the naval problem which would avoid saddling the various countries with future heavy building programmes, especially because the younger officers of the Japanese Navy were definitely opposed to the building of big ships, and were in favour of small ones.'

In fact at that very time the first rough plans for Japan's giant battleships were being drawn up. Perhaps Hirota knew about this, and was deceiving Grew. Perhaps he was deceiving himself. Perhaps he had been deceived by Kato and his cronies. Perhaps they were all practising a consummate abuse of *gekokujo* and shifting responsibility downwards. It is more than likely that these puzzles will never be unravelled; but the saddest and most pathetic possibility of all is that all of them were speaking what they believed to be the truth.

Passing through America on his way to London, Admiral Yamamoto gave a single press conference. Speaking in Japanese, he said categorically: 'I have never thought of America as a potential enemy, and the naval plans of Japan have never included the likelihood of an American-Japanese war.' Then, on 4 October, the British Admiral Chatfield remarked with foreboding: 'I think we shall have no treaty. The Japanese proposals are likely to be unacceptable to the USA. I think the sparks will be flying in a fortnight's time.' And when, on 16 October, Yamamoto arrived in Southampton, he gave an immediate press conference in English. 'Japan can no longer submit to the ratio system,' he stated. 'There is no possibility of compromise by my Government on that point.'

If one considers the American press conference, the first part of his comment was true; he, personally, had not thought of America as an enemy. The second part was patently untrue; Japanese naval plans had often been as preoccupied with anti-American Pacific strategy as American naval plans had been with anti-Japanese strategy. In the English press conference, he was saying what the cabinet had instructed him to say; and, as far as the Americans were concerned, it amounted to a direct contradiction of his previous interview. Perhaps – if one Western interpretation was correct – the two interviews were a classic example of Japanese hypocrisy and deception, and that Yamamoto had already accepted the militants' victory as inevitable. Perhaps another view was correct – that Yamamoto himself was practising the art of *gekokujo*, in the sense of initiative, setting up bargaining counters, in the hope of returning to Japan with the ratio system extant, but altered sufficiently to buy time from the militants and keep the Pacific peaceful. Either way, the admiral was running into trouble; his seeming ambiguity set American backs up, and in Japan another pamphlet appeared.

'It is possible that the naval conference will lead to a head-on collision between Japan and America and Britain,' it said. 'As this is the decisive point for the future of our whole country, we must satisfy the navy's demands at all costs. Our dignity cannot tolerate another treaty based on the ratio system. The solution of the Pacific problem and our success in China depend on naval strength.'

Reading between the lines, the message was clear: abrogation or assassination.

Over the next ten weeks, the polite fencing went on in London. 'Under the existing treaties,' said Yamamoto, 'the two navies [of Britain and America] enjoy parity in respect of all categories, but neither is satisfied. I believe that illustrates the fundamental weakness or drawback of a system of disarmament on ratios.' His principle was that, feeling insecure, navies built to the limits of categories, even if the ships in those categories were not the best for the given country's defence needs.

To overcome this problem, at the first official meeting of the Japanese and British delegates at Number 10 Downing Street, Yamamoto proposed a 'Common Upper Limit'. This, he explained, meant a limit to which all navies could legally build, with the limit set as the level which the country feeling most threatened deemed necessary for its own defence.

'Quite impossible,' said Chatfield – to Britain and America it meant either an intolerably huge Japanese Navy, or else intolerably small British and American fleets.

'It would be difficult,' wrote the Washington correspondent of *The Times*, 'to exaggerate the gravity with which the present condition of relations between Japan and the United States is considered in official circles here.' A naval officer at Japan's Washington embassy, he reported, had recently described 'in general but not detailed terms, the naval policy his country was to pursue. In brief, according to one of those present, he "rationalized the American Navy out of existence and rationalized the Japanese Navy into the status of necessary predominance at sea" – all this upon the theory that as a self-contained nation, the United States had little need of a navy'.

The same report also mentioned that Japan 'demanded' that foreign oil companies should keep six months' consumption of oil in store there – 'a device whereby Japan might compel American and foreign oil companies to guarantee her continual possession of Navy fuel for use against their countries.'

It was *The Times* again which printed on 18 October – two days after Yamamoto's arrival in Southampton – a semi-official statement from the Tokyo Foreign Office. It read:

'1. To maintain a strength sufficient to assure adequate national defence is the inalienable right of any nation, and for Japan, security in her national defence is absolutely essential for the sake of peace in the Far East.

'2. Japan seeks reduction in tonnage for each nation based on the spirit of disarmament, to render lighter the tax burdens on the peoples and to promote peaceful relations among nations.

'3. Limitations should be effected on the principle of abolition or reduction of aggressive armaments and of rendering adequate defence armaments.

'4. Japan intends to terminate the Washington Treaty and conclude a new pact.

'5. In the event of a breakdown of the Naval Conference, Japan is prepared to take proper measures to assure security, but will nevertheless maintain a serene and peaceful attitude and strive to remain on the best possible terms with the other Powers.'

A further report in the same newspaper outlined Japan's next proposals. After the common upper limit, 'on the qualitative side, the Japanese delegation would like to see "offensive" weapons – i.e. battleships, the A class of cruisers carrying guns above 6.1-inches calibre, and aircraft carriers – drastically limited in numbers, or indeed abolished altogether'. This was a real novelty; and, assuming it was genuine, universal acceptance of it would have altered the rest of the history of the twentieth century. Of course, for better or worse, it was not accepted, partly because of disagreement over what constituted an 'offensive weapon'. Japan and other nations wished to retain the submarine; but, as *The Times* said, 'the British, remembering 1917, cannot but regard the submarine as an "offensive" weapon, while the Japanese attach much more importance to the "offensive" qualities of aircraft carriers'. And the newspaper ended with an acid understatement: 'in general, the Japanese proposals do not commend themselves to the British and American delegates.'

It was all like a nightmarish poker game of bluff and counterbluff, for very high stakes. Sir Warren Fisher, the Permanent Secretary to the Treasury, voiced a thought at the back of many British minds when, on 30 October, he expressed his certainty that Germany would 'at some future date once more fight for the domination of Europe', and asked what would happen 'if on her next venture . . . she could find England distracted with a hostile Japan?'

Others were less nervous – or, perhaps, had less foresight. One of these was the British naval attaché in Tokyo, Captain Monty Legge. Hearing of the Japanese suggestion to ban aircraft carriers and reduce in size all types of warships, he thought it 'a damn clever move! Damn clever! They are the first nation to have the courage to get up and make a real effort to curb it. It proves them to be a great nation, by God it does!'

Admiral Dreyer also visited Japan aboard the flagship of his China Squadron, carefully avoiding the month of October, since then the Imperial Navy's manoeuvres were taking place. The visit, he reported, was very successful, and he was 'shown much kindness and friendship' by his Japanese hosts. While not being an invariable rule, it is notable that Westerners who actually visited or lived in Japan generally came away liking the place, and most of the people; it tended to be those who had never been there who were most fearful. By the same token, those Japanese who had never left Japan tended to be the most super-patriotic. These, by and large, were Army men, whose training did not take them beyond Japan; and one of those, a Lieutenant-Colonel Matsumoto, did the Navy the disfavour – although Kato Kanji must have loved it – of taking up what he perceived to be their cause. On 2 November, Ambassador Grew received a first-hand report of the colonel's fire-raising speech to the 'Young Men's and Ex-Soldiers' Association' in Kobe, and he paraphrased it thus:

'1. The outcome of the Naval Conference is immaterial, in that Japan now has a preponderance of warships of the classes desired, and will continue to maintain this advantage. Japan is in a position to defeat America at any time, and, in fact, any other country or combination of countries.

'2. American duplicity during former naval conferences degraded Japan, and this insult to the Imperial Navy must be *avenged*.

'3. After all, America is the one nation that stands in the way of justice, and the long list of insults from that country must be wiped out, and to establish Japan as the just ruler of the world America must be crushed.

'4. America, formerly the richest and most opulent nation in the world, has become weak and flabby through dissipation, and now is the time for Japan to prove the worth of her inheritance of the *Yamato Damashii* [the unparalleled Yamato spirit].

'5. War is surely coming, and all must be prepared so that a successful outcome may be assured. The Japanese Army is now waiting for the time to act, and the ex-servicemen and reserves must be prepared at any time to be called to the colours, which will probably be by the end of this year, or early next year. No ex-serviceman should leave his district unless on very urgent business, and then only for a very short time.

'6. Japan has never lost a war, and never will.'

In December Ambassador Grew had a long talk with the Dutch Minister in Tokyo, General Pabst – 'a shrewd and rational colleague with long experience in Japan'. In the General's opinion, 'the Japanese Navy, imbued as it is with patriotic and chauvinistic fervour and with a desire to emulate the deeds of the Army in order not to lose face with the public, would be perfectly capable of descending upon and occupying Guam at a moment of crisis, or indeed, at any other moment, regardless of the consequences'.

Grew did not entirely agree. 'I do not think such an insane step is likely,' he said, 'yet . . . the important fact is that under present circumstances, and indeed under circumstances which may continue in future . . . the armed forces of the country are perfectly capable of overriding the restraining control of the Government, and of committing what might well amount to national hara-kiri in a mistaken conception of patriotism.'

About the same time, Japan's Vice Foreign Minister Shigemitsu Mamoru expressed serious fears that the Navy would be more than willing to 'fight with the United States around 1936'; and, as the year drew to an end, on 27 December Grew, echoing Admiral Dreyer's warning in August, set down his reasons for a firm stance.

'Preparedness is a cold fact,' he stated, 'which even the chauvinists, the military, the patriots, and the ultra-nationalists in Japan, for all their bluster, can grasp and understand . . . Again, and yet again, I urge that our own country be adequately prepared to meet all eventualities in the Far East.'

Ambassador Grew liked Japan and the Japanese; but it was almost possible to hear his sigh when he noted in his diary that 'Japan is a country of paradoxical extremes, of great wisdom and great stupidity'.

He added: 'There is a swashbuckling temper in the country, largely developed by military propaganda, which can lead Japan during the next few years, or in the next few generations, to any extremes, unless the saner minds in the Government prove able to cope with it, and to restrain the country from national suicide.'

They were not. Two days later, on 29 December 1934, the sword was drawn and the pistol cocked for the national suicide when on orders from Tokyo, Admiral Yamamoto gave the delegates in London the necessary two years' notice that, at the end of 1936, Japan would cease to be bound by the treaties of naval limitation. The naval arms race – a caucus race which nobody could win – was about to start again.

18

'Clouds over the sea'

By the mid-1930s, Japanese naval technology was further advanced, qualitatively and quantitatively, than either the British Admiralty or the US Navy Department realized. The 'First Supplemental Building Programme' ended in 1935; the Second had already begun, in 1934, and by 1937 was to provide the Imperial Navy with two aircraft carriers (*Hiryu* and *Soryu*), three seaplane carriers (later to be converted to light carriers), two light cruisers of the *Tone* class (later to be converted to heavy cruisers), fourteen destroyers, eight torpedo-boats and four submarines. The Type 93 'Long Lance' torpedo was bigger, faster, more reliable and more powerful than any other in the world. The Mitsubishi Type 96 ('Nell') shore-based bomber was, in 1932, the fastest aircraft in the world, and particularly promising as a high-speed reconnaissance plane. At the same time new models of shipborne fighters and dive-bombers had been developed successfully; in 1933, under Admiral Suetsugu, highly secret work began on midget ambush submarines, and, as Commander-in-Chief Combined Fleet, Suetsugu perfected the *yogeki sakusen*, the strategy of interceptive operations. Under this system, it was estimated, repeated submarine attacks on an American fleet advancing across the Pacific would reduce the size of the enemy by 30% in the course of its passage. A decisive surface battle would then follow in or near Japan's home waters, where the proximity of shore planes, the freshness of the Combined Fleet, and the unparalleled Yamato spirit would quickly put down the aggressive American ships, just as Togo's fleet had annihilated the Russians at Tsushima. The high-speed, long-distance, aircraft-carrying Type 6 submarines would be a part of that final battle – indeed, much reliance would be placed on them throughout. As long ago as 1930, Admiral Kato Kanji had circulated among the Naval General Staff a strictly confidential memorandum in which he assessed the maximum endurance of an American submarine as two weeks, since, in his opinion, American sailors were too decadent to be suited for submarine duty. With this some Westerners tended to agree; Bywater, writing in his 1934 Pacific strategy review, said, 'It would probably be safe to assume that of two submarines of identical design, tonnage, and fuel capacity, one manned by

Japanese and the other by Westerners, the former could remain at sea 30% longer than the other boat.'

He also reckoned that 'the Japanese have many of the attributes which make for good airmanship'; but this attitude was not shared by many people outside Japan. A more common Western assessment of Japanese flying ability stemmed back to the Sempill mission of the early 1920s. Sempill himself had judged that the Japanese would 'make good airmen in time, but will probably be lacking in resource and initiative'; and, on his report, members of the British Foreign Office had scribbled some very uncomplimentary comments – 'the Japanese are not high flyers, and never will be.' 'The Japanese do not seem to be promising airmen. The Japanese does not like being taught by the foreigner. It hurts his *amour propre*. He prefers to do the thing badly by himself, and to pick up ideas on the sly.' 'What is lacking, of course, is the air policy, and it appears that nobody in the Navy Department can grasp the fact that the present state of affairs is extremely unsatisfactory . . . there are practically no Officers of Flag rank who know anything about the Air at all . . . [they] simply *will not* take the interest they should.'

By the mid-1930s the facts had altered substantially. Admiral Yamamoto's passionate belief in the fighting capabilities of aircraft had made itself felt, and the pilots of Kasumigaura were an efficient group who regarded themselves not only as an élite, but as the probable adjudicators of any future war. Early in 1935 the A5M fighter, forerunner of the Zero, was test-flown. One of its designers was an Englishman, Herbert Smith, who had been a member of the Sopwith Camel design team. Nevertheless most British and American pilots continued to believe such happy idiocies as 'the Jap can't see to fly properly – his eyes aren't the right shape'; and similar mistaken ideas existed about the fighting abilities of the Imperial Army and Navy. In late 1917, Captain Kennedy had observed that the Army used 'much the same weapons, and much the same tactics, as had been in use in the British and other Western armies in what seemed those far-off days of August 1914 . . . infantry units advanced with regimental colours unfurled and officers wearing swords, while cavalry charged in mass formation – a stirring sight, but sheer suicide . . . It was like 1853 all over again'.

Because of 'the obvious inferiority of the Japanese Army in the matters of arms, equipment, and modern methods' in 1917, other countries later committed 'the fatal mistake . . . of underrating its fighting abilities'. National stereotypes are often at least a generation behind the reality, and, despite all the observations of military attachés and civilians of many countries, this particular stereotype persisted until the 1940s blew it apart and replaced it with a new stereotype of efficiency and callous brutality.

The Imperial Navy was similarly widely underestimated – and that judgement was at least based on evidence more recent than World War One. Admiral Shiozawa's withdrawal from Shanghai after the 1932 'incident' created the impression that Japanese sailors were a jumpy lot, likely to attack if they thought they could win easily, likely to back off quickly once they found they could not, and anyway not very bright. On 18 February 1935 the British naval attaché in Tokyo, Captain Vivian, sent a report to that effect which subsequently achieved a certain notoriety.

'The Japanese have peculiarly slow brains,' he wrote. 'Teachers . . . have assured me that this is fundamentally due to the strain put on the child's brain in learning some 6,000 Chinese characters before any real education can start . . . The inertia shows itself by an inherent disability to switch the mind from one subject to another with rapidity . . . I am convinced that it is for this reason that the Japanese people are a race of specialists . . . An English master at the Naval College has described the training there as a system of over-training the boys physically, over-cramming them mentally, the finished product being a thoroughly over-tired human being . . . All the other foreign Naval Attachés are firmly convinced that the unwillingness of the authorities to show more [of their armaments] is due rather to the barrenness of the cupboard than to any secrets it may contain.'

There were advantages in the Japanese way; Yamamoto once explained that his extraordinary skill at poker and bridge was precisely because, as a child, he had had to learn so many written characters. After that, memorising the fall of fifty-two separate cards was nothing. More seriously, Vivian clearly did not consider anything other than school-work to be 'real education'; and, although there is a limited degree of justice in his report, he entirely failed to take account of the attitudes and beliefs which a Japanese child received and absorbed at every moment, and which made the adult into the kind of person he was.

And just the same sort of deadly misapprehensions existed in reverse. Japanese soldiers had heard all about the enormous numbers of prisoners taken by both sides in World War One, and, neither knowing nor understanding the Western attitude to life, death and surrender, held on for at least twenty years to this 'proof' that the armies of the West lacked any real fighting spirit; furthermore, studying the inconclusive battle of Jutland, it was not hard for young sailors in Japan to accept the same verdict on Western navies. 'What, then,' asked one, 'was radically wrong with the British Navy that it was brought to such a pass? Its traditional spirit had degenerated, and it was obsessed by the defensive instead of the offensive. We can see no other reason.'

Thus in 1935, with the knowledge that at the end of the following year the Washington and London limitation treaties would terminate, the fighting forces of the nations eyed one another with suspicion and credulity, each believing that at any moment the other side might start something, and each

– particularly the Americans and Japanese – convinced that, if something did start, the enemy would easily be vanquished.

The Imperial Navy's belief that America might well be the one to commence a war was strengthened in 1935 by two events – one was the US Navy's Pacific manoeuvres, which took place west of Hawaii, in the region of the tiny island of Midway, and which were regarded as especially provocative. The other was that, sometime in 1934 or 1935 – secrecy was such that the date is still not known – the Japanese naval attaché in Washington, Captain Yamaguchi, sent to the Naval General Staff a copy of War Plan Orange. Somehow, presumably by theft, he had obtained it from the office safe of the Secretary of the Navy; and he also got hold of the operational work sheets drawn up by the students of the US Navy War College.

On 19 July, Ambassador Grew left Japan for a well-earned holiday back home, and, just before he left, Foreign Minister Hirota told him that 'the Japanese Navy had no plan at present, and was content to let things remain as they are for the time being'. If Hirota was not an utter dupe, it is impossible to believe that he was not aware of Japan's naval plans against America. He may not have known that, as Imperial Navy's technological skills had progressed, the anticipated theatre of war had shifted steadily eastwards, ever nearer the continental United States. Originally, the Japanese naval war plan had been based in home waters, and it had by 1934 advanced to the line of the Bonin and Mariana islands, the north-south line between Tokyo and New Guinea; but, unless Hirota knew absolutely nothing at all about contemporary navy thinking, he cannot have genuinely believed that 'the Japanese Navy had no plan'. Whether or not he believed his own words, it seems obvious that on the eve of the 1935–36 London Naval Conference, someone in Japan – knowing both the American and the Japanese naval war plans – was trying, rather clumsily, to pull the wool over Grew's eyes.

As far as Grew was concerned, it worked; he went home with a light heart, and returned with an even lighter one, refreshed by his vacation.

'Life has taught me a good many things', he wrote in his diary on New Year's Day 1936, 'but nothing more definite than the fallacy of making New Year's resolutions. If you know you're going to break a treaty, it's much better not to sign one, and as I know by long experience that I am most certainly going to break all the nice resolutions made on January 1, philosophy now dictates the unwisdom of making them at all. So I no longer prepare the old charts (*à la* Benjamin Franklin) of just how many hours shall be spent in educational reading, piano practice, exercise, limitation of drinks and smokes, etc., but shamble across the threshold into the new year with a care-free thumb-nose at my New England conscience, which it has taken me all of half a century to conquer. I shall in all probability waste valuable time even more in 1936 than in 1935 – and why worry? Life is good, but only if you don't take it too seriously.' Nonetheless he ended with a note of unwilling realism – 'Yet in such a job as mine, how can life be other than serious?'

The developments in his absence had certainly been serious enough, with Navy Minister Nagano saying adamantly that 'the realization of parity is basic to our demands', and Norman H. Davis, the chief US delegate at the London Conference, retaliating with the warning that 'the USA and Great Britain will outbuild Japan, whatever she does'.

On 6 January 1936 the British Ambassador in Tokyo sent to London the disturbing confirmation that the Japanese Navy 'are absolutely determined to have a free hand and will accept no compromise to their own proposal of a common upper limit'. On 9 January, Nagano announced that, if Japan's conditions were not met, the country would withdraw from the conference table. On 13 January he received instructions from Tokyo to withdraw, and on 15 January he did so, melodramatically stalking out of the conference chamber with his entourage at his heels.

And so the London Treaty was signed without Japan taking part; Britain, America, France, Canada, Australia, New Zealand and India were all able to agree, and their delegates performed the ceremony of signature on 25 March. The offer was left open for Italy and Japan to join later, if they wished, and in April 1938, eighteen months after the treaty's ratification, Italy did subscribe. But Japan never did; and it was already clear that the country would not reconsider the abrogation of the Washington agreement.

It is odd how small the affronts sometimes are which seem to determine the fate of nations. One of the Japanese delegates, Nagai Matsuzo, complained bitterly that he had not been able to meet the British Foreign Secretary, Anthony Eden, for private talks. His repeated requests for a meeting had, he said, all been turned down, and the one time when he and Eden did meet was socially, at a party, when Eden kept the conversation strictly off politics. Nagano contrasted this with the cordial reception he had received shortly before from Ribbentrop in Germany, where they had talked privately and at length on all manner of topics; and eight months after the Japanese group left the London conference, in September 1936, Japan and Germany signed the Anti-Comintern Pact.

Yet on the personal level some of the Japanese delegates' last meetings in England were friendly enough. Captain Kennedy attended their farewell dinner on 20 January, and described its relaxed informality with pleasure. It was a memorable evening for another reason as well: for after dinner a news bulletin was brought in, one of the single most touching sentences of that inter-war period – 'The King's life is drawing peacefully to a close.' Two hours later, King George V, the sailor king, was dead, and Edward VIII, the king who would never be crowned, was monarch of Great Britain. Some time later the story began to circulate of King George's last words; it was said that his doctors, attempting to rally the dying man, had described to him the joyful possibility of recuperating in Bognor Regis. 'Bugger Bognor', he grunted, and left it to the landlubbers.

Three weeks after the king's death, Ambassador Grew sent two historic telegrams to Washington. Other lives were ending, in shattering violence.

'February 26, 10 a.m. 1936.

'The military took partial possession of the Government and city early this morning and it is reported to have assassinated several prominent men. It is impossible as yet to confirm anything. The news correspondents are not permitted to send telegrams or to telephone abroad.

'This telegram is being sent primarily as a test message, to ascertain if our code telegrams will be transmitted. Code-room please acknowledge immediately upon receipt. GREW.'

'RUSH. February 26, noon. 1936. Section 1.

'1. It now appears fairly certain that former Premier Admiral Saito, former Lord Keeper of the Privy Seal Count Makino, Grand Chamberlain Admiral Suzuki, and General Watanabe, Inspector General of Military Education, have been assassinated. It is also reported that Finance Minister Takahashi and the Chief of the Metropolitan Police Board have been wounded.

'2. The military have established a cordon around the district containing the Government administration offices and the Imperial palace and do not permit ingress without Army passes. Telephonic communication with the administrative offices has also been stopped. The stock exchange has been closed.

'Section 2.

'3. It is now reported that Premier Okada, Home Minister Goto, and former War Minister Hayashi were also assassinated and that Finance Minister Takahashi has died of his wounds. The Embassy cannot confirm any of these rumours.'

Very shortly, Grew learnt to his distress and horror that most of the rumours were true. At 5 a.m. a group of assassins had burst into the home of seventy-seven-year-old Admiral Saito, and in their frenzy had filled the old man with at least thirty-six, and perhaps as many as forty-seven, bullets. 'How we loved and admired and respected him,' the ambassador lamented in his diary. 'He had a winning smile, always, and his white hair gave him a distinction quite apart from the distinction he had won in his many high posts and useful life. Only a few hours before the assassinations he sat at our table beside Alice, jolly and gay, and his wife sat next to me, and opposite me was Admiral Suzuki, who lies at the point of death from his own [three] wounds [in head, lung and leg] . . . Who could have foreseen that he was leaving our

Embassy that night, and probably Admiral Suzuki too, to go straight to his death by bullet and bayonet in his own peaceful little Japanese home? These assassinations have stirred us terribly . . . At any rate, Saito's presence under our roof that night made no difference one way or the other; he left well before midnight and was not killed until five o'clock the next morning. It would have been doubly horrible if the murderers had invaded our Embassy, as they could easily have done so far as their force was concerned, and bayoneted him at our table; the international aspects of such a move would probably have weighed little with those young hotheads.'

Paying private tribute to Saito in particular, Grew wrote:

'It is interesting to think that he began his great career with Americans – with Admiral Schley and at the Naval Academy at Annapolis – and finished it at the American Embassy. He was a lovable character, gentle, charming, courtly, but with great wisdom and broad liberal views in an age of chauvinistic strife . . . but now his wise influence has gone and who knows what the future will bring?'

The 26 February Incident – or mutiny, as Emperor Hirohito more correctly named it – was a different operation in scale and kind to the incident of 15 May 1932, when Premier Inukai was murdered. On 26 February, it has been alleged that no less than 1,483 conspirators were involved. Only eight were civilians; all the rest were from the Army. There was no Navy involvement at all: indeed, when they learnt that admirals had been slaughtered, the fleet steamed into Tokyo Bay, and the ships' guns were trained on the area of the city taken over by the assassins. The culprits in 1932 had been, according to the *New York Times* correspondent Hugh Byas, no more than 'adolescents straying in a pink mist'; those of 1936, according to Robert Craigie (who, the next year, became Britain's ambassador in Tokyo), were 'budding totalitarians who were too impatient to wait for time to do their work for them'. The insurrection was quelled within a few days; and, like the assassins of 1932, those of 1936 claimed their actions were *gekokujo*, undertaken for the good of the nation. They probably expected the same sort of widely-publicized trials, in which they could make their views known and attempt to win supporters, and the same sort of subsequent leniency. They did not get them: the courts martial were held *in camera* and lasted only an hour each; and the ringleaders, Army and civilian, were shot.

On 8 August, in the Five Ministers' Conference, the 'Fundamentals of National Policy' were revised. Part Two of Paragraph Two now read: 'The Navy must aim at building up forces adequate to maintain ascendancy in the Western Pacific against the American fleet.' Elsewhere the new fundamentals spoke of Japanese southward expansion, saying that the country must 'as a matter of course anticipate obstruction and coercion by the United States, Britain, the Netherlands, etc., and must therefore provide for the worst by completing preparations for a resort to force'. For the first time Britain was included on the list of Japan's potential enemies; and Navy Minister Nagano demanded, and won, an allocation of up to one billion yen extra to the naval budget, for a third supplemental building programme. It would provide 66 new ships, and fourteen further flying corps.

In early September the Pakhoi Incident took place. Pakhoi is a city on the shores of the Gulf of Tonkin, on China's southern coast. A Japanese merchant was murdered, and for a short while the Naval General Staff – which now, of course, controlled the fleet's movements – contemplated taking over the island of Hainan in reprisal. Hainan lies only 300 miles south-west of Hong Kong, and the Staff fully expected its occupation would be followed by a confrontation with Britain. The Operations Section even drafted a plan for preliminary fleet mobilization, not only against China, but against Britain and America; two carrier squadrons were sent to the area, and bomber squadrons in Taiwan were placed on full alert. And, although in the end, nothing came of it, it was probably because something much more serious was already brewing in China – to be precise, in Manchuria. And when the translation of a book by Lieutenant-Commander Ishimaru Tota was published in Britain that year, the public were made as aware as they could be in peacetime of the altered attitude of the Imperial Navy. The uncompromising title was *Japan Must Fight Britain*.

It was a strange book. In parts of it Ishimaru seemed virulently anti-British; in other parts he openly acknowledged the justice of British and wider Western views of Japan. The Washington Conference, he said, 'succeeded in strangling the Alliance', which was true. But then he proceeded to see Japan's presence in Manchuria as 'broadly speaking, the natural result of the denunciation of the Alliance', which was fatuous; and he followed with the immediate contradiction that 'if these two contentions [Japan's and the League of Nations' views] were placed in the scales, a correctly adjusted instrument would assuredly go down on the foreigners' side . . . Manchuria is an area of special significance to Japan: it must be regarded as an exception. This is Japan's contention, but, for all its truth, once latitude in or exceptions to the Peace Treaties are admitted, there is no knowing where matters will stop'.

The book was published in Japan in 1935, and contained many hints of events yet to come; and, among its frequent contradictions and muddled thoughts, there were moments of considerable clarity. An Anglo-Japanese war was inevitable, he maintained, 'unless either Japan stops the policy of expansion that she has been driven to adopt under the most severe pressure, or unless England, with her excessive number of colonies, abandons her policy of the preservation of the status quo'. Emphasizing that he was not a militarist, he still believed that 'the only peaceful solution is for England to make way'; but then with greater perception he said that 'if, in any country, the soldiers and sailors control the conduct of foreign affairs, that country will be beaten in war . . . ignoring diplomacy, setting up a military despotism, or, in unnecessary haste, shouting down our diplomatists, is to repeat the mistake that led Germany to disaster: it is not the way to make our country great'.

On the naval ratios: 'a war with England must be expected to end in victory for her. In other words, we start at a disadvantage unless our naval strength is at least equal to hers.'

On the development of Singapore: 'Still thinking as they did when the dead Alliance was alive, our representatives overlooked it. Now we must wake up. With this base in existence, our ratio of 70% or of 80% is of no use against England.'

On Hong Kong: 'The harbour is large enough to take our whole Fleet. It is not strongly fortified.'

On other British possessions: 'There is a chain of bases across the Indian Ocean linking the Mediterranean with the Pacific. Going from West to East, we find Aden at the entrance to the Red Sea, Karachi and Bombay on the west coast of India, with Colombo and Trincomalee in Ceylon to the south of them. Colombo is the base of the East India Squadron. In the Bay of Bengal are Madras and Calcutta on the Indian coast and Rangoon in Burma. None of these ports is strongly fortified.'

On timing the first act of war: 'the most favourable time for us to strike the first blow would be when the [British] Fleet is at its normal peace-time stations.'

'Japan will hardly succeed in keeping [England and America] apart, and it will probably be wiser for her to devote her diplomatic energies to those European Powers that are awaiting their opportunity to deprive Britain of her supremacy.'

'When war is inevitable, but before it is declared, Japan takes time by the forelock . . . Daring has always paid in war: swift action appeals to the fighting man more than a clever and cautious plan. And, above all, the destruction of the enemy fleet is the sweet path to victory.'

'Risk is an inevitable accompaniment of war. The best way to lessen it is to attack the enemy unawares, to put fear into his heart with unlooked-for audacity, and, above all, to be swift and to strike home by the shortest path.'

Then, in describing a hypothetical attack on British ships, he became quite carried away with his own vision: 'The valour of our destroyers passes belief: their crews are supermen. No matter how many are sunk, the rest will go on, determined to close the enemy and torpedo him . . .' The Japanese Navy, in his mind, became invincible. But it was that kind of language which, along with the book's confusions and multiple standards, made it seem less threatening than it really was; and Britain, in general, ignored it.

It has been said that the Japanese language is the easiest language in the world in which to be imprecise. Further than that, some people have claimed that it is impossible to be precise in Japanese. Certainly Japanese and the languages of the West are so different that translation between them is sometimes extremely difficult, and, because of that, Ishimaru's book may have been a model of clarity in the original. But imprecision has its own virtues, and one of those is Japanese poetry, which every cultured person would practise. Probably the best-known form of this poetry in the West is the *haiku*, always containing three lines and seventeen syllables. Less well known is the *tanka*. This contains five lines and thirty-one syllables. In 1936 the Emperor Hirohito wrote a *tanka* poem. It said:

> 'As I
> was visiting
> the Shino Point in Kii,
> clouds were drifting far
> over the sea.'

It was at once an observation and a riddle, an echo of an emotion and a meditation on past, present and future. As such, it would probably have meant even less to most Westerners than Ishimaru's book. But, had Westerners been able to see one other work written in Japan in 1936, they might have found a cause for genuine concern. In November – with less than eight weeks to go before the Washington limitations ceased to exist – the Naval War College in Tokyo produced a 'Study of Strategy and Tactics in Operations against the United States'. And, amongst other things, it said:

'In case the enemy's main fleet is berthed at Pearl Harbor, the idea should be to open hostilities by surprise attacks from the air.'

PART FIVE

*Zenith
1937–1942*

*Japan challenges China again;
Germany challenges Europe again;
jointly, they challenge
America and Britain;
and the Imperial Navy appears
invincible.*

19

'Dangerous toys'

International relations must have come to a low ebb if a man could not even urinate without starting a war; yet, according to official Japanese accounts, that was exactly what happened in the summer of 1937. A minor, but often forgotten, oddity about World War Two is that it had a variety of dates of starting and ending. Ask a Pole and he will say 1 September 1939, when Hitler invaded. Ask a Briton and he will probably say 3 September, while an American is likely to cite 7 December 1941, distinguishing between the European and Pacific Wars. But ask a Japanese and he is quite likely to say 7 July 1937; for, from that day until 2 September 1945 – four months after the European War was over – Japan was at war with an ever-increasing number of countries. And those eight years of war for the Japanese all began when one of their soldiers at a border post in China slipped off into the bushes to relieve himself.

The new year found Ambassador Grew in a much more sombre mood than the previous one. This time there was no genial nose-thumbing at his New England ancestors, but an alert, sober review of the international situation. He had heard a rumour that Japan might be building 'vessels of new design, of great size (45,000 to 60,000 tons), with high gun calibres'. He speculated that 'the disadvantages to Japan of the non-treaty status may prove to outweigh the benefits . . . isolation constitutes a real danger to a country, especially in time of war . . . In the technical, naval sense, however, bearing in mind chiefly considerations of defence, it is quite possible to believe that Japan may have been the gainer, although this remains to be seen.'

The Imperial Navy was certainly a gainer: in March the Third Supplemental Building Programme commenced. Like the previous two, its details were not made public; but, for the five financial years 1937–8 to 1941–2, it provided the Navy with more than 1.1 billion yen extra – and over 80% of that was to be used for building. 837 million would produce 36 new warships – two battleships, two carriers, 18 destroyers, 14 submarines – and 34 auxiliary vessels. This was not much less than the total for the previous two programmes; and the third did not stop there. 75 million yen went for air expansion. The naval air force had taken twenty years to reach its 1936 level; in five years, the level was to be doubled.

On 7 July 1937, the Imperial Navy air force contained 219 combat-ready planes – 48 land-based attack bombers, 51 carrier-based dive-bombers, 54 carrier-based attack and torpedo bombers, and 66 carrier-based fighters. The land-based air force was divided between Taipei and Omura, ten miles north of Nagasaki. At Taipei the Kisarazu Air Corps had 30 attack bombers, while the Kanoya Air Corps had 18, as well as nine fighters. Together, these comprised the First Combined Air Flotilla. The Second Flotilla at Omura contained the 12th and 13th Air Corps; each had a dozen fighters and a dozen dive-bombers. In addition the 12th Air Corps had a dozen attack bombers, while the 13th had a dozen torpedo bombers.

As for the carrier-based air force, this totalled 90 planes, divided between the carriers *Ryujo, Hosho* and *Kaga. Hosho*, Japan's first flat-top, carried only 15 planes; *Ryujo*, only 500 tons larger, carried 27; but, of these three ships, *Kaga* was the prize. At 771 feet, she was over 200 feet longer than either of the others; she weighed 33,600 tons; and she carried a dozen *each* of fighters, dive-bombers, attack bombers and torpedo bombers. And of course, unlike the bases at Taipei and Omura, these floating airports could move anywhere their admirals chose.

On 8 July, Grew scribbled a single, hasty note in his diary; 'Fighting has broken out at the Marco Polo bridge not far from Peking between Chinese and Japanese troops. Not clear who started the trouble, but Nelson Johnson says that considering the fact that the Japanese conduct manoeuvres close to a Chinese garrison it is only surprising that such an incident had not occurred long ago.'

It is still 'not clear who started the trouble' the day before, and it probably never will be. Since the suppression of the 1900 Boxer Rebellion, various nations had had the right to station troops in China, to protect their nationals and the routes from Peking to the sea. On the night of 7 July, Japanese troops of the Naval Landing Party were conducting night manoeuvres. It was just before the roll-call at the end of these manoeuvres that one of the men discreetly moved away and performed his historic unbuttoning. Hearing a gap in the roll, the officer in charge jumped to the conclusion that the man had been abducted by Chinese troops nearby. The Chinese were challenged, and somebody started shooting. It could have been either side; it could even have been, as some Japanese believe today, a third party – perhaps Chinese Communists provoking a show-down between the Nationalists and the Japanese. Had it been left to the local commanders, it could all have been sorted out quite quickly, for in the next few days local agreements were made; but bad international communications intervened, one thing led to another, and on 26 July Tokyo issued an ultimatum that the Chinese garrison should be withdrawn from Peking. Chiang Kai-Shek refused. Three hundred Japanese reinforcements were sent in, and, on 11 August, a further thousand arrived in fifteen ships from the homeland. One of the ships was the old British-built armoured cruiser *Izumo*, now rated as a coast-defence ship and flagship of the 3rd (China) Fleet. Two days after she had discharged her human cargo at Shanghai, fighting broke out between the Chinese and Japanese troops there. Japanese intelligence reported that their garrison was surrounded by Chinese with three hundred planes. The following day, 14 August, one of those tried to bomb *Izumo*. Missing completely, it caused a heavy loss of civilian life in the International Settlement before being shot down by a Japanese scout/observation seaplane; and, that evening, the eighteen attack bombers of the Kanoya Air Corps roared in from Taipei. On 15 August the Kisarazu Corps took over; on 16 August carrier-based planes joined in.

From Taipei to Shanghai and back was a 1,250-mile round trip. 'Our aircraft constantly set new records,' wrote Horikoshi Jiro – an aeronautical engineer – and Okumiya Masatake – a flying officer – in later years. But, they added, 'despite the obvious quality of our aircraft and the calibre of our pilots, the navy air force suffered heavy losses in the early days of the incident . . . we learned – almost at once, and with devastating thoroughness – that bombers are no match for enemy fighter planes'.

The planes of the prize carrier *Kaga* in particular 'suffered disastrously'; on 17 August a flight of twelve attack bombers set off for Hangchow, a hundred miles south-west of Shanghai. One came back. *Kaga* immediately returned to Sasebo and took on a full complement of fighters. On 18 September they made their first raid on Nanking, 160 miles west of Shanghai. By 2 December they had cleared the skies of Chinese planes; and on 14 December, safe from air attack, the Japanese Army began the systematic destruction of Nanking and its inhabitants.

The rape of Naking continued for six weeks. Before World War Two it was the greatest single act of deliberate brutality ever committed. One of Chiang Kai-Shek's advisors was a prominent Nazi general, Alexander von Falkenhausen, later a member of the plot to assassinate Hitler. Of the Japanese Army in Nanking, he reported to Berlin that they 'behaved in a manner which was almost indescribable for regular troops'. After World War Two the International Military Tribunal for the Far East, sitting in Tokyo from 1946 to 1948, heard it all described, had it all recorded, and concluded that in those six weeks 20,000 women and girls were raped, while over 200,000 people – at least a quarter of them civilians, from great-grandparents to infants – had been killed by bullet, bayonet, sword and fire.

Horrible reports came from the city even while the frightful mass atrocity was going on, including the accusation – quite probably correct – that naval launches had rammed and machine-gunned boats on the Yangtze filled with fugitives. None of it was to be condoned, none of it should be forgotten – although recently attempts have been made to delete it from the history curricula of Japanese schools – and none of it should be remembered except with shame and disgust. Nevertheless, it is worth stressing that, in this hitherto unparalleled act of conscious cruelty, the Imperial Navy – despite the undoubted presence of some launches that far up river – played hardly any part; from start to finish it was an Army operation, and it was worse than bestial.

Obviously the lack of naval involvement was due at least in part to the great distance of Nanking from the sea; had the city been on the coast, perhaps the naval presence would have been larger. Had that been the case, it is impossible to say whether or not the navy men would have joined in the butchery. In the light of some later events in Manila, they might have done; but, on the whole, it seems improbable. To anyone unfamiliar with ships and the sea, the reasons for this assertion may seem implausible or even specious; to a seaman, however, or a person familiar with the history of traditional naval warfare, they are readily understandable. For hundreds of years, war at sea had been distinguished from war on land by the simple fact that a sea-battle was not fought between men, but between ships: once a ship was sunk, its opponent's next duty, if practicable, was to rescue survivors. This tradition had held good for centuries in the West, particularly in the Royal Navy, and it had broadly transferred to the Imperial Navy: the sea was an enemy common to every sailor. Massacre, in short, was not a part of the character of war at sea; and there is no great reason to suppose that the Imperial Navy would have made it a part.

Yet at the same time other events of illegal violence must be remembered – events much smaller in scale than the Nanking bloodbath, but in their potential consequences even more serious. One of them was a navy action. Their occurrence, and the manner of their settlement, showed more than ever the differences between the Imperial Army and the Navy, and the divisions within the Navy.

It was on 12 December 1937 – two days before the Nanking rape began – that the British gunboats *Ladybird* and *Bee* were fired on by Japanese shore batteries at Wuhu, sixty miles upstream from Nanking. The *Ladybird* was hit four times, and one rating killed. Later than same day, Japanese aircraft bombed British merchant ships and the gunboats *Scarab* and *Cricket* near Nanking. No one knew whether they were Army or Navy aircraft, but they were probably Army, because they all missed their targets, and Army fliers were notoriously much less expert than those of the Navy.

'We went up to Shanghai at a time when the Japanese were carrying out a good deal of bombing, and one thing and another, on the Chinese.' Royer Mylius Dick, now Rear Admiral Dick, was from 1936 to 1938 captain of the destroyer HMS *Dainty*, a part of the China Fleet. 'We certainly got the impression at that time that they were being very amateurish about what they were doing. Where the aircraft came from I don't know, I presume they were nothing to do with the Navy, but they seemed to us to be quite low grade. Indeed they may have been second-class airmen . . . but at that time one did not think of them as being a highly-trained, efficient air force. We were wrong.'

Second-class airmen or not, the attack had clearly been intentional; and, later again that same day, half-way between Nanking and Wuhu, shore batteries and naval aircraft shelled, bombed, machine-gunned and sank the American gunboat *Panay*.

'This is a black day indeed,' wrote Ambassador Grew the following morning. For a week he devoted himself to trying to sort out 'the deplorable and serious effect' of 'this indiscriminate shelling of our ships' – three American merchant ships had been attacked as well. 'I had been working for five years,' he wrote in exasperation, 'to build up Japanese-American friendship, and this incident seemed to me to risk shattering the whole structure . . . I seriously feared a breach of relations and already began to plan the details of hurried packing in case we had to leave – precisely as we began to pack in Berlin after the sinking of the *Lusitania* in 1915.'

'That incident,' he continued on 20 December, 'does seem really incredible. War never is and never can be a humane pursuit, but the action of the Japanese naval and military elements first in bombing the *Panay* and then in machine-gunning at close range and attempting to exterminate the wounded and other survivors even after they had crawled into the thicket on the shore is almost past comprehension . . . the Japanese Navy meanwhile, we learn, has recalled and retired the admiral responsible for the aeroplane bombing. It is a tense and critical moment. But never before has the fact that there are "two Japans" been more clearly emphasized.'

Back in August, a car carrying the British Ambassador to China, Sir Hughe Knatchbull-Hugessen, had been machine-gunned by a Japanese aircraft, and the ambassador himself wounded; and, on 5 October, speaking in Chicago, President Roosevelt had inserted into a prepared speech an extempore sentence that was to become famous. 'When an epidemic of physical disease starts to spread,' he said, 'the community approves and joins in a quarantine of the patients in order to protect the health of the community.' By implication he equated the militant, terrorist face of Japan with Nazi Germany and Fascist Italy. At the end of October, three British soldiers had been killed in Shanghai, probably by Japanese shells. The Imperial Navy had created a Fourth Fleet; Craigie, the British ambassador in Tokyo, feared it might be intended for the blockade of Hong Kong, while Pabst, the Dutch Minister, was equally concerned that it might be aimed at the Dutch East Indies. 'Certainly,' said Grew, 'it looks as if the Army and Navy were having their way, with very little interference on the part of the

Government'. And now, on 2 December, he received a half-demented letter from a retired naval commander which began, 'Down with Great Britain!'

'Due to Great Britain's instigation,' it continued, 'China has assumed a challenging attitude against Japan, and the consequence was the issue of the present Japan-China conflict. With the progress of military operations in China, Hong Kong has now become the centre of anti-Japanese movements. The Japanese Navy insists that Hong Kong should be taken possession of by Japan, otherwise the blockading of the China coast will be useless. We hold that Japan should occupy Hong Kong and thereby eliminate the fundamental cause of the Japan-China conflict.'

Yet while the Army and parts of the Navy cried havoc in China, and while the Oceanic Powers teetered on the brink of war, the American Embassy in Tokyo was inundated with visits from ordinary Japanese civilians of all ages and social positions 'trying to express their shame, apologies and regrets for the action of their own Navy'.

'Here we have one of the many paradoxes of Japan,' Grew reflected bitterly. 'The Army and Navy are the Emperor's "children", faithfully serving him, subject to his every wish and order – yet arbitrarily taking the bit in their teeth, running amok, and perpetrating atrocities which the Emperor himself cannot possibly desire or sanction.'

In an atmosphere of such crisis, earlier reflections took on a dreadful potential reality. Writing in 1935, R. V. C. Bodley, one of Admiral Togo's biographers, had said: 'Japan unawakened . . . might have remained a kind of primitive South Sea island or become an English colony. At any rate . . . America created Japan, and although it is just as futile to conjecture about the history of the past, may we not wonder whether this child of misadventure may not one day destroy its creator?'

In 1934 Hector C. Bywater had written that 'when the United States relieved Spain of the Philippines, she gave hostages to fortune in a sense which the American people have never fully realized. But for the acquisition of these islands they need never have maintained a powerful fleet in the Pacific or have gone to the expense of constructing great naval bases on the West Coast'.

And in a letter, a 'distinguished American naval officer' (whose identity Bywater concealed) underlined the country's vulnerability: 'The Philippines are there for Japan whenever she likes to take them, and nothing can prevent her from seizing them when she feels disposed to do so . . . If we were foolish enough to locate a fleet at Manila, the history of Port Arthur would repeat itself, with us in the role of the Russians . . . This is not merely a picture of what might happen, but of what most assuredly will happen if war breaks out within the next few years.'

The wider-ranging British Empire suffered proportionately greater fears: the possible threat was not limited to the Far East. 'There is no doubt,' said the Naval War Memorandum (Eastern) of December 1937, 'that with carefully planned supply arrangements, Japanese submarines, armed merchant cruisers and possibly one or two heavy ships could operate in the Indian Ocean and in Australian waters.'

The fear was real; the threat, however, in late 1937, was not. The pacifists in the Imperial Navy had not yet entirely given way. Nevertheless it was with considerable trepidation that Grew, on 22 December, welcomed into the Embassy study a group set up to inquire into the *Panay* sinking. The group included several members of the Embassy staff, a Japanese statesman, two colonels, a naval commander, and the Vice Minister of the Navy – Admiral Yamamoto Isoroku. For more than three hours they sat around in a circle, the floor strewn with maps; and, wrote Grew, 'we were all impressed with the apparently genuine desire and efforts of both Army and Navy to get at the undistorted facts'.

Four days later, on 26 December, came such relief that Grew could not contain himself. 'This was an eminently happy day,' he remembered, 'and it showed that wisdom and good sense of two Governments which refused to be stampeded into potential war . . . The Japanese Government had expressed the most abject apologies for the sinking of the *Panay* and we, without a moment's hesitation, accepted those apologies . . . I was so profoundly happy at the outcome that when I called on [Prime Minister] Hirota at noon I entered his room wreathed in smiles. When I had finished reading our note to him, his eyes were really filled with tears and he showed as much emotion as a Japanese is capable of showing; he said: "I heartily thank your Government and you yourself for this decision. I am very, very happy. You have brought me a splendid Christmas present." I think his relief must have been tremendous, as was mine. We have, for the moment, passed a difficult, a very difficult, hurdle. Yet,' he concluded, 'I cannot look into the future with any feeling of serenity.'

It was also in December that Yamamoto's colleague Admiral Yonai, speaking in the Diet in his official capacity as Navy Minister, stated categorically that 'the Imperial Navy has no force to match the combined strengths of Great Britain and the United States. It has no intention of building its fleet to such a level'. But, only the month before, the idea originating from Commander Ishikawa Shingo of the Kato–Suetsugu militant navy faction had started to come true: in Kure dockyard the keel was laid of the first of a new class of battleship, the giants which Ishikawa had predicted would 'at one bound raise our strength from the present ratio of 60% of US strength to a position of absolute supremacy'.

The statistics of the vessel were staggering. The ship would be 862 feet long and would weigh over 70,000 tons – at a time when the largest battleship in the world was the British, pre-Washington Treaty, HMS *Hood* of 42,000 tons. The main armament of the new super-battleship would be three turrets, each holding three guns. Each turret individually weighed 2,774 tons – as much as, or more than, a destroyer. Each of the nine guns would fire shells of 18.1 inches diameter weighing 3,200 pounds – at a time when the biggest naval shells in the world were 16 inches, and weighed 2,200 pounds – and once every ninety seconds, each gun could send one of these towards a target twenty-five miles away. Muzzle velocity would be 1,755 miles an hour; each shell would arrive at its target in less than a minute; and with nine guns, the interval between shells would be only ten seconds.

Merely being ready to imagine such a colossus showed how quickly the Japanese had learnt. Forty years earlier they had hardly known how to build a destroyer; now they tackled design problems no one had ever faced before. And of course, they were tackling those problems alone – they had to. If the ship was successful, it would in every way be the incarnation of Kato Kanji's propaganda dream of the 'unparalleled Yamato spirit'; for *Yamato* and her sisters would be unparalleled in naval history, and they would be totally Japanese.

Today the dry dock in which *Yamato* was built still exists in Kure Dockyard; close by, as part of a memorial, stands one of the gigantic shells. When building began in November 1937, the dry dock was surrounded with towering screens and covered with miles of sisal netting, and despite persistent rumours that the Imperial Navy was building something really extraordinary, secrecy was almost total. But Yonai as Navy Minister and Yamamoto as Vice Minister certainly knew what was happening – Yamamoto especially was highly critical of the whole project from the very start, frequently expressing his deep conviction that such ships were things of the past.

'Military people,' he said on one occasion, 'always carry history around with them in the shape of old campaigns. They carry obsolete weapons like swords and it is a long time before they realize they have become purely ornamental. These battleships will be as useful to Japan in modern warfare as a samurai sword.'

And on another occasion, equally bluntly, he remarked: 'These ships are like elaborate religious scrolls which old people hang up in their homes. They are of no proved worth. They are purely a matter of faith – not reality.'

That comment revealed part of the weakness of his anti-battleship, pro-air stance; for battleships *were* of proved worth, and despite the successes in China and in World War One, and General Mitchell's experiments after the war, it was still air power that was 'purely a matter of faith'. Nevertheless, these two pacifically-minded admirals knew the ships were being built, and very likely were aware of their declared purpose as well – to achieve 'absolute supremacy' over the American fleet. Given that, Yonai's unequivocal statement that Japan had 'no intention of building its fleet to such a level' seems curious, to say the least. Yet the conclusion that he was being deliberately deceitful is not necessarily correct. Some years after World War Two, when the Imperial Japanese Navy no longer existed, another officer wrote of the *Yamato*-class vessels: 'They were not built as a step towards war. Japan's aim was to enhance her international standing by becoming a great peace-time naval power.'

Obviously great naval power can contribute to the peace of the world; the century-long Pax Britannica could not have been started or maintained without the Royal Navy's global strength. Like Yamamoto, Yonai had lobbied hard against the introduction of the giant ships. Once he had been impelled to accept them, it is perfectly possible that he hoped they would actually become a force for peace; and he was, strictly speaking, correct in saying that Japan was not building 'to match the combined strengths of Great Britain and the United States.' But if, with such ships in existence; with Japan incurring the contempt and disgust of the world through her actions in China; and with Japan bound, since 25 November 1936, in the Anti-Comintern Pact with Hitler – if, under those circumstances, he hoped that peace would follow in the wake of the great ships, then it can only be said that his hope was empty and pathetic. In 1941, in his book *Sea Power in the Machine Age*, the American Bernard Brodie wrote: 'It makes a very great difference to the world what tools have been placed in the hands of the potential aggressor.' With admirals like Kato and Suetsugu in the ascendant, such tools were not likely to be used for regattas.

The last months of 1937 brought a new, critical development. On 29 September the Italian Foreign Minister, Count Galeazzo Ciano, wrote in his diary: 'The Rome-Berlin Axis is today a formidable and extremely useful reality. I shall try to draw a line from Rome to Tokyo, and the system will be complete.' On 6 November Ciano, Ribbentrop and the Japanese Ambassador to Rome, Hotta Masaaki, jointly signed Italy's accession to the Anti-Comintern Pact. 'The two Japanese military attachés, both good Fascists, were radiant,' Ciano noted happily. And on 8 November, speaking to the Old Guard in Munich, Adolf Hitler had said triumphantly: 'Germany is today no longer isolated . . . three states have come together as allies. First a European Axis, and now a great Triangle in world politics . . . And this Triangle is not composed of three feeble organizations, but of three states which are ready and determined resolutely to defend their rights and interests.'

A new year rolled round again, no less edgy, no more optimistic than the previous one; and on 4 January 1938, Vice Admiral Suetsugu stood up in the Tokyo Diet and spoke.

'The Japanese people are antagonistic towards Great Britain today,' he announced, 'because Britain is trying to block Japan's economic expansion in China. Obstacles are erected in the form of preferential treatment for British goods, and high tariffs against Japanese products, while Britain has mobilized the anti-Japanese boycott in China, and is trying to check Chinese imports from this country . . . Japan must expand economically towards China, and if London understands this and puts everything on a fair and equal basis, then the present temporary anti-British sentiment in Japan will vanish . . . Japan is fighting for her existence in Asia and the Pacific, so it is unwise for any third Power to intervene.'

In 1933 Britain's naval attaché in Tokyo, Captain Vivian, had reported that Suetsugu was 'decidedly pro-British and has a pleasant personality'. In 1938 a member of the Tokyo Diet was nearer the mark when he called Suetsugu 'a great Admiral and a great Fascist'; and the Fascists themselves, indeed Mussolini himself, made an even more accurate assessment on the very day of Suetsugu's speech. Talking to the German Ambassador in Rome, Ulrich von Hassell, the Duce said that Suetsugu 'made brutally clear the real Japanese aims, which were directed against all white peoples'.

On 1 February, Australian Intelligence reported on a recent party. 'Though particularly reserved when sober,' it said, 'they [the Imperial Navy officers present] became very garrulous after a few drinks . . . The Japanese Officers all agreed with the book *Japan Must Fight Britain*. The Japanese hope to be able to fight England alone, and consider themselves quite ready to do so. They are, however, afraid of France and USA joining England. It is their intention to dominate the whole of the coast of Eastern Asia.'

'It is difficult to understand the Eastern mentality,' wrote a puzzled Admiral Chatfield on 21 February. 'They have without reason or consideration taken up an impossible attitude for two years, which has caused intentional anxiety to all Maritime Powers.'

In the same month, the British naval base at Singapore, though unfinished, was formally opened; on 7 May Ambassador Craigie reported to the Foreign Office that yet again 'the Japanese Navy – and particularly its younger officers – are manifesting . . . strong anti-British sentiments'; and on 1 September, presumably in case any of the younger officers did not quite see why they should be anti-British, the Japanese Naval General Staff promulgated a memorandum entitled 'Why have our anti-British feelings been aggravated?' It gave both direct and indirect reasons: indirectly, 'British support or instigation lies behind the contemptuous and anti-Japanese tendencies now prevailing amongst the Chinese people'; and, directly, it found sixteen examples of definite British anti-Japanese feeling, all concerned with the fighting in China – it is surprising there were not more than sixteen – and eight examples of British treatment of Japan as a third-class nation.

Remembering his time as Captain of HMS *Dainty*, Admiral Dick recalls attitudes of the British China Fleet to the Imperial Navy.

'We all had the highest respect for the Japanese,' he says without hesitation. 'It was peculiar that whereas we went in for – and always have in the Royal Navy – having very smart ships in appearance, the Japanese were entirely utilitarian. There was very little spit and polish; everything was painted over, and they entirely concentrated on their job as sailors and as men of war. This was really very marked. But one had absolutely no doubt that we were dealing with a very highly trained, efficient and dedicated force.

'At first one saw these very drab-looking craft and one thought that they were not well looked after, which is a sign of inefficiency rather than efficiency, but what we soon realized was that that was the whole Japanese philosophy: the ships were after all much nearer to war . . . they went in for having no bright shining things about the place, and they were absolutely severely utilitarian . . . it was not that they were dirty or anything of that sort, but simply that they were entirely directed to being ready to go into action.'

It was such men, and such ships, who – as a 'prominent member' of the Italian Embassy told Grew on 27 November – 'had definitely decided to declare war, presumably in the near future.' Grew noted that if war broke out, the prominent Italian had said he ' "wouldn't give a nickel for Hong Kong." His explanation is that the Navy feels it has been merely a beast of burden for the Army, which has had all the glory since 1931; it is becoming restive in this role and has decided to take advantage of the present war pitch of the nation to remove Japan's opponents in East Asia and so complete her absolute domination in that sphere. England, as a result of the lag in her armament programme during the past fifteen years, is helpless, it is felt'.

Grew assumed that the Italian diplomat was in a position to have access to privileged information – he did not know that the comments had come from another party, in which a naval officer had got rather drunk, and started making aggressive but veiled hints to the Italian. 'My opinion,' said Grew, 'is that he may reflect the wishful thinking of the younger naval officers.'

And there was yet another party Grew did not know about – a high-class geisha evening which had taken place in the last week of July. One of the guests had been Rear Admiral Inagaki, Chief of the General Affairs Bureau of the Naval Air Force. Another was Captain Johannes Lietzmann, the German naval attaché; and, after the party, Lietzmann reported some of Inagaki's conversation to the Naval High Command in Berlin.

'Were it not for the English,' Inagaki had said, 'the war [in China] would certainly have been over long ago. For different reasons, Germany and Japan have the same interest in "smashing" England. He conceded that Germany still needed a few more years before it was well enough armed to be ready for this. Japan, too, was tied down at the moment, but in the view of the Japanese Navy, China was only a means to an end, only a step on the way to a final reckoning with *England* . . . In the event of a war in Europe, the German Navy can be sure, if this fact is of interest to it, that the Japanese Navy would stand side by side with the German Navy and would use the opportunity to advance to an attack on England.'

'I have the impression,' said Lietzmann in his own conclusion, 'that Japan will attack England as soon as the latter is involved in a serious military engagement and, depending on its own capacity to do so, just as strongly as ever it can manage.' But he was cautious enough to add his opinion that 'the Japanese naval officer corps has not taken sufficient account of a possible or probable collaboration of the United States with England'.

Considering that Japan had expropriated Germany's Pacific islands during World War One, relations between the navies of the two countries since then had been surprisingly good. Throughout the 1920s the Kawasaki shipyard at Kobe had employed several German technical specialists and a retired U-boat commander, and, using German specifications, had built ten or more ocean-going submarines. From 1925 to 1930 another German did a great deal of pioneering aeronautical work for the Imperial Navy, building spotter bi-planes for the fleet flagship *Nagato*. A decade after he left Japan, this man's name would be famous the world over – he was Ernst Heinkel, the designer of Germany's most versatile bomber, the HE 111. And, from 1926 on, the German Navy began sending training ships on cruises to the Far East, usually once every two years. The first of these was the *Hamburg*, which visited Japan between 23 July and 19 August 1926. At the end of the visit, a private farewell dinner was given. The guest list included Kato Kanji, already dreaming of a world reorganized by the forces of spirit and sea-going steel. Never one to miss a chance to speak his dreams, he declared then that, morally, Germany had been the real victor in World War One: and he looked forward to the time when the next generation of Germans and Japanese would link hands in victory.

But it was not until 1933 that these connections began to have any political significance. The very idea of co-operation between Nazi Germany, with its constant stress on racial purity, and militant Japan, with its vision of an Asia purged of the white races, seemed to many outside those two countries to be an absurd paradox, revealing the thinness of both countries' racist philosophies. However, on 29 December 1933, Maxim Litvinov, the Soviet Commissar for Foreign Affairs, gave a splendidly sardonic explanation.

'If I am not mistaken,' he said to the USSR Central Executive Committee, 'they have even recognized that they are of common race. This has become quite possible since the idea of race has ceased to be regarded as an ethnological and anthropological conception and has become something in the nature of the designation of a militant organization.'

In May 1934, a Japanese naval squadron under Vice-Admiral Matsuhita Hajime visited Germany. Matsuhita and his officers were received by Germany's highest authorities – Hermann Goering, Adolf Hitler and President von Hindenburg – and at a reception of the German-Japanese Association the admiral compared Japan's present position to that of Germany twenty years earlier, in 1914. Both countries, he believed, should work for a peace in which they had equality of status. As a Nazi writer, Johann von Leers, stated four months later: 'Every gain in Japanese strength means added involvement for the European powers in non-European territory. Only Germany is not affected by it . . . From our point of view we are vitally interested in the rise of any non-European great power. Every power of this nature ties the influence of our neighbours down and so liberates German power.'

And, lest any Aryans recall the Kaiser's 'Yellow Peril' fears, von Leers gave a conclusion in exact agreement with Litvinov's interpretation of events: 'We cannot expect that in politics all our friends will do us the favour of acquiring blue eyes and blond hair for our sake. Politics is a matter of real, popular interests, and has little connection with the ideas of racial community.'

In the same year a pamphlet entitled *The Essence of National Defence and Proposals to Strengthen It* emerged from the Japanese Army offices. Its first, memorable sentence read: 'War is the father of creation and the mother of culture.' Not much imagination was needed to see where all this might lead, but it was made explicit by a Japanese military writer, Fujita Issimarou.

'The world today contains two tinderboxes,' he remarked, 'one on the Pacific and the other around the European developments since the rise of Hitler to power. These two centres are interlocked. If the tempest breaks out in one place, it can easily extend to the other and assume a global character.'

Looking back at the years of appeasement, it is difficult not to feel that the hope of containing the world crisis was as baseless and absurd as Admiral Yonai's hope that the *Yamato* super-battleships would promote world peace. It is also easy to forget that, though they may have been unimaginative, the appeasers were not necessarily cowards, nor ignorant, nor shortsighted, but more often men of scrupulous principle, who honestly believed that a world without war was still a possibility – despite the Nazis in Vienna, the Italians in Ethiopia, and the Japanese in Manchuria and China. And so it was that in 1935 a German navy with submarines was legally re-established, and a naval technical mission promptly sent to Japan to find out how to build aircraft carriers. The Germans were given blueprints of the carrier *Akagi*, and on the basis of that and other donated Japanese data, built their own carrier *Graf Zeppelin*.

The German naval attaché in Tokyo at the time was Commander Paul Wenneker, a man of exemplary blondness and good looks. Of his Japanese counterparts he wrote: 'The target which, according to all my observations, has always been dangling in front of the Navy's eyes, is the realization of an aim which has already been set for some time – the expansion in a southerly direction by means of power politics. This is the seizure of areas which are in a position to solve two of the most urgent of Japanese problems – raw material supply and over-population.'

The following year Wenneker was permitted to inspect a large number of navy yards, bases, factories and ships. Technologically there seemed to be little that was novel, but 'on all my visits, commanding officers entered into discussions on the political situation with relish before and in the course of my inspections. From these I was able to confirm, to my surprise, that by contrast with the period of more than six months before, when the whole Japanese Navy had still, as much as ever, seemed to be fixed intently and unflinchingly on America as the only future opponent, of late a fundamental change in this attitude has come about . . . America is no longer regarded exclusively as the future enemy, but now it is primarily England'.

This discovery Wenneker found very agreeable, not least because he believed – and said firmly – that 'war between Japan and America would be complete madness'.

'Thank God for the Japanese Army,' wrote Captain Rawlings, the British naval attaché, in May 1937. 'It has preserved us from a Japanese expansion southwards until now and will go on doing so in the future. If the diversionary continental policy is given up and the bulk of the sums of money spent on Manchuria and the Army is transferred to the Navy, the consequences would be catastrophic.'

Rawlings cannot have known that the billion-yen Third Supplemental Building Programme had been authorized two months earlier. Nor, presumably, was he aware that the Navy militants profoundly regretted missing the chance in 1936 of taking over the island of Hainan, following the Pakhoi incident. Nor on 6 October 1938, would he have known of the comment made by the liaison officer of the Naval Intelligence Division to the German naval attaché – 'If we hadn't had the wretched *Panay* incident, we could have had Canton and Hainan long ago!' He may not have known, either, that on 10 February 1939 Admiral Takahashi Sankichi, an ex-Commander-in-Chief Combined Fleet, stated that 'the Japanese Navy must expand suddenly South as far as New Guinea, Celebes and Borneo'. But Rawlings, and all the rest of the world, knew what happened in Hainan that day – the Imperial Navy occupied that large, strategic island, and secured an excellent southern base for the further prosecution of the 'China Incident'.

A month later the Navy landed on and took control of the tiny, uninhabited, but French-claimed Spratly Islands in the South China Sea, exactly half-way between Indo-China and Borneo. On 6 March the Fourth Supplemental Building Programme was authorized – another 1.69 billion yen.

1.2 billion would provide 59 more warships – two battleships, a carrier, six cruisers, 24 destroyers, 26 submarines – and 24 auxiliary craft, while 300 million yen would eventually provide the navy air force with a total of 128 air groups – somewhat over 6,100 planes. Craigie made a wary and correct guess on 14 March that Japan's increase in submarines and aircraft 'may give her such a feeling of power that she might embark on adventures in the South Pacific'; and on 27 March, in discussions with the US Navy, Admiral of the Fleet Sir Roger Backhouse was definite: 'I wish also to stress the great importance it would be to us to be able to be certain of American naval intervention on our side . . . it would be impossible to exaggerate what this would mean to us in the event of a world war in which we were engaged with Germany, Italy and Japan.'

On 4 April the British Deputy Chief of Naval Staff, Admiral Sir Andrew Cunningham, warned that 'experience shows that she [Japan] fully understands the importance of getting in an early blow, and her plans are likely to be carefully prepared and put into execution simultaneously with her decision to intervene'; and the same day, Britain's naval attaché in Tokyo, Captain D. N. C. Tufnell, pointed out an ominous growth in the numbers of trainee officers at Etajima. In 1935, 1936 and 1937 the entry rate had been 243 each year; in 1938 it was 365, and in 1939, 458. At that time the period of training was four years, so Tufnell concluded 'this entry indicates an anticipated increased demand for officers in 1942 and after, which, in turn, points to a sudden increase in the Fleet at that time'.

Just over a fortnight later, on 19 April, Ambassador Grew had dinner at the Tokyo Navy Club. It was a grand occasion, organized by the Navy Minister, Admiral Yonai, whom Craigie had once characterized as 'a popular and level-headed sailor'. Grew also greatly liked Yonai, and enjoyed his evening thoroughly.

'After dinner,' he remembered, 'there was some excellent juggling by pretty girls, and then some lovely Japanese dancing. Navy officers are always better mixers than Army men, probably because they have travelled abroad, and the spirit at this dinner was splendid.'

But the most important part of the evening for Grew was a post-prandial conversation with Yonai, conducted through Counsellor of the Embassy Dooman, since the ambassador and the admiral did not speak each other's languages well enough. Via Dooman, Grew learnt from the Minister that 'my concern about the possibility of Japan's becoming involved in Europe had come to his attention and that he wished to tell me that I need have no further concern, because "Japanese policy has been decided. The element in Japan which desires Fascism in Japan and the consequent linking up with Germany and Italy had been 'suppressed' " '.

What Yonai was saying was untrue. Whether he believed it, or whether it was merely wishful thinking, is unanswerable. He recognized 'that the Navy held the balance of power in this important question', and warned Grew not to 'assume there would be no strengthening of the Anti-Comintern Pact'. Finally he talked about disarmament and naval arms limitation, 'and expressed regret that such limitation is not feasible at the present time, but navies are "dangerous toys"; the progressive increase in naval requirements could lead only to bankruptcy or a general explosion, and some day an agreement must be reached. "There must be disarmament", he repeatedly said.'

Grew was mightily encouraged by this chat – 'one of the most important and significant conversations that we have had' – and he concluded that it marked 'a new trend, indeed a milestone, in Japanese-American relations, for Yonai can be trusted'.

In May, Grew sensed that internal political pressures might shortly cause the government to fall, or to take up a full Fascist alliance; and he guessed that Yonai might become Prime Minister, which 'would still mean no totalitarian alliance'. It was fair to suppose that Admiral Yamamoto would then become Navy Minister; and, with two such men in positions of power, there would be grounds to hope that the navy militants might be kept in check. Craigie shared Grew's opinion of Yamamoto; they had met in London in 1935, when the future British Ambassador had been 'impressed by his breadth of view, constructive mind and grasp of the subject'. Japanese impressions of Yamamoto were somewhat different: the danger of his assassination was so real that Yonai felt obliged to place him and his official residence under special police guard night and day, although Yamamoto tried to refuse such protection, saying that he would 'regard it as a great honour to die for what I consider to be right'.

But, in spite of the seeming possibilities of moderation, since January 1938 the naval air force had flown constant sorties over southern and central China, and in the five months from May to September 1939 they sent twenty-two separate bombing raids to Chungking alone. And, as one of the flying officers wrote later, there were lessons to be learnt there – 'especially (1) that air groups and combat planes trained at sea for sea duty can serve successfully without special training in any air campaign over land, and (2) that the key to success in any land or sea operation depends upon command of the air.' Equally significantly, he added that 'it was also determined that pilots trained specifically for manoeuvres over land experienced great difficulty in operations over water, even in merely flying long distances over the ocean'.

Grew's sense of the domestic pressure on the government had been right. His guess of what might happen had been wrong. On 23 August Hitler concluded his pact of mutual non-aggression with Stalin, in open betrayal of the Anti-Comintern Pact. On 30 August, Admiral Yamamoto was removed from his post as Vice Navy Minister and appointed Commander-in-Chief

Combined Fleet – the Navy's highest honour, and one which no one could refuse; but it meant political castration. And, on the same day, Admiral Yonai was ousted from his position as Minister of the Navy.

Calendars turned over; Hitler's armies invaded Poland; two days later, Great Britain declared war on Germany. Japan's undeclared war with China was already two years old. The two conflicts, the war in the Far East and the war in Europe, were still separate; but, as Fujita Issimarou had prophesied in 1934, 'these two centres are interlocked. If the tempest breaks out in one place, it can easily extend to the other and assume a global character'.

Now it was only a matter of time before the prophecy came true.

20

'Paddling against the rapids'

Johannes Lietzmann, captain in the navy of the Third Reich and attaché at Germany's embassy in Tokyo from 31 August 1937 to 20 March 1940, was one of those placed in the front line of diplomatic embarrassment by the Führer's non-aggression pact with Stalin. While never mentioned explicitly, it had been perfectly obvious to everyone that the Soviet Union, and specifically Russia, was the object of the Anti-Comintern Pact. If that had not been the case, the Japanese might never have allied themselves with a nation so distant and – since the Great War – so fundamentally non-maritime as Germany. Compared to the fear of Russia, the ancient enemy, fear of Communism in Japan was slight: the idea of Japan as a Communist state was, to all except a very small minority, simply unthinkable, out of the question, the two views of society were just too different to consider their union. It was not totalitarianism that made the Japanese antagonistic towards Soviet Russia; again, had that been so, Hitler's Germany would never have been a plausible ally. Ambassador Craigie called the 1936 mutineers 'budding totalitarians'; in 1937, when Italy joined the Anti-Comintern Pact, Foreign Minister Ciano said that Japan's two military attachés in Rome were 'both good Fascists'. But Craigie then saw only what he feared, and Ciano saw only what he hoped. An article in the *Popolo d'Italia* – unsigned, but widely attributed to Mussolini – was rather closer to the truth. 'Japan,' it said, 'is not formally Fascist, but she is anti-Bolshevist, and the trend of her policy and her people brings her into the fold of the Fascist states.' The fact was that Japan was never a totalitarian dictatorship on the German and Italian models; but it always was, and still is, an authoritarian country. Political necessity, the fear of a Russian attack, meant that a pact with one of Russia's Western neighbours was desirable; Japan's authoritarian tradition meant that Germany was acceptable. The Anti-Comintern Pact was a triumph for the Imperial Army and the militants in the Navy; but the Hitler–Stalin non-aggression pact whisked the rug from under the militants' feet, leaving them looking and feeling betrayed, foolish and somewhat disenchanted with the Führer. It was this mood which, at the outbreak of the European war, Lietzmann and his diplomatic colleagues had to overcome; and they did so in a swift, professional manner. As Lietzmann said to Captain Ichimaya, senior adjutant to the Navy Minister, the pact with Stalin was 'a matter of survival for the German Reich. The decisive action of the Führer, Adolf Hitler, neutralized the serious risk of a threat from Russia to begin with and then dealt a heavy blow simultaneously to the efforts of the English and French to encircle and destroy us'.

Put like that, the Japanese could comprehend the German point of view: a matter of survival; decisive action; serious risk – they were phrases to touch a chord in any militarist heart. And, as for dealing a heavy blow to encirclement, they knew exactly the kind of thing Lietzmann meant: since 1936 at least, the American, British, Chinese and Dutch nations – the so-called ABCD ring – had been perceived as a deliberately encircling threat to Japan. 'The Navy has every sympathy for the German situation,' said Ichimaya to Lietzmann; and the German attaché was able to report that 'taken all together, at the moment one has the impression that the Navy is taking a matter-of-fact view and is waiting calmly'.

A few days later – on 2 September, the day after the Reich burst its banks and flooded Poland – Lietzmann reported that Eastern waters were running very smoothly. 'A comradely discussion with three officers of the Japanese navy' took place 'in a discreetly located tea-house', where Lietzmann learnt that 'the Japanese navy wants not only to maintain the previously friendly relationship with the German navy, but, in so far as possible, also by every means to strengthen it'. On 11 September Lietzmann congratulated Admiral Yamamoto – rather belatedly – on his promotion to Commander-in-Chief Combined Fleet, and gleefully received the Admiral's assurance that he need expect no change on Japan's relations with Germany. It did not occur to the German that Yamamoto might have been speaking with the greatest irony; and on 16 September, in a memorandum to his ambassador, General Eugen Ott, Lietzmann recorded a pleasing reassurance from Commander Yoshida of the Navy Staff – 'the Navy expects with eager anticipation that we will tan the hides off the English as much as possible. This opinion is unambiguous throughout the Navy and, moreover, is based on logic.' It is hard to see the logic, and in any case the opinion was not unambiguous; but Yoshida was speaking to the converted, and Lietzmann lapped it up.

Lietzmann certainly found ambiguity in other aspects of Navy procedure. The habit in Japan's commercial ports was to post lists of passengers boarding, in transit or disembarking. 'Obviously an un-neutral way of handling things,' Lietzmann complained; then less than a week later, in a new complaint, he said that 'the Navy Ministry . . . is slow-thinking in a noticeable way, and is rather too readily intent on an excessively correct neutrality'. The Navy Staff warned Lietzmann that some customs officers might be in the pay of the British Secret Service, who would thus know of any Germans sailing for home; and again Lietzmann complained to Yoshida, the Ministry man, 'that the neutrality practised there is clearly biassed in favour of the English'. Yoshida promptly denied the accusation: 'Any and every damage to the English,' he said, 'would be welcomed with pleasure by the Japanese navy.'

But in the late autumn and early winter of 1939 there were more serious problems on Lietzmann's mind: anchorages, oil, and propaganda. Instructed to arrange a stockpile of 10,000 tons of oil somewhere in Japan for Germany's use, he lamented on 24 October that 'there isn't a single company in Japan which will undertake to stockpile diesel oil on behalf of a third party'. It should scarcely have surprised him; the Imperial Army and Navy were busily stockpiling every drop they could get hold of for themselves, and on 27 November, 'as a result of the increased tension in relations between Japan and the USA', Yamamoto's fleet was partially mobilized.

On 14 December a telegram arrived for Lietzmann from the Navy High Command in Berlin. 'Find out which islands close to Japan, in the Aleutians and the Central Pacific are suitable as anchorages,' it said with breath-taking simplicity. 'Conditions: as far as possible uninhabited, with no cable or wireless stations in the vicinity, away from general shipping lanes, but accessible navigationally by armoured cruisers, if possible with sheltered bays and good anchoring facilities. Cable reply as soon as possible.' A very tall order, and it was made more difficult by the fact that, while Berlin could issue peremptory demands with great speed, supporting propaganda was ludicrously slow. Just then, 17 December 1939, the pocket battleship *Admiral Graf Spee* was in the middle of her final confrontation with the Royal Navy in the River Plate, and Lietzmann grumbled that 'the attitude of practically the whole of the Japanese Press, which was based from the outset primarily on enemy news, is thoroughly disagreeable, thanks to the failure of the German news to arrive on time. It seems desirable that in the future our side immediately passes on details about such events . . . especially in view of the regular up-to-the-minute English propaganda activity carried on with the greatest saturation, not least by the English naval attaché here'.

He entered the New Year with no better fortune; on 6 January 1940 the Navy Ministry regretfully informed him that it too was unable to stockpile any oil for Germany. Presumably Lietzmann had no idea about Japan's own urgent need for oil; but he must have been delighted to off-set that disappointment on 9 January, when the Navy Minister's senior adjutant, Captain Ichimaya, provided a list of five possible bases for Germany in the Pacific. One was in the Aleutians; one on Amchitka island; one in the Marshalls; two were in the Carolines; and they all fitted the Berlin bill exactly.

The list may have arrived just in time. The Prime Minister, General Abe Nobuki, had the reputation of an appeaser of the West, and on 14 January, after a motion of no confidence, his cabinet fell. Possibly Lietzmann anticipated a more pro-German successor; if so, he must have learnt with consternation that the new Premier was Admiral Yonai – hardly the man to inspire Hitler with confidence.

Sir Robert Craigie registered his pleasure: Yonai's cabinet was to him 'one of the most homogeneous and best-balanced of recent times'. After the war, he remembered that, with Yonai, 'there was now a widespread feeling that the time was ripe for Japan to return to more democratic methods of government and, had the European war taken a different course in 1940, I believe that a reaction against the extremes and follies of the last three or four years would have set in'.

Craigie had less than a week before his optimism was knocked. On 21 January HMS *Liverpool*, steaming thirty-five miles off Tokyo, stopped the passenger ship *Asama Maru* and removed from her twenty-one Germans. The reaction in Japan took Craigie aback – 'Never in my life have I known such a violent and universal outburst of vituperation,' he recalled. The ship had been boarded quite peaceably 'in the normal manner' and the German passengers removed without undue fuss. Nevertheless, Lietzmann chortled, 'the prevailing feeling amongst the Japanese is one of the deepest sense of outrage'. He thought it was 'an extraordinarily foolish act' on the part of the British, but it had its good points – it had 'created a new situation that is extraordinarily unpleasant for the Japanese. It must actually have provoked the Japanese into adopting a clear position, which can only work to our advantage'. Craigie pointed out that, since the beginning of the China Incident, there had been more than 190 cases of stop-and-search of British vessels off Hong Kong by Japanese warships; whereupon Ambassador Grew noted wryly that the national press 'shrieked with fury at the idea of comparing noble Japan with a mere colony like Hong Kong'.

'The issue is not the twenty-one Germans,' said a Navy spokesman to *The Times*' correspondent, 'but the fact that the affair occurred at Japan's front gate . . . it is very disagreeable to see British warships prowling along our coasts.'

Protesting that no insult had been intended, Craigie explained that if it had not been for exceptionally rough weather the search would have taken place much farther from the coast; and before long the affair was smoothed over, with a confidential agreement that no German reservists or technicians would be granted passage on Japanese vessels. 'This agreement,' Craigie commented, 'was observed loyally enough by the Government in Tokyo, though the same cannot be said of the Japanese Consular Officers in North and South America'; and even in Tokyo, the episode left a bad taste.

Lietzmann's tour of duty was coming to an end. His predecessor, Commander Paul Wenneker, was also to be his successor. By then Wenneker had been promoted to Rear Admiral – a measure of the new importance attached to the Tokyo posting. But, before Lietzmann departed, he managed to pull off a personal coup: in confidence, a certain Captain Kojima of the Navy Staff gave him 'the substantial document "Mercantile Convoy Regulations", i.e. the secret English convoy regulations. He [Kojima] drew particular attention to the need to keep this exchange of intelligence secret'. As well he might; for, the next day, Ambassador Ott had an interview with the Vice Foreign Minister. And, when he asked why the *Asama Maru* affair had been allowed to die down, Ott was told: 'It just had to be recognized that the English fleet controls the Pacific Ocean.'

This greatly alarmed Lietzmann, for Admiral Wenneker was coming by rail to Korea and across the Straits of Tsushima by ship; and Lietzmann was due to return by the same route. The awful thought occurred to him that either one or other or even both of them might be hijacked by the British, and in some agitation he consulted Captain Ichimaya of the Navy Ministry. Ichimaya's reaction was revealing: the thought had never entered his head, and he found it appalling. Thirty-five miles from Tokyo was bad enough; but to have such an incident take place in the Straits sanctified by Togo's victory would be quite intolerable.

In the event, however, the exchange of attachés went without a hitch; Lietzmann handed over formally to Wenneker on 20 March, and trundled away safe and sound – but no doubt very cold – all the thousands of miles overland, through the Russian winter, to Berlin.

Although it had nothing to do personally with the new naval attaché, Germany's stock in Japan began to rise sharply soon after his arrival. On 9 April Wenneker met Admiral Osumi, and amongst other things they discussed the possibility that America might come actively into the war against Germany. Osumi dismissed it 'as out of the question', Wenneker noted with satisfaction; and the same day, far off in Europe, Germany's troops invaded Denmark and Norway. Wenneker received news of the invasions while they were still going on; Denmark surrendered in twenty-four hours, and, three days later, the Ministry man Captain Ichimaya came to ask Wenneker 'as he stressed, in a purely personal capacity, about whether or not a German operation against Holland was to be anticipated soon. Manifestly, this question is one the Japanese Navy has a very great interest in, with reference to the fate of the Dutch Indies'.

In China, the undeclared war was still blazing – 'the fundamental essentials for stability and permanency, apart from Japanese bayonets, seem to be lacking,' wrote Grew – and, as it blazed, the national stockpile of oil in Japan dwindled. With the vision of a Holland ruled by Germany, the tantalizing gurgle of Dutch oil wells sounded more loudly in Imperial Navy ears, and on 15 April Wenneker recorded that: 'All newspapers uniformly concern themselves with the fate of the Netherlands Indies should Holland be drawn into the war. Their occupation by England or America can only be directed against Japan. Japan cannot tolerate the Netherlands Indies being used as a jumping-off point by England or America. Japan must reserve to itself the right to similar action as a minimum demand.'

He believed that press interest had been 'instigated by the Navy without the knowledge of the Foreign Ministry'. But he could also see the extent of the problem for Japan: 'Japan cannot consider seizing them by force as England, and especially America . . . would not tolerate such a step.' On the other hand, Japan, still technically neutral, could hardly assist England now, since that 'would mean certain defeat. It was on the cards that England, after eliminating the threat from Germany, would turn on Japan'.

Faint heart never won; yet the Imperial Navy was still divided on what should be done, as Wenneker saw for himself in two interviews on 16 April. The first, at 12.30, was with the retired Vice Admiral Kobayashi; the second, at 6.30 in the evening, was with Vice Chief of the Naval Staff Kondo. Amongst other things, Kobayashi said that 'the Navy's interest is wholly and completely fixed on the Netherlands Indies. The fleet has received an order to switch to a state of increased preparedness with effect from 1 May, and to pay attention to the possibility of a war with England and America. Everything depends upon when Holland is involved in the conflict in Europe. Then the moment will have arrived when it would be expedient for the Navy to act'.

'The European war,' Kobayashi continued, 'would provide Japan with an opportunity that would never recur to fulfil all its desires and plans . . . True Japanese patriots were extremely interested in the destruction of the British Empire. Unfortunately, there were groups which inclined towards a compromise with England . . . Such elements existed even among the senior ranks of the Japanese Navy.' Kobayashi was definitely not one of them; as he said to Wenneker, 'he and his group are attacking these "weaknesses" with vigour'.

In stark contrast to the retired Vice Admiral's rhetoric, Kondo, Vice Chief of the Navy Staff, said simply that for Japan to take the Netherlands Indies by force was 'completely out of the question. Such a step would involve war with England and America, and Japan was much too weak for that in consideration of the three-year war in China'.

The pendulum of comment swung back again on 5 May, when Wenneker had a discussion with Vice Admiral Yamagata, Chief of the Naval Air Force Bureau. Yamagata 'emphasized that for some time opinion in the Navy officer corps up to the rank of captain had been practically 100% pro-German. Some of the admirals keep on inclining towards England. That was hardly surprising because the Navy had been developed on the English model. But the spirit of the junior officers would sweep the seniors away on the tide'. In four sentences Yamagata had summarized a generation of Imperial Navy history, and had brought in *gekokujo* – 'the spirit of the junior officers' – for good measure; and in his next three sentences he revealed some fascinating technical information.

'Currently, Japan is constructing bombers with 1,000-kilogram bombs specially designed for attacks on battleships. Most Japanese aerial torpedoes have small platforms and fins which break off when the torpedo hits the water. These control the dropping of the torpedo from any height desired.'

Wenneker made no connection between this information and the American base at Pearl Harbor; there was no reason why he should have. Nor, however, did he give any clues on German plans for Holland. On 9 May he had a further naval conversation, this time with the retired Admiral Yamamoto, namesake of the Commander-in-Chief Combined Chief; and, in a kind of conclusion to the to-and-fro comments of his colleagues, Yamamoto told Wenneker that he 'firmly believes that sooner or later, all states would be drawn into the European war, whether they liked it or not'. Over the next four days, from 10 to 13 May, the German war machine invaded Holland, Belgium and Luxembourg, while in Britain Neville Chamberlain resigned and Churchill took office; and on 15 May the Dutch army capitulated.

About this time, Japan's Inland Sea was closed to foreign shipping, and Combined Fleet manoeuvres took place, with a special emphasis on air attacks. Aboard the flagship *Nagato* Yamamoto's Chief of Staff, Admiral Fukudome Shigeru, said to the Commander-in-Chief, 'It is beginning to look as if there is no way a surface fleet can elude aerial torpedoes. Is the time ripe for a decisive fleet engagement using aerial torpedo attacks as the main striking power?' The young Yamamoto paused, and replied, 'An even more crushing blow could be struck against an unsuspecting enemy force by mass torpedo attack.' He was not the only commander to have that thought at that time.

On 27 May the evacuation of the British Expeditionary Force from Dunkirk began; on 28 May Belgium surrendered to Germany; the same month the US Pacific Fleet manoeuvres were completed in Hawaii, and during June the decision was made to keep the Fleet there. 'This,' said the American Professor Arthur Marder over forty years later, 'may have been one of the biggest mistakes of the whole war.'

On 2 June the Dunkirk evacuation was complete. The principle of men before guns had been followed throughout, and hundreds of thousands of tons of supplies, weapons and ammunition had been abandoned. Now in Britain there were only five hundred guns; some of them had been brought out of museums. On the 5th the Battle of France began; on the 9th a preliminary armistice was agreed in Norway; at midnight on the 10th, Italy joined the war. On the 11th, the United States, still neutral, declared an embargo on the export of machine tools, and Captain Kojima of the Navy Staff told Wenneker frankly that Japan was 'not up to meeting the demand for these . . . the situation,' he added, 'would be extremely serious if

America also ordered an embargo on oil and scrap metal . . . In such an eventuality, there would be no alternative for Japan except to make a move to occupy the Dutch oil wells by force'. On the 13th, the first cargo ship with arms for Great Britain left the United States; on the 16th, Marshal Pétain formed his government. Almost exactly six years earlier, in July 1934, Pétain had predicted that the next war would come like a thunderclap and be over almost before anyone realized it had begun. His opinion then had been that victory would go the nation best prepared, especially if it could take the enemy by surprise. For him personally and for those of his countrymen who also gave up, the prediction had come true – negatively: for, the day after taking office, Pétain asked for an armistice with Germany, and three days later, on the 20th, for an armistice with Italy.

The Franco-German agreement was signed on 22 June; Hitler danced a jig when he heard the news. On 24 June the Franco-Italian agreement was signed; and in many parts of the world people believed that Britain must be on the point of capitulation.

In Tokyo, Admiral Wenneker basked in the Reich's reflected glory, receiving congratulations from the Navy Ministry and Navy Staff. 'Following the anticipated capitulation of England,' said Vice Chief of the Navy Staff Vice Admiral Kondo, who came to see Wenneker personally, 'circumstances would probably develop even more favourably for Japan.' And in case Wenneker wondered what more was needed to stir Japan into action – the conquest of Holland was long over, Luxembourg, Belgium, Norway, Denmark and France had fallen – the Japanese admiral told him that he 'lamented the disunity and lethargy of the Japanese political leadership, which was lacking in any decisiveness or willingness to accept responsibility'. To put it another way, Prime Minister Admiral Yonai was doing his best to prevent a full military alliance with the Axis powers. The reason was not difficult to find: Captain Ichimaya reported to Wenneker a conversation he had had with the British Naval Attaché Captain Tufnell, who 'described the situation as extremely serious for England. It was discernible from his statements that really only America can rescue the position' – and Yonai was still opposed to taking on such an antagonist.

In fact the great European dream, the conquest of Britain, was, in Hitler's version – Operation Sealion – already beginning to falter. Britain's worst weeks, the blitz of London and the Battle of Britain (in which ten per cent of the defending pilots were Polish), were about to commence, and on 30 June part of Great Britain was invaded when German troops landed on the Channel islands of Jersey and Guernsey. But, the same day that Pétain requested his armistice, Hitler had sent a message to the German Naval Headquarters which read: 'With regard to the landing in Britain, the Führer has not yet expressed any such intention, being well aware of the difficulties involved in such an operation.' Unaware of Hitler's uncharacteristic caution, astonished and vastly impressed by the tidal wave of German victories, those in the Japanese Navy who were willing for, or actively in favour of, a war with America could see less and less reason for holding back. Vice Chief of the Navy Staff Kondo came to see Wenneker again on 3 July. The Japanese naval attaché in London, he said, was no longer allowed to leave the capital, and so could not get an impression of the effects of German bombing, but was 'firmly convinced of an English defeat'. Kondo himself still did not believe it would come to a war between Japan and the joint forces of Britain and America.

'And even if it should,' he declared, 'it is manifest that the one opponent worthy of attention, America, can do practically nothing to get the better of Japan militarily. The [German] campaign in Norway has demonstrated that [the Japanese Navy] need have no fear even of a vastly superior fleet.'

But still no one was certain – not even the Americans – of what the Americans would do if Japan joined the war: whether the United States would come in and fight in the Pacific, or only in the Atlantic, or both; or whether the powerful movement for American isolation would prove superior, and keep the country out of war in either of its bordering oceans.

On 4 July, America's Independence Day, an historic presentation took place in Tokyo. Placed before the Navy General Staff was a document from the War Ministry and the Army General Staff. It was called 'Outline of the Main Principles for Coping with the Changing World Situation'. In it the Army gave way to the Navy's broad strategic preference: an advance would be made not to the north, towards continental Asia and Russia, as the Army had long wished, but to the south, to the rubber, minerals and oil fields of Malaysia, as the Navy had always advocated. The Army was now willing to co-operate with the Navy and fight if necessary, 'restricting in so far as possible its operations to Britain [i.e. British and Dutch territories] alone', and preparing to fight America, 'as it may prove impossible to avoid war with that country'. But, after years of Army arguments favouring a northern assault, the south had a price: a full alliance with the Axis.

On the same day as this plan was presented for consideration, a plot to assassinate Prime Minister Yonai was uncovered; genuine or not, it hinted at Yonai's vulnerability. And yet he did not accept the Army proposals outright, but put counter-proposals: political ties with the Axis would be strengthened but still be short of a full alliance. He stressed that the southward expansion 'must be achieved by peaceful means, if at all possible, and the use of military force must be determined with great prudence'. Curiously, at the same time but on the other side of the world, Grand Admiral Erich von Raeder in Germany was advising Hitler that Operation Sealion should only be used as a last resort. But now the Japanese Army lost patience: on 16 July the War Minister General Hata resigned from the Cabinet – which meant, of course, that Yonai's Government could not continue in office. The following day the Prime Minister admitted defeat; and after the war was over he said, 'When I received General Hata's resignation, I believed that he was forced to resign, not of his own will, but through outside influences. I am today still convinced that this was so.'

In the British Embassy, Craigie mourned; he 'had to witness at close quarters the steady disintegration of all that was decent and fair-minded in Japanese political life. The forces of greed, rapacity and oppression were carrying all before them. Time pressed if they were to snatch for themselves in the South Pacific the spoils which otherwise might fall to a victorious Germany. Now, cried the expansionists, was the great moment in Japanese history. How were they to face their ancestors should this supreme opportunity be missed?'

In the German Embassy, Wenneker pondered; if the Japanese Navy went to war, 'undoubtedly the most outstanding of the leading admirals is the present Fleet Commander-in-Chief, Admiral Yamamoto. But . . . he is closely identified with England'.

In Washington DC, Roosevelt picked up his pen and signed the Two-Ocean Expansion Act. The US Navy would grow to defend both Pacific and Atlantic.

On 1 August in the American Embassy in Tokyo, Grew assessed the new Government. Its War Minister was Lieutenant-General Tojo Hideki; its Foreign Minister was Matsuoka Yosuke, the man who, less than four weeks after Hitler's accession to power, had led the Japanese delegation out of the League of Nations for ever. 'At first sight,' said Grew, 'the Konoye Government, interpreting popular and especially military demand, gives every indication of going hell-bent towards the Axis.' The same day, a new American embargo became effective: henceforth no more aviation fuel would be exported.

6 August: the Japanese naval attaché in Berlin and the German Naval High Command exchanged plans of US battleships and heavy cruisers, and of the aircraft carrier *Yorktown*.

7 August: following the embargo, Captain Kojima told Admiral Wenneker that 'the *Navy* has very large stockpiles, with the result that it would not be seriously affected'.

15 August: in Britain, the Chiefs of Staff admitted that 'Hong Kong is not a vital interest and the garrison could not long withstand Japanese attack'.

22 August: Wenneker recorded a conversation with Captain Ichimaya, more realistic than Kojima's comment – 'Oil was a matter of life and death for Japan, and if she could not obtain it by peaceful means, no one need be surprised about this latter solution' – meaning the proposed southern expansion. From a post-war perspective, the gathering impetus rings doubly tragic: in 1979, Japan imported 281 million tons of oil. In 1940, the whole stake was only 6 million tons.

September came, and with it the first anniversary of the start of the war in Europe, the United States and Japan still technically neutral. On 2 September an Anglo-American agreement was announced whereby Britain received fifty urgently-needed American destroyers in return for a ninety-nine year lease on air bases in Newfoundland and the West Indies. On 6 September Admiral Oikawa Koshiro, thought to be a moderate, became Navy Minister; his Vice Minister was the brilliant Vice Admiral Toyoda Teijiro. Toyoda in 1905 had been top of his class of 171 cadets, and, in the British naval attaché's estimation, was 'one of the best friends of England among Japanese flag officers'. Craigie had met him at the London Naval Conference of 1930, and remembered him as 'one of the pleasantest but also one of the most uncompromising members of the Delegation'. Toyoda was so pro-Royal Navy that once, when talking about it, he had referred to it as 'our Navy'. With luck, it seemed that he and Oikawa might yet influence events for peace; but, on 12 September, Craigie reported that 'this moderation may at any moment turn to advocacy of a forward policy if and when the Navy should have the power and material to carry out this policy, because it is not to be supposed that the Navy should be essentially less anxious to acquire an overseas empire for their country than any other section of the population'. He was right; the following day both Oikawa and Toyoda signed their agreement to a full Tripartite Pact with the Axis.

Now the Navy was caught in an ultimately fatal dilemma. As one officer said: 'Although the Navy demands priority to complete its armaments against the United States, it does not desire to go to war with that country. But it cannot say it is absolutely opposed to war either, for others will retort that in that event armaments against the United States are unnecessary.' What, the Army could quite legitimately have asked, had been the point of naval priority for steel and oil, if not to fight the enemy across the seas? Protestations of unreadiness, after years of high budgets, could only sound like cowardice. In 1940 naval officers who feared a war they believed they could not win learnt a new fear: that the sound of cowardice would prompt a severe Army reaction – in short, civil war. 'You should give approval to the Pact,' said Yamamoto to Navy Minister Oikawa, 'it can't be helped. There is no other means left to prevent a great internal upheaval.'

On 14 September a Liaison Conference of Army, Navy and Foreign Office Staff approved the Tripartite Pact. Next day, at a meeting of top navy officers, Yamamoto stated that signing the Pact could mean eventual war with America, for which the Navy was not ready; but he was not forceful – it was already too late to stem the flow. In a speech at his old Middle School in Nagaoka shortly before, his lecture to the students had been more direct.

'Most people think,' he said then, 'that Americans love luxury and that their culture is shallow and meaningless. It is a mistake to regard the Americans as luxury-loving and weak. I can tell you' – and he knew, for he had lived long in the United States – 'Americans are full of the spirit of justice, fight and adventure; and their thinking is very advanced and scientific . . . Do not forget American industry is much more developed than ours – and unlike us they have all the oil they want. Japan cannot beat America – therefore she should not fight America.'

In Britain, Naval Intelligence had passed figures on the Japanese Navy to the Prime Minister; and, the same day that Yamamoto registered his penultimate protest, Churchill wrote: 'I am very doubtful whether the Japanese figures are correct. The Naval Intelligence Branch are very much inclined to exaggerate Japanese strength and efficiency.'

And amongst those who knew the strength and efficiency of the Imperial Navy – the senior officers themselves – there were still many unwilling to ally with the Axis powers. Uncertain of the future, they could see themselves slowly losing control over the situation which they had helped to create; and they could give each other no consolation. On 19 September, during an Imperial Conference, Chief of the Naval Staff Prince Fushimi said: 'The Navy cannot carry on a protracted war on the basis of its own stockpiles. I would like to know where we will get the additional oil necessary for a very long war.' 'Any way we can,' answered the Director of the Planning Board. 'May I interpret this,' Fushimi asked, 'to mean that there is, in general, no assurance that additional oil can be obtained? I will add that we cannot count on supplies from the Soviet Union. In the end, we will need to get oil from the Netherlands East Indies. There are two ways of getting it – by peaceful means, and by the use of force. The Navy very much prefers peaceful means.'

'You can't carry on a war without oil,' said Hara Yoshimichi, President of the Privy Council. It was the central paradox of the Imperial Navy – 'If we ever get into a war with the United States,' Fushimi remarked, 'the Navy will be fighting on the front line' – and yet Japan could not provide the one thing its front-line defence needed.

On 27 September, the Tripartite Pact was signed in Berlin. Considering that it was aimed at Britain and America, there was one rather piquant absurdity: the Pact was written in English, since that was the only language shared by the three nations' delegates.

'Our opposition to the alliance,' said Admiral Yonai glumly, 'was like paddling against the rapids only a few hundred yards upstream from Niagara Falls.' He took no comfort from Ribbentrop's declaration that the Pact 'will, in any event, serve the restoration of peace'; nor from Oikawa's belief that 'the Tripartite Pact is a defensive, not an offensive alliance'; nor from Matsuoka's claim that 'the object of the Pact is to prevent the United States from encircling us . . . the only thing that can prevent an American encirclement policy is a firm stand on our part at this time'; nor yet from the words of Japan's ambassador in London, who called it 'a pact of peace' which 'arose only out of the desire of Japan to limit the conflict'. But he might have found some wry humour in Ambassador Craigie's comment that the Pact 'completely miscarried in its primary political purpose, which was to frighten the United States . . . resentment against Japan's action spread throughout the United States'. In fact, Craigie concluded, 'Matsuoka could not have done us a better turn'.

21

'I shall run wild'

Just two days before the Tripartite Pact was signed in Berlin, a remarkable break-through was made in the United States – a step so extraordinary that still today there are many people in Japan who do not accept that it came about by pure inspiration. Yet it was also the result of twenty months of hard work; and those months in turn were the fruit of at least as many years. On 25 September 1940, American cryptologists recovered their first fully-intelligible, ungarbled text from Japan's PURPLE naval code machine.

It was not until August 1940 that the Americans had tumbled to the way it worked. From the basis of the earlier so-called RED machine it had taken them only a few weeks to reconstruct what they reckoned to be 25% of the new machine; but, after that, almost nothing. A few bits and pieces of telegrams were broken over eighteen months of intensive work; and then in the nineteenth month one of the cryptographic team had a blinding flash of understanding – a Japanese Buddhist would have called it *satori*, a moment of enlightenment. The young man's name was Harry Lawrence Clark. He expressed himself simply: 'I wonder if those monkeys used stepping switches instead of discs in the cryptographic element of the unit?' No one else had considered such a possibility, and it was the answer. Within two days the fundamental functions had been understood; before the end of September Japanese secrets were appearing in clear English. With an echo of imperial Rome, the Americans named the machine PURPLE; as a sign of their own astonishment, they named the whole operation MAGIC. This stood for the recovering of all the diplomatic codes – PURPLE, RED, and others – and the individual messages recovered were known as 'magics', with a small m. Today, Washington's National Archives bulge with magics, as more and more are slowly declassified with the passage of time. Already there are thousands of boxes, each containing many hundreds of sheets. Sorted only by date and indexed very roughly – for there are far too many to index in detail – they are a researcher's nightmare and a historian's potential treasure-trove, mute but eloquent witnesses to the industry and effectiveness of America's pre-war and wartime intelligence drive.

In October 1940 – as the blitz continued over London, and German armies, eager for oil, entered Romania; as Hitler abandoned Operation

Sealion and the RAF bombed the Kiel naval base; as Hitler met Pétain and Mussolini invaded Greece, and as Britain refused Japan's request to close the Burma Road and cease supplying Chiang Kai-Shek – it seemed to America's code-breakers that no secret message could resist their skill for long. But these, it must be remembered, were all diplomatic codes; the US Navy still handled the naval codes. And on 1 November, ahead of schedule, Japan's Admirals' Code was changed – so radically that 'the most difficult as well as the most important system the Japanese Navy was using' remained proof against all cracking, until close to the end of the Pacific War.

On 10 November 1940, almost the entire Italian fleet was assembled in the harbour of Taranto, on the Western or inner coast of the heel of Italy. It was a small but deadly group built around a heart of six battleships. Around the vessels hung torpedo-nets; above them floated barrage balloons, tethered to earth by wires that could tear off the wing of an aircraft. The fleet had every reason to feel secure.

Early in the evening of 11 November, 180 miles away, the Royal Navy aircraft carrier *Illustrious* took up position, escorted by four cruisers and four destroyers. The first wave of aircraft – obsolete Swordfish bi-planes, nicknamed 'Stringbags' – took off at 8.30 p.m., the second wave an hour later; at 10 p.m. the last straggler left, delayed from the first wave by technical troubles, but refusing to be left out. Twenty-one took off in total; nineteen returned, after dodging the flak and the barrage wires; and next day a spotter plane from Malta photographed the result of their flight. Their torpedoes had damaged the 23,600-ton battleship *Cavour* so badly she would have to be beached. The battleship *Duilio* had already dragged herself on to the sand; *Italia* was down by the bows and gushing oil; the cruiser *Trento* was bombed out of commission; two destroyers were damaged, two supply vessels sunk, and, not least important, the Taranto oil depot had almost entirely burnt down. A few months earlier the Italian fleet had tried the same manoeuvre in Alexandria, using aircraft-launched torpedoes against the cruiser HMS *Gloucester*. That attack had failed: in the shallow harbour, their torpedoes had plunged into the mud. Now half their own battle fleet had been knocked out of the war in a single night.

On 22 November, Churchill wrote to the First Lord of the Admiralty and the First Sea Lord. 'Should Japan enter the war on one side,' he said, 'and the United States on ours, ample naval forces will be available to contain Japan by long-range controls in the Pacific. The Japanese Navy is not likely to venture far from its home bases so long as a superior battle-fleet is maintained at Singapore or Honolulu.'

On 1 October, Ambassador Grew had written in his diary: 'It may be admitted that the security of the United States has rested to a certain extent upon the British Fleet, which in turn has had its support, and can only have its support, from the British Empire . . . if, by a firm policy, we can maintain conditions in the Pacific *in statu quo* until such time as Britain may be successful in the European war, Japan will be confronted with a situation which will render it impossible for the present outlook of opportunism to remain dominant.'

But the Ambassador had also once written: 'To threaten the Japanese is merely to increase their own determination.' Now on both sides of the Pacific there was 'a firm policy', an experiment in brinkmanship and deterrence; yet, for different reasons, neither side was deterred. In Admiral Yamamoto's words, the American economic embargoes following the Tripartite Pact had left Japan 'stunned, enraged and discomfited'. For the Government to react in such a way 'at this belated hour', he wrote to Admiral Shimada Shigetaro, 'is like a schoolboy who unthinkingly acts on the impulse of the moment'. The Pact had not had a warm reception from the Japanese public; 'something,' wrote the newspaper *Hochi*, 'must be done to set the people's blood to boiling. The Tripartite Pact is a stirring march for Japan, not an elegy!' But it brought with it the near-inevitability of a southward advance, peaceful or not; and Yamamoto's letter to Shimada continued: 'The southern operations, unlike the operations in China, will determine the nation's rise or fall, for they will lead to a war in which the nation's very fate will be at stake.'

The lessons of Taranto had not been ignored. The maximum depth of its harbour was 42 feet; that of Pearl was 45 feet. Navy Secretary Frank Knox wrote to Army Secretary Henry L. Stimson: 'The success of the British aerial torpedo attack against ships at anchor suggests that precautionary measures be taken immediately to protect Pearl Harbor against a surprise attack in the event of war between the United States and Japan. The greatest danger will come from aerial torpedoes.'

Just before Christmas, however, the commander of the US fleet, Admiral Husband E. Kimmel, vetoed such protection: 'Anti-torpedo nets at Pearl Harbor,' he pronounced, 'would restrict boat traffic by narrowing the channel.' It was during that same week, aboard the flagship *Nagato*, that Admiral Yamamoto remarked to his Chief of Staff Admiral Fukudome Shigeru: 'An air attack on Pearl Harbor might be possible now, especially as our air training has turned out so successfully.'

To evade the Pact would probably have brought civil war to Japan. To sign it would probably bring external war. Now that it was signed, a new mood began to take hold of Yamamoto and all those navy men who had opposed external war: they would accept a foreign conflict, if the alternative was war at home; and they would do their best to win. But they still were fearful of the outcome. In September, Prime Minister Prince Konoye had asked

Yamamoto what he felt Japan's chances were in a long war. The Admiral's reply had been brief and memorable:

'If I am told to fight regardless of the consequences, I shall run wild considerably for the first six months or a year; but I have utterly no confidence in the second and third years.'

The American ambassador received a card bearing good wishes for Christmas and the New Year. The sender was an Army man, a General Haraguchi, who was a Christian. His card began with a poem he had written himself, in English:

> 'Grant all your hopes a singing breeze,
> Happy harbour safe to win;
> Quick upon untroubled seas
> May your ships sail in!'

It was a pretty and very creditable attempt, 'worthy', as Grew noted, 'of something more than mere derision'; but Haraguchi must have been almost alone in facing 1941 with such faithful hope of peace. On 4 January, at the eighth meeting of the Chiefs of Staff, Vice Admiral Sir Tom Phillips, Vice Chief of the Naval Staff, plainly stated the implications for Britain of a war in the Far East: 'Without USA co-operation with us, the stark fact was that we had not got the ships to take on the German, Italian and Japanese fleets at the same time. We should either have to let the Eastern Mediterranean or the Far East go.'

In Berlin, Ribbentrop predicted that Britain would be 'wiped out by autumn of this year at the latest'. On 7 January, on board *Nagato* in Hiroshima Bay, Yamamoto wrote to Navy Minister Oikawa, saying: 'In case the enemy main force comes out from Hawaii before our attack and keeps coming at us, [we] must encounter it with all our decisive force to destroy it at one stroke.' In London on the same day, Churchill wrote: 'If Japan goes to war, there is not the slightest chance of holding Hong Kong or of relieving it.' And the following day the German naval record stated: 'Regarding Japanese interests in Singapore, the Führer feels that the Japanese should be given a free hand, even if this may entail the risk that America is thus forced to take drastic steps.'

During January, Japanese sea-planes reconnoitred the coast of Kota Bharu, just inside the northern border of British-held Malaya, and only 300 miles north-north-west of Singapore.

'Should hostilities break out between Japan and the United States,' wrote Yamamoto in a letter on 26 January, 'it would not be enough that we take Guam and the Philippines, nor even Hawaii and San Francisco. To make victory certain, we would have to march into Washington and dictate the terms of peace in the White House.'

Such a thing, he knew, was manifestly impossible; but he was incautious in his choice of correspondent, an ultranationalist on whom the sarcasm was lost. An edited version of the letter was published, and reported in America, in which Yamamoto's 'dictated terms' were received as declared Japanese policy. One more warning had been misunderstood; to some people, American and Japanese, it was beginning to seem as though anything might be possible.

'There is a lot of talk around town,' Grew noted on 27 January, 'to the effect that the Japanese, in case of a break with the United States, are planning to go all out in a surprise mass attack on Pearl Harbor. Of course I informed the Government.' The message was passed to Kimmel in Hawaii by the Division of Naval Intelligence with the comment that they placed 'no credence in these rumours. Furthermore based on known data regarding the present disposition and deployment of Japanese naval and army forces no move against Pearl Harbor appears imminent or planned for the foreseeable future'.

It now appears that Yamamoto's planning specifically for a strike on Pearl began in December 1940; and, on 30 January 1941, his friend and colleague Admiral Inoue Shigemi, head of Naval Aviation Headquarters, submitted a detailed memorandum to the Navy Minister. Its title was 'On New Armaments Plans', and its gist may be given in one of its sentences: 'who commands the air commands the sea'. Inoue prophesied that a war with the United States would revolve around possession of the islands in the South Pacific. Technological advances had been so great that he believed the very basis of Japan's broad Pacific strategy needed radical revision; as far as sea-power was concerned, he was convinced that the country's 'ratio neurosis' had led it into building the wrong kind of navy for a modern war: instead of ships and guns, it should be almost entirely carriers and planes.

But the stupendous super-battleship *Yamato* had already been launched, on 8 August 1940, and was within a year of completion. Huge sums of money had already been spent on her; the second of her giant class, *Musashi*, had been launched on 1 November 1940; the third, *Shinano*, and the unnamed fourth had been commenced. Looking at the expenditure and investment, no minister would have sanctioned the scrapping of the programme; and, looking at the colossal hulls and the superstructures taking shape in Kure, Nagasaki and Yokosuka, there were not many admirals – in any part of the world – who would have wanted to scrap them either. They already looked like, and in all naval orthodoxy they promised to be, sea-power incarnate. They were going to be the biggest battleships in history; Britain could certainly have done with one or two; the Imperial Japanese Navy was intending to have four at least. The debate on the virtues of big ships and big guns versus aircraft had not been resolved and could not be, until put to the test of actual modern war. As the American author Bernard Brodie wrote at that time: 'Even if it were established that battleships could be sunk by aerial attack, the questions would still remain: Under what circumstances? At what cost?' Five years earlier, R. V. C. Bodley had given the opposite, and farther-sighted view:

'Nothing will avail after a host of aeroplanes carrying tons of bombs have passed over the finest sea force in the world. Even if the Navy manages to escape from an aerial attack, it will be of no further use if the country from which it originates has been reduced to ashes by bombs from the skies . . . in a few years' time battleships will be as obsolete as bows and arrows . . . anything which moves comparatively slowly will be at the mercy in the near future of anything which flies in the air.'

Yet, to all except the most convinced supporter of air power – such as Inoue and Yamamoto – the mere sight of such splendid ships as *Yamato* and *Musashi* would sweep away all doubts: the age of the battleship was not only unfinished, it had yet to reach its climax. Inoue's tightly-reasoned arguments could be dismissed as the last-ditch attempt of an eccentric serviceman to get money and metal for his pet theory.

But Inoue was not alone; nor, in February 1941, was Yamamoto. On the first day of the month the Commander-in-Chief outlined his proposal for an air attack on Pearl Harbor to Rear Admiral Onishi Takijiro, Chief of Staff of the 11th Air Fleet. Onishi in turn showed the plan to his best pilot, Commander Genda Minoru, a member of the crew of the aircraft carrier *Kaga*. Aboard the carrier, Genda studied the plan for ten days, and then delivered his opinion. As he expressed it after the war, he felt 'that the attack would be extremely hazardous but would have a reasonable chance of success'. It is interesting to note that, after the 1921 Sempill mission from the Royal Navy, the Royal Air Force had lent an air commodore to the Imperial Navy as an air fighting instructor for six months in 1930–31. His name was R. W. Chappell; and Genda was his 'star pupil'.

Between Britain and the United States there was little agreement over Pacific and Far East strategy, partly because the two countries put different priorities on the areas that should be defended, and partly because, with the isolationist lobby still strong, President Roosevelt would not and could not give a definite commitment as to when, or even whether, America would support Britain.

'I think I ought to let you know,' Churchill telegraphed Roosevelt on 15 February, 'that the weight of the Japanese Navy, if thrown against us, would confront us with situations beyond the scope of our naval resources . . .

Everything you can do to inspire the Japanese with the fear of a double war may avert the danger. If however they come in against us and we are alone, the grave character of the consequences cannot easily be overstated.'

Essentially, the British wished that the American Pacific Fleet should be based at Singapore, while the Americans were unwilling to move it so far from the continental United States. Not the least powerful of their motives was the reluctance – despite Grew's pointed comment about the ultimate source of present American security – to contribute to the defence of an empire seen by many as an outdated political concept. On 19 February the US Staff Committee expressed its view that even if Malaysia were lost, 'this loss need not have a decisive effect upon the issue of the war'. Unofficially, however, the US Navy Department had said on 4 December 1940 that Singapore was a vital part of the defence of the British Isles. Grew endorsed this energetically, saying on 7 February that 'Britain is in no position today, and presumably will not be in the near future, to part with important naval units for the defence of Singapore. In conformity with our admitted policy of aiding Britain, we must see to it that this strategically important base does not become the possession of a hostile power . . . the taking of Singapore would necessarily have grave repercussions upon Chinese morale [which was more interesting to many American businesses than British morale] as well as upon Britain's position in the Near East and in the eastern Mediterranean'.

On 5 February the British Joint Planners had begun to feel they might have to resort to bluff: 'the stronger the line we take, the more likely are the Japanese to believe that the United States are behind us. In any case we would be instilling doubt and hesitation into their minds.' Yet something neither they nor Grew could have known was told to Hitler by Grand Admiral Raeder on 18 March: Japanese naval officers had indicated that there would be no attack on Singapore until and unless German forces landed in Britain.

Elsewhere, the concern was with neither Britain nor Singapore. Admiral Patrick L. Bellinger, Air Defence Officer of Pearl Harbor, in collaboration with Major-General Frederick L. Martin, commanding officer of the Army Air Force in Hawaii, produced an estimate of probable Japanese strategy in the event of war. It was dated 31 March, and it stated that most probably Japanese surface forces would approach Hawaii from the north, where there were no regular trade routes; would launch planes from 350 miles away; and would attack at dawn.

'In the past Japan has never preceded hostile actions by a declaration of war. Japanese submarines and a fast raiding force may arrive in Hawaiian waters with no prior warning from the US intelligence service. A successful raid against the ships and naval installations in Oahu might prevent effective action by their forces in the West Pacific for a long period.'

In short, they agreed with the results of Admiral Yarnell's 'raid' in 1932; both predicted accurately the turn of future events; and both were ignored in their country as effectively as Inoue's plea for naval reorganization was ignored in his.

Churchill also tried the logical approach. On 2 April he sent a list of eight questions to Japan's volatile Foreign Minister Matsuoka, questions which, if answered honestly and accurately, pointed out Japan's inability to wage successful war against a combination of British and American forces. No such combination formally existed yet, but Churchill was hardly going to tell Matsuoka that. Looking at the list again after the war was over, the Prime Minister said disarmingly: 'I was rather pleased with this when I wrote it, and I don't mind the look of it now.' Matsuoka's reply was a masterpiece of non-committal ambiguity. Written in a train crossing Siberia and dated 22 April, it thanked Churchill and said:

'Your Excellency may rest assured that the foreign policy of Japan is determined upon after an unbiased examination of all the facts and a very careful weighing of all the elements of the situation she confronts, always holding steadfastly in view the great racial aim and ambition of finally bringing about the conditions envisaged in what she calls Hakko-ichiu, the Japanese conception of a universal peace under which there would be no conquest, no oppression, no exploitation of any and all peoples. And, once determined, I need hardly tell Your Excellency that it will be carried out with resolution but with utmost circumspection, taking in every detail of changing circumstances.'

It was all true, but it said nothing. 'A barren reply,' Churchill grunted disdainfully.

Matsuoka's purpose in Russia had been very particular: now that a decision had been made for southward rather than northward expansion, he needed to secure Japan's northern front. And he had been successful, signing a non-aggression pact with Stalin on 13 April. At his departure, he and the burly dictator had embraced warmly in a scene which the *Manchester Guardian* described as the 'most touching since the Walrus and the Carpenter wept like anything before they ate the oysters'. Admiral Yamamoto was equally cynical – six months earlier he had observed: 'Even if a non-aggression pact is concluded with Russia, she cannot be relied upon entirely. While we are fighting the United States, who can guarantee she will observe the pact and not attack us from the rear?' No one, was the answer; but it was a risk which would have to be taken.

'Now is the time' – said Captain Ishikawa, the originator of the *Yamato* project, when Matsuoka returned in April – 'Now is the time to strike; we won't be defeated.' On 11 June, at the 29th Liaison Conference – after Hess had parachuted into Britain, the *Bismarck* had been sunk, and 16,583 British, Australian and New Zealander troops and sailors had died defending Crete – Matsuoka declared: 'From the point of view of diplomacy, I would like to go on a sudden rampage, but I won't because the Supreme Command tells me not to' – to which Admiral Nagano Osami, Chief of the Naval Staff, replied decisively: 'We must build bases in French Indo-China and Thailand in order to launch military operations. We must resolutely attack anyone who tries to stop us. We must resort to force if we have to.'

A fortnight later, at the 32nd Conference, Navy Minister Admiral Oikawa was more cautious.

'On behalf of the Navy', he began, 'I want to say something about diplomacy in the future. I'm not questioning the past. Given the delicate international situation at the present time, you shouldn't talk about the distant future without consulting the Supreme Command. The Navy is confident about a war with the United States and Britain, but is not confident about a war against the United States, Britain and the Soviet Union. Suppose the Soviets and the Americans get together, and the United States builds naval bases, air bases, radar stations, etc., on Soviet soil. In order to avoid a situation of this kind, don't tell us to strike at Soviet Russia and also to strike south. The Navy doesn't want the Soviet Union stirred up.'

The theoretical possibility was, after all, there; and Matsuoka replied with extraordinary obtuseness: 'You say you are not afraid of a war with the United States and Britain, so why is it that you do not wish to see the Soviets enter the war?' The answer was blindingly obvious, but Oikawa gave it nonetheless: 'If the Soviets come in, it means fighting another country, doesn't it?'

Three days later, at the 35th Conference on 28 June, an Army comment on the minutes showed some exasperation: 'Although the Navy has expressed the view that it is absolutely opposed to entering the war, it will not say so openly – so it is difficult to see exactly what the Navy wants.' On 2 July the situation was clarified. The scene was the second Imperial Conference; the agreed resolution read:

'For the sake of her self-sufficiency and self-defence, Japan shall continue necessary diplomatic negotiations with nations concerned in the southern regions, and shall promote other necessary measures . . . In order to achieve these purposes, Japan shall not decline war with Britain and the United States.'

'In accordance with the established policy,' the resolution continued, 'every effort, diplomatic and otherwise, shall be made to restrain the United States from entering the war. Should the United States nevertheless do so, Japan shall act in accordance with the Tripartite Pact; but the timing and method of resort to arms shall be independently decided.'

Impatience was growing, for as time passed the risks increased. At the 41st Liaison Conference, on 24 July, Admiral Nagano voiced the impatience: 'As for a war with the United States, although there is now a good chance of achieving victory, the chances will diminish as time goes on. By the latter half of next year it will already be difficult for us to cope with the United States . . . If we could settle things without war, there would be nothing better. But if we conclude that conflict cannot ultimately be avoided, then I would like you to understand that as time goes by we will be in a disadvantageous position.' And he concluded, rather weakly, 'I believe our defences in the South Sea Islands are strong, and that we could put up a good fight there.'

A spokesman for the Navy Ministry, Captain Hiraide Hideo, was saying the same thing, but more positively, when he described the Navy in July 1941 as 'never having been in better shape'. But the reason for Nagano's cautious haste was that, the day he spoke, Japanese troops had entered French Indo-China. There was a basis of legality to the operation: an agreement had been made with Pétain's 'government' in Vichy, which was hardly in a position to refuse. By the end of the month, 40,000 Japanese troops were in French Indo-China; and there was some considerable doubt as to how other countries, particularly America, would react. Roosevelt did not keep them in suspense: within twenty-four hours all Japanese assets in the United States had been frozen, and all trade, including oil, had been halted. The same happened in Britain, and again in the Netherlands East Indies on the 28th. To speak of putting up a good fight, as Nagano had done on the 24th, did not sound promising; and on 30 July, in a private audience, Emperor Hirohito asked Nagano the obvious, direct question – 'Is it certain that we will win?' To his Emperor, Nagano could only give the honest reply – 'No, it is not.' According to one source, Hirohito then murmured: 'I fear our entry into the war will mean fighting in despair.'

Such a comment would have been defeatist in the extreme; and it may have been what Hirohito meant. But for this exchange, because of the difficulties of translation, there is more than one version. In another, the dialogue from Emperor to Navy Chief of Staff was:

'Will you win a great victory?'

'I am sorry, but that will not be possible.'

'Then', said Hirohito, 'the war will be a desperate one.' Superficially the two versions are similar; but the implication of the latter is quite different to that of the former. To say a 'great victory' will not be possible is not the same as saying winning is uncertain; to say a war will be desperate is not the same as saying one will fight in despair. In one there is resolution and defiance; in the other there is nothing but the expectation of defeat.

On the last day of July, an incident took place which in Grew's words brought his country and Japan within 'eight yards of war'. At Chungking, far up the Yangtze, 'with what seemed to me the utmost stupidity', a naval plane attempted to bomb the US gunboat *Tutuila*. The action was quite deliberate; the bomb, however, fell eight yards short of the vessel. Yamamoto, then Acting Vice Minister for Foreign Affairs, immediately went to see the American ambassador to apologize, and the affair was smoothed over; but, Grew felt, 'once again the Japanese have been playing with fire'.

Again the reason for Yamamoto's prompt apology is open to speculation, and cannot be finally determined; either he was still trying to avert war, especially in the light of the Indo-Chinese crisis; or perhaps he was merely trying to delay war. For, since early July, the Fleet, as Craigie observed, 'had been fully mobilized; later in the month was a large-scale mobilization of the Army which was not completed until the middle of August'. And, since the late spring, naval aircraft had been undergoing special training in Japan's deep south. The training was aerial torpedo-bombing; and the location, chosen by Yamamoto, was Kagoshima Bay – the site, back in 1863, of the British Admiral Kuper's bombardment, in 'a precedent . . . inconceivably disastrous to mankind'. It is possible the historical connection – the ancient grudge, one could say – played some part in Yamamoto's choice of this bay; but, far more important, far more practical, was the fact that Kagoshima Bay bears a fair resemblance to Pearl Harbor.

In Britain, a second Far Eastern tragedy was brewing. On 25 August, in a letter to the First Lord of the Admiralty and the First Sea Lord, Churchill put his case for sending out a small deterrent force: 'We have only to remember all the preoccupations which are caused us by the *Tirpitz* – the only capital ship left to Germany against our fifteen or sixteen battleships and battle-cruisers – to see what an effect would be produced upon the Japanese Admiralty by the presence of a small but very powerful and fast force in Eastern waters.' Four days later he amplified this: '*Tirpitz* is doing to us exactly what a *K.G.V.* [a *King George V*-class battleship] in the Indian Ocean would do to the Japanese Navy. It exercises a vague general fear and menaces all points at once. It appears, and disappears, causing immediate reactions and perturbations on the other side.'

Meanwhile, though, amid doubts of his sanity, Japan's Foreign Minister Matsuoka had been replaced – he had refused to resign, and to get rid of him, the entire cabinet had had to resign. It had then been reinstated without him. The new Foreign Minister was Admiral Toyoda Teijiro, and about the time that Churchill was preparing to send a deterrent force eastwards, Toyoda made a remark to Craigie which neatly summed up the dead-end when deterrence fails: 'If we both think that our countries are being threatened, we won't get anywhere.'

But, as the mutual deterrents grew, so did the refusal of either side to be deterred; and so did Japan's concern over her own ability to fight at all if the fight was delayed any further.

'It is exceedingly doubtful whether Japan could provide arms, equipment, and other necessities for her naval and military forces on a war footing for a longer period than twelve months if foreign supplies ceased to be available . . . By strictly rationing her stocks of steel and other essential material she might be able for a time to cope with the demands of her Navy and Army, but she would certainly not be in a position to embark, for instance, on a large emergency programme of naval construction.'

Hector Bywater wrote that in 1934; the words were different, but the sense was virtually identical to Yamamoto's statement in September 1940 that he would 'run wild considerably for six months or a year; but I have utterly no confidence in the second and third years'. By August 1941 the message was getting through even to the Army: at a liaison conference in the last week of the month, Colonel Iwakuro Hideo gave his frightening ratios of American:Japanese war capability. They were: steel, 20:1; coal, 10:1; planes, 5:1; labour force, 5:1; shipping, 2:1; and oil – 100:1. Overall, Iwakuro estimated, the United States' war potential was ten times greater than that of Japan.

'The Empire is losing materials,' said Navy Chief of Staff Nagano at the 50th Liaison conference on 3 September. 'That is, we are getting weaker. By contrast, the enemy is getting stronger. With the passage of time, we will get increasingly weaker, and we won't be able to survive . . . We hope the enemy will come out for a quick showdown; in that event there will be a decisive battle in waters near us, and I anticipate that our chances of victory would be quite good. But I do not believe the war would end with that.'

Three days later, at a two-hour Imperial Conference, he emphasized his misgivings to the Emperor in person:

'If they [the United States] should aim for a quick war leading to an early decision, send their principal naval units, and challenge us to an immediate war, this would be the very thing we hope for . . . However, even if our Empire should win a decisive naval victory, we will not thereby be able to bring the war to a conclusion. We can anticipate that America will attempt to prolong the war, utilizing her impregnable position, her superior industrial power, and her abundant resources. Our Empire does not have the means to take the offensive, overcome the enemy, and make them give up their will to fight.'

Speaking on behalf of the Emperor – who, custom decreed, was always silent in such conferences, simply approving their final resolutions with a nod – President of the Privy Council Hara Yoshimichi voiced Hirohito's worries.

'After the China Incident was expanded, it was said that our hundred million people were completely united; but reality betrays this assertion. Even at the present time, some people are opposed to the adjustment of relations between Japan and the United States' – the reference was to recent ultranationalist outrages, including a plot to assassinate Prime Minister

Prince Konoye, which attempted to ruin any hopes of a diplomatic settlement – 'they might be patriots, but I feel a great anxiety when I see that some people are opposed to what the Government is doing . . . At the time of the Russo-Japanese war the people really were of one mind . . . now, despite the fact that we are engaged in war [in China], acts of terror are perpetrated. I wonder if the decisions of this Conference in the presence of the Emperor can be put into effect?'

It was an extraordinary question; the Emperor was in effect asking the Government if they were capable of ruling. But then something yet more extraordinary, a complete break with precedent, took place: in case there was any doubt of the Imperial will in his Ministers' minds, Hirohito spoke for himself. The minutes of the Conference were written by an Army man, who said merely: 'Finally, the Emperor graciously made some remarks.' He did not note the remarks, nor the electrifying effect that the Emperor's voice, normally never heard, had upon all present; and it seems fair to assume that he deleted those points from the record because Hirohito's words, veiled as they were, were the opposite of Army wishes. The Emperor's short, historic speech was a poem composed by his grandfather, Emperor Meiji. It read:

> 'The four seas
> are brothers to one another;
> Why then do the waves seethe
> and the winds rage?'

No one present could mistake his meaning; it was a plea for peace. And yet the resolution remained: 'In the event that there is no prospect of our demands being met by the first ten days of October through the diplomatic negotiations . . . we will immediately decide to commence hostilities against the United States, Britain and the Netherlands.'

'The 2 July Imperial Conference decision' – ('Japan will not decline war') – 'had made a Pacific War inescapable,' said the wartime Foreign Minister, Togo Shigenori, in 1956. 'That of 6 September made it definite.'

22

'The proper application of overwhelming force'

In 1940 Japan's annual rate of domestic oil production was somewhat over 400,000 tons. At the same time, the country's annual rate of oil consumption was five million tons. In 1937 the Synthetic Oil Industry Law started a seven-year plan of expansion which aimed at producing 7.8 million barrels in 1941. Actual production of synthetic oil for that year was 1.2 million barrels. To glance forward, production of 14 million barrels had been planned for 1943; achieved production was just over 1 million. In the Netherlands East Indies, the annual rate of oil production in 1940 topped eight million tons – 60% more than Japan's total needs. A simple sum promised independence, and was an irresistible lure – the more so after the international oil embargo of 26 July 1941 had stopped almost all oil coming into Japan from abroad. By the autumn the country's total oil reserves were 43 million barrels, of which the Navy had 21.7 million. Two years earlier the national reserve had been 51 million; under conditions of war, what remained could not be expected to last for more than two years at most; and, as Churchill pointed out later, at the outbreak of war, the Imperial Navy had used four months' worth of its reserve, with nothing coming in. And yet rivalry between the Army and Navy was so great that this dire state of affairs was not mutually revealed until October 1941 – 'this disunity,' said the German naval attaché Admiral Wenneker, 'was quite amazing to me.'

But it was also quite traditional. Wenneker could have found an almost exact parallel to his own times in the diary of Major-General Iguchi. In 1903, just before the Russo-Japanese War, the General had written: 'There is no harmony between the Army and the Navy. The Army and Navy ministers, especially Yamamoto . . . are blind to opportunities. They have no resolution to fight a decisive battle' – which went to show, again, how little Japanese fighting thought had altered in almost forty years.

On 12 October 1941, in what was subsequently described as his 'last chance', Navy Minister Oikawa refused to come out against war, but also refused to support war; instead, taking the line of least resistance, he left the Navy's decision one way or the other to the Prime Minister. And two days later, equally unable to bear the weight of such a choice, Konoye resigned again – this time for good. Oikawa could have resigned himself and, in the old tradition, brought down the cabinet and thus deferred the decision. There is some mystery about this; after the war he was asked why he did not resign, and would make no reply. But even if he had resigned it would probably have made little difference; the Army would have seen to it that the next Navy Minister was more malleable.

Such a man could certainly have been found; if he had not been too junior, it might have been Captain Hiraide Hideo, navy spokesman *extraordinaire*, who, the day after Konoye's resignation, announced that 'the Imperial Navy is prepared for the worst and has completed all necessary preparations. In fact, the Imperial Navy is itching for action when needed'.

The infamous General Tojo Hideki became Prime Minister on 18 October. In the footsteps of Toyoda Teijiro, another Toyoda was suggested as his Navy Minister: Toyoda Soemu. Tojo would not accept him – 'I don't care for him. He is quite unpopular with the Army leaders, and he lacks a co-operative attitude.' But Toyoda Soemu's non-appearance was made memorable by his comment: 'I don't like khaki,' he said, and, calling the Army 'horseshit and landlubbers', he promptly returned to Kure. This was not sour grapes on his part; he had loathed the Army for years, and was by no means the only sailor to feel that way.

The man who became Navy Minister under Tojo, and served until July 1944, was Admiral Shimada Shigetaro. Yamamoto thought him a 'simpleton'; he had the reputation of being weak and subservient, ready to do as he was told – the wrong man at the wrong time, if ever a time had been right for him; but he was ideal for Tojo.

The day after the Prime Minister's installation another resignation was threatened – one which, had it been followed through, would certainly have changed the world. On 19 October Admiral Yamamoto's plan to attack Pearl Harbor was rejected by the Naval Staff: it was too unorthodox, too risky, too far removed from the strategy of attrition that had been accepted for years. The risks were obvious enough; firstly, to make the operation worthwhile, the majority of the US Fleet would have to be sitting undefended; secondly, the attacking fleet would have to be undetected throughout the long voyage to Hawaii – a voyage which, by the shortest route, was 3,389 miles. The Admiral had long ago understood and accepted those risks – in January he said that, should the US Fleet come out and advance, his ships would 'encounter it with all our decisive force to destroy it at one stroke'. His pilots were thoroughly trained professionals, each with an average of 800 hours' flying experience. Yamamoto believed in them and was convinced of the value of his plan; and, when it was rejected, he wrote an impassioned letter to Nagano – who, as a civil servant rather than a politician, had survived Konoye's resignation and was still Chief of the Naval Staff.

'The presence of the US Fleet in Hawaii,' Yamamoto wrote, 'is a dagger pointed at our throats. Should war be declared, the length and breadth of our southern operations would immediately be exposed to a serious threat on its flank. The Hawaiian operation is absolutely indispensable . . . the numerous difficulties of this operation do not make it impossible . . . Should the Hawaiian operation by chance end in failure, that would merely imply that fortune is not on our side. That should also be the time for definitely halting all operations.'

And in the formal third person he declared that 'unless it is carried out, Admiral Yamamoto has no confidence that he can fulfil his assigned responsibility'.

It was a tribute to his status and acknowledged ability that, despite their doubts and his own previously unswerving anti-war attitude, the Naval Staff gave way; on 20 October the plan was accepted.

November began with a stormy Liaison Conference – the 66th. It lasted seventeen hours, ending at 1.30 a.m. The 10 October dead-line for decision had long passed with no decision, as the diplomats in Washington stumbled along their dark and stony road. Something had to be done, and soon.

'If we go along as at present, without war,' said Finance Minister Kaya Okonori, 'and three years hence the American Fleet comes to attack us, will the Navy have a chance of winning or won't it?' (The Army secretary noted that 'he asked this several times'.) Nagano replied, simply, 'Nobody knows.' Kaya altered his question – 'Will the American Fleet come to attack us or won't it?' 'I don't know,' Nagano answered. 'I think the chances are about 50-50.' Kaya disagreed: 'I don't think they will come. But, if they should come, can we win the war on the seas?' ('He could not very well ask the Supreme Command if we would lose,' the secretary noted.) 'I too,' said Foreign Minister Togo Shigenori, 'cannot believe that the American Fleet would come and attack us. I don't believe there is any need to go to war now.' 'There is a saying,' Nagano reminded him, ' "Don't rely on what won't come." The future is uncertain; we can't take anything for granted. In three years enemy defences in the south will be strong, and the number of enemy warships will also increase.' 'Well then,' Kaya asked again, 'when can we go to war and win?' And suddenly something seemed to snap in Nagano. 'Now!' he burst out. 'The time for war will not come later!'

'He said this with great emphasis,' the secretary noted dourly.

The following day Ambassador Grew telegrammed the Secretary of State: 'Action by Japan which might render unavoidable an armed conflict with the United States may come with dangerous and dramatic suddenness.' It was an intelligent guess rather than an informed prediction; but, the same day, Imperial General Headquarters sent Naval Order No. 1 to Yamamoto.

'In view of the great possibility of being compelled to go to war against the United States, Great Britain and the Netherlands,' it read, 'Japan has decided to complete various operational preparations within the first ten days of December . . . the Commander-in-Chief will make the necessary operational preparations.'

A minor part of this involved the briefing of Toyoda Soemu. When it was over, he snorted out another memorable remark – 'Was the Navy *serious* about a war with the United States?'

There could not be much doubt about that now. While Toyoda was grumbling in disbelief, another Imperial Conference was in session.

'Hereafter,' said Admiral Nagano, 'we will go forward steadily with our war preparations, expecting the opening of hostilities in the early part of December . . . it is very important that we carry out our initial operations ahead of the enemy and with courageous decisiveness. Consequently the concealment of our war plans has an important bearing on the outcome of the war.'

On the Emperor's behalf, President of the Privy Council Hara sounded one cautionary note: 'Don't let hatred of Japan become stronger than hatred of Hitler, so that everybody will in name and in fact gang up on Japan.' No one else appeared to have had that thought; but for very many people, especially in America, it was exactly what came to pass.

On 10 November orders were given to a large, but very select, part of the Navy. Six of Japan's ten aircraft carriers, accompanied by two battleships, two heavy cruisers, one light cruiser and nine destroyers were to weigh anchor at intervals and proceed under strict radio silence to remote Hitokappu Bay, far north in the Kurile Islands – a suitably discreet rendezvous, closer to Kamchatka than to Tokyo. As they left, their call-signs would be taken over by shore stations and other ships broadcasting more frequently, to cover what would otherwise be a suspicious silence. The operation was now almost irrevocably under way; and the next day Yamamoto wrote with a certain poignancy to his friend Vice Admiral Hori Teikichi, one of the victims of the 'Osumi purge'. 'I find my present position extremely odd,' said the Commander-in-Chief, 'obliged to make up my mind to pursue unswervingly a course that is precisely the opposite of my personal views.'

'How can we let the United States continue to do as she pleases,' demanded Prime Minister Tojo at the 67th Liaison Conference on 12 November, 'even if there is some uneasiness? Two years from now we will have no petroleum left for military use. Ships will stop moving.' The Navy was using 12,000 tons of fuel daily; Tojo was not exaggerating. 'When I think about the strengthening of American defences in the south-west Pacific, the expansion of the American fleet, the unfinished China Incident, and so on, I see no end to difficulties. We can talk about austerity and suffering, but can our people endure such a life for a long time? The situation is not the same as it was during the Sino-Japanese War. I fear that we would become a third-class nation after two or three years if we just sit tight . . . As to what our moral basis for going to war should be, there is some merit in making it clear that Great Britain and the United States represent a strong threat to Japan's self-preservation.'

'Some uneasiness' must be one of the most understated euphemisms for war; but Tojo was correct in feeling there was 'some merit' in making clear the 'moral basis' that he and most Japanese had, or believed they had, for going to war. There still is some merit in the clarification. In March, Ambassador Grew had written: 'To what extent the intelligent Japanese were guilty of intellectual dishonesty, or to what extent they arrive at honest convictions from the propaganda with which they are fed, is always to me an open question.' And it is therefore worth emphasizing that by November 1941, if not long before, a very great number of intelligent Japanese people sincerely and firmly believed that their country was facing the most serious threat of its long history, and that that threat was the deliberate creation of America, Britain and Holland.

'The formidable cordon of naval and air bases which America has developed around Japan in concert with Britain, the Netherlands East Indies, Australia and Chungking constitutes a direct threat against the Japanese Empire,' said the editorial of the *Japan Times and Advertiser* on 18 November. 'If America desires no war in this part of the world, it should realize that it holds in its own hands the key to the solution of the whole situation.'

'Typical of the view-point here,' Grew complained, much more sour than before. 'It is always we who threaten; it is always we who are the potential aggressor, never Japan.'

'In Japan's funeral march of aggression,' said Britain's Ambassador Craigie, 'ambition has been the leitmotiv, fear a recurrent undertone. We should make a mistake if in our analysis of Japanese war psychology we were to leave fear out of account.'

'The main driving force,' he added, 'has been a primitive lust for power and dominion . . . I do not suggest that this primitive lust for conquest is confined to the Army; but the Army is unquestionably its spiritual home, and, but for Army influence in the State, it would never have played such a part in the shaping of Japan's destinies.'

The newspaper editorial came out in the morning; at dusk on the same day, five of Japan's largest submarines – numbers 16, 18, 20, 22 and 24 of the I-class, C(1) type – left Kure harbour. Destination: Pearl Harbor. They were large vessels, over 350 feet long at the waterline, each weighing over 2,100 tons – submerged they weighed over 3,500 tons – and capable of over 23 knots on the surface, eight knots submerged. Each carried twenty torpedoes, a 5.5-inch gun, and two 25-millimetre anti-aircraft guns; each had a crew of one hundred and one. And, for the Pearl Harbor run, each had a midget submarine fitted on deck.

As part of the war preparations, all of Japan's merchant ships were being summoned home; and, on 23 November, the British Far East Combined Bureau – or, less modestly, British intelligence – came up with a remarkable forecast. The method was simplicity itself: a graph was made with a calendar on one axis and the number of Japanese merchant ships not yet home on the other. But the deduction it produced could hardly have been more accurate: all Japanese merchant ships would have returned to Japan by the first week of December; and at that time, or shortly after, war would break out.

On 28 November the US Navy Department similarly predicted that an aggressive Japanese move would come in the next few days; but *no one could say where*. Most thought it would be the Philippines, or the Kra Isthmus which links Thailand and Malaya to Burma, or possibly Borneo. No one considered Hawaii.

On 26 November, right on schedule, the Pearl Harbor Task Force weighed anchor in Hitokapu Bay. And, as a final example of the chronic lack of Army–Navy and forces–civilian communication that plagued Japan, it is worth noting that Prime Minister Tojo, who was also the Minister of War, had not yet been told and did not know until after the war that at that moment the Task Force was on its way. Foreign Minister Togo Shigenori was equally in the dark. On 29 November at the 74th 'Liaison' Conference, he asked Nagano: 'Is there enough time left so that we can carry on diplomacy?' 'We do have enough time,' replied Nagano guardedly. 'Tell me what zero hour is,' Togo pressed him. 'Otherwise, I can't carry on diplomacy.' 'Well, then,' Nagano answered reluctantly, 'I will tell you. The zero hour is' – and for some extraordinary reason, as if they might hear him in Oahu, he whispered: '*December the eighth*' – which would be 7 December in Hawaii, the other side of the International Date Line. 'There is still time,' he finished in a normal voice, 'so you had better resort to the kind of diplomacy that will be helpful in winning the war.'

As Navy Minister in 1936 – five long years ago – Nagano had once said: 'It is for the sake of the morale and training of our forces that we make the outward pretence of some day conducting operations against America and Britain. But in reality I wish to guide the Navy towards friendly relations with those powers.' In November 1941 a disgusted Army Staff officer realized this and wrote: 'The Navy's whole attitude and preparations to date have been directed towards the simple aim of expanding itself!' And, privately, ex-Prime Minister Admiral Yonai commented sadly that, whatever happened next, the Navy had only itself to thank.

On 1 December, in a further Imperial Conference, Nagano spoke again.

'In this most serious crisis since the founding of our country,' he said, 'all of the officers and men in the task forces of the Army and Navy have extremely high morale, and are prepared to lay down their lives for their country. Once the Imperial Command is given, they will undertake the assignments. I hope Your Majesty will feel assured on this point.'

Three days afterwards, at the 75th Liaison Conference, Foreign Minister Togo informed his colleagues: 'We have time to send one last statement, but no more. If we rework this draft communication to sever diplomatic relations, send it by wire tomorrow afternoon, the 5th, and allow the 6th for translation, it will be delivered on the right day.'

To this, someone, whose name was not recorded, replied: 'The Foreign Minister can word the text on the basis of the draft. As for the time when it should be delivered to them: if it is too early, it will allow them time to get ready; on the other hand, if it is too late, there will be no point in delivering the note. At any rate, the most important thing now is to win the war.'

On 7 December, Tokyo time, Rear Admiral Ugaki Matome – Chief of Staff to Admiral Yamamoto – wrote in his diary: 'When we concluded the Tripartite Alliance and moved into Indo-China, we had already burnt the bridges behind us on our march towards the anticipated war.'

At the same time the submarine I-24 was moving forward quietly on the surface of the sea, a few miles away from Pearl Harbor. Illuminated signs were clearly visible; music was clearly audible. *Déjà vu, déjà entendu*; Port Arthur was well within living memory, a mere thirty-seven years ago.

Grew was awakened by the telephone at 7 a.m. on 8 December. He was requested to come and see Foreign Minister Togo as soon as possible. Thirty minutes later the two men were facing each other. Togo, 'grim and formal', handed Grew a thirteen-page memorandum. Its final paragraph read:

'The Japanese Government regrets to have to notify hereby the American Government that, in view of the attitude of the American Government, it cannot but consider that it is impossible to reach an agreement through further negotiations.'

Togo politely showed the Ambassador to the door; and 'not a word was said about Pearl Harbor'. The first that Grew learnt of it was from his daily newspaper.

At 7.45 a.m. Craigie's telephone rang. Again it was an invitation to see the Foreign Minister at once.

'In view of the early hour, the urgency of the message and the political situation I assumed I was being summoned to receive a declaration of war.'

None was forthcoming; he too was given a long memorandum, but 'discerned there was not a word in it about war – merely a rambling series of assertions and false accusations'. He left Togo's office and returned to the Embassy. His wife – who had the delightful name of Lady Pleasant – met him. She had just heard on the radio that war had begun.

At Chequers, the British Prime Minister's official country residence, Churchill was relaxing after dinner with Averell Harriman, and the American ambassador John G. Winant. Just after 9 p.m. on 7 December – 4 p.m. on the 7th in Washington, 11 a.m. on the 7th in Hawaii and noon of the 8th in Tokyo – Churchill switched on the wireless. The news had already begun. He was sleepy after his meal and paid little attention. Then one of his guests said he had heard something about a Japanese attack. Sawyers, the butler, confirmed it: 'It's quite true. We heard it ourselves outside.'

Wide awake, Churchill left the table, and, closely followed by Ambassador Winant, went to his office across the hall and picked up the telephone.

'In two or three minutes Mr Roosevelt came through. "Mr President, what's this about Japan?" "It's quite true," he replied. "They have attacked us at Pearl Harbor. We are all in the same boat now."

Churchill handed the telephone to Winant, who listened, 'at first saying "Good," "Good" – and then, apparently graver, "Ah!"'

Churchill took the telephone again and said to Roosevelt, 'This certainly simplifies things. God be with you.'

In the dining room once more, his American guests 'wasted no words in reproach or sorrow. In fact, one might almost have thought they had been delivered from a long pain'.

They left, and in private Churchill contemplated the future with more hope than he had dared for many months. In June 1934 his predecessor Chamberlain had said: 'We ought to know by this time that the USA will give us no understanding to resist by force any action by Japan, short of an attack on Hawaii or Honolulu.' Now it had happened; and Churchill rejoiced.

'No American,' he wrote, 'will think it wrong of me if I proclaimed that to have the United States on our side was to me the greatest joy. I could not foretell the course of events. I do not pretend to have measured accurately the martial might of Japan, but now at this very moment I knew the United States was in the war, up to the neck and in to the death. So we had won after all! . . . we should not be wiped out . . . Hitler's fate was sealed. Mussolini's fate was sealed. As for the Japanese, they would be ground to powder. All the rest was merely the proper application of overwhelming force.'

23

'The Imperial Navy takes this Territory'

On 6 December 1941, twenty-two-year-old Lee Benbrooks, a radio operator in the US Army Air Force, was promoted to sergeant. He was a native of Arkansas, and had managed to get posted to Hawaii. On the morning of Sunday 7 December he was sitting on his bunk on the third, the top, floor of the newly-built barracks at Hickam Air Field, a couple of miles south-east of Pearl Harbor. Almost all his squadron were on the base, because there had been a beer party the night before in one of the hangars. Even so, most people were up early, and by 7.30 had had breakfast. Newly-promoted Sergeant Benbrooks was contentedly sewing the extra chevron on his shirt-sleeve when he heard aircraft passing overhead. They sounded very much like SOC3s, Curtis-Rye floatplanes used by the Navy as scouts for heavy cruisers. Army planes never flew on Sundays, but Navy ones did, so there was nothing unusual in hearing engines. Nevertheless, Benbrooks and his young colleagues were all interested in aircraft, and he went to the window, with two or three others, to watch the planes go by. There were three, flying in a V-formation at about ten thousand feet. As the young men watched, they saw the aircraft go into a dive.

'This was unusual, but we really thought' – like so many others in Oahu that morning – 'that the Navy was carrying on some kind of an exercise. And so we watched these guys, and they went through a long dive and pulled out at – oh, maybe a couple of thousand feet; and a short while later we saw a sort of whitish smoke, not really very dense smoke. The general comment was, "Gee whiz, they must have awfully big spotting charges in those practice bombs", but at that point neither myself nor anyone standing at the window had any thought that there was a hostile action under way.'

The barracks window faced Pearl, but with navy buildings and dry docks in the way it was not possible actually to see the ships in the harbour. The aircraft vanished; 'and then we saw another airplane, the fourth, which came in from the West, so we had a broadside view. We thought it was a float-plane, because there was a long thing underneath the airplane which looked like a float. He came in – must have been around 500 feet, I guess – and while we watched, he dropped to an even lower altitude. And while he was out of sight, after . . . perhaps ten or fifteen seconds, we saw an enormous geyser of water, which we all knew could only have come from a torpedo exploding against the side of a ship.'

They had hardly time to register the thought before the first three aircraft reappeared 'directly over the barracks; and of course we saw the markings on the wings and on the fuselage. I can remember right now, to this day, distinctly, the sort of feeling of revulsion that I felt when I saw those big red emblems – and we knew immediately what we were doing'.

Benbrooks had a troop of one to command, his assistant radio operator Bill Hamilton. They and the others ran outside in case the barracks was bombed – 'once a thing like that starts, who knows what's going to happen?' In the street, the only cover was the edge of the sidewalk. 'I can remember lying in the street with my head flat on the ground as I could get it, and one eye was above the kerb, and I could see this guy coming across the barracks shooting. So I said to Bill, "This doesn't seem like the right place." ' They ran to the hangars a block away, where the guns were stored. The armoury was locked and no one had the key. A staff sergeant shot the lock away; Benbrooks took a machine-gun and Hamilton a can of a hundred rounds of ammunition, and together they ran down the runway to where some old B-18s were parked. 'God, it seemed to me that day it was a mile, but it was probably half a mile . . . we took off across the runway and down towards those B-18s, ran and ran, my lord, I thought I would die – in those days nobody ran for exercise like today . . . I guess we stopped and walked.' By then there seemed to be aircraft everywhere. Anti-aircraft shells were bursting 500 feet above – 'big black puffs of smoke, anti-aircraft shell fragments falling all over; fuses about the size of a cantaloupe would come down all in one piece – you could see this junk lying all over the ground.' Hamilton reeled as a fragment hit him on the head – fortunately he 'had gotten an old World War One wash-pan type helmet' from somewhere, and carried on. 'And in the midst of all this, while we were running down there, all of a sudden there appeared a [flight of] brand new B-17, D-model airplanes; these were the 28 airplanes that had come in from somewhere on the coast, and of course these guys didn't know what in the world was going on. I later talked to some of the crew – the guns were [sealed] in Cosmoline, they had no ammunition on board, and they arrived right in the middle of a shooting war! And there were these dive-bombers going all around, and the Navy was shooting at *everything* that was in the air . . .'

Benbrooks and Hamilton made it to the parked planes 'just *out* of breath, and – typical military thing – there was a gun in the rear turret, there was a gun in the nose turret, there was ammunition; we'd brought this enormous load down there and we didn't need it'.

They took a turret each, turned towards Honolulu, and as if on cue an enemy aircraft appeared, only fifty feet above the ground. 'When he was – oh, I don't know, three hundred yards away, it's hard to tell – it was always hard to estimate range really, when an aircraft was coming head on – we began firing at him.' Every fifth round of ammunition should have been a tracer, 'so you had some kind of an idea, aside from the sights, of where your fire was going'; but Benbrooks' ammunition had no tracers, 'and the ammunition that Bill had seemed to have been *all* tracers, or every other round – when he shot that gun, it was like somebody taking a garden hose, because it was just *hosing* tracers down towards that airplane.' It passed over – 'you could have hit him with a rock, he was that low' – but they never knew if they had hit him, 'because immediately behind him there was another one. The first guy was not aware, I think, until he was too close that we were shooting at him, because he never returned the fire. The second guy obviously saw the tracers . . . the vivid memories you get from a thing like this – I can see how it looked: this guy was coming up, and I guess about the time we began firing at him I remember off the wing-roots of the airplane this yellowish smoke came out, and I looked at that for a moment; then I realized – that son of a bitch is shooting at us. That's the first time I'd ever been shot at. And you can't hear anything, you just see the smoke coming out of the muzzles of the guns. He kept coming on, we kept shooting at him, he kept shooting at us' – and then on the ground below Benbrooks saw a huge crowd. 'I'll bet there was five hundred people, and they were all running, just like a big army, and for an instant I thought: if I shoot, the spent bullets that miss that guy can't help hitting somebody down there. Well, you only have a fraction of a second to make your decision, and in that instant the guy was gone . . . I guess I'll wonder till my dying day what I should have done. This guy was so close I could almost see the pilot's features; I had the gun; I was ready to shoot. What happened I really don't know: I'm sure we damaged the airplanes, but whether we damaged them enough so that they didn't get back to their carrier – in that kind of a situation one really can't tell. We asked some of the others back at the hangar later and somebody said, Oh yeah, we saw one of them burn; but who knows? I've never really placed much credence in that.'

In fact by drawing the enemy fire Benbrooks probably saved lives in the running crowd, because the Japanese was 'a dead shot – that guy had shot that old B-18 from one wing-tip to the other. A 20-mm shell had gone off about three feet behind me – they were contact fuses – when it hit the side; there was a hole about a foot in diameter right behind where I'd been. I never even *heard* it, and received no damage whatever'.

The attack ended as swiftly and unexpectedly as it had begun. Benbrooks and Hamilton remained at their self-appointed station for a long time – 'Bill and I thought the airplanes were going to keep showing up all day long, and so we'd stay until the ammunition was gone.' But there were no more. The lightning strike was over, and nothing remained but to count the cost and assess the implications. The two young men were amongst the lucky ones:

the barracks, from which they had watched the first aircraft had been burnt out; inside one particular hangar 75 or 80 men died, crushed when the construction imploded, not exploded, under a direct hit; every squadron had lost many aircraft, mostly in a peculiar way – bullets had set fire to the flares stored in the centre of the planes. The aircraft had buckled, and folded in two, but they had not burnt out; their fuel tanks had not ignited, and their engines were recoverable.

Lee Benbrooks lost all his personal possessions in the barrack blaze – all except one thing. On the lawn outside the smoking ruin he found a shirt with his name on it, and a new sergeant's chevron on the sleeve. It was the one he had been sewing after breakfast.

So, for one man, ended one of the most startling openings of any war, one of the most famous attacks in history. Benbrooks is modest about his own part, and about his account – 'it sounds in retrospect sketchy, but that's what it was like for one man watching the action from the ground.' Many others who survived that day, both Japanese and American, have recounted their memories, and Pearl Harbor must be one of the most frequently-described battles there have ever been. In 1950 Winston Churchill was already able to say 'the story has now been exhaustively recorded', and in the decades since there have been many ever more detailed moment-by-moment accounts. This, however, is the first time Lee Benbrooks has committed his memories to print.

Hickam Field had been destroyed. So had the airfields of Wheeler, Ford Island and Kaneohe; and so, in Pearl Harbor itself, had some 300,000 tons of shipping – eight battleships, three cruisers, two auxiliary craft, a minelayer and a target ship. Over 3,600 Americans were killed or wounded, including 400 buried alive in the battleship *Arizona*. For all those people, Pearl Harbor today is their memorial.

There were phrases used that day which also became famous, such as President Roosevelt's 'a date that will live in infamy'. Listening today to the archive recording the President's high-pitched sternly controlled emotion is audible, and gives his words a faintly priestlike quality, like the intonation of a creed. Then there was the comment of Secretary of State Cordell Hull when, after an unintended delay due to problems with the Japanese Embassy's translation and typing, he was presented with the memorandum which Craigie and Grew saw in Tokyo. 'In all my fifty years of public service,' Hull declared, 'I have never seen a document that was more crowded with infamous falsehoods and distortions – infamous falsehoods and distortions on a scale so huge that I never imagined until today that any government on this planet was capable of uttering them.' His rhetoric was grander than

Roosevelt's – and much less effective. The third phrase born from that day was the simplest, and it was extremely effective: 'Remember Pearl Harbor!' It is not often that a modern nation should have one single rallying war-cry, but the words became exactly that, a most potent challenge and demand.

'This surprise attack on Pearl Harbor,' wrote America's official naval historian, Admiral Samuel E. Morison, 'far from being "a strategic necessity" as the Japanese claimed even after the war, was a strategic imbecility. One can search military history in vain for an operation more fatal to the aggressor. On a tactical level Pearl Harbor was wrongly concentrated on ships rather than permanent installations and oil tanks. On a strategic level it was idiotic, on the high political level it was disastrous.'

All that was true, despite its wounded, defensive tone; but a comment made by Shigemitsu Mamoru, Japan's Foreign Minister from 1943 and after the war, was equally true, and immediately after Pearl Harbor would have appeared much more accurate:

'The secret intelligence gained by the enemy from their ability to decipher our telegrams [makes] the great success of the attack all the more outstanding, for the raiding squadron had a vast ocean to cross: a bold attack indeed. The enemy were caught napping.'

Naturally a great deal has been made of the treacherous nature of the strike at Pearl, even though that treachery turned out to be less than fully intended: as is well known, the document breaking off diplomatic talks was delayed in its delivery until after the attack had taken place. Despite that, and despite the fact that it was not a declaration of war, Americans could have counted themselves lucky to have received anything at all. The British received nothing; and a minor fact that is now generally forgotten is that Pearl was not Japan's first aggressive action in what became the Pacific War. That action took place some twenty hours before the first bombs began to drop on Pearl. About eighty miles south of Cape Cambodia, a Japanese naval force steaming towards the Kra Isthmus and bearing troops for the subsequent invasion was sighted by a British Catalina flying-boat from Singapore. The plane was promptly shot down by ten Army fighters based in French Indo-China. It is a technicality, but true to say that from that moment Britain and Japan were in a state of war; and Pearl Harbor was still peaceful.

Yet it was not until more than twenty-four hours had passed since the Catalina shooting that, at 4.15 a.m. London time on 8 December, the British Admiralty telegrammed Singapore: 'Commence hostilities at once.' And by then, roughly noon on 8 December Singapore time, Japanese troops had been on Malayan soil for twelve hours. The Philippines had suffered their first air raid, Hong Kong had been bombed; and the way was being cleared for Britain's first great tragedy in the Pacific War – the Imperial Navy's first, and completely successful, attack against its old tutor, the Royal Navy.

After sharing so much in the past, the two navies still had many attitudes in common when at last they came to blows. Amongst these, one very small one was a predilection for the letter Z. The Pearl Harbor strike had been named Operation Z; towards the end of the task force's voyage, the Z flag had been raised – the very same one which had been raised at Tsushima. It still meant the same – 'The fate of the Empire depends on this battle. Let every man do his utmost' – and it was accompanied by stirring speeches and emotional scenes. And at 5.35 p.m. on 8 December Singapore time – around midnight on the 7th Hawaiian time, when Oahu was settling in for a sleepless night, electric with rumours, and the smoke of the battleships still hung in the air – Admiral Tom Phillips set sail from Singapore with Britain's Force Z.

Churchill had had his way, despite considerable opposition within the Admiralty. There had been no definite American commitment to join Britain until forty-eight hours before the Pearl attack, and the lack had seriously cramped British Far Eastern naval strategy. Convinced that a small force was better than none, and that a small fast force could have a disproportionate effect on Japan, the British Prime Minister had bulldozed through the decision to send out HMS *Prince of Wales*, a 36,727-ton battleship, believed to be the most modern of its kind in the world. She was joined in Singapore by HMS *Repulse*, a 33,250-ton veteran of World War One, and should also have been joined by a brand-new aircraft carrier, HMS *Indomitable*. But *Indomitable*'s captain had run her on to a Jamaican reef on 3 November; no other carrier could be spared; and Force Z became an inadequate, unbalanced force. The battleships' sole escort was a group of four destroyers, one of which had to be sent back to Singapore not long after sailing. Nor were the battleships ideal for their situation: *Repulse* did not have the arms or the armour to withstand an air attack, and *Prince of Wales*, designed for use in northern waters, had very poor ventilation, which easily brought on heat exhaustion in her crew. She did at least have the reputation of being unsinkable; but many other ships have had that reputation, and they have all sunk.

On 8 December, when Force Z left Singapore, the weather in the South China Sea was squally and overcast. It was the only real protection the ships had from air attack, and twenty-four hours later it had gone; the skies were clear – mercifully, of aircraft as well as cloud. There was however some suspicion that the small fleet might have been sighted from the air, and on receiving a report of Japanese landings at Kuantan, over 150 miles south of Kota Bharu, Admiral Phillips turned his ships that way, in the fair hope that with the change of course, any chance, earlier Japanese sighting of his ships would thus prove useless. In fact there had been no earlier sighting; but, before dawn on 10 December, a submarine saw them heading south. From their base near Saigon a search party of nine Japanese aircraft took off at 6 a.m.; at 7 a.m., in nine separate waves, a total of 34 high-level bombers and 51 torpedo-bombers followed.

Force Z found nothing at Kuantan; the report had been mistaken. Nor did the Japanese Navy air fleet find Force Z – at first; they searched as far south as Singapore, until their fuel approached the half-way mark, before turning back. It was then, as Churchill wrote, that 'fortune was hard'; for quite by chance a wandering scout plane spotted the fleet, and at once began to shadow it.

'We'd been looking for the British ships for two days – we had no real idea of where they were,' said Furusawa Keiichi, an observer in one of the torpedo-bombers. On 9 December 1981 – one day before the fortieth anniversary of the battle – his memory took him back to the year when he was twenty-one, and his voice and face brought to life the intense excitement and pride that he and all his colleagues felt when they sighted the battleships far below.

'Each of our torpedo bombers was armed with a single torpedo; it weighed one ton, and had 800 kilos of explosive. There was a seven-man crew in each plane, I was observer in mine. When we spotted the ships on the 10th we'd already flown over the limit of safety, we'd used more than half our fuel and were returning to base when there they were! Two thousand metres below us, and about 20 kilometres away. They looked so small, especially the destroyers – like toys. We dived, and approached at about 160 miles an hour; we dropped our torpedoes about a kilometre from them, flying at 20 metres above the waves. I remember we went so low we seemed to be below their deck-level – I'm fairly sure their guns could not go low enough to hit us. But after dropping the torpedo we had to pull out immediately, because we were approaching so fast – my plane skimmed over the ship, just missing the mast, and we were so close I could see the sailors on deck – and I think some of them were firing rifles, or even hand-guns, at us, as well as the anti-aircraft barrage, which was very thick. We climbed to a safe altitude; I couldn't see if our torpedo hit – I think it did. But we were leaking oil somehow, and had to return to base a little before the others, and even then we didn't get all the way back. A car came out from the base to pick us up, and one of the senior officers was in it. "Well done," he said, "both the battleships are sunk." "*BANZAI! BANZAI!*" we shouted, all together – ah, so happy, so proud – we had been part of the first Imperial Navy attack on the Royal Navy; and *we had won.*'

Asked if he has any regrets, Furusawa shrugs his shoulders: 'No; I am still proud of it. It was war, and we did well. I don't think there is any reason to be sorry in peace.'

Winston Churchill was in bed, still working, 'when the telephone at my bedside rang. It was the First Sea Lord. His voice sounded odd. He gave a sort of cough and gulp, and at first I could not hear quite clearly. "Prime Minister, I have to report to you that the *Prince of Wales* and the *Repulse* have both been sunk by the Japanese – we think by aircraft. Tom Phillips is drowned." "Are you sure it's true?" "There is no doubt at all." So I put the telephone down. I was thankful to be alone. In all the war I never received a more direct shock. As I turned over and twisted in bed the full horror of the news sank in upon me. There were no British or American capital ships in the Indian Ocean or the Pacific except the American survivors of Pearl Harbor, who were hastening back to California. Over all this vast expanse of waters Japan was supreme, and we everywhere were weak and naked.'

Furusawa's pride in victory is legitimate; yet not all his colleagues shared it unequivocally then, nor do they all share it now. 840 British officers and men had died, and some of the Japanese had seen them go down. Some of the aircrews felt that somehow it had been wrong to sink such ships with such cheap but superior weapons as torpedoes; and many of them remembered and responded to the Japanese tradition which holds that an enemy who dies after fighting bravely is no longer an enemy.

'We were overjoyed when we learnt of our success,' said Flight Petty Officer 1st Class Tahira Ei, 'and yet, when we read about all those English seamen who shared the fate of their ships, we prayed for their souls.'

A Japanese colonel, Tsuji Masanobu, wrote in an official report of the action: 'It was the golden opportunity of a thousand years', and gave a harrowing description of the battle. But then, in a manner totally different to the trite cheers of victory, he suddenly added: 'Battered as the ships were, they kept on fighting in the true British naval tradition.'

In the Imperial Navy, so unlike the Army, there was still room for honour and respect for the foe. At his base near Saigon, Lieutenant Iki Haruki sent one of his men out to buy two bouquets of flowers; and then, in a gesture so unexpected it became world-famous, he flew back to the site of the battle and dropped one bouquet each over the places where the ships went down. Four Japanese planes had been lost, and, as he explains today, he wished to honour the dead of both nations, the men who now lay equal beneath the waves.

Some of the Japanese survivors do not like to talk about it at all. One such is Lieutenant Commander Miyauchi Hichiro, senior officer of the attacking force. The memory to him is like something from another life. Today he lives in Hiroshima, and runs a kindergarten. Choosing such an occupation in such a place, he has deliberately turned his back on all the Pacific War, from Japan's stunning early victories to its final shattering defeat.

But perhaps the farewell to the *Prince of Wales* and the *Repulse* should be left to another of the airmen, Uchida Manabu. A few days after the battle he confided his thoughts to his diary, using an old-fashioned Japanese word, *appare*. It is a part of Japan's written vocabulary, rarely used in speech, and rather difficult to translate. It conveys a sense of praise and surprise in a somewhat archaic manner; the best English equivalent would be something like 'gallantly done'. He wrote:

'. . . then the British battleships caught fire and began to sink; but the men did not leave their positions until the last moment. This is an honourable memory for the Royal Navy and for Anglo-Saxon history. Gallantly done, Royal Navy men! I wish you peaceful sleep, although you were my enemies.'

'If the [Anglo-Japanese] alliance ends,' the British army captain Malcolm Kennedy had written in 1921, 'it is a thousand to one that Germany will step in and form a Japan-Germany alliance . . . If that happens, there is going to be hell for the world in a few years.' It had taken twenty years, but he had won his bet.

The leaders of the Imperial Navy, however, were still far from certain that they could raise hell for the world, or even that they wanted to. In August 1939, asked if a combination of the German, Italian and Japanese navies could beat a combination of the British, French, Dutch and American navies, Admiral Yonai had stated categorically: 'We would have absolutely no chance of winning. The Japanese Navy is not *made* to fight against the United States and England, to begin with. As for the Italian and German navies, they would be no help at all.' In October 1940, Admiral Yamamoto had said: 'It is my opinion that in order to fight the United States we must be ready to challenge almost the entire world . . . I shall exert myself to the utmost but I expect to die on the deck of my flagship . . . It is indeed a perplexing situation. We have come to such a pass that our fate is inescapable.' And after the outbreak of war he said on one occasion: 'If I had been the Chief of the Navy General Staff, or the Navy Minister, I would clearly have stated that the Navy had no prospect of defeating the United States.' This was after Pearl Harbor, of course, when he might have been expected to be more optimistic; yet he deprecated the victory in a letter to a friend, not through modesty but realism, saying: 'This war will give us much trouble in the future. The fact that we have had a small success at Pearl Harbor is

Japanese battleship *HIEI*, 5 December 1939 *(Imperial War Museum MH 6159)*

Japanese battleship *TAMATO*, 30 October 1941 *(Imperial War Museum MH 6174)*

Japanese cruiser *MOGAMI (Imperial War Museum MH 6208)*

Japanese aircraft carrier *KAGA*, circa 1936 *(Imperial War Museum MH 6489)*

Japanese aircraft carrier *SORYU*, January 1938 *(Imperial War Museum MH 6490)*

Japanese aircraft carrier *HIRYU*, 6 June 1942 *(Imperial War Museum MH 6492)*

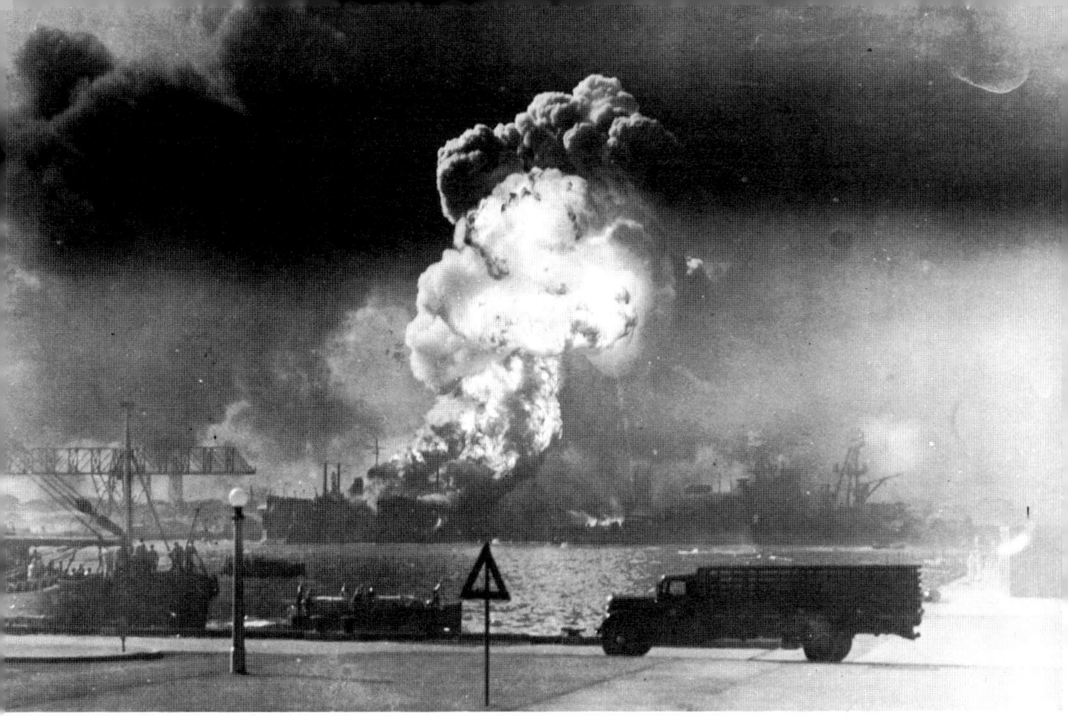

Pearl Harbor – the destroyer *Shaw* in flames: 'A bold attack indeed. The enemy were caught napping' *(Mansell Collection)*

Pearl Harbor – too little was destroyed: 'One can search military history in vain for an operation more fatal to the aggressor' *(Mansell Collection)*

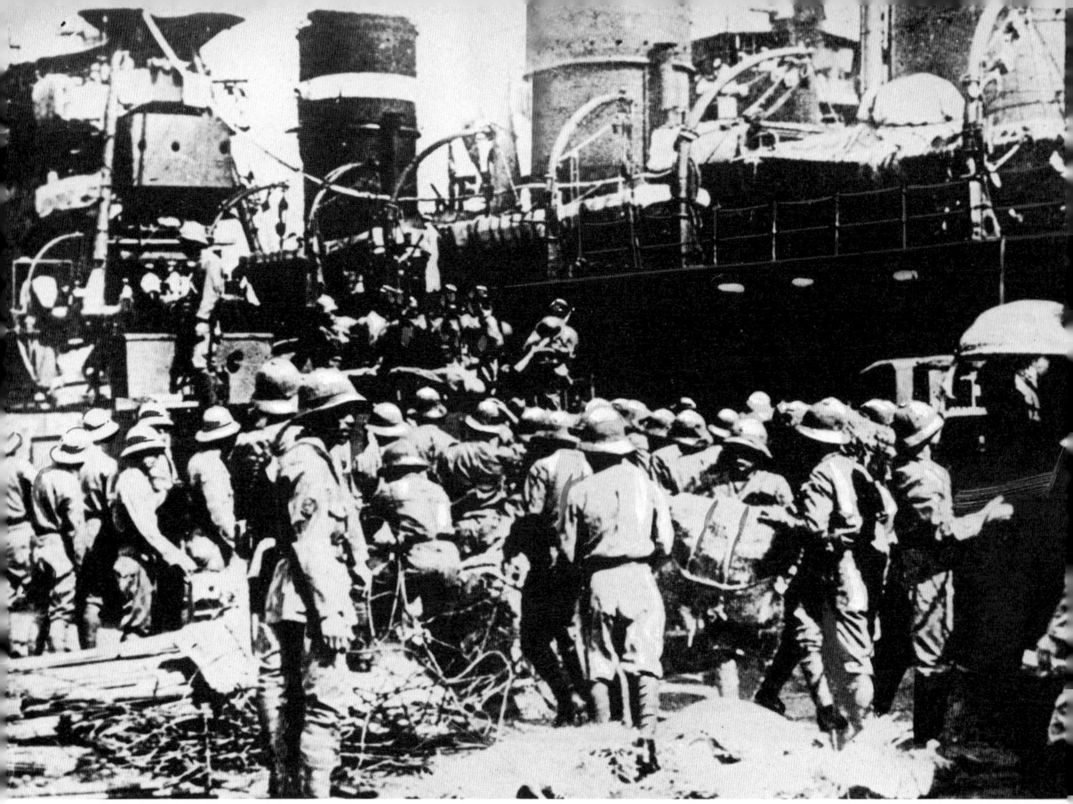

The Imperial Army embarking: 'Again we have to live uncomfortably in ships. It is disgusting just to think of it' *(Mansell Collection)*

The Imperial Army invading: 'All we have to do is attack where we are ordered to attack . . . and then die' *(Mansell Collection)*

Port Darwin 1942 – left, an Australian vessel explodes; right, a British vessel burns; foreground, an American destroyer approaches to rescue survivors: 'The great dream of invading Australia looked set to become reality' *(Mansell Collection)*

l Sea 7-8 May 1942 – the 674-foot aircraft carrier *Shoho* blazes furiously before ng. Arrows pinpoint two American aircraft *(Mansell Collection)*

Midway — the bursting of the steel balloon. Crew-members gather on the stern of a burning *Mogami*-class heavy cruiser: 'an ill-starred family' *(Mansell Collection)*

Midway — under a heavy protective anti-aircraft barrage, USS *Yorktown* lists to port, while on the horizon at extreme left, smoke marks the end of a Japanese aircraft: 'a decisive battle *had* taken place' *(Mansell Collection)*

uadalcanal – to avoid the anti-aircraft barrage, Japanese torpedo-bombers skim the surface of the sea: 'the Japanese . . . fought back with the rage of the dispossessed' *(Mansell Collection)*

Osaka 1945: 'Osaka, the heart of our national industry, would not be beyond an enemy's reach . . .' *(Mansell Collection)*

'Debris all over the country greets our eyes... Not one single thing but reminds us vividly of defeat, defeat and defeat' (*Mansell Collection*)

nothing. The fact that we have succeeded so easily has pleased people. Personally I do not think it is a good thing to whip up propaganda to encourage the nation. People should think things over and realize how serious the situation is.'

The official declaration of war had been issued in the form of an Imperial Rescript on 8 December. Paradoxically, it stated that one of Japan's war aims was 'to ensure the stability of East Asia and to contribute to world peace'. The old belief that to attack a stronger nation was to act defensively, not aggressively, still held good. As long ago as 1907 the newspaper *Tokyo Keizai Shinpo* had protested that 'suspicious nations often look at us as an aggressive people . . . they completely misunderstand us. Where can one find an instance in the two thousand years of our history when Japan started an aggressive war with another country? During the past fifty years Japan's diplomatic posture has always been defensive. It is beyond contention the recent two wars have been forced upon us and were motivated by self-defence'.

In 1916 a semi-official naval journal had corroborated this view: 'To impute aggressive motives to us is unjust. Our Fleet is not a sword but a shield; its function is not offensive but defensive . . . Our frontiers are the sea, and if we cannot defend them we shall assuredly become the prey of foreign enemies . . . be the burden what it may, the people of Japan will continue cheerfully to make sacrifices for the Navy so long as they believe it to be the one vital guarantee of their country's safety and welfare.'

And although Emperor Hirohito added a sentence of his own to the draft declaration of war – a sentence which read, 'It has been truly unavoidable and far from Our wishes that Our Empire has now been brought to cross swords with America and Britain' – nevertheless, *after* the war, General Tojo said with insistence to the Allies' tribunal: 'I believe firmly and will contend to the last that it was a war of self-defence and in no manner a violation of presently acknowledged international law.' He was hanged, even so.

At the beginning of 1942, however, such retribution was a long way off. The super-battleship *Yamato* had been completed on 16 December 1941, and, as the ultimate embodiment of the Imperial Navy's fighting spirit, and indeed of all Japan, became Admiral Yamamoto's flagship. On 29 December Hitler had sent a cheery New Year's message to Mussolini – 'Above all, Duce,' he said, 'it often seems to me that human development has only been interrupted for fifteen hundred years and is now about to resume its former character.' Presumably he meant the character of the fifth-century Attila, King of the Huns. On 18 January 1942, the spheres of influence of Germany, Italy and Japan were delineated in Berlin. Japan's section included 'the waters eastward from about 70° E. longitude to the west coast of the American continent, as well as the continent and islands – Australia, the

Netherlands East Indies, and New Zealand – which are situated in these waters'. By any standards that covered a very sizeable chunk of the world; but, in Churchill's opinion, Pearl Harbor alone meant that 'the mastery of the Pacific had passed into Japanese hands, and the strategic balance of the world was for the time being fundamentally changed'. And the Imperial Forces were swift to capitalize on the change. In 1934 Hector Bywater had foretold that 'within a fortnight after the beginning of hostilities, the United States would find herself bereft of her insular possessions in the West Pacific, and consequently without a single base for naval operations in those waters'.

It took longer than Bywater's predicted fortnight, but not a great deal longer. Over the last weeks of 1941 and the first months of 1942 the expanding ring of Japanese victory and conquest spread visibly, almost daily, over the map of south-east Asia and the chart of the west and south-west Pacific: a steel balloon, swelling outwards from the home islands of Japan, and, almost without check, pushing everything out of its way.

The day of the Royal Navy's blooding, 10 December, the Imperial Navy suffered a small, temporary setback 3,500 miles further east at the small American-owned island of Wake, roughly half-way between Taiwan and Hawaii. As a potential base for ships and aircraft, Wake was one of those islands whose position gave it a strategic importance out of all proportion to its physical size. On 10 December the light cruiser *Yubari* – completed in 1923, and instantly recognizable to the Americans from her curious two-legged smoke stack, which they thought looked like a sailor dancing a hornpipe – closed the island, escorted by six destroyers, two patrol boats and two troop transports. The American forces on the island allowed her to approach to within three miles before they opened fire. They sank two destroyers and the remainder withdrew; but the Imperial Navy learned a lesson more valuable than two destroyers, and, ever after, always preceded such attacks by heavy air raids.

But to the now official yet still unfamiliar allies, Britain, Holland and America, that small success was as swiftly extinguished as a match lit in a hurricane. On 14 December, the heavy cruisers *Myoko* and *Nachi*, along with two destroyers, supported troops landing at Luzon in the Philippines; and, in Malaya, Penang fell. Two days later landings took place at Sarawak and Brunei in Borneo; two days after that, half of Hong Kong was in Japanese hands; two days later again, the invasion of Mindanao, the second largest Philippine island, began. On 21 December, 43,000 troops started the invasion of Luzon in earnest; next day Wake was attacked again, by a fleet of destroyers, two heavy cruisers and two aircraft carriers. On 23 December the American forces on the island gave up the impossible struggle and surrendered; and, on Christmas Day, Hong Kong followed suit.

Writing home from Wake, one of the Japanese recorded his contempt and amazement: 'Extravagance and hedonism are, as you know, a part of the

American soldier, but I was astonished to see that every soldier had a crude woman's picture pinned on the walls when I went round the barracks. How can they fight the war with this kind of spirit? The annihilation of this kind of people before long is most certain.'

On 29 December the attack commenced on America's island fortress of Corregidor in the entrance to Manila Bay, south of the Bataan peninsula; and on 31 December Japanese troops entered Manila.

By 21 January 1942 the Emperor's soldiers and sailors were established throughout Malaysia, and as far south-east as the Bismarck Archipelago, where Rabaul in New Britain and Kavieng in New Ireland were taken. On 24 January the flag of the Rising Sun was raised at Balikpapan in Borneo – a major oil port, and an invaluable resource for the prosecution of war. This was exactly the kind of conquest most wanted by the Navy; and, only six days afterwards, the naval base of Amboina, in the Moluccas, fell. The Japanese Navy was within 700 miles of Australia. It had taken them just five weeks.

On 31 January the British withdrawal from Malaya to Singapore was finished; on 1 February, when America's Vice Admiral Halsey and Rear Admiral Fletcher led attacks on Japanese air bases in the Marshall Islands and Gilbert Islands, the carrier *Enterprise* was damaged by a new and particularly unpleasant form of retaliation: a suicide bomber. On 10 February a Japanese landing at Makassar in the Celebes took place; on 15 February Singapore surrendered and 70,000 Allied troops were taken prisoner.

'Replacing the White Ensign, the dazzling, fluttering Rising Sun Ensign was, indeed, an emotional sight,' said an Imperial GHQ communiqué. 'If this wasn't a symbol of the shining dawn of Great East Asia, what was it?'

The next day Allied forces withdrew from Palembang in Sumatra – another great prize, for they did not even have time to destroy the oil refinery there. By 25 February Amboina was entirely in Japanese hands; and on the 26th, actually in the Indian Ocean, an American support ship – USS *Langley* – was sunk by Japanese aircraft. More important than the loss of the vessel was the destruction of her cargo: 32 aircraft destined for Java. It was a loss that would be sorely felt; the following day, 27 February, the battle of the Java Sea took place.

The Dutch Rear Admiral Karel Doorman was in command of a motley collection of Allied ships of all countries: there was his flagship, the Dutch cruiser *De Ruyter*; the British cruiser *Exeter* and the American cruiser *Houston*; the Australian light cruiser *Perth* and the Dutch light cruiser *Java*; and ten destroyers from three countries. Their task was to seek out and repel a Japanese fleet heading to invade Java – if the invasion were successful it would complete Japan's grip on the coveted Netherlands East Indies. The size of the Imperial fleet reflected the importance of the operation: 14 destroyers, the light cruisers *Jintsu* and *Naka*, and the heavy cruisers *Nachi* and *Haguro*, all under the overall command of Admiral Tokagi Sokichi, and protecting no less than 97 transports.

After several days' fruitless search, running low on fuel and with (in Doorman's words) his men's 'exhaustion point far exceeded' – they had been at action stations for thirty-seven unbroken hours – the Japanese approach was finally reported. There was no real alternative but to give battle, and Doorman did so – a cruiser versus cruiser engagement, and the biggest surface battle since Jutland, a generation earlier. It was the British cruiser *Exeter*, scouting ahead, which sighted *Jintsu* and the first seven destroyers. It was a naked-eye contact – *Exeter* was the only Allied ship to have radar. None of the Japanese vessels had radar either, but they did have aircraft – six float planes which proved invaluable spotters. At first, to the Allied fleet, the balance seemed fairly even; but then the two heavy cruisers were seen, and the conclusion became almost inevitable. *Nachi* and *Haguro* were powerful sisters. Originally completed in 1928 and 1929, at Kure and Nagasaki respectively, they had both been modernized in 1941. Now they weighed nearly 15,000 tons each and could do almost 34 knots. Between them, apart from the aircraft, they boasted sixteen torpedo tubes, sixteen anti-aircraft guns, sixteen five-inch guns and twenty eight-inch guns. It was those guns, and the torpedoes, which tipped the balance decisively: Doorman's cruisers had only twelve eight-inchers, and the Japanese torpedoes were Long Lance – altogether there was more power, more punch and more range in the Japanese armament; and, in a series of engagements which lasted until the morning of 29 February, eleven of the fifteen Allied warships were sunk – six destroyers, and all the cruisers. All nationalities acknowledged Doorman's personal bravery; but he died with *De Ruyter*, and the invasion of Java went ahead unimpaired.

The island fell on 7 March; by 9 March the whole of the Dutch East Indies was under Japanese control. The conquest of that oil-rich territory, contemplated for so long with such wary greed, such yearning apprehension, had taken three months and one day from the initial strike at Pearl. It had been far easier than expected – perhaps too easy. But rapid conclusions were dear to the Japanese heart, and the concept of the decisive battle was central to naval emotions, fed by youthful games at Etajima and the glorious memory of Rozhdestvenski's downfall. Swift victory was an inherent part of the Imperial Naval tradition; Pearl and the succeeding months had proved that the new navy was a worthy descendant of the old. The erstwhile ally, Britain, was being fought as effectively as the ancient enemies China and Russia had been fought in their day; and few Japanese now questioned the ease of achievement, or doubted that the steel balloon could expand yet further, and engulf more than had ever been imagined in the beginning.

On 10 March troops landed at Finschhafen, New Guinea, and aircraft raided Port Moresby in Papua – little more than 300 miles from Australia.

The same day, arching eastwards from the Bismarcks, Buka in the Solomon Islands was invaded; the following day, some 3,000 miles north-west, America's General Douglas MacArthur left Luzon. In 1904 he, with his father, had observed the Japanese army at war with Russia; now, too valuable to be allowed to surrender, he became an unwilling evacuee, and swore his famous oath that one day he would return.

On 13 March Japanese troops in New Guinea were replaced by navy personnel, while the Fourth Fleet, issuing from its new base at Rabaul in New Britain, oversaw the completion of the North Solomons conquest. Ten days later, far off in the Bay of Bengal, the Andaman Islands were occupied, and on 30 March the first landing was made on Christmas Island, south of Java. The possibilities of the Indian Ocean were being explored: political unrest in India itself could be made wartime capital, and, since Vichy France was the nominal owner of Madagascar, there was every chance that Britain's ocean supply lines from the Empire could be cut – *and* that Russia's overland supply lines through Persia could be cut as well. On 31 March news came to Admiral Sir James Somerville of the Allies' India Squadron that a heavy attack on his fleet's base in Ceylon was imminent. He had 15 destroyers, eight cruisers (including two Dutch ones), five old battleships and three carriers. One of those was the *Indomitable*, which should have been around four months earlier, protecting Force Z.

Against these, from Kendari in the Celebes, Admiral Kondo Nobutake was sailing with a fleet of twenty-one warships; but, despite the smaller number of units, Kondo's fleet would easily match Somerville's. He had nine destroyers, the light cruiser *Abukuma*, the twin heavy cruisers *Tone* and *Chikuma*, four crack battleships and five aircraft carriers. The carriers were most terrible of all: their names were *Akagi*, *Soryu*, *Hiryu*, *Shokaku* and *Zuikaku*, and their crews did not need to be told that they could beat anything in the world; for they were all veterans of Pearl.

Prudently, Admiral Somerville withdrew his squadron towards a secret base in the Maldives. On 3 April, four days after his departure, Japanese aircraft bombed Mandalay. On the 4th Kondo's squadron was off Colombo. On the 5th, 200 miles south of Ceylon, and believing that Somerville was still in Colombo, Kondo launched 200 bombers, dive-bombers and fighters against the port. Twelve torpedo planes replied, all of which were shot down. The port installations were destroyed, and, south-west of the island, two British cruisers – *Cornwall* and *Dorsetshire* – were found and sunk. On the 6th the bombers began to raid India, while in the distant Admiralty Islands, north of New Guinea, Japanese troops invaded. On the 9th the American forces in Luzon surrendered; the horrors of the Bataan Death March commenced as the Imperial Army herded 76,000 men, including 12,000 Americans, north towards San Fernando; and, in the Indian Ocean, Kondo's fleet attacked Trincomalee in Ceylon, found and sank the British destroyer *Vampire*, the undefended British carrier *Hermes* and a 10,000-ton transport, while a squadron of six heavy cruisers and a light carrier under Vice Admiral Kurita Takeo entered the Bay of Bengal and sank 135,000 tons of shipping with no loss to itself.

The following day, 10 April, the Royal Navy ships in the Indian Ocean retreated north and west: the ocean lay defenceless.

'I must revert,' wrote Churchill to Roosevelt on 15 April, 'to the grave situation in the Indian Ocean arising from the fact that the Japanese have felt able to detach nearly a third of their battle fleet and half their carriers, which forces we are unable to match for several months. The consequences of this may easily be:

(a) The loss of Ceylon.
(b) Invasion of Eastern India, with incalculable internal consequences to our whole war plan, including the loss of Calcutta and of all contact with the Chinese through Burma.

But this is only the beginning. Until we are able to fight a fleet action there is no reason why the Japanese should not become the dominating factor in the Western Indian Ocean. This would result in the collapse of our whole position in the Middle East, not only because of the interruption to our convoys to the Middle East and India, but also because of the interruption to the oil supplies from Abadan, without which we cannot maintain our position either at sea or on land in the Indian Ocean area. Supplies to Russia via the Persian Gulf would also be cut. With so much of the weight of Japan thrown upon us we have more than we can bear.'

And yet there was no Japanese attack eastward. The Imperial Navy's 'Strike South' motto, ingrained over many years, seemed to prevail again: the wide wild wastes of the Indian Ocean could have been the Imperial Navy's own, bringing immense benefits to the Axis and the direst possible effects to the Allies. Secure bases in Madagascar were there for the asking; Ceylon could not have endured long. The Persian Gulf, the Red Sea and Suez would probably have succumbed, the link would have been established with Germany in Egypt and the South Caucasus, and from the Mediterranean to the Marshalls the 'unparalleled Yamato spirit' could have ruled the waves; but it did not. Instead the Imperial Navy turned again towards its old preoccupation, the islands of the west and south-west Pacific. It is easier to see crucial moments in events than in non-events, but Britain's Ambassador Craigie was right when, after the war, he said that the 'failure of the Japanese to exploit resolutely their initial advantages in these waters [the Indian Ocean] was one of the great turning-points of the war'. And Germany's military attaché in Tokyo, Kretschner, was also right when he complained after the war that 'all my urgings for closer co-operation between German and Japanese High Commands were in vain. Both Supreme Headquarters seemed to be intent on waging their own wars'.

This is scarcely surprising; despite all the protestations of mutual regard and esteem, the alliance between Japan on the one hand and Germany and Italy on the other never blossomed. There were several reasons for this, one of which Goebbels expressed in his private diary. On 27 January 1942 he wrote: 'Our position with Japan and the problems of East Asia is rather precarious, since we are uncompromising in our racial views', and three days later he added: 'The Führer profoundly regrets the heavy losses sustained by the white race in East Asia, but that isn't our fault.' And, if it were not sufficiently lunatic that Hitler preferred his sworn mortal enemies to his own allies, the Führer was also reported to have declared on 22 March that he would be pleased to send the English twenty divisions of troops, if it would help throw back the yellow men.

But it was not just the racism, which was mutual, nor the geograpical obstacles, which weakened the Axis from the start. There was the obstacle of language, which the Allies did not have to overcome; there was the obvious paradox of two nations on one side believing themselves superior to the other, or any other; and most basic of all there was the huge gulf of culture. Germany and Japan were not natural allies; they had nothing of importance in common, except opportunism. By contrast, the majority of the Allies – leaving aside Russia – had a good deal of common culture, and a common democratic method of living. It meant, quite simply, that despite all their quarrels and arguments and the rude comments they made about each other, the Allied nations all had the same objective: to preserve the democratic way of life they knew in peace, and to share the world rather than dominate it. And, because of that, they were able to perceive the European and Pacific wars as parts of a single conflict, and tackle them accordingly, whereas the Axis nations fought two almost totally separated wars.

Pearl, Churchill had seen, had fundamentally altered the world's strategic balance. On 18 April 1942 a materially small but psychologically enormous step was taken towards the restoration. It was the celebrated Doolittle raid, when Lieutenant-Colonel J. H. Doolittle of the 8th US Air Force took off with sixteen B25s from the deck of USS *Hornet*, 750 miles off Japan, zoomed in over the inviolate homeland, bombed Tokyo, Kobe, Yokohama, Nagoya and Yokosuka, and zoomed out again towards the continental coast. Physical effects were slight; mental effects were huge on both sides. The British and American Ambassadors were interned along with their staffs in their respective embassies; but, as Grew noted, 'We were all very happy and proud in the Embassy, and the British told us later that they drank toasts all day to the American fliers.' Craigie cheerfully endorsed this; the sound of the bombs, he said, was 'music'. In Tokyo, to counter Doolittle's moral blow, Japan's conquest of the island of Cebu in the Philippines was promptly announced, and the facts still bore out the morale-boosting propaganda. By 20 April, Hitler's fifty-third birthday, the Japanese were in virtually complete control of the central Philippines; and, on scores of islands from the edge of the Indian Ocean to the west Pacific, civilians read the official message of Imperial GHQ. What was happening to them was not war, but liberation.

'*NOTICE.*
1. His Imperial Majesty the Emperor of Japan, of boundless mercy, benevolence and unrivalled might in the world, has commanded His Imperial Forces to relieve the oppression and pain which law-abiding citizens have suffered under Britain and America.
2. The Imperial Japanese Navy takes this Territory, occupies it completely, and places it under military law.
3. All persons who do not raise their hats or salute when confronting officers, units, patrols or sentries of the Imperial Forces, must be dealt with as enemies.
4. The Imperial Forces respect and lovingly protect life and property of law-abiding citizens. Pursue your occupations without worry.
5. It is strictly forbidden for anyone to prejudice public peace, conceal weapons, or commit any action against our operations. Anyone breaking these regulations will be severely dealt with according to military law.'

On 28 April came the start of the assault on Mindanao; two days later, the whole of central Burma was Japanese; on 4 May alone, in the climax of the seventeen-week battle for Corregidor, sixteen thousand bombs and shells were dropped on the beleaguered island fortress; and on 5 May Japanese troops landed on the island.

But it was on that day too that the moves began which, in less than a month, would burst the steel balloon.

24

'The enemy is unaware of our presence'

Officially, the men of the Imperial Forces thought and acted like superhuman beings, performing deeds of audacity and endurance far beyond the powers of other races. The claim often came close to the truth, when even the most unwilling warriors, like Admiral Yamamoto, suppressed their convictions and gave all they had to the national cause. The image still remains firmly implanted in Japanese and Western minds of the soldier or sailor who would face death or take his own life rather than surrender. Three British survivors of the *Prince of Wales* and *Repulse* 'laughed happily', a Tokyo newspaper report noted in astonishment, 'even though they were prisoners'. The article pointed out that 'considered from a Japanese point of view, these men were very, very unfortunate; but, considered from the John Bull viewpoint, these men would probably be looked upon as being lucky'. But very privately, in their personal diaries, some men of the Imperial Forces revealed attitudes far from the official ideal.

One such was Second-Class Seaman Kamimura Tsuneya of Yokosuka Naval Barracks. From 3 January to 10 December 1941 he kept a personal journal, adding to it almost every day with comments which, had they been read by his seniors, would have earned him even more punishments than those he recorded. There was some excuse for his attitudes – he was chronically ill with what was diagnosed as 'neuritis of the ribs' – but he must have been a nightmare to his petty officers.

'I slept the whole day in the powder magazine,' he noted on 7 January. 'Just barely escaped being discovered by the deck guard. As usual I felt the pain in my chest. Can't sleep at night.'

11 January: 'Had combat drills. Could not discover cause of sickness. It still pains. My head feels heavy. I do not feel well.'

12 January: 'Borrowed book, "Imperial Navy", from friend Fukai and read. Uninteresting.'

Other entries underlined his almost permanent boredom: 'At gunnery drill we had ammunition supplying drill. Salvo firing interval is 18 seconds. Nobody can do it in time by himself. But the senior NCO unconcernedly reprimanded me for being slow. That thoughtless, noisy fellow! My shoulder has turned purple . . . Cleaned portholes in morning. Had clothing inspection in the afternoon. Assembly on deck. Was slapped twice. We had a squad party afterwards and I got drunk. Got slapped by the Section Leader . . . We had a movie but it was uninteresting . . . Got paid today, 17 yen, 20 sen. Money left over, 2 yen. Very hopeless, indeed! . . . Was reprimanded by the squad leader because I had powder on my hat. That misunderstanding fool! . . . There is no place so dirty and unpleasant as Yokosuka. In the morning we cleaned the ship's bottom. In the afternoon I didn't fall in for work, but slept . . . received punishment. This is quite frequent nowadays. Think nothing of it . . . Struck by 1st class seaman Uyehara. Today's blow was especially felt. This is the 8th one today . . . As night settled over the peaceful sea, I felt the pang of old memories. It must be my youth. I feel like drinking liquor. No money, no time. Oh what a meaningless life!'

In every sentence it was apparent that he loathed being in the Navy; but such are the feelings of many soldiers and sailors during peacetime. The first time his ship joined the Combined Fleet, he began to change his mind: 'It is a magnificent sight! We seem to overpower the South Pacific Ocean. At night we had another drill. The two submarines accompanying us present a beautiful sight.' And during the night of 19 June 1941 he 'learned that Germany and Russia are at war. For the first time since the enlistment, felt it worthwhile being in the Navy. Hope there will be a war because it will be much more exciting than getting a scolding every day'. He still did not stop complaining and misbehaving – '24 July: While smoking in the latrine, discovered by an officer of the watch and struck . . . Look at my face, my swollen cheek . . . There is no more wretched place than the streets of Yokosuka. Each time we arrive at Yokosuka there is nothing there to give us enjoyment or pleasure' – but at least he could look forward to the end of the mind-sapping boredom of routine work. One might wonder how many millions of other young men have gone to war for no better reason.

On 22 October the youthful seaman had an experience which probably altered his attitude more than any slaps or blows: he took part in a wrestling tournament, and, 'after a furious bout with my opponent Tasaka, I came out victorious. Received a writing pad as a prize. One gets a pleasant sensation from winning'. It seems he had never realized that before; and within a few weeks the change was complete. On 24 November 1941 he noted: 'Henceforth I'll write my diary in more detailed form. After all, it is a valuable record of a day gone by.'

30 November: 'We anchored at Truk at 0800 hours . . . The South Sea Islands have undergone a complete transformation into gigantic fortifications. Rows of barracks are standing. The sound of dynamite detonating can be heard throughout the islands.' 1 December: 'It was 1300 hours when I had taken the Admiral back in his launch. My 23rd year will pass into oblivion with this month.' 2 December: 'Left Truk at 0900 hours . . . today is the 5th day of preparations and dispositions have been completed. It is rumoured

that on the 6th day the Navy is to advance on a simultaneous general attack. Can it be a fact? Though I try to consider it calmly, my eyes and body reveal the state of excitement.' 3 December: 'Will it be possible for me to see my native land again? Any thoughts of leaving the Navy have vanished from my mind.' 7 December: 'In the morning, after inspection of our division was concluded, the ship's captain gave us an address and read the Imperial message. We were instructed that action would commence on 0000 hours [midnight] on the morning of the eighth. I was very excited on hearing that Japan would declare war . . . After anchoring, I drank beer and got drunk.'

It was not a bad way to go to war. Whether he did ever see his homeland again is another of those unanswered fragments; but it seems unlikely. It also seems unlikely that his seniors ever saw his secret thoughts. The diary became more sporadic; its last entry was made on 26 June 1943, with a reference to Milne Bay; and some time after that, tattered and torn, it was found by an American who sent it home. Today its translation is part of the National Archives in Washington, a minor but very human memory.

The Army also had some members whose diaries revealed the unofficial straying of their thoughts. One was Takamura Jiro, a member of an unidentified signal unit. As with Second-Class Seaman Kamimura, whether he survived the war or not is unknown, but he too kept a diary which ran from 15 December 1941 to 6 December 1942, and which finally found its way into a cardboard box in Washington. Dating his translation 30 August 1943 and heading it SECRET – BRITISH MOST SECRET, the anonymous Allied translator commented: 'This diary reveals how the human and naive reactions of some Japanese soldiers break through the crust of regimentation. However, in spite of his disgust with officialdom, the writer fought to the end.'

Takamura's diary began in Guam. Presumably he had never left his homeland before; certainly he found the tropical island idyllic.

'Coconut trees, and other trees that I do not recognize, grow in wild profusion. South Seas cities are indeed very beautiful and romantic. There is such a romantic atmosphere about a figure sitting on a stool on a wide balcony of a native hut, built on high stilts painted a pure white and in the midst of a coconut grove. Flowers of wild and gaudy colours do not seem so disagreeable here in this southern land. This village . . . is peaceful and a wonderful place in which to live. It is not very large, but the largest on the island. It does not seem possible that enemy troops were here only a few days before.'

He learnt from his Medical Officer how the Americans had planned the natural extinction of the natives by not administering satisfactory treatment for venereal disease; the small number of children and old people seemed to him to bear this out. He saw with astonishment that the natives chewed tobacco instead of smoking it; he heard with horror that the Americans had been cultivating typhus bacilli on the island; he complained at the lack of fresh vegetables; and he listened to 'a musical programme given by the natives at the public square. It was very good. Despite all, it is a wonderful thing to listen to a band of young people brought up in the American way of life'.

'Natives,' he mused to himself. 'I always thought of natives as being primitive, but their culture is not very much different from that of the Japanese . . . Probably the reason why the natives do not have a sense of nationality is that the means of earning a living is easy.'

Hong Kong fell, and Takamura took part in signal manoeuvres. 'Didn't understand a thing about signal work, and so it was uninteresting.' Tragedy in one theatre of war; tedium in another.

On 30 December 1941 American troops retired to the last prepared defence line in front of Bataan. On the Eastern Front, Russian troops began an amphibious operation against the east Crimea. In Malaya Japanese troops threatened Kuantan. In Guam, Takamura wrote: 'Can't think of this as a combat zone. Went to buy beer for the New Year . . . beer isn't considered a form of liquor here, but a beverage.'

With little to do, he was able to worry about his family; but all too soon he had to leave the island paradise and go south of the equator to New Britain. The transport convoy was escorted by navy vessels and aircraft; altogether there were over 30 ships. On 23 January 1942 a landing was made in almost pitch darkness, broken only by enemy flares and the glow of a smouldering volcano. But opposition seemed slight – 'we couldn't imagine that this was an opposed landing' – and, later that same day, he entered Rabaul.

His first impression was that 'the island was different from Guam'; and, inside a month, one of its most pernicious differences was found. 'The number of dengue patients increased all at once, but upon examination later, they were found to have tropical malaria. There have been two deaths caused by this sickness . . . Combatting malaria by taking pills and burning down the grass in the vicinity to destroy the breeding places of mosquitoes. 150 gallons of aviation gasoline was used to burn the grass. A very extravagant thing to do in view of the situation.'

On 19 February, the Nagumo Task Force – the veterans of Pearl – successfully raided Darwin in north Australia. Port installations were wrecked and twelve warships, including an American destroyer, were sunk. The great dream of invading Australia looked set to become reality, and if it did, Takamura would be part of it; but on 20 February he noted the receipt of an accurate intelligence report.

'An American Naval Fleet, including an aircraft carrier, had attacked the

Marshall Islands, and was headed towards Rabaul. Our Navy planes took off to search for the enemy and attack him. It seems that the enemy plans to deal a crushing aerial blow with over 100 planes, and to augment this with gunfire from the warships.'

This was exactly the American intention. 25 February: 'At night there was another enemy air attack, bombs dropping on the airfield and blowing up the gasoline dump and destroying four fighter planes. The enemy planes are now heavy bombers. Our planes are no match for theirs.' The enemy aircraft came from the carrier *Lexington*. 'The south airfield was attacked by enemy planes. Damage was heavy . . . One enemy recce plane flew over very early this morning, and for the first time, anti-aircraft fire brought it down . . . Received a wireless message at night from the *China Maru* [*maru* signified an auxiliary vessel] that the *Yokohama Maru* taking part in the New Guinea Operations was sunk by 40 enemy planes . . . Do not know the details of the attack, but I think that there must have been quite a number of casualties . . . At 1200 hours, two enemy planes attacked and dropped bombs . . . by the time our fighter planes took to the air, they had gone. The Navy is useless. They give an air-raid warning when enemy planes are already overhead, then they open fire in great confusion. The Fourth Fleet is useless.'

It was typical Army carping; the Japanese naval air attacks had been heavier than Takamura knew – heavy enough to prevent the Americans from dislodging the men in Rabaul. Yet Japan's New Guinea operation had to be postponed; for almost the first time, a Japanese advance did not go according to plan. Takamura was not very disappointed – when the plan was revived in late April, he wrote: 'Again we have to live uncomfortably in ships. It is disgusting just to think of it.' And, in any case, he had begun to make friends in the most unexpected quarter: amongst the prisoners of war.

'The commander of this island [Rabaul], Colonel Scanlon, was interrogated. Looked at his record . . . and was surprised at the resolute answers he made, even though he is a reserve officer. After all, if one becomes a commander, one must have considerable ability.' It was not simply a trite observation; somehow it is very easy to feel that, in comparison to one's own, the leaders of other armies and navies are bound to be less professional. Takamura found that Scanlon 'manifested the ideal that the Englishmen have of respecting appearance by wearing his service uniform and by requesting special quarters. He has altogether different ideas from the Japanese'.

Later Takamura 'borrowed a prisoner to help repair a Ford truck along with a wireless technician and five mechanics'. He 'borrowed' the same prisoners again the next day, and began to like and admire them. 'I was surprised at [their] intricate knowledge of these things, and at [their] mechanical ability . . . there is an exceedingly able telephone mechanic among the prisoners. It is interesting to watch him repair one damaged phone after another. Mechanics and wireless men among the prisoners are all excellent. They work hard with little rest. I felt sorry for them. They probably do not get much to eat . . . at least while they are here I do all I can for them . . . they put the food that is left over into empty cans and take it back to their comrades. That feeling of brotherly love is the same everywhere. Tears welled up in my eyes. I go around to see how the work is getting along. It is pretty much of a strain for me because of my weak leg, but when I think of the prisoners, I forget my leg . . . there are no mosquito nets in the prisoners' stockade, and there are a number of malaria patients. There is no medicine, they are given only aspirin tablets.'

When the time came for his 'borrowed' prisoners to be relieved by another group, Takamura 'felt sorry for them, so I sent Mochizuki to the stockade to see what could be done. It would be too bad if they had to work on road construction. I suppose they do not want to leave here because they can get vegetables and food to their heart's content here . . . If it were not for the prisoners, I would be bored'.

But, as if to remind him that he was at war, Allied planes continued their raids on Rabaul: on 18 April – the same day as the Doolittle raid – 'an enemy plane suddenly flew over low and made a direct hit on the *Komaki Maru* (8,500 tons) just when they were unloading at the pier. There was a direct hit on the No. 2 hatch, containing aviation gasoline, and a terrific explosion was followed by fire . . . the fire spread from the forward part of the ship to the stern, and at about 2000 hours, there was a terrific explosion as the 800 kilos of explosives in the stern of the ship blew up. The fire at once spread to the warehouse on the pier and burned up the crated planes within. Then it spread to the ammunition and oil in the vicinity and seemed to endanger the entire city . . .' and, amid rumours that the prisoners of war would be sent to Japan, Takamura received orders to prepare to leave Rabaul. 'Next objective is probably Port Moresby.'

Thinking he would never see them again, he wrote his last thoughts about the prisoners: 'It is a wonder that only 6 men could do so much work in little over a month's time. This is not all. Spiritually, we have gained a lot from them. They never left a job unless it was completed.'

The Port Moresby operation, delayed from February, was code-named MO. On 2 May 'those sections to be attached to the first position squads for the MO operation boarded ships today' and were promptly subjected to another Allied air raid. 'Several men were killed.' 3 May: 'preparations are completed.' 4 May: 'The *Asakasan Maru* put into port on schedule. Unloading of 1500 drums of heavy oil began immediately. The squad is to embark during tomorrow morning.' 5 May: 'Total personnel embarked by 1200 hours. Left Rabaul Harbour at 1700 hours.'

The fifth of May 1942 – to Takamura Jiro, it was just a busy, sweaty, hot tropical morning. Somewhere on shore, beyond the burnt-out warehouses, 'his prisoners went into naval custody. Somewhere on the ship, we might imagine glimpsing him, pushing others aside to make himself a space, settling for a short while, crowding the rail to watch the ship move off and the shore recede – one individual in a multitude, where each man had his own story, his own memories of home and family and battle. Most would have shared Takamura's feelings – excitement at moving on, nervousness and matter-of-fact preparation at the prospect of battle, regret at leaving a comfortable billet, nostalgia with thoughts of home, optimism over the course of the war, perhaps even anticipation of Japan's conquest of Australia, in which each of them would have a small part. But as Rabaul receded, as darkness fell and the island of New Britain vanished astern, none of them knew what else had happened that day. They were only soldiers, and good, bad or indifferent, liking their prisoners or loathing them, no one would have told them that, if they wanted to win the war, they were going in the wrong direction. Still absorbed by the goal of the Pacific, still fighting a war almost completely distinct from that of their Axis partners, the Imperial Navy was intent on breaking the America-Australia supply line. Now their long neglect of the far more vulnerable Indian Ocean presented its account to the Axis; for while Takamura was boarding his transport ship in Rabaul, a British naval squadron invaded Madagascar and took part of the island from the Vichy French. The spacious harbour of Diego Suarez rapidly became an important naval base, matched by an air base in its hinterland. In Tokyo, Craigie cheered and called the operation 'that magnificent stroke'; now there was to be no second chance of a Japanese-dominated Indian Ocean. The steel balloon could have expanded westwards indefinitely; instead it was swelling east and south-east, and was about to burst. While Takamura's ship steamed towards New Guinea – 'sailing at a terrific speed in order to catch up with the convoy that left earlier' – Imperial GHQ Naval Order No. 18 told Combined Fleet Commander-in-Chief Admiral Yamamoto to 'carry out the occupation of Midway Islands and key points in the western Aleutians'. Midway and the Aleutians were codenamed MI and AO; victory there looked a good probability, and Port Moresby, MO, looked a certainty. But all the plans were being 'purpled', read by US intelligence. In the north, AO, and the centre, MI, American defences were being prepared; in the south, MO, they were ready.

Takamura had little idea of what was going on. 'The ship is always changing its course from west to north or to the south,' he wrote on 8 May. 'Do not know where we are heading. At 1000 hours the escort fleet assembled to starboard and sailed off. According to stories, an enemy task force was discovered south-east of Samarai, and they went to attack it.'

The 'stories' were correct, and Takamura would just miss taking part in history. Samarai lies at the south-eastern tip of Papua-New Guinea; south-east of Samarai lies the Coral Sea; and, while the troop transports wondered which way to turn, the Battle of the Coral Sea was fought – history's first engagement of carriers versus carriers.

The transports had been escorted by Japan's Fourth Fleet, under Vice Admiral Takagi Takeo. Altogether this fleet included two heavy carriers, the Pearl Harbor veterans *Shokaku* and *Zuikaku*; the light carrier *Shoho*; eight cruisers; seventeen destroyers; seven submarines; three gunboats, a sea-plane transport, a minelayer and two tankers. But, waiting for them in the Coral Sea were America's 17th and 44th Task Forces. Rear Admiral Frank Fletcher commanded TF 17; TF 44 was under the British Rear Admiral J. C. Crace; and between them they had two carriers (*Lexington* and *Yorktown*), seven heavy cruisers, a light cruiser, thirteen destroyers, a seaplane support ship and two tankers.

Takamura heard an outline of what happened, not from rumours but from official communiqués: 'One aircraft carrier besides the *Saratoga*, one British warship and one American cruiser were sunk, and one American warship was seriously damaged . . . In the present operations we had one of two plans to carry out, the annihilation of the British-American fleet in the Solomons area or the carrying out of an opposed landing at Port Moresby. Since the enemy fleet had been destroyed, the operation was a success . . . we lost one destroyer, one carrier, and 37 planes. This naval victory is second only to that achieved in the Hawaii Naval Battle.'

Put like that, it sounded like a highly satisfactory outcome, even if no one had previously known that there were two alternative targets. Takamura like everyone else accepted the communiqué. But, as his transport once more picked up speed in a definite direction, he noted down his own view of things: 'We are just like decoy ships now. Four enemy heavy bombers attacked us. They dropped bombs perilously close . . . the convoy scattered, and each ship went its own way. What a sight. The anti-aircraft on our ships belched forth. It is a case of eat or be eaten. At night heard that the ship was heading back for Rabaul . . . Seems we will stay for a while.'

In fact the communiqué was less accurate than the rumours beforehand had been. The American carrier *Saratoga* had not even been in the Coral Sea – the vessel mistaken for her was a tanker, which had not been sunk, although she had been hit seven times. The *Lexington had* gone down, and *Yorktown* had been severely damaged. But the Japanese believed her to be sunk, and so it was a considerable shock to the Imperial Navy when she reappeared in later months. As for the other warships reported sunk and damaged, only one of them, a destroyer, had actually been lost. And, on the Japanese side, losses were greater than the 'one destroyer, one carrier and 37 planes' claimed. Some 70 aircraft had gone, including the majority of those from *Zuikaku*. Although the ship herself had escaped serious damage, the loss of pilots meant that until they were replaced she was effectively non-combatant; and already the Imperial Navy Air Arm was running short of fully-trained pilots. Of the other two carriers, it was true to say that only one was lost, the light *Shoho* – the first Japanese carrier sunk in the Pacific War; but the third, *Shokaku*, was so badly damaged that, after struggling home to Kure, she needed a month's repairs. In short, as a result of the Coral Sea action, not one but *three* carriers were lost to the Imperial Navy for several crucial weeks.

As with the Battle of Jutland, both sides, with some justice, claimed a victory. Physically, American losses had been greater than Japanese, and for Japan it was a tactical victory; but it was certainly an American strategic victory. The US Task Forces had not been annihilated, as the Japanese communiqués claimed; the Imperial Navy carrier strength had been badly impaired; and there never had been two alternative targets for the Japanese operation. The idea that a return to Rabaul meant naval success was a pure invention conjured out of thin air, a useful myth to cover retreat.

None of this meant anything to signalman Takamura. Back on Rabaul, after finding that 'the Navy had taken the good furniture and the refrigerator' from his 'former abode', he 'borrowed the same prisoners and had a good time talking to them . . . Had a lot of fun with the prisoners all day long. They are just like one of us . . . In China there were only lamps and candles, here everything is run by electricity. Viewed from the eyes of a "have-not" country, Japan, these things . . . are to be marvelled at. In China we were proud of our culture when compared to that of the enemy, but now, we learn from the culture of the enemy countries . . . Did we not consider it as something new, the knowledge which they considered as only a common everyday experience? There is definitely a lot for us to learn, even though we may have false pride in ourselves. To utilize the knowledge gained from them, and to lead as comrades . . . would require a great amount of effort. When we show a lacking in this effort, the fruits of all this work will be difficult to obtain.'

These private meditations of a young soldier stuck away on a distant South Sea island showed more insight and wisdom than most of the policies and projects worked out by the Supreme Command in Tokyo. Despite the total loss of *Shoho* and the temporary loss of *Shokaku* and *Zuikaku*, Naval Order No. 18 still stood: the preparations for the operation to occupy Midway and the western Aleutians were making good progress.

On 27 May 1942 – Navy Day, the thirty-seventh anniversary of Tsushima – a signal was hoisted to the masthead of the carrier *Akagi*, lying at anchor in Hashirajima Bay. 'Sortie as scheduled,' it commanded; and with slow certainty the anchors of twenty-one warships were raised. Twelve destroyers and a light cruiser; two heavy cruisers; two battleships; and four carriers, the four Pearl Harbor veterans still active. *Akagi* was the flagship, as before; and, as before, Vice Admiral Nagumo Chuichi commanded the fleet. Since

Pearl Harbor the force under his command had ranged over fifty thousand miles of sea, and everywhere it had gone, it had conquered. The occupation of Midway would be one more victory credited to this invincible group, and as they steamed towards their objective, officers read Nagumo's intelligence report: 'The enemy is unaware of our presence in this area and will remain so until after our initial attacks on the island.'

Before Pearl Harbor, the assessment would have been no more than the truth. Before Midway, it was little less than a fantasy.

PART SIX

The Tropical Twilight
1942–1945

*The six months of running wild
are over.
For Japan's navy, the rest
of World War Two is a
catalogue of defeat and disaster;
victories are rare and minor.
The super-battleships are destroyed,
and the Imperial Navy loses
almost every ship it possesses.*

25

'These bright ministers of death'

The twenty-one warships moved over the Pacific in a single line ahead. Had they been sailing ships in sight of an enemy, such a formation would have been unexceptional; for a carrier-centred fleet, however, it sounds eccentric. If an enemy *had* been in sight, it would have been a suicidal file – the ships offered each other virtually no protection. But not only could the ships see no enemy, they could not even see one another. A week out of Hashirajima they had run into a dense and apparently unending bank of fog. It began as a light sea-mist, and for a few hours the fleet had proceeded in battle order – the four carriers forming a square in the middle, the two battleships and two heavy cruisers in a larger square around them, and, surrounding the two boxes, a ring of the twelve destroyers led by the single light cruiser. But, as visibility dropped, the risk of collision grew. The ships were sailing dumb: radio silence was essential to maintain the mission's secrecy, and, as the fog thickened, flag- and light-signals slowly became useless. So, before it was too late, they moved into line ahead, each ship trailing a buoy astern for the next ship to follow. The buoys did not remain visible for long. Searchlights were turned on and directed astern, converting the fog into a white wall; from the ship ahead, a faint glow could be made out. Now they were sailing almost blind as well as dumb – radar would have revealed the invisible vessels to each other, but they had none.

Aboard his flagship *Akagi*, Admiral Nagumo must have yearned for the chance to escape the fog by changing course, or at least to reduce its dangers by dropping his speed, but he could do neither. If his force were to succeed in this strike, as it had succeeded in every other one for the past six months, not only secrecy but rigorous punctuality was imperative. And it was not only the ships under his immediate command which depended on his exact timing: north, south and west of him were other fleets whose victory, whose very survival, hinged on him. It was the largest single operation the Imperial Navy had ever undertaken; for its execution, what was reputed to be the largest armada in history had been assembled, under the personal overall command of Admiral Yamamoto. Estimates of the total number of ships involved vary wildly, from less than 200 to over 350; but the central objective of this sledgehammer collection was to take possession of the two minute islands halfway across the Pacific, close to the International Date Line, which made up the atoll of Midway. Aeons ago, some submarine earthquake or volcano had thrown up the peaks which, piercing the ocean's surface, became the Hawaiian chain; Midway's two islands, Sand and East, were among its final fragments. The atoll was six miles across, with only two square miles of dry land; if it had been forty feet lower, it would have been a submerged rock, a hazard to shipping and nothing more. But in 1942, eleven hundred miles from Pearl Harbor and thirty-nine feet above sea-level at its highest point, Midway was the most westerly possession of the United States still in American hands; and that gave the barren little outcrops a strategic value out of any proportion to their physical size.

Possessing Midway, Japan could attack Hawaii easily; could threaten American's West Coast; could dominate the central as well as the west Pacific, crack American communication lines to the East, and – in Yamamoto's now dearest wish, the one move he calculated could bring a final Japanese victory in this Pacific war – could draw out the United States fleet for the ultimate showdown, the decisive battle on which all Imperial Naval doctrine was based.

No war has been less aptly named than that of the Pacific; but few islands have been better named than Midway, and still fewer battles. The rigorously-educated Admirals Nagumo and Yamamoto, and the members of Imperial GHQ may have read the dramatic tragedies of ancient Greece; yet if they had, they did not apply those unities to themselves. But any one of the Greek tragedians given the plot of Midway would have instantly recognized its two fundamental qualities, long known in Athens but discounted and ignored in Tokyo – hubris and nemesis: overwhelming pride and confidence, leading to cataclysmic downfall. Afterwards – too late – the Imperial Navy and the Japanese nation recognized this mortal weakness, and called it the victory disease. The phrase has become a proverb, and, over-used as they are, proverbs express a culture's broad bases. The Anglo-Saxons, with their cultures founded on Greece and Rome, had known for centuries that pride comes before a fall. After the war against the Chinese, after Port Arthur and Tsushima, a light burden in the First World War and swift and easy victories in the Second, the old wisdom of hubris and nemesis was something Japan had forgotten, or had yet to learn.

The trouble was that nations, like individuals, need to be defeated, or suffer a severe setback, at least once – and to remember that setback – in order to remain more or less level-headed; and the Japanese had had no real setbacks for a very long time. The pilots of the Nagumo Force in particular had never experienced a collective defeat, and as their ships steamed through the fog they were thoroughly optimistic and full of confidence. Aboard ship they had few responsibilities; their duties lay in the air, and in transit from the homeland to the scene of their next battle they had only to remember their past to be ready for the future; and they were always ready. Even Admiral Nagumo, who, just before the Pearl Harbor strike, had appeared morose and nervous, now seemed to share some of the confidence. It was his personal misfortune to be very much in the wrong job commanding carriers – he was a torpedo expert, and due to the vagaries of the Imperial Navy's system of promotion (strictly through seniority and performance at Etajima rather than through aptitude or ability) Nagumo had been given his command, although he knew little about aerial warfare. That his Force had been so successful in the six months since Pearl was more a tribute to the pilots' ability and the lack of opposition than to his own skill. He had succeeded through the simple, and to him natural, method of doing exactly what his orders stipulated, and by taking advice from his two ace pilots, Genda Minoru and Fuchida Mitsuo; and, fortunately, both advice and orders had been good. After months of uninterrupted victory, he could legitimately feel he had grasped a good deal of the necessary knowledge, and that he could trust advice and orders. But, as his ships surged on through the unrelenting fog, any doubts he may have felt were well-founded. His advisors, Fuchida and Genda, were with him, but both were ill; and, for once, the orders from Yamamoto were inadequate. They were so precise that paradoxically they were ambiguous; and they left open the unwelcome possibility that Nagumo might have to take a serious decision on his own responsibility.

Broadly speaking, the Japanese forces involved in the operation were divided into four branches. Approaching Midway from the south-west were a host of transports, bearing some 5,000 troops for the invasion of the islands. These would land when the Nagumo Force had pulverized any American defences. Far to the north other groups of ships would perform a diversionary attack on the Aleutians; and coming in behind the Nagumo Force was Admiral Yamamoto with the fleet's Main Body. Centred around the magnificent sister ships *Yamato* and *Musashi*, Yamamoto's plan anticipated that the Main Body, with himself in personal command, would administer the final *coup de grâce* to the American navy, as Togo had done to the Russians in 1905.

Looking at the plan on paper, Yamamoto might well have thought the same as Nelson before Trafalgar: 'It was singular – it was simple! It must succeed.' In theory the aphorism was appropriate; but the reality was neither singular nor simple, but multiple and complex. The enormous forces at Yamamoto's disposal were scattered far and wide, and a successful outcome to the grand strategy depended on their clock-work co-ordination, which in turn depended on the assumption that the American fleet would do just what it was expected to do. Starting from the premise that the enemy had no idea of the imminent storm, it followed that Midway would be only lightly defended. Nagumo would subdue the island and troops would invade while the northern force attacked the Aleutians; torn between two fronts, the US navy would sortie from Pearl and divide, whereupon Nagumo would circle round and come between the enemy and his base, while Yamamoto's Main Body would close the trap and annihilate. As Admiral Chester Nimitz, Commander-in-Chief of the US Pacific Fleet, said later, 'There was nothing petty in Japanese planning.'

With his ruddy complexion, white hair and piercing blue eyes, Nimitz looked like the American flag come to life. His approach to the coming battle was, essentially, as direct as Yamamoto's was complicated. 'You will be governed by the principle of calculated risk,' he told his tactical commanders, Rear Admirals Frank Fletcher and Raymond Spruance. 'This means the avoidance of exposure of your force to attack by superior enemy forces without good prospects of inflicting greater damage on the enemy.' In other words, wait for the chance, and when it came, go in and knock them on the head. Nimitz's attitude had a lot more of 'the Nelson touch' than had Yamamoto's: 'The business of an English Commander-in-Chief,' said Nelson, was 'first to bring an enemy's fleet to battle on the most advantageous terms to himself . . . and secondly to continue them there, without separating, until the business is decided . . . In case Signals can neither be seen nor perfectly understood, no Captain can do very wrong if he places his ship alongside that of an Enemy.' And, perhaps above all, both Nelson and Nimitz allowed for something which Yamamoto's plan simply did not include. The English admiral's words could have been just as aptly said by the American: 'Something must be left to chance; nothing is sure in a sea fight beyond all others. Shot will carry away the masts and yards of friends as well as foes; but I look with confidence to a Victory before the Van of the Enemy could succour their Rear.'

No one today could truthfully claim to know Yamamoto's innermost thoughts at that time; and this is a pity, because, able man though he was, his Midway plan was studded with inconsistencies. It gave no thought to the chance of something going wrong with its timetable. It gave no contingency arrangement to cover circumstances other than those anticipated. It assumed that Japanese intelligence was accurate and American intelligence deficient. With relatively little immediate surface assistance, it placed Nagumo's carriers in a potentially very vulnerable position, and, in the intended destruction of the American fleet, it put the emphasis on the super-battleships' surface power. This was especially uncharacteristic of Yamamoto, renowned as a believer in naval air. All this is puzzling, but stranger still was the way in which the war-games testing the operation were conducted: only eight years previously, Hector Bywater had stressed that 'naval manoeuvres are invariably conducted with as much realism as possible, and the umpires take immense pains to reach an accurate decision on every point, however insignificant'. In the first four days of May, table-top manoeuvres aboard *Yamato* had attempted to determine the elements of chance and probability in the operation; but, when the Red team, representing the American fleet, caught Nagumo's Blue team by surprise and 'sank' two of his carriers, the hitherto scrupulously-observed rules suddenly went by the board. As if the very idea of such a loss was inadmissible, one of the carriers was allowed to pop up again in the next stage of the game, miraculously raised from the sea-bed and fighting fit.

Yamamoto had the reputation of a gambler prepared to risk high odds; yet it was unlike him to set up a game with dice loaded against him. For some of these inconsistencies there are partial explanations, of which the most circumstantial – but nonetheless the most cogent – is tradition: the division of forces, the pincer movement, the envelopment, were all long-standing elements of Japanese naval thought. Similarly, despite Yamamoto's own convictions about air-power, despite Pearl and subsequent victories, the all-big-gun lobby was still strong in the Imperial Navy. To this emotional allegiance, the mere existence of *Yamato* and *Musashi* lent immeasurable weight, far beyond the ability of any one man or minority to overturn. So, in his arrangement of forces, Yamamoto seems to have been trapped by tradition; and, ironically, he himself had released his enemies from the same trap. The fortunate absence of the American carriers on 7 December had forced the US Navy willy-nilly over to the side of air-power development – a position which the Japanese admiral had long and earnestly desired for his own navy, and which he would never have the opportunity to realize.

But, if tradition partially dictated Yamamoto's distribution of his ships, there was no tradition to explain his over-ready acceptance of favourable intelligence reports. When the Main Body left the Inland Sea, it was observed – and *knew* it was observed – by at least two American submarines, and the following day learned from intercepts of Allied radio messages that there must be at least a dozen other shadowing spies; yet even that did not seem to dent the Admiral's certainty that the Americans knew nothing of what was going on.

In fact they knew almost everything – or, at least, almost everything they needed to know: the size, directions and probable dates of the movements of the different forces moving eastwards from Japan. Only a very few senior US Navy officers were aware that a certain cellar in Pearl Harbor housed their own top-secret Combat Intelligence Unit; but in that cellar, working under Commander Joseph Rochefort, was a team of expert code-breakers. With a combination of inspiration and sheer toil they were steadily ploughing through the Imperial Navy's radio-broadcast orders, instructions, questions and answers, building up a picture of Yamamoto's intentions. Today, perhaps nothing brings home more clearly the extent and effectiveness of this intelligence drive than the enormous collections in Washington's National Archives. Eventually the Americans knew almost as much of what

Yamamoto was going to do as he did himself; for instance, document number SRN 000217 records a message dated 26 April 1942 from the Second Fleet to the Works Bureau in Tokyo:

'The following charts are requested for delivery by middle of May for the use of this command's headquarters and ships under this command: charts of . . . and . . . west of 140° West, east of 65°' – the translator added, 'Seems like it should be 165°; possible that the hundred is supplied or not as needed – south of 61° North and north of 50° North.'

All that was necessary was to glance at an atlas. The section requested covered the Gulf of Alaska, part of the Alaskan coast, and the eastern Aleutians. Few intercepts were as clear as that, however. AL, AO, AOB and AF were all coded place-names that appeared again and again. The Combat Intelligence Unit knew that A stood for the Pacific; AL, AO and AOB were parts of the Aleutians, and on the evidence of SRN 000217 many believed that the major part of the Japanese offensive was going to fall on Alaska, or even the West Coast. It was Commander Rochefort who discovered the identity of AF, in an episode whose simplicity made it part of the legend of US Naval intelligence – the celebrated 'fresh water' message.

Personally convinced that AF was Midway, and that the atoll was the prime objective of the coming Japanese offensive, Rochefort persuaded Admiral Nimitz to test his conviction. The method was an elementary intelligence snare: a message was broadcast from Midway in plain language, not in code, stating that the garrison's fresh-water plant had broken down and that a serious shortage of drinking water was developing. After the broadcast, Rochefort sat back and waited; and, sure enough, two days later his unit intercepted an Imperial naval report. AF, it said, was running short of fresh water. Rochefort's belief was confirmed, and on 14 May – thirteen days before the Nagumo Force weighed anchor from Hashirajima – Admiral Nimitz began preparations to oppose invasion.

It was certainly astonishingly lax of the Japanese to fall for such a ploy; but laxity was one more symptom of hubris, the victory disease. The incident confirmed the Imperial Navy's faith in its own security and the secrecy of the Midway operation. It also gives credit to the assertion that Yamamoto's seemingly reckless planning – planning that took no heed of unfavourable intelligence and disregarding the possibility of ill luck – was based on a desperate need to believe in victory. This time it really was all or nothing, and anything less than total success at Midway would condemn Japan to the long-drawn-out war he had sought to avoid. Playing a game he had not wanted to join, knowing the rules and the likelihood of loss, a gambler's faith in the winning streak allowed the admiral to play on into double-or-quits, staking all he had won on the turn of a single card.

There is much validity in that interpretation; but it misses something out, something revealed in the newly-released documents at the National Archives. In mid-November 1941, members of the Japanese Embassy in Washington had travelled by flying-boat to Guam, Hawaii, Midway and Wake for the purposes of assessing American defences. On 18 November they sent their findings in a report entitled 'The State of American Alert' to the Navy Vice Minister and the Vice Chief of the Naval General Staff in Tokyo. Intercepted by American intelligence, the report now rests in Washington, numbered SRNA 000175.

'In Guam and Hawaii,' they said, 'no special precautions were taken in regard to passengers. At Midway and Wake curtains were drawn over the windows of the plane before landing on the water, and over the windows of the boat in which we went ashore.'

They were not really able to do very much; they could walk around, but not entirely freely. 'The passengers were not permitted to leave the premises of the hotel, which was built at a place where one could see only part of the sea.' They managed to go out that evening, and 'went to the Marine barracks, but since it was night, and raining, we could not see anything along the way'. They could only guess at building operations; they could only hear coastal battery practice, and saw some anti-aircraft firing practice. All in all it was a pretty futile attempt at reconnaissance; but in their paragraph 4 (c) they recorded one definite point worth noting:

'We noticed the lack of pure water on Wake and Midway. For drinking water, filtered fresh water was used; for miscellaneous purposes, sea-water was used.'

So Rochefort had not been shooting entirely in the dark. He and his unit were already aware that the Japanese knew very little about Midway, and that one of the few things they did know was that the islands lacked 'pure water'. To use that piece of information for his snare broadcast was not just serendipity; and, when the Japanese swallowed the bait, it was not just gullibility, but because Rochefort had sent out the one message about Midway which they knew could easily be true.

'The enemy is expected to attempt the capture of Midway in the near future,' said Nimitz's Operation Plan No. 29-42 on 27 May. 'For this purpose it is believed that the enemy will employ approximately the following: 2–4 fast battleships; 4–5 carriers; 8–9 heavy cruisers; 16–24 destroyers; 8–12 submarines; a landing force with sea-plane tenders'. Thanks to Rochefort and his colleagues, here was a good assessment of the opposition; but it underestimated some sections considerably. The actual numbers of warships mustered against Midway – excluding the Aleutians force – totalled four heavy carriers and two light ones; seven battleships; twelve heavy and light cruisers; sixteen submarines; and 46 destroyers. In only one class was there a slight American preponderance: Nimitz could gather 19 submarines. But, for all the rest, the total available to him was lower in every class – three carriers, eight cruisers, and only 19 destroyers. On the face of it, Yamamoto's gamble was still a fair risk.

The Nagumo Force broke out of the fog at dawn on 4 June. They had navigated through it successfully for six hundred miles; now their target lay another six hundred miles ahead. At one point in the all-concealing murk the admiral had had to alter course, and with lights and flags useless had reluctantly authorized a brief short-range transmission. It was his first departure from orders, and he did not like it; despite reassurances from his officers, he had a needling suspicion that the two words – 'Course 125' – could have been picked up by enemy eavesdroppers. In fact, by some freak of weather, it *had* been overheard by the Main Body's flagship *Yamato*, four hundred miles further back. But it never reached American ears, and to the Commander-in-Chief, Admiral Yamamoto, the unscheduled transmission was good news – the Force was on schedule.

Six hundred miles south-west of Nagumo, the Transport Group, carrying the invasion troops, was also on schedule. During the first half of that morning – 3 June by American dates, west of the International Date Line – the Nagumo Force, the Transport Group, and Midway atoll itself formed an almost perfect equilateral triangle, a triangle that slowly grew smaller and smaller as the three points converged.

In the welcome freshness of the morning light, Nagumo's ships took up their battle order once again, the carriers four-square inside their protective screens. The Admiral gave his estimate of the situation: 'It is assumed that there are no enemy carriers in the waters adjacent to Midway.' By 'the waters adjacent to Midway' he would have meant a circle with a radius of a thousand miles or so; but, at that time, the three American carriers of Task Forces 16 and 17 were a trifling 300 miles from the atoll. Cordons of Japanese submarines should have spotted them as they left Pearl, and the submarines were backed up by a flying-boat reconnaissance team based at French Frigate Shoals, halfway between Hawaii and Midway. Nagumo expected to receive warning from these observers of any early American sortie. Nothing had come through from them or from far-distant Yamamoto, and so Nagumo could only conclude that all was going well, indeed superbly well, with the ambitious enterprise.

But the submarines had been delayed leaving Japan, and took up their positions two days late. There they stayed until it was all over, staring hopefully towards Hawaii – the wrong direction: the American Task Forces had already passed by, and the submarines had not seen them at all. And

Operation K, the flying-boat reconnaissance at French Frigate Shoals, was cancelled before it began, for the Americans had got there first. Thus, there was no effective Japanese surveillance of the Hawaii-Midway sealanes; but there was very effective American surveillance of all the seas around the atoll. Just a few hours after Nagumo emerged from the fog, land-based aircraft from Midway located the Transport Group, looking so impressively large that at first it was mistaken for the Main Body. Before the end of the day other aircraft had followed the sighting and attacked; Yamamoto, receiving the news, was forced to conclude that at least part of his plan was discovered; and yet none of this information was passed to Nagumo. With an agreeable sense of present security and future victory, his Force steamed on at 24 knots, preparing to deliver its attack. The moment of launch for the first aircraft was fast approaching.

By Nagumo's calendar it was 0430 on 5 June when the First Air Striking Force took off. Conditions were ideal: calm sea, clear sky, a light south-easterly breeze. It took only a quarter of an hour to launch 108 planes – 36 level bombers, 36 dive-bombers and a fighter escort of 36 Zeros. Ninety-three aircraft were kept aboard the carriers, just in case any enemy ships should appear, despite all the favourable indications; and, as a check that the surrounding sea actually was as empty as it looked, a search mission of seven float-planes was flown off at the same time as the Striking Force. But only three got off promptly – those from the carriers *Akagi* and *Kaga* and battleship *Haruna*. The heavy cruisers *Tone* and *Chikuma* sent two planes each, but *Chikuma*'s were delayed by engine trouble in one, while on *Tone* it was suddenly found that the launching catapult was malfunctioning. 'Luckily for us!' said the US Navy's historian Samuel Morison. The belated search-planes wasted half an hour, an apparently minor delay; but those thirty minutes turned out to be an invaluable gift to the Americans, and one of the last they would need.

For just over an hour, as the sky slowly lightened, the First Air Striking Force roared towards Midway; and far above them, completely undetected, a US flying-boat shadowed them. Its warning was received on the atoll, and at about 0550 ground radar on Midway made contact with the approaching enemy. Instantly the aircraft on the island began taking off; and there were not sixty as Nagumo still believed, but 115.

The battle over Midway lasted for twenty-five minutes, with more than a ton of bombs falling on the islands every minute. Fuel storage tanks blazed up; hangars were destroyed; the airstrip was damaged and 24 people on the ground were killed. But this was not the total obliteration called for by Yamamoto's plan, and at 0700 Nagumo received a message from the leader of the Striking Force: 'There is need for a second attack.' But there was never going to be a second chance.

At 0710 the first wave of American counter-attackers zoomed in at

Nagumo's ships – ten torpedo-bombers. Not one of them scored a hit, and only two survived. Yet the retaliation had begun, and it showed all too clearly that Midway was not subdued. At 0715 Nagumo gave the order to make ready for a second attack; and on that decision the battle hinged.

The 93 reserve planes were armed with torpedoes, ready to repel and sink the ships that were expected to rally to Midway's aid. Now, for a land attack, they had to be taken down from the flight-deck to the hangar-deck, their torpedoes had to be taken off and replaced with bombs, and the planes had then to be returned to the flight-deck. Altogether it was likely to take an hour of hard work, and it had no more than begun when, at 0728, the fatefully-delayed search-plane from *Tone* radioed: 'Ten ships, apparently enemy, sighted in position bearing 10° distance 240 miles from Midway. Course 150°, speed over 20 knots.' If the plane had got off punctually, or if her pilot's message had been clearer, the 93 reserves would have been ready and waiting. Now Nagumo, the torpedo expert in charge of Japan's crack carrier squadron, had to make a fast, vital decision: to continue rearming with bombs and carry out a second attack on Midway, or to reverse his previous order, have the torpedoes replaced, and hit the enemy ships. Yamamoto's tight schedule demanded pre-invasion obliteration of land forces on Midway; it also demanded an engagement, the long-awaited decisive battle, with the American fleet. Nagumo had always feared the enemy ships might appear ahead of schedule; now he knew for certain that his nightmare was coming true, and that a wrong decision could spell disaster for the operation, and even for the Combined Fleet. Any commander in wartime faces such moments and so it is possible to feel sympathy for the unfortunate Nagumo: his training and expertise was for another branch of the service, and he should never have been placed in command of *Akagi*.

But there was no time for idle reflection: much depended on the nature of those ten ships. Urgently, the scout was asked to be more explicit, and replied only that the enemy had changed course. Asked again, the answer came back: 'Enemy ships are five cruisers and five destroyers.' Relief flooded *Akagi*'s bridge – cruisers and destroyers could be picked off at leisure. Eleven more minutes passed and the rearming was nearing completion. A second American air attack of sixteen glide-bombers had been beaten off – eight of the machines were shot down, and six of the eight which returned to Midway were irreparably damaged. A third attack, by fifteen high-level B-17 Flying Fortresses, dropped 58 tons of bombs from 20,000 feet without a single hit on the fast-manoeuvring vessels below; then at 0820 three things happened at once. The fourth American attack wave droned in – eleven slow-speed Vindicator bombers, two of which were shot down. At the same moment, to the astonishment of everyone – including its captain – an American submarine surfaced right in the middle of the fleet; and also at the same moment the scout-plane radioed a new message: 'Enemy is accompanied by what appears to be a carrier.'

Minutes later came another shock from the scout: 'Two additional enemy ships sighted, apparently cruisers.' Whatever the exact composition of this force, by then it was certain that it was bound to contain a carrier; and it was 200 miles away, almost within the range of Nagumo's ships. And they were almost within its range too.

The submarine stayed on the surface long enough to fire one torpedo, which missed, then hurriedly dived, followed by an avalanche of depth charges. A destroyer, *Arashi*, was detailed to hunt and kill, but compared with the now undoubted presence of an American carrier, the submarine was a minor irritation. The change of armament on the reserve planes, from torpedoes to bombs, had to be reversed. Down they went to the hangar again; and just about then a screening destroyer signalled that it had sighted over a hundred aircraft approaching. After a few moments of frantic barrage, someone realized that the aircraft were their own First Air Striking Force returning from the atoll. Some had been damaged over Midway; all were low on fuel and needed to land as soon as possible. With many aircraft aboard wrongly armed, many others above virtually unarmed and still to land safely, and an enemy carrier within striking range, Admiral Nagumo could have been forgiven for feeling that things were getting out of hand. By 0905 the recovery of the First Air Striking Force was still incomplete, but the agitated Admiral had made up his mind: he would go for the carrier. 'We plan to contact and destroy the enemy Task Force,' he signalled, and ordered a 90° change of course. At 0917, recovery complete, the change was made. Hangars and decks were littered with planes being refuelled and rearmed, and in their haste the crews simply stacked bombs anywhere; and in the midst of this chaos, with the carriers excruciatingly vulnerable, another wave of fifteen American torpedo bombers appeared. But they had no fighter cover – somewhere the two groups had lost each other – and every one of the fifteen planes was shot down, with only one man out of thirty surviving. Hard on their heels came yet another wave, fourteen this time, also unprotected; ten were shot down, and none scored a hit. Then thirteen more, with six fighters – all the fighters fell, and six of the thirteen torpedo bombers. Of all the dozens of American aircraft lost, not one had damaged the Japanese ships; but the wave on wave of torpedo bombers had had two unexpected consequences – by forcing the ships to manoeuvre constantly, no additional aircraft had been flown off the carriers, and the Zeros that were in the air were all low down near the water. And, at the same time as the Zeros were beating off the torpedo bombers, the Americans were given the one stroke of luck they needed – the chance which in the space of six minutes, turned the battle for them from a slow defeat into one of the most spectacular naval victories ever known.

Nagumo's 90° change of course had confused and disoriented some of the waves of attacking aircraft. One group of 35 bombers, with fighter cover, missed the Japanese fleet entirely, but extended its search for so long that the aircraft were unable to return to their home carrier, *Hornet*, and had either to ditch in the sea, land at Midway, or – in the case of two which ran out of fuel a moment too soon – splash down in the atoll's lagoon. Another group, a double squadron of 37 Dauntless dive-bombers from the carrier *Enterprise*, was also wandering around above an empty ocean. Like the Japanese aircraft which had sunk the *Prince of Wales* and *Repulse* seven long months ago, these American planes were already over their safe limit of fuel endurance when, 19,000 feet below, at 0955, they spotted the wake of a single ship. It was the destroyer *Arashi*, calling off the fruitless hunt for the submarine which had surfaced in the middle of the Nagumo Force, and now making full speed directly back to join the pack. Even though he had no idea why a solitary ship should be down below, the squadron leader, Lieutenant-Commander Clarence McClusky, immediately decided it was obvious where she was heading. Equally obvious was the risk that all his planes might run out of gas if they gave chase. But there was a chance of success, and McClusky went for it.

And, in a few minutes, there they were – not one lone destroyer, but the whole Nagumo Force, the victors of Pearl and Trincomalee and all the other battles, now scattered by rapid manoeuvres, a loosely-formed unit sprinkled over the ocean, their mutual gun protection reduced, the screening Zeros close down by the water, the flight-decks cluttered with aircraft and fuel-hoses, the invisible hangar decks littered with bombs. McClusky turned his aircraft almost onto its nose and led his squadron into a screaming 70° dive, their engines hurtling them down at 280 knots. Five or ten minutes more and the first freshly-fuelled Zeros would have been taking off – their engines were warming up, the carriers were turning into the wind, and aboard *Akagi*, with Nagumo gazing down from the bridge, the Air Officer had just given the signal to commence launch. At that moment the klaxons whooped out a warning – for many sailors and airmen it was the last sound they heard on earth. Automatically they glanced upward, saw the plummeting silhouettes, registered the black shapes that fell almost lazily from their wings, watched for long fractions of a slow-motion second the bombs floating gentle and sinister in the bright Pacific sunshine – then came their shrill shrieking wail, the snap back to reality.

Sailors on every ship fell to the deck; *Akagi* and *Kaga* shook with crashing explosions; and, even as McClusky's men flashed over and past, another squadron – seventeen dive-bombers from the carrier *Yorktown*, ghost survivor of the Coral Sea – plunged in towards *Soryu*. The *Enterprise* pilots had made six direct hits, four on *Kaga*, two on *Akagi* – the *Yorktown* men, under Lieutenant Commander Maxwell Leslie, hit *Soryu* three times; and every ship became an instant volcano, as aircraft blazed, fuel-tanks exploded, and the carelessly-unloaded bombs blew up. It was the sound and sight of hell – and then suddenly, unexpectedly, as startling as the uproar, there came a lull: the Americans – 'these bright ministers of death', as Morison called them – were gone, the guns had stopped; and, on the ships, those who had survived could see what was left.

Amidships on *Agaki*'s flight deck, just astern of the elevator, there was an enormous void. The elevator itself hung twisted in the hole. The second bomb had hit the flight deck port side – another gaping emptiness, pouring smoke and flame. Charred and scorched bodies, living and dead, lay on all sides, everywhere metal plates were wrenched out of shape, and under the feet of those who could move and run the body of the ship herself heaved with internal explosions as fire reached the magazines. Topside, the flaring planes ignited ammunition in machine-guns and anti-aircraft guns, and in a final macabre slaughter, unmanned, undirected, the thump and rattle of artillery began again, as the guns brought unintentional death to those they should have protected. On *Kaga* and *Soryu* the scene was similar; on all three ships even the paint was burning, so that the very metal seemed on fire; and on the bridge of *Akagi*, in rage and deep shock, Admiral Nagumo refused to move.

Admiral Wenneker sent a telegram to his superiors at home. '9 June 1942 – Kriegsmarine Berlin – (From: Tokyo) – 1.95 SECRET – (To: Berlin) – Jap Navy reports the following: 1) Own losses at Midway: One large carrier sunk, 2 badly damaged; American losses: 2 carriers sunk. 2) Several of the Aleutian Islands were occupied.'

The day before he had telegrammed a complaint that 'it has been impossible to get any details on the Midway battle from the Jap Navy. The Army maintains that the landings were successful'. He might have been grateful for the news he received on 9 June; as he must have guessed, it was wrong, but it was closer to the truth than the information publicly released in Japan. After trying to get confirmation, he reported on 10 June that:

'The Jap Navy has remained stubbornly silent on the subject of the strategy underlying the Battle of Midway. The following can be assembled from various utterances: the Jap Fleet with transports assembled at the Marshall Islands with the intention of landing on Midway. The approach was reported prematurely by American subs and the attack was accordingly interrupted. The American pilots were tenacious beyond expectation.'

On the same day, signalman Takamura Jiro in Rabaul noted in his diary that 'according to the 1900 hours news, our forces made an opposed landing at Dutch Harbour in the Aleutians on 8 June. Navy planes bombed Midway

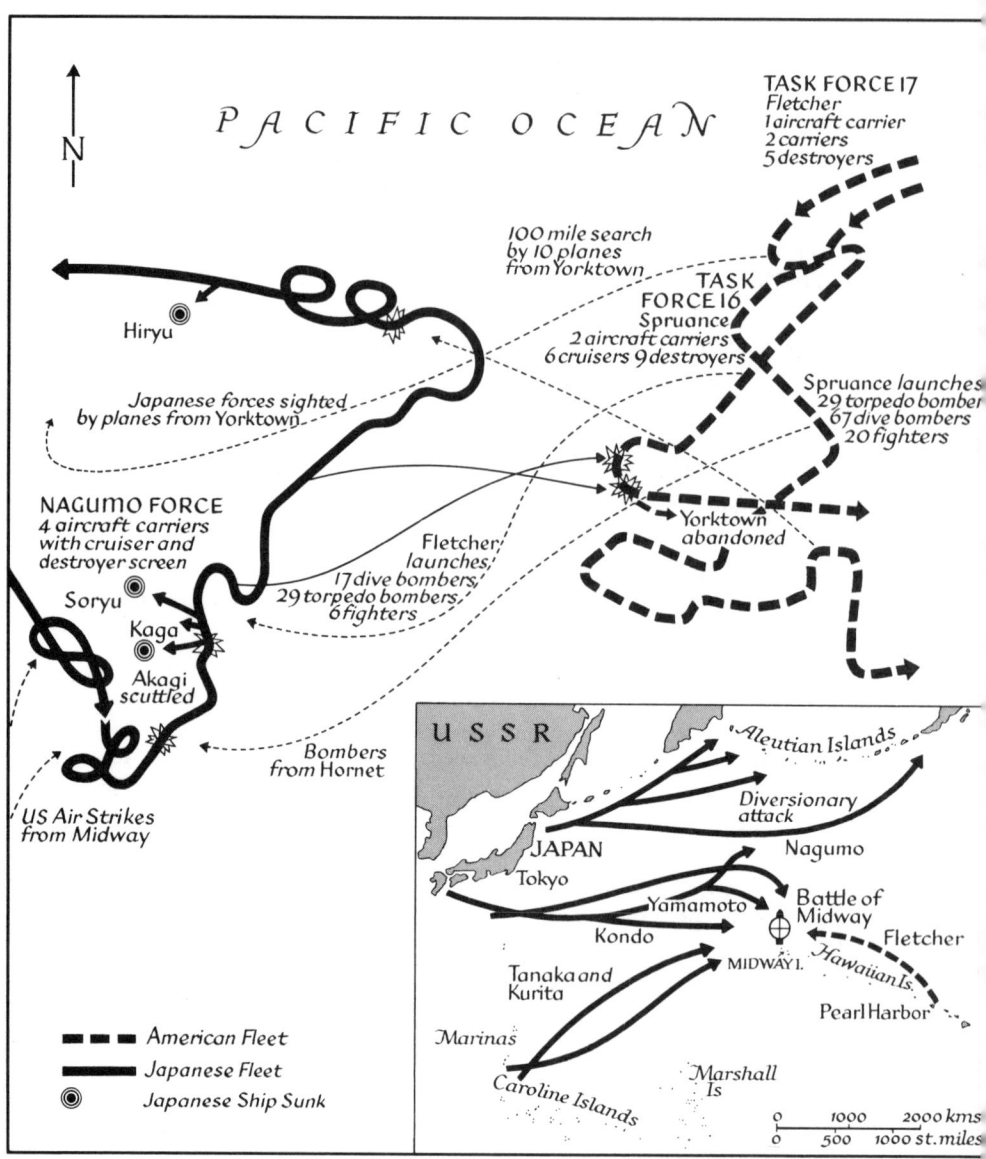

and sank two enemy aircraft carriers. The front line has spread from north to south and has taken in half the world. The American Navy has lost most of its carriers which must have hindered the mobility of their fleet. We lost one aircraft carrier, while another carrier and a cruiser were seriously damaged. Even though we did sustain some loss, we succeeded in decreasing the manoeuvrability of the enemy'.

'The operations have not yet been ended,' Wenneker continued, 'and a more favourable outcome is expected.'

The following day Second-Class Seaman Wada Noboru, a member of the Transport Group, recorded a different view: 'Due to the somewhat unfavourable results of the Main Fleet's action, and the ineffective bombing of Midway, it became evident that a landing, even by our invincible landing party, would be difficult. Therefore, the capturing of Midway was postponed.'

At the time of writing, his ship, the *Brazil Maru*, was heading for Guam, after being 'ordered to flee from enemy's aerial attacks'. And his use of the past tense – 'the capturing of Midway was postponed' – was correct: barely seventeen hours after McClusky and Leslie's squadrons began their dive, and five full days before Wenneker's report that 'operations have not yet been ended', Admiral Yamamoto had made what must have been the most painful decision of his professional life. Broadcast to all ships, for fleet ears only, at five minutes to three in the morning of 6 June, Tokyo time, the Commander-in-Chief's message was more than a postponement. It stated flatly and without excuse that 'the Midway operation is cancelled'.

Admiral Nagumo had survived the battle, forced by his junior officers to quit *Akagi*'s burning wreck. His defeat and humiliation – the unnecessary fruits of a wrong system, and of wrong decisions not his own, more than the consequences of personal misjudgements – were completed when, the battle still in progress, he was relieved of his command. Just over two years later, on 6 July 1944, he died by his own hand; but, after Midway, the burden of apology to the Emperor rested with Yamamoto alone. There was no real excuse except the truth, which could hardly be voiced – that entering the war had been a mistake from the very beginning. The Commander-in-Chief had given clear and ample warning then, and had lived to see his prophecy fulfilled: there had been six glorious months of running wild. After that, there could be no guarantee.

A tally of the first months gave the picture in glaring clarity. 7 December 1941, Pearl; 10 December, the *Prince of Wales* and *Repulse*; January 1942, the Netherlands East Indies operation begun; 15 February, the fall of Singapore; 27 February, the battle of the Java Sea; in March, the penetration of the Indian Ocean, and the Netherlands East Indies in Japanese hands; in April, Bataan, and in May, Corregidor. The list was a constant elaboration of Japanese victory. Then, in May, the Coral Sea, a two-sided victory – a draw, in effect; and in June, in search of the elusive decisive battle, Midway. Those in Japan who knew its true results could not escape the admission that a decisive battle *had* taken place, and that without any doubt they had lost. All four of the carriers had gone, *Akagi*, *Kaga* and *Soryu* first, victims of that almost unbelievable six-minute attack. *Hiryu*, whose name meant 'Flying Dragon', had become somewhat separated from the others in the manoeuvring under early American attacks, and that separation gave her a few hours' respite. Roaring, twisting and spitting fire like the dragon for which she was named, it was *Hiryu* that sent out the one really successful Japanese assault, an air strike which found and fatally hit *Yorktown*. The American Navy had also lost a destroyer, *Hammann*; 150 aircraft; and 300 officers and men. Yet, beyond the four carriers, the Japanese Navy had lost a heavy cruiser, *Mikuma*; 322 aircraft; and some 5,000 officers and men. Various other ships, including *Mikuma*'s sister *Mogami*, had been seriously damaged; but in the final unhappy accounting, it was the loss of the trained men which weighed most heavily. The steel balloon, Japan's outer defence perimeter, had at last been pierced. Hollow within, no patch could completely repair it; and, although the defeat of the Imperial Navy was still bitterly contested and slow, nevertheless it was, in the end, complete.

26

'Change target!'

Five months had gone by since the sinking of the carriers. Some survivors were still in hospital, isolated as totally as if they had the plague – which, in a sense, they did have. Newsreels and papers had not revealed to the ordinary Japanese the extent of the defeat, or even that a defeat had taken place. In those months the focus of Pacific fighting had switched southwards again, to the Solomon Islands, and in particular to the steamy seas and stinking jungles of the island of Guadalcanal. On 7 August American forces landed there, and on the neighbouring islands of Florida, Tulagi, Tanambogo and Gavutu. Further bounded by Savo Island, the gulf in between was the scene of the night-battle of Savo Island, 8/9 August, and after that night earned its macabre nickname of Ironbottom Sound. By morning four Allied heavy cruisers lay on its bed, and over a thousand Allied dead. They had been accompanied on the surface by two further heavy cruisers, two light cruisers and eight destroyers. The opposing Japanese force had been smaller – only five heavy cruisers, two light ones and a single destroyer – yet not a single one of those ships had been sunk, only three had been slightly damaged, and the total of dead and wounded was 111. Signalman Takamura, still in Rabaul, dutifully wrote down the communiqué from Imperial GHQ: 'The victory is next only to the Coral Sea.'

On 10 August the heavy cruiser *Kako*, returning from the site of the battle, was sighted and torpedoed by an American submarine; but no one could say yet that the Imperial Navy had lost its war.

That point came suddenly closer on 24 August, in the Battle of the Eastern Solomons. The opposing fleets were both very large: three carriers, a battleship, five heavy and two light cruisers, 254 aircraft and eighteen destroyers made up the three combined American Task Forces under Vice Admiral Frank Fletcher, promoted since his command of Task Force 17 at Midway. As at Midway, Japanese strategic and tactical commands were divided; strategic command remained with Yamamoto aboard *Yamato*, now in Truk, while tactical command devolved upon Vice Admiral Kondo Nobutake. Kondo's fleet included three aircraft carriers – *Shokaku, Zuikaku* and *Ryujo*; three battleships; no less than 13 heavy and three light cruisers; 31 destroyers; a dozen submarines, a seaplane transporter, and four troop transports for the relief of Guadalcanal. But Kondo, despite his enormous surface and submarine superiority, could call on only 168 aircraft; and, in the battle, ninety of these were lost, along with a light cruiser, a destroyer, a troop transport – and, most importantly, a carrier.

The victim was *Ryujo*, originally completed in 1931 and modernized in 1934–36. At the beginning of the year, the Imperial Navy had had ten carriers totalling just over 238,800 tons; *Ryujo* was the sixth to go down. But six others were commissioned in the course of the whole year, and it was not difficult to suppose that the supply from Japan's shipyards would keep pace with demand: once, in 1918, they had even established a world record by building a 5,800-ton merchant ship in only twenty-nine days. Yet, hearing Admiral Kondo's report, Yamamoto must have known that the picture was far bleaker than it appeared superficially. Altogether, nearly 150,000 tons of carrier shipping had been lost; only a little over 123,000 tons had been built. With *Ryujo* gone, there was a net loss of nearly 26,500 tons – more than nine per cent in four months – and, far worse, the replacement ships were all conversion jobs. Two had been submarine support vessels, four passenger liners; all were a long way below the standard of purpose-built ships; and, with the war only nine months old, the navy was already having to scratch around and take what it could get for carriers. In the Mitsubishi shipyard at Nagasaki, in mid-November 1942, Commander Chihaya Masataka reflected that, if the Commander-in-Chief had been right in saying this war would be won or lost by air power, then Japan needed to make a huge effort, her greatest effort ever, to maintain the impetus of those first wonderful months.

If, on the other hand, battleships still proved worthy of their traditional role, the national effort was well-placed. Chihaya had served upon several top-class surface ships, and he knew his business. His early career had been typical of many naval officers: graduating from Etajima in 1930, he had made a training voyage to Europe, via Suez, had been promoted ensign on his return in 1931, and in 1932 had seen action at Shanghai as assistant navigating officer on his squadron's flagship, the cruiser *Yubari*. Then followed a posting to the first-class destroyer *Nagatsuki*, and a second European voyage, this time as instructor, not pupil; service on *Chokai*, flagship of the Second Fleet under Vice Admiral Yonai; and eighteen months of gunnery training, specializing in anti-aircraft gunnery. When war broke out in Europe, he had been anti-aircraft officer on the battleship *Fuso*; in 1940 the same aboard the cruiser *Chikuma*; and then again aboard the battleship *Nagato*, flag of the Combined Fleet under Admiral Yamamoto himself. Chihaya had also been in charge of the Combined Fleet's air defence until the autumn of 1941; and, from then until the summer of 1942, he had been a key member in the fitting out of the Imperial Navy's second super-battleship, *Musashi*. It was impossible not to be impressed and overawed by that great war-vessel. *Musashi* had been completed at Nagasaki on 5 August, and Chihaya privately named her 'the Hope of Japan'. If anything could swing the balance, it was surely a ship such as this.

'This is finally farewell to Rabaul,' wrote Signalman Takamura on 16 August, four months after landing there. 'All we have to do is to attack where we are ordered to attack, and do what we are ordered to do. Travel by government expense – that is what I think of the whole thing. Go where I can go, see new lands, and then die.'

His 'borrowed' prisoners of war had been shipped to Japan. After seeing them off personally and watching the ship until it vanished over the horizon – 'the least I can do for them' – he had endured a public reprimand by his company commander. 'I have no intention of stamping out my own will, regardless of the fact that this is the Army,' the signalman snorted. 'This is an army where rank is respected, but I do not want to be a slave to rank. If they think I will become restrained and docile because they reprimanded me in front of the company, they are badly mistaken.'

Loaded up and ready to go, he groaned at the weight of his equipment – 'how can one march 250 miles with all of this?' – but in New Guinea, for the first time in his life, he had to face up properly to the realities of war.

'While preparing mess, it started to rain. The fire would not burn. The tent leaked. Did not sleep most of the night. It rains every day towards evening and at night . . . Our equipment gets wet and becomes heavier. Our bodies smell of the rain and of sweat. This is the perfume of war . . . Just a little more patience now. Batteries were inspected and some of them, which were useless, were discarded because of exposure to the rain. If we do not get rid of some of the load, our bodies will not last . . . Running short of tobacco. At this rate we will run short of rice, too . . . The fighting is getting fiercer and casualties are mounting . . . there is such heavy enemy fire that the dead cannot be brought in.'

It is extraordinary that under the circumstances he continued to write his diary. By 15 September the supplies whose weight he had complained of were becoming more valuable than bullets – 'Food is our first objective now . . . The 6-House [an American-occupied building] has fallen. Towards evening everyone rushed up to the 6-House position but could not find anything to eat. The enemy took all of his provisions to the rear . . . From tomorrow we will have to live off the land.'

On 19 September, 'I am so hungry,' he wrote, 'that it is an effort just to move.' Two days later he 'tried to climb to the 6-House, but was so weak I could not. We are just like sick men, no colour in our faces. We are like dead men walking around . . . No-one expressed it in words, but we may starve to death'.

Two more days went by, and then: 'The co-ordinated operations of the army and navy in the Tulagi-Samarai and Moresby areas are not going as planned. The MO operations of this corps apparently have been abandoned.' And at last on 24 September, to his own unexpected disappointment, 'the MO operations have been temporarily stopped. It has been decided that the corps is to withdraw . . . it is a pity that we have to withdraw after coming so far. Do not know whether I can make it in my condition'.

As the land and sea battles of the south-west Pacific campaign raged on, a new catch-phrase began to circulate amongst Japanese soldiers and sailors – 'if only they'd give us a month!' For them, every Allied attack came a month too early. It had been so since the start of the campaign, when American forces landed on Guadalcanal and seized the airfield. Named Lunga by the Japanese, it 'had been built by the navy's civil engineering squad after two months of indescribable struggles with epidemics and all imaginable hardships', as Chihaya wrote in a private manuscript after the war. The American seizure took place on 7 August; and 'the following day, August 8th, we were to celebrate its completion'. In memory of a marine torpedo plane leader killed at Midway, Major Lofton Henderson, the newly-finished strip was promptly named Henderson Field by its captors, and while Yamamoto's retaliation was prompted solely by strategic considerations, the Japanese on Guadalcanal itself fought back with the rage of the dispossessed.

Like Midway, Henderson was a worthless stretch of mud in peacetime; but in wartime, squashed flat by bulldozers and floored with steel mats, its geographical location made it invaluable, and for six months it became the focal point of battering assaults and counter-assaults. To sustain and reinforce the Japanese troops, the near-legendary 'Tokyo Express' was invented – blockade-breaking flotillas of destroyers running swift and low down New Georgia Sound, 'the Slot' in the middle of the Solomons. Bombed and bombarded from air, land and sea, uncountable tons of high explosive fell on and around the airstrip – in one night alone, the cruisers *Maya* and *Myoko* fired 1,500 shells at it. Rain, disease, and fatigue all took the incalculable death-toll higher still for Japanese and American; but, once they had got it, the Americans kept the ridiculous, horrible and priceless place – and kept it operational.

Thirty miles away, over the night of 11–12 October and throughout the day of the 12th, American ships exacted their revenge for Savo Island in the Battle of Cape Esperance. Three Japanese destroyers and the heavy cruiser *Furutaka* mirrored, to the north-west of Savo, the American wrecks to the south-east in Ironbottom Sound. But two days later the battleships *Kongo* and *Haruna*, under Vice Admiral Kurita Takeo, blasted to pieces 48 of the 90 US aircraft at Henderson. At Buna in New Guinea, Second-Class Seaman Wada scribbled, 'News: fall of Guadalcanal is only a question of time. Our fleet shelled the island with 15-inch guns. Aerodromes and barracks were destroyed.' On 20 October he added: 'It seems that victory is already in our hands'; five days later: 'only a few enemy planes are operating over Guadalcanal. The air is practically controlled by our forces.' And on 27 October: 'Results of the naval battle near Santa Cruz at 0630 – News: Our Navy encountered a strong enemy force north of Santa Cruz Island. Sunk – 4 aircraft carriers, 1 battleship, 1 unidentified vessel. Considerably damaged – 1 battleship, 3 cruisers, 3 destroyers. Destroyed – over 200 planes. Our losses – Two aircraft carriers and 1 cruiser slightly damaged. Forty of our planes failed to return.'

'This battle will be known as "South Pacific Sea Battle",' Wada noted. The Allies called it the Battle of Santa Cruz, and it was, as Wada believed, a considerable Japanese victory. But it was not nearly as great as he thought. The figures he recorded were partly accurate, partly exaggerated – a typical jumble of truth, confused reporting and morale-boosting hope. Against the two-hundred-plus American planes he was told were lost, the true figure was 74; against the forty Japanese, the true figure was nearer one hundred. The damage figures for American vessels were correct; but the figures for American vessels sunk were optimistic at best. No American battleship had been sunk, and only a single carrier, the *Hornet* – the four carriers claimed sunk did not even exist for, besides *Hornet*, *Enterprise* was the only other US carrier present. And the outcome of the battle was scarcely surprising, for in the Japanese fleet there *had* been four carriers, as well as four battleships to the American two; nine heavy cruisers to the American four; four light cruisers to the American five; 31 destroyers to the American 19; and a dozen submarines where the Americans had none. But the most curious and prophetic fact of the battle was that each side had had exactly the same number of aircraft – 412 – and, there, it was the Japanese who had suffered the greater loss.

On 20 October in New Guinea 'at about 1200 hours, the situation in the front suddenly changed,' wrote Takamura. 'Casualties continuously poured in. At 1230 the corps was ordered to withdraw a little. As it is, we have more patients on our hands than we can take care of. The continuous pouring in of the wounded and dead means only complete defeat. At 1500 hours concentrated at the 3-forked road on a plateau in the rear. Were given one bag of hardtack. This is a pitiful battle no matter how we look at it. There are still quite a number of wounded at the front waiting to be sent back. The troops on the front to withdraw at 1800 hours. In this signal company, the equipment has been damaged and the personnel killed or wounded. The corps cannot fight any more. When is the relief corps coming? Cannot hold out until the 25th. How are we to fight for the next five days?'

Wounded, ill and half-starved, the corps continued to hold out, and on 25 October learned that relief was still at least a week away. His company retreated further, and on the 29th saw friendly planes dropping supplies. It was the first time they had seen Japanese aircraft since landing seventy-three days before. Now they were under almost continuous attack, being strafed and bombed daily. 2 November: 'Most of my friends have been killed.' 8 November: 'Bullets ripped through the tents and trees . . . regimental HQ surrounded on three sides . . .' Next day he began to give way to despair: 'The enemy completely cut off our rear, and the supply route is severed. Cannot send one single wounded to the rear. Rifle shots around Papaki. Rifle fire near Yazawa corps area. Seems the enemy are gradually being reinforced' – and now he and his surviving colleagues were surrounded on all sides.

In Truk, at the end of October, Chihaya Masataka joined *Hiei*, flagship of the 11th Battleship Division, as staff officer in charge of the division. Santa Cruz – strangely similar to Midway, with its ratio of two American carriers against four Japanese – had temporarily put both fleets out of the war: not only had *Hornet* been sunk and *Enterprise* sufficiently damaged to force her return to New Caledonia, but *Shokaku*, *Zuikaku* and *Zuiho* had all been damaged as well. The Americans were always faster at repairing their ships than the Japanese, and, despite the greater severity of her damage, *Enterprise* was back on the scene sooner than the Imperial carriers. On 12 November she was en route again for the Solomons, repairs continuing as she steamed. But that night, under Vice Admiral Abe Hiroaki, the 11th Battleship Division, accompanied by a light cruiser and fourteen destroyers, was thundering down the Slot towards Savo, heading for Henderson and a new bombardment, and ready to try conclusions with any opposition. And the only opposition, under Rear Admiral Daniel J. Callaghan, was five cruisers and eight destroyers.

In their voyage from Truk, over a thousand miles away, *Hiei* and *Kirishima* had seen only two or three B-17 patrols, and had not been attacked. However, as they left the Pacific and penetrated the Solomons chain, a very heavy squall blew onto them. The ships were unable to see each other, and when they passed Savo – where they should have turned south-east towards Henderson – the island was completely invisible. It was not until they began to enter the Coral Sea that they realized how far they had gone beyond their turning-point. A sixteen-point change in course, a complete U-turn, was ordered. In driving rain, with poor-quality radio, it took a long time to arrange, but when it was finally done, the squall cleared at once – they had been running with it. It was already after midnight, and the bombardment of the airfield, if it took place at all, was going to be some hours behind schedule. On the bridge of *Hiei*, Chihaya and the senior staff officer of the battleship division began to argue: the senior officer wanted to call the operation off, while Chihaya wanted to press on.

'Our bombardment,' he recalls, 'was the start of the general offensive of the Combined Fleet, which would last about three days. If we did not make the bombardment, all the offensive plan would be ruined.'

It was the same tight time-tabling which had made the Midway operation so vulnerable. As the two staff officers argued, Admiral Abe came on to the bridge. He listened to them both, and decided to go ahead. The ships turned to starboard between Savo and Cape Esperance, and entered Ironbottom Sound. About twenty-five miles from Henderson, the guns were raised towards the airfield and loaded with 14-inch bombardment shells.

'Even now,' says Commander Chihaya,'I think it was about one minute before I was about to give the order to start bombarding, when, all of a sudden, the look-out on the bridge shouted "Enemy ships starboard ahead!" – I still remember it. There was no time for permission from the commanding officer. I shouted: "Change target! New target! Enemy ships starboard ahead! Start bombardment with searchlights on!"'

The battleship division had been sighted fourteen miles earlier by an American cruiser. Admiral Callaghan had drawn his inferior force into a line ahead intending to cross the Japanese T, and as *Hiei*'s searchlights stabbed through the darkness, this line was the first sight Chihaya had of the unsuspected enemy. He knew its purpose as well as anyone else, and was deeply shocked to see that a bare five miles separated the two fleets. Yet the trap did not work perfectly. Seeing the Japanese scout ships, the leading American destroyer swung unordered out of line, confused her followers, and forced the cruisers to swing as well – otherwise they would have run down their own destroyers. Nevertheless they opened fire, and as Admiral Nimitz wrote after the war, 'there followed a half-hour mêlée which for confusion and fury is scarcely paralleled in naval history'.

'The ships fought at close quarters, almost falling aboard each other,' Chihaya wrote. 'We missed the antiquated rams very badly.'

With *Hiei* in the vanguard, most of the fire was directed at her, and over fifty shells hit home. Blocked by the flagship, the rest of the Japanese fleet had to rush ahead and overtake in order to fire. Through his binoculars, Chihaya was observing from the starboard side of *Hiei*'s bridge when somewhere close by a shell exploded. Shrapnel shattered the bridge windows. The senior staff officer with whom Chihaya had argued just a few minutes earlier immediately fell dead and pain flared through Chihaya's hands. Staggering, he dropped his binoculars and could not pick them up again. Fragments of shrapnel had been deflected by the glasses and had broken both his thumbs, the top joints hanging on rags of skin. But the commander had no right to be alive – the undeflected fragments would have pierced his brain.

In the steering room another shell burst. The battleship began to circle; for some minutes they tried to steer her with the engines, but could not – somehow, repairs had to be made. She stopped, and lay rolling on the calm sea as the fight moved away. And it was then, a hundred feet above the weather-deck, at the top of her pagoda mast, that the men in the bridge found they were trapped by flames. At first they thought just the floor was on fire – then a hatch was opened, and heat and smoke billowed up from below. There was no escape down the stairs: the entire mast was ablaze. Ropes were found, hastily knotted together, made fast and flung out through the broken window. One by one, as the floor burned beneath their feet, the men eased themselves out and slid the hundred feet to safety. Chihaya, with his thumbs in pieces, could not go, but urged and encouraged the men to hurry. Seeing no chance of survival, he felt ready to accept inevitable death, and even joked with those waiting impatiently beside him. At last only he, a second officer and a signal petty officer were left – and together the other two men pushed him out of the window.

With no strength in his hands, he half-fell, half-slid to the weather deck and was picked up by willing arms. Above him the last two silhouettes came hand over hand towards him, as flames belched from the bridge and lit up the swirling smoke. Two escapes in one night – it was more than he thought possible.

Hiei was unmovable. Abe transferred his flag to the destroyer *Yukikaze*. She was known as the lucky ship of the Imperial Navy – completed at Sasebo in January 1940, she had taken part in almost every battle since Pearl Harbor, and had never suffered any appreciable damage. Her luck had held that night, and would continue to do so until close to the end of the war; but two other destroyers had gone, and *Hiei* would soon follow them down.

Drifting helplessly north of Savo, she was bombed again and again the day after the battle by planes from Henderson, and when the last sortie found nothing to bomb, they naturally reported her sunk by American hits. Others in the Imperial Navy recorded that she was scuttled; but neither of these assumptions was the case, as Commander Chihaya witnessed. The battleship was completely unmanoeuvrable, and Admiral Abe took the decision to torpedo her; but her captain, Nishida, refused to leave the ship, and no one aboard *Yukikaze* felt able to give the order that would send him to the bottom with *Hiei*. At last a message from Abe was taken over: 'This is an order. You are requested to come on board *Yukikaze* to report. If you wish, you will be sent back to *Hiei* again.'

Chihaya was sitting in a small cabin astern of *Yukikaze*'s bridge when Nishida was shown in. The captain was astonished to see him – 'I thought you were dead!' he said. And, as Chihaya began to explain, they both heard the order and felt the movement – 'Both engines ahead; prepare for torpedoing.' Nishida rushed from the cabin. Chihaya heard Nishida protesting, and then Abe's voice ordering him to be silent.

White-faced, Nishida came back into the cabin, sat down, 'and he started to cry. "This is against my will! I made up my mind to go down with my own ship – only the commanding officer instructed me to come on board *Yukikaze* to report – I came over here . . . he betrayed me!"'

Chihaya heard that in ten days Nishida was to be promoted to Rear Admiral. But he was not. Instead 'he was fired. Fired! And so was Commanding Officer Admiral Abe'.

Later that same day, 14 October, further up the Slot, on the fringe of the Coral Sea, and finally back by Savo Island, the battle picked up again and was fought hard until the early hours of the 15th. The great offensive, for which *Hiei*'s bombardment should have been the curtain-raiser, carried on regardless, and met with disaster. The Americans lost seven destroyers and two light cruisers. But *Enterprise* was now in striking range, and although shore- and carrier-based American aircraft numbered only 273 to the Japanese 310, the end result was a resounding victory for the US Navy. *Hiei*'s sister *Kirishima* went down, along with a heavy cruiser – and seven of the eleven transports the warships were guarding. Ten thousand reinforcing Japanese troops should have been landed on Guadalcanal; more than six thousand died before they got there. The price of the far south was becoming too high for Japan; and, though the land battles continued, the Imperial Navy sent no more capital ships to the Solomons.

It was no better for those in New Guinea. 'Enemy has pressed closer, attacked towards evening,' wrote Takamura on 20 November. '1 man wounded, 1 killed. Repaired trenches at night. From tomorrow, will live in trenches. Reinforcement should land on 22nd. Only 2 or 3 days to hold out.'

Nine days later: 'There have been frequent messages recently that fresh troops have landed, but there is no evidence of this.'

Six days after that: 'Concentrated enemy barrage on area as a whole, and on positions parallel to road. 4 men killed.' Takamura must have known that he too was about to die; as if in homage to their memory, he wrote down the names of all the men he knew who had been killed. There were fifty-nine. Yet again there came news that a division of reinforcements had landed; and then, on 6 December, the unexpected, final entry: 'Found out that enemy in front of our positions were Americans.'

But perhaps it is not surprising that he had never been certain who he was fighting against; for he had certainly never known why he was fighting them.

27

'Our chief object is to kill the enemy'

Admiral Yamamoto Isoroku, Commander-in-Chief of the Imperial Navy, known in America as 'the Peacock', died shortly before 10 a.m. on 18 April 1943, when the Mitsubishi aircraft carrying him was shot down in flames and crashed in the jungles of Bougainville.

He died much as he lived and fought – punctually, to a timetable. Guadalcanal had finally caved in under constant, irresistible American pressure on 9 February. On 26 March, far to the north in the archipelago of the Russian Komandorskiye Islands, the last great sea battle fought only with naval guns took place. It was the day after that when Yamamoto, the prophet of air power, sanctioned the beginning of a great air counter-offensive in the south-west Pacific. More than two hundred carrier planes were shifted to land bases scattered through the Solomon Islands. Added to the hundred-plus aircraft already there, this became the strongest single air armada mustered by the Imperial Navy. Its objective was to harass, impede, and with luck paralyze the build-up of American naval forces in the area. Action commenced on 7 April, and within a week considerable success was reported – 134 Allied planes shot down, 25 transports, two destroyers and a cruiser sunk. Under interrogation after the war, Captain Omae Toshikazu of the Naval General Staff admitted that reports from units engaged in operations 'were exaggerated after the middle of 1942, and their judgment caused much trouble'. He personally always discounted fifty per cent of shipping damage or loss claims, and operated a sliding scale of discount with aircraft claims: if less than ten were claimed shot down, he would knock off fifty per cent; between ten and fifty claimed kills, he ignored 33⅓ per cent; and over fifty he took off 25 per cent. But, he said, 'in my opinion, even after these deductions, the reports were still exaggerated'.

He was right: the week's operations by Japan's greatest-ever air fleet actually disposed of a single American destroyer, a corvette, a tanker, two transports and 25 aircraft. And that limited achievement had been won at a disproportionate cost: forty Japanese planes and their battle-seasoned crews had been lost. Yet Admiral Yamamoto appeared to accept the claimed figures at face value, and on 16 April called the operation off, believing it to have been a great success.

After Guadalcanal he had written to a friend: 'I do not know what to do next. Nor am I happy about facing my officers and men who have fought so hard without fear of death.' But that was exactly what he decided to do – to meet as many as possible of his loyal air- and sea-warriors face to face, and to show them that, whatever had happened or might happen, he was still their leader, and still ready to fight.

It was an excellent idea; the visit to the troops by a charismatic leader has always been the best inspiration. But the Admiral even now had no idea of the extent of American monitoring of Japanese radio messages, nor of the number of those messages the Americans could decode. From his flagship *Yamato*, still anchored in Truk, the precise details of his itinerary were broadcast to all interested parties, so that the airbases involved could prepare for their honoured visitor. A base which was definitely not on the list was Henderson Field in Guadalcanal, but the men there knew about Yamamoto's route almost as soon as their Japanese counterparts. For all the security it was given, the announcement might as well have been shouted from the rooftops in Washington.

Relying on Yamamoto's well-known habit of punctuality, the eighteen P-38 fighters from the long-contested Henderson Field had only to be in the right place at the right time; and the Admiral did not let them down. In his flight there were two Mistsubishi-1 aircraft, himself in one and his Chief of Staff, Admiral Ugaki Matome, in the other. Escorting them were six fighters. The two groups of planes met at 9.34 a.m. Within a minute nine aircraft were spiralling in flames towards sea and land: one P-38, and all of the Japanese flight.

'Congratulations Major Mitchell and his hunters,' Vice Admiral William F. Halsey signalled to Henderson Field when he heard the result. 'Sounds as though one of their ducks in the bag was a peacock.'

In Japan the tragedy was not announced until 21 May, when a small pot of very illustrious ashes was brought to Tokyo aboard *Yamato*'s sister-ship *Musashi*. Apart from Togo, no other admiral had achieved or would achieve such stature in the eyes of the Imperial Navy and the nation as a whole; apart from the Emperor, there was no other individual whose death would have brought greater grief. As had been calculated in Washington, the news that Yamamoto had joined his ancestors and that the stocky, confident little figure had been reduced to a jar of carbon hit the Japanese hard – as if Britons had learned of General Montgomery's death, or Americans of Nimitz's end. But the harder they were hit, the harder the Japanese believed they could hit back.

One plausible-sounding argument – reported by the American naval attaché in Santiago – asserted that 'the US has to fight on so many fronts that the production she uses to fight Japan will not be sufficient to beat us.' And in Buenos Aires, the chargé d'affaires heard from the local *Mainichi* correspondent that, when Japanese forces retreated, it was because they were 'lulling the Americans into a sense of false security . . . the Japanese are acting as though they are afraid to meet the Americans, in order to attract an even greater concentration of American force so that the blow when it comes will thus be the most effective'. Protesting somewhat too much, the correspondent continued: 'The Japanese Navy is not afraid . . . the Japanese are watching with the greatest of care for the moment to spring . . . the Japanese fleet will completely wipe out the Americans.'

Today there is a certain comic pathos in this rhetoric; but then, in 1943 Japan, it was widely, if not universally, accepted as true. The cause – one can hardly say the reason – was the retreat from reason, well established in the late 1930s, and flowing constantly stronger. With religion as much a part of society as obedience and sake, the doctrine of the 'unparalleled Yamato spirit' which would carry all before it came into full power in the years after Yamamoto's death. It had to: there was no other unlimited resource available. In 1920, when First Sea Lord, Admiral of the Fleet Lord Beatty said, 'Superiority of personnel was an asset to be kept up the sleeve, but not one to gamble with.' In Japan, long-established tradition dictated just the opposite: there was Sun Tzu; there was the eighteenth century poet Roei Sanyo, with his dictum that 'the secret of victory or defeat lies in the spirit of the men and not in their weapons'. And, in the twentieth century, there were officers such as Lieutenant General Endo Saburo, Chief of the Cabinet Bureau of Research. 'I told my men,' he said under interrogation, 'that they could fight without worrying whether they would actually win the war or lose the war: to win or lose is not of primary concern to my men; they should be willing to die gladly, knowing that it was unavoidable and that they were doing the right thing.'

Unreason had begun the war; but such single-minded, irrational determination could not have continued without a solid basis of religious belief.

'Never fail to give thanks,' a young officer named Okamoto Shigeo wrote in his note-book in New Guinea, after a particularly useful lecture. 'First of all kindness of the Empire, kindness of your parents, kindness of your leaders. Do not neglect these three. Moreover, give thanks for all things that occur in daily life. Have the same spirit with men. Give commands and orders to subordinates with the same spirit. We should be grateful for having weapons, supplies, machinery on board ship, and the like. Give thanks to everything. Foster the idea of a religious group. The soul of the invisible God becomes the true heart of the passing man.' Pride concurrent with humility; gratitude and willingness to be sacrificed – such sentiments were very close to Christian thought as well. Even gratitude for the assistance of weapons 'and the like' was not far from Christian thinking – seven hundred years earlier there had been the medieval military orders such as the Knights Templar, fighting monks in the frontline of the faith, spreading the Word on the edge of a sword; and at Pearl Harbor there had been W. H. Maguire, the navy chaplain who achieved immortality not so much by loving his enemy as by saying, 'Praise the Lord and pass the ammunition!'

And, to young Okamoto and his millions of colleagues, war without reason was wonderfully simple: 'Our chief object,' he wrote, 'is to kill the enemy.' The British naval writer Fred T. Jane would have respected the attitude: in 1906 he had tried to define something he called 'Fitness to Win'.

'A crude desire to "kill the enemy" seems ever to have been a most valuable asset,' Jane wrote. 'Nelson, when he said that a good English officer should "hate a Frenchman like the devil", was very crude, but very far-seeing. However shocking ethically, to hate the enemy with a living personal hatred is undoubtedly a most valuable practical asset . . . The Japanese tried to kill with a definite object, and the whole Japanese nation was behind them urging them to kill.'

Jane's conclusion was that 'it is probable that Fitness to Win embodies little else besides the fixed desire to kill the enemy'. The conclusion may have been valid in 1905; forty years later, much more was needed.

When American bombers and submarines began to lay mines in Japan's home waters, 'we forced shipping through regardless of the knowledge that it was dangerous'. Captain Tamura Kyuzo was head of the Imperial Navy's mine-sweeping force. 'If we suspected mines were in certain areas,' he said under interrogation, 'we stopped shipping for one day, pending sweeping operations, but then started in again, realizing full well that ships would be lost . . . the crews of the merchant ships and naval vessels were very worried and frightened by this mining, but they were all under orders and had to work through it.'

Irrational or not, such comments revealed real bravery, and, if that and determination were all that was necessary, the Japanese gamble was undertaken with two court cards in the hand. The intention was clear – to carry on to the end, no matter how bitter. 'Our one hope,' said Captain Tamura, 'was that, if we could destroy the invasion fleet when it came to actually land in Japan – although Japan could not win the war – it could hold out indefinitely for any number of years.'

But too many of the other cards were just bits of pasteboard with hurried sketches hastily coloured in. One which Tamura held was labelled 'mine counter-measures', and it said simply: 'The Navy had no department of research on mine counter-measures.' As for the experience of their German allies, 'the German attaché [Wenneker] was not a specialist . . . for that reason, when you used magnetic and pressure mines we were caught flat-footed. We had no advance notice from Germany'.

A certain Captain Yoshida held the card labelled 'navy civilian manpower': 'the Navy took second place to the Army as far as authority for the deferment of civilian workers from military service was concerned. As a result of the Army's broad authority, the Navy suffered a manpower shortage, especially in the fields of ship-building and aircraft production.'

Linked to aircraft like eggs to chickens were bombs, about which Rear Admiral Takata Toshitanea said that the Navy had originally used 500-kilo types. 'But we realized that, in order to sink certain ships, we would have to have at least 800-kilo bombs. We therefore used shells from heavy guns and turned them into 800-kilo bombs. These were the first 800-kilo bombs we used – at Pearl Harbor we used converted naval shells for bombs – and had such success with them that we settled on 800-kilo bombs as the means for sinking capital ships.' However, America's post-Pearl ships were much stronger than those at the bottom of that harbour, and demanded yet bigger bombs, but the bigger bombs were never developed. At least here there was a clear chain of cause and effect, and no chicken-and-egg mystery. Between them Admiral Takata and General Endo held the cards: Takata explained that bigger bombs were not developed because bigger planes were not developed, and Endo added that 'unlike the American set-up and also the British organization of airplanes of all different kinds, which would be very satisfactory for a country having a lot of materials, manpower, etc., in actual resources Japan was such a poor country that if we went into production of so many different types of airplanes, it would be difficult to continue production. I thought as a defensive measure we should have only fighters which we could build in Japan'.

In other words, Japan could not afford to build the materials necessary for a long war. Yamamoto had said just that for years. Now General Endo had come to the same conclusion. Unfortunately he reached it several hundred thousand lives too late.

Then there was the card labelled 'aero intelligence'. Imperial Navy Commander Yokura Sashizo held that one, and, as blunt as Tamura on mine counter-measures, Yokura stated: 'There was no real fleet intelligence.' For a nation to which intelligence-gathering was practically second nature, this was an extraordinary admission; but, far from trying to conceal it, Yokura went on to describe in some detail the near non-existence of Imperial Naval intelligence in the Pacific War. Starting as an aeronautical engineer, in 1943 he had become Air Intelligence Member of the Naval General Staff, and had remained there until July 1945. At that time he resigned – because, after many requests for assistance, he was still the only man in his section. In his unaided, thankless job, he 'received little from reconnaissance planes which were sent out by the fleet . . . I realize fully the lack of system in reconnaissance. I heard that the US had special reconnaissance squadrons and thought it was a good idea. We could not put this into practice because of shortage of planes. I made some recommendations, but no attention was paid to them'.

On anti-aircraft defences, Yokura continued, 'no study was made in my section or in the field. I knew your pilots were sent out with complete flak maps which we found in smashed planes, but we did not do this'. As for studying enemy aircraft: 'We generally knew a lot about older types, but there was a time-lag in our information. By the end of the war, we knew your 1943 airplane performance well.' It was hardly believable; but, as he concluded, 'the main reason for failure was lack of realization, both in headquarters and in the field, of the importance of intelligence . . . it was not the fault of any one person, but rather of the system which concentrated on attack and on operations. The viewpoint was not broad enough. If we had had a very broad intelligence, an organization as good as the American one, we might not have lost the war'. It did not necessarily follow; but he may have found some comfort in the thought.

The war pack was large – another one of its cards was labelled 'radar'. At Midway the Americans had employed a direction-finding system of Japanese invention; but, of the Imperial Navy's own radar, a Captain Arasawa gave an indictment that could hardly have been more comprehensive.

'We should have had more research,' he remarked. 'More research, better relations between the Army and Navy in research and production, standard nomenclature for both the Army and Navy, increased production, more distribution of radar to the field, and better training of radar personnel.'

After that, he turned to the crucial – and crucially late – development of ground control interceptors: 'We had just finished one when the war ended.' On American radar, he said that he had admired it, and had hoped in vain to capture a set; and, on relations between the Army and Navy, he was more damning still. He explained to his interrogators that the two forces did separate radar research. 'One laboratory was military and the other was Navy. The Army and Navy worked independently on radar and did not realize its use as a war weapon until too late.'

The last of the dud cards was one on which everyone – 'too late' – agreed. It was labelled 'army-navy relations'. In one of his reports, an American secret agent in Japan, codenamed 'Shark', wrote: 'Upon arrival in Japan in June 1942, I was immediately impressed with the antagonism existing between Army and Navy.' Yoshida and Arasawa had their say – 'The Navy took second place to the Army . . .'; 'Army and Navy worked independently . . .' – and now General Endo and Admiral Takata joined in.

'Army and Navy had each their own independent plan for development of air-power,' said Takata. 'On the overall policy we had no joint Chiefs of Staff.'

Endo was still more emphatic: in 1943–44, he said, the two forces 'didn't know whether they were fighting America or whether they were fighting each other'. For example he quoted the two production plants in Nakajima. One was Army, the other Navy; one had nickel, the other had not; 'but they wouldn't pass it around to make full use of it . . . I had always maintained that in case Japan would be defeated, it would be due to those fights relative to the influence of the Army and Navy – they were always fighting each other in that respect.'

With reason restored, two of the other officers were able to sum up the whole blurred pack with which they had gambled. Commander Yoshida, the air intelligence man, never received information from pilots, although 'there were many times when I wanted to issue orders along this line, and tried to do this'. As he now saw it, the trouble had been that 'our doctrine was always attack, attack, attack, and no one was too much interested in intelligence'. And Captain Tamura, the head of mine-sweeping, put a perceptive finger on his country's central weakness. 'The Japanese people,' he realized, 'were very quick to make preparations for offensive campaigns – but not for defensive campaigns.'

28

'I have grave news'

No single man could ever exercise complete moment-by-moment control over a major navy, but it has often happened that, if the lonely post of commander-in-chief was filled by a man of probity and of strong character, his navy took on something of those characteristics. It happened best not by imposition but by adoption, or absorption, or imitation: not so much when men and officers were told to behave in a particular way, but when their Admiral did, and when they respected him – or better still, loved him – and so tried to behave as he did. It was not only because of the death of Yamamoto, but after he died, the character of the Imperial Navy altered. The men who succeeded Yamamoto as commanders-in-chief were not bad men, but they lacked his charisma. Moreover, under Yamamoto, Japan's naval men had always believed at worst that they had an even chance of victory. At best, of course, he had led a navy that gave every appearance of invincibility; and the sequel to his death – although it was no more than he had prophesied – was the unwilling, leaden-footed comprehension that Japan and its navy were fighting a losing war. Or rather, a series of losing battles – 'Our navy has lost the war,' wrote Chihaya Masataka in later years, 'through battling instead of warring.' Hand-in-hand with the awful, often subconscious realization that they would lose all they had gone to war for and more, there came a kind of hysterical desperation. Sometimes with cowardice, sometimes with extreme bravery, this was the main single characteristic of the post-Yamamoto Imperial Navy; and it was made manifest in some unpleasant ways.

'I fear I have grave news to give to the House,' said Anthony Eden, Britain's Secretary of State for Foreign Affairs, in the House of Commons on 28 January 1944. 'We have a growing list of cases of brutal outrage on individuals or groups of individuals.'

His subject was the atrocities committed against British prisoners-of-war in Japanese camps. The instances he related were fairly minor in the light of post-war knowledge of Germany and Japan, but they horrified the House. All were Imperial Army responsibilities, and with the revelations of that speech the Japanese Army began to share in the loathing which the Allies had previously reserved for Nazis. The Army created for itself a reputation as unremovable as it was deserved; and, by extension, the Navy began to share that evil name. That stain remains: Japan as a fighting country is known to be brutal through and through. For the Imperial Army, the judgement is generally just – although even there, as with Signalman Takamura, there were exceptions. But again, such men, if anyone ever knew of them, were notable because they were exceptional. However, it is one of the purposes of this book to state and show that the extension of that judgement to the Navy is generally unjust: that the fundamental characteristics and attitudes of the two forces were not only vastly different, but frequently in open, mutual opposition, even when such conflicting views were not in their own or their country's interests. Fairness, and the approach to life in war and peace alike which, in the West, used to be called gentlemanly, had never been the Army's style, and they had centuries of tradition which told them so. The Navy in comparison was new, and had been taught by another navy which prided itself on being both fair and gentlemanly. Perhaps, because it was adopted, the tradition was only a veneer; certainly, because of desperation, it began to crack. Atrocities were committed by naval men, although in relation to the Army's misdeeds they were very limited, and almost incidental; but they existed and therefore they must be related. As Anthony Eden said to the Commons: 'I could not burden the House with the full tale of these. But in order to give an idea of their nature I must, I fear, quote a few typical examples.'

'At 0420 December 14th, the vessel was struck on the starboard side between Nos. 1 and 2 holds by a torpedo fired at the vessel without warning. Vessel's position at the time of attack being 195°, 16 miles, Sacramento Shoal Light House. Vessel immediately started to list and sink by the head. I ordered all boats to be lowered. The starboard forward boat was smashed in lowering and I took the double boat's complement into the port forward boat. As far as I could ascertain everyone got away from the vessel, which sank three minutes after I left her. As the vessel sank the submarine appeared about 100 yards to the North of where the vessel sank. The sub approached my boat after firing a tracer bullet at us. No words were passed and the submarine turned away but approximately three minutes later rammed my boat at an approx. speed of 16 knots, opening fire with machine guns directly after. I swam to a raft about 1½ miles away. The submarine then rammed the other two boats and machine-gunned the water over a large area. By this time 12 men were hanging onto the raft. At daylight we saw two other rafts with one man on one of them. After a struggle we got the three rafts together and I placed 4 men on each of the others, keeping 5 on my raft, one being R. Casson, a gunner who had a badly burnt and sprained

325

foot. I advised the others to endeavour to rig a sail from the awning and to keep close to my raft and we endeavoured to make westing. At midnight December 17th we landed in the Krishna River delta . . . Total number of survivors known being sixteen, ship's complement being 69 crew and 2 passengers.'

The author of that bald but convincing testimony was R. J. Weeks, Master of the steam ship *Daisy Moller*, sunk on 14 December 1943. The experience was typical of at least ten others between 27 November 1943 and 29 October 1944: all were motor vessels or merchant ships attacked by submarines, whose crews afterwards made considerable efforts to kill all survivors. Most of the sinkings were recorded by the US Naval Liaison Officer at Colombo in May 1944, and were later filed by the Office of Strategic Services – the war-time forerunner of the CIA – in confidential document number 76650. *Daisy Moller*'s death toll was not unusual, but Weeks personally was quite fortunate. He and his surviving companions reached land in less than three days; sometimes rafts drifted for six weeks or more before land was found or rescue effected; and sometimes survivors of attacks did not survive the subsequent ordeal of exposure in the Indian Ocean. The SS *British Chivalry* was torpedoed on 22 February 1944:

'After considering the chances of rescue it was decided that it would be hopeless to remain in the area. The boat in company with one raft and all available provisions moved off in an attempt to make land, using the most favourable conditions of wind, weather and currents, etc. Plans were made for making roughly a 1500-mile passage and a scale of rations calculated accordingly.

'At 11.30 p.m. on 23 February 1944, Able Seaman L. Morris, suffering from lacerations from bullet in head, and bullet hole through right forearm, lost his life by drowning. His wounds were of such a character that he had been rendered insane, and efforts were made by survivors on the raft to restrain him. He proved too violent to hold and during the struggling evaded the others, jumped overboard and disappeared from view before rescue could be effected . . . The subsequent proceedings were such as might be expected during a period of great hardship and suffering of 36 men cast adrift for 37 days in an overcrowded boat.'

Freezing by night and burning by day, supplementing rations meant for much smaller numbers with fish and sea-birds, catching rain when possible, severely short of anything but the most elementary medication – anyone who made it to a boat or raft shared the same experience. Most also shared the experience of being rammed and machine-gunned when totally defenceless; and some, the especially unlucky ones, learnt about life and death aboard the attacking submarines. One of these was P. de Jong, Chief Engineer of SS *Tjisalak*, a Dutch ship carrying 76 crew and 27 passengers, torpedoed shortly after 5.30 a.m., Sunday 26 March 1944.

'A little later the ship went down with a sigh,' said de Jong expressively; and then, with most of the others, he was taken aboard the submarine.

'With the Third Engineer I was the first one to be pointed out to the foredeck. They told us to sit there facing forward. We should in no case look back, they told us. From all around they kept us covered. When I boarded the sub they took my knife away. I had my lifebelt on and luckily they forgot to take that away. My papers were packed in the inside of my lifebelt and they did not spot it. The foreship started to fill up as they were ordering now all the people out of the boats. Two Japs were making us stand, one with a revolver and one with a coil of rope. Again and again they shouted from the tower, "Do not look back, because that will be too bad for you." I got the impression that there was little discipline. Everybody just pleased himself and they all tried to get as many souvenirs as possible. So they took watches, papers and knives . . . I got the impression that the Japs wanted to start all kinds of things at the same time. One was preparing himself to tie us up, another was fumbling with his revolver and so on . . . I felt pity for the 5th Engineer, as he was fighting, I could see, to keep himself under control, but he succeeded. It was a hard blow for him . . . he had just escaped out of occupied Holland and he was very young.

'I was very proud of every member of our crew, as I heard nobody screaming or begging for life . . . there were a few fights going on behind us, but I do not know the exact facts as I did not look behind me. Waiting was long . . . To wait all the time was unbearable. Luckily they started now. They called the 5th Engineer out and told him to start walking aft. When he was aft they shot him.

'Now it was my turn. One Jap was hanging on to my back when I walked aft. Maybe he wanted to pull off my lifebelt, maybe he wanted to prevent me from jumping overboard. Everywhere Japs were standing by with weapons. I realized that to dive with my lifebelt on would be very difficult and my chance was nil as I could not keep myself under . . . Whenever I should come up in the water I could be riddled with bullets and probably die slowly. As I had to die anyhow I preferred a sudden death. So I walked on, along the tower and on aft.

'At a distance of about 5 or 6 feet from the stern there was one Jap ready with his revolver. When I came alongside of him I stopped, as I expected him to shoot me through the head. He pointed out to me, however, that I had to carry on. When I arrived at the very end of the deck, above the propellors, I heard a bang and felt a terrific shock on my head and I toppled into the water. The Japs tried to make a good job of it indeed, as they did it above the propellors. How I missed them I do not know.'

Obviously de Jong lived on, despite the shot and the propellors, and his eventual report was long, explicit and highly critical of Allied air coverage – 'We should have some protection so that the Japs cannot repeat this slaughtering of shipwrecked people.' He and the few others who still lived were almost killed by their eventual rescuer, an American liberty ship which at first busily shelled their little craft, mistaking it for a submarine conning tower. And, although these submarine atrocities and the loss of life they involved were a very small part of the war overall, as de Jong said, 'Still it is very uncomfortable if you are included in this small percentage.'

Another distinct category of wartime atrocity involving the Imperial Navy, and which brought about a very much larger percentage of unnecessary death and suffering, was the transporting of prisoners-of-war from camps in the Southern Area to Japan and other places. The sympathetic signalman Takamura gave a terse description of the fate that thousands met. Seventeen days after he had been reprimanded for waving good-bye to the ship bearing 'his' prisoners, he wrote: 'Navy men say that the ship with the prisoners which headed for Hainan Island was sunk by an enemy submarine on the way. Probably all of the prisoners have been killed. Their compartment was locked, so none could have been saved.'

This traffic continued throughout the war, and since the ships bore no red cross or other identifying mark, they were as likely to be sunk as any other. It would be impossible to try and estimate the number of men who died as a result; but, though the greatest terror of these vessels was the prisoners' knowledge that they were enclosed, trapped under hatches and boards covering the entrance to the holds and quite unable to escape if they were sunk, nevertheless one could guess that at least as many died from the conditions of their confinement as from drowning. In the West there has only ever been one form of transport to compare, but the comparison is very close: the slave ships on which so much British and American wealth in the seventeenth and eighteenth centuries was based. The guilt of the race memory tinges the horror of these prisoners' fates; their ancestors had treated other men in the same way. Many of the men were dying before they were herded onto the ships – dysentery, beri-beri, malaria, starvation had already wasted their limbs and muscles – and, once on board, food and water were almost or completely non-existent and always foul; medical aid was what they could invent for themselves out of nothing; sanitation was usually nil, and – since they were stacked squatting on artificial inner decks of planks, fifteen men to a space six feet by six feet by three feet high – the prisoners could neither move nor see nor properly breathe. Nauseated by their diseases, their imprisonment and the motion of the ship, they had no choice but to vomit where they sat, and to remain sitting there; and, with bowels weakened by dysentery, they could not move from the puddles of infected faeces, nor avoid the dribbles from the stacks of men above. And during long passages especially, it became the crew's pastime to make the prisoners run the gauntlet on deck, staggering from one gun-butt to the next, before executions by gun or sword.

'I could not burden the House with the full tale of these'; but perhaps enough has been said 'to give an idea of their nature'.

Beyond these two broad categories – the 'slaughtering of shipwrecked people' and the active neglect, amounting to torture, of prisoners in transit on ships – there is one specific incident of naval atrocity which needs to be mentioned.

It took place in February 1945, towards the very end of the Imperial Navy's life; and it took place on land, during the battle for Manila.

Commanding the quarter-million Japanese Army troops on Luzon was Lieutenant-General Yamashita Tomoyuki. Nicknamed the 'Tiger of Malaya', it was he who had conquered Singapore. Now, as American forces advanced towards Japan, he decided to withdraw his men from the Manila-Bataan area and go up into the mountains to the north-east and north-west of Manila, to an easily-defensible area with good supplies of food and water. Only three battalions would remain in Manila itself.

But in addition to the Army forces, there were some 16,000 Navy men on Luzon, under the command of Vice Admiral Okochi Denshichi and Rear Admiral Iwabachi Sanji. Okochi accepted General Yamashita's plan, and retreated with him. Iwabachi, however, elected to remain in Manila with his men and to defend the city to the death.

Taking command of the remaining Army battalions as well as his own men, Iwabachi set about the destruction of the port's docks and wharves, then as the Americans pressed inexorably forward onto the island, the Admiral and his men fought from house to house in a slow and savage retreat. He had his orders – the 'Manila Navy Defence Force and South-Western Area Fleet Operation Orders' for 23 December 1944 to 14 February 1945. These included the paragraph: 'When killing Filipinos, assemble them together in one place, as far as possible, thereby saving ammunition and labour. The disposal of dead bodies will be troublesome, so either collect them in houses scheduled to be burned or throw them into the river.'

There was one place in the city splendidly arranged for such an operation – the old Spanish prison of Fort Santiago, at the northern end of the ancient walled Spanish town. Into this fort, Iwabachi's men herded as many Filipinos as possible. The gates were barricaded; they and the buildings were sprayed with petrol; and the whole lot was set ablaze. No one knew exactly how many Filipinos were burnt alive, nor how many were shot as they tried to escape the flames. It is not even very easy to see what the purpose of the massacre was; unarmed civilians could pose little threat, and the hideous manner of their slaughter was bound to provoke MacArthur and his men even further.

There is little point in condemning Iwabachi for the atrocity, even if, in all the dreadful pointlessness of war, these killings seem more pointless than most. After all, soldiers on the Allied side in the Pacific War behaved as badly. Thousands of Japanese soldiers were buried alive on Corregidor, sealed into the caves which were their last retreats, when they refused to surrender. The rumbling flares of flame-throwers were terrible, but common, American weapons throughout the Philippine campaign; and when nothing else could shift them, Japanese soldiers were roasted in their bunkers, petrol and diesel oil being pumped into their ventilation shafts and then set alight. Indeed, if Iwabachi had been an Army man, his action would have been scarcely more than usual; it is the fact that he was a Navy man that makes it notable, and worth some explanation. If it is difficult to see what he thought he would achieve by incinerating civilians, it is, nevertheless, fairly easy to see why he was – in Navy terms – so spectacularly brutal. Firstly, he was following orders to 'save ammunition and labour'; and secondly, he was out of his element. Perhaps, had he been at sea at that stage of the war, he would have been another of those who attacked unarmed ships and machine-gunned their survivors; but one must give him the benefit of the doubt there. On land, however, he and his men were fighting in a manner for which they were not trained: instead of other ships, their enemies were people. And there is nothing so vicious as a fighting man giving desperate battle in an alien setting – the sailor ashore or the soldier afloat feels equally out of control of his surroundings, and the defiant shout swiftly turns into the cornered rat's bad-loser snarl.

It took place in February 1945, towards the very end of the Imperial Navy's life; and it took place on land, during the Battle for Manila.

29

'The fate of the Empire'

By the time the Japanese nation knew that Yamamoto was dead, his successor had already been in office a month. The news prompted American intelligence to run an immediate profile on the new man.

Admiral Koga Mineichi was almost fifty-eight years old when he became Commander-in-Chief Combined Fleet. After an unremarkable early career, he had commanded a cruiser and a battleship; served as C-in-C of the Second Fleet in the early days of the European war; of the China Seas Fleet at the outbreak of the Pacific War; and as full admiral in 1942, he was placed in charge of Yokosuka Naval Station.

'Like his predecessor,' said the American profile, 'Admiral Koga is rated high in professional ability, but unlike Admiral Yamamoto, his position in naval circles has been a conservative one. Whereas Yamamoto was a bold and forceful innovator, to whom may be given the credit for the building up of Japanese naval aviation, Koga's career has been orthodox, and his background one almost entirely concerned with ships. Koga is held in high regard by the younger Japanese officers for his professional ability. He is said to be prudent and amiable in disposition, and in peace time, friendlily disposed towards the United States. He is well versed in international affairs, and was active as a member of technical committees at the Geneva Naval Conference.'

But the important question was how he would fight. 'The fact that a man of Koga's conservative temperament and known background should have been chosen for the top operational command of the Japanese Navy suggests the possibility of some change, defensively, in Japanese grand strategy . . . It should be borne in mind, however, that decisions regarding grand strategy lie solely within the province of Imperial Headquarters . . . The supposed cautiousness of Koga, therefore, may perhaps be reflected in operations carried out in pursuance of overall plans, but . . . the appointment in itself does not necessarily signify a complete shift to the defensive.'

In short, the men who compiled the profile had no idea how Koga might fight. But, if the newspaper headlines in Japan at the end of April were anything to go by, a shift to the defensive was far from people's minds.

'Japan plans new operations on a grand scale,' said the banner title on the

Nippon Times. 'America and Britain will surrender.' 'Greater East Asia War situation in new stage,' said the *Asahi*, 'preparations under way for grand scale new operations; enemy frantic in coping with internal struggles.' The *Yomiuri Hochi*: 'Enemy's confidence in winning shaken;' and the *Mainichi*: 'Large scale new operations are imminent; great results achieved in aerial annihilation battles; Japan secures a dominant position in south-west Pacific; enemy airbases to raid Japan destroyed.'

If the headlines sounded as though they were all written by the same person, it was because they probably had been. Looking at such clippings, the secretary of the Swiss legation in Tokyo, Robert Hausheer, commented: 'The morale of the masses is influenced by propaganda . . . Japanese propaganda is very childish, a very credulous public to which it is made.'

In fact Koga had less than a year in which to show himself cautious or aggressive: on 31 March 1944, he died, like Yamamoto, in an air crash – although this time it was accidental, and there was no ambush, but merely a storm. A divine wind, some may have said; or an infernal one.

During the forty-nine weeks of Koga's leadership, Japan's navy suffered severely. After a rapid-fire series of naval battles around the Solomons – Kolombangara, Kula Gulf, Vella Gulf, Vella Lavella – large parts of the islands had left Japan's empire for good. Rabaul, with its marvellous natural circular harbour, the bastion of Japan's south-eastward expansion, had been neutralized not by conquest but by encirclement; the Combined Fleet had been forced to withdraw from its Pearl Harbor-style base at Truk atoll, where, over 17–18 February 1944, 200,000 tons of war and supply shipping had been sunk; and, as Koga lay dead in his airplane on Mindanao, eleven carriers from America's Task Force 58 – 'the irresistible 58th', Chihaya called it – were hard at work in the Caroline Islands. In three days they sank 104,000 tons of merchant shipping, two destroyers and four escort carriers, and shot down 150 aircraft – all for the cost of twenty aircraft of their own.

Koga's record was not a happy one for Japan, but with anyone else in command – even Yamamoto – it would probably not have been much better. There is always a degree of horrible, wasteful absurdity in war; Japan's war against the Allies had been horribly, wastefully absurd from its beginning. Nakai Kazuyoshi had been in Rabaul when the first American air-raids had taken place there, dropping propaganda leaflets among the bombs. Much later his diary was found, and one entry commented: 'Enemy airplanes . . . dropped pictorial propaganda leaflets which said "What *is* the Japanese Navy doing?" It was a very clever leaflet, I thought.' Soldiers and sailors of the Imperial forces began to realize the futility of continued resistance; but even so, they fought on, always believing that there was one battle to come which would wipe out all the others and leave Japan in control of south-east Asia and the western Pacific.

They could, at least, take some comfort from the knowledge that during

1943, Japan's losses of aircraft carriers – which all but a few die-hards now saw were the vital form of shipping – had been very small compared to 1942. In 1943 only one carrier had been lost, *Chuyo*, a 20,000-ton escort vessel converted from a merchant ship; and in the same year four small carriers had been added to the fleet, giving a welcome 64,958 tons extra. And it would not have been surprising to have heard in Yokosuka Navy Yard the comment 'Just wait till they see this', for it was there that the biggest carrier in the world was taking shape: *Shinano*, 71,890-ton sister of *Yamato* and *Musashi*. Laid down as a third super-battleship in May 1940, she was now going to have an armoured flight deck above her battleship hull; and, despite being a compromise, she promised to fulfil her new role admirably. Apart from anything else, she would have an enormous capacity for the stowage of fuel and ordnance – the shell hoists where the turret barbettes should have been were made into express-rate bomb lifts – and clearly she would be able to be simultaneously a carrier in her own right, and a mother ship for other carriers, bearing their supplies inside her. She also looked very good, and (like the *Prince of Wales*, though perhaps people had forgotten that) was going to be unsinkable.

On the other hand, the net loss in oil stock was alarming: almost half the national reserve in two years – from just under 50 million barrels in 1941 to just over 25 million in 1943, while American annual production was seven hundred times larger than Japanese. But, at the current rate of consumption, Japan's stocks could last for another two years, and the war would surely be won by then. Perhaps it was better not to think of such things, but just fight.

Koga left one legacy to the Navy of which Yamamoto would have approved: plans for a radical reorganization of the Combined Fleet. Indeed Yamamoto might well have been envious, for the shuffle was going to produce the kind of navy he had long desired and never been able to realize, an air-oriented fleet in which the Main Body was composed of carriers, with battleships now relegated to a position of support. Koga died before he could carry out the grand scheme, but it went ahead nonetheless, and its inheritor was Admiral Toyoda Soemu.

Koga had taken over from Yamamoto after only two days – virtually as soon as Yamamoto's death became known. Toyoda's succession was far less smooth. Throughout the month of April 1944 it was the subject of violent arguments in Tokyo, and it was not until 3 May – nearly five weeks after Koga's death – that his appointment was agreed. It was announced two days later; yet, even before it was decided, the fleet's general future strategy had been publicized. 'All forces,' said the Navy General Staff on 2 May, 'are to be prepared to meet the enemy in the area of his main offensive and, with one blow, destroy the enemy fleet and thus thwart his offensive plans.' It amounted to no more than a restatement of the Tsushima ideal; but now the old decisive battle doctrine was being restated officially, when it should have been decently interred long before. Japanese naval strategic thought had not really developed since Tsushima; the magnitude of that victory had been too great. In the Pacific War the Japanese could have developed commerce raiding; should have developed commerce protection through convoys, should not have assumed that the southern oil-fields, once won, would not be contested; should have secured the lines of supply from the oil-fields to the homeland – but such comments, true as they are, are the easy wisdom of hindsight. Much of the clarity of hindsight came as soon as the war was over, or in the first few years of subsequent peace; it must have been waiting in the wings of the subconscious, so swift was its conscious recognition in peace. But in the pressure and passion of the moment it was hard to think so clearly and objectively, yet easy to believe that thoughts were clear and objective. Indeed one could go further, and say that, by the time Toyoda was given control of the Imperial Navy, there was no longer any actual thought in the Navy's planning, and that, instead, what passed for thought was little more than nervous reaction and automatic response, like the fly-removing twitch in a sleeping person's skin.

Toyoda, at any rate, was as committed to the notion of a single decisive battle as had been any of his predecessors. His particular problem was to determine where that battle might take place. Seemingly scattered American locations indicated three possible locations: around Palau in Polynesia; in the 'Inner South Seas' around Saipan; or somewhere north of Australia, working up towards the Philippines. Since the fleet could not be in three places at once, its new main body – the mobile fleet of carriers, supported by battleships, cruisers and destroyers – was sent to north Borneo to anchor at Tawi Tawi – a location which was close to fuel sources, but little else. This major section of the fleet was commanded by Vice Admiral Ozawa Jisaburo, while 1,644 land-based aircraft were scattered between the Carolines, the Marianas, Iwo Jima and Palau under the overall command of Vice Admiral Kakuda Kakuji. For his own part, Toyoda elected to remain aboard his rather humble flagship, the light cruiser *Oyodo*, anchored in Hiroshima Bay, 1,300 miles from the nearest likely battle site. This was a radical departure from the practice of previous Commanders-in-Chief, but it carried no imputation of cowardice. Nimitz had been using such a system for years; but to work well it did require good communications, prompt use of accurate intelligence, and the liberty of some flexibility for the commanders in the field. Recent campaigns had not shown the Imperial Navy scoring highly on any of these scales, and Toyoda's succession had not changed the rating greatly.

The battle came in June, and if in the dithering and arguing at Combined Fleet headquarters anyone was composed enough to notice, he might have pointed out that the US Navy was doing just what the Imperial Navy had hoped to do at Midway. An American assault on the island of Biak, between New Guinea and the Philippines, made the site of the forthcoming decisive conflict seem obvious. All eyes turned south, and Ozawa spent a week trying in vain to shoehorn his way back into Biak; and then, on 13 June, it became clear that Biak was no more, and no less, than a highly successful diversion. For on that day, as Okumiya Masatake wrote, 'the enemy confirmed our worst fears, and began the initial aerial bombardment against the Marianas'.

Ozawa could not have been caught more completely off balance. He was short of fuel and he was two thousand miles away from the scene of the action. American landings on Saipan did not commence until 15 June, but Ozawa was unable to arrive in the region until three days later; yet he sailed north with optimism in his heart. He knew his planes could outrange the American ones – the lightly-armed Japanese aircraft could strike from over 300 miles distance, while the Americans could manage less than 200. He would be sailing into the trade winds, and so could launch his aircraft as he advanced, whereas, to launch or land, the American carriers would have to turn away. And he anticipated that, whatever its size, the enemy fleet would be reduced by one-third by the regional shore-based aircraft. But his fleet had nine carriers with 430 aircraft, of which only 380 were operational; and Task Force 58 had fifteen carriers, with 891 aircraft. The proportions were reflected in the rest of the statistics: five Japanese battleships to seven American; thirteen Japanese cruisers to 21 American; 28 Japanese destroyers to 69 American; 43 Japanese float planes to 65 American. Ozawa was depending greatly on the attritional value of the shore-based aircraft; but he did not know that, out of those, more than 500 had been shot down, leaving only thirty or so operational. And, for all their sacrifice, the Japanese aircraft had achieved no attrition at all. The carrier aircraft were all Ozawa had to rely on, and he was going to meet a force twice the size of his own.

From Hiroshima Bay Admiral Toyoda sent out Togo's old, stirring admonition: 'The fate of the Empire depends on this battle. Let every man do his utmost.' The latter part of the message was unnecessary; no man in the Japanese fleet – or in the American, for that matter – had any intention of doing anything less than his utmost. As for the former part of the message, fate could be tempted a little too far. When the reports came in, there must have been many who secretly hoped that Toyoda had not meant what he said; for, if he had, the fate of the Empire looked to be sealed.

'Vital to every battle,' said Okumiya, 'is the indefinable element we term aggressiveness, or spirit, or *esprit de corps*.' He was trying to define the indefinable quality which Fred T. Jane, in 1906, had termed, 'Fitness to Win'; and, after the Battle of the Philippine Sea, Okumiya concluded without bitterness that 'whatever it is, the Americans had it'.

When the battle was over, the carriers *Bunker Hill* and *Wasp* and the battleship *Indiana* had been damaged; 49 American pilots and aircrew had died. But in 'The Great Marianas Turkey Shoot', as they aptly and irreverently nicknamed the conflict, the American fleet had damaged three of Ozawa's carriers and one cruiser; had sunk three further carriers, *Hiyo*, *Taiho* – Ozawa's flagship – and *Shokaku*, one of the last survivors from the days of the Nagumo Force; and had shot down or diverted into crash-landings so many of Ozawa's aircraft that in the end only 35 remained. The damaged carriers could be repaired; but a carrier stripped of its pilots was more of a liability than an asset. And, like the carriers which had been sunk, the dead pilots could not be replaced.

30

'This proud success'

Three days after the Turkey Shoot, the American secret agent in Japan codenamed 'Shark' filed this report:

'It is common knowledge in Japan,' he – or she – said, 'that they have a definite inferiority complex regarding the quality and quantity of their equipment. The realization that they cannot replace naval vessels that are lost has resulted in their hiding their fleet. High Japanese officials discuss this openly, saying they cannot afford to risk the fleet until the very last minute. There is every indication that the Japanese will play for time and hope for some miracle which may bring about a compromise peace, through an arrangement with Russia or China, before it is absolutely necessary to expose the fleet to serious losses.'

Another three days later, a message came from an agent in occupied China: 'The Jap Navy morale is on the downgrade. A few years ago a Jap sailor ashore was a far different man than the sailor who today comes ashore, gets drunk and grumbles about the inadequacy of the Navy. The activities of American subs are the chief cause of concern.'

Even before the Philippine Sea battle, B-29 Superfortresses had bombed a steelworks in Kyushu, the southernmost island of Japan proper. On 7 July, to emphasize the vulnerability of the country, came a second raid, this time directed towards naval installations at Sasebo. Guiding Japan towards its self-elected and increasingly obvious complete destruction was General Tojo, simultaneously Prime Minister and Minister of War; and on 18 July, uneasy in his embassy in Tokyo, the German Naval Attaché Admiral Wenneker sent a telegram to Berlin.

'Navy insists categorically that the Supreme Command take the view that the decision of the war will be fought out in the Pacific,' it read, 'and as a corollary demands that the present plan of allotting aircraft be changed from 50-50 to at least 30-70 in Navy's favour. General Tojo, it is said, has so far opposed this view. His retirement with entire cabinet is said to be unavoidable; a popular cabinet is demanded in order that it may be in a position to enlighten the people on the great danger impending and draw them out of their lethargy.'

Two days afterwards he sent his confirmation: 'Tojo cabinet resigned this morning . . . in composition so far determined, new cabinet indicates no improvement.'

Berlin took no immediate interest in this development: that same day, at the Wolf's Lair in East Prussia, Hitler was almost assassinated.

At the same time, on the islands of Guam and Tinian, the American air and naval bombardment – which for thirteen days had been almost continuous – became fiercer than ever; and on 5 August Wenneker cabled with matter-of-fact urgency: 'There is an imminent danger that the south area will be completely cut off.'

As far as the Imperial Navy was concerned, it could be. On 6 August came a message from Shanghai to Admiral Nimitz and General MacArthur: 'A difference of opinion has occurred between the Army and Navy supporters in Japan.' This was hardly news; but the nature of the disagreement was important. 'The Navy holds for a defence of Japan proper, while the Army holds for a defence together with the Navy of occupied areas.'

Only a week earlier the American Army and Navy, as represented by General MacArthur and Admiral Nimitz, had been going through much the same kind of 'difference of opinion'. Nimitz had argued in favour of a continuation of the by-passing strategy – the 'island-hopping' technique which, by surrounding and isolating key areas of resistance, had been so successful at Rabaul and elsewhere. The assault on Japan proper should be made, Nimitz felt, from bases seized on Formosa or the east China coast. MacArthur's passionate belief was that the advance should be made through the Philippines, and those islands used as the launching-pad for the final assault. Strategy and future political benefits mingled for him with his celebrated oath made almost three years earlier. 'I shall return' had begun as a personal commitment, and now by extension became a point of national honour as well. Accepting the General's point that an attack through heavily-fortified Formosa would entail greater casualties than one through the Philippines, where MacArthur assumed the population would prove still to be friendly, Admiral Nimitz gave way gracefully – and undoubtedly wisely. Probably MacArthur was correct in his prediction of post-war political benefits in the Philippines if they were liberated as soon as possible, but the wisdom of Nimitz's acceptance lay in realizing that a baulked MacArthur would not be as cooperative and agreeable a colleague as a MacArthur who had his way; and the eventual outcome of the war was certainly going to be the same whichever route was chosen.

Thus the General and the Admiral settled their difference of opinion and set to on a united approach; and the very unity of their approach forced a semblance of the same unity on their Japanese counterparts. The American advance was too rapid to allow anything but 'a defence together with the Navy of occupied islands.'

By 10 August America had lost 1,400 men on Guam. Japan – according to official figures – had lost over ten thousand, and the true figure may have been as much as fifty per cent higher. On 20 August American operations on Biak officially ended, with a toll of 2,555 Americans dead, wounded or missing, and almost 5,000 Japanese dead. On 25 August operations at Aitape in New Guinea ceased; Allied losses totalled three thousand, while the Japanese 18th Army had lost nearly three times that amount – 8,821 dead and 98 captured. More than two Japanese divisions had died in the vain attempts to recapture that beachhead alone; and on 31 August the American attack was launched against Iwo Jima and the Bonin Islands, little more than 500 miles south of Japan proper.

'Situation in Pacific continues practically unchanged,' Wenneker telegraphed on 1 September. 'The Americans are trying to clean out the remnants of the Jap defenders in both the Marianas and New Guinea. Otherwise except for air attacks on Palau and Yap situation is relatively quiet. Preparations of new offensives in the air of the Philippines are clearly apparent. Admiralty staff, however, lately express the opinion that it will not begin before the presidential election, as reverses would be unendurable for Roosevelt. Before that time there will at most be attempts to land on intervening occupied islands.'

The intelligence Wenneker transmitted, despite its gloomy nature for the audience in Berlin, was unbiassed and as factual as he could make it. 'The Japanese Air Force is seriously crippled,' he said on 6 October. Stressing the superiority of American air- and sea-power in the Pacific, and commenting on the effective use of radar by American artillery, he concluded that it was 'unlikely the Japs will seek decisive fleet action except under most favourable circumstances'. Telegrams back from Berlin were not always so realistic: on 17 October a personal message for Navy Minister Admiral Yonai arrived from Grand Admiral Dönitz.

'On that magnificent victory which the Imperial Japanese sea and air forces of the Navy have achieved over an attacking enemy fleet off Formosa and the Philippines,' it read, 'I extend Your Excellency my sincerest congratulations. This proud success in our common war against the unwarranted pretensions of the Anglo-Saxons is a heavy blow against the American fleet. The German Navy rejoices with me over the great victory of their Japanese comrades. It will be for us a spur to further efforts against our common foe.'

One can almost see the raised eyebrows and hear the clearing of Wenneker's throat as he wrote out the reply to this effusiveness. 'Great success must be doubted,' he said, because 'the attacks were considerably confused'.

The battle to which both men were referring was the largest single air battle of the war, the Battle off Formosa, which took place from 13–16 October. Far from being a 'magnificent victory' for Japan, it was yet another swingeing defeat. During attacks on Formosa, two American cruisers –

Canberra and *Houston* – had been badly damaged, while several others had been hit. This first stage was a night battle over 13–14 October, and the sea was lit up not only by the flames of those ships, but by what appeared to be other American wrecks as well. These were burning *Japanese* aircraft, dotting the ocean like Christmas lights, and they were mistaken by surviving Japanese pilots for American ships. Other ships *were* damaged, two destroyers, two carriers and a light cruiser amongst them, but nowhere near as badly as the rejoicing pilots believed. Picking up their gleeful messages, Admiral William Halsey arranged a simple but effective trap: with daylight, he allowed his damaged cruisers to be seen limping away. Halsey took the opportunity to sent a message that would become famous: he was 'retiring at high speed towards the enemy'. As expected, Admiral Toyoda sent out reinforcement air crews from their training in the Inland Sea to join in the joyous annihilation of the enemy fleet; and Halsey promptly jumped them, destroying at least 300 of the 600 aircraft. If this for Dönitz was still a 'proud success', the Allies had no need of victories.

And yet at that time the Allies – and in particular the US Navy, whose ships made up the overwhelming majority in the operation – were poised on the brink of their greatest battle and greatest victory. The Japanese Admiralty prediction that no new major offensive would take place in the Philippines until after the 1944 presidential election in November had been remarkably accurate: the invasion was timed for 20 December. But the prediction had been made at the beginning of September, and through that month Japanese resistance in the central Philippines was so limited that the American schedule was brought forward by two months to 20 October. By the time the election took place, the most extensive naval battle in history would itself have become a part of history, and the Imperial Japanese Navy would have come close to extinction.

31

'This ultimate assignment'

On 19 October Wenneker reported that the Japanese 'successes' off Formosa 'have given a gratifying, clearly perceptible boost in morale at stations of the armed forces'. Twenty-four hours later American forces began to land on the island of Leyte in the Philippines – exactly on their advanced schedule, and eight weeks earlier than Japan's Admiralty had originally guessed.

'The landing on Leyte was carried out as a complete surprise while a celebration of the other victory ensued in Tokyo,' said Wenneker. 'Under these considerations, the Americans achieved their purpose, even if their sacrifice was unexpectedly great . . . it will probably be very difficult, if not impossible under the circumstances, for the Japanese to force the enemy off Leyte again.'

The German was giving the facts as he knew them, but he was not entirely correct; no operation of such a size could be a complete surprise. News of it had come to Toyoda during the Tokyo celebrations, and on 18 October he issued the executive order for his counter-stroke: Operation SHO. The word means 'victory'.

There were four SHO plans, one for each of the probable areas of American attack. SHO-4 and SHO-3 covered parts of the homeland itself; SHO-2 covered Formosa and the Ryukyus, Nimitz's preferred target; SHO-1 covered MacArthur's choice, the Philippines; and all of the plans were death-or-glory last flings, the losing gambler's final throw of the dice. Win or lose, it would be done with style, and after the war Rear Admiral Takata explained why.

'By the time you had taken Saipan and had begun to land on Leyte,' he said to his Allied interrogators, 'we realized fully that it would be impossible for us to maintain a battle fleet in Japanese waters, subjected to bombing, and when the American fleet did come in close to Japan that we would be unable to oppose it with a fleet of any strength. Therefore, we decided to commit our entire fleet to the Leyte campaign, and sent every available ship down there, with the knowledge that we would lose most of them . . . but it was worth it if we could prevent conquest of the Philippines.'

Admiral Toyoda, Takata continued, 'made the decision to use his complete force because of what had happened to the Italian fleet in this war and the German fleet in the last war'. There was going to be no inglorious sinking in harbour, or scuttling in internment, for the Imperial Navy.

As for the opposition, Wenneker wrote that 'all in all, the entire American fleet seemed to be participating in the operation'. It certainly seemed so: over 200 American warships were supported by approximately 600 other vessels. Against them Toyoda could muster a total of 63 warships.

SHO-1 was an operation characteristic of the dying Imperial Navy. Forces were deliberately widely scattered, and ordered to operate far away from one another, but in conformity to a strict timetable. It had not worked at Midway; but, at least once at Leyte Gulf, one part of the fleet came close to success, and another part did succeed. The 63 ships were divided into four sections. Under Admiral Ozawa, the victim of the Turkey Shoot, was the Mobile Force – four heavy carriers, two hybrid battleship-carriers, three light cruisers and eight destroyers. Under Admiral Kurita Takeo was the Centre Force – five battleships, including both of the super-sisters, *Yamato* and *Musashi*; ten cruisers; two light cruisers; and fifteen destroyers. The remaining two groups, C and the Second Striking Force, together made up the Southern Force. C was commanded by Admiral Nishimura Shoji, and included two battleships, a cruiser and four destroyers, while Admiral Shima Kiyohide commanded the last group of two cruisers, a light cruiser and four destroyers. This allotment of command was somewhat unusual, for Shima and Nishimura were old contemporaries from naval college; Shima was six months older than Nishimura; but it was Shima who had the smaller group. It was a trivial matter, considering the circumstances; but it would have serious consequences.

Lying at anchor in Brunei Bay, the ships were still a brave sight with their Rising Sun ensigns and their bows decorated with the carved Imperial chrysanthemum; but, aboard, there was much unrest as officers and men realized the nature of SHO-1. It was not that they were going to fight a fleet far larger than their own; the cause of their concern was that their ships, of which they were still proud, might be sacrificed for a minimal prize. Tens of thousands of American troops were being landed on Leyte; if, by the time the Japanese fleets arrived there, the transports were empty, and if only cargo and munition vessels remained, there would be no worthy target. American aircraft could end the fleet's existence without it having the chance to retaliate against anything worthwhile.

Aboard his flagship, the cruiser *Atago*, Admiral Kurita called a meeting of divisional commanders and staffs and gave them a rallying speech. It was recorded; and it must rate as one of the most typically *Japanese* rallying cries of the war.

'I know that many of you are strongly opposed to this assignment,' he began. 'But the war situation is far more critical than any of you can possibly know. Would it not be a shame to have the fleet remain intact while our nation perishes? I believe that Imperial General Headquarters is giving us a glorious opportunity. Because I realize how very serious the war situation actually is, I am willing to accept even this ultimate assignment to storm into Leyte Gulf.'

It could hardly be argued that the fleet remained intact; but shame was a sure touch. Likewise 'glorious opportunity' – all the myriad debts which each of them owed to Emperor, family and nation would be repaid; and 'ultimate assignment' – there is a strong streak of attraction to melodrama in the Japanese character. As Chihaya Masataka commented, they like 'show and thrill'. So far, Kurita had got his psychology right.

Then he went on to say something which could only emphasize the suicidal pathos and grandeur of the proposed assault: 'You must all remember that there are such things as miracles.' Perhaps more than any other sentence, those words encapsulate the terrible – but impressive – refusal to give up, the moral courage which was just about all the Imperial Navy had left as a weapon.

'What man can say that there is no chance for our fleet to turn the tide of war in a decisive battle?' Many could, but none did; and one of the few who might have spoken out was a pile of ashes in Tokyo.

'We shall have a chance to meet our enemies. We shall engage his task forces. I hope that you will not carry your responsibilities lightly. I know that you will act faithfully and well.'

And they did; and they died, most of them, as they had expected, with their ships; but they believed that they had achieved something.

Toyoda's original plan for SHO-1 had been divided into two: Admiral Kurita would proceed through the Sibuyan Sea in company with Admiral Ozawa's carriers. From the Sibuyan, north-west of Leyte, they would slip through the San Bernadino Strait into the Pacific, move down the east side of Samar Island, and 'storm into Leyte Gulf' from the north-east. Meanwhile, Admiral Nishimura would take his small fleet over the Sulu Sea, south-west of Leyte, and enter the Gulf via the Surigao Strait. This would provide the diversion so beloved of the Imperial Navy; and, compared to some of the battle plans they had had, it was fairly simple.

The plan that was actually used, however, was a good deal more complex. On paper Ozawa's fleet included eight carriers with 312 aircraft; in reality there were only 108 aircraft between four carriers, and most of the pilots were raw recruits, fresh from an inadequate training course. On 19 October,

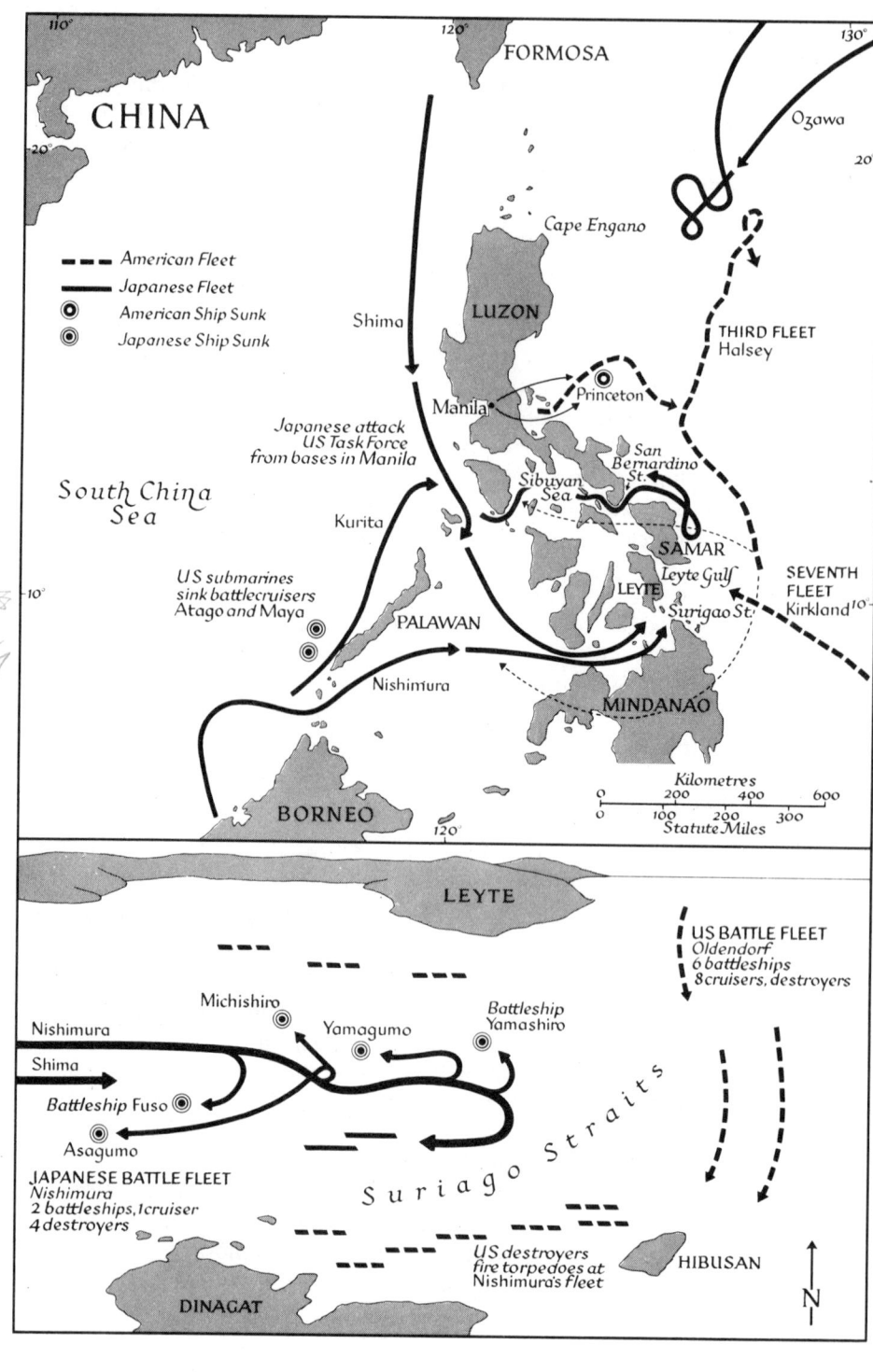

therefore, Ozawa had presented a new plan to Toyoda: 'I propose,' he said, 'to manoeuvre my ships from the *north*, in such a way that they will lure the enemy task force away from the battle area and thus reduce pressure on the Kurita fleet. I shall disregard any damage which may be inflicted on my force in this operation.'

He was offering himself, his men and his almost empty ships as a bait; and Toyoda accepted.

Then there was Shima, with his seven ships. These had not been part of the original plan at all, and were in the Pescadores. They had been a part of the force sent out to mop up Halsey's ships after the Battle off Formosa. Now Shima was detailed to follow Nishimura's 'diversionary' force. But neither was given overall command, and as men of exactly equal rank and seniority neither could assume overall command. It is said that, ever since college days, they had been open rivals; it is also said that their rivalry went so deep that they refused to talk to each other. Whether that is so or not – and it is perfectly possible – their two forces remained completely separate, mutually unhelpful, and mutually incommunicado throughout their section of the battle.

Thus there were not two approaches, as originally intended, nor three, as subsequently decided, but four; and, as at Midway and the Philippine Sea, they were all meant to work to a timetable. And, once again, the American forces blithely ignored the timetable, tackled the various fleets one by one, and did for the lot of them.

First to go was Kurita's own flagship, the cruiser *Atago*. Steaming in two tight circular formations, with even the largest ships little more than a mile from each other, the fleet had to make a zigzag passage of nearly 1,500 miles from Brunei to the Sibuyan Sea – without air cover. Less than twenty-four hours out of Brunei, however, it was not aircraft but submarines which drew first blood; and with *Atago* went a second cruiser, *Maya*, while *Atago*'s sister *Takao* was so severely damaged she had to return to base. It was hardly an auspicious start: within a day of setting out, and two days before he wanted to open the action, Admiral Kurita found himself swimming for his life. Yet even so, at least one officer maintained such professional detachment that he was heard to say, 'It's too bad our own ships can't pull off an attack like that.'

The survivors were picked up and transferred to other ships, Kurita breaking out his flag on *Yamato*. Despite constant alerts they proceeded unmolested for the rest of that day, 23 October, and by dawn next morning all four fleets were converging rapidly: Kurita approaching the Sibuyan Sea, Nishimura and Shima crossing the Sulu Sea, and Ozawa coming south-east across the Pacific towards Cape Engaño on the north-east corner of Luzon

Island. It still seemed conceivable that they might succeed; but over the next forty-eight hours all would fight and lose in four separate battles. Together the four – the Sibuyan Sea, Cape Engaño, Samar and Surigao Strait – made up the Battle for Leyte Gulf; and, by most standards of greatness in sea battles, Leyte Gulf was to be the last and greatest of them all. The area covered by the conflict was over a hundred thousand square miles, and a greater tonnage of ships and greater number of men than in any previous naval battle were used and lost. There was an historic first and another historic last as well: it was in this battle that the last classic 'crossing the T' tactic was used; and here the legendary kamikaze corps made its first appearance.

The Japanese fleets' weaknesses were manifold: numerical inferiority; a wide scattering of force; extremely limited air cover – apart from Ozawa's novices, the few additional aircraft were land-based, and would prove of limited usefulness. There was also the tremendous distance from Toyoda's central command, and the concomitant feebleness of communication. But the American fleets, too, had one glaring weakness, which came close to losing them at least part of the battle: Admiral Kinkaid's Seventh Fleet, supporting the landings, came under MacArthur's command, while Admiral Halsey's Third Fleet was under Nimitz's command. And Halsey, ever since Pearl Harbor, had had such a profound hatred of all things Japanese ('rats and barbarians' was about his kindest comment on them) and of Japanese carriers in particular, that when the chance presented itself, he could not resist taking Ozawa's carrier bait and leaving other American ships unprotected.

Nevertheless it was Halsey's aircraft which opened the first battle, that of the Sibuyan Sea. At 0810 Kurita's fleet was sighted at the entrance to the Sea, and task groups of the Third Fleet began to fly off aircraft. Before the first of them had located Kurita, and while others were preparing for fly-off, one of the task groups was caught just as Nagumo had been at Midway: with aircraft fuelling and loading, land-based Japanese planes came droning in to the attack. If they had been Nagumo's long-dead veterans, the damage would have been huge; as it was, these greenhorns had little chance. Not one of them got close enough to attack until 0930, when it appeared that all had been beaten off. But, high in the clouds, there was one remaining bomber; and, coming through, it dropped a bomb on the light carrier *Princeton*. She burned until mid-afternoon before sinking, one of the few American losses.

At 0900 Nishimura's force had been sighted, and in a skirmish shortly afterwards the old battleship *Fuso* and a destroyer were damaged; but Rear Admiral Oldendorf was merely warming up for something more spectacular.

It was 1040 when the first wave of Halsey's planes came within Kurita's range. They had to face fire from 150 anti-aircraft guns each on *Yamato* and

Musashi, and 100 each on the other capital ships. It was impossible for all the ships to survive yet, although the action lasted about an hour, none was sunk. But a cruiser was sufficiently badly damaged to force her withdrawal and return to Brunei, and, while bombs simply bounced off the sturdy decks of the two super-battleships, both were hit by torpedoes. *Yamato* took one, which made little difference to her; *Musashi* took two, followed by several successful bomb hits near her bridge, and these were more serious: the main battery synchronizers were knocked out of action.

Around noon, with the fleet still ploughing on, nearly intact, at 27 knots, the second attack wave came in – 24 heavy torpedo bombers. A dozen concentrated on the super-battleships while the others divided themselves over the rest of the fleet; and at 1325 the third wave came in, 29 planes which concentrated solely on *Musashi*. She was hit three times on the starboard bow; her speed dropped to 22 knots; thousands of tons of water flooded into her – but she kept going.

'The First Striking Force is engaged in hard fight in the Sibuyan Sea,' Kurita radioed to Toyoda. 'Enemy air attacks are expected to increase. Request land-based air force and Mobile Force to make prompt attacks on enemy carrier force.' But there was no air protection, and at 1430, as *Musashi* began to fall astern of the fleet, her bows low in the water, the fourth wave appeared – fifty planes, of which thirty gave their whole attention to the obviously dying supership. More hits brought her down to only 12 knots, and, escorted by two destroyers, she was forced to leave the battle area. The rest of the fleet could give her no more protection, and at 1510 the fifth and last attack wave came in – more than a hundred fighters and bombers. Now making only 6 knots, hit by nineteen bombs and seventeen torpedoes, *Musashi* struggled towards the distant shore, her bows awash, her forward turrets sticking out of the water.

She never made it to the beach. None of the American pilots saw her go down: the final, sudden roll to port took place at 1935.

One of the men aboard *Musashi* when she went down was Nagasue Eichi. When he heard the order to abandon ship, lined up to jump overboard, and swam in search of rescue, he reflected morosely that few men were less fortunate than he: he had been aboard *Atago* the day before. To be sunk twice in two days seemed really bad luck; in later years, however, he changed his mind. He had survived, and became a prominent member of Japan's post-war Democratic Socialist Party; but on 24 October 1944 eleven hundred of the men who had been on *Musashi* with him had died. One of those was her captain, Inoguchi Toshihira, who chose to remain on the bridge. Trained as a gunnery officer, he had always been one of those who disbelieved Yamamoto, and, until the end, saw the all-big-gun battleship as the natural final arbiter of war at sea. Now in his last report he admitted he had been wrong.

Aboard *Yamato* a young decode officer named Kojima Kiyofumi watched the pillar of smoke that remained, and felt a sudden chill of fear go through him. The feeling was an extremely unwelcome novelty; since July he had been a member of *Yamato*'s crew, and had always felt secure – she and *Musashi* were unsinkable. Now he felt as vulnerable as if he were on a cruiser or destroyer. Instinctively he glanced upwards, fearful that another attack wave would come at *Yamato*; but except for two aircraft the sky was empty, and those two aircraft were Japanese.

Thirty-seven years later, at a chance meeting in Tokyo, Kojima discovered the identity of one of those two pilots. It was Commander Iki Haruki, the veteran of that long-ago, intoxicating battle against the *Prince of Wales* and *Repulse*, the man who had returned to drop bouquets over the sites of the wrecks. The *Prince of Wales* had been called unsinkable as well. Now Iki had seen twice for himself that, without air cover, there was no such thing as a battleship proof against air attack. But there was nothing he could do, and, heavy at heart, he turned his aircraft away. The war had turned viciously against Japan since those early days, when a gesture of gallantry had not been out of place. In 1944, there were no flowers in the Philippines.

While *Musashi* was in her death throes, a message arrived for Kurita from Toyoda – the first communication from headquarters. 'Probability is great,' it said, 'that enemy will employ submarines in the approaches to San Bernadino Strait. Be alert.'

After their battering in the Sibuyan Sea, no one found anything the least bit comic in the belated warning – it was simply infuriating.

'If we continue our present course,' Kurita replied, 'our losses will increase incalculably, with little hope of success for our mission. Therefore have decided to withdraw outside the range of enemy air attack for the time being' – and he turned his ships around. One American scout plane had remained above. Seeing the fleet reverse course, it sped off eastwards and radioed that Kurita was retreating; and, far away, Halsey received the message with joy. Out of the four Japanese fleets, three had been spotted by the morning of the 24th, and, ironically, the one seen last of all was Ozawa's decoy carrier fleet. While the other admirals would have liked nothing better than to escape detection, detection was Ozawa's precise wish and intention. When he was located, his ships were 190 miles west of Cape Engaño, and the message saying so arrived on Halsey's flagship at almost the same time as the message saying that Kurita was retreating. The fleet Ozawa had hoped to protect was already badly mauled. Had he known this, Ozawa would have considered he had failed in his mission; but the inverted success he sought was coming.

'We go north,' Halsey radioed, 'and put those Jap carriers down for keeps.' Away he went, leaving the beachhead in Leyte unprotected; and a few hours later, as darkness drew in, Kurita reversed course again. With luck, he hoped a night-time dash through the San Bernadino Straits would bring him into striking range of the Gulf at dawn.

Admiral Kinkaid, in charge of the Seventh Fleet, had no idea that Halsey's whole force had gone. An earlier message had left him with the impression that Halsey was intending to leave one task group on guard; but there was nothing. So, in happy ignorance of the exposed flank, Kinkaid sent Rear Admiral Oldendorf south with the Seventh Fleet's entire Bombardment and Fire Support Group to intercept and ambush Nishimura's fleet when they came out of the Surigao Straits.

Nishimura's force, again, was composed of four destroyers, a cruiser and two battleships, and, out of those, one of the destroyers and one of the battleships had been damaged in the morning skirmish of 24 October. Oldendorf had 21 destroyers, four heavy and four light cruisers, and six battleships. Many of the ships were survivors of Pearl; one could easily imagine them seeking revenge as they cruised up and down across the mouth of the straits.

Nishimura was a thoroughly sea-going admiral of the old school. He had never held a shore post in his life, and had never wanted to; ships, and ships with guns, were what he knew and loved. He loved his son very much as well; but, though he had ships, he had lost his son earlier in the war – a fact to which some people ascribe his action in Surigao. For, knowing that his presence was detected, able to assume that there must be an enemy force ahead, nevertheless he brought his fleet through the straits in line ahead; and, shortly after 0230 in the morning of 25 October, Oldendorf crossed Nishimura's T as neatly as in a copybook exercise.

It began with a gauntlet-run of five American destroyers. Dashing into the strait, they loosed off 27 torpedoes. Eight minutes later came a series of crashing explosions: *Fuso*, the battleship already damaged, split in two. Three destroyers sank in rapid succession; and *Yamashiro*, Nishimura's flagship, staggered and slowed down as a torpedo drove into her. Then she picked up a little speed and carried on, her sole remaining companions a cruiser and a destroyer. Their primitive radar had been dazzled by the surrounding islands; and the first thing that Nishimura knew of Oldendorf's T-crossing was, at 0352, the sudden, simultaneous brilliant flashes ahead. One moment darkness; the next, a line of fire from one end of the horizon to the other.

'Every ship in the flank forces and the battle line opened up at once,' said

Oldendorf with satisfaction, 'and there was a semi-circle of fire which landed squarely on one point, which was the leading battleship.'

Yamashiro was the only battleship left, and on her Nishimura was dead. His last signal had been: 'You are to proceed and attack all ships.'

The firing did not last long; it did not need to. At 0419 *Yamashiro* turned over and went down. The remaining two ships could hardly obey their Admiral's order; the last destroyer had had her bows shot off, and limped away down the strait, while the last cruiser followed, fully ablaze and lighting up the night as she struggled to find safety. It was *Mogami*, which had lost her bows in a collision after Midway. She was not a lucky ship.

Admiral Shima, meanwhile, was coming up the strait in Nishimura's wake, also in line ahead. To support was what he had been told to do; to move in line ahead to battle was what he had been trained to do. But neither he nor Nishimura had been specifically told to co-operate, and the old rivals had steamed into the strait with an apparently adamant refusal to say anything at all to each other. Shima thus had no more idea than the unfortunate Nishimura of what lay ahead, and the first thing that happened was that a torpedo slammed into one of his two cruisers. The next was that, through the darkness and thick, swirling smoke, he sighted what appeared to be three burning wrecks. In fact there were only two: one which he rightly guessed was *Mogami*, and the two halves of *Fuso*, burning but not yet sunk. Then, thinking that he had picked up two destroyers on his radar, he fired sixteen torpedoes at an island, and while doing that managed to crash into the one clearly visible object, *Mogami*. She really was not a lucky ship. Nor was Shima much more fortunate, for that one piece of extraordinary ineptitude is the event for which he is mainly remembered. He did get away, however, laying a smoke screen as he tottered down the strait up which he had so recently and rashly steamed; and, when with daylight it became apparent that *Mogami*, trailing miserably along, was useless, his last action at Surigao was to send a torpedo through his old rival's cruiser and send her to the bottom.

At about the same time, some 200 miles to the north, Kurita's fleet was on its way down the east, Pacific, side of Samar Island. In a considerable feat of navigation, the unlit ships had successfully negotiated the narrow, pitch-dark San Bernadino Strait and had emerged into the ocean at 0335, just after Oldendorf's first destroyer attack on Nishimura. Daylight came at 0627, whereupon Kurita's men took up anti-aircraft defence stations; and only eighteen minutes later, over the distant horizon, they sighted the masts of American carriers. The range was sixteen miles; and, within a minute, Japanese shells were pluming into the water around the carrier force.

Kurita naturally assumed that he had surprised a main section of the American carrier fleet. Actually the ships were neither heavy nor even light carriers, but escort carriers – 'baby flat-tops' – under Rear Admiral Clifton Sprague. Their job by day was to guard convoys, provide air cover for amphibious attacks, and look for submarines. By night they were supposed simply to lie well clear of any land, which was just what they had been doing; and when, at 0659, *Yamato* fired her first-ever shell against an enemy ship, they were not at all well defended. Apart from their aircraft, each escort carrier had only one 5-inch gun, and beyond that the six ships were accompanied by nothing but three destroyers.

Sprague's instant reaction was to turn from Kurita and head off at top speed – a negligible 17½ knots – in order to launch his 168 planes. Within the next four minutes, in desperation, he sent a plain-language mayday call to Admiral Kinkaid; Kinkaid in turn summoned Task Force 34, the sub-group of Halsey's fleet which he believed to have stayed behind, and for the first time discovered they were not where he thought. At 0701 Sprague threw his code book and security regulations overboard. At 0706 he appealed to Kinkaid again, saying his ships were in 'the ultimate of desperate circumstances'; he estimated that within five minutes they would all be sunk. But nine minutes later they were still afloat, and at that moment a providential rain squall blew over. Gratefully, Sprague ducked his carriers into it, and the three destroyers charged towards Kurita. Each main turret on the giant *Yamato* weighed as much as any one of the destroyers, and in addition to the super-battleship, Kurita still had another three battleships, six heavy and two light cruisers, and his own outnumbering destroyers. The three American destroyers, *Hoel*, *Heermann* and *Johnston*, looked set for suicide – yet, astonishingly, they not only sank two of Kurita's cruisers, but also managed to put mighty *Yamato* to flight.

After the loss of *Musashi*, flooding may have been the danger Kurita feared most. He was within fourteen miles of Sprague's little carriers when six torpedoes were spotted hurtling towards the flagship. Evading them with a sharp turn, he found himself trapped with three on either side, running parallel to and at the same speed as *Yamato*. All he could do was to keep going until they ran out of power. It must have been intensely frustrating, and not a little nerve-wracking; but there is something irresistibly farcical about the picture, for he was heading at top speed away from the battle and, by the time he was able to turn back, he was another five miles away from Sprague. And it made a great deal of difference: he could no longer exercise any effective control over the conflict.

The heavy cruiser *Kumano* had been put out of action by one of *Johnston*'s torpedoes. Her sister *Suzuya*, slowed to 20 knots by a bomb, fell out of battle to give assistance – an ill-starred family indeed, for both were sisters to *Mogami* – and some ship, perhaps an American destroyer, perhaps the four destroyer escorts which joined in the affray, torpedoed two further heavy cruisers, *Chokai* and *Chikuma*. Sprague's aircraft used all their bombs, all their torpedoes, even all their machine-gun ammunition; and when they had no weapons left they still flew in 'dry runs', mock attacks, to distract attention from the carriers. Yet inevitably, the carriers, the destroyers and the destroyer escorts were being hit: *Hoel* received over 40 shells, was abandoned, and sank; *Johnston* took on everyone, everyone took her on, and she sank; the destroyer escort *Samuel B. Roberts* had her diminutive sides torn up by 14-inch shells – down she went; and four of Sprague's six carriers were struck. They were *White Plains*, *Kalinin Bay*, *Fanshawe Bay* and *Gambier Bay*. All but *Gambier Bay* survived. She was hit so often her damage control parties and engineers could no longer cope; losing speed, she dropped away from the others, was abandoned at 0850, and at 0907 turned over and sank.

The defence had been heroic; now there seemed little more that the Americans could do. But at 0911 Kurita gave a most unexpected order; and, as Sprague described it, 'at 0925 my mind was occupied with dodging torpedoes when near the bridge I heard one of the signalmen yell, "Goddamit, boys, they're getting away!" I could not believe my eyes, but it looked as if the whole Japanese fleet was indeed retiring. However, it took a whole series of reports from circling planes to convince me. At best, I had expected to be swimming by this time.'

Kurita actually was turning away from what could have been an easy, and should have been a certain, victory. It was incomprehensible to Sprague and his men, and until after the war – which Kurita survived – no Americans and few Japanese knew exactly why he withdrew at that moment. In America the Admiral's own limited explanation had been more generally accepted than in Japan, where critics accused him of cowardice. But such things are easily said out of the heat and stress of action. The points Kurita himself has made are valid: he believed that without air cover he was facing a major body of fleet carriers; and, after the strain of the night passage of San Bernadino Strait, the Battle of the Sibuyan Sea, the loss of his flagship *Atago*, and three days and nights without sleep, he was, in his own words, 'exhausted both physically and mentally'.

Admiral Togo might have been more charitable than those who called Kurita a coward; before Tsushima Togo had reminded his men how easy it is 'to feel that the enemy is strong and we are weak; this is because while we cannot see the damage done to the enemy's vessels, the damage to ours is always before our eyes'. And, away from the battle, proving how seriously they had been damaged, both *Chokai* and *Chikuma* sank.

For an escort carrier, two destroyers and a destroyer escort, Kurita lost three heavy cruisers and three destroyers. But, while he reformed his fleet and prepared to retrace his route through San Bernadino, the American escort carriers came under attack again.

At dawn that morning, when Kurita's men were moving to their stations, six pilots on Mindanao Island went through a simple ceremony. 'You are now as gods,' their commanding officer told them, 'free from all earthly desires.' They drank a toast in water to each other, to the homeland and the Emperor, wrapped white scarfs around their foreheads, boarded their aircraft and took off on a one-way flight to death. They were kamikaze pilots, and although there had been a few previous kamikaze attacks, these were going to be the first to find success.

While Clifton Sprague was fighting Kurita, the pilots located Rear Admiral Thomas Sprague's escort carriers in the act of flying off aircraft to assist Clifton Sprague. Down from ten thousand feet came the kamikaze, the divine wind, and two of Thomas Sprague's carriers – *Santee* and *Suwannee* – became funeral pyres for the Japanese, as the planes tore into their flight decks and exploded. The ships nevertheless survived; but shortly after, as Clifton Sprague slowly accepted the fact that Kurita had really gone, another flight found him. One suicide plane smashed into *Kitkun Bay*; two more into *Kalinin Bay*, already full of holes from Kurita's shells; and another blasted its way through the flight deck of *St Lô*. The *Bay* ships, shattered as they were, lived on; aboard *St Lô*, however, internal fires and induced explosions almost blew the ship to pieces, and shortly before midday she sank – the first vessel destroyed in such a manner.

Throughout the rest of the war some two thousand Imperial Navy men died in these suicide attacks, and between them they sank about forty ships, inflicting varying degrees of damage on at least 300 others.

'The two sources of damage are the petrol tanks in the plane and the bomb,' wrote Commander Frank Hopkins. Now Admiral Sir Frank Hopkins, he was, between September and December 1944, Royal Navy air observer attached to the US Pacific Fleet, and was present during the Battle for Leyte Gulf. Continuing his description of kamikaze damage, he said:

'The petrol tanks normally ignite on the flight deck, setting fire to the aircraft in the vicinity, and burning petrol flows through holes in the deck, starting fires among aircraft below. The bomb, being unable to penetrate the armoured hangar deck, explodes somewhere between that deck and the flight deck, usually causing considerable casualties from splinters in the various ready rooms and offices under the flight deck, and starting fires amongst planes on the hangar deck . . .

'Once the fires are well started, considerable trouble is caused from smoke. This becomes a serious handicap to firefighters and causes casualties from suffocation. The combination of burning rubber, lubricating oil and petrol makes the smoke very dense and evil-smelling. Since the air intakes for most of the ventilation are in the hangar, this smoke penetrates everywhere . . .'

It was a frightful, and frightening, form of attack. 'The only completely effective defence against crash bombing,' Hopkins continued, 'is to destroy all the attacking planes before they can deliver their attack.'

Naturally an indirect hit was far less dangerous. At about 1250 on 25 November, Task Group 38.2 came under assault from the kamikaze corps. 'The *Hancock* [a carrier] was attacked first by one plane diving from 8,000 feet out of the sun. When this plane reached about 1,000 feet it disintegrated from repeated hits by 40- and 20-mm guns. The engine fell in the sea off the starboard bow, the rear half of the fuselage hit the flight deck abaft the island, one wing and most of the forward part of the fuselage petrol tanks landed on the port side of the flight deck forward of the island and started a fire on deck. The bomb, which appeared to be about 500 pounds, fell in the sea alongside the port side abreast the island. The fire was dealt with quickly and efficiently, and flight operations were resumed within five minutes.'

At the same time, Charles Hughes-Hallett – now Vice Admiral Sir Charles – was commanding officer of HMS *Implacable*. After VE Day his ships were able to join the American ships in the Pacific.

'The real problem,' he recalls, 'came in the fact that all sorts of precautions had to be taken and had been evolved by experience against kamikazes endeavouring to get at the carriers collectively – American and British – undetected. You had well ahead of you a line of destroyers, who were there to give warning . . . well clear of the squadrons laterally there was a destroyer known as the de-lousing destroyer. Every Allied aircraft coming in from a raid had to make contact over one of these and be identified. The destroyers had a cap – a fighter unit overhead who was in touch with them – and directly the destroyers reckoned that one of the aircraft was a Japanese trying to sneak in, the cap was put down. It worked very well, but it did result in I think two occasions of the kamikaze then attacking the destroyer itself. And in one case an American destroyer was sunk; we had no trouble on the British side of it, but that was fortuitous.'

A further reason for the lesser damage to British carriers was that they had decks of 3¾-inch steel.

'The American carriers didn't in those days; they had the ordinary light wood deck, the reason they never followed our pattern being that, in hot weather, waltzing about on 3¾ inches of steel gets very bad on the feet. We reckoned that the maximum heat time occurred about three to four in the afternoon, and so my Commander Air amused himself one day by breaking an egg on the flight deck at that time. It was lightly fried – not really to eatable condition – in 7½ minutes; and that you had to walk about on. But the result was that when a kamikaze hit an American carrier, it was a three months' dockyard job; and as some put it, in the case of hitting a British carrier, you took a couple of brooms and swept the rubbish over the side. A great friend of mine, an ex-pilot who was liaison at the American headquarters in Honolulu told me that at a daily staff meeting one morning the first kamikaze attack on a British carrier – the *Formidable* – was reported. The end of her signal said: 'Expect to be in action again by four o'clock in the afternoon." The American staff around the table more or less lay back and roared with laughter, saying "Those British again!" Next morning, when they heard she *was* back in action at four o'clock in the afternoon, they changed their tune rather rapidly.'

Recollection of victory can be justifiably light-hearted; but at the time, although Hopkins, observing in the Philippines, could write the pleasant understatement that 'operations out here are being very interesting', nevertheless he had no illusions about the potential of the kamikaze.

'There does not appear to be any reason,' he noted, 'why a large force of these planes should not be able to put all the carriers in Task Force 38 out of action, provided they attacked from good cloud cover or during moonlight.'

In Tokyo, Admiral Wenneker held a similar opinion: 'now the ratio of strength is nearly balanced,' he remarked on 9 November. He, as much as the Americans, had been taken unawares by the new development, and on 3 November had sent a description to the Luftwaffe Commander-in-Chief in Berlin.

'Due to the serious situation,' he explained, 'the Navy has taken skilled volunteers from other aircraft squadrons to form special squadrons whose purpose is to destroy enemy ships by premeditated suicide . . . Fuse is at the ready before taking off, since bomb is not released. Run-in with protective escort by fighters which observe the effect of the attack at the same time. Losses during run-in are allegedly small. After reaching the ship target assigned before the take-off, dive bombers plunge almost vertically, fighters in a steep glide until the deck is hit. Sacrifice of the plane is generally sufficient to sink transport, destroyer, or possibly a light cruiser. Sinking of larger units is usually possible only with several planes, but in any case at least lasting damage is achieved . . . A continual re-formation has been provided for and can be accomplished since numerous volunteers have reported and no special training is required.'

The Germans had resorted on occasion to suicidal plane-versus-plane attacks; they had not thought of plane-versus-ship suicides, and even less of organizing a force especially for the purpose. Wenneker did not try to explain the popularity among Japanese pilots of the kamikaze corps; nor did he give any indication that he could explain it. But it is precisely that – the reason why men would willingly organize themselves for certain death – that has always lent the kamikaze corps an air of perverse fascination. 'I am afraid you cannot understand it well,' said Captain Inoguchi Rikibei to his interrogator after the war, 'or you may call it desperate or foolish.'

'Their fear', the American naval attaché in Santiago reported, 'is of the US construction on a large scale of air-plane carriers, and, therefore, they do not hesitate in making any sacrifice when an occasion for attacking one is presented.'

Inoguchi had been Chief of Staff of the First Air Fleet in the Philippines at the time of the Battle for Leyte Gulf. Commanding the later Army kamikaze aircraft in the Philippines was Lieutenant General Kawabe. After the war, he too was asked to explain the kamikaze ethos. His interrogation was long, and both he and his questioner did their best to understand one another's views of life and death; but in the end the interrogator gave up. 'We might as well stop this line of questioning here and now,' he said, admitting that 'it is true, I myself cannot understand'.

'I just wanted to explain the way I felt about it,' said Kawabe unhappily; and the explanations which he and others gave are worth listening to, and trying to understand.

Essentially, it was no more than a logical extension of ordinary warfare, an attempt to use available weapons as efficiently and effectively as possible.

'Initially,' said Inoguchi, 'the kamikaze concept was a method of coping with local situations, and not the result of an overall policy.'

'We believed probably we would lose the war and we knew we could never win the war,' Kawabe concurred, 'but we never gave up the idea of continuing the fight, using whatever special attack planes we could manufacture.'

'Although the attacks were ordered by the Commander-in-Chief First Air Fleet,' Inoguchi went on, 'in fact they were originated by the feeling of all combatants in the Philippine area. All were beginning to think that there was no way but suicide to save the situation . . . this sort of thing has to come up from the bottom. You can't order such a thing.' Gekokujo – there was a concept a student of Japan could recognize.

'We felt as follows,' remarked the persevering Inoguchi, trying to get his point across. 'We must give our lives to the Emperor and country, that is our inborn feeling. We Japanese base our lives on obedience to Emperor and Country . . . we wish for the best place in death, according to *Bushido*.'

'*Bushido*.' An anonymous writer of a fragmented, undated diary, presumed to be from the battleship *Mutsu*, explained Bushido as 'the art of seeking death. If faced with two deaths, choose the quicker one and go forth determinedly with that one purpose in mind. Greeting each morning and night with the fear that "I am going to die" means you are not giving yourself freely to Bushido. You must not stray from the path for a moment'.

'Kamikaze originates from these feelings,' Inoguchi agreed. 'It was the incarnation of these feelings. We believe in absolute obedience to the supreme authority.'

Remembering how the Japanese child was brought up, how the Japanese boy became the Japanese man, this was not so hard to comprehend.

'But did you realize at the time,' said Kawabe's interrogator, 'that the very fact that they had to resort to such measures was in effect a ready indication that ultimate defeat was on the cards? . . . Was it clear to you that the very reason you had to resort to this measure was that defeat was already in sight?'

Kawabe was adamant in his disagreement. 'No matter how you look at it, everyone who participated in these attacks died happily in the conviction that they would win the final victory by their own death.'

'When we were able to destroy your industrial capacity with B-29s,' the interrogator asked, 'yet our industrial capacity was unmolested, did you realize that the war was over because you would be deprived of your means to wage war? When did you realize that it would only be a matter of time?'

'I want to explain something to you,' Kawabe replied as patiently as he could. 'This is a very difficult thing which you may not be able to understand. The Japanese, to the very end, believed that by spiritual means they could fight on equal terms with you, yet by any other comparison it would not appear equal. We believed our spiritual conviction in victory would balance any scientific advantages, and we had no intention of giving up the fight. It seemed to be especially Japanese.'

It could have been Kato Kanji speaking, proclaiming the 'unparalleled Yamato spirit'; and Kawabe's straightforward conviction – the kind of conviction against which Yamamoto had struggled – showed how deeply such teaching had taken root: it was as basic a fact of life as breathing, and if the interrogator could not grasp such a simple truth, Kawabe could only conclude he was very dull.

'I understand,' said the interrogator – but he, naturally, was applying his own upbringing to the incomprehensible novelty he was hearing. 'You could fight to the last man, but you did that knowing perfectly well that victory would be impossible?'

'No,' Kawabe sighed. 'We still thought that that would offset the technological superiority, and that the issue was still in doubt. That's probably a contention you can't understand – that's the Japanese feeling: we'd made up our minds to fight to the very last man, and we thought we still had a chance.'

Inoguchi knew exactly what Kawabe meant. 'The only trouble with the US way of looking at it,' he remarked, 'is that if you start out on a mission with the idea of coming back you won't proceed to carry out the mission with one hundred per cent efficiency.'

The general and the captain understood each other perfectly; but there was still something which rankled with Kawabe which he desperately wanted to explain to his interrogator.

'May I point out one thing,' he said, with some dignity, to the interrogator. 'You call our kamikaze attacks "suicide" attacks. They were in no sense "suicide". The pilot did not start out on his mission with the intention of committing suicide. He looked upon himself as a human bomb which would destroy a certain part of the enemy fleet for his country. They considered it a glorious thing, while a suicide may not be so glorious.'

It seems paradoxical, and to many in the West is still a source of comedy, that many kamikaze pilots survived the war. Throughout Japan there are several hundred men who prepared themselves for the corps, and fully expected to die on the deck of an American carrier. Some who survived did so because their flights never located a target and they were forced to ditch; others, more simply, were trained too late, so that, by the time they were ready to fly, there were no planes available. One of these is Shigihara Yoshiki. Born in 1923, he was a naval air force paymaster in 1944, and it was not until March 1945 that he began kamikaze training. Wenneker had not been completely correct: there *was* some special training for the special attack force, and it was terrifying. Underneath the trainee pilot's plane a live 250-kilo bomb was roped on. Thus perilously equipped, the young man would fly to 5,000 feet and go into a dive of 30° at 250 knots. At 2,500 feet he steepened the dive to 45°; and 1,500 feet he steepened it again to 60° – still at 250 knots – and at less than 200 feet he pulled through. That is, he pulled through if he had judged the height and speed absolutely accurately: there was a fraction of a second between life and an explosive, useless death on the ground, and three of Shigihara's colleagues killed themselves accidentally.

He, like all the others, was determined to kill himself on purpose and, more than that, *for* a purpose, and the fact that he never had the chance is still, to him, a source of regret and some shame. He speaks eloquently and forcefully of those days; and he admits readily that it was a fearful thing to undertake. Each day a list would be posted bearing the names of those who were to fly their last, their only mission. Each day, as men consulted the list, fear would flutter in their stomachs; and, with every man whose name came up, Shigihara saw an identical reaction. The chosen man would stiffen, turn pale and walk away in silence; then a short time later he would be seen again, laughing, joking, doing his normal work in an utterly normal manner. It was as if the moment of death was not the impact on an enemy ship, but the icy second of recognizing his own name. Thereafter, nothing seemed to matter; and there was never any thought of altering one's allotted fate. But, when the moment of impact on an enemy ship actually came, many Americans saw the pilots throw their hands over their faces to cover the last instant.

Shigihara Yoshiki, once a member of the most unusual attack force in the world, now a notable member of the Japan Information Centre of Science and Technology, saw his name posted in the late autumn of 1945 as part of the group for the next available planes – planes which Japan could no longer supply. Now, once a month, alone in the Yasukuni shrine, and once a year with his ex-colleagues – a group with more than the usual sense of unity – he prays for the souls of all those who succeeded where he failed.

While Kurita was turning back towards the San Bernadino Strait, and while the first kamikaze were winging towards Sprague, Admiral Ozawa's decoy carriers were at last fulfilling their part. Four hundred miles south the battle which many Americans felt Halsey should have fought was almost over. Halsey himself saw it differently: 'It was not my job to protect the Seventh Fleet,' he wrote later. 'My job was offensive, to strike with the Third Fleet, and we were even then rushing to intercept a force which gravely threatened not only Kinkaid and myself, but the whole Pacific strategy.' He, at the time, certainly believed that that was the quality of the opposition; but, had he known that, by the time his fleet met Ozawa's, the Japanese Admiral had only 29 aircraft available – most of the rest had flown off to attract attention, and were unable to land again on the vessels – had Halsey known this, it is more than likely he would still have gone hell-for-leather to sink the carriers. It was his overriding ambition, and he could not easily have been persuaded to miss it; his good fortune was that his orders *were* ambiguous, that it was not his fault his messages had not all been picked up, and that the victims off Samar were not more numerous.

To Halsey – and probably also to Ozawa – the Battle off Cape Engaño, if not short, was sweet, for both got almost everything they wanted. It began at 0830 on 25 October; it continued throughout the day and into the evening; and, at the end, all four of the Japanese carriers were sunk. So were two of the cruisers and three of the destroyers; and if Ozawa managed to return to Japan, and to live for many years more, that was hardly his fault, although he had intended and expected to die. Nor was it his fault if he had failed in his self-appointed primary mission, to take the pressure off Kurita; after all, out of all the four failed fleets, his was the one which, through failure, came closest to success.

In Tokyo, Admiral Wenneker was experiencing the same frustration he had known after the Battle of Midway. On 26 October, as Kurita steamed back to Brunei and the last ships went down, Wenneker wrote: 'American reports of success fantastically exaggerated, apparently because of presidential election.' Next day he reported that 'details of the battles in and outside of Leyte Bay are impossible to get, beyond the armed forces' report. Japanese are extremely reserved about what is to be understood in regard to the fate of the Philippines and therewith the battles which are entirely decisive in the outcome of the war'. And then he said something which could have been an epitaph for the whole Pacific War – 'After initial successes the situation has become increasingly worse for the Japs.'

Within five days, however, he could be definite. The report for 1 November stated: 'Sea and air control over Leyte Gulf and approaches unquestionably remains with the enemy.'

Yet even then, sustained by the mixture of crazy unrealism and passionate self-confidence which had characterized them since Pearl Harbor, the men of the Imperial Navy still prepared to fight, and still believed they might win. The same report continued:

'Both Admiralty and General Staff regard battles about Leyte as virtually decisive for outcome of war, and are as they assert unrestrainedly determined to risk any sacrifice to drive the Americans from Leyte and Samar. A second American assault is expected shortly and with it the opportunity for a decisive decimation of the American fleet is hoped for.'

Two days later the bizarre mood had not altered: 'Admiralty staff have today expressed firm hope that the Philippine situation, which at present is still very critical, will soon be mastered. On the Japanese side, there is the advantage of shorter connection with the homeland.'

The war closed in; B-29s were in range of the industrial centres of Japan. It needed masterly sophistry – or optimism bordering on mania – to suggest that, because this meant shorter lines of communication, it was welcome.

The decisive battle, so long and so ardently desired, had taken place; the greatest sea battle in history had altered the face of naval warfare for ever; and in Japan – officially at least – no one seemed to have registered the fact at all. In America and Britain and all the Allied countries, through all the Allied armies and navies, the 'fantastically exaggerated' reports ran riot; and it must have been with great satisfaction that Admiral Nimitz wrote that 'the Imperial Japanese Navy no longer existed as a fighting force, and the United States Navy commanded the Pacific'.

32

'The fiercest serpent'

The conversion of *Shinano* from a third super-battleship to the largest aircraft carrier in the world had proceeded as fast as possible. After the Battle of the Philippine Sea and the Turkey Shoot, the need for further air power in Japan's navy became even more glaringly apparent, and on 8 October the colossal vessel was launched at Yokosuka. 71,890 tons fully laden, her flight deck had 3⅛ inches of armour all over its 840-foot length and 131¾-foot width. The hangar deck had nearly eight inches of armour; the belt around the hull was over eight inches thick, and around the magazines it was almost fourteen inches. Eleven days after launch *Shinano* was completed for her trials, but the need for her to be in use was so urgent that she was commissioned before the last tests had been administered. Her crew were virtually novices, but they were all that could be given her; and at six o'clock in the evening of 28 November she weighed anchor on her maiden voyage. Her destination was Matsuyama, opposite Hiroshima, on the southern side of the Inland Sea. By then *Musashi*, whose hull had been of the same design, was at the bottom of the Sibuyan Sea, but aboard *Shinano* Captain Abe Toshio was certain he was sailing an unsinkable ship. One can only suppose that he did not know that, in the haste to get her to the training ground in the Inland Sea, *Shinano*'s internal watertight doors had not been fitted.

She was torpedoed at twelve minutes past three in the morning of 29 November by the American submarine *Archerfish*. Just over nine hours out on her first and last voyage, she was a perfect target, a gift for a submariner, and *Archerfish* hit her four times. But four torpedoes were, or should have been, nothing to her; it had taken many more than that, and bombs as well, to kill *Musashi*. Abe continued on course, with no thought of beaching her, or of heading for the nearest port; and he was almost right. Under his feet the flooding continued; under his command the ship continued. And under his command she sank, taking him and 500 of her crew with her. 850 of the 1,400-man crew had never been on a warship before; the world's largest aircraft carrier never fired a gun or launched a plane. If she had lasted just a few hours more, she would have made it to Matsuyama, and Abe would have been vindicated; but at five minutes to eleven, less than seventeen hours after beginning her voyage, she went down, the shortest-lived capital ship ever launched. In a way it was apt; the Imperial Navy's history was full of extremes, but the life and death of *Shinano* was a record it had never achieved before.

For six months more, Admiral Wenneker's transmissions continued to provide their unique viewpoint on the Imperial Navy's last days. He was a navy man; he was living in Japan; his enemies were the enemies of Japan; but he was not Japanese. And so his reports, regularly intercepted by American intelligence, gave a frank running commentary which was simultaneously a part of, and apart from, the Navy's declining war effort. By the end of 1944, Japan had lost 2,242 ships, including 407 warships.

11 January 1945: 'As to true Japanese losses, which it goes without saying are many times greater [than Allied losses], an adamant silence is being maintained . . . In my opinion, the Jap fleet is so badly shot up that no forces worth mentioning are at present available for effective defence.'

From Berlin, a few days earlier, had come a suggestion that some German Naval officers should come to Japan for further training. 'From all appearances,' Wenneker replied, 'the Japanese fleet has been so badly mauled that on these grounds alone the Japanese are not going to burden their remaining ships with the training of outsiders. Mistrust of all whites is deeply rooted. We Germans are tolerated only as long as we are fighting on the same side and are of material use.'

In the Philippines kamikaze aircraft and their new nautical equivalent, explosive boats, were still being put to frantic, fatal work; but, if the Navy did not know where the Allies were, they could do nothing. Following American air attacks on Formosa on 9 January (when over 900 sorties were flown against the island), the disappearance of the attackers, and their subsequent re-appearance 200 miles east of Saigon on the 12th with a further 450 sorties, Wenneker remarked that 'the actuality of the appearance in the middle of the South China Sea of strong enemy naval forces, the assembling of which the Japanese were not once able to discover, is designated by the Navy itself as a source of deep shame, and has patently created a most profound impression'.

A similar impression must have been created in Wenneker's own mind when he read the message from Berlin on 8 February – 'Today's conditions – evacuation, destruction, invasion.' He himself had just sent out a message of equal gloom: 'The Japanese off Leyte lost in two weeks eight of the fourteen submarines operating. There is no danger to [Allied] submarines from the Jap air force. The latter is so feeble that if it attacks at all, it aims only at surface vessels.'

One of the most extraordinary messages from Berlin was a bitter complaint about the complete lack of Japanese co-operation in arranging frequencies and broadcasting times for mutual radio communication. 'In traffic between nations,' the reproachful message went, 'everything cannot be expressed in Z or Q abbreviations, and it is necessary to use the English language. But even with the most common English expressions no understanding can be reached with the Japanese.' And the same day, 23 February, Wenneker began to think what to any Japanese should have been unthinkable:

'Admiralty staff holds the view that direction of the American offensive will continue northward in order to give the Japs no chance to rest . . . and therefore if the occupation of Iwo Jima is accomplished, it may be expected that after suitable preparations – that is, occupation of further nearby islands and destruction of industry from the air – a landing will be made on Japan itself.'

But, by the middle of March, even the unthinkable was being prepared for Japan:

'Yonai's speech in the Diet 11 March was particularly interesting. It recounts the situation very clearly, with unusual brevity, about as follows: (1) The Navy (that is, since no floating craft to speak of are available, the Naval Air Force) is at present so weak that already three attacks by Task Forces against the homeland have had to be endured without it being possible to do any damage to enemy ships. (2) The Army and Navy, which hitherto, unfortunately, have often gone their separate ways, are now in full and definite agreement on their objective and mission. (3) Landing by enemy on the homeland is to be expected and will meet a defensive front of unexpected magnitude and determination. (4) Following newly set up air units and weapons a turn in the situation is expected soon.'

Yet the very next day Wenneker added: 'The question whether it would be possible here to strike a decisive blow at enemy landing fleet is, as is openly conceded, not considered with confidence.'

On 24 January another intelligence report had given the opinion of Chiang Kai-Shek's personal adviser – a man described as having 'a keen mind and a profound intellect' – on the future of the Imperial Navy. 'The Japanese Navy Command,' he had said, 'rather than fight an engagement that will end in the destruction of the fleet, or surrender, will take the fleet to Vladivostock and surrender to the Russians.'

Whatever basis the keen-minded adviser had for that assertion, it had no discernible link with either the historical or the cultural inheritance of Japan. On 29 March, Wenneker delivered an analysis much more in keeping with his allies' character.

'The Japanese Navy, having used only a part of its Air Force in the last Task Force attack, is determined to use its entire air power, together with the Army's, for a decisive blow at the next opportunity, presumably against the Okinawa landing. It is noteworthy that the opinion of the majority is greatly divided on the success of this action.'

He was absolutely correct as far as he went; perhaps he was unaware that it was not only the Army and Navy Air Forces which were to be used. The last remnants of the surface fleet were to be used as well.

The destroyer *Yukikaze*, to which Admiral Abe Hiroaki had transferred during the Battle of Guadalcanal, was sustaining her reputation as the lucky ship of the Imperial Navy. She had been part of the Kurita fleet at Leyte Gulf, and out of all the four fleets she was the only ship to emerge from the battle entirely unscathed. April 1945 offered her a new challenge: with nine other destroyers, the light cruiser *Yahagi* and the giant *Yamato*, little *Yukikaze* was to become a *kikusui*, a floating chrysanthemum. Flowers had always been important to the Imperial Navy: the Imperial chrysanthemum graced the ships' bows; the naval insignia was an anchor surmounted by a cherry blossom. No other navy could have had such an emblem; and, as the officers and men of the twelve ships in the *kikusui* operation made ready, they sang a song called *Doki no Sakura* – 'Cherry Blossoms of the Same Rank'.

A few other ships still existed – the battleship *Nagato* in Yokosuka, the battleship *Haruna* in dry dock, two heavy cruisers in the South Seas – but the dozen now making ready represented the sum total of ships that were still readily available.

Admiral Toyoda had issued their order on 5 April. It read: 'Second Fleet is to charge into the enemy anchorage of Kadeno, off Okinawa Island, at daybreak of 8 April. Fuel for only a one-way passage will be supplied. This is a Special Attack operation.'

'Special Attack' was a special phrase: kamikaze aircraft were Special Attack aircraft. These ships were not expected to return. Toyoda's order and the operation it set in motion have given rise to an almost irresistible legend, that the great *Yamato* was sent on her final voyage with absolutely no hope of return, and that, if she survived the passage to Okinawa, she was to be beached and used as a kind of fortress, blasting away with her 18.1-inch guns until either she was blown to pieces or her 1,080 shells were expended. It is true that that was Toyoda's basic plan, and it seems too appropriate an end to the Imperial Navy to wish to challenge it. But according to Chihaya Masataka, who was present at the meeting at which the decision was made to send the *kikusui* out, it was not so: he asserts that he and others would not agree to its authorization, and that when it went ahead, it was only because double-secret reserve oil tanks had been literally sucked dry to provide enough fuel for a return journey.

However that may be, it made no difference; the simple fact that the *kikusui* had to be undertaken without air cover meant that, with or without fuel, the ships were unlikely to come back. Only veterans were accepted into the crews for the operation; it was felt that inexperienced men might handicap whatever chance there might be. Tsukasa Tadayuki, today a noted Anglophile and an eminent businessman, was then a young ensign, intensely proud of being a member of his country's Navy. He was one of those who, not knowing her destination, saw *Yamato* depart from the Inland Sea on 6 April; and, like all those whom ships have left behind, he waved her goodbye.

In the days before the war when he had lobbied so hard for more carriers and fewer battleships, Admiral Yamamoto had often cited an apposite Japanese proverb – 'The fiercest serpent may be overcome by a swarm of ants.' *Yamato*, the last of the super-battleships, a great and graceful vessel, was overcome by swarms of American aircraft at twenty-three minutes past two in the afternoon of 7 April 1945. *Yahagi* and four of the destroyers went down as well; and one of the six surviving destroyers was *Yukikaze* – still, as ever, the Navy's lucky ship.

The plume of smoke that erupted when *Yamato* sank rose so far into the air that over a hundred miles away at Kagoshima – where Admiral Kuper had unleashed his 'inconceivably disastrous' precedent, and where Admiral Yamamoto had trained his pilots for Pearl Harbor – the death of the super-battleship that epitomized Japan could be clearly seen.

This was the true end of the Imperial Japanese Navy as a fighting force. It was no surprise when America's agent Z filed a report saying, 'The morale of the Army is bad, but the Navy's morale is even worse;' retrospectively, though, it is hardly credible that Wenneker was able to say, after speaking to Navy men, that the 'report concerning sea battle which took place was misleading. Actually an old Japanese battleship received the assignment and ran ashore there near the beachhead'. It was at least acknowledged that the 'ship was sunk by 300 American aircraft'; but the fact that she was *Yamato* they refused to recognize, and perhaps even refused to believe.

On 5 May, however, Wenneker had news for Grand Admiral Dönitz: 'Large sections of the Japanese armed forces would not regard with disfavour a suit for capitulation coming from America, even if the terms were hard, as long as they were halfway honourable.' But Dönitz was no longer interested in the fate of Japan, for the day before Germany had surrendered unconditionally to the Allies; and, while Wenneker was tapping out his signal, the Grand Admiral was ordering all troops of his nation in north-west Germany, Holland and Denmark to give up their arms.

'This is not a case of peace negotiations,' said a message from Berlin on 7 May, 'but of conversations which were carried on exclusively at the military level, and had as their aim the cessation of warlike activities.'

Another subtle distinction; but there was nothing so evasive about the message which arrived in Tokyo on 22 May. It was in plain text, and it read: 'The Allied army of occupation has forbidden radio traffic with Japan, effective immediately. Communication ends with this message.'

Wenneker's very unusual window on the Pacific War was closed. Nevertheless, a handful of ships remained in Japan. No longer even resembling a fleet, individually they fought on; and Wenneker still had a comment appropriate to one of the last episodes of the Imperial Navy's life. Back in December 1944 he had said that the Admiralty staff 'are firmly convinced that Americans would never permit British to have a share in the action, which would amount to a benefit from their (the Americans') blood sacrifice'.

Actually, although the fact is often forgotten, British ships did play an important role in the last Pacific battles; and the very last destroyer action of the Second World War was a night battle fought by a Japanese destroyer and heavy cruiser against a squadron of five British destroyers.

The cruiser was the 12,734-ton *Haguro*; the British destroyers, under Captain Manley Power, were *Saumarez, Venus, Verulam, Vigilant* and *Virago*. During the night of 16 May 1945, the small British vessels trapped *Haguro* at a point fifty-five miles west-south-west of Penang Island, just west of the Malayan peninsula. The site was peculiarly appropriate, and the end of *Haguro* even more so; for, on the other side of that same peninsula, the Imperial Navy had opened its war against the Royal Navy by sinking the *Prince of Wales*. And, during a brilliantly executed attack, the first three fatal Royal Navy torpedoes exploded simultaneously on *Haguro*'s hull in a huge triple explosion – 'very distinct,' said a witness, 'three gold-coloured splashes like a Prince of Wales' feathers, more than twice as high as her bridge'.

His description was merely accurate, not melodramatic, for no one realized the connection; but somewhere there, as a Japanese airman had written three and a half years earlier, there was 'an honourable memory for the Royal Navy', the old mentor, the old ally, the old enemy. Admiral Togo had been 'slow to learn, but very sure of what he had learned'. The Imperial Navy had been quick to learn; but, until 1945, it had not, perhaps, learnt quite enough.

EPILOGUE

*The Four Seas
in
Brotherhood*

33

'Grim reflections – ominous of change'

'After brilliance,' wrote Chihaya Masataka, 'the darkness is so much the darker. I feel now full of shame. I have survived the war, and am now a spectator of the defeated motherland . . . As a member of the defunct Imperial Navy I am not quite free from the responsibility for this utterly bottomless defeat.'

'Débris all over the country greets our eyes,' he went on. 'Then chaos and confusion. Not even assurance for tomorrow's food . . . Not one single thing but reminds us vividly of defeat, defeat and defeat.'

In the early morning of 2 September 1945, nearly two hundred warships lay quietly at anchor in Tokyo Bay – many hundreds of thousands of tons of guns and armour, silent and ghostly, unmoving in the last moments of night. As the official time of sunrise came and went, Allied ensigns were hoisted across the great expanse of the bay; but there was no real dawn. One of the memories recalled many years later was that, on that morning, no one saw the sun come up. Instead, night gave way reluctantly to a leaden light, a study of grey on grey – the cloud-covered sky above the ships, and, below them, the slow-moving sea. On the surrounding shores, there was no sign of movement. There seemed to be life only on the ships, and their flags were the only spots of colour.

Shigemitsu Mamoru, the Foreign Minister, met General Umezu Yoshijiro at the Prime Minister's official residence. With their entourages they bowed towards the Imperial palace, and set off for Yokohama.

'Not a soul was on the streets,' Shigemitsu wrote. 'As far as the eye could see, we traversed a burnt-out scene of desolation, in which survivors were to be seen here and there picking over the ruins. The scars of war were vividly present before our eyes. From Yokohama pier we embarked on an American destroyer and for an hour threaded our way through the American and British men-of-war that filled Tokyo Bay, before arriving at Nimitz's flagship *Missouri* . . . the ocean lay calm . . . we clambered up the gangway, and were saluted by the guard . . . we made our way to the upper deck, where the ceremony was to take place . . . the enclosure was thronged with enemy onlookers.'

In the port of Shimoda, eighty-nine years earlier and about eighty-nine miles south-west of *Missouri*'s anchorage, another brief ceremony had marked the opening of America's first consulate in Japan. The consul, Townsend Harris, had watched and participated with a sense of mingled pride and foreboding, and after it was over had scribbled in his diary a terse comment: 'Grim reflections – ominous of change – undoubted beginning of the end. Query – if for the real good of Japan?'

Just a few months before that, Commodore Perry had signed the first American-Japanese treaty – 'a treaty of amity and friendship'. Now, flanked by other Allied ensigns, Perry's Stars and Stripes – the very same flag – was there again, worn and threadbare, but safely encased in glass. And so it all ended as it had all begun: with an American flag, and American warships at anchor in Tokyo Bay.

'There are occasions when the soul can survive,' wrote Shigemitsu, 'only if the body dies . . . I tried to look into the future, but grief came flooding into my thoughts.'

In the days before Pearl Harbor, the Emperor had once tried to forestall war by breaking precedent in an Imperial conference, where normally he would merely listen, and speaking his thoughts aloud. He had quoted a poem written by his grandfather Emperor Meiji: 'The four seas are brothers to one another; why then do the waves seethe and the winds rage?' Now, after infinite pain, the four seas were returning to brotherhood.

In a sad shadow of his grandfather's Rescript, Emperor Hirohito wrote his own Rescript to the Armed Forces.

'We are deeply grieved,' he said, 'when we remember our dutiful and gallant officers and men who have died in action . . . we firmly believe that the faith and gallantry of you soldiers and sailors is the gem of our nation.'

'It is better,' says a Japanese proverb, 'to be a gem that is smashed to atoms than a tile which is whole.' Ninety-five per cent of the Imperial Navy had been destroyed in the Pacific War. In round figures of tonnage, the sums were: in hand in December 1941, 5,900,000 tons; built during the war, 4,100,000 tons; total, 10 million tons. Sunk during the war, 8,617,000 tons; heavily damaged, 937,000 tons; total loss, 9,554,000 tons.

Amongst those which survived was the battleship *Nagato*. She became a target in American atom-bomb experiments at Bikini atoll. There were also minesweepers; these, manned by Japanese crews, became an effective part of the American mine counter-measures in the Korean War. And, curiously, there was also a *Yamato*. All but forgotten, she was a tiny little ship of less than 1,500 tons, an unprotected cruiser launched in 1885 at Kobe. She had lived through it all, firstly as a coast defence ship, and had seen action in the Sino-Japanese war; then, decommissioned, she had become a survey vessel and finally a drill ship, continuing her humble existence when even her great namesake was defeated. But she too sank, in a storm in harbour, on 18 September 1945 – one of the first, and one of the last as well, of the Imperial Navy ships.

'The Japanese forces fought well,' said Shigemitsu Mamoru. 'In no instance was their record for courage tarnished. They showed the world of what the "Japanese spirit" was capable.' *To show the world what they could do* – from childhood upwards, for every child and for the whole nation, it had always been a matter of literally desperate importance. Aboard *Missouri*, Shigemitsu and his colleagues had to demonstrate a new capability.

'Soldiers, sailors,' said the Imperial Rescript, 'we command that you endeavour to consolidate the foundation of our State for many years to come, by acting in accordance with our wishes, standing in solidarity, and by bearing and overcoming what may seem impossible.'

'To sign the deed of surrender,' Shigemitsu wrote, 'was . . . for a soldier or sailor virtual suicide.'

Grim reflections – warships on the water, thoughts of past and future. Under a sky still overcast, the Japanese and Allied delegations assembled on *Missouri*'s deck and the formal preliminaries of national surrender were gone through. With dignity, the Japanese representatives signed away their honour. And as they were doing so, by an odd coincidence, the sun broke through the clouds, and shone on Mount Fuji.

34

'Evening faces'

The chrysanthemum is first, the Imperial flower; but next in Japan's national affection is *asagao*, the Morning Glory, with its early brilliance fading as the day passes. The cherry blossom, regarded all over the world as the epitome of things Japanese, was especially loved in the Imperial Navy, and was taken as part of its emblem; today the Maritime Self-Defence Force still uses the same insignia. A partner to the Morning Glory is *yugao*, lightly scenting the evening air. Its name means 'Evening Faces'. And, like faces slowly vanishing into the darkness, there are many farewells to the Imperial Navy. From a different context, but aptly said, there is Churchill's phrase – 'What has been the use of all this battling?' A naval victory in war may be glorious, but a navy's best distinction is the way it works in peace. Recognizing that, from the time of the China Incident, there is a comment from Okumiya Masatake.

'However brilliant these combat successes,' he said, 'no one can deny the record, for history will relate only that Japan forced her friendly neighbouring nations into an unreasonable and unnecessary war, transformed their fields and cities into battlegrounds, and visited misery and deprivation on millions of innocent people.'

From a Japanese elegy written in 1905, following the Peace of Portsmouth, there is a verse:

> 'On the wild sea, rough with waves,
> The sailors fought to their death.
> Their death for loyalty is now mere foam;
> What a pity, this blunder.'

From Manley Power, whose torpedoes brought the Prince of Wales' feathers bursting back out of the ocean, there was a description of that attack which was also an appropriate obituary for Japan's navy: it 'was a success; but it was by no means a perfect and polished performance. There is much to be learnt from it, and plenty of room for improvement.'

And from the Japanese Naval Attaché in Lisbon to his equal in Berne, there was the last message intercepted by American intelligence, the final leaf in the National Archives. Sent on 11 November 1945, it was in plain text, and it said:

'Thanks for your telegram. It's all like a dream! But we will go ahead to build up a new Japan. We are all in good health. We have made a final settlement of our affairs and are now awaiting our disposition. Muchaku, Ogishi, and Kirusaki are understood to be getting along cheerfully in their life of internment. Best wishes to Captain Nishihara and the rest. Until we meet again!'

Chronology of the Imperial Japanese Navy

1542 The Portuguese explorer, Antonio de Mota, lands in Japan. The spread of Christianity appears to threaten revolution, and in

1637 the country's borders are sealed. Only a small enclave of traders is allowed to remain; the period of defensive self-isolation begins. For 215 years Japanese society remains relatively static. Towards the end of this time, in

1847 Togo Heihachiro is born, and six years later, in

1853 *14 June*, Commodore Matthew C. Perry anchors in Edo (Tokyo) Bay, returning in

1854 to sign the first Japanese-American treaty 'of commerce and friendship'. The Japanese nation, after its long sojourn in privacy, is forced to recognize the sea as a means of defence and trade: distance is no longer a guarantee of security. A voyage to America takes place in

1860 when the *Kanrin Maru*, a 700-ton Dutch-built schooner 'crewed' by Japanese, crosses the Pacific; but there is much anti-foreign feeling in Japan. In

1863 an Englishman, Charles Richardson, is murdered. His death, and the lack of reparations for it, prompt retaliation on *14 August* by Rear Admiral Kuper, RN: the town of Kagoshima is bombarded in 'a new precedent . . . inconceivably disastrous to mankind'. The following year,

1864 Shimonoseki is similarly bombarded. The question of whether to accommodate or repel the foreigners brings civil war, shogun against emperor. In

1865 *May*, the 103-foot, 138-ton wooden gunboat *Chiyoda* is completed in Tokyo for the shogun: the first warship built in Japan.

1868 *15 April* sees the first review of an imperial fleet – six ships from seven clans supporting the Emperor. In the same year the civil war ends with the Emperor's forces victorious. By

1869 *21 July* all opposition to the Emperor has ceased. The Meiji Era, 1868–1912, brings a near-complete modernization of Japan. One of the first steps is, in

1869 a reorganization of the Navy, followed in

1872 *February* by a reorganization of the Admiralty (Kaigunsho) as a separate Department of State. A programme of buying ships abroad begins in earnest, along with a serious training programme for officers and men. This bears fruit in

1877 when the *Niigata Maru* is sailed by a Japanese crew under a British captain to London. Britain will become the source of many of Japan's ships in these early years. In

1878 *January*, the first armoured ship to be built in Britain for Japan, *Fuso*, a

	220-foot, 3,718-ton steel-hulled frigate, is completed at Poplar. For several years Japanese naval students have been coming to Britain for instruction; among them is Togo Heihachiro, and in
1879	he receives his first command. As lieutenant-commander, his ship is the *Jingei*, the last wooden paddle vessel in the Japanese Navy.
1880	introduces torpedo-boats to the Navy, with the completion of the first at Poplar.
1884	is the year of the birth of Takano Isoroku, to become C-in-C Combined Fleet Admiral Yamamoto Isoroku; and in
1885	*1 December*, the Navy's first steel cruiser is completed. *Naniwa* – 229 feet, 4,150 tons – is the most powerful cruiser in the world, and sets the tone for an abiding Japanese taste. The taste is not only for big ships but for first strikes: it is from *Naniwa*, in
1894	*25 July* that Togo – now Captain – fires the first shots of the Sino-Japanese War. On *18 August* war is declared. On *17 September* the Battle of the Yalu takes place, a resounding but incomplete Japanese victory. This gives Japan 'supremacy in the Yellow Sea at the very outset', but the war takes another seven months to win. In that time the Navy takes Talien Bay, and, in one day of fighting – *21 November* – takes Port Arthur as well. From *18 November* to
1895	*11 February* the Chinese remnants are blockaded in Wei-Hai-Wei. At last, on *17 April*, peace is restored with the Treaty of Shimonoseki, giving Japan substantial territorial gains, including the strategically invaluable Port Arthur. But these gains are immediately nullified by the 'Triple Intervention' of France, Germany and Russia: Russia wants, and gets, Port Arthur; France is an ally of Russia; and Germany joins in to avoid being sandwiched between two hostile powers. Japan is forced to give way, for she has no allies.
1897	*17 August* brings the completion in Blackwall of Japan's first battleship, the *Fuji*, 412 feet, 12,533 tons, four 12-inch guns. But the first really major coup for Japan comes with the new century, when in
1902	*30 January* the Anglo-Japanese Alliance is signed. This conclusively ends Japan's isolation; it also ends Britain's 'splendid isolation', when, for almost a century, that country had had no need of full-scale alliances with other countries. The Alliance indicates far-reaching changes in the coming century, and, very shortly after it is signed, on *1 March*, the 400-foot, 15,179-ton battleship *Mikasa* is completed at Barrow. Once again Japan possesses the largest, strongest ship of its class in the world. With such vessels, and with the Franco-Russian alliance checkmated by the Anglo-Japanese Alliance, Japan is now ready to try conclusions in the East with Russia. Diplomacy fails, for the Russians will not take the upstart nation seriously; so, in
1904	during the night of *8–9 February*, Japan's second great modern naval war begins with the surprise attack on Port Arthur. Leading the fleet on *Mikasa* is the newly-promoted C-in-C Combined Fleet, Vice Admiral Togo. The port holds out under siege conditions, high-lit by the Battle of the Yellow Sea (*10 August*) until
1905	*2 February*. By then the Russian Baltic Fleet, renamed the Second Pacific Squadron and commanded by Rear Admiral Zinovi Rozhdestvenski, is well on its way in an epic but vain voyage of rescue. After bringing his ill-formed

fleet 20,000 miles, Rozhdestvenski faces Togo in the waters of the Straits of Tsushima, between Japan and Korea, on *27 May*. The battle which ensues lasts until *28 May* and becomes one of the most notable in history: for the loss of three torpedo boats, 117 killed and 583 wounded, Admiral Togo has virtually annihilated the Russian fleet. Thirty-eight Russian ships entered the battle; nineteen were sunk; seven were captured; six were interned elsewhere; two scuttled themselves; one escaped to Madagascar; and three made it to Vladivostock. Even so, peace is a long time coming: the treaty signed at Portsmouth, New Hampshire, on *5 September* gives Japan the territory she sought, but allows no cash indemnity. The treaty is therefore unpopular in Japan, and, during the night of *11–12 September*, *Mikasa* is blown up at her moorings, perhaps as a protest. In the same year, on *1 August*, the first submarine makes its appearance in the Imperial Navy's lists, when *Holland Type No. 1* is completed in Quincy, Mass., and in

1906 on *30 March*, *Kaigun Holland No. 6* becomes the first submarine to be completed in Japan. Throughout the Russo-Japanese War the Russians mistakenly believed that the Japanese employed submarines; in fact there were none in Japan to use then. On *23 May*, *Kashima*, a 473-foot, 17,200-ton battleship, is completed at Barrow – the last battleship to be built for the Imperial Navy outside Japan. The image of Japan victorious brings unease to the white Pacific nations: Japan is overcrowded, needs population outlets, and seems belligerent. On *11 October* a ruling by the San Francisco schools board segregates Japanese students into separate schools, a move highlighting racial tensions on the West Coast; but just over one year later, in

1907 on *18 October*, America's 'Great White Fleet' is welcomed into Yokohama with even greater acclaim than that given to Togo after Tsushima. Peace seems assured.

1908 and 1909 are quiet; but

1910 brings three important events. On *25 March* the 482-foot, 19,700-ton battleship *Satsuma* is completed in Yokosuka – the first large warship built in Japan – and on *15 April Kaigun Holland No. 6* sinks off Kure with the loss of all on board. Her commander, Lieutenant Sakuma, leaves a poignant testimony to his men's endurance. In the same year Japan annexes Korea, once more stoking white Pacific fears of Japanese expansionism; but the real threat to world peace is Germany's *Hochseekriegsflotte*, built up by Tirpitz and the Kaiser.

1911 marks the beginning of the '8-8' fleet crisis in Japan: the Navy, lobbying for a greater allocation of limited funds at the Army's expense, demands the creation of a new fleet of eight battleships backed by eight cruisers, the present fleet to become a back-up force. The peculiar structure of the Constitution allows the Army to bring the government down, and a period of domestic political instability starts.

1912 sees a new step in the Navy's development, with the completion on *31 March* of the 526-foot, 21,900-ton battleship *Kawachi* at Kure. Not only is this Japan's first dreadnought, it is also the first independent Japanese design. While the 8-8 crisis continues, the Emperor Meiji dies and is succeeded by his son Yoshihito, who takes the reign-name Taisho – 'Great Righteousness'.

1913 brings a first and a last in one ship, the 704-foot, 32,200-ton battlecruiser *Kongo*, completed at Barrow on *16 August*. Combining the speed of a cruiser with the fire-power of a battleship, for the loss of some of a battleship's weight of protective armour, *Kongo* is the Imperial Navy's first battlecruiser, and its last capital ship to be built outside Japan.

1914 begins with the revelation of a vast international bribery scandal similar to the Lockheed scandal: Navy officers have taken huge 'commissions' for allocating contracts. Admiral Yamamoto Gombei's government falls. On *17 August* the Navy's first seaplane carrier, *Wakamiya*, is converted from a freighter; on *21 August* two cruisers are sent to join the British squadron at Singapore; and on 23 August Japan declares war on Germany. The siege of the German-held Chinese port of Tsingtao begins and is prosecuted by combined Welsh, Indian and Japanese forces. The surrender of the fortress on *7 November* is one of the first major Allied victories of World War One. However, Japan's interests in the war appear to be largely selfish: during September and October, the Navy takes over the ex-German Pacific Islands of the Marshall, Carolina and Mariana groups, placing a Japanese line between the American-held Philippines and the continental United States. Moreover, during

1915 on *18 January*, the infamous '21 Demands' are presented to China. Their acceptance by China in a modified form on *9 May* gives Japan considerable economic advantages in China, much to the chagrin of Western nations, as well as the Chinese themselves. Another Navy first is scored on *8 November* with the completion of a new *Fuso*. A 673-foot, 35,900-ton battleship, built at Kure, she is the first battleship to be built in Japan with Japanese materials and Japanese weapons. Japanese destroyers and cruisers assist the Royal Navy for the rest of the war in the Mediterranean and around the Cape of Good Hope; but the overall effect is that, for a very limited involvement, World War One gives Japan disproportionately high strategic and commercial benefits. Meanwhile, in

1916 Takano Isoroku – already a lieutenant-commander and a veteran of the Battle of Tsushima – graduates from Staff College and is adopted. Henceforth he will be known by his new family name: Yamamoto. Towards the end of the war, in

1918 Japanese naval and army forces take part in the Siberian Intervention, and win control of large stretches of the Russian Maritime Provinces and railways.

1919 sees Commander Yamamoto in the United States, where he studies English at Harvard until 1921, and recognizes America's enormous industrial and war potential. The War of Intervention continues, and in

1920 on *25 May* the massacre of Nikolaievsk takes place, in which several hundreds, and possibly thousands, of Japanese civilians are slaughtered by Red insurgents. In guarantee of recompense Japan takes control of the northern half of Sakhalien, whose southern half had been ceded by the Tsar after the Russo-Japanese War. The island is of great value to the Navy, since it yields good oil supplies. On *7 July* the 8-8 crisis is finally resolved, with approval of all the Navy's proposals; and on *25 November* the 708-foot, 38,500-ton battleship *Nagato* is completed at Kure – the first battleship in the world to have 16-inch guns. She is one more manifestation of the naval arms race that has beset the powers since the end of 'the war to end wars', and, ironically, now that the 8-8 plan has been approved, the Navy begins to feel it is all too expensive. The way is being paved for the

1921 Washington Naval Disarmament Conference, which begins on *21 November*. Shortly before, on *13 October*, a 541-foot, 9,630-ton ex-tanker is redesignated and becomes *Hosho*, the Navy's first aircraft depot ship. The concept of disarmament causes mixed reactions in Japan: on the plus side there is economy, on the minus side, unemployment and a feeling that Japan would somehow lose face by limiting her Navy. Two days after the Conference opens, the Prime Minister is assassinated. The Conference ends in

1922 on *6 February*, with an agreement that Britain, America and Japan should maintain their navies in a ratio of 5:5:3. But the American price of agreement has been the ending of the Anglo-Japanese Alliance, and, as Sir Robert Craigie later says, 'With it was swept away one of the main buttresses against the pursuit by Japan of a policy of adventure and aggression.' However, in

1923 there is no thought of 'adventure' in Japan, for on *1 September* a terrible earthquake strikes Tokyo, Yokohama and Yokosuka, destroying the naval bases there and killing 140,000 people. In the same year Captain Yamamoto tours America and Europe, and becomes convinced of the future role of air-power in a modern navy. He begins to voice his conviction in

1924 when he becomes second-in-command of the Kasumigaura air base; but few people agree with him, and in

1925 a sinister development takes place in the shipyards of Yokosuka, Kure, Kobe and Nagasaki. In each yard at least one cruiser is being built which will break the limits of the Washington Treaty by 20% or more. In the same year, in return for Soviet acceptance of the peace treaty concluded with the Tsar, Sakhalien reverts to Russia.

1926 sees Yamamoto in Washington at the start of a tour of duty as naval attaché. On *31 March* at Yokosuka, the 771-foot, 33,693-ton *Kaga* is completed as Japan's first flat-top carrier. In the same year the Emperor Taisho dies, after a long period of declining physical and mental health, and is succeeded on *25 December* by his son Hirohito. Hirohoto's reign-name, by which he will be known after his death, is Showa – Shining Peace. At first it seems the promise of the name might be fulfilled: in

1927 at a conference in Geneva to review the Washington Treaty, the British and American delegates find it impossible to agree, while the Japanese are the only ones to emerge with credit, and for the next two years things are quiet. But in

1930 on *21 January* the First Plenary Session of the London Naval Disarmament Conference opens with Japan demanding a ratio of 10:10:7 – an increase of 10%. The demand is all but completely granted; yet in Japan there is strong lobbying for parity, and on *7 October* the First Supplemental Building Programme is passed. A running political battle is developing between two different schools of thought, the one for abrogating the Washington and London Treaties, the other for maintaining them, and on *14 November* the Prime Minister, an advocate of treaty maintenance, is attacked and fatally wounded.

1931 brings, on *18 September*, the opening of the Manchurian Incident, rapidly followed in

1932 on *18 January* by the Shanghai Incident, in which a Japanese admiral bombs the International Settlement in reprisal for alleged Chinese outrages. In the spring of the same year the American Admiral Harry Yarnell demonstrates that the naval base at Oahu could become the victim of a surprise air attack; and militant members of the Imperial Navy set about moves which will result in the Navy being on a permanent war footing. On *15 May* 41 conspirators including 10 naval officers perpetrate the murder of the Prime Minister: the period of 'government by assassination' is well under way. The new American ambassador in Tokyo believes that 'the military are distinctly running the Government'. On *25 August* Japan recognizes the puppet state of Manchukuo; the League of Nations, of which Japan is a prominent member, refuses to follow suit; and in

1933 on *27 March* Japan announces her intention of leaving the League. On behalf of Germany, Hitler does likewise on *14 October*, and on *21 October* a plan is put forward in the Japanese Naval General Staff for giant battleships which will 'at one bound raise our strength from the present ratio of 60% of US strength to a position of absolute supremacy'. On *21 November* the British naval attaché in Tokyo notes the disturbing trend of naval appointments: the 'Osumi purge' is beginning, and those officers with a pro-Treaty attitude are being retired or placed in positions of little authority, while those opposing the Treaty are being given high office. In the same year designs are begun for midget submarines, and in

1934 in total secrecy production commences. This year also brings the preliminary talks for the 1936 London Naval Conference. Representing Japan is Vice Admiral Yamamoto, who announces that at the end of 1936 Japan will abrogate both the London and Washington Treaties. This he does against his personal inclination: he believes that Japan should not tempt war with the overwhelmingly powerful United States, but the anti-treaty faction in Japan is now the stronger. Meanwhile, on *17 April*, Japan has issued the Amau Statement, a Monroe Doctrine for the Far East with Japan as the proposed guardian of Eastern freedoms; and on *30 May* Admiral Togo, the victor of Tsushima, dies.

1936 opens with another rush of assassinations, when, on *26 February*, Army men slaughter – amongst others – ex-Prime Minister Admiral Saito. Navy indignation is great and civil war is narrowly averted.

1937 brings yet more disturbance: on *7 July* there is a skirmish between Chinese and Japanese troops stationed at the Marco Polo bridge, near Peking. This escalates into full, open but undeclared war: the 'China Incident' has begun. During August the Imperial Navy Air Force sets new records by carrying out the first-ever trans-oceanic air-raids – from Formosa and Kyushu to Shanghai and Nanking. On *12 December* the British gunboats *Ladybird* and *Bee* are attacked, and the American gunboat *Panay* is sunk. On *14 December* the Army commences the 'Rape of Nanking', the worst single atrocity recorded before the Second World War. In six weeks over 200,000 Chinese, including at least 50,000 civilians, are killed. The sinking of *Panay* brings America close to war, but Admiral Yamamoto successfully maintains peace by advising his government to make a full apology, delivered on *25 December*. In Kure, however, the keel has been laid of what will become the biggest battleship in history; and on *6 November*, Japan joined the Anti-Comintern Pact with Italy and Germany.

1938 allows no relaxation in the China Incident. From January the Naval Air Force flies constant sorties over southern and central China; and in

1939 on *10 February*, the Navy occupies Hainan Island, south of China, following that a month later with the occupation of the tiny but strategically-located Spratly Island, half-way between Borneo and Indo-China. In *mid-August* Yamamoto is removed from the post of Navy Vice Minister and made C-in-C Combined Fleet – the Navy's highest honour, but also one which prevents him from exercising any political influence. On *30 August* his colleague Admiral Yonai is removed from the post of Navy Minister; between them, these two men have had the strongest influence of any wishing to maintain peaceful relations with America and Britain, and now neither can continue that function. But in

1940 during *January*, Yonai returns to government, this time as Prime Minister. This brings great hope for peace; however Anglo-Japanese relations are disturbed on *21 January* by the *Asama Maru* affair, in which a passenger ship 35 miles off Tokyo is stopped by a British warship and 21 Germans are removed from her. 'It is very disagreeable,' says a Navy spokesman, 'to see British warships prowling along our coasts.' In *August* diplomatic pressure forces the temporary closure by Britain of the Burma Road, by which Chinese supplies are brought in; on *27 September* Japan joins the Axis, and the same day America bans the export of scrap iron and steel to Japan. On *11 November* half the Italian fleet is wrecked at its moorings in Taranto Harbour by carrier-based British torpedo-bombers. Just before *Christmas*, Admiral Husband E. Kimmel, commander of American naval forces in Pearl Harbor, vetoes the use of torpedo nets on the grounds that they would 'restrict boat traffic by narrowing the channel'.

1941 *27 January*: the American Ambassador in Tokyo notes rumours of a Japanese 'surprise mass attack on Pearl Harbor'. On *1 February* Yamamoto outlines his proposal for an air attack on Pearl. On *31 March* Admiral Patrick L. Bellinger and Major-General Frederick L. Martin produce an estimate of probable Japanese strategy in the event of war and confirm Yarnell's prediction of a carrier-based air attack. No notice is taken in America. 'As for a war with the United States,' says Admiral Nagano on *24 July*, 'although there is now a good chance of achieving victory, the chances will diminish as time goes on.' Since the late spring, Yamamoto has been training special pilots in Kagoshima Bay, the site of Kuper's 1863 bombardment, which is similar in shape to Pearl Harbor. On *26 July* an international oil embargo prevents any more oil reaching Japan. On *18 October*, after the resignation of Prime Minister Prince Konoye, General Tojo Hideki becomes Prime Minister and installs Admiral Shimada Shigetaro as Navy Minister – in Yamamoto's opinion, a 'simpleton'. On *19 October* the Naval Staff reject Yamamoto's Pearl Harbor plan as too risky. Yamamoto threatens resignation, and on *20 October* the plan is accepted. On *10 November* orders are issued to the Nagumo Force, which includes six of Japan's ten aircraft carriers. Even at this date, liaison between Army and Navy is so poor that General Tojo does not know the projected date of attack, nor how much time is left for the increasingly unpromising diplomatic negotiations in Washington to succeed or fail finally. The Navy is using 12,000 tons of fuel daily and has little more than two years' supply stockpiled. On *23 November* British Far Eastern Intelligence forecasts an aggressive move by Japan on or soon after 7 December, which forecast the US Navy Department corroborates on *28 November*; but neither can say where the blow might fall. On *7 December* Tokyo time Japan's first act of aggression in the Pacific War takes place when a British flying-boat is shot down about 80 miles south of Cape Cambodia, after sighting a naval force steaming towards the Kra Isthmus. Some twenty hours later, on *8 December* Tokyo time, Pearl Harbor is attacked. Airfields in Malaya, Singapore, the Philippines and Hong Kong are bombed next day; two days after that, on *10 December*, the British battleship *Prince of Wales* and battlecruiser *Repulse* are sunk with great loss of life, 200 miles north-east of Singapore. On *16 December* the super-battleship *Yamato* is completed – 862 feet long, 71,659 tons, she is the biggest battleship in history. By the end of the year Wake Island and Hong Kong have fallen. The new year,

1942 opens with the fall of Manila on *2 January*. Landings have already been effected in many parts of the Dutch East Indies as well as the Philippines; by the end of *January*, Japanese forces are as far south as Rabaul. On *15 February* Singapore falls, and on *19 January* Port Darwin in north Australia is raided. On *27 February* the Battle of the Java Sea takes place, a serious Allied defeat. In *March* the Indian Ocean is penetrated by the Imperial Navy with raids on Ceylon, and the Dutch East Indies – long-coveted source of oil – are in Japanese hands. In *April* Bataan falls, in *May* Corregidor; and then from *4–8 May* the Battle of the Coral Sea, first carrier-vs-carrier battle, takes place with both sides claiming the victory. Ever since Tsushima Japan has believed in the concept of a single decisive battle, and on *4–6 June* it takes place: the Battle of Midway is a decisive American victory with four Japanese carriers sunk. During *August* the American counter-offensive in the Solomons commences, and Henderson Field is captured; but during the night of *8–9 August* the Allies lose four cruisers in the Battle of Savo Island. On *24 August* a Japanese carrier is sunk and an American one damaged during the Battle of the Eastern Solomons; during September reinforcements for Japan are run in to Guadalcanal by the 'Tokyo Express'; and on *15 September* the US carrier *Wasp* is sunk by a submarine. Throughout *October* there is fierce fighting for the possession of Henderson Field; on *11–12 October*, in the Battle of Cape Esperance, a Japanese cruiser is sunk; then on *26 October*, in the Battle of Santa Cruz, a US carrier is lost. Further reinforcements for the Japanese on Guadalcanal arrive in the first week of *November*; during the night of *12–13 November* the First Battle of Guadalcanal takes place, with the loss of two US cruisers matched by the crippling and later torpedoing (by Japanese hands) of battleship *Hiei*. *14–15 November* brings the Second Battle of Guadalcanal in which battleship *Kirishima* goes down. During the year the Imperial Navy has suffered a net loss of 10% of its carriers, the replacements being converted, sub-standard ships. Very hard fighting continues on land and sea for the rest of the year, including the Battle of Tassafaronga during the night of *30 November–1 December*; and by

1943 *9 February* Guadalcanal finally caves in. Between *2–5 March* in the Battle of the Bismarck Sea, a Japanese convoy is destroyed; on *26 March* the Battle of the Komandorskiye Islands takes place – the last great sea-battle fought only with naval guns. At the beginning of *April*, Yamamoto musters Japan's largest-ever single air armada for a new offensive in the Solomons. On *16 April*, believing the operation a great success, he calls it off, and arranges to visit various bases, travelling by air. Two days later, *18 April*, his plane is shot down and he is killed. He is succeeded almost at once by Admiral Koga Mineichi, but Yamamoto's death is not announced in Japan until *21 May*, the state funeral taking place on *5 June*. Three days later, *8 June*, battleship *Mutsu* blows up in harbour. Through *July and August* there is a rapid-fire series of battles around the Solomons: *5–6 July*, Kula Gulf; *12–13 July*, Kolombangara; *6–7 August*, Vella Gulf. The series continues with *6–7 October*, the Battle of Vella Lavella; *1–2 November*, the Battle of Empress Augusta Bay; *25–26 November*, the Battle of Cape St George; and on *4 December* the carrier *Chuyo* is sunk south-east of Tokyo by a US submarine.

1944 *10 February*: the Combined Fleet is forced to evacuate its Pearl Harbor-style base at Truk atoll. A week later, *17–18 February*, more than 200,000 tons of war and supply shipping is sunk in the atoll, while close to Truk two US battleships sink a Japanese cruiser and two destroyers. On *31 March*, Admiral Koga dies like his predecessor in an air-crash, but this one is through natural causes. The question of his successor is hotly debated in Tokyo, and no replacement is made until *3 May* – almost five weeks after Koga's death – when Admiral Toyoda Soemu becomes C-in-C CF. He continues the reorganization of the Navy which Koga had put into motion, belatedly forming the fleet around a nucleus of carriers instead of battleships. By *14–15 June* American air-raids of Japan proper have begun; and during the Battle of the Philippine Sea, *19–20 June*, three Japanese carriers are sunk with no loss to the American opposition. 'The Jap Navy morale is on the downgrade,' reports an American agent in China. On *7 July* the naval installations at Sasebo are air-raided; the Navy demands greater allocation of air resources at the Army's expense; and on *18 July* Prime Minister General Tojo resigns. Together, Admiral Yonai and General Koiso form the new government, but there is still disagreement over the best strategy for Japan to pursue. Huge Japanese death-tolls are recorded in Guam, Biak and Aitape; by *31 August* American forces are little more than 500 miles south of Japan proper. On *18 August* the carrier *Taiyo* was sunk, and four weeks later on *16 September* the carrier *Unyo* follows her. The largest single air battle of the war, the Battle off Formosa, takes place from *13–16 October*, in which American forces trap Japanese and inflict a serious defeat; on *20 October* Americans land in Leyte Gulf, central Philippines; and from *24–26 October* the largest naval battle in history, the Battle for Leyte Gulf, is fought out with a near-ultimate defeat for Japan. On *19 November* the biggest aircraft carrier in the world, *Shinano* –

converted from the hull of a third *Yamato*-class battleship – is completed for trials. Ten days later, on her maiden voyage of *29 November*, she is sunk; and, on *19 December*, the carrier *Unryu* goes down. The Battle for Leyte Gulf marks the end of the Imperial Japanese Navy as a real fighting force; in the four separate battles which go to make up the whole battle, 26 Japanese warships, including the *Yamato*-class *Musashi*, are lost. But the symbolic end of the Navy comes in

1945 on *7 April* at 2.23 p.m., when the super-battleship *Yamato*, emblem of all the Imperial Navy stood for, is sunk off Okinawa. During the night of *16 May*, in the last destroyer action of World War Two, the cruiser *Haguro* is trapped and sunk by five British destroyers: it is observed that the first three of the fatal torpedoes produce 'three gold-coloured splashes like a Prince of Wales' feathers'. Oddly, and fittingly, she was sunk on the Western side of the same peninsula off which, with the sinking of HMS *Prince of Wales*, the Imperial Navy had opened its war against its old mentor, the Royal Navy.

BIBLIOGRAPHY

Many libraries could be, and indeed have been, filled with works dealing with the Imperial Japanese Navy. A complete list of such works would fill several volumes; this list, therefore, while including the majority of works consulted for this book, is no more than a selection of possible resources, and is given as a guide to some of the more interesting general and specific primary source collections and secondary materials in Western languages.

Agawa, H., *The Reluctant Admiral: Yamamoto and the Imperial Navy*, Tr. J. Bester, Kodansha International, 1979
Allen, L., *Japan: The Years of Triumph*, BPC Library of the 20th Century, 1971
Anethan, Baron d', *The d'Anethan Despatches from Japan 1894–1910*, Ed. G. A. Lensen, Sophia University and Diplomatic Press, 1967
Argyle, C. J., *Japan at War 1937–1945*, Arthur Barker Ltd., 1976
Asada, S., 'The Japanese Navy and the United States', in *Pearl Harbour as History: Japanese-American Relations 1931–1941*, Eds. D. Borg and Okumoto S. with D. K. A. Finlayson, Columbia U.P., 1973
Asakawa, K., *The Russo-Japanese Conflict, Its Causes and Issues*, Archibald Constable, 1915
Bacon, R. and McMurtrie, F. E., *Modern Naval Strategy*, Frederick Muller, 1940
Baer, J. A., 'Why Japan Wins', in *Harper's Weekly* vol. 49 (3 June 1905)
Ballard, G. A., *The Influence of the Sea on the Political History of Japan*, John Murray, 1921
Barker, J. A., *Midway: The Turning Point*, Ballantine Books, 1970
Bassett, R., *Democracy and Foreign Policy: A Case History – The Sino-Japanese Dispute, 1931–33*, Frank Cass & Co., 1968
Bateson, C., *The War with Japan*, Barrie and Rockliff, 1968
Beasley, W. G., *The Modern History of Japan*, Weidenfeld and Nicolson, 1973
Beers, B. F., *Vain Endeavour: Robert Lansing's Attempts to End the American-Japanese Rivalry*, Duke U.P., 1962
Belote, J. H. and W. M., *Titans of the Seas: The Development and Operation of Japanese and American Task Force Carriers during World War Two*, Harper and Row, 1975
Benedict, R., *The Chrysanthemum and the Sword: Patterns of Japanese Culture*, Secker and Warburg, 1947
Bergamini, D., *Japan's Imperial Conspiracy*, Heinemann, 1971
Bird, W. D., *The Strategy of the Russo-Japanese War*, Hugh Rees Ltd., 1909
Bishop, J. B., *Theodore Roosevelt and His Time*, Scribner, 1920
Bodley, R. V. C., *Admiral Togo – The Authorized Biography*, Jarrolds, 1935
Borg, D., *The United States and the Far Eastern Crisis, 1933–1938*, Harvard U.P., 1964
Braisted, W. C., *Report on Japanese Naval Medical and Sanitary Features of the Russo-Japanese War to the Surgeon-General, USN*, Government Printing Office, Washington, D.C., 1906
Brindle, E., *With Russian, Japanese and Chunchuse: The Experiences of an Englishman during the Russo-Japanese War*, John Murray, 1905
British Admiralty, *Japan: War Vessels and Torpedo Boats*, Admiralty, 1891
——, *Japan: War Vessels*, Admiralty, 1902
Brodie, B., *Sea Power in the Machine Age*, Princeton and Oxford University Presses, 1941
Brooke, Lord, *An Eyewitness in Manchuria*, Eveleigh Nash, 1905
Bullock, C., *Etajima: The Dartmouth of Japan*, Sampson, Low, Marston & Co., 1942

Burleigh, B., *Empire of the East, or, Japan and Russia at War, 1904–05*, Chapman and Hall, 1905
Busch, N. F., *A Concise History of Japan*, Cassell, 1973
Byas, H., *Government by Assassination*, Allen and Unwin, 1943
Bywater, H. C., *Sea-Power in the Pacific: A Study of the American-Japanese Naval Problem*, Constable and Co., 1934
Cannon, M. H., *Leyte: Return to the Philippines*, Dept. of the Army, Washington, D.C., 1954
Capel, A. S., 'Togo as a Youth in England' in *Strand Magazine* vol. 29 (April 1905)
Chapman, J. W. M., (Tr. and ed.) *The Price of Admiralty: The War Diary of the German naval attaché in Japan 1939–1943 – vol. 1, 25 August 1939–23 August 1940*, (two further vols. as yet unpublished), Saltire Press, 1982
Checkland, O., 'Scotland and Japan 1860–1914: A Study of Technical Transfer and Cultural Exchange' in *Bakumatsu and Meiji: Studies in Japan's Economic and Social History*, Ed. I. H. Nish, London School of Economics and Political Science, 1982
Chihaya, M., Untitled, unpublished typescript describing his part in and reactions to the Pacific War. Chihaya private possession, 1947
——, 'The Kanrin Maru goes across the Pacific', in *Japan-US Amity and Trade Centennial*, May 1960 supplement to *Shipping and Trade News*
——, 'Hard Training – A Bit of Luck – Seal Fate of Warships', in *Shipping and Trade News*, 6 February 1964
Churchill, W. S., *The Second World War*, six vols., Cassell, 1948–54
Clarke, G. S., *Russia's Seapower Past and Present, or, The Rise of the Russian Navy*, John Murray, 1898
Clifford, N. R., *Retreat from China: British Foreign Policy in the Far East 1937–1941*, Longmans, 1967
Coale, G. B., *Victory at Midway*, Farrar, 1944
Collier, B., *Japan at War*, Sidgwick and Jackson, 1975
Colomb, P. H., *Naval Warfare: Its Ruling Principles and Practice Historically Treated*, W. H. Allen and Co., 1899
Costello, J., *The Pacific War*, Rawson, Wade Publishers Inc., 1981
Couchard, P.-L., *Japanese Impressions*, Bodley Head, 1921
Craig, W., *The Fall of Japan*, Weidenfeld and Nicolson, 1967
Craigie, R., *Behind the Japanese Mask*, Hutchinson, 1946
Crewdson, W., *Japan Our Ally*, Macmillan, 1915
Crowley, J. B., *Japan's Quest for Autonomy: National Security and Foreign Policy 1930–1938*, Princeton U.P., 1966
Davis, B., *Get Yamamoto!*, Arthur Barker Ltd., 1971
Deacon, R., *A History of the Japanese Secret Service*, Frederick Muller, 1982
Dennett, T., *Roosevelt and the Russo-Japanese War*, Doubleday Page, 1925
Dept. of Agriculture and Commerce, Japan, *Japan in the Beginning of the 20th Century*, Imperial Japanese Commission, 1904
Documents on British Foreign Policy, series 1, vol. 6, Foreign Office, 1956
Documents on British Foreign Policy, 1919–1939, Second Series, vols. 18–13, Foreign Office
Doi, T., *The Anatomy of Dependence*, Kodansha International, 1973
Dull, P. S., *A Battle History of the Imperial Japanese Navy 1941–45*, P. Stephens, 1978
Dupuy, T. N., *The Naval War in the Pacific: On to Tokyo*, Edmund Ward, 1966
Dyer, H., *Japan in World Politics: A Study in International Dynamics*, Blackie and Son, 1909
Eardley-Wilmot, S., *Our Fleet Today, and Its Development during the last Half-Century*, Seeley and Co., 1900
Engely, G., *The Politics of Naval Disarmament*, Tr. H. V. Rhodes, Williams and Norgate Ltd., 1932
Esthus, R. A., *Theodore Roosevelt and Japan*, University of Washington Press, 1967
Falk, E. A., *Togo and the Rise of Japanese Seapower*, Longmans, Green and Co., 1936
Falk, S. L., *Decision at Leyte*, Norton, 1966
Farago, L., *The Broken Seal: The Story of 'Operation Magic' and the Pearl Harbour Disaster*, Arthur Barker Ltd., 1967
Field, J. A., *The Japanese at Leyte Gulf: The Sho-Operation*, Princeton U.P., 1947

Fox, J. P., *Germany and the Far East Crisis 1931–1938: A Study in Diplomacy and Ideology*, Oxford U.P./London School of Economics and Political Science, 1982
Fuchida, M. (ed. Pineau, R.), *'I led the Attack on Pearl Harbor'*, in *United States Navy Institute Proceedings*, vol. 78, no. 9, September 1952
—— and Okumiya, M., *Midway: The Battle that Doomed Japan*, U.S. Naval Institute, 1955
Gipps, G., *Journal of the Siege of Tsingtao 1914–15*, unpublished typescript held in the National Maritime Museum, NMM MSS JOD/117
Goette, J., *Japan Fights for Asia*, MacDonald and Co., 1945
Gooch, G. P. et al., *British Documents on the Origin of the War 1898–1914*, 11 vols., Foreign Office, HMSO, 1926–1938
Gray, E., *A Damned Un-English Weapon: The Story of Submarine Warfare 1914–18*, Seeley, Service and Co., 1971
Grew, J. C., *Ten Years in Japan*, Hammond, Hammond and Co., 1944
Haggie, P., *Britannia at Bay: The Defence of the British Empire against Japan, 1931–1941*, Oxford U.P., 1981
Halsey, W. F. and J. B., *Admiral Halsey's Story*, Whittesley House, 1947
Hamilton, I., *A Staff Officer's Scrap-book during the Russo-Japanese War*, Edward Arnold, 1905
Hargreaves, R., *Red Sun Rising: The Siege of Port Arthur*, J. P. Lippincott Co., 1962
Hashimoto, M., *Sunk: Japanese Submarines 1942–1945*, Cassell & Co., 1954
Hayashi, Count T., *Secret Memoirs*, Eveleigh Nash, 1915
Heiferman, R., *United States Navy in World War Two*, Hamlyn, 1978
Heinrichs, W. H., *'The Role of the United States Navy'*, in *Pearl Harbour as History: Japanese-American Relations 1931–1941*, Eds. D. Borg and Okumiya S. with D. K. A. Finlayson, Columbia U.P., 1973
Humble, R., *Japanese High Seas Fleet*, Ballantine Books, 1974
Ichihashi, Y., *The Washington Conference and After*, Stanford, 1928
Ienage, S., *Japan's Last War*, Blackwell, 1979
Ike, N., *Japan's Decision for War: Records of the 1941 Policy Conferences*, Tr., ed. and intro. by Ike, N., Stanford U.P., 1967
Ikle, F. W., *'Japanese-German Peace Negotiations during World War One'*, in *American Historical Review*, vol. 71 (1965)
Inoguchi, R. and Nakajima, T. with Pineau, R. *The Divine Wind*, Naval Institute Press, 1958
Inouye, J., *The Japan-China War, from Official and other Sources*, Kelly and Walsh, *c.* 1900
Iriye, A., *Pacific Estrangement: Japanese and American Expansion, 1897–1911*, Harvard U.P., 1972
——, *Power and Culture: The Japanese-American War 1941–45*, Harvard U.P., 1981
Ishimaru, T., *Japan Must Fight Britain*, Tr. G. V. Rayment, Hurst and Blackett, 1936
Ito, M. with Pineau, R., *The End of the Imperial Japanese Navy*, Tr. Kuroda, A. Y. and R. Pineau, Weidenfeld and Nicolson, 1962
James, D. C., *The Years of MacArthur*, three vols., Houghton, Mifflin, Co., 1970–75
James, D. H., *The Rise and Fall of the Japanese Empire*, Allen and Unwin, 1951
Jameson, W., *The Most Formidable Thing: The Story of the Submarine from its Earliest Days to the End of World War One*, Rupert Hart-Davis Ltd., 1965
Jane, F. T., *The Imperial Russian Navy*, W. Thacker and Co., 1899
——, *The Imperial Japanese Navy*, W. Thacker and Co., 1899
——, *Heresies of Sea Power*, Longmans, 1906
Japan Time and Mail, *Japan in 1938 – A Symposium*, Japan Times and Mail, 1938
Jentschura, H., Jung, D. and Mickel, P., *Warships of the Imperial Japanese Navy, 1869–1945*, Tr. A. Preston and J. D. Brown, Arms and Armour Press, 1977
Jones, F. C., *Japan's New Order in East Asia, 1937–45*, Oxford U.P., 1954
Kajima, M., *The Emergence of Japan as a World Power, 1895–1925*, Tuttle and Co., 1968
Kemp, P., (Ed.) *The Oxford Companion to Ships and the Sea*, Oxford U.P., 1976
Kennedy, M. D., *The Estrangement of Great Britain and Japan, 1917–35*, Manchester U.P., 1969
Killen, J., *A History of Marine Aviation, 1911–68*, Frederick Muller, 1969
Kirby, S. W. et al., *The War Against Japan*, five vols., H.M.S.O. 1957–69

Klado, N. L., *The Russian Navy in the Russo-Japanese War*, Hurst and Blackett, 1905
——, *The Battle of the Sea of Japan*, Tr. J. H. Dickinson and F. P. Marchant, Hodder and Stoughton, 1906
Kuropatkin, General, 'The Causes of Russia's Defeat by Japan', in *McClure's Magazine*, vol. 32
Lamb, C., *War in a Stringbag*, Cassell, 1977
Lehmann, J.-P., *The Image of Japan: From Feudal Isolation to World Power, 1850–1905*, Allen and Unwin, 1978
Lensen, G. A., *The d'Anethan Despatches from Japan 1894–1910*, Sophia University and Diplomatic Press, 1967
Liddell Hart, B. H., *History of the Second World War*, Cassell, 1970
Lissington, M. P., *New Zealand and Japan, 1900–1941*, A. R. Shearer, 1972
Lloyd, A., *Admiral Togo*, Kinkodo Publishing Co., 1905
Lord, W., *Day of Infamy*, Longmans, 1957
——, *Incredible Victory*, Harper, 1967
Lowe, P., *Great Britain and Japan 1911–15: A Study of British Far Eastern Policy*, Macmillan, 1969
——, *Great Britain and the Origins of the Pacific War: A Study of British Policy in East Asia 1937–1941*, Clarendon Press, 1977
Lu, D. J., *From the Marco Polo Bridge to Pearl Harbour*, Public Affairs Press Washington (in cooperation with Bucknell U.P), 1961
MacIntyre, D., *Leyte Gulf: Armada in the Pacific*, Ballantine Books, 1969
Mahan, A. T., 'Preparedness for Naval War', in *Harper's Weekly*, vol. XCIV, March 1897
——, 'Current Fallacies upon Naval Subjects', in *Harper's Weekly*, vol. XCVII, June 1898
Marder, A. J., *Old Friends, New Enemies: The Royal Navy and the Imperial Navy – Strategic Illusions 1936–1941*, Oxford U.P., 1981
Mars, A., *H.M.S. Thule Intercepts*, Elek Books, 1956
Martin, B., *Deutschland und Japan*, Musterschmidtverlag, 1969
Martin, C., *The Russo-Japanese War*, Abelard-Schumann, 1967
Matsuo, K., *How Japan Plans to Win*, Tr. K. K. Haan, Little, Brown and Co., 1942
McCormick, F., *The Menace of Japan*, Little, Brown and Co., 1917
Middlebrook, M. and Mahoney, P., *Battleship: The Loss of the 'Prince of Wales' and the 'Repulse'*, Allen Lane, 1977
Millard, T. F., *Democracy and the Eastern Question*, Allen and Unwin, 1919
Millot, B., *Divine Thunder: The Life and Death of the Kamikazes*, Tr. L. Bair, Macdonald, 1971
Morison, S. E., *History of the United States Naval Operations in World War Two*, fourteen vols., Oxford U.P., 1947–62
Morley, J. W., *The Japanese Thrust into Siberia, 1918*, Columbia U.P., 1957
Mosley, L. O., *Hirohito, Emperor of Japan*, Weidenfeld and Nicolson, 1966
Nakamura, K. (ed), *Admiral Togo, the Hero of the World: A Memoir*, Togo Gensui, 1937
Nakane, C., *Japanese Society*, University of California Press, 1970
Neumann, W. L., *America Encounters Japan: From Perry to MacArthur*, John Hopkins Press, 1963
Newcomb, R. F., *Savo 1942*, Constable and Co., 1963
Nimitz, C. W. and Potter, E. B., *The Great Sea War*, George Harrap, 1962
Nish, I. H., *The Anglo-Japanese Alliance: The Diplomacy of Two Island Empires 1894–1907*, Athlone Press, University of London, 1966
——, *The Story of Japan*, Faber and Faber, 1968
——, 'Admiral Jerram and the German Pacific Fleet, 1913–15', in *Mariners' Mirror*, no. 56, 1970
——, *Alliance in Decline: A Study in Anglo-Japanese Relations 1908–23*, Athlone Press, University of London, 1972
——, *Japanese Foreign Policy 1869–1942*, Routledge and Kegan Paul, 1977
Nitobe, I., et al., *Western Influences in Modern Japan*, University of Chicago Press, 1931
——, *Bushido: The Soul of Japan*, Kenkyusha, 1936
Norregaard, B. W., *The Great Siege*, Methuen, 1906
Novikoff-Priboy, A., *Tsushima*, Tr. E. and C. Paul, Allen and Unwin, 1936

Ogasawara, N., *Life of Admiral Togo*, Tr. and abbr. Inouye, J. and T., Seito Shorin Press, 1934
Ogawa, G., *Expenditures of the Russo-Japanese War*, Oxford U.P., 1923
Okamoto, S., *The Japanese Oligarchy and the Russo-Japanese War*, Columbia U.P.
Okuda, T., *'Bombardment of Kagoshima by the British Fleet, August 1863'*, in *Journal of the Royal United Service Institute*, vol. 57, November 1913
Okuma, Count S. (Ed.), *Fifty Years of New Japan*, Smith, Elder and Co., 1909
Okumiya, M., Horikoshi, J. and Caidin, M., *Zero! – The Story of the Japanese Navy Air Force, 1937–1945*, Cassell, 1957
Okumiya, M. and Horikoshi, J., *The Zero Fighter*, 1958
Pearl, C., *Morrison of Peking*, Angus and Robertson, 1967
Pelz, S. E., *Race to Pearl Harbour: The Failure of the Second London Naval Conference and the Onset of World War Two*, Harvard U.P., 1974
Politovsky, E. S., *From Libau to Tsushima*, John Murray, 1906
Posokhow, S., *'Recollections of the Battle of Tsushima, May 14–27, 1905, on Board the Cruiser Oleg'*, in *United States Navy Institute Proceedings*, April 1930
Potter, J. D., *Admiral of the Pacific: The Life of Yamamoto*, Heinemann, 1965
Prange, G. W., in collaboration with Goldstein, D. M., and Dillon, K. V., *At Dawn We Slept: The Untold Story of Pearl Harbor*, Michael Joseph, 1982
Pratt, J. W., *A History of United States Foreign Policy*, Prentice-Hall Inc., 1955
Presseisen, E. L., *Germany and Japan: A Study in Totalitarian Diplomacy 1933–1941*, Martinus Nijhoff, 1958
Preston, A., (Ed.) *Decisive Battles of the Pacific War*, Hamlyn, 1979
Pursey, C. H., *The Last Siege of Tsingtao*, unpublished typescript held in the National Maritime Museum, NMM MSS JOD/117
Reischauer, E. O., *Japan: The Story of a Nation*, Duckworth, 1970
——, *The United States and Japan*, Harvard U.P., 1965
——, *Japan Past and Present*, Duckworth, 1947
——, *The Japanese*, Harvard U.P., 1977
Repington, C.àC., *The War in the Far East 1904–05*, John Murray, 1905
Rohwer, J. and Hummelchen, G., *Chronology of the War at Sea 1939–1945*, Tr. D. Martin, two vols., Ian Allen Ltd., 1972–74
Roskill, S. W., *The War at Sea*, three vols., H.M.S.O., 1954–61
——, *The Strategy of Seapower: Its Development and Application*, Collins, 1962
——, *Naval Policy between the Wars*, two vols., Collins, 1968
Rouvier, H., (Tr. from the Japanese) *Opérations Maritimes de la Guerre Russo-Japonaise*, two vols., Libraire Militaire R. Chapelot, 1910–11
Russell of Liverpool, Lord, *The Knights of Bushido: A Short History of Japanese War Crimes*, Cassell, 1958
Salmaggi, C. and Pallavasini, A., *2194 Days of War: An Illustrated Chronology of the Second World War*, Windward, 1977
Scott, G., *The Rise and Fall of the League of Nations*, Hutchinson, 1973
Schwartz, W. L., *'Commodore Perry at Okinawa'*, in *American Historical Review*, vol. LI, June 1946
Seaman, L. L., *The Real Triumph of Japan*, Sidney Appleton, 1906
Sebald, W. J. with Brines, R., *With MacArthur in Japan*, Cresset Press, 1965
Semenov, V., *The Battle of Tsushima*, Tr. A. B. Lindsay, John Murray, 1906
——, *Rasplata: The Reckoning*, John Murray, 1909
Seymour, E. H., *My Naval Career and Travels*, Smith, Elder and Co., 1911
Shepherd, C. R., *The Case Against Japan*, Jarrolds, 1939
Shigemitsu, M., *Japan and Her Destiny: My Struggle for Peace*, Hutchinson, 1958
Smith, C. L., *Midway, 4 June 1942*, Regency, 1942
Smith, S. F., *The Battle of Leyte Gulf*, Belmont, 1961
Spurr, R., *A Glorious Way to Die: The Kamikaze Mission of the Battleship* Yamato, *April 1945*, Newmarket Press, 1981
Stead, A., *Japan, Our New Ally*, T. Fisher Unwin, 1902
——, (Ed.), *Japan by the Japanese: A Survey by its Highest Authorities*, 2 vols., Wm. Heinemann, 1904

——, *Japanese Patriotism*, Bodley Head, 1909
Steer, A. P., *The Novik*, John Murray, 1913
Stewart, A., *The Battle of Leyte Gulf*, Robert Hale, 1979
St John, S. F., *Leyte Calling*, Vanguard, 1945
Storry, R., *The Double Patriots: A Study in Japanese Nationalism*, Chatto and Windus, 1957
——, *Japan and the Decline of the West in Asia 1894–1943*, Macmillan, 1977
Suyematsu, Baron K., *The Risen Sun*, Archibald Constable, 1905
Takeuchi, T., *War and Diplomacy in the Japanese Empire*, Allen and Unwin, 1936
Taylor, A. J. P., *The Origins of the Second World War*, Hamish Hamilton, 1961
Thomas, D. A., *Java Sea 1942*, André Deutsch, 1968
——, *Japan's War at Sea: Pearl Harbour to the Coral Sea*, André Deutsch, 1978
Thorne, C., *Allies of a Kind: The United States, Britain and the War against Japan 1941–1945*, Hamish Hamilton, 1978
Tikovara, H., *Before Port Arthur in a Destroyer: The Personal Diary of a Japanese Naval Officer*, Tr. R. Grant, John Murray, 1907
Toland, J., *The Rising Sun: The Decline and Fall of the Japanese Empire 1936–1945*, Cassell, 1970
Tsunoda, R. et al., *Sources of Japanese Tradition*, Columbia U.P., 1958
Tuleja, T. V., *Climax at Midway*, Dent, 1961
Tyler, S., *The Japan-Russia War*, P. W. Ziegler Co., 1905
Unger, F. W., *The Authentic History of the War between Russia and Japan*, World Bible House, 1904
Walder, D., *The Short Victorious War: The Russo-Japanese Conflict 1904–05*, Hutchinson, 1973
Ward, A. W. and Gooch, G. P., *Cambridge History of British Foreign Policy 1783–1919*, vol. 3 1866–1919, Cambridge U.P., 1923
Warner, D. and P., *The Tide at Sunrise: A History of the Russo-Japanese War, 1904–05*, Angus and Robertson, 1975
Watts, A. J., *Japanese Warships of World War Two*, Ian Allen, 1971
—— and Gordon, B. G., *The Imperial Japanese Navy*, Macdonald
Werstein, I., *The Battle of Midway*, Crowell, 1961
Westwood, J. N., *Witnesses of Tsushima*, Sophia University Diplomatic Press, 1970
——, *The Illustrated History of the Russo-Japanese War*, Sidgwick and Jackson, 1973
White, J. A., *The Diplomacy of the Russo-Japanese War*, Princeton U.P., 1964
Wilson, H. W., *Battleships in Action*, Sampson, Low, Marston and Co., 1926
Winton, J., *The Forgotten Fleet*, Michael Joseph, 1969
——, *War in the Pacific: Pearl Harbour to Tokyo Bay*, Sidgwick and Jackson, 1978
Wiskemann, E., *The Rome–Berlin Axis*, Oxford U.P., 1949
Wohlstetter, R., *Pearl Harbor: Warning and Decision*, Stanford U.P., 1962
Woodward, C. V., *The Battle of Leyte Gulf*, Macmillan, 1947
Wright, H. C. S., *With Togo: The Story of Seven Months' Active Service under His Command*, Hurst and Blackett, 1905
Yanaga, C., *Japan Since Perry*, McGraw-Hill, 1949

Periodicals consulted, with a wide variety of dates, included: *American Historical Review*; *Army and Navy Journal*; *The Belgian Shiplover*; *Boston Post*; *Engineering*; *The Engineeer*; *Forum*; *Harper's Weekly*; *Illustrated London News*; *Japan Herald*; *Japan Society of London Transactions*; *Japan Society of New York Transactions*; *Japan Times*; *Japan–Russia War: An Illustrated Monthly Record of Operations*; *Japan Year Book*; *Journal of the Royal United Services Institute*; *Life*; *Manchester Guardian*; *Mariners' Mirror*; *McClure's Magazine*; *Navy and Army Illustrated*; *Navy International*; *Newcastle Chronicle*; *New York Times*; *Segeln*; *Shipping and Trade Weekly*; *Strand Magazine*; *Time*; *The Times*; *United States Navy Institute Proceedings*; *Washington Post*.

Archive material was gathered from: *Japan* – Bōeichō Senshibu (Historical Research Institute, Tokyo); *United States* – the Library of Congress, the National Archives, and the

Operational Branch of the Naval Historical Center (all in Washington, D.C.); *Great Britain* – the Bodleian Library (Oxford); Warwick University Library (West Midlands); the British Library, the Imperial War Museum, the Ministry of Defence Naval Historical Branch, the National Maritime Museum, the Public Records Office and the Royal Institute of International Affairs (all in London).

Index

Abbreviations: BB *battleship*, BCA *battlecruiser*, CA *cruiser*, CL *light cruiser*, CV *aircraft carrier*, CVL *light carrier*, DD *destroyer*, MTB *motor-torpedoboat*, XCV *escort carrier*; IJN, *Imperial Japanese Navy*; IRN, *Imperial Russian Navy*; RN, *Royal Navy*; USN, *United States Navy*.

Abe, H.,VAdm, IJN, 312, 313, 314–5, 364
Abe, T., Capt, IJN, 361–2
Akagi, CV, 223, 275, 287, 291, 299, 300, 302, 303, 306
Akitsushima, CA, 19, 20, 29
Aleutians, 185, 230, 285, 287, 294, 296, 297, 303
Anethan, Baron d', 34, 39, 61–3, 67, 75, 96, 102, 111
Anglo-Japanese Alliance, 21, 40, 82, 102, 115, 117, 121, 124, 126, 130, 146, 148, 149, 150, 152–3, 154, 155, 205, 206, 270, 376
Anti-Comintern Pact, 202, 219, 225, 226, 228, 381
Arashi, DD, 301, 302
Asahi, BB, 56, 74, 90
Asama Maru incident, 231–2, 381
Atago, CA, 163, 342, 345, 347, 352
Australia, 102, 106, 110–1, 116, 117, 125, 128, 220, 258, 271, 273, 274, 282, 285, 334

Bataan, 273, 275, 282, 306, 382
Bay-class ships, USN, 352–3
Beatty, D., Adm RN, 134, 146, 163–4, 175, 319
Bellinger, P. L., Adm USN, 247, 381
Benbrooks, L., Sgt USAAF, 262–5
Bodley, R. V. C., 216, 246
British Chivalry, SS, 326
British Empire, 58, 116, 117, 119, 120, 133, 148, 149, 150, 154–5, 156, 163, 216–7, 243, 275
Brodie, B., 219, 246
Brunei Bay, 342, 345, 347, 359
Bullock, C., 50, 53
Buxton, C., 10–1, 173
Byas, H., 177, 182–3, 204
Bywater, H. C., 186, 198–9, 216, 252, 272, 294

California, 103, 107, 108, 109
Callaghan, D. J., RAdm USN, 312–3
Cape Engaño, Battle of, 345, 348, 359
Caroline Islands, 124, 332, 334, 378
Ceylon, 275, 276
Chamberlain, N., 234, 261
Chatfield, Adm of the Fleet Lord, 155, 182, 193, 194, 220
Chiang Kai-Shek, 173, 212, 213, 363
Chihaya, M., Cdr IJN, 308–9, 310, 312–5, 324, 332, 343, 364, 369
Chikuma, CA, 128, 275, 299, 308, 351, 352
China, 9, 14, 19–22, 24, 25, 28, 29, 30–5, 36, 38, 40, 56, 57, 58, 62, 103, 117, 123, 126–7, 151, 162, 171–5, 181, 188, 193, 205, 212–6, 219, 220–1, 223, 224, 226, 243, 247, 274, 287, 337, 338, 362, 380
Chinhae, Bay of, 61, 89, 90
Chokai, CA, 308, 351, 352
Churchill, W. S., 124, 126, 130, 150, 161, 234, 239, 242, 244, 246–7, 248, 251, 254, 261, 265, 267, 268, 272, 276, 277, 372
Ciano, Count G., 219, 228
Coral Sea, 286–7, 306, 307; Battle of the, 312, 315, 382
Corregidor, 273, 278, 305, 382
Craigie, Sir R., 152, 155–6, 170, 204, 215, 220, 224, 225, 226, 228, 231, 237, 240, 251, 258, 260, 265, 276, 277, 285, 379
Cryptography, US, 156, 241, 242, 295–7

Daisy Moller, SS, 325–6
Dick, R. M., RAdm RN, 214–5, 220–1
Dogger Bank Incident, 83–4
Dönitz, Grand Adm, German Navy, 339–40, 365
Doolittle, J. H., Lt-Col USAF, 277, 284
Doorman, K., RAdm Dutch Navy, 273–4
Dreadnought, BB, 93, 105, 139

393

Dreyer, Sir F., Adm RN, 190, 195
Dual (Franco-Russian) Alliance, 37, 38, 40–1

Eden, Sir A., 202, 324–5
Endo, S., Lt-Gen IJArmy, 319, 321, 322, 323
Enterprise, CV, 302, 311, 312, 315
Etajima, IJN officers' academy, 44–53, 54, 166, 225, 274, 293, 308

Fisher, J., Adm RN, 93, 97, 105, 106, 116, 139, 140, 159
'Fitness to Win', 320, 335
Fletcher, F., RAdm USN, 273, 286, 294, 307
Force Z, 267–70
Formosa, 36, 96, 338, 341; Battle off, 339–40, 345, 383
Fujita, I., 223, 227
Fukudome, S., VAdm IJN, 234, 243
'Fundamentals of National Policy, the', 204–5
Furusawa, K., IJNAF observer, 268–9
Fushimi, H., Adm Prince IJN, 173, 182, 190–1, 239
Fuso (1877), 14, 24, 29, 119, 375–6; BB (1914), 119, 120, 308, 346, 349, 350, 378

Gekokujo, 191–3, 204, 356
Genda, M., Cdr IJN, 246, 293
Geneva Conference, 164–5, 331, 379
George V, King, 146, 170, 202–3
Germany, 36, 37, 38, 61, 116, 121, 123, 124, 125, 127, 129–30, 131, 132, 133, 176, 178, 180, 183, 195, 202, 215, 219, 221–3, 225, 226, 228, 229, 230, 231, 232–7, 241, 244, 247, 270, 271, 276, 277, 320–1, 324, 339, 341–2, 355, 362, 365, 377, 378
Gipps, G., 123, 124
Grew, J. C., 176, 177, 178, 181–3, 185, 188–9, 192–3, 196–7, 201–2, 203–4, 211, 212, 215–7, 221, 225–6, 232, 237, 242–3, 244–5, 247, 250–1, 256, 260, 265, 277
Grey, Lord, 128, 174–5
Guadalcanal, 307, 308, 310, 311, 315, 317–8, 364, 383; Battle of, 312–5, 382
Guam, 196, 244, 281–2, 297, 338, 383

Haguro, CA, 163, 274, 366, 384
Hainan, 205, 224, 328, 381
Haiyang, 28, 29, 30
Halsey, W. F., Adm USN, 112, 273, 318, 340, 345, 346, 348–9, 359
Hamaguchi, Prime Minister, 168, 170, 171, 172
Hamilton, W., RO USAAF, 263–4
Haruna, BB, 299, 310, 364
Hashirajima, 287, 291, 296

Hawaii, 107, 109, 110, 234, 244, 245, 247, 255, 256, 259, 261, 267, 272, 286, 292, 297, 298
Hayashi, T., 39, 40–1
Henderson Field, 310, 312, 313, 314, 318, 382
Hickam Air Field, 262, 265
Hiei (1878), 14, 24, 29; BCA (1912), 312–5, 382
Hiraide, H., Capt IJN, 250, 255
Hirohito, Emperor, 145–6, 147, 151, 159, 161, 162, 163, 171, 182, 190–1, 204, 207, 250, 252–3, 271, 305, 343, 370, 379
Hirose, T., Cdr IJN, 70–1
Hiroshima, 24, 113, 270, 334, 335, 361
Hirota, K., 192, 201, 217
Hiryu, CV, 198, 275, 306
Hitler, A., 180, 183, 211, 213, 219, 220, 226, 228, 229, 235, 236, 241–2, 244, 257, 261, 271, 277, 338, 380
Hitokappu Bay, 257, 259
Hong Kong, 31, 38, 205, 206, 215, 216, 221, 231, 237, 244, 266, 272, 282, 382
Hopkins, Sir F., Adm RN, 353–5
Hornet, CV, 302, 311, 312
Hosho, CV, 148, 212, 379
Houston, CA, 174, 273, 340
Hughes-Hallett, Sir C., VAdm RN, 354–5

Ichimaya, Capt IJN, 229, 230, 232, 235, 237
Iki, H., Lt IJNAF, 269, 348
Imperial Japanese Army, 26, 27, 28, 36, 42, 64, 108, 118, 119, 228, 236, 238, 249, 253, 258, 322, 324–5; vetoes IJN/RN co-operation, 127; and Manchurian Incident, 172, 178, 195–6; and 26 February mutiny, 203–4; and atrocities at Nanking, 213–4, 216; diaries from 281–7, 303–5, 307, 309–12, 315–6
Imperial Japanese Navy, 12, 42, 54, 56, 57, 59–60, 62, 93, 101, 103, 104, 106, 108, 110, 113, 115, 116, 117, 119, 246, 251, 252, 255, 257, 274, 276, 278, 287, 291, 295, 306, 308, 314, 315, 317–9; beginning and end, 1; made Department of State, 12, 16, 36; and Triple Intervention, 37–8; Meiji's Rescript to, 43–4, 46; at Etajima, 44–53; attacks Port Arthur, 64–5, 67–80; and '8-8' fleet crisis, 118, 140, 153, 377–9; and bribery, 122; at Kaiochow, 122–4; and von Spee, 124–5; in World War One, 126–30; 1920 tonnage, 134; 1920 personnel, 149; strategy, 135, 147, 149, 151, 160, 179–81, 236, 242, 245, 292–5, 331, 341–5; and submarines, 113–5, 136–7, 258; and aircraft, 138, 148, 199, 212–3, 214–5, 246; breaking Washington Treaty, 163; budget,

182, 211; purged, 185–6; technology, 198–9; underestimated by West, 199–200; and 26 February mutiny, 204; at Nanking, 213–4; and *Panay*, 215–6; anti-British, 219–21, 224; and IJA, 221, 225, 228, 230, 236, 238, 249, 254, 255, 259, 269, 276, 283, 322–3, 382; and oil, 158–9, 230, 232, 235, 237, 239, 250, 254, 257, 274, 333, 382; divisions in, 168, 170, 175–6, 177, 179–81, 185–7, 188, 190–4, 201, 214–9, 229, 233–4, 235–6, 238, 270–1; and *Prince of Wales* and *Repulse*, 267–70; diaries from 279–81, 332; and mine countermeasures, 320–1; and navy civilian manpower, bomb and aircraft development, aero intelligence, anti-aircraft defences, radar, 321–3; atrocities committed by, 324–30, 332–6, 360, 364–6, 369–73, 375–84; *see also under individual names of battles, ships and personnel*
India, 115, 275
Indian Ocean, 86, 128, 163–4, 269, 275, 276, 278, 285, 306, 326, 382
Inoguchi, R., Capt IJN, 355–6
Inoue, S., Adm IJN, 179, 185, 245, 246, 248
Inukai, Prime Minister, 177, 186–7, 192, 204
Ishikawa, S., Cdr IJN, 183–4, 217, 248
Ishimaru, T., Lt-Cdr IJN, 205–7
Ito, Y., Adm IJN, 28, 29–31, 32, 33, 34, 35, 37, 60

Jane, F. T., on Yalu battle, 32; 61, 82–3, 320, 335
Java Sea, Battle of, 273–4, 305, 382
Jellicoe, J. R., Adm RN, 128, 130
Jong, P. de, 326–8

Kabayama, S., VAdm IJN, 27, 28, 29
Kaga, CV, 212, 213, 299, 302, 303, 306, 379
Kagoshima, 9–11, 22, 28, 173, 251, 365, 375, 381
Kamikaze corps, origin of name, 25, 46, 346, 353–9
Kamimura, T., 2nd-class seaman IJN, 279–81
Kanto earthquake, 158–9, 160
Kato, K., VAdm IJN, 160, 168, 170, 175, 176, 179–81, 190, 196, 198, 217, 219, 222, 357
Kato, T., 121, 122, 127
Kato, T., 140, 146, 150, 151, 152, 153, 154, 156, 159–60, 171, 176, 179
Katsu, A., 12–13, 23
Kawabe, Lt-Gen IJA, 356–8
Kawachi, BB, 116, 377
Kelly, Sir H., Adm RN, 173–4
Kennedy, M. D., Capt British Army, 131, 148, 150, 152–3, 158–9, 167–8, 191, 199, 202, 270
Kiaochow, 38, 106, 121, 122–4, 125
Kimmel, H. E., Adm USN, 243, 245, 381
Kinkaid, T. C., Adm USN, 346, 349, 359
Kirishima, BB, 312, 315, 382
Koga, M., Adm IJN, 331, 332, 333, 383
Kojima, Capt IJN, 232, 234–5, 237
Kojima, K., Lt (jg) IJN, 347–8
Kondo, N., Adm IJN, 275, 307–8
Kongo, BCA, 116, 310, 378
Konoye, Prince, Prime Minister, 237, 243, 252–3, 254–5, 381
Korea, 19, 24, 25, 28, 29, 34, 36, 40, 61, 63, 67, 68, 75, 77, 105, 116, 232, 377
Koreetz, gunboat IRN, 67–8
Kota Bharu, 244, 268
Kowshing, SS, 20–1, 23, 27, 28, 32
Kra Isthmus, 259, 266
Kuantan, 268, 282
Kuper, RAdm RN, 10–11, 22, 25, 173, 251, 365, 375
Kure, 24, 44, 45, 62, 102, 116, 148, 163, 217, 218, 245, 255, 258, 274, 377
Kuriles, 86, 105, 257
Kurita, T., VAdm IJN, 276, 310, 342–3, 345–9, 350–3, 359, 364

League of Nations, 141, 174–5, 178–9, 190, 205, 380
Lenin, V., 85, 132
Leslie, M., Lt-Cdr USNAF, 302, 305
Lexington, CV, 283, 286
Leyte Gulf, Battle for, 341–60, 383
Leyte Island, 341, 342, 343, 348, 362, 383
Liaotung Peninsula, 31, 34, 36
Lietzmann, J., Capt German Navy, 221–2, 228–32
Litvinov, M., 222–3
London Naval Conference (1930), 167–70, 172, 187, 191, 379, 380
London Naval Talks (1934), 192–7
London Naval Conference (1936), 201–2
Luzon, 272, 275, 345

MacArthur, D., Genl US Army, 275, 338, 341, 346
Madagascar, 275, 276, 285
Mahan, A. T., Adm USN, 33, 107, 108–9, 117
Mainichi Shimbun, 108, 319, 332
Makaroff, S. P., Adm IRN, 37, 61, 68–74, 76
Manchuria, 58, 59, 62, 115, 151, 176, 178, 205, 223, 224
Manchurian Incident, 172, 173, 380
Manila, 214, 216, 273; naval atrocities in, 329–30, 382

Mariana Islands, 124, 201, 334, 335;'Great Marianas Turkey Shoot', 334–6, 337, 339, 342, 361, 378
Marshall Islands, 124, 273, 283, 303, 378
Martin, F. L., Maj-Genl US Army, 247, 381
Massey, W. F., 119, 148
Matsuoka, Y., 179, 237, 239–40, 248, 249
Maya, CA, 310, 345
McClusky, C., Lt-Cdr USNAF, 302, 305
Meiji, Emperor, 9, 31, 36; and the Five Articles Oath, 42; his Rescript to the Army and Navy, 43–4, 49, 54, 64, 89, 101, 118; death, 119, 145, 161, 162, 180, 186, 253, 370, 375, 377
Midway, 201, 285, 287, 288, 292, 293, 296–7, 307, 310, 312, 322, 335, 342, 345, 346, 350, 359, 382; Battle of, 298–306
Mikasa, BB, 54–5, 56, 64, 66, 73, 76, 78, 79, 86, 88, 89, 91, 101, 116, 117, 135, 376–7
Mindanao, 272, 278, 332, 353
Missouri, BB, 369, 371
Mitchell, W., Genl US Army AF, 146–7, 148, 167, 188, 218
Miyauchi, H., Lt-Cdr IJN, 269–70
Mogami-class cruisers, 171, 190, 306, 350, 351
Musashi (1884), 29; BB (1938), 245–6, 285, 293, 308, 318, 333, 342, 346–8, 351, 361, 384
Mussolini, B., 220, 228, 242, 261, 271
Mutsu, BB, 140, 356
Myoko, CA, 163, 272, 310

Nachi, CA, 163, 272, 273
Nagano, O., Navy Minister, 181, 202, 249, 250, 253, 255, 256, 259, 381
Nagasaki, 6, 148, 245, 274, 308–9
Nagato, BB, 134–5, 222, 234, 243, 244, 308, 364, 370, 378
Nagumo, C., Adm IJN, 282, 287, 288, 291, 292, 293–4, 299–303, 346
Nagumo Force, 282, 291, 292, 295, 296, 298, 382
Naniwa, CA, 15, 19, 20, 21, 22, 27, 28, 29, 59, 376
Nelson, H., Adm Lord RN, 49, 55, 60, 64, 66, 68, 91, 97, 166, 191, 293, 294
New Guinea, 124, 201, 224, 274, 275, 283, 285, 309, 310, 311, 315, 319, 335, 339
New Zealand, 102, 106, 111, 116, 117, 128, 272
Nimitz, C. W., Adm USN, 294, 296, 297, 298, 313, 318, 334, 338, 341, 346, 360, 369
Nishida, Capt IJN, 314–5
Nishimura, S., Adm IJN, 342, 343, 345, 346, 349, 350

Nomura, K., Adm IJN, 177, 179
Novik, CA, 66, 70, 71, 73, 77, 80

Oahu, 175, 248, 259, 262, 267
Oikawa, Adm IJN, Navy Minister, 238, 239, 244, 249, 254–5
Okumiya, M., 213, 335, 372
Oldendorf, J., RAdm USN, 346, 349, 350
Osumi, M., Navy Minister, 173, 181, 183, 188, 192, 232
'Osumi Purge, the', 185–6, 257, 380
Ozawa, J., VAdm IJN, 334–5, 336, 342, 343, 345, 346, 348, 359

Pacific, first Japanese voyage across, 12; Fleet, 65, 99, 102–3, 104, 105, 106, 107, 108, 109, 111, 112, 116, 117, 124–5, 126, 130, 131, 133, 150, 157, 162, 164–5, 176, 177, 183, 186, 190, 193, 198, 201, 204, 206, 211, 220, 223, 224, 230, 232, 237, 242–3, 245–6, 248, 257, 266–7, 269, 272, 276, 280, 282, 285, 287, 291, 292, 302, 307, 309, 312, 317, 321, 331, 332, 334, 338, 343, 345, 350, 359, 366
Pakenham, W., Capt RN, 76–7, 90–1, 94–5
Pakhoi Incident, 205, 224
Panay, gunboat, 215, 217, 224
Pearl Harbor, 2, 65, 136, 175, 207, 234, 243, 245, 246, 247, 251, 255, 258, 259, 266, 267, 270, 272, 274, 277, 287, 288, 292, 293, 295, 298, 302, 305, 314, 320–1, 332, 346, 349, 360, 365, 370, 381, 382, 383; attacked, 260–1, 262–5
Peking, 25, 123, 125, 212
Perry, M. C., Commodore USN, 5–9, 12, 22, 24, 25, 46, 59, 103, 189, 370, 375
Philippines, 107, 108, 109, 110, 133, 216, 244, 259, 272, 277–8, 338–9, 340, 341, 348, 355, 360, 362, 378, 382, 383
Philippine Sea, Battle of the, 334–6, 337, 345, 361
Phillips, Sir T., VAdm RN, 244, 267, 269
Port Arthur, 31, 34, 36, 37, 38, 61, 63, 64–78; first raid on, 64–5; siege of, 67–78, 84, 85, 88, 91, 95, 102, 216, 260, 292, 376
Port Moresby, 274, 284, 286, 310
Portsmouth, New Hampshire, 101, 115, 161, 372, 377
Power, M., Capt RN, 366, 372
Prince of Wales, BB, 267–70, 279, 302, 305, 333, 348, 366, 382, 384

Rabaul, 275, 282, 283–5, 286, 287, 303, 307, 309, 332, 338, 382
Raeder, E. von, Grand Adm German Navy, 236, 247
Repulse, BB, 267–70, 279, 302, 305, 348, 382
Ribbentrop, von, 202, 219, 239, 244

Richardson, C., 9, 22, 375
Robinson, V., Capt RN, 167–8
Rochefort, J, Cdr USN, 295, 296
Roosevelt, F. D., 182, 215, 237, 246, 250, 261, 265, 276, 339
Roosevelt, T., 84, 96, 106–11, 117, 133, 134
Root, E., 109, 110
Rozhdestvenski, Z. P., RAdm IRN, 82, 84–7, 89, 90, 91, 96, 101, 132, 166, 274, 376–7
Russia, 9, 11, 24, 28, 36, 37, 38, 40–1, 50, 57, 58, 59, 60, 62, 63, 87, 103, 104, 106, 108, 115, 118, 151, 161, 162, 178, 181, 189, 198, 216, 228, 248, 274, 337, 363; Navy/Baltic Fleet, 28, 29, 36, 59, 68, 77, 82, 83, 376
Russo-Japanese War, declared, 41, 58, 59, 60–102, 103, 104, 110, 126, 149, 166, 253–4
Ryujo, CV, 212, 307, 308

Saionji, K., Prince, 118–9, 161
Saito, M., Prime Minister, 160, 164, 183, 189, 203–4, 380
Sakhalien, 86, 102, 105, 133, 149, 161, 162, 378–9
Sakuma, Lt IJN, 113–5, 116, 377
Samar Islands, 343, 345, 360; Battle off, 350–2
San Bernadino Strait, 343, 348, 349, 350, 352, 359
Santa Cruz, Battle of, 311, 312, 382
Sasebo, 24, 61, 62, 89, 117, 213, 314, 337
Sato, T., Adm IJN, 117–8
Savo Island, 312, 313, 314, 315, 383; Battle of, 307, 310
Semenoff, V., Cdr IRN, 69, 70, 95
Sempill, Sir W. Forbes, 148, 199
Shanghai, 62, 87, 123, 213, 215, 308, 338
Shanghai Incident, 172–5, 176, 200, 380
Shantung Peninsula, 28, 34, 129, 161
Shidehara, Baron, at Washington Naval Conference, 152; as Foreign Minister, 161, 162, 167; as Prime Minister, 172
Shigemitsu, M., Foreign Minister, 196, 266, 369–71
Shigihara, Y., kamikaze pilot, 358
Shikishima, BB, 56, 74
Shima, K., Adm IJN, 342, 345, 350
Shimoda, 188–9, 369
Shimonoseki, bombarded, 11, 375; Treaty of, 33–4, 36, 59, 376
Shinano, CV, 245, 333, 361–2, 383–4
Shinto, 48–51, 55
Shiozawa, Adm IJN, 173–4, 200
SHO plans, 341–5
Shoho, CVL, 286, 287
Shokaku, CV, 275, 286, 287, 307, 312, 336

Siberia, 108, 149, 248
Siberian Intervention, 131–3, 378
Sibuyan Sea, 343, 345, 361; Battle of, 346–8, 352
Singapore, 162, 163–4, 206, 220, 242, 244, 247, 266, 267, 273, 305, 378
Sino-Japanese War (1894–5), declared, 16; opens, 19–22; 27, 59, 126, 370, 376; (1937–45), 212–6, 219, 220–1, 223, 224, 231–2, 233, 243, 252, 257, 372
Solomon Islands, 275, 307, 310, 312, 315, 317, 332, 382, 383
Soryu, CV, 198, 275, 302, 303, 306
Sprague, C., RAdm USN, 350–3, 359
Stalin, J., 226, 228, 229
Steer, A. P., Lt IRN, 66–7, 71, 73
Stimson, H. L., US Secretary of State, 170, 177, 243
Submarines, believed use in R-J War, 72, 93; *No. 6* tragedy, 113–5; early, 136–7; in World War One, 137, 164, 168, 170; against Pearl Harbor, 258; MI force observed by, 295, 298, 300–1, 377
Suetsugu, N., Adm IJN, CinCCF, 168, 181, 185, 190, 198, 217, 219, 220
Sulu Sea, 343, 345
Sun Tzu, Chinese strategist, 41–2, 77, 84, 319
Supplemental Building Programmes, 1st, 171, 184, 198; 2nd, 198; 3rd, 211, 224; 4th, 224
Surigao Strait, 343; Battle of, 345, 349–50
Suvoroff, BB, 87, 90, 91
Suzuki, Adm IJN, 203–4
Sydney, 110–1

Taisho, Emperor, 119, 145, 151, 162, 377
Takahashi, S., Adm IJN, CinCCF, 175, 181, 182, 190, 224
Takamura, J., Signalman IJA, 281–7, 303–5, 307, 309–12, 315–6, 325, 328
Takata, T., RAdm IJN, 321, 322–3, 341
Tamura, K., Capt IJN, 320–1, 323
Taranto, 242–3
The Times, quoted, 10–11, 13, 14, 15, 19, 27, 33, 67, 84, 109, 110–11, 194–5, 231
Tikovara, Lt IJN, 64–5, 75–6
Ting, Adm Chinese Navy, 30, 32, 34–5, 37, 38
Tjisalak, SS, 326–8
Togo, H., Adm IJN, CinCCF, 22–5, 28, 30, 44, 49, 59–61, 62, 63–4, 66–79, 84, 86–7, 97–8, 101, 103, 111, 112, 116, 140, 150, 159, 161, 166, 170, 175, 187, 198, 216, 232, 293, 318, 335, 352, 366, 375, 376–7, 380; sights Russian Baltic Fleet, 88; Order of the Day, 89–90; at Tsushima, 90–6;

Togo, H. – *cont.*
speech disbanding CF, 104–5. 108; death, 189–90
Togo, S., Foreign Minister, 253, 256, 259, 260
Tojo, H., Lt-Genl IJA, Prime Minister, War Minister, 237, 255, 257–8, 259, 271, 337–8, 381–2, 383
Tone, CA, 198, 275, 299, 300
Toyoda, S., Adm IJN, CinCCF, 255, 257, 333, 334, 335, 340, 341–3, 345–7, 364, 383
Trincomalee, 163, 206, 275, 302
Tripartite Pact, the, 238, 239, 241, 243, 249, 260
Triple Intervention, 36–7, 41, 103, 106, 121
Truk, 280, 307, 312, 318, 332
Tsarevitch, BB, 77, 79, 80
Tsingtao, 123, 124, 125, 126, 138, 378
Tsi-Yuen, BB, 19, 20, 21, 22, 25, 31
Tsuboi, K., VAdm IJN, 23, 28, 30
Tsushima, Battle of (Battle of the Sea of Japan), 89–96, 103, 104, 111, 116, 134, 136, 161, 166, 170, 181, 189, 198, 267, 287, 292, 333–4, 352, 377, 382; Straits of, 24, 86, 87, 90, 232
Tufnell, D. N. C., Capt RN, 225, 235
'Twenty-One Demands, the', 126–7, 151, 378

Ugaki, M., RAdm IJN, 260, 318
Ukhtomski, Prince, RAdm IRN, 80–1

Varyag, CA, 67–8
Vitgeft, V. K., Adm IRN, 76, 77, 78, 79, 80
Vivian, G., Capt RN, 185, 200, 220
Vladivostock, 28, 29, 36, 38, 63, 64, 69, 74, 77, 78, 85, 86, 87, 93, 131, 132, 133, 363

Wada, N., 2nd-class seaman IJN, 305, 310–11
Wakamiya, seaplane carrier, 124, 138, 378
Wake Island, 272, 297, 382
Washington Naval Conference, 150–1, 152, 153–7, 160, 164, 187, 190, 202, 205, 207, 218, 379; and 5:5:3 ratio, 154, 156; table of agreed ratios, 154–5
Wei-Hai-Wei, 29, 34, 38, 376; Battle for, 35
Wenneker, P., RAdm German Navy, 223–4, 231–5, 237, 254, 303, 305, 337–8, 339, 341–2, 355, 359, 362–4, 365–6
Wilhelm, Kaiser, 37, 106, 107, 116, 122, 223, 377
Wilson, Sir A., VAdm RN, 138–9

Yahagi, CL, 364–5
Yalu River, 28, 29, 65; Battle of the, 29–33, 60, 80, 91, 376
Yamamoto, G., Adm IJN, 110, 122, 160–1, 378
Yamamoto, I., Adm IJN, CinCCF, born Takano, 166; career to 1930, 166–7; death, 317–8; 168, 179, 180, 181, 186, 192–4, 197, 200, 217, 218, 219, 226, 229, 230, 234, 237, 238–9, 243–6, 248, 251–2, 255–7, 260, 270, 271, 279, 285, 291, 292, 293, 294, 295, 296, 298, 299, 305, 307, 308, 310, 319, 324, 331, 332, 333, 347, 357, 365, 376, 378, 379, 380, 381, 383
Yamashiro, BB, 119, 120, 349–50
'Yamato' (ancient name), 180–1, 196, 218, 276, 319, 357
Yamato, (1883) unprotected CA, 29, 370; (1937) BB, 192, 211, 217–8, 219, 223, 245–6, 248, 271, 293, 295, 298, 307, 318, 333, 342, 345, 346–8, 351, 384; sinking of BB, 364–5
Yap, 125, 339
Yarnell, H., Adm USN, 175, 248, 380, 381
Yasukuni Shrine, 49, 98, 177, 189, 358
Yellow Sea, 25, 28, 33, 77; Battle of the, 78–81, 91, 95, 376
Yokohama, 13, 111, 145, 147, 158–9, 277, 369, 377, 379
Yokosuka, 13, 54, 102, 116, 118, 147, 148, 158–9, 163, 182, 245, 277, 279, 280, 331, 333, 361, 364, 377, 379
Yonai, M., Adm IJN, 179, 180, 181, 217, 218, 219, 223, 224–6, 230, 235, 236–7, 239, 259, 270, 308, 339, 363, 381, 383
Yorktown, CV, 237, 286, 302, 306
Yoshino, CA, 16, 19, 20, 29, 30, 59
Yubari, CA, 272, 308
Yukikaze, DD, 314, 364–5

Z Flag, 91, 267
Z Force, 267–70
Zuikaku, CV, 275, 286, 287. 307, 312